Contents

"Phooey on These Juniors!"

by Abigail Van Buren

Dear Abby: Please print my letter so other mothers won't make the same mistake I did. After 19 years, I realize the error of naming our son after his father.

When he was a baby, it was no problem. We called him Billy and his father was Bill.

When he got older he decided Billy was too babyish, so he asked us to call him Bill, which wasn't too bad—we called one Big Bill and the other Little Bill. That worked out fine until Little Bill got bigger than Big Bill.

Now it's worse. It's Young Bill and Old Bill and you can imagine how thrilled father is to be Old Bill at 44.

Not only that, but their voices are identical, and they are constantly being mistaken for one another on the telephone. And their mail gets mixed up, too.

It's a pain in the neck. I should have named him Lawrence, like I wanted to. I've always loved that name. Phooey on these "Juniors."

—Too Late Now

Dear Too: Thanks. New mothers take note.

How to Name Your Baby

15 Things to Consider

1. Namesakes

Exact reproductions of a person's name, even if it is followed by Jr. or II, are often confusing to everyone involved. Parents frequently vary the middle name of a son who carries his father's first and last names, and then call the son by his middle name to distinguish him from his father; but the potential for confusion still exists. What's worse, the child never gets the satisfaction of having a name and a clear identity of his own.

Namesakes can lead to unhappy choices of names for the child, too. Somehow the name Mildred just doesn't seem to fit a little girl comfortably, even though it fits 80-year-old Aunt Mildred perfectly. Generally, it's wiser to be certain a namesake's name is one you'd choose on its own merits, quite apart from the good feelings you have for the person you're complimenting this way.

2. Nationality

If you choose a "foreign-sounding" name, be sure it's not unpronounceable or unspellable, or the name will be a burden to your child. Combinations of names from different countries, like Francois Finklebaum or Marco Mazarowski, may provoke smiles. So if you want to combine names with different ethnic roots, try them out on lots of people (see the lists of popular foreign names) before making a final decision.

3. Religion

To some parents it is important to follow religious traditions in naming a baby. Roman Catholics have traditionally chosen saints' names, sometimes using Mary as a first name for each daughter and pairing it with different middle names: Mary Rose, Mary Margaret, and so on. Jews traditionally choose Old Testament names, often the name of a deceased relative, while Protestants choose both Old and New Testament names. Muslims turn to the Koran and the names of Mohammed and his family as traditional sources of names.

4. Gender

There are two opposing lines of thought on names that can be given to boys and girls alike, whether they are changeable ones like Carol/Carroll, Leslie/Lesley, and Claire/Clair or the truly unisex names like Robin, Chris, and Terry. Some parents feel that a unisex name allows them to pick it with certainty before the baby's sex is known and that such names "type" children in sexual roles and expectations less than traditional boy-girl names do. Others argue that it's unfair and psychologically harmful to require a child to explain which sex he or she is (remember the song, "A Boy Named Sue"?). Finally, boys feel more threatened or insulted when they are presumed to be girls than girls do when they're taken to be boys.

5. Number of Names

No law requires a person to have three names, though most forms provide spaces for a first name, middle initial or name, and surname. When choosing a name for your child, you have several options: a first and last name; a first and last name and only a middle initial (Harry S Truman's S is just an S); initials for both first and middle names; or several middle names. Keep your child's lifelong use of the name in mind when you do something unusual—four middle names are going to cause space problems for your child every time he or she fills out a form!

6. Sounds

The combination of letters in a person's name can make saying the name easier or harder. Alliteration, as in Tina Turner or Pat Paulsen, is fine, but such rhymes as Tyrone Cohn or Alice Palace invite teasing. Joke names, punning names, and other displays of your wit may sound funny, but living with such a name is no laughing matter.

7. Rhythms

Most naming specialists agree that unequal numbers of syllables create pleasing rhythms. Such names as Dwight David Eisenhower or Molly Melinda Grooms fit this pattern. When first and last names have equal numbers of syllables, a middle name with a different number creates a nice effect, as in Albert Anthony Cleveland or Gail Canova Pons. Single-syllable names can be especially forceful if each name has a rather long sound, as in Mark Twain or Charles Rath.

8. Pronunciation

Nobody likes having their name constantly mispronounced. If you pick an unusual name, such as Jésus or Geneviève (Hay-soos and Zhan-vee-ev), don't expect people to pronounce them correctly. Other names with high mispronunciation potential are names that have more than one common pronunciation, as in Alicia (does the second syllable rhyme with fish or leash?) or Shana (does the name rhyme with Anna or Dana?). And if you choose a unique pronunciation of a name (for example, pronouncing Nina like Dinah), don't expect many people to get it right.

9. Spelling

In his poem *Don Juan*, Byron writes, "Thrice happy he whose name has been well spelt," and it's true that you feel a special kind of irritation when your name gets misspelled.

Ordinary spellings have the force of common sense behind them. On the other hand, a new or unusual spelling can revitalize an old name. If the name Ethel only reminds you of Ethel Mertz in the old *I Love Lucy* show, but your mate is crazy about having a daughter with that name, perhaps Ethelle will be a happy substitute. However, some people think it's silly to vary from "traditional" spelling of names and are prejudiced against any Thom, Dik, or Hari.

10. Popularity

More than 65% of all baby girls and more than 70% of all baby boys born in 1995 were given one of the 100 most popular names (see the most popular boys' and girls' names list on pages 10-13). Some names are so popular you shouldn't be surprised to find more than one child with that name in your child's classroom. A child with a very popular name may feel that he or she must "share" it with others, while a child with a very uncommon name is likely to feel that it is uniquely his or hers. However, a child with a popular name may be accepted by peers more easily than a child with a very uncommon name, which may be perceived as weird.

11. Uniqueness

Did you ever try to look in the phone book for the telephone number of someone called John Smith? You wouldn't be able to find it without also knowing the address. To avoid confusion, many people with common last names choose distinctive first and/or middle names for their children. However, a highly unusual name, such as Teague or Hestia, could be an even greater disservice to your child than Michael or Ashley.

12. Stereotypes

Most names call to mind physical or personality traits that often stem from a well-known namesake, real or fictional. Some names—Adolph and Judas, for instance—may never outlive the terrible associations they receive from a single person who bore them. Because the image of a name will affect its owner's self-image, as well as the way he or she is perceived by others, consider what associations come to mind as you make your selections (see stereotypes of names on pages 4-6).

13. Initials

Folk wisdom has it that a person whose initials spell a word—any word—is destined to be successful in life. But it can be irksome, even embarrassing, to have DUD or HAG stamped on your suitcases and jewelry. So be sure your child's initials spell "happy" words—or none at all—to avoid these problems.

14. Nicknames

Most names have shortened or familiar forms that are used during childhood or at different stages of life. For example, Michael might be called Mikey as a child, Mike as a teenager, and Michael on his college application. So, if you don't want your daughter to be called Sam, don't name her Samantha.

If you are thinking of giving your child a nickname as a legal name, remember that Trisha may grow weary of explaining that her full name is not Patricia. And consider the fact that names that sound cute for a child, as in Missy and Timmy, could prove embarrassing later in life. Can you picture Grandma Missy and Grandpa Timmy?

15. Meanings

Most people don't know the meanings of their names—first, middle, or last. But most names do have meanings, and you should at least find out what your favorite choices mean before giving them to your child. A name that means something funny or embarrassing probably won't overshadow your child's life, but if you have to choose between two names that are equally attractive to you, meanings may help tip the balance.

Stereotypes of Names

Consciously or unconsciously, we all have private pictures of the people who answer to certain names. Jackie could be sophisticated and beautiful, like Jackie Kennedy, or fat and funny, like Jackie Gleason. These pictures come from personal experience as well as from the images we absorb from the mass media and thus may conflict in interesting ways. Charlton strikes many people as a sissified, passive, whiny brat until they think of Charlton Heston. Marilyn may be the personification of voluptuous femininity until you think of your neighbor who hangs out her clothes wearing a ratty bathrobe, with curlers in her hair and a cigarette dangling out of her mouth.

Over the years researchers have been fascinated by this question of the "real" meanings of names and their effects on their bearers. When they are asked to stereotype names by age, trustworthiness, attractiveness, sociability, kindness, aggressiveness, popularity, masculinity/femininity, degree of activity or passivity, etc., people actually do tend to agree on each name's characteristics.

So if people think of Mallory as cute and likeable, does that influence a girl named Mallory to become cute and likeable? Experts agree that names don't guarantee instant success or condemn people to certain failure, but they do affect self-images, influence relationships with others, and help (or hinder) success in work and school.

Robert Rosenthal's classic experiment identified what he named the Pygmalion effect: randomly selected children who'd been labeled "intellectual bloomers" actually did bloom!

Another researcher, S. Gray Garwood, conducted a study on sixth graders in New Orleans. He found that students given names that were popular with teachers scored higher in skills tests, were better adjusted and more consistent in their self-perceptions, were more realistic in their evaluations of themselves, and more frequently expected that they would attain their goals—even though their goals were more ambitious than ones set by their peers.

A research study in San Diego suggested that average essays by Davids, Michaels, Karens, and Lisas got better grades than average essays written by Elmers, Huberts, Adelles, and Berthas. The reason? Teachers expected kids with popular names to do better (the Pygmalion effect again), and thus they assigned higher grades to those kids in a self-fulfilling prophecy.

The Sinrod Marketing Group's International Opinion panel surveyed 75,000 parents to discover their opinions about names. Results of this poll are presented in *The Baby Name Personality Survey* by Bruce Lansky and Barry Sinrod.

Their book contains the names people most often associate with hundreds of adjectives describing such personal attributes as intelligent, athletic, attractive, and nice (as well as dumb, klutzy, ugly, and nasty). It also contains personality profiles of 1,400 common and unusual boys' and girls' names and includes real or fictional famous namesakes who may have influenced people's perception of each name.

What the authors found was that most names have very clear images; some even have multiple images. The following are lists of boys' and girls' names that were found to have either positive or negative multiple images.

Girls

positive images

Alana (bright, mysterious)
Amy (educated, calm)
Ava (beautiful, dreamer)
Carla (independent, outgoing)
Christy (friendly, cute)
Courtney (mischievous, bright)
Francesca (European, exciting)
Hope (calm, gentle)
Jody (athletic, cheerful, cute)
Joy (delightful, friendly)
Joyce (friendly, fun loving)
Kate (cute, outgoing)
Linda (beautiful, sweet)
Marlo (classy, cute)
Pam (sweet, outgoing)
Randi (cute, lively)
Roxanne (feminine, enthusiastic)
Sandy (nice, fun loving)
Stacy (active, cute)
Steffi (cute, free spirited, athletic)

negative images

Augusta (old, stodgy)
Bea (heavy, grandma, old)
Beatrice (heavy, old)
Chloris (unattractive, cold)
Dolores (overweight, old)
Fifi (airhead, animal name)
Hedda (ugly, gossip)
Henrietta (fat, horrible)
Hilda (dowdy, fat, maid)
Kiki (dumb, animal name)
Marsha (average, heavy, loud)
Matilda (bossy, big)
Maud (large, opinionated)
Merry (self-centered, shallow)
Milicent (stuffy, old)
Olga (nasty, fat, strict)
Opal (weird, old)
Thelma (unattractive, old)
Twyla (dopey, strange)
Wynne (overweight, silly, whiny)

Boys

positive images	negative images

positive images

Alexander (intelligent, leader)
Allen (funny, friendly)
Bart (athletic, assertive)
Ben (strong, lovable)
Benjamin (cute, inventive)
Bradley (sensitive, fun loving)
Bronson (strong, tough)
Bud (cheerful, good personality)
Christian (well mannered, honest)
Clinton (rich/wealthy, rugged)
Danny (friendly, cute)
Dante (charming, thoughtful, rich)
David (handsome, intelligent)
Dmitri (handsome, sexy)
Douglas (handsome, strong)
Drew (attractive, independent, trim)
Joel (popular, nice, sensitive)
John (intelligent, dependable, well groomed)
Patrick (popular, happy)
Victor (handsome, sexy)

negative images

Ace (jerk, jock, stupid)
Archibald (stuffy, fat)
Boris (scary, sinister, heavy)
Bruno (rough, mean, stupid)
Butch (chubby, bully, mean)
Clem (klutz, hillbilly)
Clyde (clumsy, hillbilly)
Cyril (meek, stuffy)
Damon (evil, devil)
Dennis (brat, mischievous)
Ebenezer (mean, cranky, miserly)
Elmo (awkward, dumb)
Horton (stuffy, overweight)
Hubert (fat, old)
Norman (fat, nerd)
Percival (stuffy, snobby)
Rolf (hardheaded, rigid)
Vic (sneaky, old)
Wally (henpecked, mild mannered)
Zeke (dumb, hillbilly, dirty)

The name you select for your baby is likely to be that child's "label" for a lifetime. So consider how that name will be perceived by others before making your final choice.

Gender-Neutral Names

In the past few years, naming trends have been heading in less traditional directions. One of such trends is using gender-neutral names for both boys and girls. We have provided below a list of such popular gender-neutral names. While *all* the names below are given to both boys and girls, we have divided them into three categories: names that are used equally for both genders, names that are used more for girls, and those that are used more for boys.

used equally	used more for girls	used more for boys
Ali	Andrea	Aaron
Ariel	Angel	Adrian
Avery	Ashley	Alex
Britt	Ashton	Bobby
Brook	Aubrey	Brett
Carey	Dana	Charlie
Casey	Dominique	Christian
Dakota	Elisha	Cody
Daniele	Erin	Colby
Darcy	Jade	Corey
Devan	Jaime	Dale
Frankie	Jamie	Dallas
Jackie	Jessie	Daryl
Jan	Jodi	Devin
Jayme	Justine	Drew
Jean	Kasey	Dusty
Jody	Kelly	Evan
Kacey	Kelsey	Francis
Kayle	Leigh	Jesse
Kerry	Leslie	Joel
Kim	Lindsay	Jordan
Kirby	Lindsey	Kyle
Kristian	Lynn	Lee
Loren	Madison	Logan

used equally	used more for girls	used more for boys
Mackenzie	Robin	Micah
Marion	Sandy	Michael
Nicola	Sasha	Randall
Noel	Shannon	Riley
Paris	Tracy	Ryan
Quinn	Whitney	Shawn
Regan		Taylor
Rene		Terry
Shea		Tyler
Stevie		
Tory		

In addition, various spellings of the same name influence how that name is perceived. Below are some examples of how a slightly different spelling determines whether that name is used for girls or boys.

used for girls	used for boys
Adrienne	Adrien
Bobbie, Bobbi	Bobby
Cameron	Camron
Carie	Cary
Codi	Codey
Cori, Corie, Corrie	Cory, Corry
Frances	Francis
Gabriell	Gabriel
Kori	Korey, Kory
Randi	Randy
Ricki, Rikki	Rickey, Rickie, Ricky
Terri	Terry
Toni	Tony

The Most Popular Names

The popularity of names, like the length of hemlines and the width of ties, is subject to change every year. The changes become even more noticeable when you think about the changes in name "fashions" over longer periods.

Think about the names of your grandparents and famous entertainers of their generation: Bette Davis, Dorothy Lamour, Rhonda Fleming, Helen Hayes, Margaret O'Brien, Ralph Bellamy, Fred Astaire, Gary Cooper—none of their first names is in the list of top 100 names for 1995.

Popular entertainers of the 1950s included Debbie Reynolds, Troy Donahue, Doris Day, Rock Hudson, and Patti Page—none of their first names is in the list of top 100 names for 1995 either.

It seems that in every decade a new group of names rises in popularity, as names associated with a previous generation of babies decline. So, it is wise to consider whether a name's popularity is on the rise, decline, or is holding steady.

To help you assess name popularity trends, we are presenting the top 100 names given to baby boys and girls during 1995, in comparison to their rank during 1990. The rankings are derived from a survey of 10,000 new birth records nationwide, conducted during 1995 by the Plasman COMPAS International Research & Information Services, Saint Paul, Minnesota.

Because you may be wondering how many Michaels and Ashleys you can expect in your child's kindergarten class, we're showing the percentage of all baby boys and girls who are given each name. It may interest you to know that in 1995, 2.06 out of every 100 baby boys were named Michael and 2.05 out of very 100 baby girls were named Ashley.

By checking the percentage of all baby boys or girls who are given each name, you can also gauge the relative popularity of alternate spellings of popular names. For example, Nicholas is preferred to Nicolas by more than 6 to 1; Sarah is preferred to Sara by more than 3 to 1.

As you refer to the following data, remember that the popularity issue cuts two ways: 1) Psychologists say a child with a common or popular name seems to have better odds of success in life than a child with an uncommon name. 2.) A child whose name is at the top of the popularity poll may not feel as unique and special as a child whose name is less common.

The 100 Most Popular Girls' Names in 1995

1995 Rank	Name	% of Girls	1990 Rank
1.	Ashley	2.05%	
	Ashlee	0.13%	
	Ashleigh	0.12%	
		2.30%	4
2.	Sarah	1.55%	
	Sara	0.47%	
		2.02%	2
3.	Samantha	1.92%	10
4.	Kaitlyn	0.70%	
	Caitlyn	0.45%	
	Caitlin	0.37%	
	Kaitlin	0.31%	
	Caitlan	0.07%	
		1.90%	46
5.	Jessica	1.87%	1
6.	Brittany	1.37%	
	Brittney	0.48%	
		1.85%	3
7.	Megan	1.25%	
	Meghan	0.23%	
	Meagan	0.12%	
		1.60%	6
8.	Emily	1.60%	32
9.	Brianna	0.80%	
	Breanna	0.38%	
	Briana	0.32%	
		1.50%	na
10.	Rachel	1.17%	
	Rachael	0.18%	
		1.35%	20

1995 Rank	Name	% of Girls	1990 Rank
11.	Haley	0.62%	
	Hayley	0.50%	
	Hailey	0.20%	
		1.32%	na
12.	Kayla	1.30%	23
13.	Allison	0.77%	
	Allyson	0.23%	
	Alison	0.22%	
		1.22%	35
14.	Amanda	1.15%	5
15.	Chris	1.12%	na
16.	Nicole	0.87%	
	Nichole	0.20%	
		1.07%	16
17.	Stephanie	0.97%	21
18.	Alyssa	0.95%	54
19.	Katherine	0.40%	
	Kathryn	0.30%	
	Catherine	0.22%	
		0.92%	34
20.	Elizabeth	0.92%	7
21.	Jasmine	0.60%	
	Jasmin	0.10%	
	Jasmyn	0.10%	
	Yasmin	0.07%	
	Yazmin	0.05%	
		0.92%	na
22.	Hannah	0.82%	
	Hanna	0.08%	
		0.90%	98
23.	Taylor	0.87%	na

1995 Rank	Name	% of Girls	1990 Rank
24.	Alexis	0.82%	61
25.	Lauren	0.80%	11
26.	Victoria	0.80%	26
27.	Cody	0.77%	na
28.	Jennifer	0.77%	12
29.	Marissa	0.75%	57
30.	Alexandra	0.60%	
	Alejandra	0.10%	
		0.70%	17
31.	Chelsea	0.60%	
	Chelsey	0.10%	
		0.70%	31
32.	Michelle	0.60%	
	Michele	0.10%	
		0.70%	8
33.	Rebecca	0.60%	
	Rebekah	0.10%	
		0.70%	28
34.	Danielle	0.67%	22
35.	Kelly	0.55%	
	Kellie	0.12%	
		0.67%	14
36.	Christina	0.40%	
	Kristina	0.25%	
		0.65%	24
37.	Erica	0.40%	
	Erika	0.25%	
		0.65%	29
38.	Brooke	0.52%	
	Brook	0.10%	
		0.62%	38

1995 Rank	Name	% of Girls	1990 Rank	1995 Rank	Name	% of Girls	1990 Rank	1995 Rank	Name	% of Girls	1990 Rank
39.	Heather	0.60%	39	56.	Cassandra	0.40%		78.	Kaylee	0.25%	
40.	Melissa	0.60%	37		Kassandra	0.05%			Kayli	0.07%	
41.	Michaela	0.60%	na			0.45%	19			0.32%	na
42.	Tiffany	0.50%		57.	Linda	0.35%		79.	Krista	0.32%	95
	Tiffani	0.10%			Lynda	0.10%		80.	Vanessa	0.32%	na
		0.60%	45			0.45%	72	81.	Veronica	0.32%	na
43.	Lindsey	0.42%		58.	Kelsey	0.35%		82.	Kylie	0.30%	na
	Lindsay	0.15%			Kelsie	0.10%		83.	Leah	0.22%	
		0.57%	30			0.45%	44		Lea	0.05%	
44.	Savannah	0.57%	na	59.	Kimberly	0.42%	36			0.27%	na
45.	Jamie	0.55%	27	60.	Olivia	0.42%	79	84.	Sydney	0.27%	na
46.	Abigail	0.50%	75	61.	Andrea	0.40%	na	85.	Tara	0.27%	na
47.	Amber	0.50%	50	62.	Erin	0.40%	60	86.	Valerie	0.27%	74
48.	Crystal	0.42%		63.	Katie	0.40%	41	87.	Angela	0.25%	na
	Krystal	0.08%		64.	Kristin	0.40%	15	88.	Brandi	0.17%	
		0.50%	na	65.	Mary	0.40%	47		Brandy	0.08%	
49.	Laura	0.50%	53	66.	Natalie	0.40%	59			0.25%	na
50.	Miranda	0.50%	na	67.	Maria	0.37%	na	89.	Cassidy	0.17%	
51.	Shelby	0.42%		68.	Paige	0.37%	48		Kassidy	0.08%	
	Shelbi	0.08%		69.	Ariana	0.22%				0.25%	na
		0.50%	na		Arianna	0.13%		90.	Jenna	0.25%	na
52.	Amy	0.37%				0.35%	na	91.	Jordan	0.25%	na
	Amie	0.10%		70.	Christine	0.35%	88	92.	Alicia	0.22%	93
		0.47%	33	71.	Holly	0.35%	90	93.	Desiree	0.22%	97
53.	Courtney	0.47%	40	72.	Jacqueline	0.30%		94.	Grace	0.22%	51
54.	Madeline	0.40%			Jacquelyn	0.05%		95.	Kara	0.22%	na
	Madelyn	0.07%				0.35%	52	96.	Kendra	0.22%	82
		0.47%	na	73.	Sabrina	0.35%	na	97.	Madison	0.22%	na
55.	Anna	0.32%		74.	Alexandria	0.32%	86	98.	Natasha	0.22%	92
	Ana	0.13%		75.	Caroline	0.32%	96	99.	Rose	0.22%	na
		0.45%	76	76.	Cheyenne	0.32%	na	100.	Sierra	0.22%	na
				77.	Emma	0.32%	na				

The 100 Most Popular Boys' Names in 1995

1995 Rank	Name	% of Boys	1990 Rank
1.	Michael	2.6%	1
2.	Tyler	2.4%	12
3.	Nicholas	1.9%	
	Nicolas	0.3%	
		2.2%	7
4.	Joshua	2.1%	5
5.	Brandon	2.1%	27
6.	Jacob	2.0%	21
7.	Zachary	1.7%	
	Zachery	0.2%	
		1.9%	4
8.	Austin	1.8%	59
9.	Kyle	1.8%	19
10.	Alexander	1.7%	49
11.	Matthew	1.7%	2
12.	James	1.6%	3
13.	John	1.2%	
	Johnny	0.2%	
	Jon	0.2%	
		1.6%	34
14.	Ryan	1.5%	6
15.	Daniel	1.5%	11
16.	Andrew	1.4%	16
17.	David	1.4%	10
18.	Jonathan	1.3%	
	Jonathon	0.1%	
		1.4%	13
19.	Justin	1.3%	15
20.	Joseph	1.3%	32
21.	Steven	0.9%	
	Stephen	0.4%	
		1.3%	9
22.	Jordan	1.1%	41
23.	Robert	1.1%	20
24.	Thomas	1.1%	22
25.	Brian	0.7%	
	Bryan	0.3%	
		1.0%	18
26.	Christopher	1.0%	17
27.	William	1.0%	40
28.	Anthony	1.0%	48
29.	Eric	0.6%	
	Erik	0.2%	
	Erick	0.2%	
		1.0%	14
30.	Jason	0.9%	23
31.	Dylan	0.7%	
	Dillon	0.2%	
		0.9%	na
32.	Aaron	0.8%	54
33.	Benjamin	0.8%	35
34.	Taylor	0.8%	na
35.	Kevin	0.8%	38
36.	Christian	0.6%	na
37.	Jared	0.6%	61
38.	Patrick	0.6%	52
39.	Samuel	0.6%	47
40.	Corey	0.3%	
	Cory	0.3%	
		0.6%	51
41.	Paul	0.6%	69
42.	Derek	0.5%	
	Derrick	0.1%	
		0.6%	91
43.	Jesse	0.6%	86
44.	Cody	0.5%	30
45.	Richard	0.5%	46
46.	Travis	0.5%	33
47.	Adam	0.5%	25
48.	Dustin	0.5%	45
49.	Mark	0.3%	
	Marc	0.2%	
		0.5%	28
50.	Nathaniel	0.5%	43
51.	Nathan	0.5%	8
52.	Cameron	0.5%	na
53.	Devin	0.5%	na
54.	Connor	0.4%	na
55.	Garrett	0.4%	na
56.	Hunter	0.4%	na
57.	Isaac	0.4%	73
58.	Spencer	0.4%	82
59.	Caleb	0.4%	66
60.	Logan	0.4%	na
61.	Shelby	0.4%	na
62.	Evan	0.4%	84

1995 Rank	Name	% of Boys	1990 Rank	1995 Rank	Name	% of Boys	1990 Rank	1995 Rank	Name	% of Boys	1990 Rank
63.	Blake	0.4%	62	76.	Cole	0.3%	na	90.	Randy	0.2%	
64.	Bradley	0.4%	65	77.	Gregory	0.3%	50		Randall	0.1%	
65.	Casey	0.4%	89	78.	Morgan	0.3%	na			0.3%	na
66.	Jeffrey	0.4%	42	79.	Raymond	0.3%	75	91.	Scott	0.3%	63
67.	Timothy	0.4%	37	80.	Colin	0.2%		92.	Troy	0.3%	na
68.	Dalton	0.3%	na		Collin	0.1%		93.	Wesley	0.3%	71
69.	Kenneth	0.3%	60			0.3%	na	94.	Donald	0.2%	na
70.	Mitchell	0.3%	94	81.	Madison	0.3%	na	95.	Grant	0.2%	na
71.	Sean	0.3%	24	82.	Payton	0.3%	na	96.	George	0.2%	92
72.	Trevor	0.3%	na	83.	Peter	0.3%	68	97.	Philip	0.1%	
73.	Brendan	0.1%		84.	Edward	0.3%	na		Phillip	0.1%	
	Brenden	0.1%		85.	Frank	0.3%	na			0.2%	57
	Brendon	0.1%		86.	Gabriel	0.3%	na	98.	Shane	0.2%	na
		0.3%	56	87.	Jack	0.3%	na	99.	Tanner	0.2%	na
74.	Brett	0.3%	83	88.	Jake	0.3%	na	100.	Trent	0.2%	na
75.	Charles	0.3%	72	89.	Jeremy	0.3%	53				

The 25 Most Popular
African-American Girls' Names in 1995

1995 Rank	Name	% of Girls
1.	Briana	1.4%
	Brianna	1.4%
	Breanna	1.0%
		3.8%
2.	Jasmine	2.2%
	Jazmine	0.4%
	Jasmin	0.2%
	Jazzmin	0.2%
	Yasmine	0.2%
		3.2%
3.	Alexis	1.4%
	Alexsis	0.2%
		1.6%
4.	Brittany	0.8%
	Brittanni	0.2%
	Brittney	0.2%
	Brytteny	0.2%
		1.4%
5.	Jessica	1.2%
6.	Sierra	0.8%
	Cierra	0.4%
		1.2%
7.	Courtney	0.6%
	Kourtney	0.2%
	Kourtni	0.2%
		1.0%

1995 Rank	Name	% of Girls
8.	Danielle	1.0%
9.	Ashley	0.8%
10.	Destiney	0.4%
	Destiny	0.4%
		0.8%
11.	Diamond	0.8%
12.	Taylor	0.6%
	Teylor	0.2%
		0.8%
13.	Tiara	0.6%
	Tiarra	0.2%
		0.8%
14.	Alecia	0.4%
	Alesea	0.2%
		0.6%
15.	Alichia	0.2%
	Alicia	0.2%
	Alycia	0.2%
		0.6%
16.	Amber	0.4%
	Ambur	0.2%
		0.6%

1995 Rank	Name	% of Girls
17.	Antonia	0.4%
	Antonya	0.2%
		0.6%
18.	Asia	0.4%
	Azia	0.2%
		0.6%
19.	Kirsten	0.4%
	Kristyn	0.2%
		0.6%
20.	Latisha	0.6%
21.	Mercedes	0.6%
22.	Nykia	0.4%
	Nikiya	0.2%
		0.6%
23.	Tiana	0.4%
	Tianna	0.2%
		0.6%
24.	Whitney	0.4%
	Whitne	0.2%
		0.6%
25.	Aaliyah	0.4%

The 25 Most Popular
African-American Boys' Names in 1995

1995 Rank	Name	% of Boys
1.	Michael	2.1%
	Micheal	0.4%
		2.5%
2.	Anthony	1.9%
3.	Joshua	1.6%
4.	Nicholas	1.2%
	Nikalaus	0.2%
	Nycholas	0.2%
		1.6%
5.	Brandon	1.4%
6.	Devin	1.4%
7.	Stephen	0.6%
	Stephan	0.2%
	Stephon	0.2%
	Steve	0.2%
	Steven	0.2%
		1.4%

1995 Rank	Name	% of Boys
8.	Aaron	1.2%
9.	Christopher	1.2%
10.	David	1.2%
11.	Johnny	0.6%
	John	0.4%
	Johnnie	0.2%
		1.2%
12.	Andre	1.0%
13.	Eric	1.0%
14.	Justin	1.0%
15.	Kevin	1.0%
16.	Ryan	1.0%
17.	William	1.0%
18.	Charles	0.8%

1995 Rank	Name	% of Boys
19.	Darell	0.2%
	Darrel	0.2%
	Darrell	0.2%
	Darryl	0.2%
		0.8%
20.	James	0.8%
21.	Lawrence	0.8%
22.	Patrick	0.8%
23.	Timothy	0.8%
24.	Antonio	0.6%
25.	Daniel	0.6%

The 25 Most Popular Hispanic Girls' Names in 1995

1995 Rank	Name	% of Girls
1.	Maria	2.0%
2.	Alejandra	1.2%
	Alexandra	0.6%
		1.8%
3.	Amanda	1.8%
4.	Ashley	1.8%
5.	Jessica	1.8%
6.	Karina	1.8%
7.	Kasandra	1.6%
	Kassandra	0.2%
		1.8%
8.	Alexis	1.6%
9.	Samantha	1.6%
10.	Stephanie	1.2%
	Stepanee	0.2%
	Stephany	0.2%
		1.6%

1995 Rank	Name	% of Girls
11.	Cynthia	1.4%
12.	Jasmine	1.0%
	Jazmine	0.2%
	Yasmin	0.2%
		1.4%
13.	Sabrina	1.4%
14.	Kristina	0.6%
	Cristina	0.4%
	Christina	0.2%
		1.2%
15.	Kimberly	1.2%
16.	Valerie	1.2%
17.	Karla	0.8%
	Carla	0.2%
		1.0%

1995 Rank	Name	% of Girls
18.	Katherine	0.6%
	Catherine	0.4%
		1.0%
19.	Chris	1.0%
20.	Jennifer	1.0%
21.	Priscilla	0.6%
	Pricilla	0.2%
	Priscila	0.2%
		1.0%
22.	Rebecca	0.8%
	Rebeca	0.2%
		1.0%
23.	Vanessa	1.0%
24.	Adrian	0.8%
25.	Angel	0.8%

The 25 Most Popular Hispanic Boys' Names in 1995

1995 Rank	Name	% of Boys
1.	Juan	5.1%
2.	Jose	3.2%
3.	Eric	1.8%
	Erik	0.4%
	Erick	0.2%
		2.4%
4.	Ricardo	2.2%
5.	David	2.0%
6.	Jorge	2.0%
7.	Michael	1.8%
	Michel	0.2%
		2.0%
8.	Jonathan	1.4%
	Johnathan	0.4%
		1.8%
9.	Joshua	1.8%

1995 Rank	Name	% of Boys
10.	Anthony	1.4%
	Anthonie	0.2%
		1.6%
11.	Carlos	1.6%
12.	Christian	1.2%
	Cristian	0.4%
		1.6%
13.	Eduardo	0.8%
	Edward	0.6%
	Edwardo	0.2%
		1.6%
14.	Jesus	1.6%
15.	Luis	1.6%
16.	John	1.0%
	Jon	0.4%
		1.4%
17.	Aaron	1.2%

1995 Rank	Name	% of Boys
18.	Brandon	1.2%
19.	Jacob	1.2%
20.	Mark	1.0%
	Marc	0.2%
		1.2%
21.	Nicholas	0.8%
	Nicolas	0.2%
	Nikolas	0.2%
		1.2%
22.	Steven	0.8%
	Stephen	0.2%
	Steve	0.2%
		1.2%
23.	Hector	1.0%
24.	Javier	1.0%
25.	Joseph	1.0%

Popular Names Around the World

Family roots, foreign travel, and names in the news—all these are giving people new ideas for baby names. The following lists show the equivalents of Tom, Dick, and Harry (or Ann, Susan, and Elizabeth) from around the world. If you want information from a country not listed, check with its embassy or tourist information office. Incidentally, Mohammed (or Muhammad) is the most commonly given name in the world!

Australia

Girls	Boys
Alexandra	Adam
Alison	Alexander
Amanda	Andrew
Claire	Benjamin
Elizabeth	Bradley
Emily	Christopher
Emma	Daniel
Jennifer	David
Jessica	Jake
Kate	James
Katherine	Joshua
Lauren	Luke
Michelle	Matthew
Nicole	Michael
Rachel	Mitchell
Rebecca	Nicholas
Samantha	Ryan
Sarah	Samuel
Stephanie	Thomas
Tegan	Timothy

Canada

Girls	Boys
Amanda	Andrew
Ann(e)	Brandon
Ashley	Brian
Carol(e)	Chrisopher
Christine	Daniel
Danielle	David
Elizabeth	Derek
Jacqueline	James
Jennifer	John
Jessica	Joseph
Laura	Joshua
Linda	Kyle
Margaret	Matthew
Mary, Marie	Michael
Melissa	Pierre
Nicole	Robert
Patricia	Ryan
Sarah	Stephen
Stephanie	Tyler
Susan	William

China

Girls	Boys
Bik	Cheung
Chun	Chung
Gschu	Cong
Huan	Dong
Jai	Fai
Jing	Hung
Kwan	Keung
Lai	Kong
Lin	Mao
Ling	On
Mei	Po-Sin
Nan	Shilín
Ping	Shing
Qing	Tat
Ting	Tong
Xiaoli	Tung
Xiaomei	Wing
Xiaoying	Xiaogang
Xiong Hong	Xiaowei
Yuan	Yang

Egypt

Girls	Boys
Abeer	Abdu
Aziza	Abdulla
Efra	Ahmed
Fatima	Ali
Halima	Hisham
Hind	Hossam
Huda	Kareem
Indihar	Mahmud
Intisar	Mohammed
Maha	Moneim
Nabila	Nassir
Nadine	Omar
Nagwa	Roushdy
Nema	Saled
Ola	Sami
Rakia	Samir
Rasha	Tamer
Samira	Tewfik
Shahira	Yahiya
Sherin	Yahya

England

Girls	Boys
Alexandra	Alexander
Alice	Andrew
Amy	Charles
Anna	Christopher
Catherine	Daniel
Charlotte	David
Eleonor	Edward
Elizabeth	George
Ellen	Harry
Emily	Henry
Emma	James
Isobel	Jonathan
Lucy	Mark
Monica	Nicholas
Olivia	Oliver
Patricia	Richard
Rebecca	Robert
Sarah	Samuel
Sophie	Thomas
Victoria	William

France

Girls	Boys
Adeline	Antoine
Brigitte	Bernard
Cecile	Christophe
Charlotte	Donatien
Delphine	Eduard
Dominique	Florian
Francoise	François
Helene	Gatien
Jeanette	Guillaume
Juliette	Jacques
Laure	Jean
Marie	Jerome
Mariette	Joseph
Michelle	Luc
Nicole	Marc
Sabine	Max
Sophie	Philippe
Vanessa	Sebastian
Veronique	Stephan
Virginie	Sylvian

Germany

Girls	Boys
Anna	Alexander
Barbara	Christian
Brigitte	Claus
Claudia	Daniel
Elfie	Ernst
Franziska	Felix
Gretchen	Florian
Heidi	Gunter
Hilda	Johann
Hildegard	Kari
Jennifer	Kevin
Jessica	Lucas
Julia	Ludwig
Katharina	Marcel
Laura	Maximilian
Lisa	Paul
Maria	Peter
Mina	Thomas
Sandra	Waiter
Vanessa	Wilhelm

Greece

Girls	Boys
Aleni	Aristotle
Alexandra	Christos
Anastasia	Constantinos
Angeline	Dimitris
Aphrodite	Elias
Athena	Euripedes
Daphne	Kimon
Dimitra	Kyriako
Ekaterini	Manolis
Emalia	Nicos
Fotini	Panayiotis
Helena	Pericles
Kaliope	Platon
Katina	Staphanos
Kyriakoula	Thanasi
Marina	Thanos
Olga	Theodor
Stamata	Vasilis
Stella	Yannis
Yana	Yorgos

Iceland

Girls	Boys
Alexandra	Agust
Anna	Ari
Birna	Arni
Brynja	Bjarni
Edda	Daniel
Elin	Eggeri
Elisabet	Finnur
Erla	Geir
Erna	Gudjon
Gudrun	Gunnar
Ingibjorg	Halldor
Johanna	Haukur
Julia	Johann
Katrin	Jon
Kristin	Magnus
Lara	Olafur
Lilja	Omar
Nina	Pall
Sigridur	Petur
Sigrun	Sigurdur

Ireland

Girls	Boys
Alana	Brendan
Breana	Charles
Bridget	Colin
Caitlin	Curran
Cassidy	Darcy
Ciarda	Devin
Colleen	Dillon
Dacey	Fionn
Edana	John
Eileen	Joseph
Erin	Liam
Kathleen	Neal
Keara	Owen
Kelley	Patrick
Kerry	Quinn
Kyla	Seamus
Maureen	Sean
Megan	Thomas
Sinead	Trace
Tara	Troy

Israel

Girls	Boys
Aviva	Alon
Carmela	Benyamin
Dalia	Boaz
Daphne	David
Efrat	Doron
Galit	Gal
Hagit	Leor
Hila	Moshe
Michal	Ofer
Micki	Omer
Mirav	Oren
Nua	Roee
Ora	Ronen
Orit	Shai
Ronit	Shimon
Sharon	Tal
Smadar	Yaakov
Talia	Yaron
Tamar	Yigal
Yael	Yonatan

Italy

Girls	Boys
Angelina	Alessandro
Annabella	Antonio
Assuntina	Carmine
Beatrice	Dario
Carmella	Davide
Catherina	Diego
Concetta	Eugenio
Costanzia	Fabrizio
Dominica	Francesco
Francesca	Giordano
Frederica	Giuseppe
Giovanna	Leonardo
Graziella	Liborio
Isabella	Luca
Lucia	Mauro
Maria	Pasquale
Marianna	Pietro
Roberta	Salvatore
Rosina	Santo
Teresa	Vito

Japan

Girls	Boys
Akemi	Akira
Euiko	Hiroshi
Hiroko	Joji
Junko	Jun
Kadiri	Ken
Kameko	Kenji
Keiko	Masao
Kioko	Nobuo
Kumiko	Shigeru
Mai	Sho
Manami	Tadashi
Mariko	Takashi
Megumi	Takeo
Michiko	Takeshi
Reiko	Toshio
Sachiko	Yasuo
Sakuro	Yoshio
Toshiko	Yuji
Yoko	Yujiro
Yoshiko	Yusuke

Mexico

Girls	Boys
Adriana	Alfonso
Alejandra	Alfredo
Alicia	Antonio
Alma	Arturo
Ana	Carlos
Carmen	Enrique
Claudia	Ernesto
Cristina	Fernando
Elena	Jaime
Erika	Javier
Gabriela	Jesus
Juana	José
Laura	Juan
Leticia	Louis
Maria	Marco
Marta	Mario
Monica	Pablo
Patricia	Pedro
Rosa	Raúl
Susana	Román

Nigeria

Girls	Boys
Abebi	Adebayo
Ada	Adigun
Akanke	Ajani
Alake	Akins
Amaka	Amadi
Aniweta	Ayo
Asabi	Chika
Chinwe	Chike
Chinyere	Chima
Enogi	Chinua
Fayola	Emeka
Femi	Gowon
Ijeoma	Ikenna
Limber	Ndem
Lola	Nnamdi
Nena	Okechuku
Ngozi	Okon
Nnenna	Olu
Oba	Orji
Oni	Tor

Norway

Girls	Boys
Anne	Anders
Anne-Lise	Andreas
Astrid	Christian
Berit	Christopher
Berta	Dag
Camilla	Erik
Gorun	Gunnar
Grete	Hans
Hedda	Ingvar
Hilde	Jan
Inga	Jens
Kari	Jon
Kirsti	Karl
Marianne	Olaf
Martine	Petter
Merete	Rolf
Signe	Simen
Siri	Stig
Stine	Sverre
Trine	Thomas

Philippines

Girls	Boys
Aida	Alberto
Alicia	Antonio
Ana	Armando
Aurora	Arturo
Belen	Benjamin
Carmen	Carlos
Consuela	Domingo
Elizabeth	Francisco
Elvira	Honorio
Eveline	Jose
Fermina	Juan
Gloria	Leopoldo
Isabel	Manuel
Leonor	Mariano
Maria	Pedro
Patricia	Ramon
Roario	Raúl
Socorro	Roberto
Teresa	Rolando
Teresita	Rosendo

Poland

Girls	Boys
Agata	Adam
Aniela	Andrej
Anna	Boleslaw
Beata	Dawid
Eugenia	Eugeniusz
Ewa	Franek
Franciscka	Grzegorz
Jadwiga	Heniek
Joana	Janos
Justina	Josep
Karolina	Karol
Katarzina	Krzysctof
Lucia	Lukasz
Magda	Marian
Marinna	Mateusz
Marta	Michal
Marzena	Pawal
Monika	Piotr
Stefa	Rafal
Wicktoria	Tomasz

Portugal

Girls	Boys
Ana	Americo
Clara	Antonio
Emilia	Carlos
Fatima	Edwardo
Fernanda	Fernando
Gloria	Filipe
Graca	Francisco
Helena	Germano
Ines	Henrique
Irene	Humberto
Irmelinda	João
Isabel	Joaquin
Julia	Jorge
Luisa	Luis
Manuela	Manuel
Margarida	Mario
Maria	Miguel
Rita	Paulo
Sofia	Pedro
Teresa	Ricardo

Russia

Girls	Boys
Anya	Aleksey
Anzhéla	Anatoli
Dasha	Andrei
Galina	Arkadij
Irina	Boris
Kira	Dmitrij
Larisa	Evgenij
Lera	Feodor
Marina	Georgi
Mila	Igor
Natalya	Ivan
Olga	Konstantin
Olya	Leonid
Polina	Misha
Sofia	Nikolai
Tamara	Oleg
Tatiana	Oleksandr
Vera	Sasha
Yelena	Vladimir
Yelizaveta	Yuri

Sweden

Girls	Boys
Anna	Anders
Anneka	Arne
Astrid	Axel
Birgitte	Bengt
Britta	Bjorn
Christina	Bo
Dagmar	Edvard
Elisabeth	Erik
Elsa	Ernst
Erika	Folke
Eva	Frederik
Gudrun	Greger
Helena	Gunnar
Helga	Gustaf
Inga	Hans
Ingrid	Kjell
Karin	Lars
Kerstin	Nils
Margareta	Oskar
Ulrika	Per

Baby Name Legal Guide

Shortly after your baby is born, someone on the hospital staff will ask you for information to fill out a birth certificate. If your baby is not born in a hospital, either by choice or accident, you still need to file a birth certificate. If you're on your way but don't make it to the hospital in time, the hospital will still take care of filling in the form and presenting it for your signature after you're admitted. If you plan a home birth, you will have to go to the vital statistics office and file a form there—to be certain, find out what your local laws require.

Basic facts about both parents' names, places and dates of birth, and such details about the baby as its sex, weight, length, exact time of arrival, and date of birth will be needed for a birth certificate. Questions regarding other children (if any), their ages, previous miscarriages or children's deaths, the educational levels of both parents, and so on might be asked at this time for records at your local division of vital statistics. They may not appear on the actual birth certificate, though.

The hospital staffer will type up the form and present it for the mother and doctor to sign before sending it to the vital statistics division to be recorded permanently. Once it's recorded you can request copies (needed for things like passports, some jobs, and some legal transactions).

That's what happens in the usual chain of events. But what about the technicalities and specific legal aspects of naming a child? The first thing to know is that laws that govern baby naming vary greatly throughout the country. If your choice of names is in any way unusual (such as giving your baby a hyphen-

ated surname combining the mother's maiden name with the father's name), be sure of the law before you name the baby. And sign the official birth certificate only after it has been filled out to your satisfaction.

A few of the most commonly asked questions concerning legalities are considered here but, since state and territory laws are not uniform, even these answers cannot be definite. Your local municipal health department officials can probably lead you to the proper department or official to handle your particular situation. Contact them if you need more detailed answers to your questions.

Q. Are there any restrictions on the choice of first and middle names for a baby?

A. No, with the possible exception that the baby's names should be composed of letters, not numbers. In 1978 a district court judge refused to allow a young Minneapolis social studies teacher to legally change his name to the number 1069, calling such a change "an offense to human dignity" that would "hasten that day in which we all become lost in faceless numbers."

Freedom in choosing given names is not universal. A spokesperson for the French Consulate in Chicago confirmed that an 1813 French law still governs naming practices in France. It decrees that babies must be named after Catholic saints or "persons known in ancient history."

Q. Is a choice allowed in giving the baby its surname?

A. In former generations a baby's surname was not often considered a matter for personal decision. State regulations dictated that if the parents were married, the baby took on the father's surname. If the parents were not married, the baby's surname was that of its mother.

In the past few decades such state regulations have been changing. For example, in Florida, Hawaii, and North Carolina, federal courts have ruled those three states can no longer determine the choice of a baby's surname, leaving that decision to the parent(s).

Such court rulings represent the trend prevalent in most, if not all, states to leave the choice of babies' surnames to parents. However, to be absolutely certain, be sure to check your state's regulations on this matter.

Q. Must the baby's full name be decided upon before the birth certificate can be registered?

A. In most cases no time limit exists in which given names must be recorded. However, depending on the amount of time since the birth, the evidence required to record the name varies, ranging from a letter signed by the parent to a court order.

Q. How can a baby's name be legally changed after its birth is registered?

A. More than 50,000 Americans ask courts to change their names legally every year. Some of these changes are requested by parents for their children when the names originally chosen no longer suit them.

Changes in a minor child's given names are possible in some states without a court order, with time limits ranging from a few days after birth to any time at all. In some states a simple affidavit signed by the parents or a notarized amendment is sufficient to make a name change. Others require various documents to show proof of an established new name, such as a baptismal certificate, an insurance policy, an immunization record, or the family Bible record. For older children, school records or the school census are usually allowed.

When court procedures are necessary, they involve petitions to a county probate court, a superior court, or a district court, following state laws. Often prior newspaper publication of the intended change is required. The court then issues a "change of name" order or decree. In some states new birth certificates are issued for name changes. In others, certificates are only amended.

Informal name changes can be and often are made simply through the "common law right of choice," which allows individuals to use any names they choose. Such a change is informal, though, and is not legal in official procedures.

Q. What if a mistake is made in the baby's name on the birth certificate?

A. To repeat: the best advice of all is to avoid such an occurrence by being absolutely sure that the completely filled-out certificate is correct in every detail before signing it. If a mistake is made, it is important to handle the matter quickly. Procedures for corrections on certificates vary: sometimes signatures of the parents are sufficient, but in other cases forms must be filled out or documentary evidence supplied.

Q. What are the laws for renaming adopted children?

A. An adoption decree is a court order legally obtained through basically similar procedures in all states and territories. A child's given names are selected by the adoptive parents and the surname is chosen in accordance with whatever state or territory laws exist for surnames of biological children. Then all these names are recorded in the adoption decree. In most places an entirely new birth certificate is drawn up, although the place of birth is not usually changed. Most often, the original birth certificate is sealed with the adoption papers, and the new certificate is filed in place of the original.

Q. How may a child's name be changed by a stepfather, by foster parents, or in the case of legitimization?

A. In the case of a name change by a stepfather or by foster parents, most states require that individuals follow the appropriate procedures for adoption or for legal name change.

Changing a child's surname in the case of legitimization is virtually the same as the adoption procedure in most states and territories. Some require both an affidavit of paternity and a copy of the parents' marriage license, while others do not concern themselves with the marriage of the parents. California has no procedures whatsoever, since illegitimacy is no longer defined in that state.

The Name Exchange

Celebrities' Names Before and After

Historical/Political Figures

Professional Name	Original Name
Johnny Appleseed	John Chapman
Sitting Bull	Tatanka Iyotake
Calamity Jane	Martha Jane Burke
Butch Cassidy	Robert LeRoy Parker
Gerald Ford	Leslie Lynch King, Jr.*
Mata Hari	Margareth Geertruide Zelle
Gary Hart	Gary Hartpence
Crazy Horse	Tashuna-Uitco
Sundance Kid	Harry Longbaugh
Nancy Reagan	Anne Frances Robbins
Leon Trotsky	Lev Davydovich Bronstein
Woodrow Wilson	Thomas Woodrow Wilson
Malcolm X	Malcolm Little

Sports Figures

Professional Name	Original Name
Kareem Abdul-Jabbar	Ferdinand Lewis Alcindor, Jr.
Muhammad Ali	Cassius Marcellus Clay, Jr.
Andre the Giant	Andre Roussinoff
Yogi Berra	Lawrence Peter Berra
Hulk Hogan	Terry Bodello
Pelé	Edson Arantes do Nascimento
Ahmad Rashad	Bobby Moore
Tom Seaver	George Thomas Seaver
Gene Tunney	James Joseph Tunney
Cy Young	Denton True Young

Literary Figures

Professional Name	Original Name
Pearl Buck	Pearl Comfort Sydenstricker
Truman Capote	Truman Steckfus Pearsons
Lewis Carroll	Charles Lutwidge Dodgeson
Agatha Christie	Agatha Mary Clarissa Miller
Isak Dinesen	Baroness Karen Blixen
Victoria Holt	Eleanot Burford Hibbert
Judith Krantz	Judith Tarcher
John le Carre	John Moore Carnwell
George Orwell	Eric Arthur Blair
Satchel Paige	Leroy Robert Paige
Harold Robbins	Francis Kane
Mickey Spillane	Frank Morrison
Dr. Suess	Theodore Suess Geisel
J.R.R. Tolkien	John Ronald Reuel Tolkien
Mark Twain	Samuel Clemens
Gore Vidal	Eugene Luther Vidal
Nathaniel West	Nathaniel Wallenstein Weinstein
Tennessee Williams	Thomas Lanier Williams

Entertainment Figures

Professional Name	Original Name
Eddie Albert	Edward Albert Heimberger
Alan Alda	Alphonse D'Abruzzo
Jane Alexander	Jane Quigley
Jason Alexander	Jay Scott Greenspan
Woody Allen	Allen Konigsberg
Don Ameche	Dominic Felix Amici
Julie Andrews	Julia Vernon
Ann Margret	Ann-Margret Olsson

*Gerald Ford took the name of his adoptive parents.

Professional Name	Original Name
Beatrice Arthur	Bernice Frankel
Ed Asner	Yitzak Edward Asner
Fred Astaire	Frederick Austerlitz
Lauren Bacall	Betty Joan Perske
Lucille Ball	Dianne Belmont
Anne Bancroft	Anne Italiano
John Barrymore	John Blythe
Warren Beatty	Henry Warren Beatty
Bonnie Bedelia	Bonnie Culkin
Pat Benetar	Patricia Andrejewski
Tony Bennett	Anthony Dominick Benedetto
Jack Benny	Joseph Kubelsky
Robbie Benson	Robert Segal
Ingmar Bergman	Ernst Ingmar Bergman
Milton Berle	Milton Berlinger
Irving Berlin	Israel Baline
Joey Bishop	Joseph Abraham Gottlieb
Robert Blake	Michael James Vijencio Gubitosi
Blondie	Deborah Harry
Jon Bon Jovi	John Bonjiovi
Bono	Paul Hewson
Sonny Bono	Salvatore Bono
Pat Boone	Charles Eugene Boone
Victor Borge	Borge Rosenbaum
David Bowie	David Jones
Max Brand	Gerald Kenneth Tierney
Beau Bridges	Lloyd Vernet Bridges III
Charles Bronson	Charles Buchinsky
Albert Brooks	Albert Einstein
Mel Brooks	Melvin Kaminsky
Yul Brynner	Taidje Kahn, Jr.
George Burns	Nathan Birnbaum
Ellen Burstyn	Edna Rae Gillooly
Richard Burton	Richard Jenkins
Nicholas Cage	Nicholas Coppola
Michael Caine	Maurice Micklewhite
Maria Callas	Maria Anna Sophia Cecilia Kalogeropoulos
Dyan Cannon	Samile Diane Friesen
Kate Capshaw	Kathleen Sue Nail
Vikki Carr	Florencia Bisenta de Casillas Martinez Cardona
Diahann Carroll	Carol Diahann Johnson
Ray Charles	Ray Charles Robinson
Charo	Maria Rosaria Pilar Martinez Molina Baeza
Chevy Chase	Cornelius Crane Chase
Chubby Checker	Ernest Evans
Cher	Cherilyn Sarkisian
Eric Clapton	Eric Clap
Patsey Cline	Virginia Patterson Hensley
Lee J. Cobb	Leo Jacob
Perry Como	Pierino Como
Bert Convy	Bernard Whalen Patrick Convy
Alice Cooper	Vincent Damon Furnier
David Copperfield	David Kotkin
Howard Cosell	Howard William Cohen
Elvis Costello	Declan Patrick McManus
Joan Crawford	Lucille Le Sueur
Bing Crosby	Harry Lillis Crosby
Tom Cruise	Thomas Cruise Mapother IV
Tony Curtis	Bernard Schwartz
Rodney Dangerfield	Jacob Cohen
Dawn	Joyce Elaine Vincent
Doris Day	Doris Kappelhoff
Sandra Dee	Alexandra Zuck
John Denver	Henry John Deutschendorf, Jr.
Bo Derek	Mary Cathleen Collins Derek
Danny DeVito	Daniel Michaeli
Susan Dey	Susan Smith
Marlene Dietrich	Maria von Losch
Phyllis Diller	Phyllis Driver
Kirk Douglas	Issur Danielovitch Demsky
Mike Douglas	Michael Delaney Dowd, Jr.
Patty Duke	Anna Marie Duke
Faye Dunaway	Dorothy Faye Dunaway
Bob Dylan	Robert Zimmerman

Professional Name	Original Name
Sheena Easton	Sheena Shirley Orr
Buddy Ebsen	Christian Ebsen, Jr.
Barbara Eden	Barbara Huffman
Edge	David Evans
Mama Cass Elliot	Ellen Naomi Cohen
Elvira	Cassandra Peterson
Werner Erhard	Jack Rosenberg
Dale Evans	Francis Octavia Smith
Chad Everett	Raymond Lee Cramton
Douglas Fairbanks	Julius Ullman
Morgan Fairchild	Patsy Ann McClenny
Mia Farrow	Maria de Lourdes Villiers Farrow
Farrah Fawcett	Mary Farrah Fawcett
Sally Field	Sally Mahoney
W.C. Fields	William Claude Dukenfield
Dame Margot Fonteyn	Margaret Hookham
Glenn Ford	Gwllyn Samuel Newton Ford
John Forsythe	John Freund
Jodie Foster	Alicia Christian Foster
Michael Fox	Michael Andrew Fox
Redd Foxx	John Elroy Sanford
Anthony Franciosa	Anthony Papaleo
Connie Francis	Concetta Franconero
Carlton Fredericks	Harold Casper Frederick Kaplan
Fresh Prince	Will Smith
Greta Garbo	Greta Gustafson
Ava Gardner	Lucy Johnson
Judy Garland	Frances Gumm
James Garner	James Baumgarner
Crystal Gayle	Brenda Gail Webb Gatzimos
Boy George	George Alan O'Dowd
Barry Gibb	Douglas Gibb
Whoopi Goldberg	Caryn Johnson
Cary Grant	Archibald Leach
Lee Grant	Lyova Haskell Rosenthal
Peter Graves	Peter Arness
Joel Grey	Joel Katz

Professional Name	Original Name
Robert Guillaume	Robert Williams
Buddy Hackett	Leonard Hacker
Halston	Roy Halston Frowick
Hammer	Stanley Kirk Hacker Burrell
Rex Harrison	Reginald Cary
Laurence Harvey	Lavrushka Skikne
Helen Hayes	Helen Brown
Margaux Hemingway	Margot Hemmingway
Audrey Hepburn	Audrey Hepburn-Ruston
Pee Wee Herman	Paul Rubenfeld
Barbara Hershey	Barbara Herzstine
William Holden	William Beedle
Billie Holiday	Eleanora Fagan
Bob Hope	Leslie Townes Hope
Harry Houdini	Ehrich Weiss
Rock Hudson	Roy Scherer, Jr.
Engelbert Humperdinck	Arnold Dorsey
Mary Beth Hurt	Mary Supinger
Lauren Hutton	Mary Laurence Hutton
Billy Idol	William Board
Wolfman Jack	Robert Smith
Elton John	Reginald Kenneth Dwight
Don Johnson	Donald Wayne
Al Jolson	Asa Yoelson
Tom Jones	Thomas Jones Woodward
Louis Jourdan	Louis Gendre
Boris Karloff	William Henry Pratt
Danny Kaye	David Kaminsky
Diane Keaton	Diane Hall
Michael Keaton	Michael Douglas
Chaka Khan	Yvette Stevens
Larry King	Larry Zeigler
Ben Kingsley	Krishna Banji
Nastassia Kinski	Nastassja Naksynznki
Ted Knight	Tadeus Wladyslaw Konopka
Kreskin	George Joseph Kresge Jr.
Cheryl Ladd	Cheryl Stoppelmoor
Bert Lahr	Irving Lahrheim

Professional Name	Original Name
Ann Landers	Esther "Eppie" Pauline Friedman Lederer
Michael Landon	Eugene Michael Orowitz
Stan Laurel	Arthur Stanley Jefferson Laurel
Piper Laurie	Rosetta Jacobs
Steve Lawrence	Sidney Leibowitz
Bruce Lee	Lee Yuen Kam
Gypsy Rose Lee	Louise Hovick
Peggy Lee	Norma Egstrom
Spike Lee	Shelton Jackson Lee
Huey Lewis	Hugh Cregg
Jerry Lewis	Joseph Levitch
Shari Lewis	Shari Hurwitz
Liberace	Wladziu Valentino Liberace
Hal Linden	Hal Lipshitz
Meat Loaf	Marvin Lee Aday
Jack Lord	J.J. Ryan
Sophia Loren	Sophia Scicoloni
Peter Lorre	Laszlo Loewenstein
Myrna Loy	Myrna Williams
Bela Lugosi	Bela Ferenc Blasko
Andie MacDowell	Rose Anderson MacDowell
Shirley MacLaine	Shirley Beaty
Madonna	Madonna Louise Veronica Ciccone
Lee Majors	Harvey Lee Yeary II
Karl Malden	Mladen Sekulovich
Jayne Mansfield	Vera Jane Palmer
Fredric March	Frederick Bickel
Dean Martin	Dino Crocetti
Chico Marx	Leonard Marx
Groucho Marx	Julius Henry Marx
Harpo Marx	Arthur Marx
Zeppo Marx	Herbert Marx
Walter Matthau	Walter Matuschanskayasky
Ethel Merman	Ethel Zimmerman
Paul McCartney	James Paul McCartney
Steve McQueen	Terence Stephen McQueen
George Michael	Georgious Panayiotou

Professional Name	Original Name
Joni Mitchell	Roberta Joan Anderson Mitchell
Marilyn Monroe	Norma Jean Mortenson Baker
Yves Montand	Ivo Livi
Demi Moore	Demi Gynes
Rita Moreno	Rosita Dolores Alverio
Pat Morita	Noriyuki Morita
Zero Mostel	Samuel Joel Mostel
Ricky Nelson	Eric Hilliard Nelson
Mike Nichols	Michael Igor Peschkowsky
Stevie Nicks	Stephanie Nicks
Chuck Norris	Carlos Ray
Kim Novak	Marilyn Paul Novak
Hugh O'Brian	Hugh J. Krampe
Tony Orlando	Michael Anthony Orlando Cassavitis
Peter O'Toole	Seamus O'Toole
Jack Palance	Walter Jack Palanuik
Jane Pauley	Margaret Jane Pauley
Minnie Pearl	Sarah Ophelia Colley Cannon
Gregory Peck	Eldred Gregory Peck
Bernadette Peters	Bernadette Lazarra
Christopher Pike	Kevin McFadden
Stephanie Powers	Stefania Federkiewicz
Paula Prentiss	Paula Ragusa
Priscilla Presley	Pricilla Wagner Beaulieu
♀	Prince Rogers Nelson
William Proxmire	Edward William Proxmire
Tony Randall	Leonard Rosenberg
Robert Redford	Charles Robert Redford
Donna Reed	Donna Belle Mullenger
Della Reese	Delloreese Patricia Early
Judge Reinhold	Edward Ernest Reinhold Jr.
Lee Remick	Ann Remick
Debbie Reynolds	Mary Frances Reynolds
Edward G. Robinson	Emanuel Goldenberg
Ginger Rogers	Virginia McMath
Roy Rogers	Leonard Slye
Mickey Rooney	Joe Yule, Jr.

Professional Name	Original Name
Theresa Russell	Theresa Paup
Buffy Sainte-Marie	Beverly Sainte-Marie
Susan Saint James	Susan Miller
Soupy Sales	Milton Hines
Susan Sarandon	Susan Tomaling
Leo Sayer	Gerald Sayer
John Saxon	Carmen Orrico
Jane Seymour	Joyce Frankenberg
Omar Sharif	Michael Shalhouz
Artie Shaw	Arthur Arshowsky
Charlie Sheen	Carlos Irwin Estevez
Brooke Shields	Christa Brooke Shields
Talia Shire	Talia Coppola
Dinah Shore	Frances "Fanny" Rose Shore
Beverly Sills	Belle "Bubbles" Silverman
Ione Skye	Ione Skye Leitch
Phoebe Snow	Phoebe Loeb
Suzanne Somers	Suzanne Mahoney
Elke Sommer	Elke Schletz
Ann Sothern	Harriet Lake
Sissy Spacek	Mary Elizabeth Spacek
Robert Stack	Robert Modini
Sylvester Stallone	Michael Sylvester Stallone
Jean Stapleton	Jeanne Murray
Ringo Starr	Richard Starkey
Cat Stevens (Islam Mohammed)	Steven Georgion
Connie Stevens	Concetta Anne Ingolia
Sting	Gordon Matthew Sumner
Sly Stone	Sylvester Stone
Meryl Streep	Mary Louise Streep
Donna Summer	La Donna Andrea Gaines
Max von Sydow	Carl Adolph von Sydow
Mr. T	Lawrence Tureaud
Rip Taylor	Charles Elmer Jr.
Robert Taylor	Spangler Brugh
Danny Thomas	Amos Jacobs
Tiny Tim	Herbert Buckingham Khaury
Lily Tomlin	Mary Jean Tomlin

Professional Name	Original Name
Rip Torn	Elmore Rual Torn Jr.
Randy Travis	Randy Traywick
Tina Turner	Annie Mae Bullock
Twiggy	Leslie Hornby
Rudolph Valentino	Rudolpho Alphonzo Raffaelo Pierre Filibut Guglielmo di Valentina D'Antonguolla
Rudy Vallee	Hubert Prior Vallée
Abigail Van Buren	Pauline Esther "Popo" Friedman Phillips
Nancy Walker	Ann Myrtle Swoyer
Mike Wallace	Myron Wallace
Andy Warhol	Andrew Warhola
Muddy Waters	McKinley Morganfield
John Wayne	Marion Michael Morrison
Sigourney Weaver	Susan Weaver
Raquel Welch	Raquel Tejada
Tuesday Weld	Susan Kerr Weld
Gene Wilder	Jerome Silberman
Bruce Willis	Walter Bruce Willis
Flip Wilson	Clerow Wilson
Debra Winger	Mary Debra Winger
Shelley Winters	Shirley Schrift
Stevie Wonder	Steveland Morris Hardaway
Natalie Wood	Natasha Gurdin
Jane Wyman	Sarah Jane Fulks
Tammy Wynette	Wynette Pugh
Ed Wynn	Isaiah Edwin Leopold
Loretta Young	Gretchen Young
Sean Young	Mary Sean Young

Fascinating Facts about Names

Birthrights
In some tribal societies children are not considered born until they are named. Frequently the child's name consists of a statement (that is, rather than having a pool of names as Western culture does, parents in these societies name children with a phrase that describes the circumstances of the child's birth, the family's current activities, and so on). Translated, such names might be "We are glad we moved to Memphis," or "A girl at last," or "Too little rain."

Bible Studies
It's been estimated that the majority of people in the Western hemisphere have names from the Bible. Women outnumber men, yet there are 3,037 male names in the Bible and only 181 female names. The New Testament is a more popular source of names than the Old Testament.

Change of Habit
Popes traditionally choose a new name upon their election by the College of Cardinals. The practice began in 844 A.D. when a priest whose real name was Boca de Porco (Pig's Mouth) was elected. He changed his name to Sergious II.

Saint Who?
Saints' names are a common source of names in the U.S. But saints who are popular in other countries contribute very unusual, even unpronounceable, names for children born in the U.S.—like Tamjesdegerd, Borhedbesheba, and Jafkeranaegzia.

Them Bones
Praise-God Barebones had a brother named If-Christ-Had-Not-Died-For-Thee-Thou-Wouldst-Have-Been-Damned, who was called "Damned Barebones" for short.

Hello, God?
Terril William Clark is listed in the phone book under his new name—God. Now he's looking for someone to publish a book he's written. "Let's face it," he reportedly said. "The last book with my name on it was a blockbuster."

The Status Quo

The most commonly given names in English-speaking countries from about 1750 to the present are drawn from a list with only 179 entries (discounting variations in spelling). Essentially the same practice has been followed in naming children since at least the sixteenth century, though the use of middle names has increased over the years.

It's Mainly Relative

A recent study suggests that about two-thirds of the population of the U.S. is named to honor somebody. Of the people who are namesakes, about 60 percent are named after a relative and 40 percent for someone outside the family.

Once Is Enough

Ann Landers wrote about a couple who had six children, all named Eugene Jerome Dupuis, Junior. The children answered to One, Two, Three, Four, Five, and Six, respectively. Can you imagine what the IRS, the Social Security Administration, and any other institution would do with the Dupuises?

In Sickness and Health

Tonsilitis Jackson has brothers and sisters named Meningitis, Appendicitis, and Peritonitis.

The Old College Try

A couple in Louisiana named their children after colleges: Stanford, Duke, T'Lane, Harvard, Princeton, Auburn, and Cornell. The parents' names? Stanford, Sr., and Loyola.

Peace at All Costs

Harry S Truman owed his middle name, the initial S, to a compromise his parents worked out. By using only the initial, they were able to please both his grandfathers, whose names were Shippe and Solomon.

Initials Only

A new recruit in the U.S. Army filled out all the forms he was presented with as he always had in school: R. (only) B. (only) Jones. You guessed it—from then on he was, as far as the Army cared about it, Ronly Bonly Jones, and all his records, dogtags, and discharge papers proved the point again and again.

Sticks and Stones May Break My Bones...

The nicknames children make up for each other tend to fall into four patterns: those stemming from the physical appearance of the child, those based on either real or imaginary mental traits (brains or idiocy), those based on social ranking or other relationships, and finally, those based on plays on the child's name. Children who don't conform to the values or looks of their peers are likely to pick up more nicknames than those who do. In these ways nicknames often function as instruments of social control.

The Name's the Game

John Hotvet, of Minnetonka, Minnesota, is—of course—a veterinarian. Sometimes names and occupations get inextricably interwoven. Consider these names and professions:

Dr. Zoltan Ovary, gynecologist
Mr. A. Moron, Commissioner of Education for the Virgin Islands
Reverend Christian Church and Reverend God
Mr. Thomas Crapper of Crapper, Ltd Toilets, in London, who entitled his autobiography *Flushed with Pride*
Assorted physicians named Doctor, Docter, or Doktor
Cardinal Sin, Archbishop of Manila, the Philippines
Mr. Groaner Digger, undertaker in Houston
Mr. I. C. Shivers, iceman
Ms. Justine Tune, chorister in Westminster Choir College, Princeton, New Jersey
Ms. Lavender Sidebottom, masseuse at Elizabeth Arden's in New York City
Mssrs. Lawless and Lynch, attorneys in Jamaica, New York
Major Minor, U.S. Army
Diana Nyad, champion long-distance swimmer
Mssrs. Plummer and Leek, plumbers in Sheringham, Norfolk, England
Mr. Ronald Supena, lawyer
Mrs. Screech, singing teacher in Victoria, British Columbia
Mr. Vroom, motorcycle dealer in Port Elizabeth, South Africa
Mssrs. Wyre and Tapping, detectives in New York City
Ms. A. Forest Burns, professional forester
Dr. McNutt, head of a mental hospital, and Dr. Paul Looney, psychiatrist
Mr. Vice, arrested 820 times and convicted 421 times
Dr. Slaughter, surgeon, Dr. Needles, pediatrician, and Dr. Bonebreak, chiropractor

Time Capsule Names

Celebrities and events often inspire parents in their choices of names for children. Many people are now "dated" by their World War II names, like Pearl (Harbor), Douglas (MacArthur), Dwight (Eisenhower—whose mother named him Dwight David to avoid all nicknames, but whom everyone called Ike!), and Franklin (Roosevelt). Films and film stars contribute their share of names: Scarlett O'Hara and Rhett Butler have countless namesakes whose parents were swept away by *Gone with the Wind*. Madonna, Elvis, Prince, and virtually all other big stars have their own namesakes as well.

The UN Family

One couple took the time capsule concept to an extreme and named their triplets, born on April 5, 1979, Carter, Begin, and Sadat—to honor U.S. President Jimmy Carter, Israeli Prime Minister Menachem Begin, and Egyptian President Anwar Sadat, the three principle signers of the peace treaty signed in Washington, D.C., on March 1979.

They Add Up

Dick Crouser likes to collect unusual names. Some names tell stories, like Fanny Pistor Bodganoff (although Mr. Crouser admits that he doesn't know what a "bodgan" is); some leave messages, like Hazel Mae Call; some aren't likely to add to their owner's self-esteem, like Seldom Wright and Harley Worthit; some are mere truisms, like Wood Burns; while others announce what you might call philosophies of life, like Daily Goforth and Hazel B. Good.

Truth Stranger than Fiction

Dick Neff, columnist of Advertising Age, invited his readers to contribute lists of real names they had encountered that are odd and/or funny, to say the least. Among them were the following: Stanley Zigafoose, Cigar Stubbs, Ladorise Quick, Mad Laughinhouse, Lester Chester Hester, Effie Bong, Dillon C. Quattlebaum, Twila Szwrk, Harry E. Thweatt, Benjamin E. Dymshits, Elmer Ploof, Whipple Filoon, Sweetie Belle Rufus, Peculiar Smith, John Dunwrong, All Dunn, Willie Wunn, H. Whitney Clappsaddle, W. Wesley Muckenfuss, Rudolph J. Ramstack, Sarabelle Scraper Roach, James R. Stufflebeam, Shanda Lear, Arthur Crudder, Mary Crapsey, Memory Lane, Troy Mumpower, Santa Beans, Sividious Stark, Cleveland Biggerstaff, Trinkle Bott, Cleopatra Barksdale, Spring Belch, Fairy Blessing, Royal Fauntleroy Butler, Bozy Ball, Carl W. Gigl, Joy Holy, Peenie Fase, Che Che Creech, J. B. Outhouse, Katz Meow, Stephanie Snatchole, I. O. Silver, Helen Bunpain, Birdie Fawncella Feltis, Elight Starling, Farmer Slusher, Nebraska Minor, Bill Grumbles, Peter Rabbitt, Carbon Petroleum Dubbs, Kick-a-hole-in-the-soup, Wong Bong Fong, Newton

Hooton, Sonia Schmeckpeeper, Lewie Wirmelskirchen, Lolita Beanblossom, Liselotte Pook, and Irmgard Quapp.

Popular Names?

In 1979, the Pennsylvania Health Department discovered these two first names among the 159,000 birth certificates issued in the state that year—Pepsi and Cola.

A Boy Named Sue

Researchers have found that boys who had peculiar first names had a higher incidence of mental problems than boys with common ones; no similar correlation was found for girls.

He Who Quacks Last

In a government check of a computer program, researchers turned up a real-life Donald Duck. It seems that programmers used his name to create a bogus G.I. to check out records—and found out he really existed. The Army Engineer won fame and a visit to the Johnny Carson Show as a result of this discovery.

Too-o-o-o Much

Many people dislike their own names. The most common reasons given for this dislike are that the names "sound too ugly," that they're old-fashioned, too hard to pronounce, too common, too uncommon, too long, sound too foreign, are too easy for people to joke about, and that they sound too effeminate (for men) or too masculine (for women).

What Are Parents Thinking?

It may have seemed like a good joke at the time, but did Mr. Homer Frost consider his children's future when he named them Winter Night, Jack White, Snow, Dew, Hail, and Cold (Frost)? And what was Mr. Wind thinking when he named his four children North, South, East, and West (Wind)?

For the Birds

A. Bird was the assistant manager of Britain's Royal Society for the Protection of Birds. Members of his staff were Barbara Buzzard, John Partridge, Celia Peacock, Helen Peacock, and Dorothy Rook.

Historical Irony
On July 30, 1980, *Good Morning America* announced that Richard Nixon arrested Jimmy Carter in Detroit.

Is Nothing Private Anymore?
Mr. & Mrs. Bra, a couple from South Dakota, named their two daughters Iona and Anita (Bra).

The Power of Disney
Walt Disney's popular movie *Aladdin* was released in 1992. Aladdin's love interest was named Princess Jasmine. In 1995, Jasmine is the #21 name for all girls in the U.S., the #12 name for Hispanic-American girls, and the #2 name for African-American girls.

Last But Not Least
Zachary Zzzzra has been listed in the *Guinness Book of World Records* as making "the most determined attempt to be the last personal name in a local telephone directory" in San Francisco. That happened before his place was challenged by one Vladimir Zzzzzzabakov. Zzzzra reports that he called Zzzzzzabakov and demanded to know his real name (Zzzzra's name is really his own, he says). Zzzzzzabakov told him it was none of his . . . business. At any rate, true to his reputation for determination, Zzzzra changed his name to regain his former — or latter? — position. When the new phone book appeared, he was relieved to find himself comfortably in the last place again, as Zachary Zzzzzzzzzra. Unknown to him, the contender, Zzzzzzabakov, had disappeared.

The End
One family that was not terribly successful in limiting its expansion has a series of children called, respectively, Finis, Addenda, Appendix, Supplement, and (last but not least) Errata.

Birthstones and Flowers

January

Birthstone: garnet

Flower: carnation

February

Birthstone: amethyst

Flower: violet

March

Birthstone: aquamarine

Flower: jonquil

April

Birthstone: diamond

Flower: sweet pea

May

Birthstone: emerald

Flower: lily of the valley

June

Birthstone: pearl

Flower: rose

July

Birthstone: ruby

Flower: larkspur

August

Birthstone: peridot

Flower: gladiolus

September

Birthstone: sapphire

Flower: aster

October

Birthstone: opal

Flower: calendula

November

Birthstone: topaz

Flower: chrysanthemum

December

Birthstone: turquoise

Flower: narcissus

The Baby Name List

This list will provide over 30,000 choices for you to consider as you decide what you'll name your baby. It is intended to be the most useful and contemporary list available. Here are some sample entries that explain how the list works:

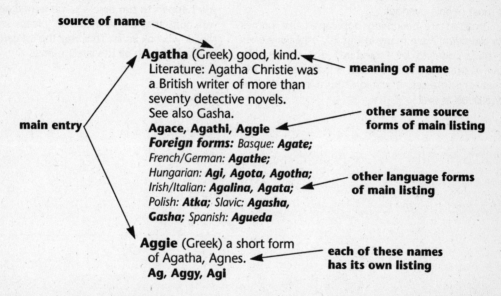

source of name

meaning of name

other same source forms of main listing

other language forms of main listing

main entry

Agatha (Greek) good, kind.
Literature: Agatha Christie was a British writer of more than seventy detective novels.
See also Gasha.
Agace, Agathi, Aggie
Foreign forms: Basque: **Agate**;
French/German: **Agathe**;
Hungarian: **Agi, Agota, Agotha**;
Irish/Italian: **Agalina, Agata**;
Polish: **Atka**; Slavic: **Agasha,
Gasha**; Spanish: **Agueda**

Aggie (Greek) a short form of Agatha, Agnes.
Ag, Aggy, Agi

each of these names has its own listing

One of the most fruitful sources of names for this list was published birth announcements in newspapers from all over the country. The names that turned up in the papers give the list a distinctively contemporary flavor that also reflects regional preferences. In the South, for instance, parents are much more apt to name a baby with what Northerners would call a nickname, like Bessie or Bobbie, while Easterners seem to favor traditional and French variants of traditional names. These birth announcements also showed that parents are creating many new variations and spellings, like Cyndie or Mychal, which are included.

Separate entries appear in this list for many names that older books note only as "nicknames," because names like Jenny, Terry, Beth, or Mickey are appearing on birth certificates all over the country! You'll notice that words like "nickname," "pet name," "diminutive," and so on are not used, to avoid suggesting that you shouldn't use a certain name because it isn't a traditional given name. Instead, you'll find more informative phrases like "a short form," "a familiar form," "a feminine form," and so on.

Some of the feminine forms of traditionally male names are identified for you, since you may not recognize the connections—Carol is a form of Charles that most people overlook.

Surnames are becoming popular as first names these days. You'll see many in this list, especially ones that have come to be "standard" first names, like Logan, Carter, Parker, and Reed. But if you're in the market for surnames, it wouldn't hurt to check your phone book as well.

Many African-American names in use today were created quite recently and are therefor not listed in most baby name books. However, you'll find them listed here with lots of interesting variations.

To help you choose the very best name from all the ones you like, note your favorites and rate them on the baby name worksheets in the back of the book. If you happen to run across some terrific new names or variations that aren't included, please send them to Meadowbrook Press. That way the list can be updated to keep up with all the latest names.

Girls'
Names

Abbey, Abbie, Abby
(Hebrew) familiar forms of
Abigail.
Abbe, Abbi, Abbye, Abia

Abebi (Yoruba) we asked for
her and we got her.

Abeer (Arabic) fragrance.

Abia (Arabic) great
Abbia, Abbiah, Abiah, Abya

Abigail (Hebrew) father's joy.
Bible: one of the wives of King
David. See also Gail.
**Abagael, Abagale, Abagil,
Abbegail, Abbegale,
Abbegayle, Abbigail,
Abbigale, Abbigayle,
Abbygail, Abbygale, Abegail,
Abegale, Abegayle, Abgail,
Abgale, Abgayle, Abigale,**

Abigayil, Avigail
Foreign forms: English:
Abagail, Abbey, Abigal, Abigel;
Irish: **Abaigeal, Abbygayle,
Abigael, Abigayle**

Abra (Hebrew) mother of
many nations. A feminine form
of Abraham.
Abree, Abri
Foreign forms: Basque:
Abarrane; *French:* **Abrielle;**
Italian) **Abriana**

Acacia (Greek) thorny.
Mythology: the acacia tree
symbolizes immortality and
resurrection. See also Casey.
Acey, Acie, Cacia, Casia, Kacia

Ada (Latin) helpful. (German)
a short form of Adelaide.
(English) prosperous; happy.
**Adabelle, Adalee, Adan,
Adda, Addia, Addie, Adia,
Adiah, Aidah, Auda, Aude**
Foreign forms: French: **Aida;**
Hebrew: **Adah**

Adalia (German, Spanish)
noble.
**Adal, Adala, Adalee, Adali,
Adalie, Adalin, Adaly, Adalyn,
Addal, Addala, Addaly**

Adama (Phoenician) woman,
humankind. (Hebrew) earth;
woman of the red earth.

A feminine form of Adam.
Adamma
Foreign forms: Spanish: **Adana,
Adanna**

Adara (Greek) beauty. (Arabic)
virgin.
**Adair, Adaira, Adaora, Adare,
Adaria, Addie, Adra**

Addie (Greek, German) a famil-
iar form of Adelaide, Adrienne.
**Adde, Addey, Addi, Addia,
Addy, Adey, Adi, Adie, Ady,
Atti, Attie, Atty**

Adelaide (German) noble and
serene. See also Ada, Adeline,
Adelle, Delia, Della, Heidi.
**Adeela, Adelade, Adelaid,
Adelei, Adelheid, Adeliade,
Aley, Elke, Laidey, Laidy**
Foreign forms: Czech: **Adelka;**
English: **Adeline;** *Hawaiian:* **Akela;**
Irish: **Ailis;** *Italian/Spanish:*
Adelaida; *Polish:* **Adelajda, Ela;**
Russian: **Adaliya**

Adeline (English) a form of
Adelaide. See also Delaney.
**Adalina, Adaline, Addie,
Adelita, Adeliya, Adelle,
Adelyn, Adelynn, Adena,
Adilene, Adina, Adinna,
Adlena, Adlene, Adlin, Adline,
Aline, Alita**
Foreign forms: French:
Adelinda, Adette; *Italian:* **Adelina**

Adelle (German, English) a short form of Adelaide, Adeline.
Adel, Adelia, Adelista, Adell, Adella
Foreign forms: French: **Adela, Adele**

Adena (Greek, Hebrew) noble; adorned.
Adeana, Adeen, Adeena, Aden, Adene, Adenia, Adina

Adrienne (Greek) rich. (Latin) dark. A feminine form of Adrian. See also Hadriane.
Addie, Adrien, Adriena, Adrienna
Foreign forms: Dutch: **Adrie;** English: **Adriane, Adrianne;** Italian: **Adriana, Adrianna**

Afra (Hebrew) young doe. (Arabic) earth color.
Affery, Affrey, Affrie, Aphra, Efra, Ofra, Ofrat

Afton (English) from Afton, England.
Aftan, Aftine, Aftyn

Agate (English) a semiprecious stone.
Aggie

Agatha (Greek) good, kind. Literature: Agatha Christie was a British writer of more than seventy detective novels.
Agace, Agathi, Aggie
Foreign forms: Basque: **Agate;** French/German: **Agathe;** Hungarian: **Agi, Agota, Agotha;** Irish/Italian: **Agalina, Agata;** Polish: **Atka;** Slavic: **Agasha, Gasha;** Spanish: **Agueda**

Aggie (Greek) a familiar form of Agatha, Agnes.
Ag, Aggy, Agi

Agnes (Greek) pure. See also Nessa, Nessie.
Aganetha, Aggie, Agneis, Agnelia, Agnella, Agnesa, Agnesina, Agness, Agnesse, Agneti, Agnetta
Foreign forms: Danish/Swedish: **Agneta;** English: **Agna, Anice, Anissa;** French: **Agnés, Agnies;** Irish: **Aignéis, Aghna, Ina, Una;** Italian: **Agnesca, Agnese, Agnola, Ines;** Lithuanian: **Agne, Agniya;** Polish: **Agnieszka;** Russian: **Inessa, Nyusha;** Spanish: **Inésita, Inez, Necha, Ynez;** Slavic: **Aneska, Neza**

Ahava (Hebrew) beloved.
Ahiva

Aiko (Japanese) beloved.

Ailani (Hawaiian) chief.

Aileen (Scottish) light bearer. (Irish) a form of Helen.
Aila, Ailean, Ailene, Aili, Ailina, Ailinn, Aleen, Aleena, Aleene, Alene, Aliana, Alianna, Alina, Aline, Allene, Alline, Allyn, Alyna, Alyne, Alynne

Aimee (Latin) an alternate form of Amy. (French) loved.
Aime, Aimée, Aimey, Aimi, Aimia, Aimie, Aimy

Ainsley (Scottish) my own meadow.
Ainslee, Ainsleigh, Ainslie, Ainsly, Ansley, Aynslee, Aynsley, Aynslie

Aisha (Swahili) life. (Arabic) woman. See also Asia.
Aesha, Aeshah, Aiesha, Aieshah, Aishah, Aishia, Aishiah, Asha, Ashia, Ayisha, Ayishah, Aysa, Ayse, Aysha, Ayshah, Ayshe, Ayshea, Ayshia, Aytza, Azia, Yiesha
Foreign forms: American: **Iesha, Isha, Ishana, Ishanda;** Persian: **Ayasha, Ayesha, Ayeshah**

Akanke (Yoruba) to meet her is to love her.

Akiko (Japanese) bright light.

Alameda (Spanish) poplar tree.

Alana, Alanna (Irish) attractive; peaceful. (Hawaiian) offering. A feminine form of Alan. See also Lana.
Alaina, Alaine, Alainna, Alainnah, Alanah, Alane, Alani, Alania, Alanis, Alanna, Alannah, Alawna, Alayna, Alayne, Allana, Allanah, Allena, Alleyna, Allyn
Foreign form: Greek: Aleni

Alba (Latin) from Alba, Italy, a city on a white hill. A feminine form of Alban.
Albina, Albine, Albinia

Alberta (German, French) noble and bright. A feminine form of Albert. See also Bertha.
Auberte
Foreign forms: English: Elberta, Elbertine; Greek: Alverta; Italian: Albertina; Latvian: Albertine; Polish: Albertyna, Albertyne, Alaka; Spanish: Bertunga

Alcina (Greek) strong minded.
Alceena, Alcine, Alcinia, Alseena, Alsinia, Alsyna, Alzina

Alea, Aleah (Arabic) high, exalted. (Persian) God's being.
Aleea, Aleeah, Alia, Alleea, Alleeah, Allia

Alethea (Greek) truth.
Alathea, Alathia, Aletha, Alethia, Aletia, Alithea, Alithia, Olethea
Foreign forms: English: Aleta; Italian/Spanish: Aletea

Alexa (Greek) a short form of Alexandra.
Alekia, Aleksa, Aleksha, Alex

Alexandra (Greek) defender of mankind. A feminine form of Alexander. History: the last czarina of Russia. See also Sandra.
Aleix, Aleka, Aleks, Alexande, Alexina, Alexine, Alexis, Alexx, Alexxandra, Alexzand, Alexzandra, Alix, Aljexi, Lexandra, Lexia, Olesia, Ritsa, Sondra
Foreign forms: Basque: Alesandese; Bulgarian: Alekko; Czech: Leska; French: Alexandre, Alexandrie, Alexandrine; Italian: Alesandra, Alessandra; Russian: Aleksandra, Aleksasha, Alla, Sasha, Shura; Spanish: Alandra, Alejandra, Xandra

Alexandria (Greek) an alternate form of Alexandra.
Alexanderia, Alexanderina, Alexanderine, Alexandrea, Alexandrena, Alexia, Alexzandrea, Alexzandria

Foreign forms: Spanish: Alexandrina, Drinka

Alexis (Greek) a short form of Alexandra.
Alexcis, Alexes, Alexi, Alexiou, Alexisia, Alexius, Alexsia, Alexus, Alexx, Alexxis, Alexys, Alexyss, Lexis

Alfreda (English) elf counselor; wise counselor. A feminine form of Alfred. See also Effie, Elfrida, Freda, Frederica.
Alfi, Alfie, Alfredda, Alfreeda, Alfrieda, Alfy

Ali (Greek) a familiar form of Alicia, Alisha, Alison.
Allea, Alli, Allie, Ally, Aly

Alice (Greek) truthful. (German) noble. See also Alisa, Alison, Alyssa, Elke.
Adelice, Aleece, Alica, Alican, Alicie, Alicyn, Aliece, Alies, Aliese, Alis, Alison, Alize, Alleece, Alles, Allesse, Allice, Allie, Allis, Allisa, Allise, Allisse, Allix, Alysa, Aluse, Alysse
Foreign forms: English: Alicia; Hawaiian: Aleeka, Aleka, Alika; Hungarian: Alisz, Aliz; Irish: Ailis; Polish: Ala; Scottish: Aili

Alicia (English) an alternate form of Alice. See also Elicia, Licia.
Aleecia, Ali, Alicea, Alicha, Alichia, Alician, Alicja, Alicya, Aliecia, Alisha, Allicea, Alycia, Ilysa
Foreign forms: American: *Aleesha, Aleisha;* Greek: *Alecea, Alecia*

Alida (Latin) small and winged. (Spanish) noble. See also Lida.
Alidia, Alita, Alleda, Allida, Allidah, Alydia, Elida, Oleda
Foreign forms: French: *Alette;* German: *Alda, Aleda, Alyda;* Greek: *Aleta;* Italian: *Aletta;* Spanish: *Adelina, Alita, Allita*

Alika (Hawaiian) truthful. (Swahili) most beautiful.
Alica, Alikah, Alike, Alikee, Aliki

Alina, Aline (Slavic) bright. (Scottish) fair. (English) a short form of Adeline.
Allyna, Allyne, Alyna, Alyne
Foreign form: Dutch: *Alene*

Alisa, Alissa (Greek) an alternate form of Alice. See also Elisa, Ilisa.
Alisia, Alise, Alisse, Alisza, Alisse, Alisza, Alyssa

Alisha (Greek) truthful. (German) noble. (English) an alternate form of Alicia. See also Elisha, Lisha.
Aleasha, Aleashea, Aleasia, Aleesha, Aleisha, Alesha, Ali, Aliesha, Alieshai, Aliscia, Alishah, Alishay, Alishaye, Alishea, Alishya, Alisia, Alissia, Alitsha, Alysha, Alysia
Foreign form: Hebrew: *Ilisha*

Alison, Allison (English) a form of Alice. See also Lissie.
Ali, Alicen, Alicyn, Alisann, Alisanne, Alisen, Alisson, Alisun, Alisyn, Alles, Allesse, Allie, Allis, Allise
Foreign form: Irish: *Allsun*

Alix (Greek) a short form of Alexandra.
Allix, Alyx

Aliya (Hebrew) ascender.
Alee, Aleea, Aleia, Aleya, Alia, Aliyah, Aly

Aliye (Arabic) noble.

Aliza (Hebrew) joyful.
Aleeza, Alieza, Aliezah, Alitza, Alizah

Allegra (Latin) cheerful.
Ali, Allie, Legra
Foreign forms: Spanish: *Alegria, Allegria*

Allie (Greek) a familiar form of Alice.
Aleni, Alenna, Aleen, Allene, Alline

Allyson, Alyson (English) alternate forms of Alison, Allison.
Allysen, Allyson, Allysun, Alyson

Alma (Arabic) learned. (Latin) soul.
Almah

Almira (Arabic) aristocratic, princess; exalted. (Spanish) from Almeíra, Spain. See also Mira.
Allmeera, Allmeria, Allmira, Almeera, Almeeria, Almeira, Almeria, Almire
Foreign form: English: *Elmira*

Althea (Greek) wholesome; healer. History: Althea Gibson was the first African-American to win a major tennis title. See also Thea.
Altheda, Altheya, Althia
Foreign forms: English: *Altha, Eltha, Elthea, Eltheya, Elthia*

Alvina (English) friend to all; noble friend; friend to elves. A feminine form of Alvin. See also Elva, Vina.
Alveanea, Alveen, Alveena,

Alvina *(cont.)*
Alveenia, Alvenea, Alvie, Alvincia, Alvine, Alvinea, Alvinesha, Alvinia, Alvinna, Alvita, Alvona, Alvyna, Alwin, Alwina, Alwyn, Elvina
Foreign forms: Dutch: **Alva;** Irish: **Ailbhe, Alvy**

Alycia (English) an alternate form of Alicia.
Allyce, Alycea, Alyse, Lycia

Alysa, Alyse, Alysse (Greek) alternate forms of Alice.
Alys, Alyss

Alisha, Alysia (Greek) alternate forms of Alisha.
Allysea, Allyscia, Alysea, Alyshia, Alysssha, Alyssia

Alyssa (Greek) rational. Botany: alyssum is a flowering herb. See also Alice, Elissa.
Alissa, Allissa, Allyssa, Ilyssa, Lyssa, Lyssah

Allysse (Greek) an alternate form of Alice.
Allys, Allyse, Allyss

Ama (African) born on Saturday.

Amada (Spanish) beloved.
Amadea, Amadi, Amadia, Amadita

Amaka (Zulu) fragrance.
Amakha

Amal (Arabic) hopeful.
Amala

Amanda (Latin) lovable. See also Manda.
Amada, Amanada, Amandah, Amandalee, Amandalyn, Amandi, Amandie, Amandy
Foreign forms: French: **Amandine;** Spanish: **Amata**

Amara (Greek) eternally beautiful. See also Mara.

Amaris (Hebrew) promised by God.
Amarissa, Maris

Amaya (Japanese) night rain.

Amber (French) amber.
Amberia, Amberise, Ambur
Foreign form: American: **Amberly**

Amberly (American) a familiar form of Amber.
Amberle, Amberlea, Amberlee, Amberlie, Amberlyn

Amelia (Latin) an alternate form of Emily. (German) hardworking. History: Amelia Earhart, an American aviator, was the first woman to fly solo across the Atlantic Ocean. See also Ima, Melia, Millie.
Amalia, Amaliya, Ameila, Ameley, Amelie, Amelina, Amelisa, Amella, Amilia, Amilina, Amilisa, Amillia, Amilyn, Amylia
Foreign forms: American: **Yamelia;** Czech: **Milka;** French: **Amélie, Ameline;** Spanish: **Amelita, Nuela**

Amelie (German) a familiar form of Amelia.
Amaley, Amalie, Amelee

Amina (Arabic) trustworthy, faithful. History: the mother of the prophet Mohammed.
Aminah, Aminda, Amindah, Aminta, Amintah

Amma (Hindi) god, godlike. Religion: another name for the Hindu goddess Shakti.

Amy (Latin) beloved. See also Emma.
Ame, Amey, Amia, Amiet, Amii, Amiiee, Amijo, Amiko, Amio, Ammie, Ammy, Amye, Amylyn
Foreign forms: English: **Amie;** French: **Aimee, Aimée, Ami, Esmé;** Italian/Spanish/Swedish: **Amada, Amata**

An (Chinese) peaceful.

Ana (Hawaian, Spanish) a form of Hannah.
Anabela

Ananda (Hindi) blissful.

Anastasia (Greek) resurrection. See also Nastasia, Stacey.
Anastacia, Anastase, Anastasha, Anastashia, Anastassia, Anastassya, Anastatia, Anastice
Foreign forms: *Czech:* **Anastazia;** *English:* **Anastace, Stacia;** *French:* **Anastacie, Anastasie;** *Irish:* **Annstás;** *Latvian:* **Anastasija;** *Spanish:* **Tasia**

Andrea (Greek) strong; courageous. (Latin) feminine. A feminine form of Andrew.
Andee, Andera, Anderea, Andi, Andra, Andrah, Andraia, Andraya, Andreah, Andreaka, Andrean, Andreane, Andreanne, Andree, Andreea, Andreia, Andreja, Andreka, Andrel, Andrell, Andrelle, Andrena, Andrene, Andreo, Andressa, Andrette, Andreya, Andriea, Andrieka, Andrienne, Andrietta, Andrija, Andrika, Andrina, Andris, Aundrea
Foreign forms: *Basque:* **Andere;** *Czech:* **Ondrea;** *English:* **Andreana, Andri, Andria, Andriana;** *French:* **Andrée;** *Irish:*

Aindrea, Andrewina, Ondrea; *Italian:* **Andreana**

Anela (Hawaiian) angel.

Angel (Greek) a short form of Angela.
Angell, Angil, Anjel

Angela (Greek) angel; messenger.
Angala, Anganita, Angel, Angelanell, Angelanette, Angele, Angelea, Angeleah, Angelee, Angeleigh, Angeles, Angeli, Angelia, Angelic, Angelica, Angella, Angelle, Angie, Anglea
Foreign forms: *English:* **Angelina, Angeline, Angelita, Angellita;** *French:* **Ange, Angèle, Angélique;** *German:* **Anjela;** *Hawaiian:* **Anakela;** *Hungarian:* **Angyalka;** *Irish:* **Aingeal;** *Polish:* **Aniela**

Angelica (Greek) an alternate form of Angela.
Angel, Angelici, Angeliki, Angellica, Angilica, Anjelica, Anjelika
Foreign form: *German:* **Angelika**

Angelina, Angeline (English) forms of Angela.
Angalena, Angalina, Angeleen, Angelena,

Angelene, Angeliana, Angeleana, Angellina, Angelyn, Angelyna, Angelyne, Angelynn, Angelynne, Anhelina, Anjelina

Angelique (French) a form of Angela.
Angeliqua, Angélique, Angilique, Anjelique

Angie (Greek) a familiar form of Angela.
Angee, Angey, Angi, Angy

Ani (Hawaiian) beautiful.

Anika (Czech) a familiar form of Anna.
Anaka, Aneeky, Aneka, Anekah, Anica, Anicka, Anik, Aniah, Anikka, Aniko, Anneka, Annik, Annika, Anouska

Anita (Spanish) a form of Ann, Anna. See also Nita.
Aneeta, Aneetah, Aneethah, Anetha, Anitha, Anithah, Anitia, Anitra, Anitte

Ann, Anne (English) gracious. A form of Hannah. See also Nan.
Ana, Anelle, Annalie, Annelisa, Annie, Anouche, Anouk
Foreign forms: *American:*

Ann, Anne (cont.)
Anetra; Basque: **Ane;** French:
Annette, Nanette; German:
Annchen; Hebrew: **Anais, Anaise;**
Hungarian: **Anci, Anikó, Anuska,
Anyu;** Latvian: **Aneta;** Lithuanian:
Anikke, Annze; Slavic: **Annik,
Annika;** Spanish: **Anita**

Anna (German, Italian, Czech,
Swedish) gracious. A form of
Hannah. Culture: Anna
Pavlova was a famous Russian
ballerina. See also Nina.
**Ana, Anah, Ania, Anika,
Annina, Annora, Anona,
Anyu, Aska**
Foreign forms: Polish: **Anka;**
Russian: **Anja, Anya, Vanya;**
Spanish: **Anica, Anita**

Annabel (English) a combina-
tion of Anna + Bel.
**Amabel, Anabel, Anabela,
Anabella, Anabelle, Annabal,
Annabell, Annabella,
Annabelle**
Foreign form: Irish: **Annabla**

Annelisa (English) a combina-
tion of Anne + Lisa.
**Analiese, Analisa, Analise,
Anelisa, Anelise, Annalisa,
Anna-Lisa, Annalise,
Anneliese**
Foreign forms: Danish:
Annelise; German: **Annaliese**

**Annemarie, Annmarie,
Anne-Marie** (English) combi-
nations of Anne + Marie.
**Annamaria, Anna-Maria,
Annamarie, Anna-Marie,
Annmaria**

Annette (French) a form of
Ann.
**Anet, Anetra, Anett, Anetta,
Anette, Anneth, Annett,
Annetta**

Annie (English) a familiar form
of Ann.
Anni, Anny

Annjanette (American) a com-
bination of Ann + Janette.
**Angen, Angenett, Angenette,
Anjane, Anjanetta, Anjani**

Annunciata (Latin) news
bearer. Religion: a holiday
celebrating the annunciation
of the Virgin Mary.
Foreign forms: Italian:
Assuntina; Spanish: **Anunciacion**

Anthea (Greek) flower.
Antha, Anthe, Anthia, Thia

Antoinette (French) a form of
Antonia. See also Nettie,
Toinette, Toni.
**Anta, Antanette, Antoinella,
Antoinet, Antonella,
Antonetta, Antonette,**

**Antonice, Antonieta,
Antonietta, Antonique**

Antonia (Greek) flourishing.
(Latin) praiseworthy. A femi-
nine form of Anthony. See also
Toni, Tonya, Tosha.
**Ansonia, Ansonya, Antania,
Antona, Antonice, Antonina,
Antonnea, Antonnia, Antonya**
Foreign forms: Basque:
Andoniñe; French: **Antoinette,
Antonine;** German: **Antonie;**
Italian: **Antoñía, Antonietta**

Antonice (Latin) an alternate
form of Antonia.
**Antanise, Antanisha,
Antonesha, Antoneshia,
Antonise, Antonisha**

Aphrodite (Greek) sea foam.
Mythology: the Greek goddess
of love and beauty who
appeared from the sea.

April (Latin) opening.
**Aprele, Aprelle, Apriell,
Aprielle, Aprila, Aprile,
Aprilette, Aprili, Aprill**
Foreign forms: English: **Apryl,
Apryle;** French: **Avril, Avrille;**
Spanish: **Abril**

Ara (Arabic) opinionated.
Arae, Arah, Ari, Aria, Arria
Foreign form: Armenian: **Aram**

Arabella (Latin) beautiful altar.
Ara, Arabele
Foreign forms: *French/German:*
Arabelle, Belle; *Italian:* **Orabella;**
Spanish: **Arabela**

Ardelle (Latin) warm; enthusiastic.
Ardelia, Ardelis, Ardella, Ardi

Arden (English) valley of the
eagle. Literature: in
Shakespeare, a romantic place
of refuge.
Ardeen, Ardeena, Ardena,
Ardene, Ardi, Ardenia, Ardin,
Ardine

Ardith (Hebrew) flowering
field.
Ardath, Ardi, Ardice, Ardie,
Ardyce, Ardys, Ardyth

Aretha (Greek) virtuous.
Areatha, Areetha, Aretina,
Arita, Aritha, Oretha, Retha,
Ritha
Foreign forms: *English:* **Areta,**
Aretta; *French:* **Arette**

Ariadne (Greek) holy.
Mythology: the daughter of
King Minos of Crete.
Ari
Foreign forms: *English:*
Arianne; *French:* **Ariane;** *Italian:*
Ariana, Arianna

Ariana, Arianna (Italian)
forms of Ariadne.
Aeriana, Aerianna, Airiana,
Arieana

Ariane (French), **Arianne**
(English) forms of Ariadne.
Aeriann, Airiann, Ari, Arianie,
Ariann, Ariannie, Arieann,
Arien, Arienne, Arieon,
Aryane, Aryanna, Aryanne

Arica (Scandinavian) an alternate form of Erica.
Aricca, Aricka, Arika, Arikka

Ariel (Hebrew) lioness of God.
Aeriale, Aeriel, Aeriela,
Aeryal, Aire, Aireal, Airial,
Ari, Aria, Arial, Ariale, Arieal,
Ariela
Foreign form: *French:* **Arielle**

Arielle (French) a form of Ariel.
Aeriell, Ariella

Arin (Hebrew) enlightened.
(Arabic) messenger. A feminine
form of Aaron. See also Erin.
Aaren, Arinn, Aryn

Arleigh (English) an alternate
form of Harley.
Arlea, Arlee, Arley, Arlie, Arly

Arlene (Irish) pledge. A feminine form of Arlen. See also
Lena, Lina.

Arla, Arlana, Arleen, Arleigh,
Arlen, Arlena, Arlenis,
Arleyne, Arliene, Arlina,
Arlinda, Arline, Arlis, Arly
Foreign forms: *American:* **Arlyn,**
Arlyne, Arlynn; *English:* **Arlette,**
Arletta

Artha (Hindi) wealthy, prosperous.

Artis (Irish) noble; lofty hill.
(Scottish) bear. (English) rock.
(Icelandic) follower of Thor. A
feminine form of Arthur.
Arthea, Athelia, Arthene,
Arthette, Arthuretta,
Arthurina, Arthurine, Arti,
Artie, Artina, Artrice

Ashanti (Swahili) from a tribe
in West Africa.
Ashanta, Ashantae, Ashante,
Ashantee, Ashaunta,
Ashauntae, Ashauntee,
Ashaunti, Ashuntae, Ashunti

Ashley (English) ash tree meadow. See also Lee.
Ashala, Ashalee, Ashalei,
Ashaley, Ashelee, Ashelei,
Asheleigh, Asheley, Ashely,
Ashla, Ashlay, Ashlea,
Ashleah, Ashleay, Ashlee,
Ashlei, Ashleigh, Ashli, Ashlie,
Ashly, Ashlye

Ashlyn, Ashlynn (English) ash tree pool. (Irish) vision, dream.
Ashlan, Ashleann, Ashleen, Ashleene, Ashlen, Ashlene, Ashliann, Ashlianne, Ashlin, Ashline, Ashling, Ashlyne, Ashlynne

Asia (Greek) resurrection. (English) eastern sunrise. (Swahili) an alternate form of Aisha.
Aisia, Asiah, Asian, Asya, Aysia, Aysiah, Aysian

Astra (Greek) star.
Astara, Astraea, Astrea
Foreign forms: Danish: **Asta;** *English:* **Aster**

Astrid (Scandinavian) divine strength.
Astri, Astrida, Astrik, Astrud, Atti, Estrid

Atalanta (Greek) mighty huntress. Mythology: an athletic young woman who refused to marry any man who could not outrun her in a footrace.
Addi, Addie, Atalaya, Atlante, Atlee, Atti, Attie
Foreign forms: English: **Atlanta;** *Hawaiian:* **Lani**

Athena (Greek) wise. Mythology: the goddess of wisdom.
Athenea, Athene, Athina, Atina

Aubrey (German) noble; bear-like. (French) blond ruler; elf ruler.
Aubary, Auberi, Aubery, Aubray, Aubre, Aubrea, Aubreah, Aubree, Aubrei, Aubreigh, Aubrette, Aubri, Aubria, Aubrie, Aubry, Aubury

Audra (French) a form of Audrey.

Audrey (English) noble strength.
Audey, Audi, Audie, Audra, Audray, Audre, Audree, Audreen, Audri, Audria, Audrianna, Audrianne, Audrie, Audrin, Audrina, Audriya, Audry, Audrye
Foreign forms: French: **Aude, Audra**

Augustine (Latin) majestic. Religion: Saint Augustine was the first Archbishop of Canterbury. See also Tina.
Augusta, Augustina, Augustyna, Augustyne, Austin

Aurelia (Latin) golden. Mythology: the goddess of dawn.
Auralea, Auralee, Auralei, Auralia, Aurea, Aureal, Aurel, Aurele, Aurelea, Aurelee, Aurelei, Aureliana, Auria, Aurie, Auriel, Aurielle, Aurilia, Aurita
Foreign forms: Basque: **Aurelne;** *English:* **Oralia;** *French:* **Aurélie;** *Hawaiian:* **Alaula**

Aurora (Latin) dawn.
Ora, Ori, Orie, Rora
Foreign form: French: **Aurore**

Austin (Latin) a short form of Augustine.

Autumn (Latin) autumn.
Autum

Ava (Greek) an alternate form of Eva. (Latin) a short form of Avis.
Avada, Avae, Ave, Aveen

Avis (Latin) bird.
Avais, Avi, Avia, Aviana, Avianca, Aviance

Aviva (Hebrew) springtime. See also Viva.
Avivah, Avivi, Avivice, Avni, Avnit, Avri, Avrit, Avy

Aya (Hebrew) bird; fly swiftly.

Ayanna (Hindi) innocent.
Ayania

Ayla (Hebrew) oak tree.
**Aylana, Aylee, Ayleen, Aylene,
Aylie**

Babe (Latin) a familiar form of
Barbara.
Babby, Bebe

Babs (American) a familiar form
of Barbara.
Bab, Babb

Bailey (English) bailiff.
**Bailee, Bailley, Bailly, Baily,
Bali, Bayla, Baylee, Baylie,
Bayly**
Foreign form: Irish: *Baillie*

Bambi (Italian) child.
Bambee, Bambie, Bamby

Baptista (Latin) baptizer.
Battista
Foreign forms: French:
Baptiste; Italian: *Batista;*
Spanish: *Bautista*

Barb (Latin) a short form of
Barbara.
Barba, Barbe

Barbara (Latin) stranger, for-
eigner.
**Babara, Babbie, Babe, Babina,
Barb, Barbara-Ann, Barbarit,
Barbarita, Barbary,
Barbeeleen, Barbie, Barbora,
Barbra, Barbraann, Barùska,
Basha, Bobbi, Bobbie**
Foreign forms: American: *Babs,
Barbie, Barby, Barbra;*
French/German: *Babette, Barbe;*
Irish: *Báirbre;* Slavic: *Varvara,
Wava;* Spanish: *Bàrbara, Bebe,
Bibi;* Swedish: *Barbro*

Barrie (Irish) spear;
markswoman. A feminine form
of Barry.
Bari, Barri

Basia (Hebrew) daughter of
God.
**Basya, Bathia, Batia, Batya,
Bitya, Bithia**

Bathsheba (Hebrew) daughter
of the oath; seventh daughter.
Bible: a wife of King David.
See also Sheba.
**Bathshua, Batsheva, Bersaba,
Bethsabee, Bethsheba**

Bea, Bee (American) short
forms of Beatrice.

Beatrice (Latin) blessed;
happy; bringer of joy. See also
Trish.
**Beata, Beatrica, Beatricia,
Beatriks, Beatris, Beatrise,
Beatriss, Beatrissa, Beattie,
Beatty, Trice**
Foreign forms: American: *Bea,
Bee, Trixie;* French: *Béatrice;*
German/Spanish: *Beatrix;* Scottish:
Beitris; Spanish: *Beatrisa,
Beatriz, Bebe, Bibi*

Becca (Hebrew) a short form of
Rebecca.
Becka, Bekka

Becky (American) a familiar
form of Rebecca.
Becki, Beckie

Bedelia (Irish) an alternate
form of Bridget.
Bedeelia, Biddy, Bidelia

Bel (Hindi) sacred wood of
apple trees. A short form of
Belinda, Isabel, Mabel.

Bela (Czech) white. (Hungarian) bright.
Belah, Belen

Belicia (Spanish) dedicated to God.
Beli, Belia, Belica

Belinda (Spanish) beautiful. Literature: a name coined by English poet Alexander Pope in *The Rape of the Lock.* See also Linda.
Bel, Belindra, Belynda
Foreign forms: American: *Blinda;* French: *Belle*

Bella (Latin) beautiful.
Bell, Bellah

Belle (French) beautiful. A short form of Arabella, Belinda, Isabel. See also Billie.
Belita, Belli, Bellina, Belva, Belvia

Belva (Latin) beautiful view.

Benecia (Latin) a short form of Benedicta.
Beneisha, Benicia, Benish, Benisha, Benishia, Bennicia

Benedicta (Latin) blessed. A feminine form of Benedict.
Bendite, Benea, Bengta, Benna, Benni, Binney
Foreign forms: French: *Benoîte;*

German: *Benedikta;* Italian: *Benedetta;* Spanish: *Benita*

Benita (Spanish) a form of Benedicta.
Benetta, Benitta, Bennita, Neeta

Benni (Latin) a familiar form of Benedicta.
Bennie, Binni, Binnie, Binny

Bente (Latin) blessed.

Berget (Irish) an alternate form of Bridget.
Bergette, Bergit, Birgit, Birgita, Birgitta

Berit (German) glorious.
Beret, Berette, Berta

Berlynn (English) a combination of Bertha + Lynn.
Berla, Berlin, Berlinda, Berline, Berling, Berlyn, Berlyne, Berlynne

Bernadette (French) a form of Bernadine. See also Nadette.
Bera, Beradette, Berna, Bernadet, Bernadett, Bernarda, Bernardette, Bernedet, Bernedette, Bernessa, Berneta
Foreign form: Italian: *Bernadetta*

Bernadine (German) brave as a bear. (English) a feminine form of Bernard.
Bernadene, Bernadin, Bernadina, Bernardine, Berni
Foreign forms: French: *Bernadette;* Italian/Spanish: *Bernardina*

Berni (English) a familiar form of Bernadine, Bernice.
Bernie, Berny

Bernice (Greek) bringer of victory. See also Bunny.
Berenike, Bernessa, Berneta, Berni, Bernise, Brona, Nixie, Vernice
Foreign form: French: *Berenice*

Bertha (German) bright; illustrious; brilliant ruler. A short form of Alberta. A feminine form of Berthold. See also Birdie.
Barta, Bartha, Berlynn, Berte, Bertita, Bertrona, Bertus
Foreign forms: French: *Berthe, Bertille;* Hawaiian: *Peke;* Italian/Spanish: *Berta;* Swedish: *Berit*

Berti (German, English) a familiar form of Gilberte, Bertina.
Bertie, Berty

Bertina (English) bright, shining. A feminine form of Bert.
Berti, Bertine

Beryl (Greek) sea green jewel.
Berri, Berrie, Berry, Beryle

Bess, Bessie (Hebrew) familiar forms of Elizabeth.
Bessi, Bessy

Beth (Hebrew, Aramaic) house of God. A short form of Bethany, Elizabeth.
Betha, Bethe, Bethia

Bethann (English) a combination of Beth + Ann.
Beth-Ann, Bethan, Bethanne, Beth-Anne

Bethany (Aramaic) house of figs. Bible: a village near Jerusalem where Lazarus lived.
Beth, Bethane, Bethanee, Bethaney, Bethani, Bethania, Bethanie, Bethann, Bethanney, Bethannie, Bethanny, Bethena, Betheny, Bethia, Bethina, Bethney

Betsy (American) a familiar form of Elizabeth.
Betsey, Betsi, Betsie

Bette (French) a form of Betty.
Beta, Beti, Betka, Bett, Betta, Betti, Bettie

Bettina (American) a combination of Beth + Tina.
Betina, Betine, Betti, Bettine

Betty (Hebrew) consecrated to God. (English) a familiar form of Elizabeth.
Bettye, Bety, Biddy, Boski, Bözsi
Foreign forms: American: **Bettyjean, Betty-Jean, Bettyjo, Betty-Jo, Bettylou, Betty-Lou;** French: **Bette**

Beulah (Hebrew) married. Bible: the Land of Beulah is a name for Israel.
Beulla, Beullah
Foreign form: English: **Beula**

Bev (English) a short form of Beverly.

Beverly (English) beaver field. See also Buffy.
Bev, Bevalee, Bevan, Bevann, Bevanne, Bevany, Beverle, Beverlee, Beverley, Beverlie, Bevlyn, Bevlynn, Bevlynne, Bevvy, Verly
Foreign form: American: **Beverlyann**

Bianca (Italian) white. See also Blanca.
Bellanca, Beonca, Beyonca, Biancha, Biancia, Bianey, Binney, Bionca, Bioncha

Foreign forms: French: **Blanche;** German: **Blanka;** Irish: **Blinnie, Bluinse;** Spanish: **Vianca**

Bibi (Latin) lively. (Arabic) lady.

Bik (Chinese) jade.

Billie (German, French) a familiar form of Belle, Wilhelmina. (English) strong willed.
Bilee, Bili, Billi, Billy, Billye

Billie-Jean (American) a combination of Billie + Jean.
Billiejean, Billyjean, Billy-Jean

Billie-Jo (American) a combination of Billie + Jo.
Billiejo, Billyjo, Billy-Jo

Bina (Hebrew) wise; understanding. (Latin) a short form of Sabina. (Swahili) dancer.
Binah, Binney, Binta, Bintah

Binney (English) a familiar form of Benedicta, Bianca, Bina.
Binnee, Binnie, Binny

Birdie (German) a familiar form of Bertha. (English) bird.
Bird, Birdee, Birdella, Birdena, Birdey, Birdi, Birdy, Byrd, Byrdey, Byrdie, Byrdy

Blaine (Irish) thin.
Blane, Blayne

Blair (Scottish) plains dweller.
Blaire, Blayre

Blaise (French) one who stammers.
Blasha, Blasia, Blaza, Blaze, Blazena

Blake (English) dark.
Blakelee, Blakeley, Blakesley

Blanca (Italian) an alternate form of Bianca.
Bellanca, Blancka

Blanche (French) a form of Bianca.
Blanch, Blancha

Bliss (English) blissful, joyful.
Blisse, Blyss, Blysse

Blondie (American) blond.
Blondee, Blondell, Blondey, Blondy

Blossom (English) flower.

Blythe (English) happy, cheerful.
Blithe, Blyth

Bo (Chinese) precious.

Bobbi, Bobbie (American) familiar forms of Barbara, Roberta.
Bauble, Bobbie-Jean, Bobbie-Lynn, Bobbie-Sue, Bobbisue,

Bobby, Bobbye, Bobi, Bobie, Bobina

Bobbi-Ann, Bobbie-Ann (American) combinations of Bobbi + Ann, Bobbie + Ann.
Bobbiann, Bobbi-Anne, Bobbianne, Bobbie-Anne, Bobbyann, Bobby-Ann, Bobbyanne, Bobby-Anne

Bobbi-Jo (American) a combination of Bobbi + Jo.
Bobbiejo, Bobbie-Jo, Bobbijo, Bobby-Jo, Bobijo

Bobbi-Lee (American) a combination of Bobbi + Lee.
Bobbie-Lee, Bobbilee, Bobbylee, Bobby-Leigh, Bobile

Bonita (Spanish) pretty.
Bonnie, Bonny

Bonnie, Bonny (English, Scottish) beautiful, pretty. (Spanish) familiar forms of Bonita. See also Bunny.
Boni, Bonie, Bonne, Bonnee, Bonnell, Bonnetta, Bonney, Bonni, Bonnin

Bonnie-Bell (American) a combination of Bonnie + Belle.
Bonnebell, Bonnebelle, Bonnibell, Bonnibelle,

Bonniebell, Bonniebelle, Bonnybell, Bonnybelle

Brandi, Brandie (Dutch) alternate forms of Brandy.
Brandice, Brandee, Brandii, Brandily, Brandin, Brandis, Brandise, Brani, Branndie

Brandy (Dutch) an after-dinner drink made from distilled wine.
Brand, Branda, Brandace, Brandaise, Brandala, Brande, Brandea, Brandee, Brandei, Brandeli, Brandell, Brandi, Brandye, Brandylee, Brandy-Lee, Brandy-Leigh, Brandyn, Brann, Brantley, Branyell

Brandy-Lynn (American) a combination of Brandy + Lynn.
Brandalyn, Brandalynn, Brandelyn, Brandelynn, Brandelynne, Brandilyn, Brandilynn, Brandilynne, Brandlin, Brandlyn, Brandlynn, Brandlynne, Brandolyn, Brandolynn, Brandolynne, Brandylyn, Brandy-Lyn, Brandylynne, Brandy-Lynne

Breana, Breanna (Irish) alternate forms of Briana.
Breanda, Bre-Anna, Breauna, Breawna, Breeana, Breeanna,

Breeauna, Breiana, Breiann, Breila, Breina

Breann, Breanne (Irish) alternate forms of Briana.
Bre-Ann, Bre-Anne, Breaunne, Bree, Breean, Breeann, Breeanne, Breelyn, Breiann, Breighann, Brieann, Brieon

Breck (Irish) freckled.

Bree (Irish) a short form of Breann. (English) broth. See also Brie.
Brea, Breah, Breay, Breea, Brei, Breigh

Breena (Irish) fairy palace.
Breina, Brena, Brina

Brenda (Irish) little raven. (English) sword. A feminine form of Brendan.
Brendell, Brendelle, Brendette, Brendie, Brendyl

Brenda-Lee (American) a combination of Brenda + Lee.
Brendalee, Brendaleigh, Brendali, Brendaly, Brendalys, Brenlee, Brenley

Brenna (Irish) an alternate form of Brenda.
Bren, Brenie, Brenin, Brenn, Brennah, Brennaugh

Brett (Irish) a short form of Brittany. See also Brita.
Bret, Bretta, Brette, Brettin, Bretton

Briana, Brianna (Irish) strong; virtuous, honorable. Feminine forms of Brian.
Brana, Breana, Breann, Bria, Briah, Briahna, Briand, Brianda, Brie-Ann, Briannah, Brianne, Brianni, Briannon, Briauna, Brina, Briona, Bryanna, Bryna
Foreign form: French: *Brienne*

Brianne (Irish) an alternate form of Briana.
Briane, Briann, Brienne, Bryanne, Bryn, Brynn, Brynne

Briar (French) heather.
Brear, Brier, Briet, Brieta, Brietta, Brya, Bryar

Bridey (Irish) a familiar form of Bridget.
Bridi, Bridie, Brydie

Bridget (Irish) strong. See also Bedelia.
Beret, Bride, Bridey, Bridger, Bridgete, Bridgett, Bridgid, Bridgot, Brietta, Brigada, Briget, Brigid, Brita, Gitta
Foreign forms: French: *Bergette, Brigitte;* Italian/Spanish: *Brigida;*

Norwegian: *Birget, Birgit;* Polish: *Bryga, Brygid;* Swedish: *Biddy, Birgitte, Birgitta*

Bridgett, Bridgette (Irish) alternate forms of Bridget.
Bridgitte, Brigette, Briggitte, Brigitta

Brie (French) a type of cheese. Geography: a region in France known for its cheese. See also Bree.
Briena, Brieon, Briette
Foreign form: French: *Brielle*

Brie-Ann (American) a combination of Brie + Ann. See also Briana.
Brieann, Brieanna, Brieanne, Brie-Anne

Brigitte (French) a form of Bridget.
Brigette, Briggitte, Brigit, Brigita

Brina (Latin) a short form of Sabrina. (Irish) a familiar form of Briana.
Brin, Brinan, Brinda, Brindi, Brindy, Briney, Brinia, Brinlee, Brinly, Brinn, Brinna, Brinnan, Briona, Bryn, Bryna

Briona (Irish) an alternate form of Briana.
Breona, Brione, Brionna, Brionne, Briony, Bryony

Brisa (Spanish) beloved. Mythology: Briseis was the Greek name of Achilles's beloved.
Breezy, Breza, Brisha, Brishia, Brissa, Bryssa

Brita (Irish) an alternate form of Bridget. (English) a short form of Brittany.
Brit, Britta

Britaney, Brittaney (English) alternate forms of Britany, Brittany.
Britanee, Britanny, Britenee, Briteny, Britianey, British, Britkney, Britley, Britlyn, Britney, Briton

Britani, Brittanie (English) alternate forms of Britany, Brittany.
Brit, Britania, Britanica, Britanie, Britanii, Britanni, Britannia, Britatani, Britia, Britini, Brittanni, Brittannia, Brittannie, Brittenie, Brittiani, Brittianni

Britney, Brittney (English) alternate forms of Britany, Brittany.
Bittney, Bridnee, Bridney, Britnay, Britne, Britnee, Britnei, Britni, Britny, Britnye, Brittnay, Brittnaye, Brittne, Brittnea, Brittnee, Brittneigh, Brittny, Brytnea, Brytni

Britni, Brittni (English) alternate forms of Britney, Britney.
Britnie, Brittnie

Britt, Britta (Latin) short forms of Britany, Brittany. (Swedish) strong.
Brett, Brit, Brita, Britte

Britany, Brittany (English) from Britain. See also Brett.
Brita, Britana, Britaney, Britani, Britanie, Britann, Britlyn, Britney, Britt, Brittainny, Brittainy, Brittamy, Brittan, Brittana, Brittane, Brittanee, Brittaney, Brittani, Brittania, Brittanica, Brittany-Ann, Brittanyne, Brittell, Britten, Brittenee, Britteney, Britteny, Brittiany, Brittlin, Brittlynn, Britton, Brittoni, Brittony, Bryttany

Britin, Brittin (English) from Britain.
Brittin, Brittina, Brittine, Brittinee, Brittiney, Brittini, Brittiny

Bronwyn (Welsh) white breasted.
Bron, Bronia, Bronney, Bronnie, Bronny, Bronwen, Bronwin, Bronwynn, Bronwynne, Bronya

Brooke (English) brook, stream. A feminine form of Brook.
Brookelle, Brookie, Brooks, Brooky

Brooklyn (American) a combination of Brooke + Lynn.
Brookellen, Brookelyn, Brooklin, Brooklynn, Brooklynne

Brunhilda (German) armored warrior.
Brinhilda, Brinhilde, Bruna, Brunhilde, Brünnhilde, Brynhilda, Brynhilde, Hilda
Foreign form: Norwegian: *Brynhild*

Bryanna, Bryanne (Irish) alternate forms of Briana.
Bryana, Bryann

Bryn, Brynn (Latin) from the boundary line. (Welsh) mound.
Brinn, Brynan, Brynee, Brynne

Bryttany (English) an alternate form of Britany, Brittany.
Brittyne, Brityn, Brityne, Bryton, Bryttani, Bryttine, Bryttney

Buffy (American) buffalo; from the plains.
Buffee, Buffey, Buffie, Buffye

Bunny (Greek) a familiar form of Bernice. (English) little rabbit. See also Bonnie.
Bunni, Bunnie

Burgundy (French) a hearty red wine. Geography: a region of France known for its burgundy wine.
Burgandi, Burgandie, Burgandy

Cachet (French) prestigious; desirous.
Cache, Cachea, Cachee, Cachée

Cady (English) an alternate form of Kady.
Cade, Cadee, Cadey, Cadi, Cadie, Cadine, Cadori, Cadye

Caeley, Cailey, Cayley (American) alternate forms of Kaylee, Kelly.
Caelee, Caelie, Cailee, Cailie, Caylee, Caylie

Cai (Vietnamese) feminine.
Cae, Cay, Caye

Cailin (American) a form of Caitlin.
Caileen, Cailene, Cailine, Cailyn, Cailynn, Cailynne, Cayleen, Caylene, Caylin, Cayline, Caylyn, Caylyne, Caylynne

Caitlin (Irish) pure. An alternate form of Cathleen. See also Kaitlin, Katelin.
Caeley, Cailey, Caitlan, Caitland, Caitlandt, Caitleen, Caitlen, Caitlene, Caitline, Caitlinn, Caitlon, Caitlyn, Caitria, Caitriona, Catlee, Catleen, Catleene, Catlin, Cayley
Foreign form: American: **Cailin**

Caitlyn (Irish) an alternate form of Caitlin. See also Kaitlyn.
Caitlynn, Caitlynne, Catlyn, Catlynn, Catlynne

Cala (Arabic) castle, fortress. See also Callie, Kala.
Calah, Calan, Calla, Callah

Calandra (Greek) lark.
Caelan, Cailan, Calan, Caleida, Calendra, Caylan, Kalan, Kalandra, Kalandria
Foreign forms: French: **Calandre;** *Spanish:* **Calandria**

Caleigh, Caley (American) alternate forms of Caeley, Kaylee, Kelly.

Cali, Calli (Greek) alternate forms of Callie. See also Kali.

Calida (Spanish) warm; ardent.
Calina, Callida, Kalida

Callie (Greek, Arabic) a familiar form of Cala, Callista. See also Cayla, Kalli.
Cal, Caleigh, Caley, Cali, Calie, Callee, Calley, Calli, Cally

Callista (Greek) most beautiful. See also Kallista.
Calesta, Calista, Callie, Calysta

Calypso (Greek) concealer. Botany: a white orchid with purple or yellow markings. Mythology: the sea nymph who held Odysseus captive for seven years.
Cally, Caly, Lypsie, Lypsy

Cam (Vietnamese) sweet citrus.
Kam

Cambria (Latin) from Wales. See also Kambria.
Camber, Camberlee, Camberleigh, Camberly, Camberry, Cambie, Cambrea, Cambree, Cambrya

Camellia (Italian) evergreen tree or shrub.
Camala, Camalia, Camallia, Camela, Camelia, Camelita, Camella, Camellita, Kamelia, Kamellia

Cameron (Scottish) crooked nose.
Camera, Cameran, Cameren, Cameri, Cameria, Camesha, Cameshia
Foreign forms: *American:* **Kameron, Kamryn**

Cami (French) a short form of Camille. See also Kami.
Camey, Camie, Cammi, Cammie, Cammy, Cammye

Camilla (Italian) a form of Camille. See also Mila.
Camia, Camila, Camillia, Chamelea, Chamelia, Chamika, Chamila, Chamilia

Camille (French) young ceremonial attendant. See also Millie.
Cami, Camill, Cammille, Cammillie, Cammilyn,

Cammyl, Cammyll, Camylle, Chamelle, Chamille, Kamille
Foreign forms: *Hungarian:* **Kamilka;** *Italian:* **Camilla;** *Slavic:* **Kamila;** *Spanish:* **Camila**

Candace (Greek) glittering white; glowing. History: the name and title of the queens of ancient Ethiopia. See also Dacey.
Cace, Canace, Canda, Candas, Candelle, Candice, Candida
Foreign forms: *American:* **Candi, Kandace;** *English:* **Candice**

Candi, Candy (American) familiar forms of Candace, Candice, Candida. See also Kandi.
Candee, Candie

Candice, Candis, Candyce (Greek) alternate forms of Candace.
Candes, Candi, Candias, Candies, Candise, Candiss, Candus, Candys, Candyse, Cyndyss

Candida (Latin) bright white.
Candeea, Candi, Candia, Candita
Foreign form: *French:* **Candide**

Candra (Latin) glowing.
Candrea, Candria, Kandra

Capri (Italian) a short form of Caprice. Geography: an island off the west coast of Italy.
Caprie, Capris
Foreign forms: *American:* **Kapri, Kaprice, Kapricia**

Caprice (Italian) fanciful.
Cappi, Caprece, Capricia, Caprina, Caprise, Capritta

Cara (Latin) dear. (Irish) friend. See also Karah.
Caragh, Carah, Caralea, Caralee, Caralia, Caralie, Caralin, Caraline, Caralyn, Caranda, Carey, Carra

Carey (Welsh) a familiar form of Cara, Caroline, Karen, Katherine. See also Carrie, Kari.
Caree, Cari, Carrey, Cary

Cari, Carie (Welsh) alternate forms of Carey, Kari.

Carina (Greek) a familiar form of Cora. (Italian) dear little one. (Swedish) a form of Karen.
Carena, Carin, Carine, Caryn

Carissa (Greek) beloved.
Carisa, Carrissa, Charisa, Charissa, Karissa
Foreign forms: *French:* **Caressa, Caresse, Karessa**

Carita (Latin) charitable.
Caritta, Charity, Karita, Karitta

Carla (Latin) an alternate form of Carol, Caroline. (German) farmer. (English) strong and womanly.
Carila, Carilla, Carle, Carleah, Carleigh, Carletha, Carlethe, Carlia, Carlicia, Carliqua, Carliyle, Carlonda, Carlreca, Carlyjo, Carlyle, Carlysle
Foreign form: Spanish: **Carlita**

Carlee, Carley (English) alternate forms of Carly.

Carlene (English) a form of Caroline.
Carlaen, Carlaena, Carleen, Carleena, Carlen, Carlena, Carlenna, Carline, Carlyn, Carlyne, Karlene

Carli, Carlie (English) alternate forms of Carly. See also Karli.

Carlin (Latin) a short form of Caroline. (Irish) little champion.
Carlan, Carlana, Carlandra, Carlen, Carlina, Carlinda, Carline, Carling, Carllan, Carllen, Carrlin

Carlissa (American) a combination of Carla + Lissa.
Carleesia, Carleeza, Carlesia,

Carlis, Carlise, Carlisha, Carlisia, Carliss, Carlisse, Carlissia, Carlista, Carlyse

Carlotta (Italian) a form of Charlotte.
Carletta, Karletta, Karlotta

Carly (English) a familiar form of Caroline, Charlotte.
Carlee, Carley, Carli, Carlie, Carlye
Foreign forms: American: **Karli, Karly**

Carmela, Carmella (Hebrew) garden; vineyard. Bible: Mount Carmel in Israel is often thought of as paradise. See also Karmel.
Carma, Carmaletta, Carmalit, Carmalla, Carmarit, Carmel, Carmeli, Carmelia, Carmelit, Carmelitha, Carmelitia, Carmelle, Carmellia, Carmellina, Carmellit, Carmellita, Carmellitha, Carmellitia, Carmesa, Carmi, Carmie, Carmiel, Carmil, Carmila, Carmilla, Leeta, Lita
Foreign forms: Italian: **Carmelina;** Spanish: **Carmalita, Carmelita, Melita**

Carmen (Latin) song. Religion: Santa Maria del Carmen— Saint Mary of Mount Carmel—

is one of the titles of the Virgin Mary.
Carma, Carmaine, Carman, Carmelina, Carmene, Carmi, Carmia, Carmin, Carmina, Carmon, Carmynn
Foreign forms: English: **Carmine, Carmita;** French: **Charmaine;** Hebrew: **Karmen;** Spanish: **Carmelita, Carmencita**

Carol (German) farmer. (French) song of joy. (English) strong and womanly. A feminine form of Carl, Charles.
Carel, Carely, Cariel, Carilis, Carilise, Carilyse, Caroleen, Carolenia, Caroll, Carolyn, Carrie, Carrol, Carroll
Foreign forms: Finnish: **Kalle, Karel, Karole;** Slavic: **Karoll;** Spanish: **Carley, Carlita, Caro, Carola, Carole, Carolinda, Caryl**

Carole (English) an alternate form of Carol.
Carolee, Karrole

Carolina (Italian) a form of Caroline.
Carilena, Carlena, Carlina, Carlita, Carrolena, Karolina

Caroline (French) little and womanly. See also Carla, Carlin.
Caralin, Caraline, Carileen, Carilene, Carilin, Cariline,

Caroline *(cont.)*
Carly, Caro, Carolann, Carolin, Carrie, Carroleen, Carrolene, Carrolin, Carroline, Cary
Foreign forms: Danish: **Kari;**
English: **Carlene, Carolyn, Charlene;** *French:* **Charlotte;**
German: **Karoline;** *Italian/Spanish:* **Carolina;** *Polish:* **Karolina;** *Slavic:* **Karoline**

Carolyn (English) a form of Caroline.
Caralyn, Caralynn, Caralynne, Carilyn, Carilynn, Carilynne, Carlyn, Carlynn, Carlynne, Carolyne, Carolynn, Carolynne, Carrolyn, Carrolynn, Carrolynne
Foreign form: American: **Karolyn**

Caron (Welsh) loving, kind hearted, charitable.
Carron, Carrone

Carrie (English) a familiar form of Carol, Caroline. See also Carey.
Carree, Carri, Carria, Carry
Foreign forms: American: **Karri, Karrie;** *Danish:* **Kari**

Caryn (Danish) a form of Karen.
Caren, Caron, Caronne, Carren, Carrin, Carron, Caryna, Caryne, Carynn

Carys (Welsh) love.
Caris, Caryse

Casey (Greek) a familiar form of Acacia. (Irish) brave. See also Kasey.
Cacy, Cascy, Casie, Cass, Casse, Cassee, Cassey, Cassye, Casy, Cayce, Cayse, Caysee, Caysy

Casie (Irish) an alternate form of Casey.
Caci, Casci, Cascie, Casi, Cass, Cayci, Caysi, Caysie, Cazzi

Cass (Greek) a short form of Cassandra.

Cassandra (Greek) helper of men. Mythology: a prophetess of ancient Greece whose prophesies were not believed. See also Kassandra, Sandra, Sandy, Zandra.
Casandera, Casandra, Casandrey, Casandri, Casandria, Casaundra, Casaundre, Casaundri, Casaundria, Casondra, Casondre, Casondri, Casondria, Cass, Cassandre, Cassandri, Cassandry, Cassaundra, Cassaundre, Cassaundri, Cassie, Cassondra, Cassondre, Cassondri, Cassondria, Cassundra,

Cassundre, Cassundri, Cassundria
Foreign form: French: **Casandre**

Cassia (Greek) spicy cinnamon.
Casia

Cassidy (Irish) clever.
Casadee, Casadi, Casadie, Cass, Cassadi, Cassadie, Cassadina, Cassady, Casseday, Cassiddy, Cassidee, Cassidi, Cassidie, Cassity
Foreign form: American: **Kassidy**

Cassie (Greek) a familiar form of Cassandra, Catherine. See also Kassie.
Cassey, Cassi, Cassy

Catalina (Spanish) a form of Catherine.
Cataleen, Catalena, Catalene, Catalin, Catalyn, Catalyna, Cateline, Kataleena, Katalina, Katalyn

Catherine (Greek) pure. (English) a form of Katherine.
Cat, Catarine, Cate, Catha, Cathann, Cathanne, Catharina, Catharine, Cathenne, Catheren, Catherene, Catheria, Catherin, Catherina, Catheryn, Cathi, Cathrine, Cathryn, Cathy, Catlaina,

Catreeka, Catrelle, Catrice, Catricia, Catrika, Catrin, Catryn, Catteeka, Cattiah
Foreign forms: Irish: *Cathleen;* Italian: *Catarina, Caterina;* Portuguese: *Catia;* Romanian: *Ecaterina;* Slavic: *Catrina;* Spanish: *Catalina*

Cathi, Cathy (Greek) familiar forms of Catherine, Cathleen. See also Kathi.
Cathe, Cathee, Cathey, Cathie

Cathleen (Irish) a form of Catherine. See also Caitllin, Katelin, Kathleen.
Cathaleen, Cathelin, Cathelina, Cathelyn, Cathi, Cathleana, Cathlene, Cathleyn, Cathlin, Cathlyn, Cathlyne, Cathy

Cathrine, Cathryn (Greek) alternate forms of Catherine.

Catrina (Slavic) a form of Catherine, Katrina.
Catina, Catreen, Catreena, Catrene, Catrenia, Catrine, Catrinia, Catriona, Catroina

Cayla (Hebrew) an alternate form of Kayla.
Cailee, Cailey, Cailie, Caily, Calee, Caly, Caylee, Cayley, Caylie, Cayly

Cecilia (Latin) blind. A feminine form of Cecil.
Cacelia, Caecilia, Cece, Ceceilia, Ceceli, Cecelia, Cecely, Cecelyn, Cecette, Cecil, Cecilea, Ceciley, Cecilija, Cecilla, Cecillia, Cecily, Ceclia, Cecylia, Cee, Ceil, Ceila, Ceilagh, Ceileh, Ceileigh, Ceilena, Cescelia, Cescelie, Cescily, Cicelia, Cilley, Secilia, Selia
Foreign forms: American: *Cissy, Sissy;* English: *Cicely;* French: *Cecile, Cecille;* German: *Cacilia, Cacilie;* Irish: *Sheila, Sisile, Sile;* Italian/Spanish: *Cecilia;* Swedish: *Celia, Cesia, Cesya*

Ceil (Latin) a short form of Cecilia.
Ceel, Ciel

Celena (Greek) an alternate form of Selena.
Celeen, Celeena, Celene, Celenia

Celeste (Latin) celestial, heavenly.
Celense, Celes, Celesia, Celesley, Celest, Celestia, Celestial, Celestin, Selestina
Foreign forms: English: *Celesta, Celestina;* French: *Celestine;* Polish: *Celestyn, Celina, Celinka, Celka;* Spanish: *Celestinia, Celestyna*

Celia (Latin) a short form of Cecilia.
Ceilia
Foreign forms: French: *Cele, Celie, Celine*

Celina (Greek) an alternate form of Celena.
Caleena, Calena, Calina, Celena, Celinda, Selina

Celine (Greek) an alternate form of Celena.
Caline, Celeen, Celene, Céline, Cellina, Cellinn

Cerella (Latin) springtime.
Cerelisa, Ceres

Cerise (French) cherry; cherry red.
Cera, Cerea, Cerese, Ceri, Ceria, Cerice, Cericia, Cerissa, Cerria, Cerrice, Cerrina, Cerrita, Cerryce, Ceryce, Cherise

Chablis (French) a dry, white wine. Geography: a region in France where wine grapes are grown.
Chabley, Chabli

Chadee (French) from Chad, a country in north central Africa. See also Sade.
Chaday, Chadday, Chade, Chadea

Chai (Hebrew) life.
Chae, Chaela, Chaeli, Chaella, Chaena

Chaka (Sanskrit) an alternate form of Chakra. See also Shaka.
Chakai, Chakia, Chakka, Chakkah

Chakra (Sanskrit) circle of energy.
Chaka, Chakara, Chakaria, Chakeitha, Chakena, Chakeria, Chakila, Chakina, Chakira, Chakrah, Chakria, Chakriya, Chakyra

Chalice (French) goblet.
Chalace, Chalcie, Chalece, Chalie, Chaliese, Chalise, Chalisk, Chalissa, Challa, Challaine, Challis, Challisse, Challysse, Chalsey, Chalyce, Chalyn, Chalyse, Chalysse

Chalonna (American) a combination of the prefix Cha + Lona.
Chalon, Chalonn, Chalonne, Shalon

Chambray (French) a light-weight fabric.
Chambre, Chambree, Chambrée

Chan (Cambodian) sweet-smelling tree.
Chanae

Chanda (Sanskrit) great goddess. Religion: the name assumed by the Hindu goddess Devi.
Chandee, Chandey, Chandi, Chandie
Foreign form: American: *Shanda*

Chandelle (French) candle.
Chandal, Chandel, Shandal, Shandel

Chandra (Sanskrit) moon. Religion: one of the names of the Hindu goddess Shakti. See also Shandra.
Chandre, Chandrea, Chandrelle, Chandria

Chanel (English) channel.
Chaneel, Chaneil, Chanell, Chanelle, Channel
Foreign form: American: **Shanel**

Chanell, Chanelle (English) alternate forms of Chanel.

Chantal (French) song.
Chandal, Chanta, Chantaal, Chantae, Chantael, Chantai, Chantale, Chantall, Chantalle, Chantara, Chantarai, Chantasia, Chantay,
Chantaye, Chanteau, Chantel, Chantil, Chantila, Chantill, Chantille, Chantle, Chantoya, Chantra, Chantri, Chantrice, Chantrill, Chaunta, Chauntay

Chantel, Chantelle (French) alternate forms of Chantal.
Chante, Chantea, Chantee, Chantée, Chanteese, Chantela, Chantele, Chantell, Chantella, Chanter, Chantey, Chantez, Chantiel, Chantielle, Chantrel, Chantrell, Chantrelle, Chantress, Chaunte, Chauntea, Chauntéa, Chauntee, Chauntel, Chauntell, Chauntelle, Chawntel, Chawntell, Chawntelle, Chontelle
Foreign form: American: *Shantel*

Chantilly (French) fine lace.
Foreign form: American: *Shantille*

Chantrea (Cambodian) moon; moonbeam.
Chantria

Chantrice (French) singer.
Chantreese
Foreign forms: American: *Shantreece, Shantrice*

Chardae, Charde (Punjabi) charitable. (French) short forms of Chardonnay. See also Shardae.
Charda, Chardai, Charday, Chardea, Chardee, Chardée, Chardese

Chardonnay (French) a dry white wine. Geography: a wine-making region in France.
Char, Chardae, Chardon, Chardonay, Chardonee, Chardonnee, Chardonnée, Shardonay, Shardonnay

Charis (Greek) grace; kindness.
Chari, Charice, Charie, Charish, Charisse

Charissa, Charisse (Greek) forms of Charity.
Charesa, Charese, Charis, Charisa, Charise, Charisha, Charissee, Charista

Charity (Latin) charity, kindness.
Carisa, Carisia, Carissa, Carita, Chariety, Charis, Charissa, Charisse, Charista, Charita, Chariti, Sharity

Charla (French, English) a short form of Charlene, Charlotte.
Char

Charlaine (English) an alternate form of Charlene.
Charlane, Charlanna, Charlayne

Charlene (English) little and womanly. A form of Caroline.
Charla, Charlaina, Charlaine, Charleen, Charleesa, Charlena, Charlesena, Charline, Charlyn, Charlyne, Charlynn, Charlynne, Charlzina
Foreign form: French: **Sharlene**

Charlie (German, English) strong and womanly.
Charla, Charle, Charlea, Charlee, Charleigh, Charley, Charli, Charyl, Chatty, Sharli, Sharlie

Charlotte (French) little and womanly. A form of Caroline. Literature: Charlotte Brontë was a British novelist and poet best known for her novel *Jane Eyre*.
Carly, Char, Chara, Charil, Charl, Charla, Charle, Charlene, Charlet, Charlett, Charletta, Charlette, Charlie, Charlisa, Charlita, Charlott, Charlotty, Charmaine, Charo, Charolet, Charolette, Charoline, Charolot, Charolotte, Lolotte

Foreign forms: American: **Karlotte, Sharlotte**; *Dutch:* **Lotje**; *English:* **Tottie**; *German:* **Karlotte, Lotta, Lotte**; *Hungarian:* **Sarolta**; *Italian:* **Carlotta**; *Spanish:* **Carlota**; *Swedish:* **Charlotta**

Charmaine (French) a form of Carmen.
Charamy, Charma, Charmain, Charmalique, Charman, Charmane, Charmar, Charmara, Charmayane, Charmeen, Charmene, Charmese, Charmian, Charmin, Charmine, Charmion, Charmisa, Charmon, Charmyn
Foreign form: American: **Sharmaine**

Charo (Spanish) a familiar form of Rosa.
Charro

Chasity (Latin) an alternate form of Chastity.
Chasa Dee, Chasadie, Chasady, Chasidy, Chasiti, Chassedi, Chassey, Chassidy, Chassie, Chassity, Chassy

Chastity (Latin) pure.
Chasity, Chasta, Chastady, Chastidy, Chastin, Chastitie, Chastney, Chasty

Chava (Hebrew) life. (Yiddish) bird. Bible: the original name of Eve.
Chabah, Chavah, Chavalah, Chavarra, Chavarria, Chave, Chavé, Chavel, Chaveli, Chavette, Chaviva, Chavvis, Hava, Kaya

Chavon (Hebrew) an alternate form of Jane.
Chavonn, Chavonna, Chavonne, Chevon, Chevonn, Chevonna, Shavon

Chaya (Hebrew) life; living.
Chaike, Chayka, Chayla, Chaylea, Chaylene, Chayra

Chelsea (English) seaport.
Chelese, Chelesia, Chelsa, Chelsae, Chelse, Chelsee, Chelsei, Chelsey, Chelsie, Chesea, Cheslee
Foreign forms: American:
Shelsea; Scottish: Kelsi

Chelsey (English) an alternate form of Chelsea. See also Kelsey.
Chelcy, Chelsay, Chelsy, Chesley
Foreign form: American:
Shelsea

Chelsie (English) an alternate form of Chelsea.
Chelcie, Chelli, Chellie,

Chellise, Chellsie, Chelsi, Chelsia, Cheslie, Chessie

Cher (French) beloved, dearest. (English) a short form of Cherilyn.
Chere, Chereen, Chereena, Cheri, Cherrelle, Sher

Cherelle, Cherrelle (French) alternate forms of Cheryl. See also Sherelle.
Charell, Charelle

Cheri, Cherie (French) familiar forms of Cher.
Chérie

Cherilyn (English) a combination of Cheryl + Lynn.
Cher, Cheralyn, Cherilynn, Cherralyn, Cherrilyn, Cherrylyn, Cherylin, Cheryline, Cheryl-Lyn, Cheryl-Lynn, Cheryl-Lynne, Cherylyn, Cherylynn, Cherylynne, Sherilyn

Cherise (French) a form of Cherish. See also Sharice.
Charisa, Charise, Cherece, Chereese, Cheresa, Cherese, Cheresse, Cherice, Cherrise

Cherish (English) dearly held, precious.
Charish, Charisha, Cheerish, Cherishe, Cherrish, Sherish
Foreign form: French: Cherise

Cherokee (Native American) a tribal name.
Cherika, Cherkita, Sherokee

Cherry (Latin) a familiar form of Charity. (French) cherry; cherry red.
Cheree, Cherey, Cherida, Cherita, Cherrey, Cherri, Cherrie, Cherrita, Cherry-Ann, Cherry-Anne, Cherrye, Chery, Cherye

Cheryl (French) beloved. See also Sheryl.
Charel, Charil, Charyl, Cherelle, Cherelle, Cheryl-Ann, Cheryl-Anne, Cheryle, Cherylee, Cherylene, Cheryll, Cherylle, Cheryl-Lee, Cheryn

Chesna (Slavic) peaceful.
Chesnee, Chesney, Chesnie, Chesny

Cheyenne (Cheyenne) a tribal name. See also Sheyenne.
Chey, Cheyan, Cheyana, Cheyann, Cheyanne, Cheyene, Cheyenna, Chi, Chi-Anna, Chie, Chyann, Chyanna, Chyanne

Chika (Japanese) near and dear.
Chikaka, Chikako, Chikara, Chikona

China (Chinese) fine porcelain. Geography: a country in eastern Asia. See also Shina.
Ciana, Chinaetta, Chinasa, Chinda, Chinea, Chinesia, Chinita, Chinna, Chinwa, Chyna, Chynna

Chinika (Swahili) God receives.
Chinarah, Chinyere

Chiquita (Spanish) little one.
Chaqueta, Chaquita, Chica, Chickie, Chicky, Chikata, Chikita, Chiqueta, Chiquila, Chiquite, Chiquitha, Chiquithe, Chiquitia, Chiquitta
Foreign form: American: *Shiquita*

Chita (Spanish) a short form of Conchita.

Chloe (Greek) blooming, verdant. Mythology: the goddess of agriculture.
Chloé, Chlöe, Chloee, Clo, Cloe, Cloey, Kloe

Chloris (Greek) pale. Mythology: the only daughter of Niobe to escape the vengeful arrows of Apollo and Artemis. See also Loris.
Cloris, Clorissa

Cho (Korean) beautiful.
Choe

Chris (Greek) a short form of Christina.
Cris
Foreign forms: American: *Kris;* English: *Chrys*

Chrissa (Greek) a short form of Christina.
Chryssa, Crissa, Cryssa
Foreign form: American: *Khrissa*

Chrissy (English) a familiar form of Christina.
Chrisie, Chrissee, Chrissie, Crissie, Khrissy

Christa (German) a short form of Christina. History: Christa McAuliffe, an American school teacher, was the first civilian on a U.S. space flight. See also Krista.
Chrysta
Foreign forms: Italian: *Crista;* Spanish: *Crysta*

Christabelle (Latin, French) beautiful Christian.
Christabella, Christable, Kristabel
Foreign form: English: *Cristabel*

Christal (Latin) an alternate form of Crystal. (Scottish) a form of Christina.
Christalene, Christalin, Christaline, Christall,

Christalle, Christalyn, Christel, Christelle

Christen, Christin (Greek) alternate forms of Christina.
Christan, Christyn, Chrystan, Chrysten, Chrystin, Chrystyn, Crestienne, Kristen
Foreign forms: Irish: *Cristen, Cristin*

Christi, Christie (Greek) short forms of Christina, Christine.
Christy, Chrysti, Chrystie, Chrysty, Kristi

Christian, Christiana (Greek) alternate forms of Christina. See also Kristian, Krystian.
Christiann, Christi-Ann, Christianna, Christi-Anne, Christianni, Christienne, Christy-Ann, Christy-Anne, Chrystyann, Chrystyanne, Crystiann, Crystianne
Foreign forms: French: *Christiane, Christianne*

Christina (Greek) Christian; anointed. See also Tina.
Chris, Chrissa, Christeena, Christella, Christena, Christi, Christiana, Christin, Christinea, Christinna, Christna, Christyna, Chrystena, Chrystina, Chrystyna, Cristy
Foreign forms: Czech: *Krista;*

Christina (cont.)
English: **Chrissy, Christy;** French:
Christine; German: **Christa,
Christiane, Kristel, Stina, Stine;**
Hungarian: **Krisztina;** Irish:
Cristiona, Cristin; Italian/Spanish:
Cristina; Russian/Scandinavian:
Khristina, Kristina; Scottish:
Cairistiona, Christal

Christine (French, English)
forms of Christina.
**Chrisa, Christeen, Christen,
Christene, Christi, Christin,
Chrystine, Cristeen, Cristene,
Cristine, Crystine**
Foreign forms: Scandinavian:
Kirsten, Kristen, Kristine

Christy (English) a short form
of Christina, Christine.
Cristy

Ciara, Cierra (Irish) black. See
also Sierra.
**Ceara, Cearaa, Cearia, Cearra,
Cera, Ciaara, Ciarda, Ciarra,
Ciarrah, Cieara, Ciearra,
Ciearria, Ciera, Cierrah**

Cinderella (French, English) little cinder girl. Literature: a
fairy tale heroine.

Cindy (Greek) moon. (Latin) a
familiar form of Cynthia.
**Cindee, Cindi, Cindl, Cynda,
Cyndal, Cyndale, Cyndall,**

**Cyndee, Cyndel, Cyndi,
Cyndia, Cyndie, Cyndle, Cyndy**
Foreign forms: American:
Sindie, Sindy, Syndi, Syndy

Claire (French) a form of Clara.
Clair, Clairette, Klaire, Klarye

Clara (Latin) clear; bright.
Music: Clara Shumann was a
famous nineteenth-century
German composer.
**Claresta, Clarette, Clarey,
Clari, Clarie, Clarina,
Clarinda, Clarine, Claritza,
Clary**
Foreign forms: English: **Clare;**
French: **Claire;** German/Hungarian:
Klara; Italian: **Chiara, Clarice,
Clarissa;** Scottish: **Sorcha;**
Spanish: **Clareta, Clarita**

Clarabelle (Latin) bright and
beautiful.
Clarabella, Claribel

Clare (English) a form of Clara.

Clarissa (Greek) brilliant.
(Italian) a form of Clara. See
also Klarissa.
**Clarecia, Claresa, Claressa,
Claresta, Clarisa, Clarissia,
Clarizza, Clarrisa, Clarrissa,
Clerissa**

Claudia (Latin) lame. A feminine form of Claude.

**Claudeen, Claudelle, Claudex,
Claudiane, Claudie, Claudie-
Anne, Claudina**
Foreign forms: American:
Klaudia; French: **Claude,
Claudette, Claudine;** Welsh:
Gladys

Clea (Greek) an alternate form
of Cleo, Clio.

Clementine (Latin) merciful. A
feminine form of Clement.
**Clemencie, Clemency,
Clementia, Clementina,
Clemenza, Clemette**
Foreign forms: French:
Clemence; German: **Klementine**

Cleo (Greek) a short form of
Cleopatra.
Clea

Cleopatra (Greek) her father's
fame. History: a great Egyptian
queen.
Cleo

Clio (Greek) proclaimer; glorifi-
er. Mythology: the muse of
history.
Clea

Coco (Spanish) coconut. See
also Koko.

Codi, Cody (English) cushion.
Coady, Codee, Codey, Codie
Foreign form: American: **Kodi**

Colby (English) coal town. Geography: a region in England known for cheese-making.
Cobi, Cobie, Colbi, Colbie
Foreign form: American: **Kolby**

Colette (Greek, French) a familiar form of Nicole.
Coe, Coetta, Coletta, Collet, Collete, Collett, Colletta, Collette, Kolette, Kollette

Colleen (Irish) girl.
Coel, Cole, Coleen, Colena, Colene, Coley, Colina, Colinda, Coline, Colleene, Collen, Collene, Collie, Collina, Colline, Colly

Concetta (Italian) pure. Religion: refers to the Immaculate Conception.
Concettina

Conchita (Spanish) conception.
Chita, Conceptia, Concha, Conciana

Concordia (Latin) harmonious. Mythology: the goddess governing the peace after war.
Con, Cordae, Cordaye

Connie (Latin) a familiar form of Constance.
Con, Connee, Conni, Conny, Konnie, Konny

Constance (Latin) constant; firm. History: Constance Motley was the first African-American woman to be appointed as a U.S. federal judge. See also Kosta.
Constancy, Constanta, Constantia, Constantine
Foreign forms: English: **Connie;** German: **Konstance, Konstanze;** Italian/Spanish: **Constancia, Constantina, Constanza, Constanzia**

Consuelo (Spanish) consolation. Religion: Santa Maria del Consuelo—Saint Mary of Consolation—is a name for the Virgin Mary.
Consolata, Consula, Konsuela, Konsuelo
Foreign forms: Italian: **Consuela, Consuella**

Cora (Greek) maiden. Mythology: the daughter of Demeter, the goddess of agriculture.
Corey, Corissa
Foreign forms: English: **Coretta, Corra, Kora;** Spanish: **Corina**

Coral (Latin) coral.
Corabel, Corabella, Corabelle, Coralee, Coralyn, Corral
Foreign forms: American: **Koral;** English: **Coraline**

Coralee (American) a combination of Cora + Lee.
Coralea, Cora-Lee, Coralena, Corella, Corilee, Koralie
Foreign form: American: **Coralie**

Corazon (Spanish) heart.

Cordelia (Latin) warm hearted. (Welsh) sea jewel. See also Delia, Della.
Cordae, Cordett, Cordette, Cordey, Cordi, Cordia, Cordie, Cordilia, Cordula, Cordy, Kordelia
Foreign forms: French: **Cordélie;** German: **Kordula**

Corey, Cory (Greek) familiar forms of Cora. (Irish) from the hollow. See also Kori.
Coree, Cori, Correy, Correye, Corry

Cori, Corie, Corrie (Irish) alternate forms of Corey.
Corian, Coriann, Cori-Ann, Corianne, Corri, Corrie-Ann, Corrie-Anne

Corina, Corinna (Greek) familiar forms of Corinne. See also Korina.
Coreena, Corinda, Correna, Corrina, Corrinna, Corynna

Corinne (Greek) maiden.
Coreen, Coren, Corin, Corina,

Corinne (cont.)
Corine, Corinee, Corinn, Correen, Corren, Corrianne, Corrin, Corrinn, Corrinne, Corryn, Coryn, Corynn

Corissa (Greek) a familiar form of Cora.
Coresa, Coressa, Corisa, Korissa

Corliss (English) cheerful; good hearted.
Corlisa, Corlise, Corlissa, Corly, Korliss

Cornelia (Latin) horn colored. A feminine form of Cornelius. See also Kornelia, Nelia, Nellie.
Carna, Carniella, Corneilla, Cornie, Cornilear, Cornisha, Corny
Foreign forms: English: **Cornela, Cornella, Cornelle;** *French:* **Cornélie**

Cortney (English) an alternate form of Courtney.
Cortnea, Cortnee, Cortneia, Cortni, Cortnie, Cortny, Corttney

Cosette (French) a familiar form of Nicole.
Cosetta, Cossetta, Cossette, Cozette

Courtenay (English) an alter-

nate form of Courtney.
Courtena, Courteney

Courtney (English) from the court. See also Kortney.
Cortney, Courtenay, Courtene, Courtnae, Courtnay, Courtnee, Courtnei, Courtni, Courtnie, Courtny, Courtonie
Foreign form: American: **Kourtney;** *French:* **Courtnée**

Crista (Italian) a form of Christa.

Cristen, Cristin (Irish) forms of Christen, Christin. See also Kristin.
Cristan, Cristyn, Crystan, Crysten, Crystin, Crystyn

Cristina (Greek) an alternate form of Christina.
Cristeena, Cristena, Cristiona, Crystina, Crystyna

Cristy (English) a familiar form of Cristina. An alternate form of Christy. See also Kristy.
Cristey, Cristi, Cristie, Crysti, Crystie, Crysty

Crystal (Latin) clear, brilliant glass.
Chrystel, Cristal, Cristalie, Cristalina, Cristalle, Cristel, Cristela, Cristelia, Cristella, Cristelle, Cristhie, Cristle,

Crystala, Crystal-Ann, Crystal-Anne, Crystale, Crystalee, Crystall, Crystaly, Crystel, Crystelia, Crysthelle, Crystl, Crystle, Crystol, Crystole, Crystyl
Foreign forms: American: **Chrystal-Lynn, Cristilyn, Crystalin, Crystalynn, Krystal;** *English:* **Christal, Chrystal**

Cybele (Greek) an alternate form of Sybil.
Cybel, Cybil, Cybill, Cybille
Foreign form: French: **Cybéle**

Cynthia (Greek) moon. Mythology: another name for Artemis, the moon goddess.
Cyneria, Cynethia, Cynithia, Cynthea, Cynthiana, Cynthiann, Cynthria, Cynthy, Cynthya, Cyntreia, Cythia, Kynthia
Foreign forms: English: **Cindy, Cynthie;** *Spanish:* **Cintia, Cyntia**

Cyrilla (Greek) ladylike. A feminine form of Cyril.
Cerelia, Cerella, Cyrella
Foreign forms: Spanish: **Cira, Cirilla**

Dacey (Greek) a familiar form of Candace. (Irish) southerner.
Dacee, Daci, Dacia, Dacie, Dacy, Daicee, Daicie, Daicy, Daycee, Daycie, Daycy

Dae (English) day.
Day, Daye

Daelynn (American) a combination of Dae + Lynn.
Daeleen, Daelena, Daelin, Daelyn, Daelynne

Daeshawna (American) a combination of Dae + Shawna.
Daeshan, Daeshanda, Daeshandra, Daeshandria, Daeshaun, Daeshauna, Daeshaundra, Daeshaundria, Daeshavon, Daeshawn, Daeshawnda, Daeshawndra, Daeshawndria, Daeshawntia,

Daeshon, Daeshona, Daeshonda, Daeshondra, Daeshondria

Dagmar (German) glorious.
Foreign forms: Czech: **Dagmara, Dasa;** Polish: **Daga**

Dagny (Scandinavian) day.
Dagna, Dagnanna, Dagne, Dagney

Dahlia (Scandinavian) valley.
Botany: a perennial flower.

Dai (Japanese) great.

Daisy (English) day's eye.
Botany: a white and yellow flower.
Daisee, Daisey, Daisi, Daisia, Daisie, Dasey, Dasi, Dasie, Dasy, Daysee, Daysie, Daysy

Dakota (Native American) tribal name.
Dakotah, Dakotha, Dekoda, Dekota, Dekotah, Dekotha

Dale (English) valley.
Daile, Daleleana, Dalena, Dalina, Dayle
Foreign forms: Dutch: **Dael;** Scandinavian: **Dahl, Dallana**

Daliah (Hebrew) branch.
Dalia, Dalialah, Daliyah

Dalila (Swahili) gentle.
Dalida, Dalilah, Dalilia

Dallas (Irish) wise.
Dalisia, Dalissia, Dallys, Dalyce, Dalys

Damaris (Greek) gentle girl.
Damar, Damara, Damarius, Damary, Damarys, Dameress, Dameris, Damiris, Dammaris, Dammeris, Damris, Demaras, Demaris

Damiana (Greek) tamer, soother. A feminine form of Damian.
Damiann, Damianna, Damianne

Damica (French) friendly.
Damee, Dameeka, Dameka, Damekah, Damicah, Damie, Damika, Damikah, Demeeka, Demeka, Demekah, Demica, Demicah

Damita (Spanish) small noblewoman.
Damee, Damesha, Dameshia, Damesia, Dametia, Dametra, Dametrah

Dana (English) from Denmark; bright as day.
Daina, Dainna, Danae, Danah, Danai, Danaia, Danalee, Danan, Danarra, Danayla,

Dana *(cont.)*
**Dane, Danean, Danee,
Daniah, Danie, Danja, Danna**
Foreign form: *Scandinavian:*
Dayna

Danae (Greek) Mythology: the
mother of Perseus.
**Danaë, Danay, Danayla,
Danays, Danea, Danee,
Dannae, Denae, Denee**

Daneil (Hebrew) an alternate
form of Danielle.
**Daneal, Daneala, Daneale,
Daneel, Daneela, Daneila**

Danelle (Hebrew) an alternate
form of Danielle.
**Danael, Danalle, Danel,
Danele, Danell, Danella,
Donelle, Donnelle**

Danessa (American) a combi-
nation of Danielle + Vanessa.
**Danesa, Danesha, Danessia,
Daniesa, Daniesha, Danisa,
Danisha, Danissa**

Danessia (American) an alter-
nate form of Danessa.
**Danesia, Danieshia, Danisia,
Danissia**

Danette (American) a form
of Danielle.
Danetra, Danett, Danetta

Dani (Hebrew) a familiar form
of Danielle.
**Danee, Danie, Danne, Dannee,
Danni, Dannie, Danny,
Dannye, Dany**

Dania, Danya (Hebrew) short
forms of Danielle.
Daniah

Danica, Danika (Hebrew)
alternate forms of Danielle.
(Slavic) morning star.
**Daneeka, Danikla, Danneeka,
Dannica, Dannika**

Danice (American) a combination of Danielle + Janice.

Daniella (Italian) a form of
Danielle.
Dannilla, Danijela

Danielle (Hebrew, French) God
is my judge. A feminine form
of Daniel.
**Daneen, Daneil, Daneille,
Danelle, Dani, Danial,
Danialle, Danica, Danie,
Daniele, Danielka, Daniell,
Danille, Danit, Danniele,
Danniell, Danniella, Dannielle**
Foreign forms: *American:*
***Danella, Danette, Danille,
Danyel, Donniella;*** *Italian:*
Daniella; *Spanish:* ***Daniela,
Danielan***

Danit (Hebrew) an alternate
form of Danielle.
**Danett, Danis, Danisha,
Daniss, Danita, Danitra,
Danitza, Daniz, Danni**

Danna (Hebrew) a short form
of Danella, Daniella. (English)
an alternate form of Dana.
**Danka, Dannae, Dannah,
Danne, Danni, Dannia,
Dannon, Danya**

Danyel, Danyell (American)
forms of Danielle.
**Daniyel, Danya, Danyae,
Danyail, Danyaile, Danyal,
Danyale, Danyea, Danyele,
Danyella, Danyelle, Danyle,
Donnyale, Donnyell, Donyale,
Donyell**

Daphne (Greek) laurel tree.
**Daphane, Daphaney,
Daphanie, Daphany,
Dapheney, Daphna, Daphnee,
Daphney, Daphnie,
Daphnique, Daphnit, Daphny**
Foreign form: *American:* ***Dafny***

Dara (Hebrew) compassionate.
**Dahra, Darah, Daraka,
Daralea, Daralee, Darda,
Darice, Darilyn, Darilyn,
Darisa, Darissa, Darja, Darra,
Darrah**

Darby (Irish) free.
(Scandinavian) deer estate.
Darb, Darbi, Darbie, Darbra

Darci, Darcy (Irish) dark.
(French) fortress.
**Darcee, Darcey, Darcie,
Darsey, Darsi, Darsie**
*Foreign forms: French:
Darcelle, Darselle*

Daria (Greek) wealthy. A femi-
nine form of Darius.
**Dari, Darian, Darianne,
Darria, Darya**

Darielle (French) an alternate
form of Daryl.
Dariel, Darriel, Darrielle

Darla (English) a short form
of Darlene.
**Darli, Darlice, Darlie, Darlis,
Darly, Darlys**

Darlene (French) little darling.
See also Daryl.
**Darlean, Darleen, Darlena,
Darlenia, Darletha, Darlin,
Darline, Darling**
*Foreign forms: American:
Darilynn; English: Darla*

Darnelle (Irish) an alternate
form of Daron.
**Darnel, Darnell, Darnella,
Darnetta, Darnette, Darnice,
Darniece, Darnita, Darnyell**

*Foreign form: American:
Darnesha*

Daron (Irish) great. A feminine
form of Darren.
**Daronica, Daronice, Darnelle,
Daryn**

Daryl (French) a short form of
Darlene. (English) beloved.
**Darelle, Darielle, Daril,
Darilynn, Darrel, Darrell,
Darrelle, Darreshia, Darryl,
Darryll**

Daryn (Greek) gifts. (Irish)
great. An alternate form
of Daron.
Daryan, Darynn, Darynne

Dashawna (American) a com-
bination of the prefix Da +
Shawna.
**Dashawn, Dashawnda,
Dashay, Dashell, Deshawna**

Dashiki (Swahili) loose-fitting
shirt worn in Africa.
**Dashi, Dashika, Dashka,
Desheka, Deshiki**

Davalynn (American) a combi-
nation of Davida + Lynn. A
form of Davina.
**Davalin, Davalinda, Davalyn,
Davalynda, Davalynne,
Davelin, Davelyn, Davelynn,
Davelynne, Davilin, Davilyn,
Davilynn, Davilynne**

Davida (Hebrew) beloved. A
feminine form of David. See
also Vida.
**Daveisha, Davesia, Daveta,
Davetta, Davette, Davika,
Davisha**
*Foreign forms: English: Davita;
Scottish: Davina*

Davina (Scottish) a form of
Davida. See also Vina.
**Dava, Davalinda, Davalynn,
Davannah, Davean, Davee,
Daveen, Daveena, Davene,
Daveon, Davey, Davi, Daviana,
Davie, Davin, Davinder,
Davine, Davineen, Davinia,
Davinna, Davonna, Davria,
Devean, Deveen, Devene,
Devina**

Davonna (Scottish, English)
an alternate form of Davina,
Devonna.
Davon, Davona, Davonda

Dawn (English) sunrise, dawn.
**Dawana, Dawandrea,
Dawanna, Dawin, Dawna,
Dawne, Dawnee, Dawnele,
Dawnell, Dawnelle, Dawnetta,
Dawnisha, Dawnlynn, Dawnn,
Dawnrae, Dawnyel,
Dawnyella, Dawnyelle**
*Foreign form: American:
Dawnisha*

Dawna (English) an alternate form of Dawn.
Dawnna, Dawnya

Deana (Latin) divine. (English) valley. A feminine form of Dean.
Deane, Deanielle, Deanna
Foreign forms: American:
Deanisha, Deena

Deandra (American) a combination of Dee + Andrea.
Deandre, Deandré, Deandrea, Deandree, Deandria, Deanndra, Diandra, Diandre, Diandrea

Deanna (Latin) an alternate form of Deana, Diana.
De, Dea, Deaana, Deahana, Deandra, Deandre, Deann, Déanna, Deannia, Deeanna, Deena

Deanne (Latin) an alternate form of Diane.
Dea, Deahanne, Deane, Deann, Déanne, Deeann, Deeanne

Debbie (Hebrew) a short form of Deborah.
Debbee, Debbey, Debbi, Debby, Debee, Debi, Debie

Deborah (Hebrew) bee. Bible: a great Hebrew prophetess.

Debbie, Debbora, Debborah, Debor, Deborha, Deborrah, Debrea, Debrena, Debria, Debrina, Debroah, Devora
Foreign forms: American:
Debra; English: **Deb, Debora, Deberah**; German: **Deboran**;
Yiddish: **Dwora**

Debra (American) a short form of Deborah.
Debbra, Debbrah, Debrah

Dedra (American) a form of Deirdre.
Deeddra, Deedra, Deedrea, Deedrie

Dee (Welsh) black, dark.
Dea, Deah, Dede, Dedie, Deea, Dee-Ann, Deedee, Dee Dee, Didi

Deena (American) a form of Deana, Dena, Dinah.

Deidra, Deidre (Irish) alternate forms of Deirdre.
Deidrea, Deidrie, Diedra, Diedre, Dierdra

Deirdre (Irish) sorrowful; wanderer.
Dee, Deerdra, Deerdre, Deidra, Deidre, Deirdree, Didi, Dierdre, Diérdre, Dierdrie
Foreign form: American: **Dedra**

Deitra (Greek) a short form of Demetria.
Deetra, Detria

Déja (French) before.
Daesha, Daija, Daisia, Daja, Dasha, Deejay, Dejanelle, Dejon

Dejon (French) an alternate form of Déja.
Daijon, Dajan, Dajona

Deka (Somali) pleasing.
Dekah, Dekka

Delana (German) noble protector.
Dalanna, Dalayna, Daleena, Dalena, Dalenna, Dalina, Dalinda, Dalinna, Delaina, Delani, Delania, Delany, Delanya, Deleena, Delena, Delenya, Delina, Dellaina

Delaney (Irish) descendant of the challenger. (English) an alternate form of Adeline.
Dalaney, Dalania, Dalene, Daleney, Daline, Del, Delainey, Delane, Delanie, Delayne, Delaynie, Deleani, Déline, Dell, Della, Dellaney
Foreign form: French: **Delaine**

Delia (Greek) visible; from Delos. (German, Welsh) a short form of Adelaide,

Cordelia. Mythology: a festival of Apollo held every five years in ancient Greece.
Dehlia, Del, Delea, Deli, Delinda, Dellia, Dellya, Delya

Delicia (English) delightful.
Delesha, Delice, Delisa, Delise, Delisha, Delisiah, Delya, Delys, Delyse, Delysia

Delilah (Hebrew) brooder. Bible: the companion of Samson. See also Lila.
Dalia, Dalialah, Dalila, Daliliah, Delila, Delilia

Della a short form of Adelaide, Cordelia, Delaney.
Del, Dela, Dell, Delle, Delli, Dellie, Dells

Delores (Spanish) an alternate form of Dolores.
Del, Delora, Delore, Deloria, Delories, Deloris, Delorise, Delorita
Foreign form: English: **Delsie**

Delphine (Greek) from Delphi.
Delfina, Delpha, Delphe, Delphi, Delphia, Delphina, Delphinia, Delvina

Delta (Greek) door. Linguistics: the fourth letter in the Greek alphabet. Geography: a triangular land mass at the mouth of a river.
Delte, Deltora, Deltoria, Deltra

Demetria (Greek) cover of the earth. Mythology: Demeter was the Greek goddess of the harvest.
Deitra, Demeta, Demeteria, Demetra, Demetrice, Demetris, Demetrish, Demetrius, Demi, Demita, Demitra, Dimitra, Dymitra

Demi (Greek) a short form of Demetria. (French) half.
Demiah

Dena (Hebrew) an alternate form of Dinah. (English, Native American) valley. See also Deana.
Deane, Deena, Deeyn, Denae, Dene, Denea, Deney, Denna

Denae (Hebrew) an alternate form of Dena.
Denaé, Denay, Denee, Deneé

Denise (French) Mythology: follower of Dionysus, the god of wine. A feminine form of Dennis.
Danice, Danise, Denese, Deney, Deni, Denica, Denie, Deniece, Denisse, Denize, Denni, Dennie, Dennise,
Denny, Dennys, Denys, Dinnie, Dinny
Foreign forms: American: **Denisha;** *English:* **Denice, Denyce, Denyse;** *Spanish:* **Denisa**

Denisha (American) a form of Denise.
Deneesha, Deneichia, Denesha, Deneshia, Deniesha, Denishia

Derika (German) ruler of the people. A feminine form of Derek.
Dereka, Derekia, Derica, Dericka, Derrica, Derricka, Derrika

Derry (Irish) redhead.
Deri, Derie

Deryn (Welsh) bird.
Derren, Derrin, Derrine, Deryne

Deshawna (American) a combination of the prefix De + Shawna.
Dashawna, Deshan, Deshanda, Deshandra, Deshane, Deshaun, Deshaundra, Deshawn, Deshawndra, Desheania, Deshona, Deshonda, Deshonna

Desi (French) a short form of
Desiree.
**Désir, Desira, Dezi, Dezia,
Dezzia, Dezzie**

Desiree (French) desired,
longed for.
**Desara, Desarae, Desarai,
Desaraie, Desaray, Desare,
Desaré, Desarea, Desaree,
Desarie, Desera, Deserae,
Deserai, Deseray, Desere,
Deseree, Deseret, Deseri,
Deserie, Deserrae, Deserray,
Deserré, Desi, Desirae,
Desirah, Desirai, Desiray,
Desirea, Desirée, Désirée,
Desirey, Desiri, Desray,
Desree, Dessa, Dessie,
Dessirae, Dessire, Dezarae,
Dezeray, Dezere, Dezerea,
Dezerie, Dezirae, Deziree,
Dezirée, Dezorae, Dezra,
Dezrae, Dezyrae**
Foreign forms: _English:_ **_Desire,
Desyre_**

Destiny (French) fate.
**Desnine, Desta, Destanee,
Destanie, Destannie, Destany,
Desteni, Destin, Destinee,
Destinée, Destiney, Destini,
Destinie, Destnie, Desty,
Destyn, Destyne, Destyni**
Foreign form: _Spanish:_ **_Destina_**

Deva (Hindi) divine. Religion:
the Hindu moon goddess.

Devi (Hindi) goddess. Religion:
the Hindu goddess of power
and destruction.

Devin (Irish) poet. An alternate
form of Devon.
**Devan, Devane, Devanie,
Devany, Deven, Devena,
Devenje, Deveny, Deveyn,
Devina, Devine, Devinne,
Devyn**

Devon (English) a short form
of Devonna.
Devonne

Devonna (English) from
Devonshire.
**Davonna, Devon, Devona,
Devonda, Devondra**

Devora (Hebrew) an alternate
form of Deborah.
Devorah, Devra, Devrah

Di (Latin) a short form of Diana,
Diane.
Dy

Diamond (Latin) precious gem.
**Diamonda, Diamonia,
Diamonique, Diamonte,
Diamontina**

Diana (Latin) divine.
Mythology: the goddess of the
hunt, the moon, and fertility.
See also Dee, Deanna,

Deanne, Dyan.
**Daiana, Daianna, Dayana,
Dayanna, Di, Dia, Dianah,
Dianalyn, Dianarose,
Dianatris, Dianca, Diandra,
Diane, Dianelis, Diania,
Dianielle, Dianita, Dianna,
Dianys, Didi, Dina**

Diane (Latin) an alternate form
of Diana.
**Deane, Deanne, Deeane,
Deeanne, Di, Dia, Diahann,
Dian, Diani, Dianie, Diann,
Dianne**

Dianna (Latin) an alternate
form of Diana.
Diahanna

Dina (Hebrew) a short form
of Dinah.

Dinah (Hebrew) vindicated.
Bible: a daughter of Jacob and
Leah.
Dina, Dyna, Dynah
Foreign form: _American:_ **_Deena_**

Dionne (Greek) divine queen.
Mythology: the mother of
Aphrodite, the goddess of love.
**Deona, Deondra, Deonia,
Deonjala, Deonna, Deonne,
Deonyia, Dion, Diona,
Diondra, Diondrea, Dione,
Dionee, Dionis, Dionna,
Dionte**

Dior (French) golden.
Diora, Diore, Diorra, Diorre

Dixie (French) tenth. (English) wall; dike. Geography: a nickname for the American South.
Dix, Dixee, Dixi, Dixy

Dodie (Greek) a familiar form of Dorothy. (Hebrew) beloved.
Doda, Dode, Dodee, Dodi, Dody

Dolly (American) a short form of Dolores, Dorothy.
Dol, Doll, Dollee, Dolley, Dolli, Dollie, Dollina

Dolores (Spanish) sorrowful. Religion: Santa Maria de los Dolores—Saint Mary of the Sorrows—is a name for the Virgin Mary. See also Lola.
Delores, Deloria, Dolorcitas, Dolorita, Doloritas
Foreign form: American: **Dolly**

Dominica, Dominika (Latin) belonging to the Lord. A feminine form of Dominic. See also Mika.
Domenica, Domenika, Domineca, Domineka, Domini, Dominixe, Domino, Dominyika, Domka, Domnicka, Domonica, Domonice, Domonika

Foreign forms: French: **Dominique, Domonique;** *Spanish:* **Dominga**

Dominique, Domonique (French) forms of Dominica, Dominika.
Domanique, Domeneque, Domenique, Domineque, Dominiqua, Domino, Dominoque, Dominuque, Domique, Domminique, Domoniqua

Donalda (English) world leader; proud ruler. A feminine form of Donald.
Donalda, Donaldina, Donaleen, Donelda, Donella, Donellia, Donette, Doni, Donita, Donnella, Donnelle

Dona, Doña (Italian) an alternate form of Donna.
Donail, Donalea, Donalisa, Donay, Donella, Donelle, Donetta, Doni, Donia, Donica, Donice, Donie, Donika, Donise, Donisha, Donishia, Donita, Donitrae

Donata (Latin) gift.
Donatha, Donatta

Donna (Italian) lady.
Dona, Donnaica, Donnalee, Donnalen, Donnay, Donnell, Donnella, Donni, Donnica,

Donnie, Donnika, Donnise, Donnisha, Donnita, Donny, Dontia, Donya
Foreign form: American: **Dondi**

Dora (Greek) gift. A short form of Eudora, Pandora, Theodora.
Doralia, Doralie, Doralisa, Doraly, Doran, Dorchen, Dorece, Doree, Doreece, Doreen, Dorella, Dorelle, Doresha, Doressa, Dori, Doriley, Dorilis, Dorinda, Dorion
Foreign forms: English: **Doralynn, Dorelia, Doretta**

Doreen (Greek) an alternate form of Dora. (Irish) moody, sullen. (French) golden.
Doreena, Dorena, Dorene, Dorina, Dorine

Dori, Dory (American) familiar forms of Dora, Doria, Doris, Dorothy.
Dore, Dorey, Dorie, Dorree, Dorri, Dorrie, Dorry
Foreign form: Spanish: **Dorinda**

Doria (Greek) from Doris, Greece. A feminine form of Dorian.
Dori, Doriana, Doriann, Dorianna, Dorianne

Doris (Greek) sea. Mythology: the wife of Nereus and mother

Doris *(cont.)*
of the sea nymphs Nereids.
**Dori, Dorice, Dorise, Dorris,
Dorrise, Dorrys, Dory, Dorys**
Foreign forms: Czech: **Dorika,
Dorka;** *English:* **Dorita;** *Hawaiian:*
Dorisa; *Hebrew:* **Dorit**

Dorothea (Greek) an alternate
form of Dorothy.
**Dorethea, Dorotha, Dorothia,
Dorotthea, Dorthea, Dorthia**

Dorothy (Greek) gift of God.
See also Dodie, Theodora.
**Do, Doa, Doe, Dolly, Dorathy,
Doretta, Dori, Doritha, Dorle,
Dorlisa, Doro, Dorolice,
Dorosia, Dorothea, Dortha,
Dorthy, Dosi, Dossiea, Dottie**
Foreign forms: Dutch: **Doortje;**
Hungarian: **Dorottya;**
Italian/Spanish: **Dorotea;** *French:*
Dorothée; *Lithuanian/Polish:*
Dorota; *Norwegian:* **Dordei,
Dordi, Dorte;** *Russian:* **Dasha,
Doroteya;** *Slavic:* **Dasya, Dosy;**
Zuni: **Lolotea**

Dottie, Dotty (Greek) familiar
forms of Dorothy.
Dot, Dottee

Drew (Greek) courageous;
strong. (Latin) a short form of
Drusilla.
Dru, Drue

Drusi (Latin) a short form of
Drusilla.
**Drucey, Drucie, Drucy, Drusey,
Drusie, Drusy**

Drusilla (Latin) descendant of
Drusus, the strong one. See
also Drew.
**Drewsila, Drucella, Drucill,
Drucilla, Druscilla, Druscille,
Drusi**

Dulcie (Latin) sweet. (Spanish)
a short form of Dulcinea.
**Delcina, Douce, Doucie, Dulci,
Dulcia, Dulcy, Dulsea**
Foreign forms: English: **Delcine,
Dulce, Dulcea, Dulciana,
Dulcibel, Dulcibella, Dulcine**

Dulcinea (Spanish) sweet.
Literature: Don Quixote's love
interest.
Dulcie

Duscha (Russian) soul; sweetheart; term of endearment.
Duschah, Dusha, Dushenka

Dustine (German) valiant
fighter. (English) brown rock,
quarry. A feminine form of
Dustin.
**Dustee, Dusti, Dustie,
Dustina, Dusty, Dustyn**

Dyan (Latin) an alternate form
of Diana. (Native American)
deer.
**Dyana, Dyane, Dyani, Dyann,
Dyanna, Dyanne**

Dyshawna (American) a com-
bination of the prefix Dy +
Shawna.
**Dyshanta, Dyshawn,
Dyshonda, Dyshonna**

Earlene (Irish) pledge. (English)
noblewoman. A feminine form
of Earl.
**Earla, Earlean, Earlecia,
Earleen, Earlena, Earlina,
Earlinda, Earline, Erla, Erlana,
Erlene, Erlenne, Erlina,
Erlinda, Erline, Erlisha**

Eartha (English) earthy.
Ertha

Easter (English) Easter time. History: a name for a child born on Easter.
Eastan, Eastlyn, Easton

Eboni, Ebonie (Greek) alternate forms of Ebony.
Ebanie, Ebonni, Ebonnie

Ebony (Greek) a hard, dark wood.
Eban, Ebanee, Ebany, Ebbony, Ebone, Ebonee, Eboney, Eboni, Ebonique, Ebonisha, Ebonnee, Ebonye, Ebonyi

Eda (Irish, English) a short form of Edana, Edith.

Edana (Irish) ardent; flame.
Eda, Edan, Edanna

Eddy (American) a familiar form of Edwina.
Eddi, Eddie, Edy

Eden (Babylonian) a plain. (Hebrew) delightful. Bible: the earthly paradise.
Ede, Edena, Edene, Edin, Edyn
Foreign forms: Spanish: **Edana, Edenia**

Edie (English) a familiar form of Edith.
Eadie, Edi, Edy, Edye, Eyde, Eydie

Edith (English) rich gift.
Eadith, Ede, Edetta, Edette, Edie, Edite, Edithe, Editta, Ediva, Edyta, Edyth, Edytha, Edythe
Foreign forms: Czech/Italian: *Edita;* German: **Editha;** Hungarian: **Edit;** Polish: **Edda, Edka;** Spanish: **Dita**

Edna (Hebrew) rejuvenation. Mythology: the wife of Enoch, according to ancient eastern legends.
Ednah, Edneisha, Ednita

Edwina (English) prosperous friend. A feminine form of Edwin. See also Winnie.
Eddy, Edina, Edweena, Edwena, Edwine, Edwyna

Effie (Greek) spoken well of. (English) a short form of Alfreda, Euphemia.
Effi, Effia, Effy, Ephie

Efrat (Hebrew) honored, distinguished.
Efrata

Eileen (Irish) a form of Helen. See also Aileen.
Eilean, Eilena, Eilene, Eiley, Eilidh, Eilleen, Eillen, Eilyn, Eleen, Elene

Elaine (French) a form of Helen. See also Laine.
Elain, Elaina, Elainia, Elainna, Elan, Elana, Elane, Elania, Elanie, Elanit, Elanna, Elauna, Elayn, Elayna, Elayne, Ellaine

Elana (Greek) a short form of Eleanor. See also Lana.
Elan, Elani, Elanie

Eldora (Spanish) golden, gilded.
Eldoree, Eldorey, Eldori, Eldoria, Eldorie, Eldory

Eleanor (Greek) light. An alternate form of Helen. History: Anna Eleanor Roosevelt was a U.S. delegate to the United Nations, a writer, and the thirty-second First Lady of the U.S. See also Elana, Ella, Lena, Leonore, Leora, Nellie, Nora, Noreen.
Elana, Elanor, Elanore, Eleanora, Eleanore, Elenor, Elenorah, Eleonor, Elianore, Elinor, Elinore, Elladine, Ellenor, Ellie, Elliner, Ellinor, Ellinore, Elna, Elnore, Elynor, Elynore
Foreign forms: Czech: **Elena;** Danish/German: **Elenore;** English: **Ellen;** French: **Eléonore;** Italian: **Elenora;** Russian: **Lenore;** Spanish: **Leanor**

Eleanora (Greek) an alternate form of Eleanor.
Elenora, Eleonora, Eleora, Elianora, Eliora, Ellenora, Ellenorah, Elnora, Elora, Elynora

Electra (Greek) shining; brilliant. Mythology: the daughter of Agamemnon, leader of the Greeks in the Trojan War.
Elektra

Elena (Greek) an alternate form of Eleanor. (Italian) a form of Helen.
Eleana, Eleen, Eleena, Elen, Elene, Eleni, Elenitsa, Elenka, Elenoa, Elenola, Elina, Ellena

Elfrida (German) peaceful. See also Alfreda, Freda.
Elfie, Elfrea, Elfredda, Elfreeda, Elfreyda, Elfryda
Foreign forms: English: **Elfreda, Elfrieda**

Eliana (Hebrew) my God has answered me. A feminine form of Eli, Elijah.
Elianna, Elianne, Elliane, Ellianna, Ellianne, Liana, Liane

Elicia (Hebrew) an alternate form of Elisha. See also Alicia.
Ellicia

Elisa (Spanish, Italian, English) a short form of Elizabeth. See also Alisa, Ilisa.
Elecea, Eleesa, Elesa, Elesia, Elisia, Elisya, Ellisa, Ellisia, Ellissa, Ellissia, Ellissya, Ellisya, Elysa, Elysia, Elyssia, Elyssya, Elysya, Lisa

Elise (French, English) a short form of Elizabeth, Elysia. See also Lisette.
Eilis, Eilise, Elese, Élise, Elisee, Elisie, Elisse, Elizé, Ellice, Ellise, Ellyce, Ellyse, Ellyze, Elsey, Elsie, Elsy, Elyce, Elyci, Elyse, Elyze, Lison
Foreign forms: American: **Lissie;** *German:* **Ilese, Ilise, Liese**

Elisha (Greek) an alternate form of Alisha. (Hebrew) consecrated to God. See also Lisha.
Eleacia, Eleasha, Elecia, Eleesha, Eleisha, Elesha, Eleshia, Eleticia, Elicia, Eliscia, Elishia, Elishua, Eliska, Elitia, Ellecia, Ellesha, Ellexia, Ellisha, Elsha, Elysha, Ilisha

Elissa, Elyssa (Greek, English) forms of Elizabeth. Short forms of Melissa. See also Alisa, Alyssa, Lissa.
Ellissa, Ellyssa, Ilissa, Ilyssa

Elita (Latin, French) chosen. See also Lida, Lita.
Elida, Elitia, Elitie, Ellita, Ellitia, Ellitie, Ilida, Ilita, Litia

Eliza (Hebrew) a short form of Elizabeth.
Aliza, Elizaida, Elizalina, Elize, Elizea

Elizabeth (Hebrew) consecrated to God. Bible: the mother of John the Baptist. See also Bess, Beth, Elsa, Libby, Lisa, Lissa, Lizzy.
Eliabeth, Elisabeta, Elisabeth, Elisabethe, Elisabette, Elise, Elisebet, Elisheba, Elisheva, Elissa, Eliz, Eliza, Elizabee, Elizabet, Elizabete, Elizebeth, Ellice, Elsabeth, Elsbet, Elschen, Elspie, Elsy, Elysabeth, Ilizzabet, Lusa
Foreign forms: American: **Betsey, Betsy, Lissie, Liza;** *Czech:* **Alzbeta;** *Danish:* **Ailsa, Helsa;** *English:* **Betty, Elyse, Elyssa, Liz, Lizabeth, Tetty;** *French:* **Lisette, Lizette;** *German:* **Elsa, Elsbeth, Else, Ilse, Ilsey, Liese, Liesel;** *Hawaiian:* **Elikapeka;** *Hungarian:* **Erzsébet, Zizi;** *Italian:* **Elisa, Elisabetta;** *Latvian:* **Lizina;** *Lithuanian:* **Elzbieta;** *Polish:* **Elka;** *Russian:* **Liza, Lizabeta, Yelisabeta;** *Scottish:* **Eilis, Elspet, Elspeth;** *Slavic:* **Elizaveta, Veta;** *Spanish:* **Isabel;** *Swedish:* **Elisabet**

Elke (German) an alternate form of Adelaide, Alice.
Elki, Ilki

Ella (Greek) a short form of Eleanor. (English) elfin; beautiful fairy-woman.
Ellamae, Ellia, Ellie, Elly

Ellen (English) a form of Eleanor, Helen.
Elen, Elenee, Eleny, Elin, Elina, Elinda, Ellan, Elle, Ellena, Ellene, Ellie, Ellin, Ellon, Ellyn, Ellynn, Elyn

Ellice (English) an alternate form of Elise.
Ellecia, Ellyce, Elyce

Ellie, Elly (English) short forms of Eleanor, Ella, Ellen.
Ele, Elie, Elli

Elma (Turkish) sweet fruit.

Elsa (Hebrew) a short form of Elizabeth. (German) noble.
Elisa, Ellse, Ellsey, Ellsie, Ellsy, Else, Elsie, Elsje, Elsy

Elsie (German) a familiar form of Elsa.
Elsi, Elsy

Elva (English) elfin. See also Alvina.
Elvenea, Elvia, Elvie, Elvina, Elvinea, Elvinia, Elvinna

Elvira (Latin) white; blond. (German) closed up. (Spanish) elfin. Geography: the town in Spain that hosted the first Ecumenical Council in 300 A.D.
Elva, Elvina, Elwira, Vira
Foreign forms: English: Elvera; French: Elvire; Polish: Wira

Elyse (English) a form of Elizabeth.

Elysia (Latin) sweet; blissful. Mythology: Elysium was the dwelling place of happy souls.
Elysha, Ilysha, Ilysia
Foreign forms: French: Elise, Ilyse

Elyssa (English) a form of Elizabeth.

Emerald (French) bright green gemstone.
Foreign forms: English: Emerant; French: Esmé; Spanish: Esmeralda

Emilee, Emilie (English) forms of Emily.
Emméie

Emilia (Italian) a form of Amelia, Emily.
Emalia, Emelia, Emila

Emily (Latin) flatterer. (German) industrious. A feminine form of Emil. See also Amelia, Emma, Millie.
Emaili, Emaily, Emalia, Emalie, Emeli, Emelia, Emelie, Emelita, Emely, Emiley, Emili, Emilienne, Emilis, Emillie, Emilly, Emmaly, Emmey, Emmie, Emmilly, Emmy, Emmye, Emyle
Foreign forms: Czech: Emilka; English: Em, Emilee, Emilie; French: Émilie, Emmaline, Emmélie; German: Emmi; Italian: Emilia; Irish: Eimile, Eimilie; Scottish: Aimal; Spanish: Amelita, Amilita

Emilyann (American) a combination of Emily + Ann.
Emileane, Emileann, Emileanna, Emileanne, Emiliana, Emiliann, Emilianna, Emilianne, Emillyane, Emillyann, Emillyanna, Emillyanne, Emliana, Emliann, Emlianna, Emlianne

Emma (German) a short form of Emily. See also Amy.
Em, Emi, Emiy, Emmi, Emmie, Emmy, Emmye
Foreign forms: French: Emeline, Emmaline; Spanish: Ema

Emmalee (American) a combination of Emma + Lee. A form of Emily.
Emalea, Emalee, Emilee,

Emmalee *(cont.)*
**Emmaleigh, Emmali,
Emmaliese, Emmalyse, Emylee**

Emmaline (French) a form of
Emily.
**Emalina, Emaline, Emelina,
Emeline, Emilina, Emiline,
Emmalina, Emmalene,
Emmeline, Emmiline**

Emmalynn (American) a com-
bination of Emma + Lynn.
**Emelyn, Emelyne, Emelynne,
Emilyn, Emilynn, Emilynne,
Emlyn, Emlynn, Emlynne,
Emmalyn, Emmalynne**

Emmanuelle (Hebrew) God is
with us. A feminine form of
Emmanuel.
Emmanuela, Emmanuella
Foreign forms: *Spanish:*
Manuela, Manuelita

Emmylou (American) a combi-
nation of Emmy + Lou.
**Emlou, Emmalou, Emmelou,
Emmilou, Emylou**

Enid (Welsh) life; spirit.

Erica (Scandinavian) ruler of all.
(English) brave ruler. A femi-
nine form of Eric. See also
Arica, Rica, Ricki.
**Ericca, Ericha, Ericka, Erikka,
Errica, Errika, Eryka, Erykka**
Foreign form: *Swedish:* ***Erika***

Erin (Irish) peace. History:
another name for Ireland. See
also Arin.
**Eran, Eren, Erena, Erene,
Ereni, Eri, Erian, Erina, Erine,
Erinetta, Erinn, Erinna,
Erinne, Eryn, Erynn, Erynne**

Erma (Latin) a short form of
Ermine. See also Irma.
Ermelinda

Ermine (Latin) noble. (German)
soldier. A feminine form of
Herman.
**Erma, Ermin, Ermina,
Erminda, Erminia, Erminie**

Ernestine (English) earnest,
sincere. A feminine form of
Ernest.
**Erna, Ernaline, Ernesia,
Ernesta, Ernestina, Ernesztina**

Eryn (Irish) an alternate form of
Erin.

Esmé (French) a familiar form
of Esmeralda. A form of Amy.
Esma, Esme, Esmée

Esmeralda (Greek, Spanish) a
form of Emerald.
**Emelda, Esmerelda,
Esmerilda, Esmiralda,
Ezmerelda, Ezmirilda**
Foreign form: *French:* ***Esmé***

Esperanza (Spanish) hope.
**Espe, Esperance, Esperans,
Esperanta, Esperanz,
Esperenza**
Foreign form: *Italian:* ***Speranza***

Essie (English) a short form of
Estelle, Esther.
Essa, Essey, Essie, Essy

Estee (English) a short form of
Estelle, Esther.
Esta, Estée, Esti

Estelle (French) a form of
Esther. See also Stella.
**Essie, Estee, Estel, Estele,
Estelina, Estelita, Estell,
Estellina, Estellita, Esthella,
Estrela, Estrelinha, Estrell**
Foreign forms: *English:* ***Estela;***
Spanish: ***Estrelle, Estrellita, Trella***

Esther (Persian) star. Bible: the
Jewish captive whom
Ahasuerus made his queen.
Essie, Estee, Esthur
Foreign forms: *Dutch:* ***Hester;***
Hungarian: ***Eszter, Eszti;*** *Italian:*
Ester; *Spanish:* ***Estella, Estrella***

Ethel (English) noble.
**Ethelda, Ethelin, Etheline,
Ethelle, Ethelyn, Ethelynn,
Ethelynne, Ethyl**

Etta (German) little. (English)
a short form of Henrietta.

Etka, Etke, Etti, Ettie, Etty, Itke, Itta

Eudora (Greek) honored gift. See also Dora.
Foreign form: French: **Eudore**

Eugenia (Greek) born to nobility. A feminine form of Eugene. See also Gina.
Eugenie, Eugenina, Eugina
Foreign forms: French: **Eugénie;** Russian: **Evgenia**

Eulalia (Greek) well spoken.
Eulalee, Eulalya, Eulia
Foreign forms: English: **Eula;** French: **Eulalie;** Spanish: **Ula**

Eunice (Greek) happy; victorious. Bible: the mother of Saint Timothy.
Euna, Eunique, Eunise, Euniss
Foreign form: English: **Unice**

Euphemia (Greek) spoken well of, in good repute. History: a fourth-century Christian martyr.
Effam, Euphan, Euphie
Foreign forms: English: **Effie, Eppie;** French: **Euphémie;** Italian/Spanish: **Eufemia**

Eurydice (Greek) wide, broad. Mythology: the wife of Orpheus.
Euridice, Euridyce, Eurydyce

Eustacia (Greek) productive. (Latin) stable; calm. A feminine form of Eustace. See also Stacey.

Eva (Greek) a short form of Evangelina. (Hebrew) an alternate form of Eve. See also Ava, Chava.
Evah, Evalea, Evalee, Evike

Evaline (French) a form of Evelyn.
Evalin, Evalina, Evalyn, Eveleen, Evelene, Evelina, Eveline

Evangelina (Greek) bearer of good news.
Eva, Evangelia, Evangelica, Evangeline
Foreign form: French: **Evangelique**

Evania (Greek) a feminine form of Evan. (Irish) young warrior.
Evana, Evann, Evanna, Evanne, Evany, Eveania, Evvanne, Evvunea, Evyan

Eve (Hebrew) life. An alternate form of Chava. Bible: the first woman created by God. (French) a short form of Evonne.
Eva, Evelyn, Evey, Evvie, Evvy, Evyn
Foreign forms: Finnish: **Eeva;**

French: **Naeva;** German: **Evy;** Hungarian: **Éva, Evi, Vica;** Polish: **Ewa;** Slavic: **Evuska, Yeva;** Spanish: **Evita**

Evelyn (English) hazelnut.
Aveline, Evaleen, Evalene, Evaline, Evalyn, Evalynn, Evalynne, Eveleen, Eveline, Evelyne, Evelynn, Evelynne, Evline
Foreign form: Hawaiian: **Ewalina**

Evette (French) an alternate form of Yvette. A familiar form of Evonne. See also Ivette.
Evett

Evline (English) an alternate form of Evelyn.
Evleen, Evlene, Evlin, Evlina, Evlyn, Evlynn, Evlynne

Evonne (French) an alternate form of Yvonne. See also Ivonne.
Evanne, Eve, Evenie, Evenne, Eveny, Evette, Evon, Evonnie, Evony

Fabia (Latin) bean grower. A feminine form of Fabian.
Fabiana, Fabiann, Fabianne, Fabiene, Fabienne, Fabiola, Fabra, Fabreanne, Fabria

Faith (English) faithful; fidelity. See also Faye.
Fayth, Faythe

Faline (Latin) catlike.
Faleen, Falena, Falene, Falina, Faylina, Fayline, Faylyn, Faylynn, Faylynne, Felina

Fallon (Irish) grandchild of the ruler.
Falan, Falen, Falin, Fallan, Fallonne, Fallyn, Falyn, Falynn, Falynne

Fancy (French) betrothed. (English) whimsical; decorative.

Fanchette, Fanchon, Fanci, Fancia, Fancie

Fanny (American) a familiar form of Frances.
Fan, Fanette, Fani, Fania, Fannee, Fanney, Fanni, Fannia, Fannie, Fanya

Farah, Farrah (English) beautiful; pleasant.
Fara, Farra, Fayre

Faren, Farren (English) wanderer.
Faran, Fare, Farin, Faron, Farrahn, Farran, Farrand, Farrin, Farron, Farryn, Farye, Faryn, Feran, Ferin, Feron, Ferran, Ferren, Ferrin, Ferron, Ferryn

Fatima (Arabic) daughter of the Prophet. History: the daughter of Muhammad.
Fatema, Fathma, Fatimah, Fatime, Fatma, Fattim

Fawn (French) young deer.
Faun, Fauna, Fawna, Fawne, Fawnia, Fawnna

Faye (French) fairy; elf. (English) an alternate form of Faith.
Fae, Fay, Fayann, Fayanna, Fayette, Fayina, Fayla, Fey, Feyla

Fayola (Nigerian) lucky.

Felecia (Latin) an alternate form of Felicia.
Flecia

Felica (Spanish) a short form of Felicia.
Falisa, Felisa, Felisca, Felissa, Feliza

Felice (Latin) a short form of Felicia.
Felece, Felise, Felize, Felysse

Felicia (Latin) fortunate; happy. A feminine form of Felix. See also Lecia.
Falecia, Falicia, Fela, Felecia, Felice, Felicie, Felicya, Felisha, Felisiana, Felita, Felixia, Felizia, Felka, Fellcia, Felysia, Fleasia, Fleichia, Flichia
Foreign forms: English: Felicity; French: Félice, Félicité; Greek: Phylicia; Spanish: Felica, Feliciana, Felicidad

Felisha (Latin) an alternate form of Felicia.
Faleisha, Falesha, Faleshia, Falisha, Falleshia, Feleasha, Feleisha, Felesha, Felishia, Fellishia, Fleishia, Flisha

Femi (French) woman. (Nigerian) love me.
Femie, Femmi, Femme

Feodora (Greek) gift of God.
Fedora, Fedoria

Fern (German) a short form of Fernanda. (English) fern.
Ferne, Ferni, Fernlee, Fernleigh, Fernley, Fernly

Fernanda (German) daring, adventurous. A feminine form of Ferdinand. See also Nan.
Andee, Ferdie, Ferdinande, Fern, Fernande, Fernandette, Nanda
Foreign forms: English:
Ferdinanda, Fernandina

Fidelia (Latin) an alternate form of Fidelity.
Fidela, Fidele, Fidelina

Fidelity (Latin) faithful, true.
Fidelia, Fidelita

Fiona (Irish) fair, white.
Fionna

Fionnula (Irish) white shouldered. See also Nola.
Fenella, Fenula, Finella, Finola, Finula, Nuala

Flair (English) style; verve.
Flaire, Flare

Flannery (Irish) redhead. Literature: Flannery O'Connor was a renowned American writer.
Flan, Flann, Flanna

Flavia (Latin) blond, golden haired.
Flavere, Flaviar, Flavie, Flavien, Flavienne, Flaviere, Flavio, Flavyere, Fulvia

Flo (American) a short form of Florence.

Flora (Latin) flower. A short form of Florence.
Fiore, Florann, Florella, Florelle, Floren, Floriana, Florianna, Florica, Florie, Florimel
Foreign forms: Basque: ***Floria;***
English: ***Floria;*** *French:* ***Fleur, Flore;*** *Italian:* ***Fiora, Fiorenza;*** *Spanish:* ***Flor***

Florence (Latin) blooming; flowery; prosperous. History: Florence Nightingale, a British nurse, is considered the founder of modern nursing.
Flora, Florency, Florendra, Florentina, Floretta, Florette, Florina
Foreign forms: American: ***Flo;*** *English:* ***Florance, Florie, Florine, Floris, Flossie;*** *German:* ***Florentia;*** *Italian:* ***Fiorenza;*** *Spanish:* ***Florencia, Florentyna, Florenza, Florida***

Florie (English) a familiar form of Florence.
Flore, Flori, Florri, Florrie, Florry, Flory

Flossie (English) a familiar form of Florence.
Floss, Flossi, Flossy

Fonda (Latin) foundation. (Spanish) inn.
Fondea, Fonta

Fontanna (French) fountain.
Fontaine, Fontana, Fontane, Fontanne, Fontayne

Fotina (Teutonic) free.
Foreign form: Italian: ***Fotini***

Fran (Latin) a short form of Frances.
Frain, Frann

Frances (Latin) free; from France. A feminine form of Francis.
Fran, Franca, France, Francena, Francess, Francesta, Franceta, Francetta, Francey, Francie, Francise
Foreign forms: American: ***Fanny, Frankie;*** *English:* ***Frannie, Franny;*** *French:* ***Francee, Francette, Francine, Françoise;*** *German:* ***Franzetta, Franziska;*** *Hungarian:* ***Franci;*** *Italian:* ***Francesca, Franchesca;*** *Polish:* ***Franciska, Franciszka;*** *Spanish:* ***Francisca, Paquita***

Francesca (Italian) a form of Frances.
Franceska, Francessca,

Francesca (cont.)
Francesta, Franchesca, Frantiska

Franchesca (Italian) an alternate form of Francesca.
Cheka, Chekka, Chesca, Cheska, Francheca, Francheka, Franchelle, Franchesa, Francheska, Franchessca, Franchesska

Francine (French) a form of Frances.
Franceen, Franceine, Franceline, Francene, Francenia, Franci, Francin, Francina, Francyne

Frankie (American) a familiar form of Frances.
Francka, Francki, Franka, Frankeisha, Frankey, Franki, Frankia, Franky

Frannie, Franny (English) familiar forms of Frances.
Frania, Franney, Franni

Freda, Freida (German) short forms of Alfreda, Elfrida, Frederica, Sigfreda.
Frayda, Fredda, Fredella, Fredia, Freeda, Freeha, Freia, Frida, Frideborg, Frieda

Freddi, Freddie (English) familiar forms of Frederica, Winifred.
Fredda, Freddy, Fredi, Fredia, Fredy, Frici

Frederica (German) peaceful ruler. A feminine form of Frederick. See also Alfreda, Ricki, Rica.
Farica, Federica, Freda, Fredalena, Fredaline, Fredericka, Frederickina, Frederika, Frederina, Frederine, Fredith, Fredora, Fredra, Fredreca, Fredreka, Fredricia, Freida, Fritzi, Fryderica
Foreign forms: English: *Freddi, Freddie;* French: *Frederique, Frédérique, Fredrica, Rike;* Norwegian: *Fredrika, Friederike;* Polish: *Freyderyka, Fryderyka*

Freja (Scandinavian) noblewoman. Mythology: the Norse goddess of love.
Fraya, Freya

Fritzi (German) a familiar form of Frederica.
Friezi, Fritze, Fritzie, Fritzinn, Fritzline, Fritzy

Gabriela, Gabriella (Italian) alternate forms of Gabrielle.
Gabriala, Gabrialla, Gabrielia, Gabriellia, Gabrila, Gabrilla

Gabrielle (French) devoted to God. A feminine form of Gabriel.
Gabielle, Gabreil, Gabrial, Gabriana, Gabriele, Gabriell, Gabrille, Gabrina, Gaby
Foreign forms: Hebrew: *Gavriella, Gavrilla;* Italian: *Gabriela, Gabriella*

Gaby (French) a familiar form of Gabrielle.
Gabbey, Gabbi, Gabbie, Gabey, Gabi, Gabie, Gavi, Gavy

Gaea (Greek) planet Earth. Mythology: the Greek goddess

of Earth.
Gaia, Gaiea, Gaya

Gail (Hebrew) a short form of Abigail. (English) merry, lively.
Gael, Gaela, Gaelen, Gaelle, Gaellen, Gaila, Gaile, Gale, Gayle

Galena (Greek) healer; calm.
Galen

Galit (Hebrew) fountain.

Garland (French) wreath of flowers.

Garnet (English) dark red gem.
Garnetta, Garnette

Gay (French) merry.
Gae, Gai, Gaye, Gaylaine, Gayleen, Gaylen, Gaylene, Gaylyn

Gayle (English) an alternate form of Gail.
Gayla, Galyn

Gemini (Greek) twin.
Gemelle, Gemima, Gemina, Geminine, Gemmina

Gemma (Latin, Italian) jewel, precious stone. See also Jemma.
Gem, Gemmey, Gemmie, Gemmy

Gen (Japanese) spring. A short form of names beginning with "Gen."
Gena, Genna

Gena (French) a form of Gina. A short form of Geneva, Genevieve, Iphigenia.
Geanna, Geenah, Gen, Genah, Genea, Geni, Genia, Genice, Genie, Genita
Foreign form: American: **Geena**

Geneen (Scottish) an alternate form of Jeanine.
Geanine, Geannine, Gen, Genene, Genine, Gineen, Ginene

Geneva (French) juniper tree. A short form of Genevieve. Geography: a city in Switzerland.
Geena, Gen, Gena, Geneive, Geneve, Genever, Genevera, Genevra, Ginevra, Ginneva, Janeva, Jeaneva, Jeneva

Genevieve (German, French) an alternate form of Guinevere. See also Gwendolyn.
Gen, Gena, Genaveve, Genavieve, Genavive, Geneva, Geneveve, Genevie, Genevíéve, Genevievre, Genevive, Genna, Genovieve, Gineveve, Ginevieve, Ginevive,
Guinevieve, Guinivive, Gwenevieve, Gwenivive
Foreign forms: Italian: **Ginevra;** Welsh: **Genevra**

Genna (English) a form of Jenna.
Gen, Gennae, Gennay, Genni, Gennie, Genny

Genovieve (French) an alternate form of Genevieve.
Genoveva, Genoveve, Genovive

Georgeanna (Latin) a form of Georgeanne. (English) a combination of Georgia + Anna.
Georgana, Georganna, Georgeana, Georgiana, Georgianna, Georgyanna

Georgeanne (English) a combination of Georgia + Anne.
Georgann, Georganne, Georgean, Georgeann, Georgianne, Georgyann, Georgyanne

Georgene (English) a familiar form of Georgia.
Georgeina, Georgena, Georgenia, Georgiena, Georgienne, Georgina, Georgine

Georgette (French) a form of Georgia.

Georgette (cont.)
**Georgeta, Georgett,
Georgetta, Georjetta**

Georgia (Greek) farmer. A feminine form of George. Art: Georgia O'Keeffe was an American painter known especially for her paintings of flowers. Geography: a southern American state; a country in Eastern Europe.
Georgi, Georgie, Giorgi
Foreign forms: American:
Jeorgia, Jorgina, Jorja; Czech:
Jirina; English: **Georgina**; *French:*
Georgette; *Italian:* **Giorgia**

Georgina (English) a form of Georgia.
**Georgena, Georgene,
Georgine, Giorgina**

Geraldine (German) mighty with a spear. A feminine form of Gerald.
**Geralda, Geraldina,
Geraldyna, Geraldyne,
Gerhardine, Gerianna,
Gerianne, Gerrilee**
Foreign forms: American: **Geri**;
English: **Jeraldine**; *French:*
Géraldine; *Italian:* **Giralda**

Geralyn (American) a combination of Geraldine + Lynn.
Geralynn, Gerilyn, Gerrilyn

Geri (American) a familiar form of Geraldine. See also Jeri.
Gerri, Gerrie, Gerry

Germaine (French) from Germany. See also Jermaine.
**Germain, Germana,
Germanie, Germaya, Germine**

Gertrude (German) beloved warrior. See also Trudy.
**Gerda, Gert, Gerta, Gertey,
Gerti, Gertie, Gertina,
Gertraud, Gertrud, Gerty**
Foreign forms: Italian:
Gertruda; *Spanish:* **Gertrudis**

Gianna (Italian) a short form of Giovanna. See also Jianna.
**Geona, Geonna, Giana,
Gianella, Gianetta, Gianina,
Giannella, Giannetta, Gianni,
Giannina, Gianny, Gianoula**

Gigi (French) a familiar form of Gilberte.
Geegee, G.G.

Gilberte (German) brilliant; pledge; trustworthy. A feminine form of Gilbert. See also Berti.
**Gilberta, Gilbertina,
Gilbertine, Gill**
Foreign form: French: **Gigi**

Gilda (English) covered with gold.
Gilde, Gildi, Gildie, Gildy

Gillian (Latin) an alternate form of Jillian.
**Gila, Gilana, Gilenia, Gili,
Gilian, Gill, Gilliana, Gilliane,
Gilliann, Gillianna, Gillianne,
Gillie, Gilly, Gillyan, Gillyane,
Gillyann, Gillyanne, Gyllian,
Lian**

Gin (Japanese) silver. A short form of names beginning with "Gin."

Gina (Italian) a short form of Angelina, Eugenia, Regina, Virginia. See also Jina.
**Gena, Gin, Ginah, Ginea, Gini,
Ginia**

Ginger (Latin) flower; spice. A familiar form of Virginia.
**Gin, Ginata, Ginja, Ginjer,
Ginny**

Ginny (English) a familiar form of Ginger, Virginia. See also Jin, Jinny.
**Gin, Gini, Ginney, Ginni,
Ginnie, Giny**

Giovanna (Italian) a form of Jane.
Giavanna, Giavonna, Giovana

Giselle (German) pledge; hostage.
**Gisel, Gisele, Gissell, Gissella,
Gisselle**

Foreign forms: *American:*
Jezella, Jiselle, Jizelle; *Czech:*
Gizela; *French:* **Giséle;** *Hungarian:*
Gizike; *Italian/Spanish:* **Gisela,**
Gisell, Gisella

Gitana (Spanish) gypsy; wanderer.

Gladys (Latin) small sword
(Irish) princess. (Welsh) a form
of Claudia. Botany: a gladiolus
flower.
Glad, Gladi, Gladis, Gladiz,
Gladness, Gladwys, Gwladys

Glenda (Welsh) a form of
Glenna.
Glanda, Glennda, Glynda

Glenna (Irish) valley, glen.
A feminine form of Glenn.
Glenetta, Glenina, Glenine,
Glenn, Glennie, Glenora,
Gleny, Glyn
Foreign forms: *American:*
Glennesha; *Welsh:* **Glenda,**
Glennis, Glennys, Glenwys,
Glenyse, Glynnis

Gloria (Latin) glory. History:
Gloria Steinem, a leading
American feminist, founded
Ms. magazine.
Gloresha, Gloriah, Gloribel,
Gloriela, Gloriella, Glorielle,
Gloris, Glorisha, Glorvina,
Glory

Foreign forms: *English:*
Gloriana, Glorianne

Glory (Latin) an alternate form
of Gloria.
Glorey, Glori, Glorie

Golda (English) gold. History:
Golda Meir was a Russian-born
politician who served as Prime
Minister of Israel.
Goldarina, Golden, Goldi,
Goldie, Goldina, Goldy

Grace (Latin) graceful.
Graca, Gracea, Graceanne,
Gracey, Graci, Gracie,
Graciela, Graciella, Gracy,
Grata, Gray, Grayce
Foreign forms: *Italian:* **Grazia,**
Graziella; *Spanish:* **Engracia,**
Gracia, Gracinha, Gratia,
Grazyna

Greer (Scottish) vigilant. A feminine form of Gregory.
Grear, Grier

Greta (German) a short form
of Gretchen, Margaret.
Greatal, Greatel, Greeta,
Gretal, Grete, Gretel, Gretha,
Grethal, Grethe, Grethel,
Gretta, Grette, Grieta, Gryta,
Grytta

Gretchen (German) a form of
Margaret.
Greta, Gretchin

Griselda (German) gray
woman warrior. See also Selda,
Zelda.
Grisel, Griseldys, Griselys,
Grissel, Grissele, Grissely,
Grizelda
Foreign forms: *Dutch:* **Griseldis,**
Grishilda, Grishilde; *Scottish:*
Grizel

Guadalupe (Arabic) river of
black stones. See also Lupe.
Guadulupe

Gudrun (Scandinavian) battler.
See also Runa.
Gudren, Gudrin, Gudrinn,
Gudruna

Guinevere (French, Welsh)
white wave; white phantom.
Literature: the wife of King
Arthur. See also Genevieve,
Jennifer, Winifred, Wynne.
Generva, Genn, Ginetta,
Guenevere, Guinivere,
Guinna, Gwen, Gwenevere,
Gwenivere, Gwynnevere
Foreign forms: *English:* **Gayna;**
Italian: **Ginevra, Guenna**

Gurpreet (Punjabi) religion.

Gussie (Latin) a short form of
Augusta.
Gus, Gussi, Gussy, Gusta,
Gusti, Gustie, Gusty

Gwen (Welsh) a short form of Guinevere, Gwendolyn. **Gwenesha, Gweness, Gweneta, Gwenetta, Gwenette, Gweni, Gwenisha, Gwenita, Gwenith, Gwenn, Gwenna, Gwennie, Gwenny, Gwyn**

Gwenda (Welsh) a familiar form of Gwendolyn. **Gwinda, Gwynda, Gwynedd**

Gwendolyn (Welsh) white wave; white browed; new moon. Literature: the wife of Merlin, the magician. See also Genevieve, Gwyneth, Wendy, Wynne. **Guendolen, Gwen, Gwendalin, Gwenda, Gwendalee, Gwendalyn, Gwendela, Gwendolene, Gwendolin, Gwendolyne, Gwendolynn, Gwendolynne, Gwendylan** *Foreign forms:* English: **Gwendaline, Gwendolen, Gwendoline**

Gwyn (Welsh) a short form of Gwyneth. **Gwinn, Gwinne, Gwynn, Gwynne**

Gwyneth (Welsh) an alternate form of Gwendolyn. See also Winnie, Wynne.

Gweneth, Gwenneth, Gwennyth, Gwenyth, Gwyn

Gypsy (English) wanderer. **Gipsy, Gypsie**

Hadassah (Hebrew) myrtle tree.

Hadley (English) field of heather. **Hadlea, Hadlee, Hadleigh**

Hadriane (Greek, Latin) an alternate form of Adrienne. **Hadriana, Hadrianna Hadrianne, Hadriene, Hadrienne**

Hagar (Hebrew) forsaken; stranger. Bible: Sarah's hand-maiden, the mother of Ishmael. **Haggar**

Hagit (Hebrew) holiday.

Hailey (English) an alternate form of Hayley. **Hailea, Hailee, Haili, Hailie, Hailley, Hailly**

Haley (Scandinavian) heroine. See also Hailey, Hayley. **Halee, Haleigh, Hali, Halie, Hallie**

Halimah (Arabic) gentle; patient. **Halima, Halime**

Halla (African) unexpected gift. **Hala, Halle**

Hallie (Scandinavian) an alternate form of Haley. **Hallee, Hallei, Halley, Halli, Hally, Hallye**

Halona (Native American) fortunate. **Haleen, Halena, Halina, Haloona, Haona**

Hana (Japanese) flower. (Arabic) happiness. (Slavic) a form of Hannah. **Hanako, Hanan, Haneen, Hania, Hanicka, Hanin, Hanita, Hanja, Hanka**

Hanna (Hebrew) an alternate form of Hannah.

Hannah (Hebrew) gracious. Bible: the mother of Samuel. See also Ann, Anna, Nina.
Chana, Hanna, Hannalore, Hanneke, Hannele, Hanni, Hannon, Honna
Foreign forms: *Czech:* ***Anezka;*** *English:* ***Ann, Anne;*** *Finnish:* ***Analee, Annalie;*** *German/Italian/ Czech/Swedish:* ***Anna;*** *Hawaiian/Spanish:* ***Ana;*** *Hungarian:* ***Anci, Nusi;*** *Polish:* ***Ania, Anka;*** *Slavic:* ***Hana;*** *Swedish:* ***Anneka***

Happy (English) happy.

Harley (English) meadow of the hare. See also Arleigh.
Harlee, Harleen, Harleigh, Harlene, Harleyann, Harli, Harlie, Harlina, Harline, Harly

Harleyann (English) a combination of Harley + Ann.
Harlann, Harlanna, Harlanne, Harleyanna, Harleyanne, Harliann, Harlianna, Harlianne

Harmony (Latin) harmonious.
Harmon, Harmoni, Harmonia, Harmonie

Harpreet (Punjabi) devoted to God.

Harriet (French) ruler of the household. (English) an alternate form of Henrietta. Literature: Harriet Beecher Stowe was an American writer noted for her novel *Uncle Tom's Cabin.*
Harri, Harrie, Harriett, Harrietta, Harriette, Harriot, Harriott, Hattie

Hasana (Swahili) she arrived first. A name used for the first-born female twin.
Huseina

Hasina (Swahili) good.
Haseena, Hasena, Hassina

Hattie (English) familiar forms of Harriet, Henrietta.
Hatti, Hatty, Hetti, Hettie, Hetty

Haviva (Hebrew) beloved.
Hava, Havah, Havalee, Havelah, Havi, Havvah, Hayah

Hayfa (Arabic) shapely.

Hayley (English) hay meadow. See also Hailey, Haley.
Haylee, Hayli, Haylie, Hayly

Hazel (English) hazelnut tree; commanding authority.
Hazal, Hazaline, Haze,

Hazeline, Hazell, Hazelle, Hazen, Hazyl
Foreign form: *French:* ***Aveline***

Heather (English) flowering heather.
Heath, Heatherlee, Heatherly

Heaven (English) place of beauty and happiness. Bible: where God and angels are said to dwell.
Heavenly, Heavin, Heavyn, Heven

Hedda (German) battler. See also Hedy.
Edda, Heda, Hedaya, Hede, Hedia, Hedwig, Heida, Hetta, Jadwiga
Foreign forms: *Czech:* ***Hedvick, Hedvig, Hedviga, Hedwiga, Hedwige***

Hedy (Greek) delightful; sweet. (German) a familiar form of Hedda.
Heddey, Heddi, Heddie, Heddy, Hedi

Heidi (German) a short form of Adelaide.
Heida, Heide, Heidie, Hidee, Hidi, Hiede, Hiedi

Helen (Greek) light. See also Eleanor, Nellie.
Elana, Halina, Hela, Hele,

Helen (cont.)
Helena, Helle, Hellen, Helli, Hellin, Hellon, Helon, Heluska
Foreign forms: *English:* **Ellen, Leanore;** *Estonian:* **Leena;** *Finnish:* **Aili;** *French:* **Elaine, Helene;** *German:* **Lene;** *Hungarian:* **Ila, Ilka, Ilona, Lenci, Onella;** *Irish:* **Aileen, Eileen, Ena, Ileene, Ilene;** *Italian:* **Elena;** *Russian:* **Alena, Alyna, Galya, Galina, Halina, Jelena, Lelya, Lena, Olena, Yalena, Yelena**

Helena (Greek) an alternate form of Helen. See also Ilena.
Halena, Helaina, Helana, Helayna, Heleana, Heleena, Helenka, Helenna, Helina, Hellanna, Hellenna, Helona, Helonna

Helene (French) a form of Helen.
Helaine, Helayne, Heleen, Hèléne, Helenor, Heline, Hellenor

Helga (German) pious. (Scandinavian) an alternate form of Olga.
Elga, Elgiva

Henrietta (English) ruler of the household. A feminine form of Henry. See also Etta, Yetta.
Harriet, Hattie, Hatty, Heneretta, Henia, Henka,

Henna, Hennrietta, Henny, Henrica, Henrie, Henrieta, Henriette, Henrique, Henriquetta, Henryetta, Henya, Hetta, Hetti, Hettie, Hetty
Foreign forms: *Dutch:* **Hendrika;** *French/German:* **Henriete, Hennriette;** *Spanish:* **Enrica;** *Swedish:* **Henrika**

Hera (Greek) queen; jealous. Mythology: the queen of heaven and the wife of Zeus.

Hermione (Greek) earthy.
Hermalina, Hermia, Hermina, Hermine, Herminia

Hermosa (Spanish) beautiful.

Hestia (Persian) star. Mythology: the Greek goddess of the hearth and home.
Hestea, Hesti, Hestie, Hesty

Hetta (German) an alternate form of Hedda. (English) a familiar form of Henrietta.
Hettie

Hila (Hebrew) greatly praised. A feminine form of Hillel.

Hilary, Hillary (Greek) cheerful, merry.
Hilaree, Hilari, Hilaria, Hilarie, Hilery, Hiliary, Hillaree, Hillari, Hillarie, Hilleary,

Hilleree, Hilleri, Hillerie, Hillery, Hillianne, Hilliary, Hillory
Foreign forms: *French:* **Alair, Allaire, Hilaire**

Hilda (German) a short form of Brunhilda, Hildegarde.
Helle, Hildey, Hildur, Hulda, Hylda
Foreign forms: *English:* **Hilde, Hildie, Hildy**

Hildegarde (German) fortress.
Hilda, Hildagard, Hildagarde, Hildegard, Hildred

Hinda (Hebrew) hind; doe.
Hindey, Hindie, Hindy, Hynda

Hiroko (Japanese) magnanimous.

Hoa (Vietnamese) flower; peace.
Ho, Hoai

Holley, Holli, Hollie (English) alternate forms of Holly.

Hollis (English) near the holly bushes.
Hollise, Hollyce, Holyce

Holly (English) holly tree.
Hollee, Holley, Holli, Hollie, Hollinda, Hollis

Hollyann (English) a combination of Holly + Ann.
Holliann, Hollianna, Hollianne, Hollyanne

Honey (Latin) a familiar form of Honora. (English) sweet.
Honalee, Hunney, Hunny

Honora (Latin) honorable. See also Nora.
Honey, Honner, Honnor, Honnour, Honor, Honorah, Honorata, Honore, Honoree, Honoria, Honorina, Honorine, Honour, Honoure, Onora

Hope (English) hope.
Hopey, Hopi, Hopie

Hortense (Latin) gardener.
Hortensia
Foreign form: Italian: Ortensia

Hoshi (Japanese) star.
Hoshie, Hoshiko, Hoshiyo

Hua (Chinese) flower.

Huda (Arabic) guidance.

Huong (Vietnamese) flower.

Hyacinth (Greek) Botany: a plant with colorful, fragrant flowers.
Hyacintha, Hyacinthia, Hycinth, Hycynth

Foreign forms: French:
Hyacinthe; *German:* **Hyacinthie;**
Italian: **Giacinta;** *Spanish:* **Jacinda**

Hye (Korean) graceful.

Ida (German) hardworking. (English) prosperous.
Idaia, Idaleena, Idaleene, Idalena, Idalene, Idamae, Idania, Idarina, Idarine, Idaya, Idette, Iduska, Idys
Foreign forms: Italian: Idalia, Idalina, Idaline, Ide; Polish: Itka; Welsh: Idelle

Iesha (American) a form of Aisha.
Ieachia, Ieaisha, Ieasha, Ieesha, Ieeshia, Ieisha, Ieishia, Ieshia

Ifeoma (Ibo) good; beautiful.
Ijeoma

Ilana (Hebrew) tree.
Ilane, Ilani, Ilainie, Illana, Illane, Illani, Ilania, Illanie, Ilanit

Ilena (Greek) an alternate form of Helena.
Ileana, Ileena, Ilina, Ilyna

Iliana (Greek) from Troy.
Ileana, Ileane, Ileanne, Ili, Ilia, Iliani, Illiana, Illiani

Ilisa (Scottish, English) an alternate form of Alisa, Elisa.
Ilissa, Illisa, Illissa, Illysa, Illyssa, Ilysa, Ilyssa

Ima (German) a familiar form of Amelia. (Japanese) presently.

Imani (Arabic) believer.
Iman

Imelda (German) warrior.
Imalda, Irmhilde, Melda

Imogene (Latin) image, likeness.
Emogen, Emogene, Imogen, Imogenia, Imojean, Imojeen, Innogen, Innogene

India (Hindi) from India.
Indi, Indie, Indy, Indya

Indigo (Latin) dark blue color.

Indira (Hindi) splendid.
Religion: the god of heaven.
History: Indira Nehru Gandi
was an Indian politician and
prime minister.
Indihar, Indra

Inga (Scandinavian) a short
form of Ingrid.
**Ingaberg, Ingaborg, Inge,
Ingeberg, Ingeborg, Ingela**

Ingrid (Scandinavian) hero's
daughter; beautiful daughter.
Inga, Inge, Inger

Intisar (Arabic) triumph.

Iola (Greek) dawn; violet col-
ored. (Welsh) worthy of the
Lord.
Iolee, Iolia
Foreign form: English: **Iole**

Iolana (Hawaiian) soaring like a
hawk.

Iona (Greek) violet flower.
Ione, Ioney, Ioni, Ionia

Iphigenia (Greek) sacrifice.
Mythology: the daughter of
the Greek leader Agamemnon.
See also Gena.

Irene (Greek) peaceful.
Mythology: the goddess of

peace. See also Rena, Rene.
**Irana, Iranda, Iranna, Irén,
Irenea, Iriana, Irien**
Foreign forms: Romanian: **Irini;**
Russian: **Ira, Irina, Jereni, Orina;**
Slavic: **Eirena, Erena, Irena,
Yarina;** Ukranian: **Iryna**

Irina (Russian) a form of Irene.
**Ira, Irena, Irenka, Irin, Irinia,
Irinka, Irona, Ironka, Irusya,
Iryna, Irynka, Rina**

Iris (Greek) rainbow.
Mythology: the goddess of the
rainbow and messenger of the
gods.
Irissa, Irita
Foreign forms: Russian: **Irisa,
Irisha**

Irma (Latin) an alternate form
of Erma.
Irmelinda, Irmina, Irminia

Isabel (Spanish) consecrated to
God. A form of Elizabeth. See
also Bel, Belle, Ysabel.
**Chavella, Isa, Isabal, Isabela,
Isabeli, Isabelita, Ishbel,
Isobel, Issi, Issie, Issy, Iza,
Izabel, Izabele**
Foreign forms: French: **Isabeau;**
German: **Isabelle;** Italian:
Isabella, Izabella

Isadora (Latin) gift of Isis.
Isidora

Isis (Egyptian) supreme goddess. Mythology: the goddess
of the moon, maternity, and
fertility.

Isolde (Welsh) fair lady.
Literature: a princess in the
Arthurian legends; a heroine in
the medieval romance *Tristan
and Isolde*. See also Yseult.
Isolda, Isolt

Italia (Italian) from Italy.
Italie

Ivana (Slavic) God is gracious.
A feminine form of Ivan. See
also Yvanna.
Iva, Ivania, Ivanka
Foreign form: English: **Ivanna**

Ivette (French) an alternate
form of Yvette. See also Evette.
**Ivete, Iveth, Ivetha, Ivetta,
Ivey**

Ivonne (French) an alternate
form of Yvonne. See also
Evonne.
Ivon, Ivonna, Iwonna, Iwonne

Ivory (Latin) made of ivory.
Ivori, Ivorine, Ivree

Ivy (English) ivy tree.
Ivey, Ivie

Jacalyn (American) a form of Jacqueline.
Jacelyn, Jacelyne, Jacelynn, Jacilyn, Jacilyne, Jacilynn, Jacolyn, Jacolyne, Jacolynn, Jacylyn, Jacylyne, Jacylynn

Jacey (Greek) a familiar form of Jacinda. (American) a combination of the initials J. + C.
Jace, Jac-E, Jacee, Jacia, Jacie, Jaciel, Jacy, Jacylin

Jacinda, Jacinta (Greek) beautiful, attractive. (Spanish) a form of Hyacinth.
Jacenda, Jacenta, Jacey, Jacinth, Jacintha, Jacinthe, Jacynth, Jakinda, Jaxine

Jackalyn (American) a form of Jacqueline.
Jackalene, Jackalin, Jackaline, Jackalynn, Jackalynne, Jackelin, Jackeline, Jackelyn, Jackelynn, Jackelynne, Jackilin, Jackilyn, Jackilynn, Jackilynne, Jackolin, Jackoline, Jackolyn, Jackolynn, Jackolynne

Jacki, Jackie (American) familiar forms of Jacqueline.
Jackee, Jackia, Jackielee, Jacky

Jacklyn (American) a short form of Jacqueline.
Jacklin, Jackline, Jacklyne, Jacklynn, Jacklynne

Jackquel (French) an alternate form of Jacqueline.
Jackquelin, Jackqueline, Jackquelyn, Jackquelynn, Jackquetta, Jackquilin, Jackquiline, Jackquilyn, Jackquilynn, Jackquilynne

Jaclyn (American) a short form of Jacqueline.
Jacleen, Jaclin, Jacline, Jaclyne, Jaclynn

Jacobi (Hebrew) supplanter, substitute. A feminine form of Jacob.
Coby, Jacobia, Jacolbi, Jacolbia, Jacolby
Foreign forms: English: *Jacobina, Jacobine;* French: *Jacoba, Jacobette*

Jacqueline (French) supplanter, substitute; little Jacqui. A feminine form of Jacques.
Jacqualin, Jacqualine, Jacqualyn, Jacqualyne, Jacqualynn, Jacqueena, Jacqueine, Jacquel, Jacqueleen, Jacquelene, Jacquelin, Jacquelyn, Jacquelynn, Jacquena, Jacquene, Jacqui, Jacquil, Jacquilin, Jacquiline, Jacquilyn, Jacquilyne, Jacquilynn, Jaquelin, Jaquelyne, Jaquelynn, Jockeline, Jocqueline
Foreign forms: American: Jacalyn, Jackalyn, Jackie, Jacklyn, Jaclyn; Spanish: Jacquenetta, Jacquenette, Jacquine, Jaqueline, Jaquelyn

Jacquelyn, Jacquelynn (French) alternate forms of Jacqueline.
Jacquelyne

Jacqui (French) a short form of Jacqueline.
Jacquay, Jacqué, Jacquee, Jacqueta, Jacquete, Jacquetta, Jacquie, Jacquise, Jaquay, Jaqui, Jaquice, Jaquie, Jaquiese, Jaquina, Jaquinta
Foreign forms: Spanish: Jacquette, Jacquita, Jaquita

Jade (Spanish) jade.
Jada, Jadah, Jadda, Jadea,
Jadeann, Jadee, Jaden, Jadera,
Jadi, Jadie, Jadielyn, Jadienne,
Jady, Jadzia, Jadziah, Jaeda,
Jaedra, Jaida, Jaide, Jaiden

Jae (Latin) jaybird. (French)
a familiar form of Jacqueline.
Jaea, Jaela, Jaya, Jayla, Jaylee,
Jayleen, Jaylyn, Jaylynn,
Jaylynne

Jael (Hebrew) mountain goat;
climber. See also Yael.
Jaela, Jaelee, Jaeleen, Jaeli,
Jaelie, Jaelle, Jaelynn, Jahla,
Jahlea

Jaffa (Hebrew) an alternate
form of Yaffa.
Jaffice, Jaffit, Jafit, Jafra

Jaime (French) I love.
Jaima, Jaimey, Jaimi, Jaimini,
Jaimmie, Jaimy
Foreign forms: English: Jaimee,
Jayme

Jaimee (French) an alternate
form of Jaime.

Jakki (American) an alternate
form of Jacki, Jackie.
Jakala, Jakea, Jakeela, Jakeida,
Jakeisha, Jakeisia, Jakeita,
Jakela, Jakelia, Jakell, Jakena,
Jakesha, Jaketta, Jakevia,

Jakia, Jakira, Jakisha, Jakiya,
Jakkia

Jalena (American) a combina-
tion of Jane + Lena.
Jalayna, Jalean, Jaleen, Jalene,
Jalina, Jaline, Jalyna, Jelayna,
Jelena, Jelina, Jelyna

Jalila (Arabic) great.
Jalile

Jamaica (Spanish) Geography:
an island in the Caribbean.
Jameca, Jameka, Jamica,
Jamika, Jamoka, Jemaica,
Jemika, Jemyka

Jamesha (American) a form
of Jami.
Jameisha, Jamese, Jameshia,
Jameshyia, Jamesia, Jamesica,
Jamesika, Jamesina, Jamessa,
Jameta, Jametta, Jamiesha,
Jamisha, Jammisha

Jami, Jamie (Hebrew) sup-
planter, substitute. (English)
feminine forms of James.
Jama, Jamay, Jamea, Jamee,
Jameka, Jamia, Jamielee,
Jamii, Jamika, Jamis, Jamise,
Jammie, Jamy, Jamya, Jamye,
Jaymee, Jaymie
Foreign form: American:
Jamesha

Jamila (Arabic) beautiful. See
also Yamila.
Jahmela, Jahmelia, Jahmil,
Jahmilla, Jamee, Jameela,
Jameelah, Jameeliah, Jameila,
Jamela, Jamelia, Jameliah,
Jamell, Jamella, Jamelle,
Jamely, Jamelya, Jamiela,
Jamilah, Jamilee, Jamilia,
Jamiliah, Jamilla, Jamillah,
Jamille, Jamillia, Jamilya,
Jamyla, Jemeela, Jemelia,
Jemila, Jemilla

Jamilynn (English) a combina-
tion of Jami + Lynn.
Jamielin, Jamieline, Jamielyn,
Jamielyne, Jamielynn,
Jamielynne, Jamilin, Jamiline,
Jamilyn, Jamilyne, Jamilynne
Foreign form: American:
Jamylin

Jamylin (American) a form
of Jamilynn.
Jamylin, Jamyline, Jamylyn,
Jamylyne, Jamylynn,
Jamylynne, Jaymylin,
Jaymyline, Jaymylyn,
Jaymylyne, Jaymylynn,
Jaymylynne

Jan (English) a short form
of Jane, Janet, Janice.
Jani, Jania, Jandy, Jannie

Jana (Slavic) a form of Jane. See
also Yana.

Janaca, Janalee, Janalisa, Janalynn, Janika, Janka, Janna, Janne

Janae, Janay (American) forms of Jane.
Janaé, Janaea, Janaeh, Janah, Janai, Janaya, Janaye, Janea, Janee, Janée, Jannae, Jannay, Jenae, Jenay, Jenaya, Jennae, Jennay, Jennaya, Jennaye

Janan (Arabic) heart; soul.
Janani, Jananie

Jane (Hebrew) God is gracious. A feminine form of John. See also Chavon, Joan.
Jaine, Jan, Janean, Janeann, Janeen, Janene, Jania, Janique, Jannie, Jayna, Jenny, Joanna, Joanne
Foreign forms: American: Janae, Janay, Jannessa; Czech: Janka, Janica, Jenka; English: Janet, Janice, Janie, Janis, Jayne; German: Johana; Irish: Seana, Shana, Shawna, Sheena, Shona, Sinead, Sinéad; Italian: Chiana, Giovanna; French: Janelle, Janine; Polish: Jasia; Romanian: Jenica; Scottish: Jean; Slavic: Jana, Janika, Jannica; Spanish: Juanita, Zaneta, Zanna

Janel, Janell (French) alternate forms of Janelle.
Jannel, Jaynel, Jaynell

Janelle (French) a form of Jane.
Janel, Janela, Janele, Janelis, Janell, Janella, Janelli, Janellie, Janelly, Janely, Janelys, Janiel, Janielle, Janille, Jannel, Jannell, Jannelle, Jannellies, Janyll, Jaynelle

Janessa (American) a form of Jane.
Janesha, Janeska, Janiesa, Janiesha, Janisha, Janissa, Jannesa, Jannesha, Jannessa, Jannisa, Jannisha, Jannissa

Janet (English) a form of Jane.
Jan, Janeta, Janete, Janett, Janetta, Janette, Janita, Janith, Janitza, Jannet, Janneta, Janneth, Jannetta, Jannette, Janot, Jante, Janyte
Foreign form: Scottish: Jessie

Janice (Hebrew) God is gracious. (English) a familiar form of Jane.
Jan, Janece, Janecia, Janeice, Janiece, Janitza, Janizzette, Jannice, Janniece, Janyce, Jynice
Foreign forms: American: Genesa, Genice, Genise, Shanece, Shaneese, Shanice, Shaneice

Janie (English) a familiar form of Jane.
Janey, Jani, Jany

Janine (French) a form of Jane.
Janeen, Janenan, Janene, Janina, Jannina, Jannine, Jannyne, Janyne, Jenine

Janis (English) a form of Jane.
Janees, Janeesa, Janesa, Janese, Janesey, Janesia, Janessa, Janesse, Janise, Janisha, Janissa, Jannis, Jannisa, Jannisha, Jannissa, Jenesa, Jenessa, Jenesse, Jenice, Jenis, Jenisha, Jenissa, Jennisa, Jennise, Jennisha, Jennissa, Jennisse

Janna (Hebrew) a short form of Johana. (Arabic) harvest of fruit.
Janaya, Janaye

Jannie (English) a familiar form of Jan, Jane.
Janney, Janny

Jardena (Hebrew) an alternate form of Jordan. (French, Spanish) garden.
Jardan, Jardane, Jarden, Jardenia, Jardine, Jardyne

Jarita (Arabic) earthen water jug.
Jara, Jari, Jaria, Jarica, Jarida, Jarietta, Jarika, Jarina, Jaritta, Jaritza, Jarixa, Jarnita, Jarrika, Jarrine

Jas (American) a short form of Jasmine.
Jass, Jaz, Jazz, Jazze, Jazzi

Jasmine (Persian) jasmine flower. See also Yasmin.
Jas, Jasma, Jasmain, Jasmaine, Jasman, Jasme, Jasmeen, Jasmeet, Jasmene, Jasmira, Jasmit, Jasmon, Jasmyn, Jassma, Jassmain, Jassmaine, Jassmin, Jassmine, Jassmit, Jassmon, Jassmyn, Jazmin
Foreign forms: English: *Jasmin, Jasmina;* French: *Jessamine*

Jaspreet (Punjabi) virtuous.
Jas, Jaspar, Jasparit, Jasparita, Jasper, Jasprit, Jasprita, Jasprite

Jatara (American) a combination of Jane + Tara.
Jataria, Jatarra, Jatori, Jatoria

Javana (Malayan) from Java.
Javanna, Javanne, Javon, Javonda, Javonna, Javonne, Javonya, Jawana, Jawanna, Jawn

Javiera (Spanish) owner of a new house. A feminine form of Javier. See also Xaviera.
Javeera, Viera

Jaya (Hindi) victory.
Jaea, Jaia, Jayla

Jaycee (American) a combination of the initials J. + C.
Jacee, Jacey, Jaci, Jacie, Jacy, Jaycey, Jayci, Jaycie, Jaycy

Jaydee (American) a combination of the initials J. + D.
Jadee, Jadey, Jadi, Jadie, Jady, Jaydey, Jaydi, Jaydie, Jaydy

Jaye (Latin) jaybird.
Jae, Jay
Foreign form: American: *Jaylene*

Jaylene (American) a form of Jaye.
Jayelene, Jayla, Jaylah, Jaylan, Jayleana, Jaylee, Jayleen

Jaylynn (American) a combination of Jaye + Lynn.
Jaelin, Jaeline, Jaelyn, Jaelyne, Jaelynn, Jaelynne, Jalin, Jaline, Jalyn, Jalyne, Jalynn, Jalynne, Jaylin, Jayline, Jaylyn, Jaylyne, Jaylynne

Jayme, Jaymie (English) alternate forms of Jami.
Jaymi, Jaymia, Jaymine, Jaymini

Jayna (Hebrew) an alternate form of Jane.
Jaynae

Jayne (Hindi) victorious. (English) a form of Jane.

Jayn, Jaynee, Jayni, Jaynie, Jaynita, Jaynne

Jazlyn (American) a combination of Jazmin + Lynn.
Jazleen, Jazlene, Jazlin, Jazline, Jazlynn, Jazlynne, Jazzleen, Jazzlene, Jazzlin, Jazzline, Jazzlyn, Jazzlynn, Jazzlynne

Jazmin, Jazmine (Persian) alternate forms of Jasmine.
Jazman, Jazmen, Jazminn, Jazmon, Jazmyn, Jazmyne, Jazzman, Jazzmen, Jazzmin, Jazzmine, Jazzmit, Jazzmon, Jazzmyn

Jean, Jeanne (Scottish) God is gracious. Forms of Jane, Joan.
Jeana, Jeanann, Jeancie, Jeane, Jeaneane, Jeaneen, Jeaneia, Jeanell, Jeanelle, Jeaneva, Jeanice, Jeanie, Jeanine, Jeanmarie, Jeanna, Jeannee, Jeanney, Jeannie, Jeannita, Jeannot, Jeanny, Jeantelle
Foreign forms: French: *Jeanette, Jeanné;* Hawaiian: *Kini*

Jeana, Jeanna (Scottish) alternate forms of Jean.

Jeanette (French) a form of Jean.
Jeanete, Jeanett, Jeanetta, Jeanita, Jeannete, Jeannett,

Jeannetta, Jeannette, Jeannita, Jenet, Jenett, Jenette, Jennett, Jennetta, Jennette, Jennita, Jinetta, Jinette
Foreign forms: *English:* **Ginette;** *Scottish:* **Jennet**

Jeanie (Scottish) a familiar form of Jean.
Jeani, Jeanny, Jeany

Jeanine, Jenine (Scottish) alternate forms of Jean.
Jeanene, Jeanina, Jeannina, Jeannine, Jennine

Jemima (Hebrew) dove.
Jamim, Jamima, Jem, Jemimah, Jemma, Jemmia, Jemmiah, Jemmy
Foreign form: *English:* **Jemmie**

Jemma (Hebrew) a short form of Jemima. (English) a form of Gemma.
Jem, Jemmia, Jemmiah

Jena (Arabic) an alternate form of Jenna.
Jenae, Jenah, Jenai, Jenal, Jenay

Jenelle (American) a combination of Jenny + Nell.
Jenall, Jenalle, Jenel, Jenell, Jenille, Jennel, Jennell, Jennelle, Jennielle, Jennille

Jenifer, Jeniffer (Welsh) alternate forms of Jennifer.

Jenilee (American) a combination of Jennifer + Lee.
Jenalea, Jenalee, Jenaleigh, Jenaly, Jenelea, Jenelee, Jeneleigh, Jenely, Jenelly, Jenileigh, Jenily, Jennely, Jennielee, Jennilea, Jennilee, Jennilie

Jenisa (American) a combination of Jennifer + Nisa.
Jenisha, Jenissa, Jennisa, Jennise, Jennisha, Jennissa, Jennisse, Jennysa, Jennyssa, Jenysa, Jenyse, Jenyssa, Jenysse

Jenna (Arabic) small bird. (Welsh) a short form of Jennifer.
Jena, Jennah, Jennat, Jennay, Jhenna
Foreign form: *English:* **Genna**

Jenni, Jennie (Welsh) familiar forms of Jennifer.
Jeni, Jenica, Jenisa, Jenka, Jenne, Jenné, Jennee, Jenney, Jennia, Jennier, Jennita, Jennora, Jensine

Jennifer (Welsh) white wave; white phantom. An alternate form of Guinevere.
Ginnifer, Jen, Jenefer, Jenifer,

Jeniffer, Jenipher, Jenna, Jennafer, Jenniferanne, Jenniferlee, Jenniffe, Jenniffer, Jenniffier, Jennifier, Jennilee, Jenniphe, Jennipher, Jenny, Jennyfer
Foreign form: *American:* **Gennifer**

Jennilee (American) a combination of Jenny + Lee.
Jennalea, Jennalee, Jennielee, Jennilea, Jennilie

Jennilynn (American) a combination of Jenni + Lynn.
Jennalin, Jennaline, Jennalyn, Jennalyne, Jennalynn, Jennalynne, Jennilin, Jenniline, Jennilyn, Jennilyne, Jennilynne

Jenny (Welsh) a familiar form of Jennifer.
Jenney, Jenni, Jennie, Jeny, Jinny

Jeri, Jerri, Jerrie (American) alternate forms of Geri.
Jera, Jerae, JeRae, Jeree, Jeriel, Jerilee, Jerilyn, Jerina, Jerinda, Jerra, Jerrece, Jerriann, Jerrilee, Jerrine, Jerry, Jerrylee, Jerryne, Jerzy

Jerica (American) a combination of Jeri + Erica.
Jerice, Jericka, Jerika, Jerreka,

Jerica (cont.)
Jerricca, Jerrice, Jerricka, Jerrika

Jerilyn (American) a combination of Jeri + Lynn.
Jeralin, Jeraline, Jeralyn, Jeralyne, Jeralynn, Jeralynne, Jerelin, Jereline, Jerelyn, Jerelyne, Jerelynn, Jerelynne, Jerilin, Jeriline, Jerilyne, Jerilynn, Jerilynne, Jerrilin, Jerriline, Jerrilyn, Jerrilyne, Jerrilynn, Jerrilynne

Jermaine (French) an alternate form of Germaine.
Jermain, Jerman, Jermane, Jermayne, Jermecia, Jermia, Jermice, Jermicia, Jermika, Jermila

Jessalyn (American) a combination of Jessica + Lynn.
Jesalin, Jesaline, Jesalyn, Jesalyne, Jesalynn, Jesalynne, Jesilin, Jesiline, Jesilyn, Jesilyne, Jesilynn, Jesilynne, Jessalin, Jessaline, Jessalyne, Jessalynn, Jessalynne, Jesselin, Jesseline, Jesselyn, Jesselyne, Jesselynn, Jesselynne

Jessamine (French) a form of Jasmine.
Jessamin, Jessamon, Jessamy, Jessamyn, Jessemin, Jessemine, Jessimin, Jessimine, Jessmin, Jessmine, Jessmon,

Jessmy, Jessmyn

Jesse, Jessi (Hebrew) alternate forms of Jessie.
Jessey

Jessenia (Arabic) flower.
Jescenia, Jesenia

Jessica (Hebrew) wealthy. A feminine form of Jesse. Literature: a name perhaps invented by Shakespeare for a character in his play The Merchant of Venice. See also Yessica.
Jesi, Jesica, Jess, Jessa, Jessaca, Jessah, Jessca, Jesscia, Jessia, Jessicca, Jessicia, Jessicka, Jessie, Jessiqua, Jessiya, Jessy, Jessyca, Jezeca, Jezica, Jezyca
Foreign forms: English:
Jessalyn, Jesseca; Italian: **Gessica**

Jessie (Hebrew) a short form of Jessica. (Scottish) a form of Janet.
Jescie, Jesey, Jess, Jesse, Jessé, Jessee, Jessi, Jessia, Jessiya, Jessy, Jessye

Jessika (Hebrew) an alternate form of Jessica.
Jesika, Jessieka, Jessika, Jessyka, Jezika

Jésusa (Hebrew) God is my salvation. (Spanish) a feminine form of Jésus.

Jetta (English) jet black gem. (American) a familiar form of Jevette.
Jetje, Jette, Jettie

Jevette (American) a combination of Jean + Yvette.
Jetta, Jeva, Jeveta, Jevetta

Jewel (French) precious gem.
Jewell, Jewelle, Jewellee, Jewellie, Juel, Jule

Jezebel (Hebrew) unexalted; impure. Bible: the wife of King Ahab.
Jessabel, Jessebel, Jez, Jezabel, Jezabella, Jezabelle, Jezebell, Jezebella, Jezebelle, Jezel, Jezell, Jezelle

Jianna (Italian) an alternate form of Gianna.
Jiana, Jianina, Jianine

Jill (English) a short form of Jillian.
Jil, Jiline, Jilli, Jillie, Jilline, Jillisa, Jillissa, Jilly, Jillyn

Jillaine (Latin) an alternate form of Jillian.
Jilaine, Jilane, Jilayne, Jillana, Jillane, Jillann, Jillanne, Jillayne

Jillian (Latin) youthful. An alternate form of Julia. See also Gillian.

Jilian, Jiliana, Jiliann, Jilianna, Jilianne, Jilienna, Jilienne, Jill, Jillaine, Jilliana, Jilliane, Jilliann, Jillianne, Jillien, Jillienne, Jillion, Jilliyn
Foreign form: Irish: **Jilleen**

Jimi (Hebrew) supplanter, substitute. (American) a feminine form of Jimmy.
Jimae, Jimaria, Jimella, Jimena, Jimetrice, Jimilonda, Jimisha, Jimiyah, Jimmeka, Jimmet, Jimmicia, Jimmie, Jimysha

Jin (Japanese) tender. (American) a short form of Ginny, Jinny.

Jina (Italian) an alternate form of Gina. (Swahili) baby with a name.
Jena, Jinae, Jinan, Jinda, Jinna, Jinnae

Jinny (Scottish) a familiar form of Jenny. (American) a familiar form of Virginia.
Jin, Jina, Jinae, Jinelle, Jinessa, Jinna, Jinnae, Jinnalee, Jinnee, Jinnell, Jinney, Jinni, Jinnie

Jo (American) a short form of Joanna, Jolene, Josephine.
Joangie, Joetta, Joette, Joey

Joan (Hebrew) God is gracious. An alternate form of Jane. History: Joan of Arc was a fifteenth-century heroine and resistance fighter. See also Jean.
Joane, Joaneil, Joanel, Joanelle, Joanie, Joanmarie, Joann, Joannanette, Joannel
Foreign forms: Czech: **Janka, Johanka;** English: **Joanna, Joanne;** German: **Johana, Johanna;** Irish: **Siobahn;** Polish: **Joanka;** Romanian: **Ioana;** Russian: **Ioanna;** Spanish: **Juanita**

Joanie (Hebrew) a familiar form of Joan.
Joani, Joanni, Joannie, Joany, Joenie, Joni

Joanna (English) a form of Joan. See also Yoanna.
Jo, Joana, Jo-Ana, Joandra, Joananna, Joananne, Jo-Anie, Jo-Anna, Joannah, Jo-Annie, Joayn, Joeana, Joeanna, Johannah

Joanne (English) a form of Joan.
Joanann, Joananne, Joann, Jo-Ann, Jo-Anne, Joeann, Joeanne

Jobeth (English) a combination of Jo + Beth.
Joby

Joby (Hebrew) afflicted. A feminine form of Job. (English) a familiar form of Jobeth.
Jobey, Jobi, Jobie, Jobina, Jobita, Jobrina, Jobye, Jobyna

Jocelyn (Latin) joyous.
Jocelin, Jocelle, Jocelynn, Jocelynne, Joci, Jocia, Joscelin, Jossalin, Josilin
Foreign forms: American: **Joycelyn;** English: **Joceline, Jocelyne, Josceline;** Spanish: **Jocinta**

Jodi, Jodie, Jody (American) familiar forms of Judith.
Jodee, Jodele, Jodell, Jodelle, Jodene, Jodevea, Jodilee, Jodi-Lee, Jodilynn, Jodi-Lynn, Jodine, Jodyne

Jodiann (American) a combination of Jodi + Ann.
Jodi-Ann, Jodianna, Jodi-Anna, Jodianne, Jodi-Anne, Jodyann, Jody-Ann, Jodyanna, Jody-Anna, Jodyanne, Jody-Anne

Joelle (Hebrew) God is willing. A feminine form of Joel.
Joela, Joelee, Joeleen, Joelene, Joeli, Joeline, Joell, Joella, Joëlle, Joellen, Joelly, Joellyn, Joelyn, Joelyne, Joelynn

Johana, Johanna (German) forms of Joan.

Johana, Johanna *(cont.)*
**Janna, Johanah, Johani,
Johanie, Johanka, Johannah,
Johanne, Johanni, Johannie,
Johonna**
Foreign forms: American:
Johnna, Jonna

Johnna, Jonna (American)
forms of Johana, Joanna.
**Jahna, Jahnaya, Jhona,
Jhonna, Jianna, Jianni,
Jiannini, Johna, Johnda,
Johneatha, Johnetta, Johni,
Johnica, Johnie, Johnita,
Johnittia, Johnnessa, Johnni,
Johnnie, Johnnielynn, Johnnie-
Lynn, Johnnquia, Johnny,
Johnquita, Jonda, Jondell,
Jondrea, Jonni, Jonnica,
Jonnie, Jonnita, Jonny,
Jonyelle, Jutta**
Foreign forms: French:
Johnette, Johnique; Slavic:
Joncie, Jonnika

Johnnessa (American) a com-
bination of Johnna + Nessa.
**Jahnessa, Johnecia, Johnesha,
Johnetra, Johnisha, Johnishi,
Johnnise, Jonyssa**

Jolanda (Greek) an alternate
form of Yolanda.
**Jola, Jolan, Jolán, Jolande,
Jolander, Jolanka, Jolánta,
Jolantha, Jolanthe, Joli**

Joleen, Joline (English) alternate forms of Jolene.

Jolene (Hebrew) God will add,
God will increase. (English) a
form of Josephine.
**Jo, Jolaine, Jolana, Jolane,
Jolanna, Jolanne, Jolanta,
Jolayne, Jole, Jolean, Joleane,
Jolee, Joleen, Jolena, Joléne,
Jolenna, Joley, Jolin, Jolina,
Jolinda, Joline, Jolinna, Jolisa,
Jolleane, Jolleen, Jollene,
Jolline, Jolye**

Jolie (French) pretty.
**Jole, Jolea, Jolee, Joleigh,
Joley, Joli, Jolibeth, Jollee,
Jollie, Jolly, Joly, Jolye**

Jolisa (American) a combination of Jo + Lisa.
Joleesa, Jolissa, Jolysa, Jolyssa

Jolynn (American) a combina-
tion of Jo + Lynn.
**Joline, Jolinn, Jolyn, Jolyne,
Jolynne**

Jonelle (American) a combina-
tion of Joan + Elle.
**Jahnel, Jahnell, Jahnelle,
Johnel, Johnell, Johnella,
Johnelle, Jonel, Jonell, Jonella,
Jynell, Jynelle**

Joni (American) a familiar form
of Joan.

**Jona, Jonae, Jonai, Jonann,
Jonati, Joncey, Jonci, Joncie,
Joneeka, Joneen, Joneika,
Joneisha, Jonelle, Jonessa,
Jonetia, Jonetta, Jonette,
Jonica, Jonice, Jonie, Jonika,
Jonilee, Joni-lee, Jonina,
Joniqua, Jonique, Jonis, Jonisa,
Jonisha, Jonit, Jony**

Jonina (Hebrew) dove. A femi-
nine form of Jonah. See also
Yonina.
**Jona, Jonika, Joniqua, Jonita,
Jonnina**

Jonita (Hebrew) an alternate
form of Jonina. See also
Yonita.
**Jonati, Jonit, Jonta, Jontae,
Jontaé, Jontaya**

Jonquil (Latin, English) Botany:
an ornamental plant with fragrant yellow flowers.
Jonquille

Jontel (American) an alternate
form of Johnna.
**Jontaya, Jontell, Jontelle,
Jontia, Jontila, Jontrice**

Jora (Hebrew) autumn rain.
Jorah

Jordan (Hebrew) descending.
**Jordain, Jordana, Jordane,
Jorden, Jordenne, Jordi,**

Jordin, Jordine, Jordon, Jordonna, Jordyn, Jordyne, Jori, Jorie

Jordana, Jordanna (Hebrew) alternate forms of Jordan.
Jordann, Jordanne, Jourdana, Jourdann, Jourdanna, Jourdanne
Foreign forms: Basque: Yordana; Italian: **Giordana**

Jori, Jorie (Hebrew) familiar forms of Jordan.
Jorai, Jorea, Joree, Jorée, Jorey, Jorian, Jorin, Jorina, Jorine, Jorita, Jorrian, Jorrie, Jorry, Jory

Joriann (American) a combination of Jori + Ann.
Jori-Ann, Jorianna, Jori-Anna, Jorianne, Jori-Anne, Jorriann, Jorrianna, Jorrianne, Jorryann, Jorryanne, Joryann, Joryanna, Joryanne

Joscelin (Latin) an alternate form of Jocelyn.
Josceline, Joscelyn, Joscelyne, Joscelynn, Joscelynne, Joselin, Joseline, Joselyn, Joselyne, Joselynn, Joselynne, Joshlyn

Josee, Josée (American) familiar forms of Josephine.
Joesee, Joesell, Joesette, Joselle, Josette, Josey, Josi,

Josiane, Josiann, Josianne, Josielina, Josina, Josy, Jozee, Jozelle, Jozette, Jozie

Joselyn, Joslyn (Latin) alternate forms of Jocelyn.
Josalene, Joselene, Joseline, Josiline, Josilyn

Josephine (French) God will add, God will increase. A feminine form of Joseph.
Fifi, Fifine, Fina, Jo, Joey, Josee, Josée, Josefena, Josephene, Josephin, Josephina, Josephyna, Josephyne, Josie, Sefa
Foreign forms: English: **Jolene**; *German:* **Josepha**; *Hebrew:* **Yosepha**; *Italian:* **Guiseppina, Josephe, Josefine, Josette**; *Spanish:* **Josefa, Josefina, Pepita**

Josette (French) a familiar form of Josephine.
Josetta

Joshlyn (Latin) an alternate form of Jocelyn. (Hebrew) God is my salvation. A feminine form of Joshua.
Jesusa, Joshalin, Joshalyn, Joshalynn, Joshalynne, Joshana, Joshann, Joshanna, Joshanne, Joshelle, Joshetta, Joshleen, Joshlene, Joshlin, Joshline, Joshlyne, Joshlynn, Joshlynne

Josie (Hebrew) a familiar form of Josephine.
Josee, Josey, Josi, Josy, Josye

Josilin, Joslin (Latin) alternate forms of Jocelyn.
Josielina, Josiline, Josilyn, Josilyne, Josilynn, Josilynne, Joslin, Josline, Joslyn, Joslyne, Joslynn, Joslynne

Jossalin (Latin) an alternate form of Jocelyn.
Jossaline, Jossalyn, Jossalynn, Jossalynne, Josseline, Jossellen, Jossellin, Jossellyn, Josselyn, Josselyne, Josselynn, Josselynne, Jossie, Josslin, Jossline, Josslyn, Josslyne, Josslynn, Josslynne

Jovanna (Latin) majestic. A feminine form of Jovan. (Italian) an alternate form of Giovanna. Mythology: Jove, also known as Jupiter, was the supreme Roman god.
Jeovana, Jeovanna, Jouvan, Jovado, Joval, Jovan, Jovana, Jovanie, Jovann, Jovanne, Joveda, Jovena, Jovian, Jovida, Jovon, Jovonda, Jovonna, Jovonne, Jowanna

Jovita (Latin) jovial.
Jovena, Joveta, Jovetta, Jovida, Jovina, Jovitta

Joy (Latin) joyous.
Joi, Joie, Joya, Joyan, Joyann, Joyanna, Joyanne, Joye, Joyeeta, Joyelle, Joyhanna, Joyhannah, Joyia, Joyvina

Joyce (Latin) joyous. A short form of Jocelyn.
Joice, Joycey, Joycie, Joyous, Joysel

Joylyn (American) a combination of Joy + Lynn.
Joyleen, Joylene, Joylin, Joyline, Joylyne, Joylynn, Joy-Lynn, Joylynne

Juanita (Spanish) a form of Jane, Joan. See also Nita.
Juana, Juandalyn, Juaneice, Juanequa, Juanesha, Juanice, Juanicia, Juaniqua, Juanisha, Juanishia, Juanna
Foreign forms: American: **Genita, Janita;** Hawaiian: **Wanika;** Zuni: **Kwanita**

Judith (Hebrew) praised. Mythology: the slayer of Holofernes, according to ancient eastern legend. A feminine form of Judah. See also Yehudit.
Judana, Jude, Judine
Foreign forms: Bulgarian: **Judita;** English: **Jodi, Jodie, Jody, Judy;** French: **Judithe;** Greek: **Ioudithe;** Hungarian: **Jucika,** **Jutka;** Italian: **Giuditta, Guila;** Lithuanian: **Judyta;** Portuguese: **Judite;** Russian: **Yudita;** Swedish: **Judit, Juditha**

Judy (Hebrew) a familiar form of Judith.
Judi, Judie, Judye
Foreign form: Hungarian: **Juci**

Judyann (American) a combination of Judy + Ann.
Judiann, Judianna, Judianne, Judyanna, Judyanne

Julia (Latin) youthful. A feminine form of Julius. See also Jillian, Sulia.
Juliann, Julica, Julina, Juline, Julisa, Julissa, Julyssa
Foreign forms: Basque: **Julene, Yulene;** Bulgarian/Romanian: **Iulia;** Czech: **Juliana, Julka;** English: **Julie;** French: **Juliet;** Hungarian: **Julianna;** Italian: **Giulia, Giulianna;** Lithuanian: **Julija;** Polish: **Jula;** Russian: **Yulia;** Spanish: **Juliana, Julita**

Juliana (Czech, Spanish), **Julianna** (Hungarian) forms of Julia.
Julliana, Jullianna

Juliann, Julianne (English) forms of Julia.
Juliane, Julieann, Julie-Ann, Julieanne, Julie-Anne

Julie (English) a form of Julia.
Juel, Jule, Julee, Juli, Julie-Lynn, Julie-Mae, Julien, Juliene, Julienne, Jullie, July

Juliet, Juliette (French) forms of Julia.
Julet, Jullet, Julliet, Jullietta
Foreign forms: Italian: **Julietta;** Spanish: **Julieta**

Jun (Chinese) truthful.

June (Latin) born in the sixth month.
Juna, Junell, Junelle, Junie, Juniet, Junieta, Junietta, Juniette, Junina, Junita
Foreign forms: English: **Junette, Junia**

Junko (Japanese) obedient.

Juno (Latin) queen. Mythology: the goddess of heaven.

Justina (Italian) a form of Justine.
Jestena, Jestina, Justinna, Justyna

Justine (Latin) just, righteous. A feminine form of Justin.
Jestine, Juste, Justi, Justie, Justinn, Justy, Justyne
Foreign forms: Italian: **Giustina, Justina**

Kacey, Kacy (Irish) brave. (American) alternate forms of Casey. A combination of the initials K. + C.
K. C., Kace, Kacee, Kaci, Kacie, Kaicee, Kaicey, Kasey, Kasie, Kaycee, Kayci, Kaycie

Kachina (Native American) sacred dancer.
Kachine

Kaci, Kacie (American) alternate forms of Kacey, Kacy.
Kasci, Kaycie, Kaysie

Kacia (Greek) a short form of Acacia.
Kaycia, Kaysia

Kady (English) an alternate form of Katy. A combination of the initials K. + D. See also Cady.

K. D., Kade, Kadee, Kadey, Kadi, Kadie, Kayde, Kaydee, Kaydey, Kaydi, Kaydie, Kaydy

Kaela (Hebrew, Arabic) beloved sweetheart. A short form of Kalila, Kelila.
Kaelah, Kayla, Kaylah, Keyla, Keylah

Kaelyn (American) a combination of Kae + Lynn. See also Kaylyn.
Kaelan, Kaelen, Kaelin, Kaelinn, Kaelynn, Kaelynne

Kai (Hawaiian) sea. (Hopi, Navaho) willow tree.

Kaila (Hebrew) laurel; crown.
Kailah, Kayla
Foreign forms: American:
Kailee, Kailey

Kailee, Kailey (American) familiar forms of Kaila. Alternate forms of Kaylee.
Kaile, Kaili

Kaitlin (Irish) pure. An alternate form of Caitlin. See also Katelin.
Kaitlan, Kaitland, Kaitleen, Kaitlen, Kaitlind, Kaitlinn, Kaitlon, Kalyn

Kaitlyn (Irish) an alternate form of Caitlyn.
Kaitlynn, Kaitlynne

Kala (Arabic) a short form of Kalila. An alternate form of Cala.

Kalani (Hawaiian) chieftain; sky.
Kailani, Kalanie, Kaloni

Kalea (Hawaiian) bright; clear.
Kahlea, Kahleah, Kailea, Kaileah, Kallea, Kalleah, Kaylea, Kayleah, Khalea, Khaleah

Kalei (Hawaiian) flower wreath.
Kahlei, Kailei, Kallei, Kaylei, Khalei

Kalena (Hawaiian) pure.
Kaleena

Kaley (American) an alternate form of Caley, Kaylee.
Kalee, Kaleigh, Kalleigh

Kali (Sanskrit) energy; black goddess; time the destroyer. (Hawaiian) hesitating. Religion: a name for the Hindu goddess Shakti. See also Cali.
Kala, Kalee, Kaleigh, Kaley, Kalie, Kallee, Kalley, Kalli, Kallie, Kally, Kallye, Kaly

Kalila (Arabic) beloved, sweetheart. See also Kelila.
Kahlila, Kala, Kaleela, Kaley, Kalilla, Kaylee, Kaylil, Kaylila,

Kalila (cont.)
Kelila, Khalila, Khalilah, Khalillah, Kyla, Kylila, Kylilah, Kylillah

Kalina (Slavic) flower. (Hawaiian) a form of Karen.
Kalinna, Kalynna

Kalinda (Hindi) sun.
Kaleenda, Kalindi, Kalynda, Kalyndi

Kalisa (American) a combination of Kate + Lisa.
Kaleesha, Kalisha, Kalissa, Kalysa, Kalyssa

Kallan (Slavic) stream, river.
Kalahn, Kalan, Kalen, Kallen, Kalin, Kallin, Kallon, Kalon, Kallyn, Kalyn

Kalli, Kallie (Greek) an alternate form of Callie. A familiar form of Kallista.
Kalle, Kallee, Kalley, Kallita, Kally

Kallista (Greek) an alternate form of Callista.
Kalesta, Kalista, Kallesta, Kalli, Kallie, Kallysta, Kaysta

Kalyn (American) an alternate form of Kaylyn.

Kama (Sanskrit) loved one. Religion: the Hindu god of love.

Kamala (Hindi) lotus.
Kamalah

Kamaria (Swahili) moonlight.
Kamara, Kamarie

Kambria (Latin) an alternate form of Cambria.
Kambra, Kambrie, Kambriea, Kambry

Kamea (Hawaiian) one and only; precious.
Kameo

Kameko (Japanese) turtle child. Mythology: the turtle symbolizes longevity.

Kameron (American) a form of Cameron.
Kamren, Kamrin, Kamron

Kami (Italian, North African) a short form of Kamila, Kamilah. (Japanese) divine aura. See also Cami.
Kammi, Kammie, Kammy, Kamy

Kamilah (North African) perfect.
Kameela, Kameelah, Kami, Kammilah

Kanda (Native American) magical power.

Kandace, Kandice (Greek) glittering white; glowing. (American) alternate forms of Candace, Candice.
Kandas, Kandess, Kandi, Kandis, Kandise, Kandiss, Kandus, Kandyce, Kandys, Kandyse

Kandi (American) a familiar form of Kandace, Kandice. See also Candi.
Kanda, Kandhi, Kandia, Kandie, Kandy

Kane (Japanese) two right hands.

Kaneisha (American) an alternate form of Keneisha.
Kaneasha, Kaneesha, Kanesha, Kaneshia, Kanisha, Kanishia

Kannitha (Cambodian) angel.

Kanya (Hindi) virgin. (Thai) young lady. Religion: a name for the Hindu goddess Shakti.
Kania

Kapuki (Swahili) first-born daughter.

Kara (Greek, Danish) pure. An alternate form of Katherine.
Kaira, Kairah, Karah, Karalea,

**Karaleah, Karalee, Karalie,
Kari**
Foreign form: French: Karielle

Karah (Greek, Danish) an alternate form of Kara. (Irish, Italian) an alternate form of Cara.
Karrah

Karalynn (English) a combination of Kara + Lynn.
Karalin, Karaline, Karalyn, Karalyne, Karalynne

Karen (Greek) pure. An alternate form of Katherine.
Kaaren, Kaarin, Kaarina, Karaina, Karan, Karena, Karna, Karon, Karren, Karrin, Karrina, Karrine, Karron, Kerrin, Kerron, Kerrynn, Kerrynne, Koren
Foreign forms: American: Karyn; Danish: Caryn; Hawaiian: Kalina; Russian: Karina, Karine; Scandinavian: Karena, Karin; Swedish: Carina; Welsh: Carey

Kari (Greek) pure. (Danish) a form of Caroline, Katherine. See also Carey, Cari, Carrie.
Karee, Karey, Kariann, Karianna, Karianne, Karie, Karrey, Karri, Karrie, Karry, Kary

Karida (Arabic) untouched, pure.
Kareeda, Karita

Karilynn (American) a combination of Kari + Lynn.
Kareelin, Kareeline, Kareelinn, Kareelyn, Kareelyne, Kareelynn, Kareelynne, Karilin, Kariline, Karilinn, Karilyn, Karilyne, Karilynne, Karylin, Karyline, Karylinn, Karylyn, Karylyne, Karylynn, Karylynne

Karimah (Arabic) generous.
Kareema, Kareemah, Karima, Karime

Karin (Scandinavian) a form of Karen.
Karina, Karine, Karinne

Karina (Russian) a form of Karen.
Karinna, Karrina, Karryna, Karyna

Karine (Russian) a form of Karen.
Karrine, Karryne, Karyne

Karis (Greek) graceful.
Karess, Karice, Karise, Karris, Karys, Karyss

Karissa (Greek) an alternate form of Carissa.

Karese, Karessa, Karesse, Karisa, Karisha, Karishma, Karisma, Karissimia, Kariza, Karrisa, Karrissa, Karyssa

Karla (German) an alternate form of Carla. (Slavic) a short form of Karoline.
Karila, Karilla, Karle, Karleen, Karleigh, Karlen, Karlena, Karlene, Karlenn, Karletta, Karley, Karlicka, Karlign, Karlin, Karlina, Karling, Karlinka, Karlisha, Karlisia, Karlita, Karlitha, Karlla, Karlon, Karlyan, Karlye, Karlyn, Karlynn, Karlynne

Karli, Karly (Latin) little and womanly. (American) forms of Carly.
Karlee, Karley, Karlie, Karlye

Karma (Hindi) fate, destiny; action.

Karmel (Hebrew) an alternate form of Carmela.
Karmeita, Karmela, Karmelina, Karmella, Karmelle, Karmiella, Karmyla
Foreign form: French: Karmielle

Karmen (Hebrew) song. A form of Carmen.
Karman, Karmencita, Karmin, Karmina, Karmine, Karmita, Karmon, Karmyn, Karmyne

Karolyn (American) a form of Carolyn.
Karalyn, Karalyna, Karalynn, Karalynne, Karilyn, Karilyna, Karilynn, Karilynne, Karlyn, Karlynn, Karlynne, Karolyna, Karolynn, Karolynne, Karrolyn, Karrolyna, Karrolynn, Karrolynne

Karri, Karrie (American) forms of Carrie.
Kari, Karie, Karry

Karyn (American) a form of Karen.
Karyna, Karyne, Karynn

Kasey, Kasie (Irish) brave. (American) forms of Casey, Kacey.
Kaisee, Kaisie, Kasci, Kascy, Kasee, Kasi, Kasy, Kasya, Kaysci, Kaysea, Kaysee, Kaysey, Kaysi, Kaysie, Kaysy

Kashawna (American) a combination of Kate + Shawna.
Kashana, Kashawn, Kashonda, Kashonna

Kashmir (Sanskrit) Geography: a state in India.
Cashmere, Kashmear, Kashmere, Kashmia, Kashmira, Kasmir, Kasmira, Kazmir, Kazmira

Kasi (Hindi) from the holy city.

Kassandra (Greek) an alternate form of Cassandra.
Kasander, Kasandria, Kasandra, Kasaundra, Kasondra, Kasoundra, Kassandr, Kassaundra, Kassi, Kazandra, Khrisandra, Krisandra, Krissandra
Foreign forms: French: Kassandre, Kassandré

Kassi, Kassie (American) familiar forms of Kassandra, Kassidy. See also Cassie.
Kassey, Kassia, Kassy

Kassidy (Irish) clever. (American) an alternate form of Cassidy.
Kassadee, Kassadi, Kassadie, Kassadina, Kassady, Kasseday, Kassedee, Kassi, Kassiddy, Kassidee, Kassidi, Kassidie, Kassity

Kate (Greek) pure. (English) a short form of Katherine.
Katy
Foreign forms: Czech: Kata, Katica; Estonian: Kati; Irish: Kaethe, Kait; Russian: Katka, Katja, Katya

Katelin, Katelyn (Irish) alternate forms of Caitlin. See also Kaitlin.

Kaetlin, Kaetlyn, Kaetlynn, Kaetlynne, Katalin, Katelan, Kateland, Kateleen, Katelen, Katelene, Katelind, Katelinn, Katelun, Katelyne, Katlyn, Kaytlin, Kaytlyn, Kaytlynn, Kaytlynne

Katharine (Greek) an alternate form of Katherine.
Katharaine, Katharin, Katharina, Katharyn

Katherine (Greek) pure. See also Carey, Catherine, Kara, Karen, Kari.
Ekaterini, Ekatrinna, Kasin, Kat, Kathann, Kathanne, Katharine, Kathereen, Katheren, Katherene, Katherenne, Katherin, Katheryn, Katheryne, Kathi, Kathyrine, Katina, Katlaina, Katreeka, Kay
Foreign forms: Czech: Katarina, Katarzina, Katerini; English: Kate, Kathryn, Kathy, Katie, Kitty; German: Katchen, Katrina; Hungarian: Kata, Kató, Katoka; Irish: Kathleen; Italian: Katerina; Norwegian: Cathrine, Katla; Polish: Kasia, Kasienka, Kassya; Romanian: Ecaterina; Russian: Ekaterina, Katya, Yekaterina; Swedish: Kolina, Kolyn

Kathi, Kathy (English) familiar forms of Katherine, Kathleen. See also Cathi.
Katha, Kathe, Kathee, Kathey, Kathi, Kathie

Kathleen (Irish) a form of Katherine. See also Cathleen.
Katheleen, Kathelene, Kathileen, Kathlyn, Kathlyne, Kathlynn, Kathy, Katleen, Katlin, Katlyn, Katlynn

Kathryn (English) a form of Katherine.
Kathren, Kathrine, Kathryne

Kati (Estonian) a form of Kate.
Katia, Katja, Katya, Katye

Katie (English) a familiar form of Kate.
Kady, Katee, Kati, Katia, Katy, Kayte, Kaytee, Kaytie

Katlyn (Greek) pure. (Irish) an alternate form of Katelin.
Kaatlain, Katland, Katlynd, Katlynn, Katlynne

Katrina (German) a form of Katherine. See also Trina.
Katreen, Katreena, Katrelle, Katrene, Katri, Katrice, Katricia, Katrien, Katrin, Katrine, Katrinia, Katriona, Katryn, Katryna, Kattiah, Kattrina, Kattryna, Katus

Foreign forms: Slavic: **Catrina, Katuska**

Katy (English) a familiar form of Kate. See also Cady.
Kady, Katey, Kayte

Kaulana (Hawaiian) famous.
Kaula, Kauna, Kahuna

Kay (Greek) rejoicer. (Teutonic) a fortified place. (Latin) merry. A short form of Katherine.
Caye, Kae, Kai, Kaye

Kaya (Hopi) wise child. (Japanese) resting place.
Kaja, Kayia

Kaycee (American) a combination of the initials K. + C.

Kayla (Arabic, Hebrew) laurel; crown. An alternate form of Kaela, Kaila. See also Cayla.
Kayle, Kaylee, Kayleen, Kaylene, Kaylia, Kaylin

Kaylee (American) a form of Kayla. See also Caeley.
Kaelea, Kaeleah, Kaelee, Kaeli, Kaelie, Kaelee, Kaeli, Kaelie, Kailea, Kaileah, Kailee, Kayle, Kaylea, Kayleah, Kaylei, Kayleigh, Kayley, Kayli, Kaylie

Kayleen, Kaylene (Hebrew) beloved, sweetheart. Alternate forms of Kayla.

Kaeleen, Kaelen, Kaelene, Kailen, Kaileen, Kailene, Kaylen

Kayleigh (American) an alternate form of Kaylee.
Kaeleigh, Kaileigh

Kaylin (American) an alternate form of Kaylyn.
Kaylan, Kaylon

Kaylyn (American) a combination of Kay + Lynn. See also Kaelyn.
Kailyn, Kailynn, Kailynne, Kayleen, Kaylene, Kaylynn, Kaylynne

Keara (Irish) dark; black. Religion: an Irish saint.
Kearia, Kearra, Keera, Keerra, Keira, Keirra, Kera, Kiara, Kiarra, Kiera, Kierra

Keeley, Keely (Irish) alternate forms of Kelly.
Kealee, Kealey, Keali, Kealie, Keallie, Kealy, Kealyn, Keela, Keelan, Keelee, Keeleigh, Keeli, Keelie, Keelin, Keellie, Keelyn, Keighla, Keilan, Keilee, Keileigh, Keiley, Keilly, Kiela, Kiele, Kieley, Kielly, Kiely, Kielyn

Keena (Irish) brave.
Keenya, Kina

Kei (Japanese) reverent.
Keiana, Keikann, Keikanna, Keionna

Keiki (Hawaiian) child.
Keikana, Keikanne

Keiko (Japanese) happy child.
Kei

Keilani (Hawaiian) glorious chief.
Keilan, Keilana

Keira (Irish) an alternate form of Kiara.
Kera

Keisha (American) a short form of Keneisha.
Keesha, Keishaun, Keishauna, Keishawn, Kesha, Keysha, Kiesha, Kisha, Kishanda

Keita (Scottish) woods; enclosed place.
Keiti

Kelila (Hebrew) crown, laurel. See also Kaela, Kalila, Kayla.
Kelilah, Kelula

Kelley (Irish) an alternate form of Kelly.

Kelli, Kellie (Irish) familiar forms of Kelly.
Keli, Kelia, Kellia, Kelliann, Kellianne, Kellisa

Kelly (Irish) brave warrior.
Keeley, Keely, Kelley, Kellyann, Kellyanne, Kelley, Kelli, Kellie, Kellye
Foreign form: American: **Caeley**

Kellyn (Irish) a combination of Kelly + Lyn.
Kelleen, Kellen, Kellene, Kellina, Kelline, Kellynn, Kellynne

Kelsey (Scandinavian, Scottish) ship island. (English) an alternate form of Chelsey.
Kelcey, Kelcy, Kelda, Kellsee, Kellsei, Kellsey, Kellsie, Kellsy, Kelsa, Kelsea, Kelsei, Kelsey, Kelsi, Kelsie, Kelsy, Keslie

Kelsi, Kelsie (Scottish) forms of Chelsea.
Kelci, Kelcie

Kenda (English) water baby. (Dakota) magical power. Astrology: a child born under Cancer, Scorpio, or Pisces.
Kendi, Kendie, Kendy, Kennda, Kenndi, Kenndie, Kenndy

Kendall (English) ruler of the valley.
Kendahl, Kendal, Kendalla, Kendalle, Kendel, Kendele, Kendell, Kendelle, Kendera, Kendia, Kendyl, Kendyle,
Kendyll, Kinda, Kindal, Kindall, Kindi, Kindle, Kynda, Kyndal, Kyndall

Kendra (English) an alternate form of Kenda.
Kendre, Kenna, Kenndra, Kentra, Kentrae, Kindra, Kyndra

Keneisha (American) a combination of the prefix Ken + Aisha.
Kaneisha, Keneesha, Kenesha, Keneshia, Kenisha, Kenishia, Kennesha, Kenneshia, Kennisa, Kennisha, Kineisha

Kenna (Irish) a short form of Kennice.
Kennia

Kennice (English) beautiful. A feminine form of Kenneth.
Kanice, Keneese, Kenese, Kennise
Foreign form: Irish: **Kenna**

Kenya (Hebrew) animal horn. Geography: a country in Africa.
Keenya, Kenia, Kenja

Kenzie (Scottish) light skinned. (Irish) a short form of Mackenzie.
Kenzy, Kinzie

Kerensa (Cornish) loving, affectionate.
Karensa, Karenza, Kerenza

Kerri, Kerrie (Irish) alternate forms of Kerry.
Keri, Keriann, Kerianne, Kerriann, Kerrianne

Kerry (Irish) dark haired. Geography: a county in Ireland.
Keree, Kerey, Kerri, Kerrie, Kerryann, Kerryanne, Kiera, Kierra

Kerstin (Scandinavian) an alternate form of Kirsten.
Kersten, Kerston, Kerstyn

Keshia (American) an alternate form of Keisha. A short form of Keneisha.
Kecia, Keishia, Keschia, Kesia, Kesiah, Kessiah

Kesi (Swahili) born during difficult times.

Kessie (Ashanti) chubby baby.
Kess, Kessa, Kesse, Kessey, Kessi, Kessia, Kessiah

Kevyn (Irish) beautiful. A feminine form of Kevin.
Keva, Kevan, Kevina, Kevone, Kevonna, Kevynn

Keziah (Hebrew) cinnamonlike spice. Bible: one of the daughters of Job.
Kazia, Kaziah, Ketzi, Ketzia, Ketziah, Kezi, Kezia
Foreign forms: American: **Kissie, Kizzie, Kizzy**

Khadijah (Arabic) trustworthy. History: Muhammed's first wife.
Khadeeja, Khadeja, Khadejha, Khadija

Khalida (Arabic) immortal, everlasting.
Khali, Khalia, Khalita

Ki (Korean) arisen.

Kia (African) season's beginning. (American) a short form of Kiana.
Kiah

Kiana (American) a combination of the prefix Ki + Ana.
Keanna, Keiana, Kiani, Kiahna, Kianna, Kianni, Kiauna, Kiandra, Kiandria, Kiauna, Kiaundra, Kiona, Kionah, Kioni, Kionna

Kiara (Irish) little and dark. A feminine form of Kieran.

Kiaria, Kiarra, Kichi (Japanese) fortunate.

Kiele (Hawaiian) gardenia; fragrant blossom.
Kiela, Kieley, Kieli, Kielli, Kielly

Kiera, Kierra (Irish) alternate forms of Kerry.
Kierana, Kieranna, Kierea

Kiki (Spanish) a familiar form of names ending in "queta."

Kiku (Japanese) chrysanthemum.
Kiko

Kiley (Irish) attractive; from the straits.
Kilee, Kilie, Kylee, Kyli, Kylie

Kim (Vietnamese) needle. (English) a short form of Kimberly.
Kimba, Kimbra, Kimee, Kimette, Kimme, Kimmee, Kimmi, Kimmie, Kimmy, Kimy, Kym

Kimana (Shoshone) butterfly.

Kimberlee, Kimberley (English) alternate forms of Kimberly.
Kimbalee, Kimberlea, Kimberlei, Kimberleigh, Kimbley

Kimberly (English) chief, ruler.
**Cymbre, Kim, Kimba,
Kimbely, Kimber, Kimbereley,
Kimberely, Kimberlee,
Kimberli, Kimberlie,
Kimberlyn, Kimbery, Kimbria,
Kimbrie, Kimbry, Kymberly**

Kimi (Japanese) righteous.
**Kimia, Kimika, Kimiko,
Kimiyo**

Kina (Hawaiian) from China.

Kineisha (American) an alternate form of Keneisha.
**Kineesha, Kinesha, Kineshia,
Kinisha, Kinishia**

Kinsey (English) offspring; relative.
Kinsee

Kioko (Japanese) happy child.
Kiyo, Kiyoko

Kiona (Native American) brown hills.

Kira (Persian) sun. (Latin) light. A feminine form of Cyrus.
Kiran, Kiri, Kiria

Kirima (Eskimo) hill.

Kirsta (Scandinavian) an alternate form of Kirsten.

Kirsten (Greek) Christian; annointed. (Scandinavian) a form of Christine.
**Karsten, Keirstan, Kerstin,
Kiersten, Kirsteni, Kirsta,
Kirstan, Kirsteen, Kirstene,
Kirstin, Kirston, Kirsty,
Kirstyn, Kjersten, Kursten,
Kyrsten**

Kirstin (Scandinavian) an alternate form of Kirsten.
Karstin, Kirstien, Kirstine

Kirsty (Scandinavian) a familiar form of Kirsten.
**Kerstie, Kirsta, Kirstee, Kirsti,
Kirstie, Kjersti, Kyrsty**

Kishi (Japanese) long and happy life.

Kita (Japanese) north.

Kitty (Greek) a familiar form of Katherine.
**Ketter, Ketti, Ketty, Kit,
Kittee, Kitteen, Kittey, Kitti,
Kittie**

Klarissa (German) clear, bright. (Italian) an alternate form of Clarissa.
**Klarisa, Klarise, Klarrisa,
Klarisza, Klarysa, Kleresa**

Koffi (Swahili) born on Friday.
Kaffe, Kaffi, Koffe, Koffie

Koko (Japanese) stork. See also Coco.

Kona (Hawaiian) lady. (Hindi) angular. Astrology: born under the sign of Capricorn.
Koni, Konia

Konstance (Latin) an alternate form of Constance.
**Konstantina, Konstantine,
Konstanza, Konstanze**

Kora (Greek) an alternate form of Cora.
**Kore, Koren, Korey, Kori,
Korie, Kory, Korra, Korri,
Korrie, Korry**
Foreign forms: Spanish:
**Korella, Koressa, Koretta,
Korilla**

Kori (American) a short form of Korina. See also Corey, Cori.
**Koree, Korey, Koria, Korie,
Korri, Korrie, Korry, Kory**

Korina (Greek) an alternate form of Corina.
**Koreen, Koreena, Korena,
Korin, Korine, Korinna,
Korreena, Korrin, Korrina,
Korrine, Korrinna, Korrinne,
Koryn, Koryna**
Foreign form: American: **Kori**

Kornelia (Latin) an alternate form of Cornelia.

Kornelia (cont.)
Karniela, Karniella, Karnis, Kornelija, Kornelis, Kornelya, Korny

Kortney (English) an alternate form of Courtney.
Kortnay, Kortnee, Kortni, Kortnie, Kortny

Kosta (Latin) a short form of Constance.
Kostia, Kostusha, Kostya

Koto (Japanese) harp.

Kourtney (American) a form of Courtney.
Kourtni, Kourtny, Kourtynie

Kris (American) a short form of Kristine. An alternate form of Chris.
Khris, Krissy

Krissy (American) a familiar form of Kris.
Krissey, Krissi, Krissie

Krista (Czech) a form of Christina. See also Christa.
Khrissa, Khrista, Khryssa, Khrysta, Krissa, Kryssa
Foreign form: Polish: **Krysta**

Kristen (Greek) Christian; annointed. (Scandinavian) a form of Christine.

Christen, Kristan, Kristin, Krysten
Foreign form: Czech: **Krystin**

Kristi, Kristie (Scandinavian) short forms of Kristine.
Christi

Kristian, Kristiana (Greek) Christian; anointed. Alternate forms of Christian.
Khristian, Kristian, Kristiann, Kristi-Ann, Kristianna, Kristianne, Kristi-Anne, Kristien, Kristienne, Kristiin, Kristyan, Kristyana, Kristy-Ann, Kristy-Anne

Kristin (Scandinavian) an alternate form of Kristen. See also Cristen.
Kristyn

Kristina (Greek) Christian; annointed. (Scandinavian) a form of Christina. See also Cristina.
Khristina, Kristeena, Kristena, Kristiana, Kristianna, Kristinka, Krysteena, Krystena, Krystiana, Krystianna, Krystina
Foreign forms: Polish: **Krystyna, Krystynka**

Kristine (Scandinavian) a form of Christine.
Kristeen, Kristene, Kristi,

Kristiane, Kristie, Kristy, Krystine, Krystyne

Kristy (American) a familiar form of Kristine, Krystal. See also Cristy.
Kristi, Kristia, Kristie, Krysia, Krysti

Krysta (Polish) a form of Krista.
Krystka

Krystal (American) clear, brilliant glass. A form of Crystal.
Kristabel, Kristal, Kristale, Kristall, Kristel, Kristell, Kristelle, Kristill, Kristl, Kristle, Kristy, Krystalann, Krystalanne, Krystale, Krystall, Krystel, Krystelle, Krystil, Krystle, Krystol

Krystalee (American) a combination of Krystal + Lee.
Kristalea, Kristaleah, Kristalee, Krystalea, Krystaleah, Krystlea, Krystleah, Krystlee, Krystlelea, Krystleleah, Krystlelee

Krystalynn (American) a combination of Krystal + Lynn.
Krystaleen, Krystalina, Kristaline, Kristalyn, Kristalynn, Kristilyn, Kristilynn, Kristlyn, Krystalin, Krystalyn

Krystian, Krystiana (Greek) alternate forms of Christian.
Krystiana, Krystianne, Krysty-Ann, Krystyan, Kristyana, Krystyanna, Krystyanne, Krysty-Anne, Krystyen

Krystin (Czech) a form of Kristen.

Krystle (American) an alternate form of Krystal.
Krystl, Krystyl

Kumiko (Japanese) girl with braids.
Kumi

Kyla (Irish) attractive. (Yiddish) crown; laurel.
Kylen, Kylene, Kylia, Kylynn

Kyle (Irish) attractive.
Kial, Kiele, Kylee, Kylene, Kylie

Kylee (Irish) a familiar form of Kyle.
Kylea, Kyleah, Kyleigh, Kylie

Kylene (Irish) an alternate form of Kyle.
Kylen, Kylyn

Kylie (West Australian Aboriginal) curled stick; boomerang. (Irish) a familiar form of Kyle.

Keiley, Keilley, Keilly, Keily, Kiley, Kye, Kylee

Kymberly (English) an alternate form of Kimberly.
Kymberlee, Kymberley, Kymberlie, Kymberlyn

Kyoko (Japanese) mirror.

Kyra (Greek) ladylike. An alternate form of Cyrilla.
Keera, Keira, Kira, Kyrah, Kyrene, Kyria, Kyriah, Kyriann, Kyrie

Lacey, Lacy (Greek) a familiar form of Larissa. (Latin) cheerful.
Lacee, Laci, Lacie

Lachandra (American) a combination of the prefix La + Chandra.
Lachanda, Lachandice

Laci, Lacie (Latin) alternate forms of Lacey.
Lacia, Laciann, Lacianne

Lacrecia (Latin) an alternate form of Lucretia.
Lacrasha, Lacreash, Lacreasha, Lacreashia, Lacresha, Lacreshia, Lacresia, Lacretia, Lacricia, Lacrisha, Lacrishia

Lada (Russian) Mythology: the goddess of beauty.

Ladasha (American) a combination of the prefix La + Dasha.
Ladaisa, Ladaishia, Ladaseha, Ladashia, Ladassa, Ladaysha, Ladesha

Ladonna (American) a combination of the prefix La + Donna.
Ladon, Ladona, Ladonne, Ladonya

Laela (Arabic, Hebrew) an alternate form of Leila.
Layla, Laylah

Laila (Arabic) an alternate form of Leila.
Laili, Lailie

Laine (French) a short form of Elaine.
Laina, Lainee, Lainey, Layney

Lajuana (American) a combination of the prefix La + Juana.
Lajuanna, Lawana, Lawanna, Lawanne, Lawanza, Lawanze, Laweania

Lakeishia (American) a combination of the prefix La + Keisha. See also Lekasha.
Lakaiesha, Lakaisha, Lakasha, Lakecia, Lakeesh, Lakeesha, Lakesha, Lakeshia, Lakeshya, Lakesia, Laketia, Lakeysha, Lakeyshia, Lakezia, Lakicia, Lakiesha, Lakieshia, Lakisha, Lakitia

Lakendra (American) a combination of the prefix La + Kendra.
Lakanda, Lakedra

Lakenya (American) a combination of the prefix La + Kenya.
Lakeena, Lakeenna, Lakeenya, Lakena, Lakenia, Lakin, Lakinja, Lakinya, Lakwanya, Lekenia, Lekenya

Lakesha, Lakeshia, Lakisha (American) alternate forms of Lakeishia.
Lakecia, Lakeesha, Lakeseia, Lakiesha

Laketa (American) a combination of the prefix La + Keita.
Lakeeta, Lakeetah, Lakeita,
Lakeitha, Lakeithia, Laketha, Laketia, Laketta, Lakietha, Lakita, Lakitra, Lakitri, Lakitta

Lakia (Arabic) found treasure.
Lakita

Lakresha (American) a form of Lucretia.
Lacresha, Lacreshia, Lacresia, Lacretia, Lacrisha, Lakreshia, Lakrisha, Lekresha, Lekresia

Lallie (English) babbler.
Lalli, Laily

Lamesha (American) a combination of the prefix La + Mesha.
Lamees, Lameise, Lameshia, Lamisha, Lemisha

Lana (Latin) woolly. (Irish) attractive, peaceful. A short form of Alana, Elana. (Hawaiian) floating; bouyant.
Lanae, Lanata, Lanay, Laneetra, Lanette, Lanna, Lannah, Lanny

Lane (English) narrow road.
Laina, Laney, Lanie, Lanni, Lanny, Lany, Layne

Laneisha (American) a combination of the prefix La + Keneisha.
Lanecia, Laneesha, Laneise, Lanesha, Laneshe, Lanessa, Lanesse, Lanisha

Lani (Hawaiian) sky; heaven. A short form of Atalanta, Leilani.
Lanita, Lannie

Laqueena (American) a combination of the prefix La + Queenie.
Laqueen, Laquena, Laquenetta

Laquinta (American) a combination of the prefix La + Quintana.
Laquanta, Laqueinta, Laquenda, Laquenta, Laquinda, Laquita

Laquisha (American) a combination of the prefix La + Queisha.
Laquasha, Laquaysha, Laqueisha, Laquesha, Laquiesha

Laquita (American) a short form of Laquinta.
Laqeita, Laqueta, Laquetta, Laquia, Laquiata, Laquitta

Lara (Greek) cheerful. (Latin) shining; famous. Mythology: the daughter of the river god Almo. A short form of Laraine,

Lara *(cont.)*
Larissa, Laura.
Larah, Laretta, Larette

Laraine (Latin) an alternate form of Lorraine.
Lara, Laraene, Larain, Larayne, Larein, Lareina, Lareine, Larena

Larina (Greek) seagull.
Larena, Larine

Larissa (Greek) cheerful. See also Lacey.
Laris
Foreign forms: Russian: **Larisa, Laryssa**

Lark (English) skylark.

Lashanda (American) a combination of the prefix La + Shanda.
Lashana, Lashanay, Lashandra, Lashane, Lashanna, Lashannon, Lashanta, Lashante

Lashawna (American) a combination of the prefix La + Shawna.
Lashaun, Lashauna, Lashaune, Lashaunna, Lashaunta, Lashawn, Lashawnd, Lashawnda, Lashawndra, Lashawne, Lashawnia, Leshawn, Leshawna

Lashonda (American) a combination of the prefix La + Shonda.
Lachonda, Lashaunda, Lashaundra, Lashon, Lashona, Lashond, Lashonde, Lashondia, Lashondra, Lashonna, Lashonta, Lashunda, Lashundra, Lashunta, Lashunte, Leshande, Leshandra, Leshondra, Leshundra

Latanya (American) a combination of the prefix La + Tanya.
Latana, Latandra, Latania, Latanja, Latanna, Latanua

Latara (American) a combination of the prefix La + Tara.

Latasha (American) a combination of the prefix La + Tasha.
Latacha, Latacia, Latai, Lataisha, Latashia, Lataysha, Letasha, Letashia, Leteshia, Letasiah, Leteisha

Lateefah (Arabic) pleasant. (Hebrew) pat, caress.
Latifa, Latifah, Latipha

Latesha (American) a form of Letitia.
Lataeasha, Lateashia, Latecia, Lateesha, Lateicia, Lateisha, Latesa, Lateshia, Latessa, Latisa, Latissa

Latia (American) a combination of the prefix La + Tia.
Latea, Lateia

Latisha (Latin) joy. An alternate form of Leticia. (American) a combination of the prefix La + Tisha.
Laetitia, Laetizia, Latashia, Latia, Latice, Laticia, Lateasha, Lateashia, Latecia, Lateesha, Lateicia, Lateisha, Lateshia, Latiesha, Latishia, Latissha, Latitia

Latonya (American) a combination of the prefix La + Tonya.
Latona, Latoni, Latonia, Latonna, Latonshia

Latoria (American) a combination of the prefix La + Tori.
Latorio, Latorja, Latorray, Latorreia, Latory, Latorya, Latoyra, Latoyria

Latosha (American) a combination of the prefix La + Tosha.
Latoshia, Latosia

Latoya (American) a combination of the prefix La + Toya.
Latoia, Latoira, Latoiya, LaToya, Latoyia, Latoye, Latoyia, Latoyita, Latoyo, Latoyra, Latoyria

Latrice (American) a combination of the prefix La + Trice.
Latrece, Latreece, Latreese, Latresa, Latrese, Latressa, Letreece, Letrice

Latricia (American) a combination of the prefix La + Tricia.
Latrecia, Latresh, Latresha, Latreshia, Latrica, Latrisha, Latrishia

Laura (Latin) crowned with laurel. A feminine form of Laurence.
Lara, Lauralee, Laureana, Laurel, Laurelen, Laurella, Lauriana, Laurina, Lorinda, Lorina, Lorna, Loura
Foreign forms: American: **Lorelle, Loren, Lori;** Bulgarian: **Lora;** English: **Lauren, Laurie, Lorena, Loretta, Lolly;** French: **Laurette;** Italian: **Lauricia, Lorenza;** Polish: **Laurka;** Russian: **Lavra;** Spanish: **Lauriane, Lorinda, Lorita**

Laurel (Latin) laurel tree.
Laural, Laurell, Laurelle, Lorel, Lorelle

Lauren (English) a form of Laura.
Laureen, Laurena, Laurene, Laurin, Lauryn, Laurynn, Loren

Laurie (English) a familiar form of Laura.
Lari, Larilia, Laure, Lauré, Lauri, Lawrie, Lori

Lavena (Latin) an alternate form of Lavina. (Irish, French) joy.

Laverne (Latin) springtime. (French) grove of alder trees. See also Verna.
Laverine, Lavern, Laverna, La Verne

Lavina (Latin) purified; woman of Rome. See also Vina.
Lavena, Lavenia, Lavinia, Lavinie, Levenia, Levinia, Livinia, Louvinia, Lovina, Lovinia

Lavonna (American) a combination of the prefix La + Yvonne.
Lavon, Lavonda, Lavonder, Lavondria, Lavone, Lavonia, Lavonica, Lavonn, Lavonne, Lavonnie, Lavonya

Lawanda (American) a combination of the prefix La + Wanda.
Lawynda

Layla (Hebrew, Arabic) an alternate form of Leila.
Layli, Laylie

Le (Vietnamese) pearl.

Lea (Hawaiian) Mythology: the goddess of canoe makers.

Leah (Hebrew) weary. Bible: the wife of Jacob. See also Lia.
Lea, Léa, Leea, Leeah, Leia
Foreign forms: English: **Lee, Leigh**

Leala (French) faithful, loyal.
Lealia, Lealie, Leial

Lean, Leanne (English) forms of Leeann, Lian.
Leana, Leane, Leann, Leanna

Leandra (Latin) like a lioness.
Leanda, Leandre, Leandrea, Leandria, Leeanda, Leeandra

Leanna (English) an alternate form of Liana.
Leana

Leanore (Greek) an alternate form of Eleanor. (English) a form of Helen.
Leanora, Lanore

Lecia (Latin) a short form of Felecia.
Leecia, Leesha, Leesia, Lesha, Leshia, Lesia

Leda (Greek) lady. Mythology: the Queen of Sparta and the mother of Helen of Troy.

Leda *(cont.)*
Ledah, Lida, Lidah, Lita, Litah, Lyda, Lydah

Lee (Chinese) plum. (Irish) poetic. (English) meadow. A short form of Ashley, Leah.
Lea, Leigh

Leeann, Leeanne (English) a combination of Lee + Ann. A form of Lian.
Leane, Leanna, Leean, Leeanna, Leian, Leiann, Leianna, Leianne

Leeza (American) an alternate form of Lisa, Liza.

Lei (Hawaiian) a familiar form of Leilani.

Leigh (English) an alternate form of Lee.
Leigha, Leighann, Leighanna, Leighanne

Leila (Hebrew) dark beauty; night. (Arabic) born at night. Literature: the heroine of the epic Persian poem *Leila and Majnum*. See also Laela, Layla, Lila.
Laila, Layla, Leela, Leelah, Leilah, Leilia, Lela, Lelah, Leland, Lelia, Leyla

Leilani (Hawaiian) heavenly flower; heavenly child.
Lani, Lei, Lelani, Lelania

Lekasha (American) an alternate form of Lakeishia.
Lekeesha, Lekeisha, Lekesha, Lekeshia, Lekesia, Lekicia, Lekisha

Lelia (Greek) fair speech.
Lelie, Lelika, Lelita, Lellia

Lena (Greek) a short form of Eleanor. (Hebrew) dwelling or lodging. (Latin) temptress. (Norwegian) illustrious. Music: Lena Horne, a well-known African-American singer.
Lenah, Lene, Lenea, Lenee, Lenette, Leni, Lenka, Lina

Leneisha (American) a combination of the prefix Le + Keneisha.
Lenece, Lenesha, Lenisa, Lenise, Lenisha

Lenita (Latin) gentle.
Leneta

Leona (German) brave as a lioness. A feminine form of Leon. See also Lona.
Lenia, Leoine, Leola, Leolah, Leone, Leonia, Leonice, Leonicia, Leonissa, Liona
Foreign forms: *English:* **Leonelle, Leonine;** *French:* **Léonie**

Leonore (Greek) an alternate form of Eleanor. See also Nora.
Leonor, Leonora, Leonorah, Léonore

Leontine (Latin) like a lioness.
Leontyne, Léontyne

Leora (Greek) a familiar form of Eleanor. (Hebrew) light.
Leorah, Leorit, Liora

Lera (Russian) a short form of Valerie.
Lerka

Lesley (Scottish) gray fortress.
Leslea, Leslee, Leslie, Leslye, Lezlee, Lezley, Lezli, Lezly

Leslie (Scottish) an alternate form of Lesley.
Lesli, Lesslie

Leta (Latin) glad. (Swahili) bringer.
Lita, Lyta

Leticia (Latin) joy. See also Latisha, Tisha.
Leisha, Leshia, Let, Leta, Letha, Lethia, Letice, Letisia, Letita, Letiticia, Loutitia
Foreign forms: *American:* **Latesha;** *English:* **Letty;** *French:* **Léetice;** *Hungarian:* **Leticia;** *Italian:* **Letiza, Letizia;** *Polish:* **Letisha, Letycia**

Letty (English) a familiar form of Leticia.
Letta, Letti, Lettie

Levana (Hebrew) moon; white. (Latin) risen. Mythology: the goddess of newborn babies.
Lévana, Levania, Levanna, Levenia, Lewana, Lewanna, Livana

Levina (Latin) flash of lightning.
Levene

Levona (Hebrew) spice, incense.
Leavonia, Levonat, Livona

Lexandra (Greek) a short form of Alexandra.
Lisandra

Lexi (Greek) a familiar form of Alexandra.
Leksi, Leska, Lesya, Lexa, Lexane, Lexey, Lexia, Lexie, Lexina, Lexine, Lexy

Leya (Spanish) loyal. (Tamil) the constellation Leo.
Leyla

Lia (Greek) bringer of good news. (Hebrew, Dutch, Italian) dependent. See also Leah.
Liah

Lian (Chinese) graceful willow. (Latin) a short form of Gillian, Lillian.
Lean, Leeann, Liane

Liana (Hebrew) a short form of Eliana. (Latin) youth. (French) bound, wrapped up; tree covered with vines. (English) meadow.
Leanna, Liane, Lianna, Lianne

Liane, Lianne (English) forms of Lian.
Liana

Libby (Hebrew) a familiar form of Elizabeth.
Lib, Libbee, Libbey, Libbie

Liberty (Latin) free.

Licia (Greek) a short form of Alicia.
Licha, Lisha, Lishia, Lisia, Lycia

Lida (Greek) happy. (Latin) a short form of Alida, Elita. (Slavic) loved by people.
Leeda, Lyda

Lidia (Greek) an alternate form of Lydia.
Lyda
Foreign forms: *Hungarian:* **Lidi;** *Polish:* **Lidka**

Lien (Chinese) lotus.
Lienne

Lila (Arabic) night. (Hindi) free will of god. (Persian) lilac. A short form of Dalila, Delilah, Lillian. See also Leila.
Lilah, Lilia, Lyla, Lylah

Lilibeth (English) a combination of Lilly + Beth.
Lilibet, Lillibeth, Lillybeth, Lilybet

Lilith (Arabic) of the night; night demon. Mythology: the first wife of Adam, according to ancient eastern legends.
Lillis, Lilly, Lily

Lillian (Latin) lily flower.
Lian, Lila, Lilas, Lileana, Lileane, Lilian, Liliana, Liliane, Lilias, Liliha, Lilja, Lilla, Lillia, Lillianne, Liuka
Foreign forms: *English:* **Lil,** *French:* **Lis;** *Slavic:* **Lilijana, Lilka;** *Spanish:* **Lilia**

Lily (Latin, Arabic) a familiar form of Lilith, Lillian.
Lil, Líle, Lilie, Liliosa, Lilium, Lille, Lilli, Lillie, Lilly
Foreign forms: *Estonian:* **Lilli;** *German:* **Lili;** *Hungarian:* **Lilika, Lilike**

Lillyann (Latin) an alternate form of Lilian. (English) a combination of Lily + Ann.
Lillyan, Lillyanne, Lilyan, Lilyann, Lilyanne

Limber (Tiv) joyful.

Lin (Chinese) beautiful jade. (English) a short form of Lynn.
Linn, Lyn

Lina (Greek) light. (Latin) an alternate form of Lena. (Arabic) tender.
Lin, Linah

Linda (Spanish) pretty.
Lin, Lind, Lindee, Lindey, Lindi, Lindie, Linita
Foreign forms: American: Lynda; English: Lindy

Lindsay (English) an alternate form of Lindsey.
Lin, Lindsi, Lyndsaye, Linsay
Foreign forms: American: Lindsi, Lyndsay, Lyndsay

Lindsey (English) linden tree island; camp near the stream.
Lin, Lind, Lindsea, Lindsee, Linsey, Lyndsey
Foreign forms: American: Lindsi, Lynsey

Lindsi (American) a familiar form of Lindsay, Lindsey.
Lin, Lindsie, Lindsy, Lindzy

Linette (Welsh) idol. (French) bird.
Lanette, Lin, Linet, Linnet, Linnetta, Linnette
Foreign form: English: Lynette

Ling (Chinese) delicate, dainty.

Linnea (Scandinavian) lime tree. History: the national flower of Sweden.
Lin, Linea, Linnaea, Lynea, Lynnea

Linsey (English) an alternate form of Lindsey.
Lin, Linsi, Linsie, Linsy, Linzee, Linzey, Linzi, Linzy, Lynsey

Liora (Hebrew) light.

Lisa (Hebrew) consecrated to God. (English) a short form of Elizabeth.
Leesa, Liisa, Lisanne, Litsa, Liza, Lysa
Foreign forms: American: Leeza; Dutch: Liesje; Finnish: Lusa; French: Lisette; German: Liesa, Lise; Slavic: Lisenka, Liszka

Lise (German) a form of Lisa.

Lisette (French) a form of Lisa. (English) a familiar form of Elise, Elizabeth.
Liseta, Lisetta, Lisettina, Lissette

Lisha (Hebrew) a short form of Alisha, Elisha. (Arabic) darkness before midnight.
Lishe

Lissa (Greek) honey bee. A short form of Elissa, Elizabeth, Melissa, Millicent.
Lissi, Lyssa

Lissie (American) a familiar form of Alison, Elise, Elizabeth.
Lissee, Lissey, Lissi, Lissy, Lissye

Lita (Latin) a familiar form of names ending in "lita."
Leta

Litonya (Moquelumnan) darting hummingbird.

Liv (Latin) a short form of Livia, Olivia.

Livana (Hebrew) an alternate form of Levana. Astrological: born under the sign of Cancer.
Livna, Livnat

Livia (Hebrew) crown. A familiar form of Olivia. (Latin) olive.
Levia, Liv, Livie, Livy, Livya, Livye

Liviya (Hebrew) brave lioness; royal crown.
Leviya, Levya, Livya

Livona (Hebrew) an alternate form of Levona.

Liz (English) a short form of Elizabeth.
Lizanka, Lizanne, Lizina

Liza (American) a short form of Elizabeth.
Leeza, Lizete, Lizette, Lizka, Lizzie, Lyza

Lizzy (American) a familiar form of Elizabeth.
Lizzie

Lois (German) famous warrior. An alternate form of Louise.

Lola (Spanish) a familiar form of Carlota, Dolores, Louise.
Lolita

Lolita (Spanish) sorrowful. A familiar form of Lola.
Lita, Lulita

Lona (Latin) lioness. (German) a short form of Leona. (English) solitary.
Lonna
Foreign form: American: **Loni**

Loni (American) a form of Lona.
Lonee, Lonie, Lonni, Lonnie

Lora (Latin) crowned with laurel. (American)

a form of Laura.
Lorah, Lorane, Lorann, Lorra, Lorrah, Lorrane

Lorelei (German) alluring. Mythology: the sirens of the Rhine River who lured sailors to their deaths. See also Lurleen.
Loralee, Loralie, Loralyn, Lorilee, Lorilyn

Loren (American) an alternate form of Lauren.
Loreen, Lorena, Lorin, Lorine, Lorne, Lorren, Lorrin, Lorryn, Loryn, Lorynn, Lorynne

Lorena (English) an alternate form of Lauren, Loren.
Loreen, Lorene, Lorenia, Lorenna, Lorrina, Lorrine

Loretta (English) a familiar form of Laura.
Larretta, Lauretta, Laurette, Loretah, Lorette, Lorita, Lorretta, Lorrette

Lori (Latin) crowned with laurel. (French) a short form of Lorraine. (American) a familiar form of Laura.
Laurie, Loree, Lorey, Loria, Lorianna, Lorianne, Lorie, Lorree, Lorrie, Lory

Loris (Greek) a short form of Chloris. (Latin) thong. (Dutch) clown.
Laurice, Laurys, Lorice

Lorna (Latin) crowned with laurel. An alternate form of Laura. Literature: probably coined by Richard Blackmore in his novel *Lorna Doone*.
Lorrna

Lorraine (Latin) sorrowful. (French) from Lorraine. See also Rayna.
Laraine, Lauraine, Laurraine, Lorain, Loraine, Lorayne, Lorein, Loreine, Lori, Lorine, Lorrain, Lorraina, Lorrayne, Lorreine

Lotus (Greek) lotus.

Lou (American) a short form of Louise, Luella.

Louisa (English) a familiar form of Louise. Literature: Louisa May Alcott was an American writer and reformer best known for her novel *Little Women*.
Heloisa, Louisian, Louisane, Louisina, Louiza, Lujza, Lula, Lulita
Foreign forms: Italian: **Eloisa;** Polish: **Ludovica, Ludwiga;** Slavic: **Lujzika;** Spanish: **Luisa, Luiza**

Louise (German) famous warrior. A feminine form of Louis. See also Lois, Luella, Lulu.
Aloisa, Loise, Louisette, Louisiane, Louisine, Lovisa, Lowise, Loyce, Loyise, Lu, Ludovika, Luise
Foreign forms: American: **Lou;** *English:* **Louisa;** *French:* **Eloise, Heloise, Héloïse;** *Spanish:* **Lola**

Love (English) love; kindness; charity.
Lovely, Lovena, Lovewell, Lovey, Lovie, Lovina, Lovy, Luv, Luvvy

Luann (Hebrew, German) graceful woman warrior. (Hawaiian) happy; relaxed. (American) a combination of Louise + Anne.
Lewanna, Louann, Louanna, Louanne, Lu, Lua, Luan, Luana, Luane, Luanne, Luanni, Luannie, Luwana

Lucerne (Latin) lamp; circle of light. Geography: a lake in Switzerland.
Lucerna

Lucia (Italian, Spanish) a form of Lucy.
Luciana, Lucianna

Lucie (French) a familiar form of Lucy.

Lucille (English) a familiar form of Lucy.
Lucila, Lucile, Lucilla

Lucinda (Latin) a familiar form of Lucy. See also Cindy.
Lucka, Lucky

Lucine (Basque) a form of Lucy. (Arabic) moon.
Lucina, Lucyna, Lukene, Lusine, Luzine

Lucretia (Latin) rich; rewarded.
Lacrecia, Lucrece, Lucreecia, Lucresha, Lucreshia, Lucrisha, Lucrishia
Foreign forms: American: **Lakresha;** *French:* **Lucrèce;** *Italian:* **Lucrezia;** *Spanish:* **Lucrecia**

Lucy (Latin) light; bringer of light. A feminine form of Lucius.
Luce, Luci, Lucida, Lucija, Lucinda, Luciya, Luzca
Foreign forms: Basque: **Lucine;** *English:* **Lu, Lucetta, Lucille;** *French:* **Lucie, Lucienne;** *German:* **Luzi;** *Hungarian:* **Luca;** *Italian/Spanish:* **Lucia, Lucita, Luz;** *Polish:* **Lucya;** *Slavic:* **Lucika**

Ludmilla (Slavic) loved by the people. See also Mila.
Ludie, Ludka, Ludovika, Lyuba, Lyudmila
Foreign form: German: **Ludmila**

Luella (German) a familiar form of Louise. (English) elf.
Loella, Lou, Louella, Lu, Ludella, Luelle, Lula, Lulu

Luisa (Spanish) a form of Louisa.

Lulani (Polynesian) highest point of heaven.
Foreign form: Spanish: **Lali**

Lulu (Arabic) pearl. (German) a familiar form of Louise, Luella. (English) soothing, comforting. (Native American) hare.
Loulou, Lula, Lulie

Luna (Latin) moon.
Lunetta, Lunette, Lunneta, Lunnete

Lupe (Latin) wolf. (Spanish) a short form of Guadalupe.
Lupita

Lurleen, Lurlene (German) alternate forms of Lorelei. (Scandinavian) war horn.
Lura, Lurette, Lurline

Lusela (Moquelumnan) like a bear swinging its foot when licking it.

Luz (Spanish) light. Religion: Santa Maria de Luz is another name for the Virgin Mary.
Luzi, Luzija

Lycoris (Greek) twilight.

Lyda (Greek) a short form of Lidia, Lydia.

Lydia (Greek) from Lydia, an ancient land once ruled by Midas. (Arabic) strife.
Lidi, Lidiya, Lyda, Lydië
Foreign forms: French: **Lydie;**
Italian/Spanish: **Lidia;** *Russian:*
Lida, Lidija, Lidka, Lidochka

Lyla (French) island. (English) a feminine form of Lyle.
Lila, Lilah

Lynda (Spanish) pretty. (American) a form of Linda.
Lyndall, Lynde, Lyndee, Lyndi, Lyndy, Lynnda, Lynndie, Lynndy

Lyndsay (American) a form of Lindsay.

Lyndsey (English) linden tree island; camp near the stream. (American) a form of Lindsey.
Lyndsea, Lyndsee, Lyndsi, Lyndsie, Lyndsy, Lynndsie

Lynelle (English) pretty.
Linel, Linell, Linnell, Lynell

Lynette (Welsh) idol. (French) a form of Lynn.
Lynett, Lynetta, Lynnet, Lynnette

Lynn, Lynne (English) waterfall; pool below a waterfall.
Lin, Lina, Linn, Lyn, Lyndel, Lyndell, Lyndella, Lynlee, Lynley, Lynna, Lynnell
Foreign form: French: **Lynette**

Lynnell (English) an alternate form of Lynn.
Linell, Linnell, Lynell, Lynella, Lynelle, Lynnelle

Lynsey (American) an alternate form of Lyndsey.
Lynnsey, Lynnzey, Lynsie, Lynsy, Lynzey, Lynzi, Lynzie, Lynzy

Lyra (Greek) lyre player.
Lyre, Lyris

Lysandra (Greek) liberator. A feminine form of Lysander.
Lisandra, Lytle

Mab (Irish) joyous. (Welsh) baby. Literature: the name of the Fairy Queen in Edmund Spenser's epic romance *The Faerie Queene.*
Mabry

Mabel (Latin) lovable.
Amabel, Mab, Mable, Mabyn, Maybel, Maybelle, Maybull
Foreign forms: French: **Mabelle;**
Irish: **Maible**

Mackenzie (Irish) daughter of the wise leader. See also Kenzie.
Macenzie, Mackensi, Mackensie, Mackenzee, Mackenzi, Mackenzia, Mackenzy, Mekenzie, Mykenzie
Foreign form: Scottish:
McKenzie

Maddie (English) a familiar form of Madeline.
Maddi, Maddie, Maddy, Mady

Madeleine (French) a form of Madeline.
Madelaine, Madelayne, Madelon

Madeline (Greek) high tower. (English) from Magdala, England. An alternate form of Magdalen. See also Maud.
Mada, Madailéin, Madalaina, Madaleine, Madaline, Maddie, Madel, Madelena, Madelene, Madelia, Madella, Madelle, Madelyn, Madge, Madlin, Madline, Madoline, Maida, Malena
Foreign forms: French: Madeleine; German/Polish: Lena, Madlen; Italian: Maddalena, Madelina; Spanish: Madalena, Magdalena

Madelyn (Greek) an alternate form of Madeline.
Madalyn, Madalynn, Madalynne, Madelynn, Madelynne, Madlyn, Madolyn

Madge (Greek) a familiar form of Madeline, Margaret.
Madgi, Madgie, Mady

Madison (English) good; son of Maud.

Madisen, Madissen, Madisyn, Madysen, Madyson

Madonna (Latin) my lady.
Madona

Madrona (Spanish) mother.
Madre, Madrena

Mae (English) an alternate form of May. History: Mae Jemison was the first African-American woman in space.
Maelea, Maeleah, Maelen, Maelle, Maeona

Maegan (Irish) an alternate form of Megan.
Maeghan

Maeko (Japanese) honest child.
Mae, Maemi

Maeve (Irish) joyous. History: a first-century queen of Ireland. See also Mavis.
Maevi, Maevy, Maive, Mayve

Magan, Magen (Greek) short forms of Margaret.

Magdalen (Greek) high tower. Bible: Magdala was the home of Saint Mary Magdalen. See also Madeline.
Magdalina, Magdaline, Magdalyn, Magdelana, Magdelane, Magdelene, Magdeline, Magdelyn,

Magdlen, Maggie, Mahda, Maighdlin, Makda, Mala, Malaine, Maudlin
Foreign forms: English: Mada, Magdala, Magdalene; Hungarian: Magdolna; Polish: Magdelina; Slavic: Magda, Marlene; Spanish: Magdalena, Magola; Swedish: Malena

Maggie (Greek) pearl. (English) a familiar form of Magdalen, Margaret.
Mag, Magge, Maggee, Maggen, Maggey, Maggi, Maggia, Maggiemae, Maggin, Maggy, Mags

Magnolia (Latin) flowering tree.
Nola
Foreign form: English: Nollie

Maha (Arabic) wild cow.

Mahal (Filipino) love.

Mahala (Arabic) fat, marrow; tender. (Native American) powerful woman.
Mahalah, Mahalar, Mahalla, Mahela, Mahila, Mahlah, Mahlaha, Mehala, Mehalah
Foreign form: American: Mahalia

Mahalia (American) a form of Mahala.

**Mahaliah, Mahelea,
Maheleah, Mahelia, Mahilia,
Mehalia**

Mahogony (Spanish) rich;
strong.
**Mahagony, Mahogani,
Mahoganie, Mahogny,
Mohogany, Mohogony**

Mai (Japanese) brightness.
(Vietnamese) flower. (Navajo)
coyote.

Maia (Greek) mother; nurse.
(English) kinswoman; maiden.
Mythology: the loveliest of the
Pleiades, the seven daughters
of Atlas, and the mother of
Hermes. See also Maya.
**Maiah, Maie, Maya, Mayam,
Mya**

Maida (Greek) a short form of
Madeline. (English) maiden.
**Maidel, Maidie, Mayda,
Maydena, Maydey**
*Foreign forms: German: **Mady,
Magd, Magda***

Maja (Arabic) splendid.
**Majal, Majalisa, Majalyn,
Majalynn, Majida, Majidah**

Makala (Hawaiian) myrtle.

Makana (Hawaiian) gift,
present.

Makani (Hawaiian) wind.

Makara (Hindi) born during
the lunar month of Capricorn.

Makayla (American) a form
of Michaela.
Mikayla

Mala (Greek) a short form of
Magdalen.
Malana, Malee, Mali

Malana (Hawaiian) bouyant,
light.

Malaya (Filipino) free.
Malayna, Malea

Malha (Hebrew) queen.
**Maliah, Malkah, Malkia,
Malkiah, Malkie, Malkiya,
Malkiyah, Miliah**

Mali (Thai) jasmine flower.
(Hungarian) a short form of
Malika.
Malea, Malee, Maley

Malia (Hawaiian, Zuni) a form
of Mary. (Spanish) a form of
Maria.
**Malea, Maleah, Maleia,
Maliaka, Maliasha, Malie,
Maliea, Malli, Mally**

Malika (Hungarian) industrious.
Maleeka, Maleka, Mali

Malina (Hebrew) tower.
(English) from Magdala,
England. (Native American)
soothing.
**Malin, Maline, Malina,
Malinna, Mallie**

Malinda (Greek) an alternate
form of Melinda.
Malinde, Malinna, Malynda

Malini (Hindi) gardener.
Religion: the Hindu god of the
earth.

Malissa (Greek) an alternate
form of Melissa.

Mallorie (French) an alternate
form of Mallory.

Mallory (German) army coun-
selor. (French) unlucky.
**Malerie, Maliri, Mallari,
Mallary, Mallauri, Mallerie,
Mallery, Malloree, Malloreigh,
Mallorey, Mallori, Mallorie,
Malori, Malorie, Malorym,
Malree, Malrie, Mellory,
Melorie, Melory**
*Foreign forms: American:
Malley, Mallie*

Malvina (Scottish) a form of
Melvina. Literature: a name
created by the eighteenth-cen-
tury romantic poet James
MacPherson.
Malva, Malvane, Malvi

Manda (Latin) a short form of Amanda. (Spanish) woman warrior.
Mandee, Mandy

Mandara (Hindi) calm. Religion: a Hindu mythical tree that makes worries disappear.

Mandeep (Punjabi) enlightened.

Mandisa (Xhosa) sweet.

Mandy (Latin) lovable. A familiar form of Amanda, Manda, Melinda.
Mandee, Mandi, Mandie

Mani (Chinese) a mantra repeated in Tibetan Buddhist prayer to impart understanding.
Manee

Manon (French) a familiar form of Marie.

Manpreet (Punjabi) mind full of love.

Mansi (Hopi) plucked flower.
Mancey, Manci, Mancie, Mansey, Mansie, Mansy

Mara (Greek) a short form of Amara. (Slavic) a form of Mary.
Mahra, Marah, Marra

Foreign forms: English: ***Damara, Maralina, Maraline***

Marcella (Latin) martial, warlike. Mythology: Mars was the Roman god of war. A feminine form of Marcellus.
Mairsii, Marca, Marce, Marceil, Marcele, Marcelia, Marcell, Marcello, Marcena, Marchella, Marciella, Marcile, Marcilla, Marcille, Marella, Marsella, Marsiella
Foreign forms: American: ***Mrciann, Marcyanna;*** English: ***Marcelen, Marcelline, Marci, Marcie;*** French: ***Marcelle, Marchelle, Marselle;*** Italian: ***Marcelina, Marcellin, Marcellina, Marcelyn;*** Spanish: ***Marcela***

Marcena (Latin) an alternate form of Marcella, Marcia.
Maracena, Marceen, Marcene, Marcenia, Marceyne, Marcina

Marci, Marcie (English) familiar forms of Marcella, Marcia.
Marcee, Marcita, Marcy, Marsi, Marsie

Marcia (Latin) martial, warlike. An alternate form of Marcella.
Marcena, Marchia, Marci, Marciale, Marcsa, Martia
Foreign forms: English: ***Marsha, Mercia;*** French: ***Marcie;*** Spanish: ***Marquita***

Marcilynn (American) a combination of Marci + Lynn.
Marcilen, Marcilin, Marciline, Marcilyn, Marcilyne, Marcilynne, Marcylen, Marcylin, Marcyline, Marcylyn, Marcylyne, Marcylynn, Marcylynne

Marcy (English) an alternate form of Marci.
Marsey, Marsy

Mardi (French) born on Tuesday. (Aramaic) a familiar form of Martha.

Maren (Latin) sea. (Aramaic) a form of Mary. See also Marina.
Marena, Marin, Miren, Mirena

Margaret (Greek) pearl. History: Margaret Hilda Thatcher served as British prime minister. See also Peggy, Rita.
Madge, Maergrethe, Maggie, Maretha, Margalide, Margalit, Margalith, Margalo, Marganit, Margara, Margarett, Margaretta, Margarette, Margaro, Margeret, Margeretta, Margerette, Margerie, Margerite, Marget, Margetta, Margette, Margiad, Margisia
Foreign forms: American: ***Mamie;*** Armenian: ***Margarid;***

Basque: **Errita;** Czech: **Margareta, Markita;** English: **Maretta, Marge, Margie, Meg;** Estonian: **Marga, Reatha, Reet;** French: **Margaux, Margo, Margot, Marguerite;** German: **Greta, Gretchen, Margret, Margrita, Meta;** Hungarian: **Margit;** Irish: **Megan;** Italian/Spanish: **Margarita;** Polish: **Gita;** Portuguese: **Margarida;** Scottish: **Maisie, Maisey, Marjorie, Mayzie**

Margarita (Italian, Spanish) a form of Margaret. **Margarit, Margaritis, Margaritt, Margaritta, Margharita, Margherita, Margrieta, Margrita, Marguarita, Marguerita, Margurita**

Marge (English) a short form of Margaret, Marjorie. **Margie**

Margie (English) a familiar form of Marge, Margaret. **Margey, Margi, Margy**

Margo, Margot (French) forms of Margaret. **Mago, Margaro**

Marguerite (French) a form of Margaret. **Margarete, Margaretha,** **Margarethe, Margarite, Margerite, Marguaretta, Marguarette, Marguarite, Marguerette, Margurite**

Mari (Japanese) ball. (Spanish) a form of Mary.

Maria (Hebrew) bitter; sea of bitterness. (Italian, Spanish) a form of Mary. **Malia, Marea, Mareah, Mariabella, Mariae, Mariesa, Mariessa, Mariha, Marija, Mariya, Marja** *Foreign forms:* French: **Maree, Marie;** Slavic: **Marya**

Mariah (Hebrew) an alternate form of Mary. See also Moriah. **Maraia, Maraya, Mariyah, Marriah, Meriah**

Marian (English) an alternate form of Maryann. **Mariane, Mariann, Mariene, Marrian, Marriann, Marrianne** *Foreign forms:* French: **Marianne;** Italian: **Marianna;** Spanish: **Mariana**

Mariana (Spanish) a form of Marian. **Marriana, Marrianna, Maryana, Maryanna**

Maribel (French) beautiful. (English) a combination of Maria + Bell. **Marabel, Marbelle, Mariabella, Maribella, Maribelle, Maridel, Marybel, Marybella, Marybelle**

Marie (French) a form of Mary. **Manon, Maree, Marrie** *Foreign forms:* Italian: **Maretta, Marietta, Marrietta**

Mariel (German, Dutch) a form of Mary. **Marial, Marieke, Mariela, Mariele, Marieline, Mariella, Marielle, Mariellen, Marielsie, Mariely, Marielys**

Marigold (English) Botany: a plant with yellow or orange flowers. **Marygold**

Marika (Dutch, Slavic) a form of Mary. **Marica, Marieke, Marija, Marijke, Marike, Marikia, Mariska, Mariske, Marrika, Maryk, Maryka, Merica, Merika**

Mariko (Japanese) circle.

Marilee (American) a combination of Mary + Lee. **Marrilee, Marylea, Marylee, Merrilee, Merrili, Merrily**

Marilyn (Hebrew) Mary's line or descendants. See also Merilyn.
Maralin, Maralyn, Maralyne, Maralynn, Maralynne, Marelyn, Marillyn, Marilynn, Marilynne, Marlyn, Marolyn, Marralynn, Marrilin, Marrilyn, Marrilynn, Marrilynne, Marylinn, Marylyn, Marylyne, Marylynn, Marylynne
Foreign forms: English: Marilin, Marylin

Marina (Latin) sea. See also Maren.
Marena, Marinda, Marindi, Marine, Marrina, Maryna, Merina
Foreign forms: Slavic: Marenka, Marinka

Marini (Swahili) healthy; pretty.

Marion (French) a form of Mary.
Marrion, Maryon, Maryonn

Maris (Latin) sea.
Maries, Marise, Marris, Marys, Meris

Marisa (Latin) sea.
Amaris, Mariesa, Mariessa, Marisela, Marissa, Marrisa, Marysa
Foreign forms: Dutch: Maryse,

Merisa; *German:* **Maritza, Maryssa;** *Russian:* **Mariza;** *Spanish:* **Marita**

Marisha (Russian) a familiar form of Mary.
Marishenka, Marishka, Mariska

Marisol (Spanish) sunny sea.
Marise, Marizol

Marissa (Latin) an alternate form of Maris, Marisa.
Maressa, Marisa, Marisse, Marrissa, Marrissia, Merissa, Morissa

Marit (Aramaic) lady.
Marita

Maritza (Arabic) blessed.

Mariyan (Arabic) purity.
Mariya

Marjie (Scottish) a familiar form of Marjorie.
Marje, Marjey, Marji, Marjy

Marjolaine (French) marjoram.

Marjorie (Greek) a familiar form of Margaret. (Scottish) a form of Mary.
Majorie, Margeree, Margerey, Margerie, Margery, Margorie, Margory, Marjarie, Marjary, Marjerie, Marjery, Marjie,

Marjorey, Marjori, Marjory
Foreign form: English: **Marge**

Markeisia (English) a combination of Mary + Keisha.
Markesha, Markesia, Markiesha, Markisha, Markishia

Markita (Czech) a form of Margaret.
Marka, Markeda, Markee, Markeeta, Marketa, Marketta, Markia, Markie, Markieta, Markita, Markitha, Markketta

Marla (English) a short form of Marlena, Marlene.
Marlah, Marlea, Marleah

Marlana (English) a form of Marlene.
Marlania, Marlanna

Marlee (English) a form of Marlene.
Marlea, Marleah

Marlena (German) a form of Marlene.
Marla, Marlaina, Marleena, Marlina, Marlinda, Marlyna, Marna

Marlene (Greek) high tower. (Slavic) a form of Magdalen.
Marlaine, Marlane, Marlayne,

Marleen, Marlenne, Marline, Marlyne
*Foreign forms: English: **Marla, Marlana, Marlee, Marley;** German: **Marlena***

Marley (English) a familiar form of Marlene.
Marlee, Marli, Marlie, Marly

Marlis (English) a combination of Maria + Lisa.
Marles, Marlisa, Marlise, Marlys, Marlyse, Marlyssa

Marnie (Hebrew) a short form of Marnina.
Marna, Marne, Marnee, Marney, Marni, Marnja, Marnya

Marnina (Hebrew) rejoice.

Marquise (French) noble-woman.
Markese, Marquees, Marquese, Marquice, Marquies, Marquiese, Marquisa, Marquisee, Marquiste

Marquita (Spanish) a form of Marcia.
Marqueda, Marquedia, Marquee, Marqueita, Marquet, Marqueta, Marquetta, Marquette, Marquia, Marquida,

Marquietta, Marquitra, Marquitia, Marquitta

Marsala (Italian) from Marseille, Italy.
Marsali, Marseilles

Marsha (English) a form of Marcia.
Marcha, Marshae, Marshay, Marshayly, Marshel, Marshele, Marshell, Marshia, Marshiela

Marta (English) a short form of Martha, Martina.
Martá, Martä, Marte, Marttaha, Merta

Martha (Aramaic) lady; sorrow-ful. Bible: a sister of the Virgin Mary. See also Mardi.
Martaha, Marth, Marthan, Marthina, Marthine, Marthy, Marti, Marticka
*Foreign forms: English: **Marta, Marti, Mattie, Matty;** French: **Marthe;** Hungarian: **Martuska;** Polish: **Masia;** Spanish: **Maita, Maite, Marthena, Martita, Martus***

Marti (English) a familiar form of Martha, Martina.
Martie, Marty

Martina (Latin) martial, war-like. A feminine form of Martin. See also Tina.

Martel, Martella, Martelle, Martene, Marthena, Marthina, Marthine, Martinia, Martino, Martisha, Martiza, Martosia, Martoya, Martricia, Martrina, Martyna, Martyne, Martynne
*Foreign forms: English: **Marta, Marti;** French: **Martine***

Maru (Japanese) round.

Marvella (French) marvelous.
Marva, Marvel, Marvela, Marvele, Marvelle, Marvely, Marvetta, Marvette, Marvia, Marvina

Mary (Hebrew) bitter; sea of bitterness. An alternate form of Miriam. Bible: the mother of Jesus. See also Mariah, Miriam, Muriel.
Marella, Marelle, Marian, Maridel, Mariquilla, Maritsa, Maryla, Marynia, Marysia, Meridel, Merrili, Mirja, Morag
*Foreign forms: Aramaic: **Maren;** Basque: **Mendi, Molara;** Dutch/Slavic: **Marika;** English: **Marlo, Marlow;** Estonian: **Marye;** Finnish: **Maija, Marja;** French: **Manette, Manon, Maree, Marie, Marion, Maryse, Mérane;** German: **Mariel, Marilla, Mitzi;** Greek: **Maroula;** Hawaiian/Zuni: **Malia;** Irish: **Maira, Maire, Mare, Maura, Maureen, Molly,***

Mary (cont.)
Moira, Moya; Italian: Maria,
Marice; Polish: Manka, Marjan;
Rumanian: Maricara; Russian:
Manya, Marisha, Mariya,
Masha; Scottish: Marjorie,
Mhairie, Muire; Slavic: Mara,
Mavra; Spanish: Mari, Maria,
Mariquita, Maruca; Swedish:
Marja

Marya (Arabic) purity; bright whiteness.

Maryann, Maryanne (English) combinations of Mary + Ann.
Mariann, Marianne,
Maryanna

Marybeth (American) a combination of Mary + Beth.
Maribeth, Maribette

Maryellen (American) a combination of Mary + Ellen.
Mariellen

Maryjo (American) a combination of Mary + Jo.
Marijo

Marylou (American) a combination of Mary + Lou.
Marilou, Marilu

Mathena (Hebrew) gift of God. (English) a feminine form of Matthau.
Mäite, Marité

Matilda (German) powerful battler. See also Tilda, Tillie.
Máda, Mahaut, Malkin, Mat,
Mathilda, Mathilde, Matylda
Foreign forms: English: Mattie,
Matty, Maud; French: Matilde;
Irish: Maitilde; Italian: Matelda;
Slavic: Matya; Spanish: Matusha,
Matuxa

Matsuko (Japanese) pine tree.

Mattea (Hebrew) gift of God.
Matea, Mathea, Matia, Matte,
Mattia
Foreign forms: English: Mathia,
Matthea, Matthia

Mattie, Matty (English) familiar forms of Martha, Matilda.
Matte, Mattey, Matti, Mattye

Maud, Maude (English) short forms of Madeline, Matilda.
Maudie, Maudine, Maudlin

Maura (Irish) dark. An alternate form of Mary, Maureen. See also Moira.
Maure, Maurette, Mauricette,
Maurita

Maureen (French) dark. (Irish) a form of Mary.
Maura, Maurine, Mo, Morene,
Morine, Morreen, Moureen
Foreign forms: English:
Maurene, Moreen; Italian:
Maurizia; Spanish: Morena

Maurelle (French) dark; elfin.
Mauriel, Mauriell, Maurielle

Maurise (French) dark skinned; moor; marshland. A feminine form of Maurice.
Maurisa, Maurissa, Maurita

Mauve (French) violet colored.
Malva

Mavis (French) song thrush bird. See also Maeve.
Mavies, Mavin, Mavine,
Mavon, Mavra

Maxine (Latin) greatest. A feminine form of Maximillian.
Max, Maxa, Maxeen, Maxena,
Maxene, Maxi, Maxie,
Maxima, Maxime,
Maximiliane, Maxina, Maxna,
Maxy, Maxyne

May (Latin) great. (Arabic) discerning. (English) flower; month of May. See also Mae, Maia.
Maj, Mayberry, Maybeth,
Mayday, Maydee, Maydena,
Maye, Mayela, Mayella,
Mayetta, Mayrene

Maya (Hindi) God's creative power. (Greek) mother; grandmother. (Latin) great. An alternate form of Maia.

Maybeline (Latin) a familiar form of Mabel.
Maybel, Maybelle

Maylyn (American) a combination of May + Lynn.
Mayelene, Mayleen, Maylen, Maylene, Maylin, Maylon, Maylynn, Maylynne

Mayoree (Thai) beautiful.
Mayra, Mayree, Mayariya

Maysa (Arabic) walks with a proud stride.

Mazel (Hebrew) lucky.
Mazal, Mazala, Mazella

McKenzie (Scottish) a form of Mackenzie.
McKensi, McKinzie

Mead, Meade (Greek) honey wine.

Meagan (Irish) an alternate form of Megan.
Maegan, Meagain, Meagann, Meagen, Meagin, Meagnah, Meagon

Meaghan (Welsh) a form of Megan.
Meaghann, Meaghen, Meahgan

Meara (Irish) mirthful.

Meda (Native American) prophet; priestess.

Medea (Greek) ruling. (Latin) middle. Mythology: a sorceress who helped Jason get the Golden Fleece.
Medeia

Medina (Arabic) History: the site of Muhammed's tomb.

Medora (Greek) mother's gift. Literature: a character in Lord Byron's poem "Corsair."

Meena (Hindi) blue semiprecious stone; bird.

Meg (English) a familiar form of Margaret, Megan.
Meggi, Meggie, Meggy

Megan (Greek) pearl; great. (Irish) a form of Margaret.
Maegan, Magan, Meagan, Magen, Megean, Megen, Meggan, Meggen, Megyn, Meygan
Foreign forms: English: *Meg;* Welsh: *Meaghan, Meghan*

Megara (Greek) first. Mythology: Hercules's first wife.

Meghan (Welsh) a form of Megan.
**Meeghan, Meehan, Megha,
Meghana, Meghane, Meghann, Meghanne, Meghean, Meghen, Mehgan, Mehgen**

Megumi (Japanese) blessing; merry; charity.

Mehadi (Hindi) flower.

Mehira (Hebrew) speedy; energetic.
Mahira

Mehitabel (Hebrew) benefited by trusting God.
Mehetabel, Mehitabelle, Hetty, Hitty

Mehri (Persian) kind; lovable; sunny.

Mei (Chinese) a short form of Meiying. (Hawaiian) great.
Meiko

Meira (Hebrew) light.
Meera

Meiying (Chinese) beautiful flower.

Meka (Hebrew) a familiar form of Michaela.

Mel (Portuguese, Spanish) sweet as honey.

Melanie (Greek) dark skinned.
**Malania, Malanie, Meila,
Meilani, Meilin, Meladia,
Melaine, Melainie, Melane,
Melanee, Melaney, Melania,
Melanney, Melannie, Melanya,
Melayne, Melenia, Mella,
Mellanie, Melya, Melyn,
Melyne, Melynn, Melynne
Foreign forms:** *American:*
Melonie; *English:* **Melani,
Melany;** *French:* **Mélanie;** *Polish:*
Mela; *Russian:* **Melana, Melanka,
Melashka, Melasya, Milena,
Milya**

Melantha (Greek) dark flower.

Melba (Greek) soft; slender.
(Latin) mallow flower.
Malva, Melva

Mele (Hawaiian) song; poem.

Melesse (Ethiopian) eternal.
Mellesse

Melia (German) a short form
of Amelia.
**Melcia, Melea, Meleah,
Meleia, Meleisha, Meli,
Meliah, Melida, Melika,
Mema, Milia, Milica, Milka**

Melina (Latin) canary yellow.
(Greek) a short form of
Melinda.
Melaina, Meleana, Meleena,

**Melena, Meline, Melinia,
Melinna, Melynna**

Melinda (Greek) honey. See
also Linda, Melina, Mindy.
**Maillie, Malinda, Melinde,
Melinder, Mellinda, Melynda,
Milinda, Milynda, Mylinda,
Mylynda**

Meliora (Latin) better.
**Melior, Meliori, Mellear,
Melyor, Melyora**

Melisande (French) a form
of Melissa, Millicent.
**Lisandra, Malisande,
Malissande, Malyssandre,
Melesande, Melisandra,
Melisandre, Mélisandré,
Melisenda, Melissande,
Melissandre, Mellisande,
Melond, Melysande,
Melyssandre**

Melissa (Greek) honey bee.
See also Elissa, Lissa, Millicent.
**Malissa, Mallissa, Melesa,
Melessa, Meleta, Melisa,
Mélisa, Melise, Melisha,
Melishia, Melisia, Melisse,
Melissia, Meliza, Melizah,
Mellisa, Mellissa, Melosa,
Milissa, Molissia, Mollissa,
Mylisa, Mylisia, Mylissa,
Mylissia
Foreign forms:** *American:* **Melly;**
English: **Millie, Milly, Missy;**
French: **Melisande, Mélissa**

Melita (Greek) an alternate
form of Melissa. (Spanish)
a short form of Carmela.
**Malita, Meleeta, Melitta,
Melitza, Melletta, Molita**

Melly (American) a familiar
form of names beginning with
"Mel." See also Millie.
Meli, Melie, Melli, Mellie

Melonie (American) an alter-
nate form of Melanie.
**Melloney, Mellonie, Mellony,
Melonee, Meloney, Meloni,
Melonie, Melonnie, Melony**

Melody (Greek) melody.
**Melodee, Melodey, Melodi,
Melodia, Melodie, Melodye**

Melosa (Spanish) sweet;
tender.

Melvina (Irish) armored chief.
A feminine form of Melvin.
See also Malvina.
**Melevine, Melva, Melveen,
Melvena, Melvene, Melvonna**

Mercedes (Latin) reward, payment. (Spanish) merciful.
Merced, Mercede, Mersade

Mercy (English) compassionate,
merciful. See also Merry.
**Mercey, Merci, Mercie,
Mercille, Mersey**

Meredith (Welsh) protector of the sea.
Meredithe, Meredy, Meredyth, Meredythe, Meridath, Merideth, Meridie, Meridith, Merridie, Merridith, Merry

Meri (Finnish) sea. (Irish) a short form of Meriel.

Meriel (Irish) shining sea.
Meri, Merial, Meriol, Meryl

Merilyn (English) a combination of Merry + Lynn. See also Marilyn.
Merelyn, Merlyn, Merralyn, Merrelyn, Merrilyn

Merle (Latin, French) blackbird.
Merl, Merla, Merlina, Merline, Merola, Murle, Myrle, Myrleen, Myrlene, Myrline

Merry (English) cheerful, happy. A familiar form of Mercy, Meredith.
Merie, Merree, Merri, Merrie, Merrielle, Merrile, Merrilee, Merris, Merrita

Meryl (German) famous. (Irish) shining sea. An alternate form of Meriel, Muriel.
Meral, Merel, Merrall, Merrell, Merril, Merrill, Merryl, Meryle, Meryll

Mesha (Hindi) born in the lunar month of Aries.
Meshal

Mia (Italian) mine. A familiar form of Michaela, Michelle.
Mea, Meah, Miah

Micah (Hebrew) a short form of Michaela. Bible: one of the Old Testament prophets.
Mica, Mika, Myca, Mycah

Michaela (Hebrew) who is like God? A feminine form of Michael.
Machaela, Meecah, Micaela, Michael, Michaelann, Michealia, Michaelina, Michaeline, Michaell, Michaelle, Michaelyn, Michaila, Michal, Michala, Micheal, Micheala, Michelia, Michelina, Michely, Michelyn, Micheyla, Micheline, Micquel, Mikaela, Miquelle, Mycala, Mychal
Foreign forms: American: ***Makayla, Micki Mychaela;*** French: **Michelle;** Italian: **Mia, Michaella, Michele;** Russian: **Misha;** Spanish: **Miguela, Miguelita, Miquela**

Michala (Hebrew) an alternate form of Michaela.
Michalann, Michale, Michalene, Michalin,

Mchalina, Michalisha, Michalla, Michalle, Michayla, Michayle

Michele (Italian) a form of Michaela.
Michela

Michelle (French) who is like God? A form of Michaela. See also Shelley.
Machealle, Machele, Machell, Machella, Machelle, Mechelle, Meichelle, Meschell, Meshell, Meshelle, Mia, Michel, Michele, Michèle, Michell, Michella, Michellene, Michellyn, Mischel, Mischelle, Mishae, Mishael, Mishaela, Mishayla, Mishell, Mishelle, Mitchele, Mitchelle

Michi (Japanese) righteous way.
Miche, Michee, Michiko

Micki (American) a familiar form of Michaela.
Mickee, Mickeeya, Mickia, Mickie, Micky, Mickya, Miquia

Midori (Japanese) green.

Mieko (Japanese) prosperous.
Mieke

Mignon (French) cute; graceful.
Mignonette, Minnionette,

Mignon (*cont.*)
**Minnonette, Minyonette,
Minyonne**

Mika (Hebrew) an alternate
form of Micah. (Latin) a short
form of Dominica, Dominika.
(Russian) God's child. (Native
American) wise racoon.
Mikah

Mikaela (Hebrew) an alternate
form of Michaela.
**Mekaela, Mekala, Mekayla,
Mickael, Mickaela, Mickala,
Mickalla, Mickayla, Mickeel,
Mickell, Mickelle, Mikail,
Mikaila, Mikal, Mikalene,
Mikalovna, Mikalyn, Mikayla,
Mikayle, Mikea, Mikeisha,
Mikeita, Mikel, Mikela,
Mikele, Mikell, Mikella,
Mikesha, Mikeya, Mikie,
Mikiela, Mikkel, Mikyla**
Foreign forms: American:
Mikhaela, Mykaela

Mikhaela (American) a form
of Mikaela.
**Mikhail, Mikhaila, Mikhala,
Mikhalea, Mikhelle**

Miki (Japanese) flower stem.
**Mika, Mikia, Mikiala, Mikie,
Mikita, Mikiyo, Mikka, Mikki,
Mikkie, Mikkiya, Mikko, Miko**

Mila (Italian, Slavic) a short
form of Camilla, Ludmilla.
(Russian) dear one.
Milah, Milla

Milada (Czech) my love.
Mila, Milady

Milagros (Spanish) miracle.
**Mila, Milagritos, Milagro,
Milagrosa, Mirari**

Milana (Italian) from Milan,
Italy.
**Mila, Milan, Milane, Milani,
Milanka, Milanna, Milanne**

Mildred (English) gentle coun-
selor.
**Mil, Mila, Mildrene, Mildrid,
Millie, Milly**

Milena (Greek, Hebrew,
Russian) a form of Ludmilla,
Magdalen, Melanie.
**Mila, Milène, Milenia,
Milenny, Milini, Millini**

Milia (German) industrious.
A short form of Amelia, Emily.
**Mila, Mili, Milica, Milika,
Milla, Milya**

Miliani (Hawaiian) caress.
Mila, Milanni, Mililani

Milissa (Greek) an alternate
form of Melissa.
Milisa, Millisa, Millissa

Millicent (Greek) an alternate
form of Melissa. (English)
industrious. See also Lissa.
**Melicent, Meliscent,
Mellicent, Mellisent, Melly,
Milicent, Milisent, Millie,
Millisent, Milly, Milzie, Missie,
Missy**
Foreign forms: French:
Melisande; Spanish: *Melisende*

Millie, Milly (English) familiar
forms of Amelia, Camille,
Emily, Melissa, Mildred,
Millicent.
**Mili, Milla, Millee, Milley,
Millie**

Mina (German) love. (Persian)
blue sky. (Hindi) born in the
lunar month of Pisces. (Arabic)
harbor. (Japanese) south. A
short form of names ending in
"mina."
Meena, Mena, Min

Minda (Hindi) knowledge.

Mindy (Greek) a familiar form
of Melinda.
**Mindee, Mindi, Mindie,
Mindyanne, Mindylee, Myndy**

Minerva (Latin) wise.
Mythology: the goddess of
wisdom.
**Merva, Minivera, Minnie,
Myna**

Minette (French) faithful defender.
Minnette, Minnita

Minna (German) a short form of Wilhelmina.
Mina, Minnie, Minta

Minnie (American) a familiar form of Mina, Minerva, Minna, Wilhelmina.
Mini, Minie, Minne, Minni, Minny

Mio (Japanese) three times as strong.

Mira (Latin) wonderful. (Spanish) look, gaze. A short form of Almira, Mirabel, Miranda.
Mirae, Mirra, Mirah

Mirabel (Latin) beautiful.
Mira, Mirabell, Mirabella, Mirabelle, Mirable
Foreign forms: English:
Marabel, Marabelle

Miranda (Latin) strange; wonderful; admirable. Literature: the heroine of Shakespeare's *The Tempest*. See also Randi.
Maranda, Marenda, Meranda, Mira, Miran, Miranada, Mirandia, Mirinda, Mirindé, Mironda, Mirranda, Muranda, Myranda

Mireil (Hebrew) God spoke. (Latin) wonderful.
Mirella, Mirelle, Mirelys, Mireya, Mireyda, Mirielle, Mirilla, Myrella, Myrilla

Miriam (Hebrew) bitter, sea of bitterness. Bible: the original form of Mary.
Mairona, Mairwen, Marca, Marcsa, Mariam, Mariame, Maruja, Meryem, Miram, Mirham, Miriain, Miriama, Miriame, Mirian, Mirit, Mirjana, Mirra, Mirriam, Mirrian, Miryam, Miryan
Foreign forms: American:
Myriam; Finnish: **Mirjam;** French:
Mimi; German: **Mitzi;** Greek:
Maroula; Gypsy: **Miri;** Polish:
Macia; Russian: **Maruska,
Masha;** Spanish: **Maruca**

Missy (English) a familiar form of Melissa, Millicent.
Missi, Missie

Misty (English) shrouded by mist.
Missty, Mistee, Mistey, Misti, Mistie, Mistin, Mistina, Mistral, Mistylynn, Mystee, Mysti, Mystie

Miya (Japanese) temple.
Miyana, Miyanna

Miyo (Japanese) beautiful generation.
Miyoko, Miyuki, Miyuko

Miyuki (Japanese) snow.

Mocha (Arabic) chocolate-flavored coffee.
Moka

Modesty (Latin) modest.
Modeste, Modestie, Modestina, Modestus
Foreign forms: French:
Modestine; Italian: **Modesta;**
Spanish: **Modestia**

Mohala (Hawaiian) flowers in bloom.
Moala

Moira (Irish) great. A form of Mary. See also Maura.
Moirae, Moirah, Moire, Moya, Moyra, Moyrah

Molly (Irish) a familiar form of Mary.
Moll, Mollee, Molley, Molli, Mollie, Mollissa

Mona (Greek) a short form of Monica, Ramona, Rimona. (Irish) noble.
Moina, Monah, Mone, Monea, Monna, Moyna

Monet (French) Art: Claude Monet was a leading French

Monet (cont.)
impressionist remembered for
his paintings of water lilies.
Monae, Monay, Monee

Monica (Greek) solitary. (Latin)
advisor.
**Mona, Monee, Monia, Monic,
Monice, Monicia, Monicka,
Monise, Monn, Monnica,
Monnie, Monya**
Foreign forms: French:
Monique; German: **Monika;** Irish:
Monca

Monika (German) a form
of Monica.
**Moneeke, Moneik, Moneka,
Monieka, Monike, Monnika**

Monique (French) a form
of Monica.
**Moniqua, Moniquea,
Moniquie, Munique**

Montana (Spanish) mountain.
Montanna

Mora (Spanish) blueberry.
Morea, Moria, Morita

Morela (Polish) apricot.

Morgan (Welsh) seashore.
Literature: Morgan Le Fay was
the half-sister of King Arthur.
**Morgana, Morgance,
Morgane, Morganetta,**

**Morganette, Morganica,
Morgann, Morganna,
Morganne, Morgen, Morgyn,
Morrigan**

Moriah (Hebrew) God is my
teacher. (French) dark skinned.
Bible: the name of the moun-
tain on which the temple of
Solomon was built. See also
Mariah.
**Moria, Moriel, Morit, Morria,
Morriah**

Morie (Japanese) bay.

Morrisa (Latin) dark skinned;
moor; marshland. A feminine
form of Morris.
Morisa, Morissa, Morrissa

Moselle (Hebrew) drawn from
the water. A feminine form of
Moses. (French) a white wine.
Mozelle

Mosi (Swahili) first-born.

Mura (Japanese) village.

Muriel (Arabic) myrrh. (Irish)
shining sea. A form of Mary.
See also Meryl.
**Merial, Meriol, Merrial,
Merriel, Muriell, Murielle**
Foreign forms: English: **Meriel,
Murial;** Scottish: **Muireal**

Musetta (French) little bagpipe.
Musette

Mya (Burmese) emerald.

Mykaela (American) a form
of Mikaela.
**Mykael, Mykal, Mykala,
Mykaleen, Mykel, Mykela**

Myla (English) merciful.

Mylene (Greek) dark.
**Mylaine, Mylana, Mylee,
Myleen, Mylenda, Mylinda**

Myra (Latin) fragrant ointment.
A feminine form of Myron.
Myrena, Myria

Myriam (American) a form
of Miriam.
Myriame, Myryam

Myrna (Irish) beloved.
Merna, Mirna, Morna, Muirna

Myrtle (Greek) dark green
shrub.
**Mertis, Mertle, Mirtle, Myrta,
Myrtia, Myrtias, Myrtice,
Myrtie, Myrtilla, Myrtis**

Nabila (Arabic) born to nobility.
Nabeela, Nabiha, Nabilah

Nadette (French) a short form of Bernadette.

Nadia (French, Slavic) hopeful.
Nada, Nadea, Nadenka, Nadie, Nadine, Nadiya, Nadja, Nadka, Nadusha, Nady, Nadya
Foreign form: Russian: *Nadezhda*

Nadine (French, Slavic) an alternate form of Nadia.
Nadean, Nadeana, Nadeen, Nadena, Nadene, Nadien, Nadina, Nadyne, Naidene, Naidine

Nadira (Arabic) rare, precious.
Nadirah

Naida (Greek) water nymph.
Naia, Naiad, Naya, Nayad, Nyad

Naila (Arabic) successful.
Nailah

Najila (Arabic) brilliant eyes.
Naja, Najah, Najia, Najla

Nakeisha (American) a combination of the prefix Na + Keisha.
Nakeesha, Nakesha, Nakeshea, Nakeshia, Nakeysha, Nakiesha, Nakisha, Nekeisha

Nakeita (American) a form of Nikita.
Nakeeta, Nakeitha, Nakeithra, Nakeitra, Nakeitress, Nakeitta, Nakeittia, Naketta, Nakieta, Nakitha, Nakitia, Nakitta, Nakyta

Nakia (Arabic) pure.
Nakea, Nakeia

Nakita (American) a form of Nicole, Nikita.
Nakia, Nakkita, Naquita

Nalani (Hawaiian) calm as the heavens.
Nalanie, Nalany

Nami (Japanese) wave.
Manami, Namika, Namiko

Nan (German) a short form of Fernanda. (English) an alternate form of Ann.
Nana, Nanette, Nani, Nanice, Nanine, Nanna, Nannie, Nanny, Nanon

Nana (Hawaiian) spring.

Nancy (English) gracious.
Nainsi, Nance, Nancee, Nancey, Nanci, Nancie, Nancine, Nancsi, Nancye, Nanice, Nanine, Nanncey, Nanncy, Nanouk, Nansee, Nansey, Nanuk, Noni, Nonie
Foreign forms: French: *Nanete, Nanette, Nannette*

Nani (Greek) charming. (Hawaiian) beautiful.
Nanni, Nannie, Nanny

Naomi (Hebrew) pleasant, beautiful. Bible: a friend of Ruth.
Naomia, Naomie, Naomy, Navit, Noemie, Noma, Nomi, Nyome, Nyomi
Foreign forms: English: *Naoma, Noami;* Spanish: *Neoma, Neomi, Noemy*

Nara (Greek) happy. (English) north. (Japanese) oak.
Narah

Narcissa (Greek) daffodil. A feminine form of Narcissus. Mythology: the youth who fell in love with his own reflection. **Narcisa, Narcisse, Narcyssa, Narkissa**

Narelle (Australian) woman from the sea.

Nari (Japanese) thunder. **Nariko**

Nashawna (American) a combination of the prefix Na + Shawna. **Nashana, Nashanda, Nashauna, Nashaunda, Nashawn, Nashounda, Nashuana**

Nastasia (Greek) an alternate form of Anastasia. **Nastasha, Nastashia, Nastasja, Nastassa, Nastassia, Nastassiya, Nastassja, Nastassya, Nastasya, Nastazia, Nastisija, Nastusya**
Foreign forms: Russian: Nastka, Nastya

Nasya (Hebrew) miracle. **Nasia**

Nata (Sanskrit) dancer. (Latin) swimmer. (Polish, Russian) a form of Natalie. (Native American) speaker; creator. See also Nadia. **Natia, Natka, Natya**

Natalia (Russian) a form of Natalie. See also Talia. **Nacia, Natala, Nataliia, Natalja, Natalka, Natallia, Natalya, Nathalia, Natka**

Natalie (Latin) born on Christmas day. See also Talia. **Nat, Natalea, Natalee, Natalene, Natali, Nataline, Nataly, Natalya, Natalyn, Natelie, Nathalia, Nathalie, Nathaly, Nati, Natie, Natilie, Natlie, Nattalie, Natti, Nattie, Nattilie, Nattlee, Natty**
Foreign forms: French: Natalène, Natalle, Natallie; Polish: Nata, Natalina; Russian: Natalia, Natasha

Natane (Arapaho) daughter. **Natanne**

Natania (Hebrew) gift of God. A feminine form of Nathan. **Natée, Nathania, Nathenia, Netania, Nethania**

Natara (Arabic) sacrifice.

Natasha (Russian) a form of Natalie. See also Stacey, Tasha. **Nahtasha, Natacha, Natachia, Natacia, Natasa, Natascha, Natashah, Natashea, Natashenka, Natashia, Natashiea, Natashja, Natashka, Natasia, Natassija, Natassja, Natasza, Natausha, Natawsha, Nathasha, Nathassha, Naticha, Natisha, Natishia, Natosha, Natoshia, Netasha, Netosha, Notasha, Notosha**
Foreign forms: American: Nitasha, Nitishia

Natesa (Hindi) godlike; goddess. Religion: another name for the Hindu goddess Shakti. **Natisa, Natissa**

Neala (Irish) an alternate form of Neila. **Nayela, Naylea, Naylia, Nealee, Nealia, Nealie, Nealy, Neela, Neelia, Neeli, Neelie, Neely, Neila**

Neci (Hungarian) fiery, intense. **Necia, Necie**

Neda (Slavic) born on Sunday. **Nedi**

Nedda (English) prosperous guardian. A feminine form of Edward. **Neddi, Neddie, Neddy**

Neely (Irish) a familiar form of Neila, Nelia.

Neelee, Neeley, Neelia, Neelie, Neili, Neilie

Neema (Swahili) born during prosperous times.

Neila (Irish) champion. A feminine form of Neil. See also Neala, Neely.
Neile, Neilla, Neille, Nia

Nekeisha (American) an alternate form of Nakeisha.
Nechesa, Neikeishia, Nekesha, Nekeshia, Nekiesha, Nekisha, Nekysha

Nelia (Spanish) yellow. (Latin) a familiar form of Cornelia.
Neelia, Neely, Neelya, Nela, Neli, Nelka, Nila

Nelle (Greek) stone.

Nellie (English) a familiar form of Cornelia, Eleanor, Helen, Prunella.
Nel, Neli, Nell, Nelley, Nelli, Nellianne, Nellice, Nellis, Nelly, Nelma
*Foreign forms: Russian: **Nella, Nelya***

Neola (Greek) youthful.

Neona (Greek) new moon.

Nerine (Greek) sea nymph.
Nereida, Nerida, Nerina, Nerita, Nerline

Nerissa (Greek) sea nymph. See also Rissa.
Narice, Narissa, Nerice, Nerisse, Nerys, Neryssa

Nessa (Greek) a short form of Agnes. (Scandinavian) promontory. See also Nessie.
Nesa, Nesha, Neshia, Nesiah, Nessia, Nesta, Nevsa, Neya, Neysa, Nyusha

Nessie (Greek) a familiar form of Agnes, Nessa, Vanessa.
Nese, Neshie, Nesho, Nesi, Ness, Nessi, Nessy, Nest, Neys

Neta (Hebrew) plant, shrub.
Netia, Netta, Nettia

Nettie (French) a familiar form of Annette, Antoinette.
Neti, Netie, Netta, Netti, Netty, Nety

Neva (Spanish) snow. (English) new. (Russian) Geography: a river in Russia.
Neiva, Nevada, Neve, Nevein, Nevia, Nevin, Neyva, Nieve

Nevada (Spanish) snow. Geography: a western American state.
Neiva, Neva

Nevina (Irish) worshipper of the saint. A feminine form of Nevin. History: a well-known Irish saint.
Nevena, Nivena

Neylan (Turkish) fulfilled wish.
Neya, Neyla

Ngozi (Ibo) blessing.

Nichelle (American) a combination of Nicole + Michelle. Culture: Nichelle Nichols was the first African-American woman featured in a television drama *(Star Trek)*.
Nichele, Nishelle

Nichole (French) an alternate form of Nicole.
Nichol, Nichola

Nicki (French) a familiar form of Nicole.
Nicci, Nickey, Nickeya, Nickia, Nickie, Nickiya, Nicky, Niki

Nicola (Italian) a form of Nicole.
Nacola, Necola, Nichola, Nickola, Nicolea, Nicolla, Nikkola, Nikola, Nikolia, Nykola

Nicole (French) victorious people. A feminine form of Nicholas. See also Colette, Cosette.
Nacole, Necole, Nica, Nichole,

Nicole (cont.)
Nicholette, Nicia, Nicki, Nickol, Nickole, Nicol, Nicolette, Nicoli, Nicolie, Nicoline, Nicolle, Niquole, Nocole
Foreign forms: American: **Nakita, Nikki;** Italian: **Nicola;** Russian: **Nikita**

Nicolette (French) an alternate form of Nicole.
Nettie, Nicholette, Nicoletta, Nikkolette, Nikoleta, Nikoletta, Nikolette

Nicoline (French) a familiar form of Nicole.
Nicholine, Nicholyn, Nicoleen, Nicolene, Nicolina, Nicolyn, Nicolyne, Nicolynn, Nicolynne, Nikolene, Nikolina, Nikoline

Nicolle (French) an alternate form of Nicole.
Nicholle

Nida (Omaha) Mythology: an elflike creature.

Nidia (Latin) nest.
Nidi, Nidya

Niesha (Scandinavian) an alternate form of Nissa. (American) pure.
Neisha, Neishia, Neissia, Nesha, Neshia, Nesia, Nessia, Niessia, Nisha

Nika (Russian) belonging to God.

Nike (Greek) victorious. Mythology: the goddess of victory.

Niki (Russian) a short form of Nikita.
Nikia

Nikita (Russian) victorious people. A form of Nicole.
Niki, Nikkita, Niquita, Niquitta
Foreign forms: American: **Nakeita, Nakita, Nikki**

Nikki (American) a familiar form of Nicole, Nikita.
Nicki, Nikia, Nikka, Nikkey, Nikkia, Nikkie, Nikky

Nikole (French) an alternate form of Nicole.
Nikkole, Nikola, Nikole, Nikolle

Nila (Latin) Geography: the Nile River in Egypt. (Irish) an alternate form of Neila.
Nilesia

Nima (Hebrew) thread. (Arabic) blessing.
Nema, Nimali

Nina (Hebrew) a familiar form of Hannah. (Spanish) girl.

(Native American) mighty.
Neena, Nena, Ninacska, Nineta, Ninete, Ninetta, Ninette, Ninita, Ninja, Nynette
Foreign forms: English: **Ninnetta, Ninnette;** French: **Ninon;** Russian: **Ninochka, Ninoshca**

Nirel (Hebrew) light of God.

Nisa (Arabic) woman.

Nisha (American) an alternate form of Niesha, Nissa.

Nishi (Japanese) west.

Nissa (Hebrew) sign, emblem. (Scandinavian) friendly elf; brownie. See also Nyssa.
Nisha, Nisse, Nissie, Nissy

Nita (Hebrew) planter. (Spanish) a short form of Juanita. (Choctaw) bear.
Nitika

Nitza (Hebrew) flower bud.
Nitzah, Nitzana, Nitzanit, Niza, Nizah

Nixie (German) water sprite.

Nizana (Hebrew) an alternate form of Nitza.
Nitzana, Nitzania, Zana

Noel (Latin) Christmas.
Noël, Noela, Noeleen, Noelene, Noelia, Noeline, Noelyn, Noelynn, Noleen, Novelenn, Novelia, Nowel, Noweleen, Nowell
Foreign form: French: Noelle

Noelani (Hawaiian) beautiful one from heaven.
Noela

Noelle (French) Christmas. A form of Noel.
Noell, Noella, Noelleen, Noellyn

Noemi (Hebrew) an alternate form of Naomi.
Noemie, Nohemi, Nomi

Nokomis (Dakota) moon daughter.

Nola (Latin) small bell. (Irish) famous; noble. A short form of Fionnula. A feminine form of Nolan.
Nuala

Noleta (Latin) unwilling.
Nolita

Nona (Latin) ninth.
Nonah, Noni, Nonia, Nonie, Nonna, Nonnah, Nonya

Nora (Greek) light. A familiar form of Eleanor, Honora, Leonore.
Norah
Foreign form: Irish: Noreen

Noreen (Irish) a form of Eleanor, Nora. (Latin) a familiar form of Norma.
Noorin, Noreena, Noren, Norene, Norina, Norine, Nureen

Norell (Scandinavian) from the north.
Narell, Narelle, Norelle

Nori (Japanese) law, tradition.
Noria, Norico, Noriko, Norita

Norma (Latin) rule, precept.
Noreen, Normi, Normie
Foreign form: Hawaiian: Noma

Nova (Latin) new. A short form of Novella, Novia. (Hopi) butterfly chaser. Astronomy: a star that releases bright bursts of energy.

Novella (Latin) newcomer.
Nova, Novela

Novia (Spanish) sweetheart.
Nova, Novka, Nuvia

Nu (Burmese) tender. (Vietnamese) girl.
Nue

Nuna (Native American) land.

Nunciata (Latin) messenger.
Nunzia

Nura (Aramaic) light.
Noor, Nour, Noura, Nur, Nureen

Nuria (Aramaic) the Lord's light.
Nuri, Nuriel, Nurin

Nurita (Hebrew) Botany: a flower with red and yellow blossoms.
Nurit

Nuru (Swahili) daylight.

Nydia (Latin) nest.
Nyda

Nyoko (Japanese) gem, treasure.

Nyree (Maori) sea.
Nyra, Nyrie

Nyssa (Greek) beginning. See also Nissa.
Nisha, Nissi, Nissy, Nysa

Oba (Yoruba) Mythology: the goddess who rules the rivers.

Oceana (Greek) ocean. Mythology: Oceanus was the god of water.
Ocean, Oceanne, Oceon

Octavia (Latin) eighth. A feminine form of Octavio. See also Tavia.
Octavice, Octavienne, Octavise, Octivia
Foreign forms: French: **Octavie**; Italian: **Ottavia**

Odele (Greek) melody, song.
Odela, Odelet, Odelette, Odella, Odelle

Odelia (Greek) ode; melodic. (Hebrew) I will praise God. (French) wealthy. A feminine form of Odell.
Oda, Odeelia, Odele, Odeleya, Odelina, Odell, Odelyn, Odila, Odile
Foreign forms: English: **Odelinda, Odilia**; German: **Odetta**

Odella (English) wood hill.
Odelle, Odelyn

Odessa (Greek) odyssey, long voyage.

Odetta (German, French) a form of Odelia.
Oddetta, Odette

Okalani (Hawaiian) heaven.
Okilani

Oki (Japanese) middle of the ocean.

Ola (Greek) a short form of Olesia. (Scandinavian) ancestor. A feminine form of Olaf.

Olga (Scandinavian) holy. See also Helga.
Olia, Olva
Foreign forms: Czech: **Olina**; English: **Olivia**; Estonian: **Olli, Olly**; Polish: **Ola**; Russian: **Olenka, Olya**

Olina (Hawaiian) filled with happiness.

Olinda (Greek) an alternate form of Yolanda. (Latin) scented. (Spanish) protector of property.

Olive (Latin) olive tree.
Oliff, Oliffe, Olivet, Olivette

Olivia (Latin) olive tree. (English) a form of Olga.
Oliva, Olive, Olivea, Olivianne, Oliwia, Ollye, Olyvia
Foreign forms: French: **Olivette, Ollie, Olva**; Hebrew: **Livia**

Olympia (Greek) heavenly.
Foreign forms: French: **Olympe**; German: **Olympie**; Italian: **Olimpia**

Oma (Hebrew) reverent. (German) grandmother. (Arabic) highest. A feminine form of Omar.

Ondine (Latin) an alternate form of Undine.
Ondina, Ondyne

Oneida (Native American) eagerly awaited.
Onida, Onyda

Oni (Yoruba) born on holy ground.

Oona (Latin, Irish) an alternate form of Una.
Ona, Onna, Onnie, Oonagh, Oonie

Opa (Choctaw) owl.

Opal (Hindi) precious stone.
Opale, Opalina, Opaline

Ophelia (Greek) helper.
Literature: Hamlet's love inter-
est in the Shakespearean play
Hamlet.
Filia, Ofeelia, Ophilia, Phelia
Foreign forms: *English:* **Ofelia,**
Ofilia; *French:* **Ophélie**

Oprah (Hebrew) an alternate
form of Orpah.
Ophra, Ophrah, Opra

Ora (Greek) an alternate form
of Aura. (Hebrew) light. (Latin)
prayer. (Spanish) gold.
(English) seacoast.
Orabel, Orabelle, Orah, Orlice,
Orra

Oralee (Hebrew) the Lord is
my light.
Orali, Oralit, Orlee, Orli, Orly

Oriana (Latin) dawn, sunrise.
(Irish) golden.
Orania, Orelda, Orelle, Ori,
Oria, Oriane, Orianna
Foreign form: *French:* **Oraine**

Orinda (Hebrew) pine tree.
(Irish) light skinned, white. A
feminine form of Oren.
Orenda

Oriole (Latin) golden; black
and orange bird.
Auriel, Oriel, Oriella, Oriola

Orlanda (German) famous
throughout the land. A feminine form of Orlando.
Orlantha

Orli (Hebrew) my light.
Orlice, Orlie, Orly

Ormanda (Latin) noble.
(German) mariner, seaman. A
feminine form of Orman.
Orma

Orpah (Hebrew) runaway. See
also Oprah.
Orpa, Orpha, Orphie

Orsa (Greek) an alternate form
of Ursula. (Latin) bearlike. A
feminine form of Orson. See
also Ursa.
Orsaline, Orse, Orsel,
Orselina, Orseline, Orsola

Osanna (Latin) praise the Lord.

Owena (Welsh) born to nobility; young warrior. A feminine
form of Owen.

Oz (Hebrew) strength.

Ozara (Hebrew) treasure,
wealth.

Paca (Spanish) a short form
of Pancha. See also Paka.

Page (French) young assistant.
Padget, Padgett, Pagen,
Paget, Pagett, Pagi, Payge

Paige (English) young child.

Paisley (Scottish) patterned
fabric made in Paisley,
Scotland.
Paisleyann, Paisleyanne

Paka (Swahili) kitten. See also
Paca.

Pallas (Greek) wise.
Mythology: another name for
Athena, the goddess of wis-
dom.

Palma (Latin) palm tree.
Pallma, Pallmirah, Pallmyra,
Palmer
Foreign forms: English:
Palmira, Palmyra

Paloma (Spanish) dove.
Aloma, Palloma, Palometa,
Palomita, Peloma

Pamela (Greek) honey.
Pama, Pamala, Pamalla,
Pamelia, Pamilla, Pammela,
Pammi, Pammie, Pamula
Foreign forms: English: Pam,
Pamelina, Pamella, Pammy

Pancha (Spanish) free; from
France. A feminine form of
Pancho.
Paca, Panchita

Pandita (Hindi) scholar.

Pandora (Greek) highly gifted.
Mythology: a young woman
who received many gifts from
the gods, such as beauty, wis-
dom, and creativity. See also
Dora.
Pandi, Pandorah, Pandorra,
Pandorrah, Pandy, Panndora,
Panndorah, Panndorra,
Panndorrah

Pansy (Greek) flower; fragrant.
(French) thoughtful.
Pansey, Pansie

Panya (Swahili) mouse; tiny
baby. (Russian) a familiar form
of Stephanie.

Paola (Italian) a form of Paula.
Paolina

Pari (Persian) fairy eagle.

Paris (French) Geography: the
capital of France. Mythology:
the Trojan prince who started
the Trojan war by abducting
Helen.
Parice, Paries, Parisa, Pariss,
Parissa, Parris

Pascale (French) born on
Easter or Passover. A feminine
form of Pascal.
Pascalette, Pascaline,
Pascalle, Paschale, Paskel

Pasha (Greek) sea.
Palasha, Pashel, Pashka

Pat (Latin) a short form of
Patricia, Patsy.

Pati (Moquelumnan) fish bas-
kets made of willow branches.

Patia (Latin, English) a familiar
form of Patience, Patricia.
(Gypsy, Spanish) leaf.

Patience (English) patient.
Paciencia, Patia, Patty

Patrice (French) a form of
Patricia.
Patrease, Patrece, Patresa,
Patriece, Patryce, Pattrice

Patricia (Latin) noblewoman.
A feminine form of Patrick. See
also Trisha, Trissa.
Patia, Patreece, Patreice,
Patrica, Patriceia, Patricja,
Patricka, Patrickia, Patrisha,
Patrishia, Patsy
Foreign forms: English: Pat,
Patty; French: Patrice; Irish:
Payton; Italian: Patrizia,
Patrizzia

Patsy (Latin) a familiar form
of Patricia.
Pat, Patsey, Patsi

Patty (English) a familiar form
of Patricia.
Patte, Pattee, Patti

Paula (Latin) small. A feminine
form of Paul. See also Polly.
Pali, Paliki, Paulane, Paulann,
Pauli, Paulie, Pauline, Paulla,
Pauly
Foreign forms: Bulgarian:
Paulina; Czech: Pavla; French:
Paule, Paulette; Italian/Spanish:
Paola, Paolina; Polish: Pawlina;
Russian: Pavia, Polina

Paulette (French) a familiar
form of Paula.
Pauletta, Paulita, Paullette

Pauline (Latin) a familiar form of Paula.
Pauleen, Paulene, Paulyne

Peace (English) peaceful.

Pearl (Latin) jewel. See also Peninah.
Pearla, Pearle, Pearleen, Pearlena, Pearlene, Pearlette, Pearlie, Pearline, Perlette, Perlie, Perline, Perlline, Perry

Peggy (Greek) a familiar form of Margaret.
Peg, Pegeen, Pegg, Peggey, Peggi, Peggie, Pegi

Penelope (Greek) weaver. Mythology: the clever and loyal wife of Odysseus, a Greek hero.
Penna, Pennelope, Penny, Pinelopi, Popi
Foreign forms: English: Pen, Penina; Polish: Pela, Penelopa

Peni (Hebrew) a short form of Peninah. (Carrier) mind.

Peninah (Hebrew) pearl.
Peni, Penina, Peninit, Peninnah, Penny

Penny (Greek) a familiar form of Penelope, Peninah.
Penee, Penney, Penni, Pennie

Peony (Greek) flower.
Peonie

Pepper (Latin) condiment from the pepper plant.

Perdita (Latin) lost. Literature: a character in the Shakespearean play *The Winter's Tale*.
Perdida, Perdy

Peri (Greek) mountain dweller. (Persian) fairy or elf.
Perita

Perlie (Latin) a familiar form of Pearl.
Pearley, Pearly, Perl, Perla, Perle, Perley, Perli, Perly, Purley, Purly

Pernella (Greek, French) rock. (Latin) a short form of Petronella.
Parnella, Pernel, Pernelle

Perri (Greek, Latin) small rock; traveler. (French) pear tree. (Welsh) daughter of Harry. A feminine form of Perry.
Perrey, Perriann, Perrie, Perrin, Perrine, Perry

Persephone (Greek) spring-time. Mythology: the goddess of spring.

Peta (Blackfoot) golden eagle.

Petra (Greek, Latin) small rock. A short form of Petronella. A feminine form of Peter.
Pet, Peta, Petena, Peterina, Petrice, Petrina, Petrine, Petrova, Petrovna
Foreign forms: French: Pier, Pierette, Pierrette; Italian: Pietra

Petronella (Greek) small rock. (Latin) of the Roman clan Petronius.
Pernella, Peternella, Petra, Petrona, Petronela, Petronella, Petronelle, Petronia, Petronija, Petronilla
Foreign form: German: Petronille

Petula (Latin) seeker.
Petulah

Petunia (Native American) flower.

Phaedra (Greek) bright.
Faydra, Phae, Phaidra, Phe, Phedre

Pheodora (Greek, Russian) an alternate form of Feodora.
Phedora, Phedorah, Pheodorah, Pheydora, Pheydorah

Philana (Greek) lover of mankind. A feminine form of Philander.

Philana (cont.)
Phila, Philene, Philiane, Philina, Philine

Philantha (Greek) lover of flowers.

Philippa (Greek) lover of horses. A feminine form of Philip.
Philippe, Phillipina, Phillie, Philly, Pippy
*Foreign forms: English: **Phil, Philipa, Pippa;** French: **Phillippine;** Italian: **Filippa;** Spanish: **Felipa;** Zuni: **Pelipa***

Philomena (Greek) love song; loved one. Bible: a first-century saint.
Mena, Philomina
*Foreign forms: French: **Philomène;** Italian: **Filomena***

Phoebe (Greek) shining.
Phaebe, Pheba, Phebe, Pheby, Phoebey

Phylicia (Greek) a form of Felicia. (Latin) fortunate; happy.
Philica, Philycia, Phylecia, Phylesia, Phylisha, Phylisia, Phyllecia, Phyllicia, Phyllisia

Phyllida (Greek) an alternate form of Phyllis.
Fillida, Philida, Phillida, Phillyda

Phyllis (Greek) green bough.
Filise, Fillys, Fyllis, Philis, Phillis, Philliss, Philys, Philyss, Phylis, Phyllida, Phyllis, Phylliss, Phyllys
*Foreign form: Italian: **Filide***

Pia (Italian) devout.

Pilar (Spanish) pillar, column. Religion: honoring the Virgin Mary, the pillar of the Catholic Church.
Peelar, Pilár

Ping (Chinese) duckweed. (Vietnamese) peaceful.

Pinga (Hindi) bronze; dark. Religion: another name for the Hindu goddess Shakti.

Piper (English) pipe player.

Pippi (French) rosy cheeked.
Pippen, Pippie, Pippin, Pippy

Pita (African) fourth daughter.

Placidia (Latin) serene.
Placida

Polla (Arabic) poppy.
Pola

Polly (Latin) a familiar form of Paula.
Paili, Poll, Pollee, Polley, Polli, Pollie

Pollyam (Hindi) goddess of the plague. Religion: the Hindu name invoked to ward off bad spirits.

Pollyanna (English) a combination of Polly + Anna. Literature: an overly optimistic heroine created by Eleanor Poiter.

Poloma (Choctaw) bow.

Pomona (Latin) apple. Mythology: the goddess of fruit and fruit trees.

Poni (African) second daughter.

Poppy (Latin) poppy flower.
Poppey, Poppi, Poppie

Porsche (German) a form of Portia.
Porcha, Porchai, Porcsha, Porcshe, Porscha, Porsché, Porschea, Porschia, Pourche

Porsha (Latin) an alternate form of Portia.
Porshai, Porshay, Porshe, Porshia

Portia (Latin) offering. Literature: the heroine of Shakespeare's play *The Merchant of Venice*.
Porsha, Portiea
*Foreign form: German: **Porsche***

Precious (French) precious; dear.

Prima (Latin) first, beginning; first child.
Primalia, Primetta, Primina, Priminia

Primavera (Italian, Spanish) spring.

Primrose (English) primrose flower.
Primula

Princess (English) daughter of royalty.
Princetta, Princie
Foreign forms: French: *Princesa;* Italian: *Princessa*

Priscilla (Latin) ancient.
Cilla, Piri, Precilla, Prescilla, Pricila, Pricilla, Prisca, Priscella, Priscila, Priscill, Priscille, Prisella, Prisila, Prisilla, Prissilla, Prissy, Prysilla
Foreign form: English: *Pris*

Prissy (Latin) a familiar form of Priscilla.
Prisi, Priss, Prissi, Prissie

Pru (Latin) a short form of Prudence.
Prue

Prudence (Latin) cautious; discreet.
Pru, Prudencia, Prudy

Prudy (Latin) a familiar form of Prudence.
Prudee, Prudi, Prudie

Prunella (Latin) brown; little plum. See also Nellie.
Prunela

Psyche (Greek) soul. Mythology: a beautiful mortal loved by Eros, the Greek god of love.

Pualani (Hawaiian) heavenly flower.
Pua, Puni

Purity (English) purity.
Pura, Pureza, Purisima

Qadira (Arabic) powerful.
Kadira

Qamra (Arabic) moon.
Kamra

Qing (Chinese) blue.

Qitarah (Arabic) fragrant.

Quaneisha (American) a combination of the prefix Qu + Aisha.
Quanecia, Quanesha, Quanesia, Quanisha, Quanishia, Quansha, Quarnisha, Queisha, Quenisha, Quenishia, Qynisha

Quanika (American) a combination of the prefix Qu + Nika.
Quanikka, Quanikki,

Quanika *(cont.)*
Quanique, Quantenique, Quawanica

Qubilah (Arabic) agreeable.

Queenie (English) queen. See also Quinn.
Queen, Queena, Queenation, Queeneste, Queenetta, Queenette, Queenika, Queenique, Queeny, Quenna

Queisha (African) a short form of Quaneisha.
Qeysha, Queshia

Quenby (Scandinavian) feminine.

Quenna (English) an alternate form of Queenie.
Quenell, Quenessa, Quenetta

Querida (Spanish) dear; beloved.

Questa (French) searcher.

Queta (Spanish) a short form of names ending in "queta" or "quetta."

Quiana (American) a combination of the prefix Qu + Anna.
Quian, Quianna

Quinby (Scandinavian) queen's estate.

Quincy (Irish) fifth.
Quinci, Quincie

Quinella (Latin) an alternate form of Quintana.
Quinetta, Quinette, Quinita, Quinnette

Quinn (German, English) queen. See also Queenie.
Quin, Quinna

Quintana (Latin) fifth. (English) queen's lawn. A feminine form of Quentin, Quintin. See also Quinella.
Quinntina, Quinta, Quintanna, Quintara, Quintarah, Quintia, Quintila, Quintilla, Quintina, Quintona, Quintonice

Quintessa (Latin) essence. See also Tess.
Quintice

Quisha (African) excellence of mind; physical and spiritual beauty.

Quita (Latin, French) tranquil.
Quiterie

Rabi (Arabic) breeze.
Rabiah

Rachael (Hebrew) an alternate form of Rachel.
Rachaele

Rachel (Hebrew) female sheep. Bible: the wife of Jacob. See also Rae, Rochelle.
Racha, Rachael, Rachal, Racheal, Rachela, Rachelann, Rackel, Raechel, Raechele, Rahela, Raycene, Rey
Foreign forms: Bulgarian: **Rahil;** English: **Ray;** French: **Rachelle, Racquel, Raquel;** German: **Rahel;** Hawaiian: **Lahela;** Italian: **Rachele;** Russian: **Rakhil;** Swedish: **Rakel;** Yiddish: **Ruchel**

Rachelle (French) a form of Rachel.

Rachalle, Rachell, Rachella, Raechell, Raechelle, Raeshelle, Rashel, Rashele, Rashell, Rashelle, Raychell, Rayshell, Rochell, Ruchelle

Racquel (French) a form of Rachel.
Racquell, Racquella, Racquelle

Radinka (Slavic) full of life; happy, glad.

Radmilla (Slavic) worker for the people.

Rae (English) doe. (Hebrew) a short form of Rachel.
Raeda, Raedeen, Raeden, Raeh, Raelene, Raena, Raenah, Raeneice, Raeneisha, Raesha, Raewyn, Ralina, Ray, Raye, Rayetta, Rayette, Rayma, Rayna, Rayona, Rey

Raeann (American) a combination of Rae + Ann. See also Rayanne.
Raea, Raeanna, Reanna, Raeanne

Raelene (American) a combination of Rae + Lee.
Raela, Raelee, Raeleen, Raeleigh, Raeleigha, Raelene, Raelesha, Raelina, Raelyn, Raelynn

Rafa (Arabic) happy; prosperous.

Rafaela (Hebrew) an alternate form of Raphaela.
Rafaelia, Rafaella

Ragnild (Scandinavian) Mythology: a warrior goddess.
Ragna, Ragnell, Ragnhild, Rainell, Renilda, Renilde

Ráidah (Arabic) leader.

Raina (German) mighty. (English) a short form of Regina. See also Rayna.
Raenah, Raheena, Raine, Rainna, Reanna

Rainbow (English) rainbow.
Rainbeau, Rainbeaux, Rainbo, Raynbow

Raine (Latin) a short form of Regina. An alternate form of Raina, Rane.
Rainey, Raini, Rainie, Rainy

Raja (Arabic) hopeful.
Raia

Raku (Japanese) pleasure.

Rama (Hebrew) lofty, exalted. (Hindi) godlike. Religion: another name for the Hindu goddess Shiva.
Ramah

Ramona (Spanish) mighty; wise protector. See also Mona.
Raymona, Romona, Romonda
Foreign form: English: *Ramonda*

Ran (Japanese) water lily. (Scandinavian) destroyer. Mythology: the sea goddess who destroys.

Rana (Sanskrit) royal. (Arabic) gaze, look.
Rahna, Rahni, Rani

Randall (English) protected.
Randa, Randah, Randal, Randalee, Randel, Randell, Randelle, Randi, Randilee, Randilynn, Randlyn, Randy, Randyl

Randi, Randy (English) familiar forms of Miranda, Randall.
Rande, Randee, Randeen, Randene, Randey, Randie, Randii

Rane (Scandinavian) queen.
Raine

Rani (Sanskrit) queen. (Hebrew) joyful. A short form of Kerani.
Rahni, Ranee, Rania, Ranice, Ranique

Ranita (Hebrew) song; joyful.
Ranata, Ranice, Ranit, Ranite, Ranitta, Ronita

Raphaela (Hebrew) healed by God. Bible: one of the four archangels.
Foreign forms: Italian: Rafaella; Spanish: Rafaela

Raquel (French) a form of Rachel.
Rakel, Rakhil, Rakhila, Raqueal, Raquela, Raquella, Raquelle, Rockell
Foreign forms: American: Rickquel, Ricquel, Ricquelle, Rikell, Rikelle

Rasha (Arabic) young gazelle.
Rahshea, Rahshia, Rashea

Rashawna (American) a combination of the prefix Ra + Shawna.
Rashana, Rashanda, Rashani, Rashanta, Rashaunda, Rashaundra, Rashawn, Rashon, Rashona, Rashonda, Rashunda

Rashida (Swahili, Turkish) righteous.
Rahshea, Rahsheda, Rahsheita, Rashdah, Rasheda, Rashedah, Rasheeda, Rasheeta, Rasheida, Rashidi

Rashieka (Arabic) descended from royalty.
Rasheeka, Rasheika, Rasheka, Rashika, Rasika

Rasia (Greek) rose.

Ratana (Thai) crystal.
Ratania, Ratanya, Ratna, Rattan, Rattana

Raula (French) wolf counselor. A feminine form of Raoul.
Raoula, Raulla, Raulle

Raven (English) blackbird.
Raveen, Raveena, Ravena, Ravennah, Ravi, Ravin, Ravine, Ravyn, Rayven, Rayvin

Rawnie (Gypsy) fine lady.
Rawna, Rhawnie

Raya (Hebrew) friend.
Raia, Raiah, Ray, Rayah

Rayanne (American) an alternate form of Raeann.
Ray-Ann, Rayan, Rayana, Rayann, Rayanna, Rayona, Reyana, Reyann, Reyanna, Reyanne

Rayleen (American) a combination of Rae + Lyn.
Rayel, Rayele, Rayelle, Raylena, Raylene, Raylin, Raylona, Raylyn, Raylynn, Raylynne

Raymonde (German) wise protector. A feminine form of Raymond.
Rayma, Raymae, Raymie

Rayna (Scandinavian) mighty. (Yiddish) pure, clean. (French) a familiar form of Lorraine. (English) king's advisor. A feminine form of Reynold. See also Raina.
Rayna, Rayne, Raynell, Raynelle, Raynette, Rayona, Rayonna, Reyna

Rayya (Arabic) thirsty no longer.

Razi (Aramaic) secretive.
Rayzil, Rayzilee, Raz, Razia, Raziah, Raziela, Razilee, Razili

Rea (Greek) poppy flower.
Reah

Reanna (German, English) an alternate form of Raina. (American) an alternate form of Raeann.
Reannah

Reanne (American) an alternate form of Raeann, Reanna.
Reana, Reane, Reann, Reannan, Reanne, Reannen, Reannon, Reeana

Reba (Hebrew) fourth-born child. A short form of Rebecca. See also Reva, Riva.
Rabah, Reeba, Rheba

Rebecca (Hebrew) tied, bound. Bible: the wife of Isaac. See also Becca, Becky.
Rabecca, Rabecka, Reba, Rebbecca, Rebeccah, Rebeccea, Rebeccka, Rebecha, Rebecka, Rebeckah, Rebecky, Rebi, Riva, Rivka
Foreign forms: American: *Becky;* French: *Rébecca, Rebeque;* German: *Rebekke;* Rumanian: *Reveca;* Slavic: *Reveka;* Spanish: *Rebeca;* Yiddish: *Rifka*

Rebekah (Hebrew) an alternate form of Rebecca.
Rebeka, Rebekha, Rebekka, Rebekkah, Revecca, Revekka

Rebi (Hebrew) a familiar form of Rebecca.
Rebbie, Rebe, Reby, Ree, Reebie

Reena (Greek) peaceful.
Reen, Reenie, Rena, Reyna

Reganne (Irish) little ruler. A feminine form of Regan.
Ragan, Reagan, Regin

Regina (Latin) queen. (English) king's advisor. A feminine form of Reginald. Geography: the capital of Saskatchewan.
Ragina, Raine, Rega, Regena, Regennia, Reggi, Reggie, Reggy, Regi, Regia, Regie, Regiena, Regin, Reginia, Regis
Foreign forms: French: *Reine, Reinette;* German: *Regine;* Hebrew: *Rena;* Italian: *Gina, Reina;* Norwegian: *Rane;* Polish: *Renia;* Spanish: *Raina*

Rei (Japanese) polite, well behaved.
Reiko

Reina (Spanish) a short form of Regina. See also Reyna.
Reiny, Reiona, Rina

Remi (French) from Rheims.
Remee, Remie, Remy

Ren (Japanese) arranger; water lily; lotus.

Rena (Hebrew) song; joy. A familiar form of Irene, Regina, Renata, Sabrina, Serena.
Reena, Rina, Rinna, Rinnah

Renae (French) an alternate form of Renée.
Renay

Renata (French) an alternate form of Renée.
Ranata, Rena, Renada, Renita, Renyatta, Rinada, Rinata
Foreign forms: English: *Renie, Rennie;* German: *Renate*

Rene (Greek) a short form of Irene, Renée.
Reen, Reenie, Renae, Reney, Rennie

Renée (French) born again.
Renae, Renata, Renay, Rene, Renell, Renelle

Renita (French) an alternate form of Renata.
Reneeta, Renetta, Renitza

Reseda (Spanish) fragrant mignonette blossom.

Reshawna (American) a combination of the prefix Re + Shawna.
Resaunna, Reshana, Reshaunda, Reshawnda, Reshawnna, Reshonda, Reshonn, Reshonta

Reta (African) shaken.
Reeta, Retta, Rheta, Rhetta

Reubena (Hebrew) behold a daughter. A feminine form of Reuben.
Reubina, Reuvena, Rubena,

Reubena *(cont.)*
Rubenia, Rubina, Rubine, Rubyna

Reva (Latin) revived. (Hebrew) rain; one-fourth. An alternate form of Reba, Riva.
Ree, Reeva, Revia, Revida

Rexanne (American) queen. A feminine form of Rex.
Rexan, Rexana, Rexann, Rexanna

Reyhan (Turkish) sweet-smelling flower.

Reyna (Greek) peaceful. (English) an alternate form of Reina.
Reyne

Reynalda (German) king's advisor. A feminine form of Reynold.

Rhea (Greek) brook, stream. Mythology: the mother of Zeus.
Rheá, Rhéa, Rhealyn, Rheana, Rheann, Rheanna, Rheannan, Rheanne, Rheannon

Rhiannon (Welsh) witch; nymph; goddess.
Rhian, Rhiana, Rhianen, Rhianna, Rhianne, Rhiannen, Rhianon, Rhianwen, Rhiauna, Rhinnon, Rhyan, Rhyanna,

Rian, Riana, Riane, Riann, Rianna, Rianne, Riannon, Rianon, Riayn

Rhoda (Greek) from Rhodes.
Rhode, Rhodeia, Rhodie, Rhody, Roda, Rodi, Rodie, Rodina

Rhona (Scottish) powerful, mighty. (English) king's advisor. A feminine form of Ronald.

Rhonda (Welsh) grand.
Rhondelle, Rhondene, Rhondiesha, Rhonnie, Ronda, Ronelle, Ronnette

Ria (Spanish) river.
Riah

Riana (Irish) a short form of Briana.
Reana, Reanna, Rianna

Rica (Spanish) a short form of Erica, Frederica, Ricarda. See also Sandrica, Terrica, Ulrica.
Ricca, Rieca, Riecka, Rieka, Rikka, Riqua, Rycca

Ricarda (Spanish) rich and powerful ruler. A feminine form of Richard.
Rica, Richanda, Richarda, Richi
Foreign forms: *American:* **Ricki, Rikki;** *French/German:* **Richelle**

Richael (Irish) saint.

Richelle (German, French) a form of Ricarda.
Richel, Richela, Richele, Richell, Richella, Richia

Ricki, Rikki (American) familiar forms of Erica, Frederica, Ricarda.
Rica, Rici, Ricka, Rickia, Rickie, Rickilee, Rickina, Rickita, Ricky, Ricquie, Riki, Rikia, Rikita, Rikky

Rida (Arabic) favored by God.

Rihana (Arabic) sweet basil.
Rhiana, Rhianna, Riana, Rianna

Rika (Swedish) ruler.

Riley (Irish) valiant.
Rileigh, Rilie

Rilla (German) small brook.

Rima (Arabic) white antelope.
Reem, Reema, Rema, Remah, Rim, Ryma

Rimona (Hebrew) pomegranate. See also Mona.

Rin (Japanese) park. Geography: a Japanese village.
Rini, Rynn

Rina (English) a short form of names ending in "rina."
Reena, Rena

Rinah (Hebrew) joyful.
Rina

Riona (Irish) saint.

Risa (Latin) laughter.
Reesa, Resa

Risha (Hindi) born during the lunar month of Taurus.
Rishah, Rishay

Rishona (Hebrew) first.

Rissa (Greek) a short form of Nerissa.
Risa, Rissah, Ryssa, Ryssah

Rita (Sanskrit) brave; honest. (Greek) a short form of Margarita.
Reatha, Reda, Reeta, Reida, Reitha, Rheta, Riet, Ritamae, Ritamarie

Ritsa (Greek) a familiar form of Alexandra.
Ritsah, Ritsi, Ritsie, Ritsy

Riva (Hebrew) a short form of Rebecca. (French) river bank. See also Reba, Reva.
Rivalee, Rivana, Rivi, Rivvy

River (Latin, French) stream, water.
Rivana, Rivers, Riviane

Rivka (Hebrew) a short form of Rebecca.
Rivca, Rivcah, Rivkah

Riza (Greek) a short form of Theresa.
Riesa, Rizus, Rizza

Roanna (American) a combination of Rose + Anna.
Ranna, Roana, Roanda, Roanne

Roberta (English) famous brilliance. A feminine form of Robert. See also Bobbi, Robin.
Robbi, Robbie, Robby, Robena, Robertena, Robertina
Foreign forms: American:
Bobbi, Bobetta, Bobbette;
Czech: ***Roba;*** *French:* ***Robine;***
German: ***Rupetta;*** *Spanish:*
Robertha, Ruperta

Robin (English) robin. An alternate form of Roberta.
Robann, Robbi, Robbie, Robbin, Robby, Robena, Robina, Robinette, Robinia, Robinn, Robinta, Robyn

Robinette (English) a familiar form of Robin.
Robernetta, Robinet, Robinett, Robinita

Robyn (English) an alternate form of Robin.
Robbyn, Robyne, Robynn, Robynne

Rochelle (Hebrew) an alternate form of Rachel. (French) large stone.
Roch, Rochele, Rochell, Rochella, Rochette, Rockelle, Roshele, Roshell, Roshelle

Roderica (German) famous ruler. A feminine form of Roderick.
Rica, Rika, Rodericka, Roderika, Rodreicka, Rodricka, Rodrika

Rohana (Hindi) sandalwood. (American) a combination of Rose + Hannah.
Rochana, Rohena

Rohini (Hindi) woman.

Rolanda (German) famous throughout the land. A feminine form of Roland.
Ralna, Rolaine, Rolene, Rollande, Rolleen
Foreign forms: French:
Rolande; *Italian:* ***Orlanda***

Roma (Latin) from Rome.
Romeise, Romeka, Romelle, Romesha, Rometta, Romi, Romie, Romilda, Romilla, Romina, Romini, Romma, Romonia

Romaine (French) from Rome.
Romana, Romanda, Romanelle, Romanique, Romayne

Romy (French) a familiar form of Romaine. (English) a familiar form of Rosemary.
Romi

Rona (Scandinavian) a short form of Rhona.
Rhona, Roana, Ronalda, Ronalee, Ronella, Ronelle, Ronna, Ronne, Ronni, Ronsy

Ronda (Welsh) an alternate form of Rhonda.
Rondai, Rondel, Rondelle, Rondesia, Rondi, Ronelle, Ronndelle, Ronnette, Ronni

Roneisha (American) a combination of Rhonda + Aisha.
Ronecia, Ronee, Roneeka, Roneice, Roneshia, Ronessa, Ronichia, Ronicia, Roniesha, Ronisha, Ronnesa, Ronnesha, Ronni, Ronnise, Ronnisha, Ronnishia

Ronelle (Welsh) an alternate form of Rhonda, Ronda.
Ranell, Ranelle, Ronella, Ronnella, Ronnelle

Ronli (Hebrew) joyful.
Roni, Ronia, Ronice, Ronit, Ronlee, Ronlie, Ronni

Ronnette (Welsh) a familiar form of Rhonda, Ronda.
Ronetta, Ronita, Ronni

Ronni, Ronnie, Ronny (American) familiar forms of Veronica and names beginning with "Ron."
Ronee, Roni, Ronnee, Ronney

Rori, Rory (Irish) famous brilliance; famous ruler. Feminine forms of Robert, Roderick.

Ros, Roz (English) short forms of Rosalind, Rosalyn.
Rozz, Rozzey, Rozzi, Rozzie, Rozzy

Rosa (Italian, Spanish) a form of Rose. History: Rosa Parks inspired the American civil rights movement by refusing to give up her bus seat to a white man in Montgomery, Alabama.
*Foreign forms: Slavic: **Roza, Ruza, Ruzha***

Rosabel (French) beautiful rose.
Rosabella, Rosabelle

Rosalba (Latin) white rose.

Rosalie (English) a form of Rosalind.
Rosalea, Rosalee, Rosaleen, Rosalene, Rosalia, Roselia, Rosilee, Rosli, Rozali, Rozalie, Rozália, Rozele

Rosalind (Spanish) fair rose.
Ros, Rosalina, Rosalinda, Rosalinde, Rosalyn, Rosalynd, Rosalynde, Roselind, Rosie, Rozalind
*Foreign form: English: **Rosalie***

Rosalyn (Spanish) an alternate form of Rosalind.
Ros, Rosaleen, Rosalin, Rosaline, Rosalyne, Rosalynn, Rosalynne, Roseleen, Roselin, Roseline, Roselyn, Roselynn, Roselynne, Rosilyn, Roslin, Roslyn, Roslyne, Roslynn, Rozalyn, Rozland, Rozlyn

Rosamond (German) famous guardian.
Rosamund
*Foreign forms: Dutch: **Rozamond**; French: **Rosemonde**; Italian: **Rosmunda**; Spanish: **Rosamunda***

Rosanna, Roseanna (English) combinations of Rose + Anna.
Ranna, Roanna, Rosana, Rosannah, Roseana, Roseannah, Rosehanah, Rosehannah, Rosie, Rossana, Rossanna, Rozana, Rozanna

Rosanne, Roseanne (English) combinations of Rose + Ann.
Roanne, Rosan, Rosann, Roseann, Rose Ann, Rose Anne, Rossann, Rossanne, Rozann, Rozanne

Rosario (Filipino, Spanish) rosary.
Roario

Rose (Latin) rose.
Rada, Rasia, Rasine, Rosella, Roselle, Roseta, Rosse
Foreign forms: Basque: **Arrosa**; Czech: **Ruzena**; English: **Rosie, Rosina, Rozina**; French: **Róise, Rosette**; Hungarian: **Rozsi, Ruzsa**; Irish: **Rois**; Italian/Spanish: **Rosetta, Rosa**; Lithuanian: **Rozele, Rozyte**; Russian: **Raisa, Raiza**; Slavic: **Roza, Ruzha**; Spanish: **Chalina, Charo, Rosita**; Yiddish: **Raizel**

Roselani (Hawaiian) heavenly rose.

Rosemarie (English) a combination of Rose + Marie.
Romy, Rosemaria, Rose Marie

Rosemary (English) a combination of Rose + Mary.
Romi, Romy

Rosetta (Italian) a form of Rose.

Roshan (Sanskrit) shining light.

Roshawna (American) a combination of Rose + Shawna.
Roshan, Roshanda, Roshani, Roshanna, Roshanta, Roshaun, Roshaunda, Roshawn, Roshawnda, Roshawnna, Roshona, Roshonda

Rosie (English) a familiar form of Rosalind, Rosanna, Rose.
Rosey, Rosi, Rosio, Rosse, Rosy, Rozy

Rowan (English) tree with red berries. (Welsh) an alternate form of Rowena.

Rowena (Welsh) fair haired. (English) famous friend. Literature: Ivanhoe's love interest in Sir Walter Scott's novel *Ivanhoe.*
Ranna, Ronni, Row, Rowan, Rowe, Roweena, Rowina

Roxana, Roxanna (Persian) alternate forms of Roxann, Roxanne.
Rocsana

Roxann, Roxanne (Persian) sunrise. Literature: the heroine of Edmond Rostand's play *Cyrano de Bergerac.*
Rocxann, Roxana, Roxane, Roxanna, Roxianne, Roxy

Roxy (Persian) a familiar form of Roxann.
Roxi, Roxie

Royale (English) royal.
Royal, Royalle, Ryal, Ryale

Royanna (English) queenly, royal. A feminine form of Roy.
Roya, Royalene, Roylee, Roylene

Rozene (Native American) rose blossom.
Rozena, Rozina, Rozine

Ruana (Hindi) stringed musical instrument.
Ruan, Ruon

Rubena (Hebrew) an alternate form of Reubena.
Rubenia, Rubina, Rubine, Rubinia, Rubyn, Rubyna

Ruby (French) precious stone.
Rubetta, Rubette, Rubey,

Ruby *(cont.)*
Rubi, Rubiann, Rubyann, Rubye
Foreign forms: *English:* **Rubia, Rubie**

Rudee (German) famous wolf. A feminine form of Rudolph.
Rudeline, Rudell, Rudella, Rudi, Rudie, Rudina, Rudy

Rudra (Hindi) seeds of the rudraksha plant.

Rue (German) famous. (French) street. (English) regretful; strong-scented herbs.
Ru, Ruey

Ruffina (Italian) redhead.
Rufeena, Rufeine, Rufina, Ruphyna

Rula (Latin, English) ruler.

Ruri (Japanese) emerald.
Ruriko

Rusti (English) redhead.
Russet, Rustie, Rusty

Ruth (Hebrew) friendship. Bible: friend of Naomi.
Rutha, Ruthalma, Ruthe, Ruthella, Ruthetta, Ruthie, Ruthina, Ruthine, Ruthven, Ruthy

Ruthann (American) a combination of Ruth + Ann.
Ruthan, Ruthanne

Ruthie (Hebrew) a familiar form of Ruth.
Ruthey, Ruthi, Ruthy

Ruza (Czech) rose.
Ruzena, Ruzenka, Ruzha, Ruzsa

Ryann (Irish) little ruler. A feminine form of Ryan.
Raiann, Raianne, Rhyann, Riana, Riane, Ryana, Ryanna, Ryanne, Rye, Ryen, Ryenne

Ryba (Czech) fish.

Rylee (Irish) valiant.
Rye, Ryley, Rylie, Rylina, Ryllie, Rylly, Rylyn

Ryo (Japanese) dragon.
Ryoko

Saarah (Arabic) princess.

Saba (Greek) a form of Sheba. (Arabic) morning.
Sabah, Sabbah

Sabi (Arabic) young girl.

Sabina (Latin) History: the Sabine were a tribe in ancient Italy. See also Bina.
Sabienne, Sabinna, Sabiny, Saby, Sabyne, Savina, Sebina, Sebinah
Foreign forms: *French/German:* **Sabine;** *Slavic:* **Sabinka**

Sabiya (Arabic) morning; eastern wind.
Saba, Sabaya

Sable (English) sable; sleek.
Sabel, Sabela, Sabella

Sabra (Hebrew) thorny cactus fruit. History: a name for native-born Israelis, who were said to be hard on the outside and soft and sweet on the inside. (Arabic) resting.
Sabira, Sabrah, Sabriya, Sebra

Sabrina (Latin) boundary line. (Hebrew) a familiar form of Sabra. (English) princess. See also Brina, Rena.
Sabre, Sabreena, Sabrinia, Sabrinna, Sabryna, Sebree, Sebrina
Foreign forms: American: Zabreena, Zabrina, Zabryna

Sacha (Russian) an alternate form of Sasha.

Sachi (Japanese) blessed; lucky.
Sachiko

Sada (Japanese) chaste. (English) a form of Sadie.
Sadá, Sadako

Sade (Hebrew) an alternate form of Chadee, Sarah, Shardae, Sharday.
Sáde, Sadé, Sadee

Sadie (Hebrew) a familiar form of Sarah.
Sadah, Sadella, Sadelle, Sady, Sadye, Saidee, Saydie, Sydel, Sydell, Sydella, Sydelle
Foreign form: English: Sada

Sadira (Persian) lotus tree. (Arabic) star.
Sadra

Sadiya (Arabic) lucky, fortunate.
Sadi, Sadia, Sadya

Saffron (English) Botany: a plant with purple or white flowers whose orange stigmas are used as a spice.

Sage (English) wise. Botany: an herb with healing powers.
Sagia, Saige, Salvia

Sahara (Arabic) desert; wilderness.
Sahar, Saharah

Saida (Hebrew) an alternate form of Sarah. (Arabic) happy; fortunate.
Saidah

Sakaë (Japanese) prosperous.

Sakura (Japanese) cherry blossom; wealthy, prosperous.
Sakuro

Sala (Hindi) sala tree. Religion: the sacred tree under which Buddha died.

Salama (Arabic) peaceful. See also Zulima.

Salima (Arabic) safe and sound; healthy.
Saleema, Salema, Salim, Salimah, Salma

Salina (French) solemn, dignified.
Salena, Saleena, Salinda

Salliann (English) an alternate form of Sally.
Sallian, Sallianne, Sallyann, Sally-Ann, Sallyanne, Sally-Anne

Sally (English) princess. A familiar form of Sarah. History: Sally Ride, an American astronaut, became the first U.S. woman in space.
Sal, Salaid, Sallee, Salletta, Sallette, Salley, Salli, Salliann, Sallie

Salome (Hebrew) peaceful. History: Salome Alexandra was a ruler of ancient Judea. Bible: the sister of King Herod.
Salomey
Foreign forms: English: Saloma, Salomi; French: Salomé

Salvadora (Spanish) savior.

Salvia (Latin) a form of Sage. (Spanish) healthy; saved.
Sallvia, Salviana, Salviane, Salvina, Salvine

Samala (Hebrew) asked of God.
Samale, Sammala

Samantha (Aramaic) listener. (Hebrew) told by God.
Sam, Samana, Samanath, Samanatha, Samanitha, Samanithia, Samanta, Samanth, Samanthe, Samanthi, Samanthia, Sami, Sammanth, Sammantha, Sammatha, Semantha, Simantha, Smanta, Smantha, Symantha

Samara (Latin) elm tree seed.
Sam, Samaria, Samarie, Samarra, Samera, Sameria, Samira, Sammar, Sammara, Samora

Sameh (Hebrew) listener. (Arabic) forgiving.
Samaiya, Samaya

Sami (Hebrew) a short form of Samantha, Samuela. (Arabic) praised.
Samia, Samiha, Samina, Sammey, Sammi, Sammijo, Sammy, Sammyjo, Samya, Samye

Samira (Arabic) entertaining.
Sami

Samuela (Hebrew) heard God, asked of God. A feminine form of Samuel.
Samala, Samelia, Samella, Samielle, Samille, Sammile, Samuella, Samuelle

Sana (Arabic) mountaintop; splendid; brilliant.
Sanaa, Sanáa

Sancia (Spanish) holy, sacred.
Sanceska, Sancha, Sancharia, Sanchia, Sancie, Santsia, Sanzia

Sandeep (Punjabi) enlightened.

Sandi (Greek) a familiar form of Sandra.
Sandee, Sandia, Sandie, Sandiey, Sandine, Sanndie

Sandra (Greek) defender of mankind. A short form of Alexandra, Cassandra. History: Sandra Day O'Connor was the first woman appointed to the U.S. Supreme Court. See also Zandra.
Sahndra, Sandi, Sandira, Sandrea, Sandria, Sandrica, Sandy, Shandra, Sondra
Foreign form: English: *Saundra*

Sandrea (Greek) an alternate form of Sandra.
Sandreea, Sandreia, Sandrell,

Sandrenna, Sandria, Sandrina, Sandrine, Sanndra, Sanndria

Sandrica (Greek) an alternate form of Sandra. See also Rica.
Sandricka, Sandrika

Sandy (Greek) a familiar form of Cassandra, Sandra.
Sandya, Sandye

Santana (Spanish) saint.
Santa, Santaniata, Santanna, Santanne, Santena, Santenna, Santina
Foreign form: American:
Shantana, Shantanika

Santina (Spanish) little saint.
Santinia

Sanya (Sanskrit) born on Saturday.

Sanyu (Luganda) happiness.

Sapphire (Greek) blue gemstone.
Saffire, Saphyre, Sapphira

Sara (Hebrew) an alternate form of Sarah.
Saralee, Sarra

Sarah (Hebrew) princess. Bible: the wife of Abraham and mother of Isaac. See also Sadie, Saida, Saree, Sharai, Zara.

Sahra, Sara, Saraha, Sarahann, Sarai, Sarann, Sarina, Sarita, Sarrah, Sayre
Foreign forms: English: **Sally;** French: **Sarotte;** Hungarian: **Sarolta, Sasa, Shari;** Irish: **Sorcha;** Spanish: **Zarita**

Saree (Hebrew) a familiar form of Sarah. (Arabic) noble.
Sareeka, Sareka, Sari, Sarika, Sarka, Sarri, Sarrie, Sary

Sarila (Turkish) waterfall.

Sarina (Hebrew) a familiar form of Sarah.
Sareen, Sarena, Sarene, Sarinna, Sarinne

Sarita (Hebrew) a familiar form of Sarah.
Saretta, Sarette, Saritia, Sarolta, Sarotte

Sasa (Hungarian) a form of Sarah, Sasha. (Japanese) assistant.

Sasha (Russian) defender of mankind. A short form of Alexandra. See also Zasha.
Sacha, Sahsha, Sasa, Sascha, Saschae, Sashah, Sashana, Sashel, Sashenka, Sashia, Sashira, Sashsha, Sasjara, Sasshalai, Sausha, Shasha, Shashi, Shashia, Shura, Shurka

Satara (American) a combination of Sarah + Tara.
Sataria, Satarra, Sateriaa, Saterra, Saterria

Satin (French) smooth, shiny.
Satinder

Sato (Japanese) sugar.
Satu

Saundra (English) a form of Sandra, Sondra.
Saundee, Saundi, Saundie, Saundy

Saura (Hindi) sun worshiper. Astrology: born under the sign of Leo.

Sass (Irish) Saxon.
Sassie, Sassoon, Sassy

Savannah (Spanish) treeless plain.
Sahvannah, Savana, Savanah, Savanha, Savanna, Savannha, Savauna, Sevan, Sevanah, Sevanh, Sevann, Sevanna, Svannah

Scarlett (English) bright red. Literature: Scarlett O'Hara is the heroine of Margaret Mitchell's novel *Gone with the Wind.*
Scarlet, Scarlette, Scarlotte, Skarlette

Scotti (Scottish) from Scotland. A feminine form of Scott.
Scota, Scotia, Scottie, Scotty

Seana (Irish) a form of Jane. See also Shauna, Shawna.
Seaana, Seandra, Seane, Seanette, Seann, Seanna, Seannalisa, Seanté, Seantelle, Sina

Sebastiane (Greek) venerable. (Latin) revered. (French) a feminine form of Sebastian.
Sebastene, Sebastia, Sebastienne
Foreign form: English: **Sebastiana**

Secilia (Latin) an alternate form of Cecilia.
Saselia, Sasilia, Sesilia, Sileas

Secunda (Latin) second.

Seema (Greek) sprout. (Afghani) sky; profile.
Seemah, Sima, Simah

Seki (Japanese) wonderful.
Seka

Selam (Ethiopian) peaceful.

Selda (German) a short form of Griselda. (Yiddish) an alternate form of Zelda.
Seldah, Selde, Sellda, Selldah

Selena (Greek) moon. Mythology: Selene was the goddess of the moon. See also Celena.
Saleena, Sela, Selen, Séléné, Selenia, Sena, Syleena, Sylena
Foreign forms: English: **Selene, Selina**

Selia (Latin) a short form of Cecilia.
Seel, Seelia, Seil, Sela

Selima (Hebrew) peaceful. A feminine form of Solomon.
Selema, Selemah, Selimah

Selina (Greek) an alternate form of Celina, Selena.
Selia, Selie, Selina, Selinda, Seline, Selinka, Selyna, Selyne, Sylina

Selma (German) devine protector. (Irish) fair, just. (Scandinavian) divinely protected. (Arabic) secure. A feminine form of Anselm. See also Zelma.
Sellma, Sellmah, Selmah

Sen (Japanese) Mythology: a magical forest elf that lives for thousands of years.

Sequoia (Cherokee) giant redwood tree.
Sequora, Sequoya, Sikoya

Serafina (Hebrew) burning; ardent. Bible: Seraphim are the highest order of angels.
Sarafina, Seraphe, Seraphin, Seraphina, Seraphita, Serapia, Serofina
Foreign forms: English: **Serafine, Seraphine**

Serena (Latin) peaceful. See also Rena.
Sarina, Saryna, Sereena, Serenah, Serene, Serenity, Serenna, Serina, Serrena, Serrin, Serrina, Seryna

Sevilla (Spanish) from Seville.
Seville

Shada (Native American) pelican.
Shadae, Shadea, Shadeana, Shadee, Shadi, Shadia, Shadiah, Shadie, Shadiya, Shaida, Shaiday

Shadrika (American) a combination of the prefix Sha + Rika.
Shadreka, Shadrica, Shadricka

Shae (Irish) an alternate form of Shea.
Shaeen, Shaeine, Shaela, Shaelea, Shaelee, Shaeleigh, Shaelie, Shaely, Shaelyn, Shaena, Shaenel, Shaeya, Shaia

Shaelyn (Irish) an alternate form of Shea.
Shaeleen, Shaelene, Shaelin, Shaeline, Shaelynn, Shaelynne

Shafira (Swahili) distinguished.

Shahar (Arabic) moonlit.
Shahara, Shahira

Shahina (Arabic) falcon.
Shaheen, Shaheena, Shahi, Shahin

Shahla (Afghani) beautiful eyes.
Shaila, Shailah, Shalah

Shaina (Yiddish) beautiful.
Shaena, Shainah, Shaine, Shainna, Shajna, Shanie, Shayna, Shayndel, Sheina, Sheindel

Shajuana (American) a combination of the prefix Sha + Juanita. See also Shawanna.
Shajuan, Shajuanda, Shajuanita, Shajuanna, Shajuanza

Shaka (Hindi) an alternate form of Shakti. A short form of names beginning with "Shak." See also Chaka.
Shakah, Shakha, Shikah, Shikha

Shakarah (American) a combination of the prefix Sha + Kara.
Shacara, Shacari, Shaccara, Shaka, Shakari, Shakkara, Shikara

Shakeena (American) a combination of the prefix Sha + Keena.
Shaka, Shakeina, Shakeyna, Shakina, Shakyna

Shakeita (American) a combination of the prefix Sha + Keita. See also Shaqueita.
Shaka, Shakeeta, Shakeitha, Shakeithia, Shaketa, Shaketha, Shakethia, Shaketia, Shakita, Shakitra, Sheketa, Shekita, Shikita, Shikitha

Shakia (American) a combination of the prefix Sha + Kia.
Shakeeia, Shakeeyah, Shakeia, Shakeya, Shakiya, Shekeia, Shekia, Shekiah, Shikia

Shakila (Arabic) pretty.
Shaka, Shakeela, Shakeena, Shakela, Shakilah, Shekila, Shekilla, Shikeela
Foreign forms: *American:*
Shaquilla, Shequela, Shequele

Shakira (Arabic) thankful. A feminine form of Shakir.
Shaakira, Shaka, Shakera, Shakerah, Shakeria, Shakeriay, Shakeyra, Shakir, Shakirah, Shakirat, Shakirra, Shakyra, Shekiera, Shekira, Shikira

Shakti (Hindi) divine woman. Religion: the Hindu goddess who controls time and destruction.
Sakti, Shaka, Sita

Shalana (American) a combination of the prefix Sha + Lana.
Shalaina, Shalaine, Shaland, Shalanda, Shalane, Shalann, Shalaun, Shalauna, Shallan, Shalyn, Shalyne, Shelan, Shelanda

Shaleah (American) a combination of the prefix Sha + Leah.
Shalea, Shalee, Shaleea

Shaleisha (American) a combination of the prefix Sha + Aisha.
Shalesha, Shalesia, Shalicia, Shalisha

Shalena (American) a combination of the prefix Sha + Lena.
Shaleana, Shaleen, Shalen, Shálena, Shalene, Shalené, Shalenna, Shelayna, Shelayne, Shelena

Shalisa (American) a combination of the prefix Sha + Lisa.
Shalesa, Shalese, Shalice, Shalise, Shalisia, Shalisse, Shalys, Shalyse

Shalita (American) a combination of the prefix Sha + Lita.
Shaleta, Shaletta, Shalida, Shalitta

Shalonda (American) a combination of the prefix Sha + Ondine.
Shalonde, Shalondine

Shalona (American) a combination of the prefix Sha + Lona.
Shálonna, Shalonne

Shalyn (American) a combination of the prefix Sha + Lynn.
Shalin, Shalina, Shalinda, Shaline, Shalyna, Shalynda, Shalynn, Shalynne

Shamara (Arabic) ready for battle.
Shamar, Shamarah, Shamari, Shamaria, Shamarra, Shamarri, Shammara, Shamora, Shamorra, Shamorria

Shameka (American) a combination of the prefix Sha + Meka.
Shameca, Shamecca, Shamecha, Shameeka, Shameika, Shameke, Shamekia

Shamika (American) a combination of the prefix Sha + Mika.
Shamica, Shamicia, Shamicka, Shamieka, Shamikia

Shamira (Hebrew) precious stone. A feminine form of Shamir.
Shamir, Shamiran, Shamiria

Shana (Hebrew) God is gracious. (Irish) a form of Jane.
Shaana, Shan, Shanae, Shanay, Shane, Shanna, Shannah, Shauna, Shawna
Foreign forms: American: **Shanda**; English: **Shandi**

Shanae (Irish) an alternate form of Shana.
Shanea

Shanda (American) a form of Chanda, Shana.
Shandah

Shandi (English) a familiar form of Shana.
Shandee, Shandeigh, Shandey, Shandi, Shandice, Shandie

Shandra (American) an alternate form of Shanda. See also Chandra.
Shandrea, Shandreka, Shandri, Shandria, Shandriah, Shandrice, Shandrie, Shandry

Shane (Irish) an alternate form of Shana.
Shanea, Shanee, Shanée, Shanie

Shaneisha (American) a combination of the prefix Sha + Aisha.
Shanesha, Shaneshia, Shanessa, Shanisha, Shanissha

Shaneka (American) an alternate form of Shanika.
Shanecka, Shaneikah, Shanekia, Shanequa, Shaneyka

Shanel, Shanell, Shanelle (American) forms of Chanel.
Schanel, Schanell, Shanella, Shannel, Shenel, Shenela, Shenell, Shenelle, Shonelle, Shynelle

Shaneta (American) a combination of the prefix Sha + Neta.
Shaneeta, Shanetha, Shanethis, Shanetta, Shanette

Shani (Swahili) marvelous.

Shanika (American) a combination of the prefix Sha + Nika.
Shanica, Shanicca, Shanicka, Shanieka, Shanike, Shanikia, Shanikka, Shanikqua, Shanikwa, Shaniqua, Shanique, Shenika

Shanita (American) a combination of the prefix Sha + Nita.
Shanitha, Shanitra, Shanitta

Shanley (Irish) hero's child.
Shanlee, Shanleigh, Shanlie, Shanly

Shanna (Irish) an alternate form of Shana, Shannon.
Shanea, Shannah, Shannda, Shannea

Shannon (Irish) small and wise.
Shanan, Shann, Shanna, Shannan, Shanneen, Shannen, Shannie, Shannin, Shannyn, Shanon

Shanta, Shantae, Shante (French) alternate forms of Chantal.
Shantai, Shantay, Shantaya, Shantaye, Shantea, Shantee, Shantée

Shantara (American) a combination of the prefix Sha + Tara.
Shantaria, Shantarra, Shantera, Shanteria, Shanterra, Shantieria, Shantira, Shantirea

Shanteca (American) a combination of the prefix Sha + Teca.
Shantecca, Shanteka, Shantika, Shantikia

Shantel, Shantell (American) song. Forms of Chantel.
Shanntell, Shanta, Shantal, Shantae, Shantale, Shante, Shanteal, Shanteil, Shantele, Shantella, Shantelle, Shantrell, Shantyl, Shantyle, Shauntel, Shauntell, Shauntelle, Shauntrel, Shauntrell, Shauntrella, Shentel, Shentelle, Shontal, Shontalla, Shontalle

Shantesa (American) a combination of the prefix Sha + Tess.
Shantese, Shantice, Shantise, Shantisha

Shantia (American) a combination of the prefix Sha + Tia.
Shanteya, Shanti, Shantida, Shantie, Shaunteya, Shauntia

Shantina (American) a combination of the prefix Sha + Tina.
Shanteena

Shantora (American) a combination of the prefix Sha + Tory.
Shantoia, Shantori, Shantoria, Shantory, Shantorya, Shantoya, Shanttoria

Shaquanda (American) a combination of the prefix Sha + Wanda.
Shaquan, Shaquana, Shaquand, Shaquandra, Shaquanera, Shaquani, Shaquanna, Shaquantia, Shaquonda

Shaqueita (American) an alternate form of Shakeita.
Shaqueta, Shaquetta, Shaquita, Shequida, Shequita, Shequittia

Shara (Hebrew) a short form of Sharon.
Shaara, Sharal, Sharala, Sharalee, Sharlyn, Sharlynn, Sharra

Sharai (Hebrew) princess. An alternate form of Sarah. See also Sharon.
Sharae, Sharaé, Sharah, Sharaiah, Sharay, Sharaya

Sharan (Hindi) protector.
Sharaine, Sharanda, Sharanjeet

Shardae, Sharday (Punjabi) charity. (Yoruba) honored by royalty. (Arabic) runaway. An alternate form of Chardae.
Sade, Shadae, Sharda, Shar-Dae, Shardai, Shar-Day, Sharde, Shardea, Shardee, Shardée, Shardei, Shardeia, Shardey

Sharee (English) a form of Shari.
Shareen, Shareena, Sharine

Shari (French) beloved, dearest. An alternate form of Cheri. (Hungarian) a form of Sarah. See also Sharita, Sheree, Sherry.
Shara, Sharian, Shariann, Sharianne, Sharie, Sharra, Sharree, Sharrie, Sharry, Shary
Foreign form: English: Sharee

Sharice (French) an alternate form of Cherise.
Shareese, Sharese, Sharica, Sharicka, Shariece, Sharis, Sharise, Shariss, Sharisse
Foreign forms: American: Sharesa, Sharissa, Sharisha, Shereeza

Sharik (African) child of God.

Sharita (French) a familiar form of Shari. (American) a form of Charity. See also Sherita.
Shareeta, Sharrita

Sharla (French) a short form of Sharlene, Sharlotte.

Sharlene (French) little and womanly. A form of Charlene.
Scharlane, Scharlene, Shar, Sharla, Sharlaina, Sharlaine, Sharlane, Sharlanna, Sharlee, Sharleen, Sharleine, Sharlena, Sharleyne, Sharline, Sharlyn, Sharlynn, Sharlynne, Sherlean, Sherleen, Sherlene, Sherline

Sharna (Hebrew) an alternate form of Sharon.
Sharnae, Sharnay, Sharne, Sharnea, Sharnease, Sharnee, Sharneese, Sharnell, Sharnelle, Sharnese, Sharnett, Sharnetta, Sharnise

Sharon (Hebrew) desert plain. An alternate form of Sharai.
Shaaron, Shara, Sharai, Sharan, Shareen, Sharen, Shari, Sharin, Sharna, Sharonda, Sharran, Sharren, Sharrin, Sharron, Sharrona, Sharyn, Sharyon, Sheren, Sheron, Sherryn

Sharonda (Hebrew) an alternate form of Sharon.
Sharronda, Sheronda, Sherrhonda

Sharrona (Hebrew) an alternate form of Sharon.
Sharona, Sharone, Sharonia, Sharony, Sharronne, Sheron, Sherona, Sheronna, Sherron, Sherronna, Sherronne, Shirona

Shatara (Hindi) umbrella. (Arabic) good; industrious. (American) a combination of Sharon + Tara.
Shataria, Shatarra, Shataura, Shateira, Shaterah, Shateria, Shatherian, Shatierra, Shatiria

Shatoria (American) a combination of the prefix Sha + Tory.
Shatora, Shatorria, Shatorya, Shatoya

Shauna (Hebrew) God is gracious. (Irish) an alternate form of Shana.
Shaun, Shaunah, Shaune, Shaunee, Shauneen, Shaunelle, Shaunette, Shauni, Shaunice, Shaunicy, Shaunie, Shaunika, Shaunisha, Shaunna, Shaunnea, Shaunua, Shaunya

Shaunda (Irish) an alternate form of Shauna. See also Shanda, Shawnda, Shonda.
Shaundal, Shaundala, Shaundel, Shaundela, Shaundell, Shaundelle, Shaundra, Shaundrea, Shaundree, Shaundria, Shaundrice

Shaunta (Irish) an alternate form of Shauna. See also Shawnta.
Schunta, Shauntae, Shauntay, Shaunte, Shauntea, Shauntee, Shauntée, Shaunteena, Shauntei, Shauntia, Shauntier, Shauntrel, Shauntrell, Shauntrella

Shavonne (American) a combination of the prefix Sha + Yvonne. See also Siobhahn.
Schavon, Schevon, Shavan, Shavana, Shavanna, Shavaun, Shavon, Shavonda, Shavondra, Shavone, Shavonn, Shavonna, Shavonni, Shavontae, Shavonte, Shavonté, Shavoun, Shivani, Shivaun, Shivawn, Shivonne, Shyvon, Shyvonne

Shawanna (American) a combination of the prefix Sha + Wanda. See also Shawna.
Shawana, Shawanda, Shawante

Shawna (Hebrew) God is gracious. (Irish) a form of Jane. An alternate form of Shana, Shauna.
Sawna, Shawn, Shawnai, Shawnaka, Shawne, Shawnee, Shawneen, Shawneena, Shawnequa, Shawneika, Shawnell, Shawnette, Shawni, Shawnicka, Shawnie, Shawnika, Shawnna, Shawnra, Sheona, Siân, Siana, Sianna

Shawnda (Irish) an alternate form of Shawna. See also Shanda, Shaunda, Shonda.
Shawndai, Shawndala, Shawndan, Shawndel, Shawndra, Shawndrea, Shawndree, Shawndreel, Shawndrell, Shawndria

Shawnta (Irish) an alternate form of Shawna. See also Shaunta, Shonta.
Shawntae, Shawntay, Shawnte, Shawnté, Shawntee, Shawntell, Shawntelle, Shawnteria, Shawntia, Shawntil, Shawntile, Shawntill, Shawntille, Shawntina, Shawntish, Shawntrese, Shawntriece

Shay (Irish) an alternate form of Shea.

Shaya, Shayda, Shaye, Shayha, Shayia, Shey, Sheye

Shayla (Irish) an alternate form of Shay.
Shay, Shaylagh, Shaylah, Shaylain, Shaylan, Shaylea, Shaylee, Shayley, Shayli, Shaylie, Shaylin, Shaylla, Shayly, Shaylyn, Shaylynn, Sheyla, Sheylyn

Shayna (Hebrew) beautiful. A form of Shaina.
Shaynae, Shayne, Shaynee, Shayney, Shayni, Shaynie, Shayny

Shea (Irish) fairy palace.
Shae, Shay, Shealy, Shealyn, Sheana, Sheann, Sheanna, Sheannon, Sheanta, Sheaon, Shearra, Sheatara, Sheaunna, Sheavon

Sheba (Hebrew) a short form of Bathsheba. Geography: an ancient country of South Arabia.
Sabah, Shebah, Sheeba
Foreign form: Greek: Saba

Sheena (Hebrew) God is gracious. (Irish) a form of Jane.
Sheenagh, Sheenah, Sheenan, Sheeneal, Sheenika, Sheenna, Sheina, Shena, Shiona

Sheila (Latin) blind. (Irish) a form of Cecelia.
Seelia, Seila, Selia, Shaylah, Sheela, Sheelagh, Sheelah, Sheilagh, Sheilah, Sheileen, Sheiletta, Sheilia, Sheillynn, Sheilya, Shela, Shelagh, Shelah, Shelia, Shiela, Shila, Shilah, Shilea, Shyla
Foreign form: Basque: Zelizi

Shelby (English) ledge estate.
Schelby, Shel, Shelbe, Shelbee, Shelbey, Shelbi, Shelbie, Shellby

Shelee (English) an alternate form of Shelley.
Shelee, Sheleen, Shelena, Sheley, Sheleza, Sheli, Shelia, Shelica, Shelicia, Shelina, Shelinda, Shelisa, Shelise, Shelisse, Shelita, Sheliza

Shelley, Shelly (English) meadow on the ledge. (French) a familiar form of Michelle.
Shelee, Shell, Shella, Shellaine, Shellana, Shellany, Shellee, Shellene, Shelli, Shellian, Shellie, Shellina

Shena (Irish) an alternate form of Sheena.
Shenada, Shenae, Shenay, Shenda, Shene, Shenea, Sheneda, Shenee, Sheneena,

Shena *(cont.)*
Shenica, Shenika, Shenina, Sheniqua, Shenita, Shenna

Shera (Aramaic) light.
Sheera, Sheerah, Sherae, Sherah, Sheralee, Sheralle, Sheralyn, Sheralynn, Sheralynne, Sheray, Sheraya

Sheree (French) beloved, dearest. An alternate form of Shari.
Scherie, Sheeree, Shere, Shereé, Sherrelle, Shereen, Shereena

Sherelle (French) an alternate form of Cherelle, Sheryl.
Sherrell

Sheri, Sherri (French) alternate forms of Sherry.
Sheria, Sheriah, Sherian, Sherianne, Shericia, Sherie, Sheriel, Sherrie, Sherrina

Sherice (French) an alternate form of Sherry.
Scherise, Sherece, Shereece, Sherees, Shereese, Sherese, Shericia, Sherise, Sherisse, Sherrish, Sherryse, Sheryce

Sherika (Punjabi) relative. (Arabic) easterner.
Shereka, Sherica, Shericka, Sherrica, Sherricka, Sherrika

Sherissa (French) a form of Sherry, Sheryl.
Shereeza, Sheresa, Shericia, Sherrish

Sherita (French) a form of Sherry, Sheryl. See also Sharita.
Shereta, Sheretta, Sherette, Sherrita

Sherleen (French, English) an alternate form of Sheryl, Shirley.
Sherileen, Sherlene, Sherline

Sherry (French) beloved, dearest. An alternate form of Shari. A familiar form of Sheryl. See also Sheree.
Sherey, Sheri, Sherissa, Sherrey, Sherri, Sherria, Sherriah, Sherrie, Sherye, Sheryy

Sheryl (French) beloved. An alternate form of Cheryl. A familiar form of Shirley. See also Sherry.
Sharel, Sharil, Sharilyn, Sharyl, Sharyll, Sheral, Sherell, Sheriel, Sheril, Sherill, Sherily, Sherilyn, Sherissa, Sherita, Sherleen, Sherral, Sherrel, Sherrell, Sherrelle, Sherril, Sherrill, Sherryl, Sherylly

Sherylyn (American) a combination of Sheryl + Lynn. See also Cherilyn.
Sharlyne, Sharolin, Sharolyn, Sharyl-Lynn, Sheralyn, Sherilyn, Sherilynn, Sherilynne, Sherralyn, Sherralynn, Sherrilyn, Sherrilynn, Sherrilynne, Sherrylyn, Sherryn, Sherylanne

Shevonne (American) a combination of the prefix She + Yvonne.
Shevaun, Shevon, Shevonda, Shevone

Sheyenne (Cheyenne) an alternate form of Cheyenne.
Sheyen, Shi, Shiana, Shianda, Shiana, Shiane, Shiann, Shianna, Shianne, Shiante, Shyan, Shyana, Shyann, Shyanne, Shye, Shyenna

Shifra (Hebrew) beautiful.
Schifra, Shifrah

Shika (Japanese) gentle deer.
Shi

Shilo (Hebrew) God's gift. Geography: a site near Jerusalem. Bible: a sanctuary for the Israelites where the Ark of the Covenant was kept.
Shiloh

Shina (Japanese) virtuous; wealthy. (Chinese) an alternate form of China.
Shine, Shineeca, Shineese, Shinelle, Shinequa, Shineta, Shiniqua, Shinita, Shiona

Shino (Japanese) bamboo stalk.

Shira (Hebrew) song.
Shirah, Shiray, Shire, Shiree, Shiri, Shirit

Shirlene (English) an alternate form of Shirley.
Shirleen, Shirline, Shirlynn

Shirley (English) bright meadow. See also Sheryl.
Sherlee, Sherleen, Sherley, Sherli, Sherlie, Shir, Shirelle, Shirl, Shirlee, Shirlena, Shirlene, Shirlie, Shirlina, Shirly, Shirlyn, Shirlly, Shurlee, Shurley

Shizu (Japanese) silent.
Shizue, Shizuka, Shizuko, Shizuyo

Shona (Irish) a form of Jane. An alternate form of Shana, Shauna, Shawna.
Shonagh, Shonah, Shonalee, Shonda, Shone, Shonee, Shonelle, Shonetta, Shonette, Shoni, Shonna, Shonneka, Shonnika, Shonta

Shonda (Irish) an alternate form of Shona. See also Shanda, Shaunda, Shawnda.
Shondalette, Shondalyn, Shondel, Shondelle, Shondi, Shondia, Shondie, Shondra, Shondreka, Shounda

Shonta (Irish) an alternate form of Shona. See also Shaunta, Shawnta.
Shontá, Shontae, Shontai, Shontal, Shontalea, Shontara, Shontasia, Shontavia, Shontaviea, Shontay, Shontaya, Shonte, Shonté, Shontecia, Shontedra, Shontee, Shontel, Shontelle, Shonteral, Shonteria, Shontessia, Shonti, Shontia, Shontina, Shontol, Shontoy, Shontrail, Shontrice, Shountáe

Shoshana (Hebrew) lily. An alternate form of Susan.
Shosha, Shoshan, Shoshanah, Shoshane, Shoshanha, Shoshann, Shoshanna, Shoshannah, Shoshauna, Shoushan, Sosha, Soshana

Shu (Chinese) kind, gentle.

Shula (Arabic) flaming, bright.
Shulah

Shulamith (Hebrew) peaceful. See also Sula.
Shulamit, Sulamith

Shunta (Irish) an alternate form of Shonta.
Shuntae, Shunté, Shuntel, Shuntia

Shyla (English) an alternate form of Sheila.

Sibley (Greek) an alternate form of Sybil. (English) sibling; friendly.
Sybley

Sidonia (Hebrew) enticing.

Sidonie (French) from Saint Denis, France. Geography: an ancient Phoenician city. See also Sydney.
Sidaine, Sidanni, Sidelle, Sidney, Sidoine, Sidona, Sidonia, Sidony

Sierra (Irish) black. (Spanish) saw toothed. Geography: a rugged range of mountains that, when viewed from a distance, has a jagged profile. See also Ciara.
Seara, Searria, Seera, Seiarra, Seira, Seirra, Siara, Siarah, Siarra, Sieara, Siearra, Siera, Sieria, Sierrah, Sierre

Sigfreda (German) victorious peace. See also Freda.
Sigfreida, Sigfrida, Sigfrieda, Sigfryda

Signe (Latin) sign, signal. (Scandinavian) a short form of Sigourney.
Sig, Signa, Signy, Singna, Singne

Sigourney (English) victorious conquerer.
Sigourny, Sigrun
Foreign form: *Scandinavian:* **Signe**

Sigrid (Scandinavian) victorious counselor.
Siegrid, Siegrida, Sigridur, Sigritt

Siko (African) crying baby.

Silvia (Latin) an alternate form of Sylvia.
Silivia, Silva, Silvaine, Silvanna, Silvi, Silviane, Silva, Silvy

Simcha (Hebrew) joyful.

Simone (Hebrew) she heard. (French) a feminine form of Simon.
Siminie, Simmi, Simmie, Simmona, Simmone, Simoane, Simona, Simonetta,
Simonette, Simonia, Simonina, Simonne, Somone, Symona, Symone

Siobhan (Irish) a form of Joan. See also Shavonne.
Shibahn, Shibani, Shibhan, Shioban, Shobana, Shobha, Shobhana, Siobahn, Siobhana, Siobhann, Siobhon, Siovaun, Siovhan

Sirena (Greek) enchanter. Mythology: sirens were half-woman, half-bird creatures whose singing so enchanted sailors, they crashed their ships into nearby rocks.
Sireena, Sirene, Sirine, Syrena, Syrenia, Syrenna, Syrina

Sita (Hindi) an alternate form of Shakti.
Sitah, Sitarah, Sitha, Sithara

Siti (Swahili) respected woman.

Skye (Arabic) water giver. (Dutch) a short form of Skyler. Geography: an island in the Hebrides, Scotland.
Sky

Skyler (Dutch) sheltering.
Schuyla, Schuyler, Schuylia, Schyler, Skila, Skilah, Skye, Skyla, Skylar, Skylee, Skylena, Skyllar, Skylynn, Skyra

Sloane (Irish) warrior.
Sloan

Socorro (Spanish) helper.

Sofia (Greek) an alternate form of Sophia.
Sofeea, Sofeeia, Soffi, Sofie, Sofija
Foreign forms: *German:* **Sofi;** *Russian:* **Sofiya;** *Spanish:* **Chofa, Soficita;** *Turkish:* **Sofya**

Solana (Spanish) sunshine.
Solande, Solanna, Soleil, Solena, Solene, Soléne, Soley, Solina, Solinda

Solange (French) dignified.

Soledad (Spanish) solitary.
Sole, Soleda

Solenne (French) solemn, dignified.
Solaine, Solène, Solenna, Solina, Soline, Solonez, Souline, Soulle

Soma (Hindi) lunar. Astrological: born under the sign of Cancer.

Sommer (English) summer; summoner. (Arabic) black. See also Summer.
Sommar, Sommara

Sondra (Greek) defender of mankind. A short form of Alexandra.
Saundra, Sondre, Sonndra, Sonndre

Sonia (Russian, Slavic) an alternate form of Sonya.
Sonica, Sonida, Sonita, Sonni, Sonnie, Sonny

Sonja (Scandinavian) a form of Sonya.
Sonjae, Sonjia

Sonya (Greek) wise. (Russian, Slavic) a form of Sophia.
Sonia, Sunya
Foreign form: Scandinavian: Sonja

Sophia (Greek) wise.
Sofia, Sophie, Sophronia
Foreign forms: Hungarian: Zsofi, Zsofia; Russian: Sonya; Slavic: Sofka, Zofia, Zofka

Sophie (Greek) a familiar form of Sophia.
Sophey, Sophi
Foreign forms: English: Sophy; Polish: Zocha

Sora (Native American) chirping songbird.

Soraya (Persian) princess.
Suraya

Sorrel (French) reddish brown. Botany: a wild herb.

Soso (Native American) tree squirrel dining on pine nuts; chubby-cheeked baby.

Souzan (Persian) burning fire.

Spring (English) springtime.

Stacey, Stacy (Greek) resurrection. (Irish) a short form of Anastasia, Eustacia, Natasha.
Stace, Stacee, Staceyan, Staceyann, Staicy, Stayce, Staycee
Foreign forms: Czech: Stasa; English: Staci; Russian: Stasya

Staci (Greek) an alternate form of Stacey.
Stacci, Stacia, Stacie, Stayci

Stacia (English) a short form of Anastasia.
Stasia, Stasya, Staysha

Starleen (English) an alternate form of Starr.
Starleena, Starlena, Starlene, Starlin, Starlyn, Starlynn, Starrlen

Starling (English) bird.

Starr (English) star.
Star, Staria, Starisha, Starla, Starle, Starlee, Starleen,

Starlet, Starlette, Starley, Starlight, Starly, Starri, Starria, Starrika, Starrsha, Starsha, Starshanna, Starskysha, Startish

Stasya (Greek) a familiar form of Anastasia. (Russian) a form of Stacey.
Stasa, Stasha, Stashia, Stasia, Stasja, Staska

Stefanie (Greek) an alternate form of Stephanie.
Stafani, Stafanie, Staffany, Stefaney, Stefani, Stefania, Stefanié, Stefanija, Stefannie, Stefany, Stefcia, Stefenie, Steffane, Steffani, Steffanie, Steffany, Steffi
Foreign forms: Czech/Polish: Stefka; English: Stefa

Steffi (Greek) a familiar form of Stefanie, Stephanie.
Stefa, Stefcia, Steffie, Stefi, Stefka, Stepha, Stephi, Stephie, Stephy

Stella (Latin) star. (French) a familiar form of Estelle.
Steile, Stellina

Stephanie (Greek) crowned. A feminine form of Stephan. See also Stevie, Zephania.
Stamata, Stamatios, Stefanie, Steffie, Stephaija, Stephaine,

Stephanie *(cont.)*
Stephanas, Stephane,
Stephanee, Stephaney,
Stephani, Stephanine,
Stephann, Stephannie,
Stephany, Stephene,
Stephenie, Stephianie,
Stephney, Stevanee
Foreign forms: English:
Stephana; French: **Stéphanie;**
Russian: **Panya, Stepania,**
Stepanida, Stephania, Stesha,
Steshka

Stephene (Greek) an alternate
form of Stephanie.
Stephina, Stephine, Stephyne

Stephenie (Greek) an alternate
form of Stephanie.
Stephena

Stephney (Greek) an alternate
form of Stephanie.
Stephne, Stephni, Stephnie,
Stephny

Stevie (Greek) a familiar form
of Stephanie.
Steva, Stevana, Stevanee,
Stevee, Stevena, Stevey, Stevi,
Stevy, Stevye

Stockard (English) stockyard.

Stormy (English) impetuous by
nature.
Storm, Storme, Stormi,
Stormie

Sue (Hebrew) a short form
of Susan, Susanna.
Suann, Suanna, Suanne,
Sueanne, Suetta

Suela (Spanish) consolation.
Suelita

Sugar (American) sweet as
sugar.
Shug

Suki (Japanese) loved one.
(Moquelumnan) eagle eyed.
Sukie

Sula (Greek, Hebrew) a short
form of Shulamith, Ursula.
(Icelandic) large seabird.

Sulia (Latin) an alternate form
of Julia.
Suliana

Sumi (Japanese) elegant,
refined.
Sumiko

Summer (English) summer-
time. See also Sommer.
Sumer, Summar,
Summerbreeze, Summerhaze,
Summerlee

Sun (Korean) obedient.
Suncance, Sunday, Sundee,
Sundeep, Sundi, Sundip,
Sundrenea, Sunta, Sunya

Sunee (Thai) good.
Suni

Sun-Hi (Korean) good; joyful.

Suni (Zuni) native; member of
our tribe.
Sunita, Sunitha, Suniti,
Sunne, Sunni, Sunnie, Sunnilei

Sunny (English) bright, cheerful.
Sunni, Sunnie

Sunshine (English) sunshine.

Suri (Todas) pointy nose.
Suree, Surena, Surenia

Surya (Pakistani) sun god.
Surra

Susan (Hebrew) lily. See also
Shoshana.
Sawsan, Sosana, Sue, Suesan,
Sueva, Suisan, Susann,
Susanna, Susen, Suson, Sussi,
Suzan, Suzane, Suzzane
Foreign forms: American: **Susie;**
Czech/Polish: **Zusa;** English:
Suzanne; French: **Susanne,**
Susette, Suzette; Hawaiian: **Suke,**
Sukey, Suse; Hungarian: **Zsa Zsa;**
Irish: **Sosanna;** Scottish: **Siusan**

Susanna, Susannah (Hebrew)
alternate forms of Susan.
Sonel, Sue, Suesanna,

Susanah, Susanka, Suzana, Suzanna
Foreign forms: *American:* **Susie;** *Brazilian:* **Xuxa;** *English:* **Zanna;** *French:* **Susette;** *Hungarian:* **Zsuzsa, Zsuzsanna;** *Spanish:* **Susana**

Susie (American) a familiar form of Susan, Susanna.
Suse, Susey, Susi, Sussy, Susy, Suze, Suzi, Suzie, Suzy

Suzanne (English) a form of Susan.
Susanne, Suszanne, Suzane, Suzann, Suzzann, Suzzanne

Suzette (French) a form of Susan.
Susetta, Susette, Suzetta

Suzu (Japanese) little bell.
Suzue, Suzuko

Suzuki (Japanese) bell tree.

Svetlana (Russian) bright light.
Sveta, Svetochka

Sybil (Greek) prophet. Mythology: sibyls were oracles who relayed the messages of the gods. See also Cybele, Sibley.
Sebila, Sibbel, Sibbella, Sibbie, Sibbill, Sibel, Sibilla, Sibyl, Sibylline, Sybila, Sybilla, Sybille, Syble

Foreign forms: *Dutch:* **Sibylla;** *English:* **Sib, Sibby, Sybella;** *French:* **Sibylle;** *Irish:* **Sibeal**

Sydney (French) from Saint Denis, France. A feminine form of Sidney. See also Sidonie.
Sy, Syd, Sydania, Sydel, Sydelle, Sydna, Sydnee, Sydni, Sydnie, Sydny, Sydnye, Syndona, Syndonah, Syndonia

Sylvana (Latin) forest.
Sylva, Sylvaine, Sylvanna, Sylvi, Sylvie, Sylvina, Sylvinnia, Sylvonna

Sylvia (Latin) forest. Literature: Sylvia Plath was a well-known American writer and poet. See also Silvia.
Sylvana, Sylvette, Sylwia
Foreign forms: *French:* **Sylvie;** *Greek:* **Xylia**

Syreeta (Hindi) good traditions. (Arabic) companion.

Tabatha (Greek, Aramaic) an alternate form of Tabitha.
Tabathe, Tabathia, Tabbatha

Tabby (English) a familiar form of Tabitha.
Tabbee, Tabbey, Tabbi, Tabbie

Tabia (Swahili) talented.

Tabina (Arabic) follower of Muhammed.

Tabitha (Greek, Aramaic) gazelle.
Tabatha, Tabbetha, Tabbitha, Tabetha, Tabithia, Tabotha, Tabtha, Tabytha
Foreign form: *English:* **Tabby**

Taci (Zuni) washtub.
Tacia, Taciana, Tacie

Tacita (Latin) silent.
Tace, Tacy, Tacye
Foreign forms: English: **Tacey, Taci**

Tadita (Omaha) runner.
Tadeta, Tadra

Taesha (Latin) an alternate form of Tisha. (American) a combination of the prefix Ta + Aisha.
Taheisha, Tahisha, Taiesha, Taisha, Taishae, Teisha, Tesha, Tyeisha, Tyeishia, Tyeshia, Tyeyshia, Tyieshia, Tyishia

Taffy (Welsh) beloved.
Taffia, Taffine, Taffye, Tafia, Tafisa, Tafoya

Tahira (Arabic) virginal, pure.
Taheera, Taheria

Taima (Native American) loud thunder.
Taimy

Taite (English) cheerful.
Tate, Tayte

Taja (Hindi) crown.
Taiajára, Taija, Teja, Tejah, Tejal

Taka (Japanese) honored.

Takala (Hopi) corn tassel.

Takara (Japanese) treasure.
Takra

Takeisha (American) a combination of the prefix Ta + Keisha.
Takecia, Takesha, Takeshia, Takesia, Takisha, Takishea, Takishia, Tekeesha, Tekeisha, Tekeshi, Tekeysia, Tekisha, Tikesha, Tikisha, Tokesia, Tykeisha, Tykeshia, Tykeza, Tykisha

Takenya (Hebrew) animal horn. (Moquelumnan) falcon. (American) a combination of the prefix Ta + Kenya.
Takenia, Takenja

Taki (Japanese) waterfall.
Tiki

Takia (Arabic) worshiper.
Takeiyah, Takeya, Takija, Takiya, Takiyah, Takkia, Taqiyya, Taquaia, Taquaya, Taquiia, Tekeyia, Tekiya, Tikia, Tykeia, Tykia

Takira (American) a combination of the prefix Ta + Kira.
Takara, Takarra, Takeara, Takiria, Taquera, Taquira, Tekeria, Tikara, Tikira, Tykera, Tykira

Tala (Native American) stalking wolf.

Talasi (Hopi) corn tassel.
Talasea, Talasia

Taleah (American) a combination of the prefix Ta + Leah.
Talaya, Talea, Taleéi, Talei, Talia, Tylea, Tylee

Taleisha (American) a combination of the prefix Ta + Aisha.
Taileisha, Taleesha, Taleise, Talesa, Talesha, Taleshia, Talesia, Talicia, Taliesha, Talisa, Talisha, Tallese, Tallesia, Talysha, Teleisia, Teleshia, Telesia, Telicia, Telisa, Telisha, Telishia, Tellisa, Telsa, Tilisha, Tyleasha, Tyleisha, Tylicia, Tylisha, Tylishia

Talena (American) a combination of the prefix Ta + Lena.
Talayna, Talihna, Talin, Talina, Talinda, Taline, Tallenia, Talná, Tilena, Tilene, Tylena, Tylina, Tyline

Talia (Greek) blooming. (Hebrew) dew from heaven. (Latin, French) birthday. A short form of Natalie, Taleah. See also Thalia.
Tahlia, Tali, Taliah, Talieya, Taliya, Talley, Tallia, Tallie,

Tally, Tallya, Talya, Talyah, Tylia

Talitha (Arabic) young girl.
Taleetha, Taletha, Talethia, Taliatha, Talita, Talithia, Telita, Tiletha

Tallis (French, English) forest.
Tallys

Tallulah (Choctaw) leaping water.
Talley, Tallie, Tallou, Tally, Talula

Tam (Vietnamese) heart.

Tama (Japanese) jewel.
Tamaa, Tamah, Tamaiah, Tamala

Tamaka (Japanese) bracelet.
Tamaki, Tamako, Timaka

Tamar (Hebrew) a short form of Tamara. (Russian) History: Tamar was a twelfth-century Georgian queen.
Tamer, Tamor, Tamour

Tamara (Hebrew) palm tree. See also Tammy.
Tamar, Tamará, Tamarah, Tamaria, Tamarin, Tamarla, Tamarra, Tamarria, Tamarrian, Tamarsha, Tamary, Tamer, Tamera, Tamerai, Tameria, Tameriás,

Tamma, Tammara, Tammera, Tamora, Tamoya, Tamra, Tamura, Tamyra, Temara, Temarian, Thama, Thamar, Thamara, Thamarra, Thamer, Timara, Timera, Tomara, Tymara

Tamassa (Hebrew) an alternate form of Thomasina.
Tamasin, Tamasine, Tamsen, Tamsin, Tamzen, Tamzin

Tameka (Aramaic) twin.
Tameca, Tamecia, Tamecka, Tameeka, Tamekia, Tamiecka, Tamieka, Temeka, Timeeka, Timeka, Tomeka, Tomekia, Trameika, Tymeka, Tymmeeka, Tymmeka

Tamesha (American) a combination of the prefix Ta + Mesha.
Tameshia, Tameshkia, Tamisha, Tamishia, Tamnesha, Temisha, Timesha, Timisha, Tomesha, Tomiese, Tomise, Tomisha, Tramesha, Tramisha, Tymesha

Tamiko (Japanese) child of the people.
Tami, Tamica, Tamieka, Tamika, Tamike, Tamikia, Tamikka, Tamiqua, Tamiyo, Timika, Timikia, Tomika, Tymika, Tymmicka

Tamila (American) a combination of the prefix Ta + Mila.
Tamala, Tamela, Tamelia, Tamilla, Tamille, Tamillia, Tamilya

Tammi, Tammie (English) alternate forms of Tammy.
Tameia, Tamia, Tamiah, Tamie, Tamijo, Tamiya

Tammy (Hebrew) a familiar form of Tamara. (English) twin.
Tamilyn, Tamlyn, Tammee, Tammey, Tammi, Tammie, Tamy, Tamya

Tamra (Hebrew) a short form of Tamara.
Tammra, Tamrah

Tana (Slavic) a short form of Tanya.
Taina, Tanae, Tanaeah, Tanah, Tanairi, Tanairy, Tanalia, Tanara, Tanas, Tanasha, Tanashea, Tanavia, Tanaya, Tanaz, Tanea, Tania, Tanna, Tannah

Tandy (English) team.
Tanda, Tandalaya, Tandi, Tandie, Tandis, Tandra, Tandrea, Tandria

Taneisha, Tanesha (American) a combination of the prefix Ta + Nesha.

Taneisha, Tanesha (cont.)
Tahniesha, Tanasha, Tanashia, Taneesha, Taneshea, Taneshia, Tanesia, Tanesian, Tanessa, Tanessia, Taniesha, Tanneshia, Tanniecia, Tanniesha, Tantashea

Tangia (American) a combination of the prefix Ta + Angela.
Tangela, Tangi, Tangie, Tanja, Tanji, Tanjia, Tanjie

Tani (Japanese) valley. (Slavic) stand of glory. A familiar form of Tania.
Tahni, Tahnie, Tanee, Taney, Tanie, Tany

Tania (Russian, Slavic) fairy queen. A form of Tanya, Titania.
Taneea, Tanija, Tanika, Tanis, Taniya, Tannia, Tannica, Tannis, Tanniya, Tannya, Tarnia

Taniel (American) a combination of Tania + Danielle.
Taniele, Tanielle, Teniel, Teniele, Tenielle

Tanis, Tannis (Slavic) forms of Tania, Tanya.
Tanesa, Tanese, Taniese, Tanisa, Tanissa, Tanka, Tannesa, Tannese, Tanniece, Tanniese, Tannisa, Tannise,

Tannus, Tannyce, Tenice, Tenise, Tennessa, Tonise, Tranice, Tranise, Tranissa, Tynice, Tyniece, Tyniese, Tynise

Tanisha (American) a combination of the prefix Ta + Nisha.
Tahniscia, Tahnisha, Tanicha, Taniesha, Tanish, Tanishah, Tanishia, Tanitia, Tannicia, Tannisha, Tenisha, Tenishka, Tinisha, Tonisha, Tonnisha, Tynisha

Tanita (American) a combination of the prefix Ta + Nita.
Taneta, Tanetta, Tanitra, Tanitta, Teneta, Tenetta, Tenita, Tenitta, Tyneta, Tynetta, Tynette, Tynita, Tynitra, Tynitta

Tanith (Phoenician) Mythology: the goddess of love.
Tanitha

Tansy (Greek) immortal. (Latin) tenacious, persistent.
Tancy, Tansee, Tansey, Tanshay, Tanzey

Tanya (Russian, Slavic) fairy queen. A short form of Tatiana.
Tahnee, Tahnya, Tana, Tanaya, Taneia, Taneya, Tania,

Tanis, Taniya, Tanka, Tannis, Tanoya, Tany, Tanyia, Taunya, Tawnya, Thanya

Tao (Chinese, Vietnamese) peach.

Tara (Aramaic) throw; carry. (Irish) rocky hill. (Arabic) a measurement.
Taira, Tairra, Taraea, Tarah, Taráh, Tarai, Taralee, Tarali, Taralyn, Taran, Tarasa, Tarasha, Taraya, Tarha, Tari, Tarra, Taryn, Tayra, Tehra

Taree (Japanese) arching branch.
Tarea, Tareya, Tari, Taria

Tari (Irish) a familiar form of Tara.
Taria, Tarika, Tarila, Tarilyn, Tarin, Tarina, Taris, Tarisa, Tarise, Tarisha, Tarissa, Tarita

Tarra (Irish) an alternate form of Tara.
Tarrah

Taryn (Irish) an alternate form of Tara.
Taran, Tareen, Tareena, Taren, Tarene, Tarin, Tarina, Tarren, Tarrena, Tarrin, Tarron, Tarryn, Taryna

Tasha (Greek) born on Christmas day. (Russian) a short form of Natasha. See also Tosha.
Tacha, Tachia, Tachiana, Tachika, Tahsha, Tasenka, Tashana, Tashka, Thasha, Tysha
Foreign forms: Italian: *Tazia;* Latvian: *Taska;* Slavic: *Tashi, Tasia*

Tashana (American) a combination of the prefix Ta + Shana.
Tashanda, Tashani, Tashanika, Tashanna, Tashiana, Tishana, Tishani, Tishanna, Tishanne, Toshanna, Toshanti, Tyshana

Tashawna (American) a combination of the prefix Ta + Shawna.
Tashauna, Tashawanna, Tashonda, Tashondra, Tiashauna, Tishawn, Tishunda, Tishunta, Toshauna, Toshawna, Tyshauna, Tyshawna

Tasheena (American) a combination of the prefix Ta + Sheena.
Tasheeni, Tashena, Tashenna, Tashina, Tisheena, Tosheena, Tysheana, Tysheena, Tyshyna

Tashelle (American) a combination of the prefix Ta + Shelley.
Tachell, Tashell, Techell, Techelle, Teshell, Teshelle, Tochell, Tochelle, Toshelle, Tychell, Tychelle, Tyshell, Tyshelle

Tashi (Slavic) a form of Tasha. (Hausa) a bird in flight.
Tashia, Tashiana, Tashika, Tashima, Tashina, Tashira

Tasia (Slavic) a familiar form of Tasha.
Tasiya, Tassi, Tassia, Tassiana, Tassie, Tasya

Tate (English) a short form of Tatum. An alternate form of Taite, Tata.

Tatiana (Slavic) fairy queen. A feminine form of Tatius. See also Tanya.
Taitiann, Taitianna, Tata, Tatania, Tatanya, Tati, Tatia, Tatie, Tatihana, Tatjana, Tatyana, Tatyanah, Tatyanna, Tiana, Tiatiana

Tatum (English) cheerful.
Tate, Tatumn

Taura (Latin) bull. Astrology: Taurus is a sign of the zodiac.
Taurina

Tavia (Latin) a short form of Octavia.
Taiva, Tauvia, Tava, Tavah, Tavie, Tavita
Foreign form: Polish: *Tawia*

Tavie (Scottish) twin. A feminine form of Tavish.

Tawanna (American) a combination of the prefix Ta + Wanda.
Taiwana, Taiwanna, Taquana, Taquanna, Tawan, Tawana, Tawanda, Tawanne, Tequana, Tequanna, Tequawna, Tewanna, Tewauna, Tiquana, Tiwanna, Tiwena, Towanda, Towanna, Tywania, Tywanna

Tawny (Gypsy) little one. (English) brownish yellow, tan.
Tahnee, Tany, Tauna, Tauné, Tauni, Taunia, Taunisha, Tawna, Tawnee, Tawnesha, Tawney, Tawni, Tawnia, Tawnie, Tawnyell, Tiawna, Tiawni

Tawnya (American) a combination of Tawny + Tonya.

Taye (English) a short form of Taylor.
Tay, Taya, Tayah, Tayana, Tayiah, Tayna, Tayra, Taysha, Taysia, Tayva, Tayvonne,

Taye *(cont.)*
Teyanna, Teyona, Teyuna, Tiaya, Tiya, Tiyah, Tiyana, Tye

Taylor (English) tailor.
Tailor, Taiylor, Talor, Talora, Taye, Tayla, Taylar, Tayler, Tayllor, Taylore

Teagan (Welsh) beautiful, attractive.
Taegen, Teaghen, Teegan, Teeghan, Tega, Tegan, Teghan, Tegin, Tegwen, Teigan, Tejan, Tiegan, Tigan, Tijan, Tijana

Teal (English) river duck; blue green.
Teala, Teale, Tealia, Tealisha

Teanna (American) a combination of the prefix Te + Anna. An alternate form of Tina.
Teana, Teann, Teanne, Teaunna, Teena, Teuana

Tecla (Greek) God's fame.
Foreign form: Swedish: Tekla

Teddi (Greek) a familiar form of Theodora.
Tedde, Teddey, Teddie, Teddy

Tedra (Greek) a short form of Theodora.
Teddra, Teddreya, Tedera, Teedra, Teidra

Temira (Hebrew) tall.
Temora, Timora

Tempest (French) stormy.
Tempeste, Tempestt, Tempistt, Tempress, Tempteste

Tenesha (American) a combination of the prefix Te + Nesha.
Tenecia, Teneesha, Teneisha, Tenesha, Teneshia, Tenesia, Tenessa, Teneusa, Tenezya, Teniesha

Tennille (American) a combination of the prefix Te + Nellie.
Taniel, Tanille, Teneal, Teneil, Teneille, Teniel, Tenille, Tenneal, Tenneill, Tenneille, Tennia, Tennie, Tennielle, Tennile, Tineal, Tiniel, Tonielle, Tonille

Tequila (Spanish) an alcoholic cocktail.
Taquela, Taquella, Taquila, Taquilla, Tequilia, Tequilla, Tiquila, Tiquilia
Foreign forms: American: Takelia, Takella, Takeyla, Takila, Tekilaa

Tera, Terra (Latin) earth. (Japanese) swift arrow.
Teria, Terria

Teralyn (American) a combination of Terri + Lynn.
Teralyn, Teralynn, Terralin, Terralyn

Teresa (Greek) reaper. An alternate form of Theresa. See also Tressa.
Taresa, Tarese, Taress, Taressa, Taris, Tarisa, Tarise, Tarissa, Terasa, Tercza, Tereasa, Tereatha, Tereese, Tereka, Terese, Teresea, Teresha, Tereson, Teress, Teressa, Teretha, Terez, Terezinha, Terezsa, Teri, Teris, Terisa, Terisha, Teriza, Terrasa, Terresa, Terresia, Terrosina, Terza
Foreign forms: Hungarian: Teca, Tereza, Teruska; Polish: Tereska; Russian: Terezilya; Spanish: Teresia, Teresita, Teté

Teri (Greek) reaper. A familiar form of Theresa.
Terie

Terrelle (Greek) an alternate form of Theresa.
Teral, Terall, Terel, Terell, Teriel, Terral, Terrall, Terrell, Terrella, Terriel, Terrill, Terryl, Terryll, Terrylle, Teryl, Tyrell, Tyrelle

Terrene (Latin) smooth. A feminine form of Terrence.

**Tareena, Tarena, Teran,
Teranee, Tereena, Terena,
Terencia, Terene, Terenia,
Terentia, Terina, Terran,
Terren, Terrena, Terrin,
Terrina, Terron, Terrosina,
Terryn, Terun, Teryn, Teryna,
Terynn, Tyreen, Tyrene**

Terri (Greek) reaper. A familiar
form of Theresa.
Terree, Terria, Terrie

Terriann (American) a combi-
nation of Terri + Ann.
**Terian, Teriana, Teriann,
Terianna, Terianne, Terria,
Terrian, Terrianna, Terrianne,
Terriyanna**

Terrica (American) a combina-
tion of Terri + Erica. See also
Rica.
**Terica, Tericka, Terika,
Terreka, Terricka, Terrika,
Tyrica, Tyricka, Tyrika,
Tyrikka**

Terry (Greek) a short form of
Theresa.
**Tere, Teree, Terelle, Terene,
Teri, Terie, Terrey, Terri,
Terrie, Terrye, Tery**

Terry-Lynn (American) a com-
bination of Terry + Lynn.
**Terelyn, Terelynn, Terri-Lynn,
Terrilynn, Terrylynn**

Tertia (Latin) third.
**Tercia, Tercina, Tercine,
Terecena, Tersia, Terza**

Tess (Greek) a short form of
Quintessa, Theresa.

Tessa (Greek) reaper. A short
form of Theresa.
**Tesa, Tesha, Tesia, Tessia,
Tezia**

Tessie (Greek) a familiar form
of Theresa.
Tessey, Tessi, Tessy, Tezi

Tevy (Cambodian) angel.
Teva

Thaddea (Greek) courageous.
(Latin) praiser. A feminine
form of Thaddeus.
Thada, Thadda

Thalassa (Greek) sea, ocean.

Thalia (Greek) an alternate
form of Talia. Mythology: the
Muse of comedy.
Thaleia, Thalie, Thalya

Thana (Arabic) happy occasion.
Thaina

Thanh (Vietnamese) bright
blue. (Punjabi) good place.
Thantra, Thanya

Thao (Vietnamese) respectful of
parents.

Thea (Greek) goddess. A short
form of Althea.
Theo

Thelma (Greek) willful.
Thelmalina

Thema (African) queen.

Theodora (Greek) gift of God.
A feminine form of Theodore.
See also Dora, Dorothy.
**Taedra, Teddy, Tedra,
Teodory, Theda, Thedrica,
Theo, Theodosia, Theodra**
Foreign forms: Czech: **Teodora;**
Italian: **Teodosia;** Russian:
Feodora; Spanish: **Theadora**

Theone (Greek) gift of God.
Theondra, Theoni, Theonie

Theophania (Greek) God's
appearance. See also Tiffany.
Theo, Theophanie

Theophila (Greek) loved by
God.
Theo

Theresa (Greek) reaper. See
also Riza, Tracey, Tracy.
**Teresa, Terri, Terry, Tess,
Tessa, Tessie, Thereza, Thersa,
Thersea, Tresha, Tressa, Trice**
Foreign forms: Czech: **Reza,**

Theresa (cont.)
Terezia, Terezie, Terezka; French:
Thérèse; German: **Resi;**
Hungarian: **Teca;** Italian: **Teresina,**
Tersa, Theresina; Russian: **Zilya;**
Spanish: **Theresita, Theressa**

Therese (Greek) an alternate
form of Theresa.
Terese, Terise, Terrise,
Theresia, Theressa, Therra,
Therressa, Thersa

Theta (Greek) Linguistics: a letter in the Greek alphabet.

Thetis (Greek) disposed.
Mythology: the mother of
Achilles.

Thi (Vietnamese) poem.
Thia, Thy, Thya

Thirza (Hebrew) pleasant.
Therza, Thirsa, Thirzah,
Thursa, Thurza, Thyrza,
Tirshka, Tirza

Thomasina (Hebrew) twin.
A feminine form of Thomas.
See also Tamassa, Tammy.
Thomasa, Thomasia,
Thomasin, Thomazine,
Thomencia, Thomethia,
Thomisha, Thomsina, Toma,
Tomasa, Tomina, Tommie,
Tommina
Foreign forms: English:
Thomasine, Tomasina, Tomasine

Thora (Scandinavian) thunder.
A feminine form of Thor.
Thordia, Thordis, Thorri,
Thyra, Tyra

Thuy (Vietnamese) gentle.

Tia (Greek) princess. (Spanish)
aunt.
Ti, Téa, Teah, Teeya, Teia,
Tiaisha, Tiakeisha, Tialeigh,
Tiamarie, Tianda, Tiandria,
Tianeka, Tianika, Tiante,
Tiashauna, Tiawanna, Tiia

Tiana (Greek) princess. (Latin)
a short form of Tatiana.
Teana, Teanna, Tia, Tiahna,
Tianna, Tiaon

Tiara (Latin) crowned.
Teair, Teaira, Teairra, Teara,
Téare, Tearra, Tearia, Tearria,
Teearia, Teira, Teirra, Tiaira,
Tiairra, Tiarra, Tiera, Tiéra,
Tierra, Tierre, Tierrea, Tierria,
Tyara, Tyarra

Tiberia (Latin) Geography: the
Tiber River in Italy.
Tib, Tibbie, Tibby

Tida (Thai) daughter.

Tierney (Irish) noble.
Tiernan

Tiff (Latin) a short form of
Tiffanie, Tiffany.

Tiffani, Tiffanie (Latin) alter-
nate forms of Tiffany.
Tephanie, Tifanee, Tifani,
Tifanie, Tiff, Tiffanee,
Tiffayne, Tiffeni, Tiffenie,
Tiffennie, Tiffiani, Tiffianie,
Tiffine, Tiffini, Tiffinie, Tiffni,
Tiffy, Tiffynie, Tifni, Tiphani,
Tiphanie

Tiffany (Greek) a short form of
Theophania. (Latin) trinity.
Taffanay, Taffany, Tifaney,
Tifany, Tiff, Tiffaney, Tiffani,
Tiffanie, Tiffanny, Tiffeney,
Tiffiany, Tiffiney, Tiffiny,
Tiffnay, Tiffney, Tiffny, Tiffy,
Tiphany, Triffany
Foreign forms: American:
Tyfany, Tyfanny, Tyffani, Tyffini,
Typhanie, Typhany

Tiffy (Latin) a familiar form of
Tiffani, Tiffany.
Tiffey, Tiffi, Tiffie

Tijuana (Spanish) Geography:
a border town in Mexico.
Tajuana, Tajuanna, Thejuana,
Tiajuana, Tiawanna

Tilda (German) a short form of
Matilda.
Tilde, Tildie, Tildy, Tylda,
Tyldy

Tillie (German) a familiar form
of Matilda.
Tilli, Tilly, Tillye

Timi (English) a familiar form of Timothea.
Timia, Timie, Timmi, Timmie

Timothea (English) honoring God. A feminine form of Timothy.
Thea

Tina (Spanish, American) a short form of Augustine, Martina, Christina, Valentina.
Teanna, Teena, Teina, Tena, Tenae, Tine, Tinnia, Tyna, Tynka

Tinesha (American) a combination of the prefix Ti + Nesha.
Timnesha, Tinecia, Tinesha, Tineshia, Tiniesha, Tinsia

Tipper (Irish) water pourer.

Tira (Hindi) arrow.
Tirah, Tirea, Tirena

Tirza (Hebrew) pleasant.
Thersa, Thirza, Tierza, Tirsa, Tirzah, Tirzha, Tyrzah

Tisa (Swahili) ninth-born.
Tisah, Tysa, Tyssa

Tish (Latin) an alternate form of Tisha.

Tisha (Latin) joy. A short form of Leticia.
Taesha, Tesha, Teisha, Tiesha,

Tieshia, Tish, Tishal, Tishia, Tysha, Tyshia

Tita (Greek) giant. (Spanish) a short form of names ending in "tita." A feminine form of Titus.

Titania (Greek) giant. Mythology: the Titans were a race of giants.
Tania, Teata, Tita, Titanna, Titanya, Titianna, Tiziana, Tytan, Tytania

Tivona (Hebrew) nature lover.

Tobi (Hebrew) God is good. A feminine form of Tobias.
Tobe, Tobee, Tobey, Tobie, Tobit, Toby, Tobye, Tova, Tovah, Tove, Tovi, Tybi, Tybie

Toinette (French) a short form of Antoinette.
Toinetta, Tonetta, Tonette, Toni, Toniette, Twanette
Foreign form: Polish: Tola

Toki (Japanese) hopeful.
Toko, Tokoya, Tokyo

Tomi (Japanese) rich.
Tomie, Tomiju

Tommie (Hebrew) a short form of Thomasina.
Tomme, Tommi, Tommia, Tommy

Tomo (Japanese) intelligent.
Tomoko

Tonesha (American) a combination of the prefix To + Nesha.
Toneisha, Toneisheia, Tonesha, Tonesia, Toniece, Toniesha, Tonisa, Tonneshia

Toni (Greek) flourishing. (Latin) praiseworthy. A short form of Antoinette, Antonia, Toinette.
Tonee, Toney, Tonia, Tonie, Tony

Tonia (Latin, Slavic) an alternate form of Toni, Tonya.
Tonja, Tonje, Tonna, Tonni, Tonnia, Tonnie, Tonnja

Tonya (Slavic) fairy queen.
Tonia, Tonnya, Tonyetta

Topaz (Latin) golden yellow gem.

Topsy (English) on top. Literature: a slave in Harriet Beecher Stowe's novel *Uncle Tom's Cabin*.
Toppsy, Topsey, Topsie

Tora (Japanese) tiger.

Tori (Japanese) bird. (English) an alternate form of Tory.
Toria, Toriana, Torie, Torri, Torria, Torrie, Torrina, Torrita

Toriana (English) an alternate form of Tory.
Torian, Toriann, Torianna, Torianne

Torilyn (English) an alternate form of Tory.
Torilynn, Torrilyn, Torrilynn

Tory (Latin) a short form of Victoria. (English) victorious.
Torey, Tori, Torrey, Torreya, Torrye, Torya, Torye
Foreign forms: Spanish: Toia, Toya

Tosha (Punjabi) armaments. (Polish) a familiar form of Antonia. (Russian) an alternate form of Tasha.
Toshea, Toshia, Toshiea, Toshke, Tosia, Toska

Toshi (Japanese) mirror image.
Toshie, Toshiko, Toshikyo

Totsi (Hopi) moccasins.

Tovah (Hebrew) good.
Tova, Tovia

Tracey (Greek) a familiar form of Theresa. (Latin) warrior.
Trace, Tracee, Tracell, Traci, Tracie, Tracy, Traice, Trasey, Treesy

Traci, Tracie (Latin) alternate forms of Tracey.

Tracia, Tracilee, Tracilyn, Tracilynn, Tracina, Traeci

Tracy (Greek) a familiar form of Theresa. (Latin) warrior.
Treacy

Tralena (Latin) a combination of Tracy + Lena.
Traleen, Tralene, Tralin, Tralinda, Tralyn, Tralynn, Tralynne

Tranesha (American) a combination of the prefix Tra + Nesha.
Traneice, Traneis, Traneise, Traneisha, Traneshia

Trava (Czech) spring grasses.

Tresha (Greek) an alternate form of Theresa.
Trescha, Trescia, Treshana, Treshia

Tressa (Greek) a short form of Theresa.
Treaser, Tresa, Tresca, Trese, Tresha, Treska, Tressia, Tressie, Trez, Treza, Trisa

Trevina (Irish) prudent. (Welsh) homestead. A feminine form of Trevor.
Treva, Trevanna, Trevenia, Trevonna

Triana (Greek) an alternate form of Trina. (Latin) third.
Tria, Triann, Trianna, Trianne

Trice (Greek) a short form of Theresa.
Treece

Tricia (Latin) an alternate form of Trisha.
Trica, Tricha, Trichelle, Tricina, Trickia

Trilby (English) soft hat.
Tribi, Trilbie, Trillby

Trina (Greek) pure. A short form of Katrina. (Hindi) points of sacred kusa grass.
Treena, Treina, Trenna, Triana, Trinia, Trinchen, Trind, Trinda, Trine, Trinette, Trinica, Trinice, Triniece, Trinika, Trinique, Trinisa, Trinnette, Tryna

Trinity (Latin) triad. Religion: the Father, the Son, and the Holy Spirit.
Trini, Trinita

Trish (Latin) a short form of Beatrice, Trisha.
Trishell, Trishelle

Trisha (Latin) noblewoman. A familiar form of Patricia. (Hindi) thirsty. See also Tricia.

Treasha, Trish, Trishann, Trishanna, Trishanne, Trishara, Trishia, Trishna, Trissha

Trissa (Latin) a familiar form of Patricia.
Trisa, Trisanne, Trisia, Trisina, Trissi, Trissie, Trissy, Tryssa

Trista (Latin) a short form of Tristen.
Trisatal, Tristess, Tristia, Trysta, Trystia

Tristen (Latin) bold. A feminine form of Tristan.
Trista, Tristian, Tristiana, Tristin, Tristina, Tristine, Trystan

Trixie (American) a familiar form of Beatrice.
Tris, Trissie, Trissina, Trix, Trixi, Trixy

Troya (Irish) foot soldier.
Troi, Troia, Troiana

Trudy (German) a familiar form of Gertrude.
Truda, Trude, Trudessa, Trudey, Trudi, Trudie
Foreign form: Dutch: Trudel

Tuesday (English) second day of the week.
Tuesdey

Tula (Hindi) born in the lunar month of Capricorn.
Tulah, Tulla, Tullah, Tuula

Tullia (Irish) peaceful, quiet.
Tulia, Tulliah

Turquoise (French) blue green, semi-precious stone originally brought to Europe through Turkey.
Turkois, Turkoise, Turkoys, Turkoyse

Twyla (English) woven of double thread.
Twila, Twilla

Tyanna (American) a combination of the prefix Ty + Anna.
Tya, Tyana, Tyann, Tyanne

Tyesha (American) a combination of the prefix Ty + Aisha.
Tyisha

Tyler (English) tailor.
Tyller, Tylor

Tyne (English) river.
Tine, Tyna, Tynelle, Tynessa, Tynetta

Tynesha (American) a combination of the prefix Ty + Nesha.
Tynaise, Tynece, Tyneicia, Tynesa, Tynesha, Tyneshia, Tyniesha, Tynisha, Tyseisha

Tyra (Scandinavian) battler. Mythology: Tyr was the god of battle.
Tyraa, Tyrah, Tyran, Tyree, Tyrell, Tyrelle, Tyrena, Tyrene, Tyresa, Tyresia, Tyria, Tyrica, Tyricka, Tyrikka, Tyrina, Tyronica

Udele (English) prosperous.
Uda, Udella, Udelle, Yudelle

Ula (Basque) the Virgin Mary. (Irish) sea jewel. (Spanish) a short form of Eulalia. (Scandinavian) wealthy.
Uli, Ulla

Ulani (Polynesian) cheerful.
Ulana, Ulane

Ulima (Arabic) astute; wise.
Ullima

Ulla (Latin) a short form of Ursula. (German, Swedish) willful.
Ulli

Ulrica (German) wolf ruler; ruler of all. A feminine form of Ulric. See also Rica.
Ulka, Ullrica, Ullricka, Ullrika, Ulrika, Ulrike

Ululani (Hawaiian) heavenly inspiration.

Uma (Hindi) mother. Religion: another name for the Hindu goddess Shakti.

Umeko (Japanese) plum blossom child; patient.
Ume, Umeyo

Una (Latin) one; united. (Irish) a form of Agnes. (Hopi) good memory. See also Oona.
Unna, Uny

Undine (Latin) little wave. Mythology: the Undines were water sprites. See also Ondine.
Undeen, Undene

Unique (Latin) only one.
Unica, Uniqua

Unity (English) unity.
Unita, Unitee

Urania (Greek) heavenly. Mythology: the Muse in charge of astronomy.
Urainia, Uranie, Uraniya, Uranya

Urika (Omaha) useful to everyone.

Ursa (Greek) a short form of Ursula. (Latin) an alternate form of Orsa.
Ursey, Ursi, Ursie, Ursy

Ursula (Greek) little bear. See also Sula, Ulla.
Ursa, Ursala, Ursel, Ursela, Ursella, Ursely, Ursilla, Ursillane, Urszuli, Urzula
Foreign forms: English: **Ursuline;** French: **Ursule;** Italian: **Orsola;** Latvian: **Urszula;** Spanish: **Ursulina, Ursola**

Ushi (Chinese) ox. Astrology: a sign of the zodiac.

Uta (German) rich. (Japanese) poem.
Utako

Vail (English) valley.
Vale, Vayle

Val (Latin) a short form of Valentina, Valerie.

Valarie (Latin) an alternate form of Valerie.
Valaria

Valda (German) famous ruler. A feminine form of Valdemar.
Valida, Velda

Valencia (Spanish) strong. Geography: a region in eastern Spain.
Valecia, Valence, Valenica, Valentia, Valenzia

Valene (Latin) a short form of Valentina.
Valaine, Valean, Valeda, Valeen, Valen, Valena,

Valeney, Valien, Valina, Valine, Vallan, Vallen

Valentina (Latin) strong. History: Valentina Tereshkova, a Soviet cosmonaut, was the first woman in space. See also Tina, Valene, Valli.
Val, Valantina, Vale, Valentijn, Valentin, Valiaka, Valtina, Valyn, Valynn
Foreign forms: English: Valentine, Valida, Velora

Valerie (Latin) strong.
Vairy, Val, Valarae, Valaree, Valarey, Valari, Valarie, Vale, Valeree, Valeri, Valeriane, Valery Vallarie, Valleree, Valleri, Vallerie, Vallery, Valli, Vallirie, Valora, Valry, Veleria, Velerie
Foreign forms: English: Valaria, Valerye; French: Valérie; Italian: Valeria; Polish: Waleria; Russian: Lera, Valera, Valka, Valya; Spanish: Valeriana

Valeska (Slavic) glorious ruler. A feminine form of Vladislav.
Valese, Valeshia, Valezka, Valisha

Valli (Latin) a familiar form of Valentina, Valerie. Botany: a plant native to India.
Vallie, Vally

Valma (Finnish) loyal defender.

Valonia (Latin) shadow valley.
Vallon, Valona

Valora (Latin) an alternate form of Valerie.
Valori, Valoria, Valorie, Valory, Valorya

Vanda (German) an alternate form of Wanda.
Vandana, Vandella, Vandetta, Vandi, Vannda

Vanessa (Greek) butterfly. Literature: a name invented by Jonathan Swift as a nickname for Esther Vanhomrigh. See also Nessie.
Van, Vanassa, Vanesa, Vanesha, Vaneshia, Vanesia, Vanesse, Vanessia, Vanessica, Vaneza, Vaniece, Vaniessa, Vanisa, Vanissa, Vanita, Vanna, Vannessa, Vanneza, Vanni, Vannie, Vanny, Varnessa, Venessa
Foreign forms: English: Vanetta; Slavic: Vania, Vanija, Vanika, Vanya

Vanity (English) vain.
Vanita, Vanitty

Vanna (Greek) a short form of Vanessa. (Cambodian) golden.
Vana, Vanae, Vannah, Vannalee, Vannaleigh

Vanora (Welsh) white wave.
Vannora

Vantrice (American) a combination of the prefix Van + Trice.
Vantrece, Vantricia, Vantrisa, Vantrissa

Varda (Hebrew) rose.
Vadit, Vardia, Vardice, Vardina, Vardis, Vardit

Vashti (Persian) lovely. Bible: the wife of Ahasuerus, king of Persia.
Vashtee, Vashtie

Veda (Sanskrit) wise. Religion: the Vedas are the sacred writings of Hinduism.
Vedad, Vedis, Veeda, Veida, Veleda, Vida, Vita

Vedette (Italian) sentry; scout. (French) movie star.
Vedetta

Vega (Arabic) falling star.

Velma (German) a familiar form of Vilhelmina.
Valma, Vellma, Vilma, Vilna

Velvet (English) velvety.

Venecia (Italian) from Venice.
Vanecia, Vanetia, Veneise, Venesa, Venesha, Venesher,

Venecia *(cont.)*
Venesse, Venessia, Venetia, Venette, Venezia, Venice, Venicia, Veniece, Veniesa, Venise, Venisha, Venishia, Venita, Venitia, Venize, Vennesa, Vennice, Vennisa, Vennise, Vonitia, Vonizia

Venessa (Latin) a form of Vanessa.
Venesa

Venus (Latin) love. Mythology: the goddess of love and beauty.
Venis, Venusa, Vinny

Vera (Latin) true. (Slavic) faith. A short form of Veronica. See also Verena.
Vara, Veera, Veira, Veradis, Vere, Vira
Foreign forms: Czech: **Verka, Viera;** *English:* **Verla;** *Polish:* **Wera;** *Russian:* **Verasha**

Verda (Latin) young, fresh.
Verdi, Verdie, Viridiana, Viridis

Verena (Latin) truthful. A familiar form of Vera, Verna.
Verene, Verenis, Vereniz, Verina, Verine, Virna
Foreign forms: Russian: **Verinka, Veroshka, Verunka, Verusya**

Verity (Latin) truthful.
Verita, Veritie

Verlene (Latin) a combination of Veronica + Lena.
Verleen, Verlena, Verlin, Verlina, Verlinda, Verline, Verlyn

Verna (Latin) springtime. (French) a familiar form of Laverne. See also Verena.
Verne, Vernese, Vernesha, Verneshia, Vernessa, Vernetia, Vernetta, Vernette, Vernia, Vernice, Vernis, Vernisha, Vernisheia, Vernita, Verusya, Viera, Virida, Virna, Virnell

Vernice (Latin) a form of Bernice, Verna.
Vernica, Vernicca, Vernique

Veronica (Latin) true image. See also Ronni.
Varonica, Verhonica, Verinica, Verohnica, Veron, Verone, Veronic, Véronic, Veronice, Veronika, Veronne, Veronnica, Vironica, Vonni, Vonnie, Vonny, Vron, Vronica
Foreign forms: Czech: **Verona;** *French:* **Veranique, Verenice, Veronique, Véronique;** *German:* **Veronike;** *Polish:* **Weronika;** *Russian:* **Veruszhka;** *Slavic:* **Vera**

Veronika (Latin) an alternate form of Veronica.
Varonika, Veronick, Véronick, Veronik, Veronka, Veronkia, Veruka

Veronique, Véronique (French) forms of Veronica.

Vesta (Latin) keeper of the house. Mythology: the goddess of the home.
Vessy, Vest, Vesteria

Vi (Latin, French) a short form of Viola, Violet.
Vye

Vianna (American) a combination of Vi + Anna.
Viana, Viann, Vianne

Vicki (Latin) a familiar form of Victoria.
Vic, Vicci, Vicke, Vickee, Vickiana, Vickie, Vickilyn, Vickki, Vicky, Vika, Viki, Vikie, Vikki

Vicky (Latin) a familiar form of Victoria.
Viccy, Vickey, Viky, Vikkey, Vikky

Victoria (Latin) victorious. See also Tory.
Vicki, Vicky, Victoriana, Victorie, Victorina, Victorine,

Victory, Viktoria, Vyctoria
Foreign forms: Czech:
Viktorka; French: **Victoire;** Italian:
Vittoria; Polish: **Wicktoria,**
Wisia; Spanish: **Vitoria**

Vida (Sanskrit) an alternate
form of Veda. (Hebrew) a
short form of Davida.
Vidamarie

Vienna (Latin) Geography: the
capital of Austria.
Veena, Vena, Venna, Vienette,
Vienne, Vina

Viktoria (Latin) an alternate
form of Victoria.
Viktorie, Viktorina, Viktorine
Foreign form: Dutch: **Viktorija**

Vilhelmina (German) an alternate form of Wilhelmina.
Velma, Vilhelmine, Vilma

Villette (French) small town.
Vietta

Vilma (German) a short form
of Vilhemina.

Vina (Hebrew) a short form of
Davina. (Hindi) Mythology: a
musical instrument played by
the Hindu goddess of wisdom.
(Spanish) vineyard. See also
Lavina. (English) a short form
of Alvina.
Veena, Vena, Viña, Vinesha,

Vinessa, Vinia, Viniece,
Vinique, Vinisha, Vinita,
Vinna, Vinni, Vinnie, Vinny,
Vinora, Vyna

Vincentia (Latin) victor, con-
queror. A feminine form of
Vincent.
Vicenta, Vincenta,
Vincentena, Vincentina,
Vincentine, Vincenza, Vincy,
Vinnie

Viñita (Spanish) an alternate
form of Vina.
Viñeet, Viñeeta, Viñetta,
Viñette, Viñitha, Viñta, Viñti,
Viñtia, Vyñetta, Vyñette

Viola (Latin) violet; stringed
instrument in the violin family.
Literature: the heroine of the
Shakespearean play *Twelfth
Night*.
Vi, Violaine, Violanta, Viole,
Violeine

Violet (French) Botany: a plant
with purplish blue flowers.
Vi, Violette, Vyolet, Vyoletta,
Vyolette
Foreign forms: Italian: **Violetta;**
Spanish: **Violante, Violeta**

Virgilia (Latin) rod bearer, staff
bearer. A feminine form of
Virgil.
Virgillia

Virginia (Latin) pure, virginal.
Literature: Virginia Woolf was a
well-known British writer. See
also Ginger.
Ginia, Verginia, Verginya,
Virge, Virgen, Virgenia,
Virgenya, Virgie, Virgine,
Virginio, Virginnia, Virgy,
Virjeana
Foreign forms: American: **Jinny;**
Dutch: **Virginië;** English: **Ginny;**
French: **Virginie;** Hawaiian:
Wilikina; Italian: **Gina**

Viridis (Latin) green.
Virdis, Virida, Viridia,
Viridiana

Vita (Latin) life.
Veeta, Veta, Vitaliana,
Vitalina, Vitel, Vitella, Vitia,
Vitka, Vitke

Viv (Latin) a short form of
Vivian.

Viva (Latin) a short form of
Aviva, Vivian.
Vica, Vivan, Vivva

Viveca (Latin) an alternate form
of Vivian.
Viv, Vivecca, Vivecka, Viveka,
Vyveca

Vivian (Latin) full of life.
Vevay, Vevey, Viv, Viva,
Viveca, Vivee, Vivi, Vivia,

Vivian (cont.)
Viviane, Vivie, Vivina, Vivion, Vivyan, Vyvyan
Foreign forms: French: **Vivien, Vivienne;** Italian: **Viviana**

Viviana (Latin) an alternate form of Vivian.
Viv, Viviann, Vivianna, Vivianne, Vivyana, Vivyann, Vivyanne, Vyvyana, Vyvyann, Vyvyanne

Vondra (Czech) loving woman.
Vonda, Vondrea

Voneisha (American) a combination of Yvonne + Aisha.
Voneishia, Vonesha, Voneshia

Vonna (French) an alternate form of Yvonne.
Vona, Vonni, Vonnie, Vonny

Vontricia (American) a combination of Yvonne + Tricia.
Vontrece, Vontrese, Vontrice, Vontriece

Wakana (Japanese) plant.

Wakanda (Dakota) magical power.
Wakenda

Wakeisha (American) a combination of the prefix Wa + Keisha.
Wakeishia, Wakesha, Wakeshia, Wakesia

Walda (German) powerful; famous. A feminine form of Waldo.
Waldina, Waldine, Walida, Wallda, Welda

Walker (English) cloth; walker.
Wallker

Wallis (English) from Wales. A feminine form of Wallace.
Wallie, Walliss, Wally, Wallys

Wanda (German) wanderer. See also Wendy.
Wahnda, Wandah, Wandely, Wandi, Wandie, Wandis, Wandy, Wannda, Wonda, Wonnda
Foreign forms: Czech: **Vanda;** Polish: **Wandzia;** Swedish: **Wanja**

Waneta (Native American) charger.
Waneeta, Wanita, Wanite, Wanneta, Waunita, Wonita, Wonnita, Wynita

Wanetta (English) pale face.
Wanette, Wannetta, Wannette

Warda (German) guardian. A feminine form of Ward.
Wardia, Wardine

Waynette (English) wagon maker. A feminine form of Wayne.
Waynel, Waynelle, Waynlyn

Weeko (Dakota) pretty girl.

Wehilani (Hawaiian) heavenly adornment.

Wenda (Welsh) an alternate form of Wendy.
Wendaine, Wendayne

Wendelle (English) wanderer.
Wendaline, Wendall,

Wendalyn, Wendeline, Wendella, Wendelline

Wendi (Welsh) an alternate form of Wendy.
Wendie

Wendy (Welsh) white; light skinned. A familiar form of Gwendolyn, Wanda.
Wenda, Wende, Wendee, Wendey, Wendi, Wendye

Weslee (English) western meadow. A feminine form of Wesley.
Weslea, Weslene, Wesley, Weslia, Weslie, Weslyn

Whitley (English) white field.
Whitely

Whitney (English) white island.
Whiteney, Whitne, Whitné, Whitnee, Whitneigh, Whitnie, Whitny, Whitnye, Whittany, Whitteny, Whittney, Whytne, Whytney, Witney

Whitnie (English) an alternate form of Whitney.
Whitani, Whitnei, Whitni, Whittnie, Whytnie

Whoopi (English) happy; excited.
Whoopie, Whoopy

Wilda (German) untamed. (English) willow.
Willda, Wylda

Wilhelmina (German) determined guardian. A feminine form of Wilhelm, William. See also Billie, Minna.
Helma, Vilhelmina, Willa, Willamina, Willamine, Willemina, Williamina, Willmina, Willmine, Wilma, Wimina, Winnie
Foreign forms: *American:* *Minnie;* *Danish:* ***Wilhelmine;*** *English:* ***Wileen, Willette, Willie;*** *French:* ***Guillelmine;*** *Polish:* ***Minka;*** *Spanish:* ***Guillerma***

Willa (German) a short form of Wilhelmina.
Willabella, Willette, Williabelle

Willette (English) a familiar form of Wilhelmina, Willa.
Wiletta, Wilette, Willetta, Williette

Willow (English) willow tree.

Wilma (German) a short form of Wilhelmina.
Williemae, Wilmanie, Wilmayra, Wilmetta, Wilmette, Wilmina, Wilmyne, Wylma

Wilona (English) desired.
Willona, Willone, Wilone

Win (German) a short form of Winifred.
Wyn

Winda (Swahili) hunter.

Windy (English) windy.
Windee, Windey, Windi, Windie, Wyndee, Wyndy

Winema (Moquelumnan) woman chief.

Winifred (German) peaceful friend. (Welsh) an alternate form of Guinevere. See also Freddi, Una, Winnie.
Win, Winafred, Winefred, Winefride, Winfreda, Winfrieda, Winiefrida, Winifrid, Winifryd, Winnafred, Winnefred, Winniefred, Winnifred, Winnifrid, Wynafred, Wynifred, Wynnifred

Winna (African) friend.
Winnah

Winnie (English) a familiar form of Edwina, Gwyneth, Winnifred, Winona, Wynne. History: Winnie Mandela kept the anti-aparteid movement alive in South Africa while her

Winnie *(cont.)*
husband, Nelson Mandela, was imprisoned. Literature: the lovable bear in A. A. Milne's children's story *Winnie the Pooh*.
Wina, Winne, Winney, Winni, Winny, Wynnie

Winola (German) charming friend.
Wynola

Winona (Lakota) oldest daughter.
Wanona, Wenona, Wenonah, Winnie, Winonah, Wynnona, Wynona

Winter (English) winter.
Wintr, Wynter

Wren (English) wren, songbird.

Wyanet (Native American) legendary beauty.
Wyaneta, Wyanita, Wynette

Wynne (Welsh) white, light skinned. A short form of Guinivere, Gwyneth.
Winnie, Wyn, Wynn

Wyoming (Native American) Geography: a western American state.
Wy, Wye, Wyoh, Wyomia

Xandra (Greek) an alternate form of Zandra. (Spanish) a short form of Alexandra.
Xander, Xandrea, Xandria

Xanthe (Greek) yellow, blond. See also Zanthe.
Xanne, Xantha, Xanthia, Xanthippe

Xanthippe (Greek) an alternate form of Xanthe. History: Socrates's wife.
Xantippie

Xaviera (Basque) owner of the new house. (Arabic) bright. A feminine form of Xavier. See also Javiera.
Xavia, Xavière, Xavyera
Foreign form: *Spanish:* ***Zaviera***

Xela (Quiché) my mountain home.

Xenia (Greek) hospitable. See also Zena, Zina.
Xeenia
Foreign forms: *English:* ***Xena;*** *French:* ***Chimene***

Xiang (Chinese) fragrant.

Xiaoli (Chinese) small and beautiful.

Xiaoying (Chinese) small flower.

Xiu Mei (Chinese) beautiful plum.
Xiaomei

Xuan (Vietnamese) spring.

Yael (Hebrew) strength of God. See also Jael.
Yaeli, Yaella, Yeala

Yaffa (Hebrew) beautiful. See also Jaffa.
Yafeal, Yaffit, Yafit

Yalanda (Greek) an alternate form of Yolanda.
Yalando, Yalonda, Ylana, Ylanda

Yamila (Arabic) an alternate form of Jamila.
Yamile, Yamilla, Yamille

Yaminah (Arabic) right, proper.
Yamina, Yamini, Yemina, Yeminah, Yemini

Yamuna (Hindi) sacred river.

Yana (Slavic) an alternate form of Jana.
Yanae, Yanah, Yanet, Yaneth, Yanik, Yanina, Yanis, Yanisha, Yanitza, Yanixia, Yanna, Yannah, Yannica, Yannick, Yannina

Yáng (Chinese) sun.

Yasmin, Yasmine (Persian) alternate forms of Jasmine.
Yashmine, Yasiman, Yasimine, Yasma, Yasmain, Yasmaine, Yasmeen, Yasmene, Yasmina, Yasminda, Yasmon, Yasmyn, Yazmen, Yazmin, Yazmina, Yazmine, Yesmean, Yesmeen, Yesmin, Yesmina, Yesmine, Yesmyn

Yasu (Japanese) resting, calm.
Yasuko, Yasuyo

Yehudit (Hebrew) an alternate form of Judith.
Yudit, Yudita, Yuta

Yeira (Hebrew) light.

Yemena (Arabic) from Yemen.
Yemina

Yen (Chinese) yearning; desirous.
Yeni, Yenih, Yenny

Yeo (Korean) mild.
Yee

Yepa (Native American) snow girl.

Yera (Basque) Religion: a name for the Virgin Mary.

Yesenia (Arabic) flower.
Yesnia, Yessena, Yessenia, Yissenia

Yessica (Hebrew) an alternate form of Jessica.
Yessika, Yesyka

Yetta (English) a short form of Henrietta.
Yette, Yitta

Yín (Chinese) silver.

Yoanna (Hebrew) an alternate form of Joanna.
Yoana, Yohana, Yohanka, Yohanna, Yohannah

Yoki (Hopi) bluebird.
Yokie

Yoko (Japanese) good girl.
Yo

Yola (Greek) a short form of Yolanda.
Yoley, Yoli, Yolie, Yoly

Yolanda (Greek) violet flower. See also Jolanda, Olinda.
Yalanda, Yolaine, Yolana, Yoland, Yolane, Yolanna,

Yolanda *(cont.)*
Yolantha, Yolanthe, Yolette, Yolonda, Yorlanda, Youlanda, Yulanda, Yulonda
Foreign forms: *English:* **Iolanthe;** *French:* **Yolande;** *Spanish:* **Yola**

Yon (Burmese) rabbit. (Korean) lotus blossom.
Yona, Yonna

Yoné (Japanese) wealth; rice.

Yonina (Hebrew) an alternate form of Jonina.
Yona, Yonah

Yonita (Hebrew) an alternate form of Jonita.
Yonat, Yonati, Yonit

Yoomee (Coos) star.
Yoome

Yori (Japanese) reliable.
Yoriko, Yoriyo

Yoshi (Japanese) good; respectful.
Yoshie, Yoshiko, Yoshiyo

Ysabel (Spanish) an alternate form of Isabel.
Ysabell, Ysabella, Ysabelle, Ysbel, Ysbella, Ysobel

Ysanne (American) a combination of Ysabel + Ann.
Ysande, Ysann, Ysanna

Yseult (German) ice rule. (Irish) fair; light skinned. (Welsh) an alternate form of Isolde.
Yseulte, Ysolt

Yuana (Spanish) an alternate form of Juana.
Yuan, Yuanna

Yuk (Chinese) moon.

Yuki (Japanese) snow.
Yukie, Yukiko, Yukiyo

Yuri (Japanese) lily.
Yuriko, Yuriyo

Yvanna (Slavic) an alternate form of Ivana.
Yvan, Yvana, Yvannia

Yvette (French) a familiar form of Yvonne. See also Evette, Ivette.
Yavette, Yevett, Yevette, Yevetta, Yvetta

Yvonne (French) young archer. (Scandinavian) yew wood; bow wood. A feminine form of Ivar. See also Evonne, Ivonne, Vonna, Yvette.
Yavanda, Yavanna, Yavanne, Yavonda, Yavonna, Yavonne, Yveline, Yvon, Yvone, Yvonna, Yvonny
Foreign forms: *Polish:* **Iwona, Iwonka;** *Portuguese:* **Ivone;** *Russian:* **Ivona**

Zacharie (Hebrew) God remembered. A feminine form of Zachariah.
Zacari, Zacceaus, Zacchaea, Zachoia, Zackeisha, Zackery, Zakaria, Zakaya, Zakeshia, Zakiah, Zakir, Zakiya, Zakiyah, Zechari

Zada (Arabic) fortunate, prosperous.
Zaida, Zayda, Zayeda

Zafirah (Arabic) successful; victorious.

Zahavah (Hebrew) golden.
Zachava, Zachavah, Zechava, Zechavah, Zehava, Zehavi, Zehavit, Zeheva, Zehuva

Zahra (Swahili) flower. (Arabic) white.
Zahara, Zahrah

Zakia (Swahili) smart. (Arabic) chaste.
Zakiah, Zakiyah

Zalika (Swahili) born to royalty.
Zuleika

Zandra (Greek) an alternate form of Sandra.
Zahndra, Zandrea, Zandria, Zandy, Zanndra, Zondra

Zanna (Spanish) a form of Jane. (English) a short form of Susanna.
Zana, Zanella, Zanette, Zannah, Zannette

Zanthe (Greek) an alternate form of Xanthe.
Zanth, Zantha

Zara (Hebrew) an alternate form of Sarah, Zora.
Zaira, Zarah, Zaree, Zareen, Zareena, Zaria

Zasha (Russian) an alternate form of Sasha.
Zascha, Zashenka, Zashka, Zasho

Zaynah (Arabic) beautiful.
Zayn, Zayna

Zea (Latin) grain.

Zelda (German) a short form of Griselda. (Yiddish) gray haired. See also Selda.
Zelde, Zella, Zellda

Zelene (English) sunshine.
Zeleen, Zelena, Zeline

Zelia (Spanish) sunshine.
Zele, Zelene, Zelie, Zélie, Zelina

Zelma (German) an alternate form of Selma.

Zemirah (Hebrew) song of joy.

Zena (Greek) an alternate form of Xenia. (Ethiopian) news. (Persian) woman. See also Zina.
Zeena, Zeenat, Zeenet, Zeenia, Zeenya, Zein, Zeina, Zenah, Zenana, Zenea, Zenia, Zenya

Zenda (Persian) sacred; feminine.

Zenobia (Greek) sign, symbol. History: a queen who ruled the city of Palmyra in the Arabian desert.
Zeba, Zeeba, Zenovia
Foreign form: French: *Zénobie*

Zephania, Zephanie (Greek) alternate forms of Stephanie.
Zepania, Zephanas, Zephany

Zephyr (Greek) west wind.
Zefiryn, Zephra, Zephria, Zephyer, Zephyrine

Zera (Hebrew) seeds.

Zerlina (Latin, Spanish) beautiful dawn. Music: a character in Mozart's opera *Don Giovanni*.
Zerla, Zerlinda

Zeta (English) rose. Linguistics: the last letter in the Greek alphabet.
Zayit, Zetana, Zetta

Zetta (Portuguese) rose.

Zeynep (Turkish) jewel, precious stone.
Zeyno

Zhen (Chinese) chaste.

Zia (Latin) grain. (Arabic) light.
Zea

Zihna (Hopi) one who spins tops.

Zilla (Hebrew) shadow.
Zila, Zillah, Zylla

Zilpah (Hebrew) dignified. Bible: Jacob's wife.
Zilpha, Zylpha

Zimra (Hebrew) song of praise.
Zamora, Zemira, Zemora, Zimria

Zina (Greek) an alternate form of Xenia, Zena. (African) secret spirit. (English) hospitable.
Zinah, Zine

Zinnia (Latin) Botany: a plant with beautiful, rayed, colorful flowers.
Zinia, Zinny, Zinnya, Zinya

Zipporah (Hebrew) bird. Bible: Moses' wife.
Zipora, Ziporah, Zipporia, Ziproh

Zita (Spanish) rose. (Arabic) mistress. A short form of names ending in "sita" or "zita."
Zeeta, Zyta, Zytka

Ziva (Hebrew) bright; radiant.
Zeeva, Ziv, Zivanka, Zivit

Zoe (Greek) life.
Zoé, Zoë, Zoee, Zoelie, Zoeline, Zoelle, Zoey, Zoie, Zooey
Foreign forms: *Slavic: Zoia, Zoya*

Zohreh (Persian) happy.
Zahreh, Zohrah

Zola (Italian) piece of earth.
Zoela

Zona (Latin) belt, sash.
Zonia

Zondra (Greek) an alternate form of Zandra.
Zohndra

Zora (Slavic) aurora; dawn. See also Zara.
Zorah, Zorana, Zoreen, Zoreena, Zorna, Zorra, Zorrah, Zorya

Zorina (Slavic) golden.
Zorana, Zori, Zorie, Zorine, Zorna, Zory

Zuleika (Arabic) brilliant.
Zeleeka, Zul, Zulay, Zulekha, Zuleyka

Zulima (Arabic) an alternate form of Salama.
Zuleima, Zulema, Zulemah, Zulimah

Zuri (Basque) white; light skinned. (Swahili) beautiful.
Zuria, Zurisha

Boys'
Names

Aaron (Hebrew) enlightened. (Arabic) messenger. Bible: the brother of Moses and the first high priest of the Jews.
Aahron, Aaran, Aaren, Aareon, Aarin, Aaronn, Aarron, Aaryn, Aeron, Aharon, Ahran, Ahren, Aranne, Aren, Ari, Arin, Aron, Aronek, Arran, Arron
Foreign forms: German/Italian: Aronne; Polish: Arek; Russian: Aronos

Abbey (Hebrew) a familiar form of Abe.
Abbie, Abby

Abbott (Hebrew) father; abbot.
Ab, Abba, Abbah, Abbán, Abbot
Foreign forms: French: Abbé, Abott; Spanish: Abad

Abdul (Arabic) servant.
Abdal, Abdeel, Abdel, Abdoul, Abdu, Abdual, Abul

Abdulaziz (Arabic) servant of the Mighty.
Abdelazim, Abdelaziz, Abdulazaz, Abdulazeez

Abdullah (Arabic) servant of Allah.
Abdalah, Abdalla, Abdallah, Abdualla, Abdulah, Abdulahi

Abdulrahman (Arabic) servant of the Merciful.
Abdelrahim, Abdelrahman, Abdirahman, Abdolrahem, Abdularahman, Abdurrahman, Abdurram

Abe (Hebrew) a short form of Abel, Abraham.
Abey

Abel (Hebrew) breath. (Assyrian) meadow. (German) a short form of Abelard. Bible: Adam and Eve's second son.
Abe, Abele, Abell, Able, Adal, Avel

Abelard (German) noble; resolute.
Ab, Abalard, Abelhard, Abilard, Adalard, Adelard

Abi (Turkish) older brother.

Abiah (Hebrew) God is my father.
Abia, Abiel, Abija, Abijah, Abisha, Abishai, Aviya, Aviyah

Abie (Hebrew) a familiar form of Abraham.

Abner (Hebrew) father of light. Bible: the commander of King Saul's army.
Ab, Avner
Foreign form: English: Ebner

Abraham (Hebrew) father of many nations. Bible: the first Hebrew patriarch. See also Avram, Bram.
Abarran, Abe, Aberham, Abey, Abhiram, Abie, Abrahim, Abrahm, Abram
Foreign forms: Arabic: Ibrahim; Italian: Abrahamo, Abramo; Portuguese: Abrão; Spanish: Abrahán, Abrán; Swahili: Arram

Abram (Hebrew) a short form of Abraham. See also Bram.
Abrams, Avram

Absalom (Hebrew) father of peace. Bible: the son of King David.
Absalon, Avshalom
Foreign form: Scandanavian: Axel

Ace (Latin) unity.
Acer, Acie
Foreign form: English: **Acey**

Achilles (Greek) Mythology: a hero of the Trojan war. Literature: the hero of Homer's epic *The Iliad*.
Achill, Achille, Achillea, Achillios, Akil, Akili, Akilles

Ackerley (English) meadow of oak trees.
Accerley, Ackerlea, Ackerleigh, Ackersley, Acklea, Ackleigh, Ackley, Acklie

Acton (English) oak-tree settlement.

Adair (Scottish) oak-tree ford.
Adaire, Adare

Adam (Phoenician) man; mankind. (Hebrew) earth; man of the red earth. Bible: the first man created by God. See also Adamson, Addison, Macadam.
Adama, Adas, Addam, Addams, Addy, Adem, Adham, Adné, Adomas
Foreign forms: Czech: **Adamec**; English: **Ad**; Italian: **Adamo**; Polish: **Adok**; Portuguese: **Adão**; Scottish: **Adhamh, Keddy**; Slavic: **Damek**; Spanish: **Adan**

Adamson (Hebrew) son of Adam.
Adams, Adamsson, Addamson

Adar (Syrian) ruler, prince. (Hebrew) noble; exalted.
Addar

Addison (English) son of Adam.
Addis, Adison, Adisson

Addy (Hebrew) a familiar form of Adam, Adlai. (German) a familiar form of Adelard.
Addey, Addi, Addie, Ade, Adi

Ade (Yoruba) royal.

Adebayo (Yoruba) he came in a joyful time.

Adelard (German) noble; courageous.
Adal, Adalar, Adalard, Addy, Adel, Adél, Adelar

Adigun (Yoruba) righteous.

Adlai (Hebrew) my ornament.
Ad, Addy, Adley

Adler (German) eagle.
Ad, Addler, Adlar

Adolf (German) noble wolf. History: Adolf Hitler led Germany to defeat in World War II. See also Dolf.

Ad, Adolfus, Adolph
Foreign form: Italian/Spanish: **Adolfo**

Adolph (German) an alternate form of Adolf.
Adulphus
Foreign forms: French: **Adolphe**; Italian/Spanish: **Adolpho**; Swedish: **Adolphus**

Adonis (Greek) highly attractive. Mythology: the attractive youth loved by Aphrodite.
Adon, Adonnis, Adonys

Adrian (Greek) rich. (Latin) dark. (Swedish) a short form of Hadrian.
Adarian, Ade, Adorjan, Adrain, Adreian, Adreyan, Adri, Adriaan, Adriane, Adrion, Adron, Adryan, Adryon
Foreign forms: French: **Adrien**; Italian: **Adriano**; Russian: **Adrik**

Adriano (Italian) a form of Adrian.
Adrianno

Adriel (Hebrew) member of God's flock.
Adrial

Adrien (French) a form of Adrian.
Adriene

Aeneas (Greek) praised. Literature: the Trojan hero of Virgil's epic *Aeneid*.
Foreign forms: French: **Enne;** Spanish: **Eneas**

Afton (English) from Afton, England.
Affton

Agamemnon (Greek) resolute. Mythology: the King of Argos who led the Greeks in the Trojan War.

Ahab (Hebrew) father's brother. Literature: the captain of the *Pequod* in Herman Melville's novel *Moby Dick*.

Ahearn (Scottish) lord of the horses. (English) heron.
Ahearne, Aherin, Ahern, Aherne, Hearn

Ahmad (Arabic) most highly praised. See also Muhammad.
Achmad, Achmed, Ahamad, Ahamada, Ahamed, Ahmaad, Ahmaud, Amad, Amahd, Amed

Ahmed (Swahili) praiseworthy.

Ahsan (Arabic) charitable.

Aidan (Irish) fiery.
Aden, Adin, Aiden, Aydan, Ayden, Aydin

Aiken (English) made of oak.
Aicken, Aikin, Ayken, Aykin

Aimery (German) an alternate form of Emery.
Aime, Aimerey, Aimeric, Amerey, Aymeric, Aymery

Ainsley (Scottish) my own meadow.
Ainsleigh, Ainslie, Ansley, Aynslee, Aynsley, Aynslie

Ajani (Yoruba) one who takes possession after a struggle.

Ajay (Punjabi) victorious; undefeatable. (American) a combination of the initials A. + J.
Aj, Aja, Ajai, Ajaz, Ajit

Akar (Turkish) flowing stream.
Akara

Akbar (Arabic) great.

Akil (Arabic) intelligent. Geography: a river in the Basque region.
Ahkeel, Akeel, Akeyla, Akhil, Akiel, Akili

Akim (Hebrew) a short form of Joachim.
Achim, Ackeem, Ackim, Ahkieme, Akeam, Akee, Akeem, Akiem, Akima, Arkeem

Akins (Yoruba) brave.

Akira (Japanese) intelligent.
Akihito, Akio, Akiyo

Akiva (Hebrew) an alternate form of Jacob.
Akiba, Kiva

Aksel (Norwegian) father of peace.

Al (Irish) a short form of Alan, Albert, Alexander.

Aladdin (Arabic) height of faith. Literature: the hero of a story in the *Arabian Nights.*
Ala, Alaa, Alaaddin, Aladean, Aladino

Alain (French) a form of Alan.
Alaen, Alainn, Alayn, Allain

Alaire (French) joyful.

Alan (Irish) handsome; peaceful.
Ailin, Al, Alair, Aland, Alani, Alanson, Allan, Allen, Alon, Alun
Foreign forms: French: **Alain;** Italian/Spanish: **Alano;** Portuguese: **Alao;** Scottish: **Ailean**

Alaric (German) ruler of all. See also Ulrich.
Alarick, Alarik, Aleric, Allaric, Allarick, Alric, Alrick

Foreign forms: Italian: Alarico;
Swedish: Alrik

Alastair (Scottish) a form of
Alexander.
**Alaisdair, Alaistair, Alaister,
Alasdair, Alasteir, Alaster,
Alastor, Aleister, Alester,
Alistair, Allaistar, Allastair,
Allaster, Allastir, Allysdair,
Alystair**

Alban (Latin) from Alba, Italy, a
city on a white hill.
**Albain, Albany, Albean,
Albein, Alby, Auban**
Foreign forms: French: Aubin;
Italian: Albino

Albert (German, French) noble
and bright. See also Ulbrecht.
**Adelbert, Al, Alberts, Albie,
Albrecht, Alvertos, Aubert**
Foreign forms: Czech: Albertik;
English: Elbert; Italian: Alberto;
Scottish: Ailbert

Alberto (Italian) a form of
Albert.
Berto

Albie, Alby (German, French)
familiar forms of Albert.

Albin (Latin) an alternate form
of Alvin.
**Alben, Albeno, Albinek,
Albino, Albins, Albinson,
Alby, Auben**

Albion (Latin) white cliffs.
Geography: a reference to the
white cliffs in Dover, England.

Alcott (English) old cottage.
**Alcot, Alkot, Alkott, Allcot,
Allcott, Allkot, Allkott**

Alden (English) old; wise
protector.
Aldin, Elden
Foreign form: German: Aldous

Alder (German, English) alder
tree.

Aldo (Italian) old; elder.

Aldred (English) old; wise
counselor.
Alldred, Eldred

Aldrich (English) wise coun-
selor.
**Aldric, Aldrick, Aldridge,
Aldrige, Aldritch, Alldric,
Alldrich, Alldrick, Alldridge,
Eldridge**
Foreign form: French: Audric

Alec (Greek) a short form of
Alexander.
Aleck, Alek, Alekko, Alic
Foreign form: Hungarian: Elek

Alejándro (Spanish) a form of
Alexander.
Alejándra, Aléjo, Alexjándro

Aleric (German) an alternate
form of Alaric.
Alerick, Alleric, Allerick

Alessandro (Italian) a form of
Alexander.
Alessand, Allessandro

Alex (Greek) a short form of
Alexander.
Alax, Alix, Allax, Allex
Foreign form: Hungarian: Elek

Alexander (Greek) defender of
mankind. History: Alexander
the Great was the conquerer
of the Greek Empire. See also
Xan, Zander.
**Alec, Alecsandar, Alekos,
Aleksandar, Aleksander,
Aleksandras, Aleksandur,
Alex, Alexandar, Alexandor,
Alexandr, Alexandros, Alexis,
Alexxander, Alexzander,
Alisander, Alixander,
Alixandre**
Foreign forms: Afgani:
Iskander; English: Alistair, Lex,
Sander, Sandy; Estonian: Leks;
French: Alexandre; German:
Alick; Hungarian: Sándor; Irish:
Al; Italian: Alessandro, Sandro;
Polish: Olés; Russian: Aleksandr,
Aleksei, Aleksey, Oleksandr,
Sasha; Scottish: Alastair; Spanish:
Alejandro, Jando; Yiddish: Zindel

Alexandre (French) a form of Alexander.

Alexandros (Greek) an alternate form of Alexander.
Alexandras, Alexandro, Alexandru

Alexis (Greek) a short form of Alexander.
Alexei, Alexes, Alexey, Alexi, Alexie, Alexio, Alexios, Alexius, Alexiz, Alexy

Alfie (English) a familiar form of Alfred.
Alfy

Alfonso (Italian, Spanish) a form of Alphonse.
Alfonsus, Alfonza, Alfonzo, Alfonzus

Alford (English) old river ford.

Alfred (English) elf counselor; wise counselor. See also Fred.
Alf, Alfeo, Alfie, Alured
Foreign forms: Irish: Ailfrid, Ailfryd; Italian/Spanish: Alfredo

Alfredo (Italian, Spanish) a form of Alfred.
Alfrido

Alger (German) noble spearman. (English) a short form of Algernon. See also Elger.
Algar, Allgar

Algernon (English) bearded, wearing a moustache.
Algenon, Alger, Algie, Algin, Algon

Algie (English) a familiar form of Algernon.
Algy

Ali (Arabic) greatest. (Swahili) exalted.
Aly

Alim (Arabic) scholar.

Alisander (Greek) an alternate form of Alexander.
Alisander, Alissander, Alissandre, Alsandair, Alsandare, Alsander

Allan (Irish) an alternate form of Alan.
Allayne

Allard (English) noble, brave.
Ellard
Foreign form: French: Alard

Allen (Irish) an alternate form of Alan.
Alen, Alley, Alleyn, Alleyne, Allie, Allin, Allon, Allyn

Alon (Hebrew) oak.

Alonzo (Spanish) a form of Alphonse.
Alano, Alanzo, Alon, Alonso, Alonza, Elonzo, Lon, Lonnie

Aloysius (German) famous warrior. An alternate form of Louis.
Alaois, Alois, Aloisius, Aloisio

Alphonse (German) noble and eager.
Alf, Alphons, Alphonsa, Alphonza, Alphonzus, Fonzie
Foreign forms: French: Alfonse; Irish: Alphonsus; Italian/Spanish: Alfonso, Alonzo, Alphonso; Portuguese: Affonso; Swedish: Alfons

Alphonso (Italian) a form of Alphonse.
Alphanso, Alphonzo, Fonso

Alroy (Spanish) king.

Alston (English) noble's settlement.
Allston

Altair (Greek) star. (Arabic) flying eagle.

Altman (German) old man.
Altmann, Atman

Alton (English) old town.
Alten

Alva (Hebrew) sublime.

Alvaro (Spanish) just; wise.

Alvin (Latin) white; light skinned. (German) friend to all; noble friend; friend of elves. See also Albin.
Alvan, Alven, Alvie, Alvy, Alvyn, Alwin
Foreign forms: English: **Elvin;** French: **Aloin, Aluin;** Italian: **Alvino;** Spanish: **Aluino**

Alwin (German) an alternate form of Alvin.
Ailwyn, Alwyn, Alwynn, Aylwin

Amadeus (Latin) loves God. Music: Wolfgang Amadeus Mozart was a famous eighteenth-century Austrian composer.
Amad, Amadeaus, Amadei, Amadio, Amadis, Amado, Amador, Amadou, Amedeo, Amodaos
Foreign forms: French: **Amadée, Amando;** Italian: **Amadeo**

Amal (Hebrew) worker. (Arabic) hopeful.

Amandeep (Punjabi) light of peace.
Amandip, Amanjit, Amanjot, Amanpreet

Amar (Punjabi) immortal. (Arabic) builder.

Amari, Amario, Amaris, Amarjit, Amarpreet, Ammar, Ammer

Amato (French) loved.

Ambrose (Greek) immortal.
Ambie, Ambrus, Amby
Foreign forms: Dutch/German/Swedish: **Ambrosius;** French: **Ambroise;** Irish: **Ambros;** Italian: **Ambrosi;** Spanish: **Ambrosio**

Amerigo (Teutonic) industrious. History: Amerigo Vespucci was the explorer for whom America is named.
Americo

Ames (French) friend.

Amiel (Hebrew) God of my people.
Ammiel

Amin (Hebrew, Arabic) trustworthy; honest. (Hindi) faithful.

Amir (Hebrew) proclaimed. (Punjabi) wealthy; king's minister. (Arabic) prince.
Ameer

Amit (Punjabi) unfriendly. (Arabic) highly praised.
Amitan, Amreet, Amrit

Amory (German) an alternate form of Emory.
Amery, Amor

Amos (Hebrew) burdened, troubled. Bible: an Old Testament prophet.

An (Chinese, Vietnamese) peaceful.
Ana

Anand (Hindi) blissful.
Ananda, Anant, Ananth

Anastasius (Greek) resurrection.
Anas, Anastagio, Anastas, Anastase, Anastasi, Anastasio, Anastasios, Anastice, Anastisis, Anaztáz, Athanasius

Anatole (Greek) east.
Anatol, Anatoli, Anatolijus, Anatolio, Anatoly, Anitoly

Anders (Swedish) a form of Andrew.
Ander, Andersen, Anderson

André (French) a form of Andrew.
Andra, Andrae, Andre, Andrecito, Andree, Aundré

Andreas (Greek) an alternate form of Andrew.
Andries

Andres (Spanish) a form of
Andrew.
Andras, Andrés, Andrez

Andrew (Greek) strong; manly;
courageous. Bible: one of the
Twelve Apostles. See also
Evagelos.
**Andery, Andonis, Andreas,
Andrews, Andru, Andrue,
Andy, Anndra, Antal, Audrew
Foreign forms:** *Bulgarian/
Romanian/Russian:* **Andrei;** *Czech:*
Ondro; *Danish:* **Anker;** *English:*
Drew; *French:* **André;** *Hungarian:*
Andor, András, Bandi, Endre;
Irish: **Aindrea;** *Lithuanian:*
Andrius; *Scottish:* **Kendew;**
Spanish: **Andres;** *Swedish:* **Anders**

Andros (Polish) sea. Mythology: the god of the sea.
Andris, Andrus

Andy (Greek) a short form
of Andrew.
Andino, Andis, Andje

Aneurin (Welsh) honorable;
gold. See also Nye.
Aneirin

Angel (Greek) angel. (Latin)
messenger.
**Ange, Angell, Angie, Angy
Foreign forms:** *German:*
Gotzon; *Italian/Spanish:* **Angelo**

Angelo (Italian) a form of
Angel.
Angelito, Angelos, Anglo

Angus (Scottish) exceptional;
outstanding. Mythology:
Angus Og was the Celtic god
of laughter, love, and wisdom.
See also Ennis.
Aeneas, Aonghas

Anh (Vietnamese) peace; safety.

Anil (Hindi) wind god.
Aneel, Anel, Aniel, Aniello

Anka (Turkish) phoenix.

Ansel (French) follower of a
nobleman.
Ancell, Ansa, Ansell

Anselm (German) divine
protector.
**Anse
Foreign forms:** *French:*
Anselme; *Italian:* **Anselmi;** *Latin:*
Elmo; *Spanish:* **Anselmo**

Ansley (Scottish) an alternate
form of Ainsley.
**Anslea, Anslee, Ansleigh,
Anslie, Ansly, Ansy**

Anson (German) divine.
(English) Anne's son.
Ansun

Anthony (Latin) praiseworthy.
(Greek) flourishing. See also
Tony.
**Anathony, Andonios, Andor,
András, Anothony, Anfernee,
Anferny, Anthawn, Anthey,
Anthian, Anthino, Anthoney,
Anthoni, Anthonie, Anthonio,
Anthonu, Anthoy, Anthyoine,
Anthyonny, Antony
Foreign forms:** *Arabic:* **Antwan;**
French: **Antoine;** *Hungarian:*
Antal; *Irish:* **Anntoin;** *Italian:*
Antonio; *Lithuanian:* **Antavas;**
Polish: **Antonin;** *Slavic:* **Anton,
Anthonysha;** *Spanish:* **Antjuan**

Antoan (Vietnamese) safe,
secure.

Antoine (French) a form of
Anthony.
Antionne, Antoiné, Atoine

Anton (Slavic) a form of
Anthony.
Antone, Antons, Antos

Antonio (Italian) a form of
Anthony. See also Tino.
**Antinio, Antonello, Antoino,
Antonín, Antonino, Antonnio,
Antonios, Antonius, Antonyia,
Antonyio, Antonyo**

Antony (Latin) an alternate
form of Anthony.
Antin, Antini, Antius,

Antoney, Antoni, Antonie, Antonin, Antonios, Antonius, Antonyia, Antonyio, Antonyo, Anty

Antwan (Arabic) a form of Anthony.
Antaw, Antawan, Antawn, Anthawn, Antowine, Antowne, Antowyn, Antwain, Antwaina, Antwaine, Antwaion, Antwane, Antwann, Antwanne, Antwarn, Antwaun, Antwen, Antwian, Antwine, Antwion, Antwoan, Antwoin, Antwoine, Antwon, Antwone, Antwonn, Antwonne, Antwuan, Antwyon, Antyon, Antywon

Anwar (Arabic) luminous.
Anour, Anouar, Anwi

Apollo (Greek) manly. Mythology: the god of prophecy, healing, music, poetry, truth, and the sun. See also Polo.
Appollo, Apolinar, Apolinario, Apollos, Apolo, Apolonio

Aquila (Latin, Spanish) eagle.
Acquilla, Aquil, Aquilas, Aquilla, Aquillino

Aram (Syrian) high, exalted.
Ara, Aramia, Arra

Aramis (French) Literature: one of the title characters in Alexandre Dumas's novel *The Three Musketeers*.
Airamis, Aramith, Aramys

Archer (English) bowman. See also Ives.
Archie

Archibald (German) bold.
Arch, Archibold, Archie
Foreign forms: *French:* **Archaimbaud, Archambault;** *Russian:* **Arkadij, Arkady;** *Spanish:* **Archibaldo**

Archie (German, English) a familiar form of Archer, Archibald.
Archy

Ardell (Latin) eager; industrious.

Arden (Latin) ardent; fiery.
Ard, Ardie, Ardin, Arduino

Ardon (Hebrew) bronzed.

Aren (Danish) eagle; ruler.

Argus (Danish) watchful, vigilant.
Agos

Ari (Greek) a short form of Aristotle. (Hebrew) a short form of Ariel.

Aria, Arias, Arie, Arih, Arij, Ario, Arri

Aric (German) an alternate form of Richard. (Scandinavian) an alternate form of Eric.
Aaric, Areck, Arick, Arik, Arric, Arrick, Arrik

Ariel (Hebrew) lion of God. Bible: another name for Jerusalem. Literature: the name of a spirit in the Shakespearean play *The Tempest*.
Airel, Arel, Areli, Ari, Ariya, Ariyel, Arrial, Arriel

Aries (Greek) Mythology: Ares was the Greek god of war. (Latin) ram.
Arie, Ariez

Arion (Greek) enchanted. Mythology: a magic horse. (Hebrew) melodious.
Arian, Ariane, Arien, Arrian

Aristides (Greek) son of the best.
Aris, Aristidis

Aristotle (Greek) best; wise. History: a third-century B.C. philosopher who tutored Alexander the Great.
Ari, Aris, Aristito, Aristo, Aristokles, Aristotelis

Arkin (Norwegian) son of the eternal king.
Aricin, Arkeen, Arkyn

Arledge (English) lake with the hares.
Arlidge, Arlledge

Arlen (Irish) pledge.
Arlan, Arland, Arlend, Arlin, Arlyn, Arlynn
Foreign form: Scandinavian:
Arles

Arley (English) a short form of Harley.
Arleigh, Arlie, Arly

Arlo (German) an alternate form of Charles. (Spanish) barberry. (English) fortified hill. See also Harlow.

Arman (Persian) desire, goal.
Armaan

Armand (Latin) noble. (German) soldier. An alternate form of Herman.
Armad, Armanda, Armands, Armanno, Armaude, Armenta, Armond
Foreign forms: Italian/Spanish:
Armando; Polish: Mandek;
Russian: Arman

Armando (Spanish) a form of Armand.
Armondo

Armon (Hebrew) high fortress, stronghold.
Arman, Armen, Armin, Armino, Armoni, Armons

Armstrong (English) strong arm.

Arne (German) an alternate form of Arnold.
Arna, Arnel, Arnell

Arnette (English) little eagle.
Arnat, Arnet, Arnot, Arnott

Arnie (German) a familiar form of Arnold.
Arney, Arni, Arnny, Arny

Arno (German) eagle wolf. (Czech) a short form of Ernest.
Arnou, Arnoux

Arnold (German) eagle ruler.
Arnald, Arne, Arnie, Arnoll, Arndt
Foreign forms: French: Arnaud;
Irish: Ardal; Italian: Arno,
Arnoldo; Spanish: Arnaldo

Aron, Arron (Hebrew) alternate forms of Aaron.

Arsenio (Greek) masculine; virile. History: Saint Arsenius was a teacher in the Roman Empire.
Arsen, Arsène, Arsenius, Arseny, Arsinio

Art (English) a short form of Arthur.

Artemus (Greek) gift of Artemis. Mythology: Artemis was the goddess of the hunt and the moon.
Artemas, Artemio, Artemis, Artimas, Artimis, Artimus

Artie (English) a familiar form of Arthur.
Arte, Artian, Artis, Arty, Atty

Arthur (Irish) noble; lofty hill. (Scottish) bear. (English) rock. (Icelandic) follower of Thor.
Art, Arth, Arther, Arthor, Artie, Artor, Aurthar, Aurther, Aurthur
Foreign forms: French: Artus;
Italian/Spanish: Arturo, Turi;
Polish: Artek; Russian: Artur;
Scottish: Artair

Arturo (Italian) a form of Arthur.
Arthuro, Artur

Arun (Cambodian, Hindi) sun.
Aruns

Arundel (English) eagle valley.

Arve (Norwegian) heir, inheritor.

Arvid (Hebrew) wanderer. (Norwegian) eagle tree.

See also Ravid.
**Arv, Arvad, Arve, Arvie,
Arvind, Arvinder, Arvydas**
Foreign form: Hungarian:
Arpad

Arvin (German) friend of the
people; friend of the army.
**Arv, Arvie, Arvind, Arvinder,
Arvon, Arvy**

Asa (Hebrew) physician, healer.
(Yoruba) falcon.
Ase

Asád (Arabic) lion.
**Asaad, Asad, 'Asid, Assad,
Azad**

Ascot (English) eastern cottage;
style of necktie. Geography: a
famous racetrack near Windsor
castle.

Ash (Hebrew) ash tree.
Ashby

Ashby (Scandinavian) ash-tree
farm. (Hebrew) an alternate
form of Ash.
Ashbey

Asher (Hebrew) happy;
blessed.
Ashar, Ashor, Ashur

Ashford (English) ash-tree ford.
Ash, Ashtin

Ashley (English) ash-tree
meadow.
**Ash, Asheley, Ashelie, Ashely,
Ashlan, Ashleigh, Ashlen,
Ashlie, Ashlin, Ashling,
Ashlinn, Ashlone, Ashly,
Ashlyn, Ashlynn, Aslan**

Ashon (Swahili) seventh-born
son.

Ashton (English) ash-tree
settlement.
Ashtin

Ashur (Swahili) Mythology: the
principle Assyrian deity.

Aston (English) eastern town.
Asten, Astin

Atherton (English) town by a
spring.

Atlas (Greek) lifted; carried.
Mythology: Atlas was forced
to carry the world on his
shoulders as a punishment for
feuding with Zeus.

Atley (English) meadow.
**Atlea, Atlee, Atleigh, Atli,
Attley**

Attila (Gothic) little father.
History: the Hun leader who
conquered the Goths.
Atalik, Atilio, Atiya

Atwater (English) at the
water's edge.

Atwell (English) at the well.

Atwood (English) at the forest.

Atworth (English) at the farmstead.

Auberon (German) an alternate form of Oberon.
Auberron, Aubrey

Aubrey (German) noble; bear-
like. (French) a familiar form of
Auberon.
**Aubary, Aube, Aubery, Aubry,
Aubury**
Foreign forms: English: *Avery;*
Swedish: *Alberik*

Auburn (Latin) reddish brown.

Auden (English) old friend.

Audie (German) noble; strong.
(English) a familiar form of
Edward.
Audi, Audiel, Audley

Audon (French) old; rich.
Audelon

Audric (English) wise ruler.

Audun (Scandinavian) desert-
ed, desolate.

Augie (Latin) a familiar form of August.
Auggie, Augy

August (Latin) a short form of Augustine, Augustus.
Augie

Augustine (Latin) majestic. Religion: Saint Augustine was the first Archbishop of Canterbury. See also Austin, Tino.
Agostino, Agoston, August, Agustin, Augustin
Foreign forms: French: **Auguste;** Irish: **Aguistin;** Italian: **Agosto;** Spanish: **Augusto**

Augustus (Latin) majestic; venerable. History: a name used by Roman emperors such as Augustus Caesar.
August

Aurek (Polish) golden haired.

Aurelius (Latin) golden. History: Marcus Aurelius Antoninus was a second-century A.D. philosopher and emperor of Rome.
Arelian, Areliano, Aurélien, Aurey, Auriel, Aury
Foreign forms: Czech: **Aurel;** French: **Aurele, Aurèle;** Italian: **Aurelio;** Polish: **Aureli;** Russian: **Avreliy**

Austin (Latin) a short form of Augustine.
Astin, Austen, Austine, Auston, Austyn
Foreign forms: Irish: **Oistin, Ostin**

Avent (French) born during Advent.
Aventin, Aventino

Averill (French) born in April. (English) boar-warrior.
Ave, Averel, Averell, Averiel, Averil, Averyl, Averyll, Avrel, Avrell, Avrill, Avryll

Avery (English) a form of Aubrey.
Avary, Aveary, Averey, Averie, Avry

Avi (Hebrew) God is my father.
Avian, Avidan, Avidor, Aviel, Avion

Aviv (Hebrew) youth; springtime.

Avner (Hebrew) an alternate form of Abner.
Avneet, Avniel

Avram (Hebrew) an alternate form of Abraham, Abram.
Arram, Avraham, Avrom, Avrum

Axel (Latin) axe. (German) small oak tree; source of life. (Scandinavian) a form of Absalom.
Aksel, Ax, Axe, Axell, Axil, Axill

Aydin (Turkish) intelligent.

Ayers (English) heir to a fortune.

Azad (Turkish) free.

Azeem (Arabic) an alternate form of Azim.
Aseem, Asim

Azi (Nigerian) youth.

Azim (Arabic) defender.

'Aziz (Arabic) strong.

Azizi (Swahili) precious.

Azriel (Hebrew) God is my aid.

Baden (German) bather.
Bayden

Bailey (French) bailiff, steward.
**Bail, Bailie, Bailio, Baillie,
Baily, Bayley, Bayly**

Bain (Irish) a short form of
Bainbridge.
Bayne

Bainbridge (Irish) fair bridge.
**Bain, Baynbridge,
Baynebridge**

Baird (Irish) bard, traveling
minstrel; poet.
Bairde, Bard

Baker (English) baker. See also
Baxter.

Baldemar (German) bold;
famous.
**Baldemer, Baldomero,
Baumar**
Foreign form: French: *Baumer*

Balder (Scandinavian) bald.
Mythology: the Norse god of
light, summer, and innocence.
Baldier, Baldur
Foreign form: French: *Baudier*

Baldric (German) brave ruler.
Baldrick
Foreign form: French: *Baudric*

Baldwin (German) bold friend.
**Bald, Baldwinn, Baldwyn,
Baldwynn, Balldwin**
Foreign forms: Danish/Swedish:
Balduin; French: *Baudoin;* Italian:
Baldovino

Balfour (Scottish) pasture land.
Balfor, Balfore

Balin (Hindi) mighty soldier.
Bali, Valin

Ballard (German) brave;
strong.
Balard

Balthasar (Greek) God save
the king. Bible: one of the
Three Wise Men.
**Badassare, Baltazar,
Balthasaar, Balthazar,**

**Baltsaros, Belshazar,
Boldizsár**
Foreign forms: German:
Baltasar; Hebrew: *Belshazzar;*
Italian: *Baldassare*

Bancroft (English) bean field.
**Ban, Bancrofft, Bank,
Bankroft, Banky, Binky**

Banner (Scottish, English) flag
bearer.
Bannor, Banny

Banning (Irish) small and fair.
Banny

Barak (Hebrew) lightning bolt.
Bible: the valiant warrior who
helped Deborah.
Barrak

Barclay (Scottish, English)
birch tree meadow.
**Bar, Barcley, Barklay, Barkley,
Barklie, Barrclay, Berkeley**

Bard (Irish) an alternate form
of Baird.
Bar, Bardia, Bardiya, Barr
Foreign form: French: *Barde*

Bardolf (German) bright wolf.
Literature: the name of a
drunken fool who appeared in
four Shakespearean plays.
Bardo
Foreign forms: English:

Bardolf (cont.)
Bardolph, Bardulf, Bardulph;
French: **Bardou, Bardoul**

Bardrick (Teutonic) axe ruler.
Bardric, Bardrik

Barker (English) lumberjack;
advertiser at a carnival.

Barlow (English) bare hillside.
Barlowe, Barrlow, Barrlowe

Barnabas (Greek, Hebrew,
Aramaic, Latin) son of the mis-
sionary. Bible: disciple of Paul.
Barnabus, Barnebus
Foreign forms: English: **Barnaby,
Barney;** *French:* **Barnabé;**
Hawaiian: **Bane;** *Hungarian:*
Barna; *Italian:* **Barnaba;** *Spanish:*
Bernabé, Barnebas

Barnaby (English) a form of
Barnabas.
**Barnabee, Barnabey,
Barnabie, Burnaby**

Barnes (English) bear; son of
Barnett.

Barnett (English) nobleman;
leader.
**Barn, Barnet, Barney,
Baronet, Baronett, Barrie,
Barron, Barry**

Barney (English) a familiar
form of Barnabas, Barnett.
Barnie, Barny

Barnum (German) barn; stor-
age place. (English) baron's
home.
Barnham

Baron (German, English)
nobleman, baron.
**Baaron, Baronie, Barrion,
Barron, Baryn**

Barrett (German) strong as
a bear.
**Bar, Baret, Barrat, Barret,
Barrette, Barry**

Barrington (English)
Geography: a town in
England.

Barry (Welsh) son of Harry.
(Irish) spear, marksman.
(French) gate, fence.
**Baris, Barri, Barrie, Barris,
Bary**

Bart (Hebrew) a short form of
Bartholomew, Barton.
Barrt, Bartel, Bartie, Barty

Bartholomew (Hebrew) son
of Talmaí. Bible: one of the
Twelve Apostles.
**Balta, Barth, Barthélmy,
Bartho, Bartholomieu,
Bartimous, Bartolommeo,
Bartome**
Foreign forms: Czech: **Bartek,
Bartz;** *English:* **Bart, Bartlet,**
Bat; *French:* **Barthélemy,
Bartholome, Bartolomé;**
German: **Barthel, Bartholomaus;**
Hawaiian: **Bane;** *Italian:* **Bartholo,
Bartholomeo, Bartolo,
Bartolomeo;** *Portuguese:*
Bartolomeô; *Scottish:* **Parlan;**
Slavic: **Jerney;** *Spanish:* **Barto,
Bartoli, Bartolome;** *Swedish:*
Barthelemy, Bartholomeus

Barton (English) barley farm;
Bart's town.
Barrton, Bart

Bartram (English) an alternate
form of Bertram.
Barthram

Baruch (Hebrew) blessed.
Boruch

Basil (Greek, Latin) royal, king-
ly. Religion: a saint and lead-
ing scholar of the early
Christian Church. Botany: an
herb used in cooking. See also
Vasilis.
Base, Baseal, Basel, Bassel
Foreign forms: Czech: **Bazil;**
Dutch/Swedish: **Basilius;** *English:*
Bas; *French:* **Basile;** *German:*
Basle; *Hungarian:* **Bazel;** *Italian:*
Basilio; *Polish:* **Bazek;** *Russian:*
Bazyli, Wasili; *Spanish:* **Basilios**

Basir (Turkish) intelligent,
discerning.

Bashar, Basheer, Bashir, Bashiyr, Bechir, Bhasheer

Bassett (English) little person.
Basett, Basset

Bastien (German) a short form of Sebastian.
Baste, Bastiaan

Baxter (English) an alternate form of Baker.
Bax, Baxie, Baxty, Baxy

Bay (Vietnamese) seventh son. (French) chestnut brown color; evergreen tree. (English) howler.

Bayard (English) reddish brown hair.
Bay, Bayerd, Bayrd
Foreign form: Italian: Baiardo

Beacher (English) beech trees.
Beach, Beachy, Beech, Beecher, Beechy

Beale (French) an alternate form of Beau.
Beal, Beall, Bealle, Beals

Beaman (English) beekeeper.
Beamann, Beamen, Beeman, Beman

Beamer (English) trumpet player.

Beasley (English) field of peas.

Beattie (Latin) blessed; happy; bringer of joy. A masculine form of Beatrice.
Beatie, Beatty, Beaty

Beau (French) handsome.
Beale, Bo

Beaufort (French) beautiful fort.

Beaumont (French) beautiful mountain.

Beauregard (French) handsome; beautiful; well regarded.

Beaver (English) beaver.
Beav, Beavo, Beve, Bevo

Bebe (Spanish) baby.

Beck (English, Scandinavian) brook.
Beckett

Bede (English) prayer. Religion: the patron saint of scholars.

Bela (Czech) white. (Hungarian) bright.
Béla, Belal, Bellal

Belden (French, English) pretty valley.
Beldin, Beldon, Bellden, Belldon

Bell (French) handsome. (English) bell ringer.

Bellamy (French) beautiful friend.
Belamy, Bell, Bellamey, Bellamie

Bello (African) helper or promoter of Islam.

Bem (Tiv) peace.
Behm

Ben (Hebrew) a short form of Benjamin.
Behn, Benio, Benn, Benne, Benno

Ben-ami (Hebrew) son of my people.
Baram, Barami

Benedict (Latin) blessed.
Bendick, Bendict, Bendix, Benedick, Benedictus
Foreign forms: French: Benoit; German/Slavic: Benedikt; Greek: Venedictos; Hungarian: Benci, Benedik, Benke; Italian: Benedetto, Benito; Russian: Venya; Scandinavian: Bengt; Spanish: Benedicto

Benito (Italian) a form of Benedict. History: Benito Mussolini led Italy during World War II.

Benito *(cont.)*
Benedo, Benino, Benno, Beno, Betto

Benjamin (Hebrew) son of my right hand.
Behnjamin, Bejamin, Bemjiman, Ben, Benejamen, Benjaim, Benjamaim, Benjaman, Benjamen, Benjamine, Benjamino, Benjamon, Benjamyn, Benjemin, Benjermain, Benji, Benjie, Benjiman, Benjimen, Benjjmen, Benjy, Benny, Benyamin
Foreign forms: *Basque:*
Benkamin; *Bulgarian:* **Veniamin;**
Ethiopian: **Beniam;** *Hawaiian:*
Peniamina; *Italian:* **Beniamino;**
Lithuanian: **Benejaminas;** *Spanish:*
Benja, Mincho; *Yiddish:* **Binyamin**

Benjiro (Japanese) enjoys peace.

Bennett (Latin) little blessed one.
Benet, Benett, Bennet

Benny (Hebrew) a familiar form of Benjamin.
Bennie

Beno (Hebrew) son. (Mwera) band member.

Benoit (French) a form of Benedict. (English) Botany: a yellow, flowering rose plant.
Berne

Benson (Hebrew) son of Ben. A short form of Ben Zion.
Bensen, Benssen, Bensson

Bentley (English) moor; coarse grass meadow.
Bent, Bentlea, Bentlee, Bentlie, Lee

Benton (English) Ben's town; town on the moors.
Bent

Ben Zion (Hebrew) son of Zion.
Benzi

Berg (German) mountain.
Berdj, Bergh, Berje

Bergen (German, Scandinavian) hill dweller.
Bergin, Birgin

Berger (French) shepherd.

Berk (Turkish) solid, rugged.

Berkeley (English) an alternate form of Barclay.
Berk, Berkie, Berkley, Berklie, Berkly, Berky

Berl (German) an alternate form of Burl.

Bern (German) a short form of Bernard.
Berne

Bernal (German) strong as a bear.
Bernald, Bernaldo, Bernel, Bernhald, Bernhold, Bernold

Bernard (German) brave as a bear.
Bear, Ber, Berend, Bern, Bernabé, Bernardel, Bernardus, Bernardyn, Bernarr, Bernat, Bernel, Bernerd, Bernhard, Bernhards, Bernhardt, Bernie, Burnard
Foreign forms: *Czech:* **Bernek,** *French:* **Barnard, Bernardin;** *Irish/Scottish:* **Bearnard;** *Lithuanian:* **Bernadas;** *Polish:* **Benek;** *Russian:* **Berngards;** *Scandanavian:* **Bjorn;** *Spanish:* **Bernal, Bernardo**

Bernardo (Spanish) a form of Bernard.
Barnardino, Barnardo, Barnhardo, Benardo, Bernhardo, Berno, Burnardo, Nardo

Bernie (German) a familiar form of Bernard.
Berney, Berni, Berny, Birney, Birnie, Birny, Burney

Berry (English) berry; grape.

Bert (German, English) bright, shining. A short form of Berthold, Berton, Bertram, Bertrand.
Bertie, Bertus, Birt, Burt

Berthold (German) bright; illustrious; brilliant ruler.
Bert, Bertold, Bertolde
Foreign form: French: Berthoud

Bertie (English) a familiar form of Bert.
Bertie, Berty, Birt, Birtie, Birty

Bertín (Spanish) distinguished friend.
Berti

Berton (English) bright settlement; fortified town.
Bert

Bertram (German) bright; illustrious. (English) bright raven. See also Bartram.
Beltran, Bert, Berton
Foreign forms: Italian: Beltrano; Spanish: Beltrán

Bertrand (German) bright shield.
Bert, Bertran
Foreign forms: Italian: Bertrando, Bertranno

Berwyn (English) harvest son; powerful friend. Astrology: a name for babies born under the signs of Virgo, Capricorn, and Taurus.
Berwin, Berwynn, Berwynne

Bevan (Welsh) son of Evan.
Beavan, Beaven, Beavin, Bev, Beve, Beven, Bevin, Bevo, Bevon

Beverly (English) beaver meadow.
Beverlea, Beverleigh, Beverley, Beverlie

Bevis (French) from Beauvais, France; bull.
Beauvais, Bevys

Bickford (English) axe-man's ford.

Bijan (Persian) ancient hero.
Bihjan, Bijann

Bill (German) a short form of William.
Bil, Billijo, Byll, Will

Billy (German) a familiar form of Bill, William.
Bille, Billey, Billie, Billy, Bily, Willie

Bing (German) kettle-shaped hollow.

Binh (Vietnamese) peaceful.

Binky (English) a familiar form of Bancroft, Vincent.
Bink, Binkie

Birch (English) white; shining; birch tree.
Birk, Burch

Birger (Norwegian) rescued.

Birkey (English) island with birch trees.
Birk, Birkie, Birky

Birkitt (English) birch-tree coast.
Birk, Birket, Birkit, Burket, Burkett, Burkitt

Birley (English) meadow with the cow barn.
Birlee, Birlie, Birly

Birney (English) island with a brook.
Birne, Birnie, Birny, Burney, Burnie, Burny

Birtle (English) hill with birds.

Bishop (Greek) overseer. (English) bishop.
Bish

Bjorn (Scandinavian) a form of Bernard.
Bjarne, Bjarni

Blackburn (Scottish) black brook.

Blade (English) knife, sword.
Blae, Blaed, Blayde

Blaine (Irish) thin, lean. (English) river source.
Blane, Blaney, Blayne, Blayney

Blair (Irish) plain, field. (Welsh) place.
Blaire, Blayr, Blayre

Blaise (French) a form of Blaze.
Ballas, Balyse, Blaisot, Blase, Blasi

Blake (English) attractive; dark.
Blakely, Blakeman, Blakey

Blakely (English) dark meadow.
Blakelee, Blakeleigh, Blakeley, Blakelie, Blakeny

Blanco (Spanish) light skinned, white, blond.

Blaze (Latin) stammerer. (English) flame; trail mark made on a tree.
Balázs, Blaise, Blaize, Blayze
Foreign forms: German: **Blasien;** Italian: **Biaggio, Biagio;** Spanish: **Blas;** Swedish: **Blasius**

Blayne (Irish) an alternate form of Blaine.
Blain, Blaine, Blane

Bliss (English) blissful; joyful.

Bly (Native American) high.

Blythe (English) carefree; merry, joyful.
Blithe, Blyth

Bo (English) a form of Beau, Beauregard.

Boaz (Hebrew) swift; strong.
Bo, Boas, Booz, Bos, Boz

Bob (English) a short form of Robert.
Bobb, Bobby, Rob
Foreign form: Czech: **Bobek**

Bobby (English) a familiar form of Bob, Robert.
Bobbey, Bobbi, Bobbie, Boby

Boden (Scandinavian) sheltered. (French) messenger, herald.
Bodee, Bodie, Bodin, Bodine, Boe, Boedee

Bodil (Norwegian) mighty ruler.

Bogart (German) strong as a bow. (Irish, Welsh) bog, marshland.
Bo, Bogey, Bogie, Bogy

Bonaro (Italian, Spanish) friend.
Bona, Bonar

Bond (English) tiller of the soil.
Bondie, Bondon, Bonds, Bondy

Boniface (Latin) do-gooder.
Bonifacy
Foreign forms: Dutch/German/Swedish: **Bonifacius;** Italian: **Bonifacio**

Booker (English) bookmaker; book lover; Bible lover.
Bookie, Books, Booky

Boone (Latin, French) good. History: Daniel Boone was an American frontiersman.
Bon, Bone, Bonne, Boonie, Boony

Booth (English) hut. (Scandinavian) temporary dwelling.
Boot, Boote, Boothe

Borak (Arabic) lightning. Mythology: the horse that carried Muhammed to seventh heaven.

Borden (French) cottage. (English) valley of the boar; boar's den.
Bord, Bordie, Bordy

Borg (Scandinavian) castle.

Boris (Slavic) battler, warrior. Religion: the patron saint of Moscow.

Boriss, Borja, Borris, Borya, Boryenka, Borys

Borka (Russian) fighter.
Borkinka

Bosley (English) grove of trees.

Botan (Japanese) blossom, bud.

Bourne (Latin, French) boundary. (English) brook, stream. See also Burne.
Byrn

Bowen (Welsh) son of Owen.
Bow, Bowe, Bowie

Bowie (Irish) yellow haired. History: Colonel James Bowie was an American scout.
Bow, Bowen

Boyce (French) woods, forest.
Boice, Boise, Boy, Boycey, Boycie

Boyd (Scottish) yellow haired.
Boid, Boyde

Brad (English) a short form of Bradford, Bradley.
Bradd, Brade

Bradburn (English) broad stream.

Braden (English) broad valley.
Bradan, Bradden, Bradin, Bradine, Bradyn, Braeden, Braiden, Brayden

Bradford (English) broad river crossing.
Brad, Braddford, Ford

Bradley (English) broad meadow.
Brad, Bradlay, Bradlea, Bradlee, Bradleigh, Bradlie, Bradly, Bradney

Bradly (English) an alternate form of Bradley.

Bradon (English) broad hill.
Braedon, Braidon, Braydon

Bradshaw (English) broad forest.

Brady (Irish) spirited. (English) broad island.
Bradey

Braham (Hindi) creator.
Braheem, Braheim, Brahiem, Brahima, Brahm

Brainard (English) bold raven; prince.
Brainerd

Bram (Hebrew) a short form of Abraham, Abram. (Scottish)

bramble, brushwood.
Bramm, Bramdon

Bramwell (English) bramble-bush spring.
Brammel, Brammell, Bramwel, Bramwyll

Branch (Latin) paw; claw; tree branch.

Brand (English) firebrand; sword. A short form of Brandon.
Brandall, Brande, Brandel, Brandell, Brander, Brandley, Brandol, Brandt, Brandy, Brann

Brandeis (Czech) dweller on a burned clearing.
Brandis

Branden (English) beacon valley.

Brandon (English) beacon hill.
Brand, Brandan, Branddon, Brandin, Brandone, Brandonn, Brandyn, Branndan
Foreign forms: Irish: **Bran, Brannon**

Brandt (English) an alternate form of Brant.

Brandy (Dutch) brandy.
Brandey, Brandi, Brandie

Brannon (Irish) a form of Brandon.
Branen, Brannan, Branon

Branson (English) son of Brandon, Brant.
Bransen, Bransin, Brantson

Brant (English) proud.
Brandt, Brannt, Brantley, Brantlie

Brawley (English) meadow on the hillside.
Brawlee, Brawly

Braxton (English) Brock's town.

Breck (Irish) freckled.
Brec, Breckie, Brexton

Brede (Scandinavian) iceberg, glacier.

Brendan (Irish) little raven. (English) sword.
Breandan, Bren, Brenden, Brendis, Brendon, Brenn, Brennan, Brenndan, Bryn

Brenden (Irish) an alternate form of Brendan.
Bren, Brendene, Brendin, Brendine

Brennan, Brennen (English, Irish) alternate forms of Brendan.
Bren, Brennin, Brennon

Brent (English) a short form of Brenton.
Brendt, Brentson

Brenton (English) steep hill.
Brent, Brentan, Brenten, Brentin, Brentton, Brentyn

Bret, Brett (Scottish) from Great Britain.
Bhrett, Braten, Braton, Brayton, Breton, Brette, Bretten, Bretton, Brit

Brit, Britt (Scottish) alternate forms of Bret, Brett.
Brit, Britain, Briton, Brittain, Brittan, Britten, Britton, Brityce

Brewster (English) brewer.
Brew, Brewer, Bruwster

Brian (Irish, Scottish) strong; virtuous; honorable. History: Brian Boru was the most famous Irish king.
Briant, Briante, Brien, Brience, Brient, Brin, Briny, Brion, Bryan
Foreign forms: Hawaiian: Palaina; Italian: Briano

Brice (Welsh) alert; ambitious. (English) son of Rice.
Bricen, Briceton, Bryce

Brick (English) bridge.
Brickman, Brik

Bridger (English) bridge builder.
Bridd, Bridgeley, Bridgely

Brigham (English) covered bridge. (French) troops, brigade.
Brig, Brigg, Briggs, Brighton

Brock (English) badger.
Broc, Brocke, Brockett, Brockie, Brockley, Brockton, Brocky, Brok, Broque

Brod (English) a short form of Broderick.

Broderick (Welsh) son of the famous ruler. (English) broad ridge. See also Roderick.
Brod, Broddie, Broddy, Broderic, Brodric, Brodrick, Brodryck

Brodie (Irish) an alternate form of Brody.
Brodi

Brody (Irish) ditch; canal builder.
Brodee, Broden, Brodey, Brodie, Broedy

Bromley (English) brushwood meadow.

Bron (Afrikaans) source.

Bronislaw (Polish) weapon of glory.

Bronson (English) son of Brown.
Bransen, Bransin, Branson, Bron, Bronnie, Bronnson, Bronny, Bronsen, Bronsin, Bronsonn, Bronsson, Bronsun

Brook (English) brook, stream.
Brooke, Brooker, Brookin, Brooklyn

Brooks (English) son of Brook.
Brookes, Broox

Brown (English) brown; bear.

Bruce (French) brushwood thicket; woods.
Brucey, Brucy, Brue, Bruis

Bruno (German, Italian) brown haired; brown skinned.
Brunon, Bruns

Bryan (Irish) strong; virtuous; honorable. An alternate form of Brian.
Bryant, Bryen

Bryant (Irish) an alternate form of Bryan.
Bryent

Bryce (Welsh) an alternate form of Brice.

Brycen, Bryceton, Bryson, Bryston

Bryon (German) cottage. (English) bear.

Bryson (Welsh) son of Brice.

Bubba (American) good old boy.

Buck (German, English) male deer.
Buckie, Buckley, Buckner, Bucko, Bucky

Buckley (English) deer meadow.
Bucklea, Bucklee

Buckminster (English) preacher.

Bud (English) herald, messenger.
Budd
Foreign form: American: *Buddy*

Buddy (American) a familiar form of Bud.
Budde, Buddey, Buddie

Buell (German) hill dweller. (English) bull.

Buford (English) ford near the castle.
Burford

Burgess (English) town dweller; shopkeeper.
Burg, Burges, Burgh, Burgiss, Burr

Burke (German, French) fortress, castle.
Berk, Berke, Birk, Bourke, Burk, Burkley

Burl (German) a short form of Berlyn. (English) cup bearer; wine servant; knot in a tree.
Burley, Burlie, Burlin, Byrle

Burleigh (English) meadow with knotted tree trunks.
Burlee, Burley, Burlie, Byrleigh, Byrlee

Burne (English) brook. See also Bourne.
Beirne, Burn, Burnell, Burnett, Burney, Byrne

Burney (English) island with a brook. A familiar form of Rayburn.

Burr (Swedish) youth. (English) prickly plant.

Burris (English) town dweller.

Burt (English) an alternate form of Bert. A short form of Burton.
Burrt, Burtt, Burty

Burton (English) fortified town.
Berton, Burt

Busby (Scottish) village in the thicket; tall, military hat made of fur.
Busbee, Buzby, Buzz

Butcher (English) butcher.
*Foreign form: American: **Butch***

Buster (American) hitter, puncher.

Buzz (Scottish) a short form of Busby.
Buzzy

Byford (English) by the ford.

Byram (English) cattleyard.

Byrd (English) birdlike.
Bird, Birdie, Byrdie

Byrne (English) an alternate form of Burne.
Byrn, Byrnes

Byron (French) cottage. (English) barn.
Beyren, Beyron, Biren, Biron, Buiron, Byram, Byran, Byrann, Byren, Byrom, Byrone

Cable (French, English) rope maker.

Cadao (Vietnamese) folk song.

Cadby (English) warrior's settlement.

Caddock (Welsh) eager for war.

Cade (Welsh) a short form of Cadell.

Cadell (Welsh) battler.
Cade, Cadel, Cedell

Cadmus (Greek) from the east. Mythology: the founder of the city of Thebes.

Caelan (Scottish) a form of Nicholas.
Cael, Caelin, Cailan, Cailean, Cailen, Cailin, Caillan, Caillin,
Calan, Caleon, Caley, Calin, Callan, Callen, Callon, Calyn, Caylan, Cayley

Caesar (Latin) long haired. History: a title for Roman emperors.
Caezar, Caseare, Ceasar, Seasar
*Foreign forms: French: **César**, German: **Kaiser**; Italian: **Ceseare**; Russian: **Czar, Kesar**; Slavic: **Cezar**; Spanish: **Cesar, Sarito***

Cahil (Turkish) young, naive.

Cain (Hebrew) spear; gatherer. Bible: Adam and Eve's oldest son. See also Kane.
Cainan, Caine, Caineth
*Foreign form: Turkish: **Kabil***

Cairn (Welsh) landmark made of piled-up stones.
Cairne, Carn, Carne

Cairo (Arabic) Geography: the capital of Egypt.
Kairo

Cal (Latin) a short form of Calvert, Calvin.

Calder (Welsh, English) brook, stream.

Caldwell (English) cold well.

Cale (Hebrew) a short form of Caleb.

Caleb (Hebrew) dog; faithful. (Arabic) bold, brave. Bible: a companion of Moses and Joshua. See also Kaleb.
Caeleb, Calab, Cale
Foreign form: Irish: Caley

Calhoun (Irish) narrow woods. (Scottish) warrior.
Colhoun, Colquhoun

Callahan (Irish) Religion: a Catholic saint.
Calahan, Callaghan

Callum (Irish) dove.
Callam, Calum, Calym

Calvert (English) calf herder.
Cal, Calbert, Calvirt

Calvin (Latin) bald. See also Kalvin, Vinny.
Cal, Calv

Cam (Gypsy) beloved. (Scottish) a short form of Cameron.
Camm, Cammie, Cammy, Camy

Camden (Scottish) winding valley.

Cameron (Scottish) crooked nose. See also Kameron.

Cam, Camar, Camaron, Cameran, Camerson, Camiren, Camron

Camilo (Latin) child born to freedom; noble.
Camiel, Camillus
Foreign forms: French: Camille; Italian: Camillo

Campbell (Latin, French) beautiful field. (Scottish) crooked mouth.
Cam, Camp, Campy

Camron (Scottish) a short form of Cameron.
Camren

Candide (Latin) pure; sincere.
Candid, Candido, Candonino

Cannon (French) church official; large gun.
Cannan, Canning, Canon

Canute (Latin) white haired. (Scandinavian) knot. History: an ancient Danish king who won a battle at Knutsford. See also Knute.
Cnut, Cnute

Cappi (Gypsy) good fortune.

Car (Irish) a short form of Carney.

Carey (Greek) pure. (Welsh) castle; rocky island. See also Karey.
Care, Cary

Carl (German) farmer. (English) strong and manly. An alternate form of Charles. A short form of Carlton. See also Carroll, Karl.
Carle, Carles, Carless, Carlis, Carll, Carlson, Carlston, Carlus, Carolos
Foreign forms: Hawaiian: Kale; Italian: Carlo; Scandinavian: Kalle; Spanish: Carlos

Carlin (Irish) little champion.
Carlan, Carlen, Carley, Carlie, Carling, Carlino, Carly

Carlisle (English) Carl's island.
Carlyle, Carlysle

Carlo (Italian) a form of Carl, Charles.
Carolo

Carlos (Spanish) a form of Carl, Charles.

Carlton (English) Carl's town.
Carl, Carleton, Carliton, Carlston, Carltonn, Carltton, Charlton

Carmel (Hebrew) vineyard, garden.

Carmel (cont.)
Carmello, Carmelo, Karmel
Foreign form: Italian: **Carmine**

Carmichael (Scottish) follower
of Michael.

Carmine (Latin) song; crimson.
(Italian) a form of Carmel.
Carman, Carmen, Carmon

Carnell (English) defender of
the castle.

Carney (Irish) victorious.
(Scottish) fighter. See also
Kearney.
Car, Carny, Karney

Carr (Scandinavian) marsh.
See also Kerr.
Karr

Carrick (Irish) rock.
Carooq, Carricko

Carroll (German) an alternate
form of Carl. (Irish) champion.
**Carel, Carell, Cariel, Cariell,
Carol, Carole, Carolo, Carols,
Carollan, Carolus, Carrol,
Cary, Caryl**

Carson (English) son of Carr.
Carrson

Carter (English) cart driver.
Cart

Cartwright (English) cart
builder.

Carvell (French, English) village
on the marsh.
Carvel

Carver (English) wood-carver;
sculptor.

Case (Irish) a short form of
Casey. (English) a short form
of Casimir.

Casey (Irish) brave.
**Case, Casie, Casy, Cayse,
Caysey, Kacey**

Cash (Latin) vain. (Slavic) a
short form of Casimir.
Cashe

Casimir (Slavic) peacemaker.
Cas, Cash, Casimirer
Foreign forms: English: **Case,
Castime;** *German:* **Kasimir;** *Polish:*
Kazio; *Spanish:* **Cachi, Casimiro,
Cashi**

Casper (Persian) treasurer.
(German) imperial. See also
Kasper.
Caspar, Cass
Foreign forms: English: **Jasper;**
French: **Gaspar, Gaspard;** *Italian:*
Gasparo

Cass (Irish, Persian) a short
form of Casper, Cassidy.

Cassidy (Irish) clever; curly
haired.
Cass, Cassady, Cassie, Kassidy

Cassie (Irish) a familiar form of
Cassidy.
Casi, Casie, Cassy

Cassius (Latin, French) box;
protective cover.
Cassia, Cassio
Foreign form: American: **Cazzie**

Castle (Latin) castle.
Cassle, Castel

Castor (Greek) beaver.
Astrology: one of the twins in
the constellation Gemini.
Mythology: one of the patron
saints of sailors.
Caston

Cater (English) caterer.

Cato (Latin) knowledgeable,
wise.
Caton, Catón

Cavan (Irish) handsome. See
also Kevin.
Caven, Cavin

Cecil (Latin) blind.
Cecill, Celio
Foreign forms: Dutch: **Cecilius;**
English: **Cece;** *French:* **Cécile;** *Irish:*
Siseal; *Italian:* **Cecilio**

Cedric (English) battle chieftain. See also Kedrick, Rick.
Cad, Caddaric, Ced, Cedrec, Cédric, Cedrick, Cedryche
Foreign form: Irish: *Sedric*

Cedrick (English) an alternate form of Cedric.
Cederick, Cedirick, Cedrik

Ceejay (American) a combination of the initials C. + J.
Cejay, C.J.

Cemal (Arabic) attractive.

Cephas (Latin) small rock. Bible: the term used by Jesus to describe Peter.
Cephus

Cerdic (Welsh) beloved.
Caradoc, Caradog, Ceredig, Ceretic

Cerek (Greek) an alternate form of Cyril. (Polish) lordly.

Cesar (Spanish) a form of Caesar.
Casar, César, Cesare, Cesareo, Cesario, Cesaro

Chad (English) warrior. A short form of Chadwick. Geography: a country in north-central Africa.
Ceadd, Chaad, Chadd, Chaddie, Chaddy, Chade,

Chadleigh, Chadler, Chadley, Chadlin, Chadlyn, Chadmen, Chado, Chadron, Chady

Chadrick (German) mighty warrior.
Chaderick, Chadric

Chadwick (English) warrior's town.
Chad, Chadvic, Chadwyck

Chaim (Hebrew) life.
Chai, Chaimek, Khaim
Foreign form: English: *Hyman*

Chal (Gypsy) boy; son.
Chalie, Chalin

Chalmers (Scottish) son of the lord.
Chalmer, Chalmr, Chamar, Chamarr

Cham (Vietnamese) hard worker.
Chams

Chan (Sanskrit) shining. (Spanish) an alternate form of Juan.
Chann, Chano, Chayo

Chanan (Hebrew) cloud.

Chance (English) a short form of Chancellor, Chauncey.
Chanc, Chancey, Chancy, Chanse, Chansy, Chants, Chantz, Chanz

Chancellor (English) record-keeper.
Chance, Chancelen

Chander (Hindi) moon.
Chand, Chandan, Chandany, Chandara, Chandaravth, Chandon

Chandler (English) candle maker.
Chand, Chandlan

Chane (Swahili) dependable.

Chaney (French) oak.
Chayne, Cheney, Cheyn, Cheyne, Cheyney

Channing (English) wise. (French) canon; church official.
Chane, Chann

Chante (French) singer.
Chant, Chantha, Chanthar, Chantra, Chantry, Shantae

Chapman (English) merchant.
Chap, Chappie, Chappy

Charles (German) farmer. (English) strong and manly. See also Carl.
Charl, Charle, Charlen, Charlie, Charlzell, Chick, Chip
Foreign forms: American: *Chuck;* Basque: *Xarles;* French: *Charlot;* Irish: *Searles;* Italian:*

Charles (cont.)
Carlo; Scottish: **Tearlach**; Spanish: **Carlos**

Charlie (German, English) a familiar form of Charles.
Charley, Charly

Charlton (English) an alternate form of Carlton.
Charlesten, Charleston, Charleton, Charlotin

Charro (Spanish) cowboy.

Chase (French) hunter.
Chasen, Chason, Chass, Chasten, Chaston, Chasyn

Chauncey (English) chancellor; church official.
Chan, Chance, Chancey, Chaunce, Chauncei, Chauncy

Chayton (Lakota) falcon.

Chaz (English) a familiar form of Charles.
Chas, Chazwick, Chazz

Ché (Spanish) a familiar form of José. History: Ché Guevarra was a revolutionary who fought at Fidel Castro's side in Cuba.
Chay

Chen (Chinese) great, tremendous.

Cherokee (Cherokee) people of a different speech.

Chester (English) a short form of Rochester.
Ches, Cheslav, Cheston, Chet

Chet (English) a short form of Chester.

Cheung (Chinese) good luck.

Chevalier (French) horseman, knight.
Chev, Chevy

Chevy (French) a familiar form of Chevalier. Geography: Chevy Chase is a town in Maryland. Culture: a short form of Chevrolet, an American automobile.
Chev, Chevi, Chevie, Chevvy

Chi (Chinese) younger generation. (Nigerian) personal guardian angel.

Chick (English) a familiar form of Charles.
Chic, Chickie, Chicky

Chico (Spanish) boy.

Chik (Gypsy) earth.

Chike (Ibo) God's power.
Chika

Chiko (Japanese) arrow; pledge.

Chilton (English) farm by the spring.
Chil, Chill, Chilt

Chim (Vietnamese) bird.

Chinua (Ibo) God's blessing.
Chino, Chinou

Chioke (Ibo) gift of God.

Chip (English) a familiar form of Charles.
Chipman, Chipper

Chris (Greek) a short form of Christian, Christopher. See also Kris.
Chriss, Christ, Chrys, Cris, Crist

Christian (Greek) follower of Christ; anointed. See also Khristian, Kit, Kristian.
Chris, Christa, Christai, Christain, Christé, Christen, Christensen, Christiaan, Christiana, Christianos, Christin, Christino, Christion, Christon, Christos, Christyan, Chritian, Cristian
Foreign forms: Dutch: **Kerstan**; Estonian: **Jaan**; French: **Chrétien**; Italian/Spanish: **Christiano**; Polish: **Chrystian, Crystek, Krystian**; Swedish: **Krister**

Christophe (French) a form of Christopher.
Christoph

Christopher (Greek) Christ-bearer. Religion: the patron saint of travelers and drivers. See also Kit, Kristopher, Topher.
Chris, Chrisopherson, Christafer, Christepher, Christhoper, Christifer, Christipher, Christofer, Christofper, Christoher, Christoper, Christopherr, Christophoros, Christorpher, Christos, Christpher, Christphere, Christpor, Christrpher
Foreign forms: Danish: **Christoffer**; English: **Kester**; Finnish: **Risto**; French: **Christophe**; German: **Christoph, Stoffel**; Italian: **Christoforo, Cristoforo**; Portuguese: **Christovao**; Russian: **Christoff**; Spanish: **Christobal, Tobal**

Christophoros (Greek) an alternate form of Christopher.
Christoforos, Christophor, Christophorus, Christphor, Cristopher

Christos (Greek) an alternate form of Christopher. See also Khristos.

Chuck (American) a familiar form of Charles.
Chuckey, Chuckie, Chucky

Chui (Swahili) leopard.

Chul (Korean) firm.

Chuma (Ibo) having many beads, wealthy. (Swahili) iron.

Chung (Chinese) intelligent.
Chungo, Chuong

Churchill (English) church on the hill. History: Sir Winston Churchill served as British prime minister and won a Nobel Prize for literature.

Cian (Irish) ancient.
Céin, Cianán, Kian

Cicero (Latin) chickpea. History: a famous Roman orator and statesman.
Cicerón

Cid (Spanish) lord. History: an eleventh-century Spanish soldier and national hero.
Cyd

Clancy (Irish) red-headed fighter.
Clancey, Claney

Clare (Latin) a short form of Clarence.
Clair, Clarey, Clary

Clarence (Latin) clear; victorious.
Clarance, Clare, Clarrance, Clarrence, Clearence

Clark (French) cleric; scholar.
Clarke, Clerc, Clerk

Claude (Latin, French) lame.
Claud, Claudan, Claudel, Claudell, Claudian, Claudianus, Claudien, Claudin
Foreign forms: Dutch/German: **Claudius**; Italian/Spanish: **Claudio**

Claudio (Italian) a form of Claude.

Clay (English) clay pit. A short form of Clayborne, Clayton.

Clayborne (English) brook near the clay pit.
Claiborn, Claiborne, Clay, Clayborn, Claybourne, Clayburn

Clayton (English) town built on clay.
Clay

Cleary (Irish) learned.

Cleavon (English) cliff.

Clem (Latin) a short form of Clement.
Cleme, Clemmy, Clim

Clement (Latin) merciful. Bible: a disciple of Paul.
Clem, Clemmons
Foreign forms: Bulgarian: **Kliment;** Czech: **Klement;** Danish: **Clemens;** Dutch: **Clementius;** French: **Clément;** German: **Klemens, Menz;** Italian/Spanish: **Clemente, Clemento, Clemenza;** Polish: **Klimek**

Cleon (Greek) famous.
Kleon

Cletus (Greek) illustrious. History: a Roman pope and martyr.
Cledis, Cleotis, Cletis

Cleveland (English) land of cliffs.
Cleaveland, Cleavland, Cleavon, Cleve, Clevelend, Clevelynn, Clevey, Clevie, Clevon

Cliff (English) a short form of Clifford, Clifton.
Clif, Clift, Clive, Clyff, Clyph

Clifford (English) cliff at the river crossing.
Cliff, Cliford, Clyfford

Clifton (English) cliff town.
Cliff, Cliffton, Clift, Cliften, Clyfton

Clint (English) a short form of Clinton.

Clinton (English) hill town.
Clint, Clinten, Clintton, Clynton

Clive (English) an alternate form of Cliff.
Cleve, Clivans, Clivens, Clyve

Clovis (German) famous soldier. See also Louis.

Cluny (Irish) meadow.

Clyde (Welsh) warm. (Scottish) Geography: a river in Scotland.
Cly, Clywd

Coby (Hebrew) a familiar form of Jacob.
Cob, Cobe, Cobey, Cobie

Cochise (Apache) History: a famous Apache warrior and chief.

Coco (French) a familiar form of Jacques.
Coko, Koko

Codey (English) an alternate form of Cody.
Coday

Cody (English) cushion. History: William Cody (Buffalo Bill) was

a sharpshooter and showman in the American "Wild" West. See also Kody.
Code, Codee, Codell, Codey, Codi, Codiak, Codie, Coedy

Coffie (Ewe) born on Friday.

Colbert (English) famous seafarer.
Cole, Colt, Colvert, Culbert

Colby (English) dark; dark haired.
Colbey, Collby, Kolby

Cole (Greek) a short form of Nicholas. (Latin) cabbage farmer. (English) a short form of Coleman.
Colet, Coley, Colie

Coleman (Latin) cabbage farmer. (English) coal miner.
Cole, Colemann, Colm, Colman

Colin (Greek) a short form of Nicholas. (Irish) young cub.
Colan, Cole, Colen, Colyn
Foreign form: Scottish: **Collin**

Colley (English) black haired; swarthy.
Collie, Collis

Collier (English) miner.
Colier, Collayer, Collie, Collyer, Colyer

Collin (Scottish) a form of Colin, Collins.
Cailean, Collen, Collon, Collyn

Collins (Greek) son of Colin. (Irish) holly.
Collin, Collis
Foreign form: Scottish: **Collin**

Colson (Greek, English) son of Nicholas.
Coulson

Colt (English) young horse; frisky. A short form of Colter, Colton.

Colter (English) herd of colts.
Colt

Colton (English) coal town.
Colt, Colten, Coltin, Coltrane, Kolton

Columbus (Latin) dove. History: Cristopher Columbus was an Italian explorer who is credited with the discovery of America in 1492.
Columbo, Columba

Colwyn (Welsh) Geography: a river in Wales.
Colwin, Colwinn

Conall (Irish) high, mighty.
Connell

Conan (Irish) praised; exalted. (Scottish) wise.
Conant, Conary, Connie, Connor, Conon

Conary (Irish) an alternate form of Conan.
Conaire

Conlan (Irish) hero.
Conlen, Conley, Conlin, Conlyn

Connie (English, Irish) a familiar form of Conan, Conrad, Constantine, Conway.
Con, Conn, Conney, Conny

Connor (Scottish) wise. (Irish) an alternate form of Conan.
Conner, Conor, Konnor

Conor (Irish) an alternate form of Connor.

Conrad (German) brave counselor.
Konrad
Foreign forms: English: **Connie;** French: **Conrade;** Italian/Spanish: **Conrado, Corrado**

Conroy (Irish) wise.
Conry, Roy

Constant (Latin) a short form of Constantine.

Constantine (Latin) firm, constant. History: Constantine the Great was one of the most famous Roman emperors.
Constadine, Constandine, Constandios, Constanstine, Constant, Constantinos, Constantios, Costa
Foreign forms: Greek: **Dinos;** English: **Connie;** French: **Constantin;** German/Russian: **Konstantin;** Italian/Spanish: **Constantino, Stancio**

Conway (Irish) hound of the plain.
Connie, Conwy

Cook (English) cook.
Cooke

Cooper (English) barrel maker.
Coop, Couper
Foreign forms: German: **Keefer, Keiffer**

Corbett (Latin) raven.
Corbet, Corbit, Corbitt

Corbin (Latin) raven.
Corban, Corben, Corbey, Corbie, Corby
Foreign form: English: **Korbin**

Corcoran (Irish) ruddy.

Cordaro (Spanish) an alternate form of Cordero.

Cordaro (cont.)
Coradaro, Cordairo, Cordara, Cordarell, Cordareo, Cordarin, Cordario, Cordarius, Cordarrel, Cordarrell, Cordarro, Cordarrol, Cordarryl, Cordaryal, Corddarro, Corrdarl

Cordell (French) rope maker.
Cord, Cordae, Cordale, Corday, Cordeal, Cordel, Cordelle, Cordie, Cordy
Foreign form: English: **Kordell**

Cordero (Spanish) little lamb.
Cordaro, Cordeal, Cordeara, Cordearo, Cordeiro, Cordelro, Cordera, Corderall, Corderro, Corderun, Cordiaro, Cordy, Corrderio

Corey (Irish) hollow. See also Kory.
Core, Coreaa, Cori, Corian, Corie, Corio, Correy, Corria, Corrie, Corry, Corrye, Cory

Cormac (Irish) raven's son. History: a third-century king of Ireland who founded schools.
Cormack, Cormick

Cornelius (Greek) cornel tree. (Latin) horn colored. See also Kornel, Kornelius.
Carnelius, Conny, Cornealous, Corneili, Corneilius, Corneliaus, Cornelious, Cornelis, Corneliu, Cornellis, Cornellius, Cornelus, Corney, Cornie, Corniellus, Corny, Cournelius, Nelius
Foreign forms: English: **Nellie**; *French:* **Cornell**; *Italian/Spanish:* **Cornelio**; *Polish:* **Nelek**

Cornell (French) a form of Cornelius.
Carnell, Cornall, Corney, Cornie, Corny

Cornwallis (English) from Cornwall.

Corrigan (Irish) spearman.
Corrigon, Corrigun, Korrigan

Corrin (Irish) spear carrier.

Corry (Irish) an alternate form of Corey.

Cort (German) bold. (Scandinavian) short. (English) a short form of Courtney.
Cortie, Corty, Kort

Cortez (Spanish) conqueror. History: Hernando Cortez was an explorer who conquered the Aztecs in Mexico.
Cartez, Cortes, Courtez

Corwin (English) heart's companion; heart's delight.
Corwinn, Corwyn, Corwynn

Cory (Latin) a form of Corey. (French) a familiar form of Cornell.

Corydon (Greek) helmet, crest.
Coridon, Corradino, Cory, Coryden, Coryell

Cosgrove (Irish) victor, champion.

Cosmo (Greek) orderly; harmonious; universe.
Cos, Cozmo, Kosmo
Foreign forms: French: **Cosme, Cosmé**; *Italian/Spanish:* **Cosimo**

Costa (Greek) a short form of Constantine.
Costandinos, Costantinos, Costas, Costes

Coty (French) slope, hillside.
Cotee, Cotey, Cotie, Cotty

Courtland (English) court's land.
Court, Courtlana, Courtlandt, Courtlin, Courtlyn

Courtney (English) court.
Cort, Cortnay, Cortne, Cortney, Court, Courteney, Courtnay, Curt

Cowan (Irish) hillside hollow.
Coe, Cowey, Cowie

Coy (English) woods.
Coyie, Coyt

Coyle (Irish) leader in battle.

Coyne (French) modest.
Coyan

Craddock (Welsh) love.
Caradoc, Caradog

Craig (Irish, Scottish) crag;
steep rock.
**Crag, Craige, Craigen,
Craigery, Craigon, Creag,
Cregg, Creig, Criag, Kraig**

Crandall (English) crane's
valley.
**Cran, Crandal, Crandell,
Crendal**

Crawford (English) ford where
crows fly.
Craw, Crow, Ford

Creed (Latin) belief.
Creedon

Creighton (English) town near
the rocks.
**Cray, Crayton, Creighm,
Creight, Creighto, Crichton**

Crispin (Latin) curly haired.
Crispian
Foreign forms: English: **Cris;**
French: **Crepin;** *German:* **Krispin;**
Italian: **Crispino;** *Spanish:* **Crispo**

Cristian (Greek) an alternate
form of Christian.

**Crétien, Cristhian, Cristiano,
Cristino, Cristle, Criston,
Cristos, Cristy, Crystek**

Cristopher (Greek) an alternate form of Christopher.
Cristaph, Cristofer, Cristoval
Foreign forms: French:
Cristophe; *German:* **Cristoph;**
Italian: **Cristoforo;** *Portuguese:*
Cristovao; *Spanish:* **Cristóbal,
Cristobál**

Crofton (Irish) town with
cottages.

Cromwell (English) crooked
spring, winding spring.

Crosby (Scandinavian) shrine
of the cross.
Crosbey, Crosbie, Cross

Crosley (English) meadow of
the cross.
Cross

Crowther (English) fiddler.

Cruz (Portuguese, Spanish)
cross.
Kruz

Cullen (Irish) handsome.
Cull, Cullan, Cullie, Cullin

Culley (Irish) woods.
Cullie, Cully

Culver (English) dove.
Colver, Cull, Cullie, Cully

Cunningham (Irish) village of
the milk pail.

Curran (Irish) hero.
**Curan, Curr, Currey, Currie,
Curry**

Curt (Latin) a short form of
Courtney, Curtis. See also Kurt.

Curtis (Latin) enclosure.
(French) courteous. See also
Kurtis.
Curt, Curtice, Curtiss, Curtus
Foreign forms: Spanish: **Curcio,
Currito**

Cuthbert (English) brilliant.

Cutler (English) knife maker.
Cut, Cuttie, Cutty

Cy (Persian) a short form of
Cyrus.

Cyprian (Latin) from the island
of Cyprus.
Ciprien, Cyprien
Foreign form: Spanish: **Cipriano**

Cyrano (Greek) from Cyrene,
an ancient Greek city.
Literature: *Cyrano de Bergerac*
is a play by Edmond Rostand
about a great swordsman
whose large nose prevented

Cyrano *(cont.)*
him from pursuing the woman he loved.

Cyril (Greek) lordly.
Cerek, Cerel, Ceril, Ciril, Cyra, Cyrel, Cyrell, Cyrelle
Foreign forms: Basque: **Kuiril**; *Danish/Swedish:* **Cyrillus**; *French:* **Cyrille**; *German:* **Cyrill**; *Italian:* **Cirillo**; *Slavic:* **Kiril**

Cyrus (Persian) sun. Historial: Cyrus the Great was a king in ancient Persia.
Cy, Cyris
Foreign forms: Bulgarian: **Kir**; *Italian/Spanish:* **Ciro**

Dabir (Arabic) tutor.

Dacey (Latin) from Dacia, an area now in Romania. (Irish) southerner.

Dace, Dache, Dacian, Dacias, Dacio, Dacy, Daicey, Daicy

Dada (Yoruba) curly haired.
Dadi

Dag (Scandinavian) day; bright.
Daeg, Daegan, Dagen, Dagny, Deegan

Dagan (Hebrew) corn; grain.
Dagon

Dagwood (English) shining forest.

Dai (Japanese) big.

Dajuan (American) a combination of the prefix Da + Juan. See also Dejuan.
Da Jon, Da-Juan, Dawan, Dawaun, Dawawn, Dawon, Dawoyan, Dijuan, Diuan, D'Juan, D'juan, Dujuan, Dwaun

Dakarai (Shona) happy.

Dakota (Dakota) friend; partner; tribal name.
Dac, Dack, Dacoda, Dacota, DaCota, Dak, Dakoata, Dakotah, Dakotha, Dekota, Dekotes

Dalal (Sanskrit) broker.

Dalbert (English) bright, shining. See also Delbert.

Dale (English) dale, valley.
Dael, Dal, Dalen, Daley, Dallan, Daly, Dayl, Dayle
Foreign form: Czech: **Dalibor**

Dalen (English) an alternate form of Dale.
Daelan, Daelen, Daelin, Dailin, Dalan, Dalian, Dalin, Dalione, Dalyn, Daylan, Daylen, Daylin, Daylon

Daley (Irish) assembly. (English) a familiar form of Dale.
Daily, Daly, Dawley

Dallan (English) an alternate form of Dale.
Dallen, Dallin, Dallon, Dallyn

Dallas (Scottish) Geography: a town in Scotland; a city in Texas.
Dal, Dalieass, Dall, Dalles, Dallis, Dalys, Dellis

Dalston (English) Daegel's place.
Dalis, Dallon

Dalton (English) town in the valley.
Dal, Dallton, Dalt, Dalten

Dalziel (Scottish) small field.

Damian (Greek) tamer; soother.
Daemean, Daemon, Daemyen, Daimean, Daimen, Daimon, Daimyan, Damaiaon, Dame, Damean, Dameion, Dameon, Dameone, Damián, Damiann, Damianos, Damien, Damion, Daymian
Foreign forms: Hungarian: *Damján;* Italian: *Damiano;* Russian: *Damyan, Dema, Demyan*

Damien (Greek) an alternate form of Damian. Religion: Father Damien spent his life serving the leper colony on Molokai island, Hawaii.
Daemien, Daimien, Damie, Damyen

Damion (Greek) an alternate form of Damian.
Damin, Damyon

Damon (Greek) constant, loyal. (Latin) spirit, demon.
Daemen, Daemon, Daemond, Daimon, Daman, Damen, Damonn, Damonta, Damontez, Damontis, Daymon, Daymond

Dan (Hebrew) a short form of Daniel. (Vietnamese) yes.
Dahn, Danh, Danne

Dana (Scandinavian) from Denmark.
Dain, Daina

Dandin (Hindi) holy man.

Dandré (French) a combination of the prefix De + André.
Dandrae, Dandras, Dandray, Dandre, D'André, D'andrea, Dondrea

Dane (English) from Denmark. See also Halden.
Daine, Danie, Dhane
Foreign form: Scandinavian: *Dayne*

Danial (Hebrew) an alternate form of Daniel.
Danal, Daneal, Danieal

Daniel (Hebrew) God is my judge. Bible: a great Hebrew prophet. See also Danno.
Dacso, Dan, Daneel, Daneil, Danial, Daniël, Daniell, Daniels, Danielson, Daniyel, Dan'l, Dannel, Danniel, Dannil, Danno, Danny, Danyel, Dayne, Deniel, Doneal, Doniel
Foreign forms: Basque: *Danel;* Czech: *Dano;* English: *Danforth;* French: *Donois;* Hawaiian: *Kanaiela;* Hungarian: *Dasco;* Lithuanian: *Danielus, Danukas;* Polish: *Danek;* Russian: *Danila,*

Danilka; Scottish: *Dániel;* Serbian: *Dusan;* Spanish: *Danilo, Nelo*

Daniele (Hebrew) an alternate form of Daniel.

Danior (Gypsy) born with teeth.

Danno (Hebrew) a familiar form of Daniel. (Japanese) gathering in the meadow.
Foreign form: American: *Dannon*

Dannon (American) a form of Danno.
Daenan, Daenen, Dainon, Danaan, Danen, Danon

Danny (Hebrew) a familiar form of Daniel.
Dani, Dannee, Dannie, Dannye, Dany

Dante (Latin) lasting, enduring.
Danatay, Danaté, Dant, Danté, Dauntay, Dauntaye, Daunté, Dauntrae, Deanté, De Anté, Deaunta
Foreign forms: American: *Dontae, Donté*

Danyel (Hebrew) an alternate form of Daniel.
Danya, Danyal, Danyale, Danyele, Danyell, Danyiel, Danyl, Danyle, Danylets, Danylo, Donyell

Daquan (American) a combination of the prefix Da + Quan.
Daquain, Daquann, Daquawn, Daqwan, Dequain, Dequan, Dequann, Dequaun

Dar (Hebrew) pearl.

Dara (Cambodian) stars.

Daran (Irish) an alternate form of Darren.
Darann, Darawn, Darian, Darran, Dayran, Deran

Darby (Irish) free. (English) deer park.
Dar, Darb, Darbee, Darbey, Darbie, Derby

Darcy (Irish) dark. (French) from Arcy.
Dar, Daray, D'Aray, Darce, Darcee, Darcel, Darcey, Darcio, D'Arcy, Darsey, Darsy

Dareh (Persian) wealthy.

Darell (English) a form of Darrell.
Daralle, Dareal

Daren (Irish) an alternate form of Darren. (Hausa) born at night.
Dare, Dayren, Dheren

Darick (German) an alternate form of Derek.
Daric, Darico, Darek, Darik

Darin (Irish) an alternate form of Darren.
Darian, Darien, Darion, Darrian, Darrin, Daryn, Darynn, Dayrin, Dearin, Dharin

Dario (Spanish) affluent.

Darius (Greek) wealthy.
Dairus, Dare, Darieus, Darioush, Darrias, Darrious, Darris, Darrius, Darrus, Derrious, Derris, Derrius

Darnell (English) hidden place.
Dar, Darn, Darnall, Darnel

Daron (Irish) an alternate form of Darren.
Darron, Dayron, Dearon, Dharon, Diron

Darrell (French) darling, beloved; grove of oak trees.
Dare, Darel, Darral, Darrel, Darrill, Darrol, Darryl, Derrell
Foreign form: English: **Darell**

Darren (Irish) great. (English) small; rocky hill.
Daran, Dare, Daren, Darin, Daron, Darran, Darrian, Darrien, Darrience, Darrin, Darrion, Darron, Darryn, Darun, Daryn, Dearron, Deren, Dereon, Derren, Derron

Darrick (German) an alternate form of Derek.
Darrec, Darrik, Darryk

Darrion (Irish) an alternate form of Darren.
Darian, Darien, Darion, Darrian, Darrien, Derrian, Derrion

Darryl (French) darling, beloved; grove of oak trees. An alternate form of Darrell.
Dahrll, Darryle, Darryll, Daryl, Daryle, Daryll, Derryl

Darshan (Hindi) god; godlike. Religion: another name for the Hindu god Shiva.

Darton (English) deer town.
Dartel, Dartrel

Darwin (English) dear friend. History: Charles Darwin was the naturalist who established the theory of evolution.
Darwyn, Derwin, Derwynn, Durwin

Daryl (French) an alternate form of Darryl.
Darel, Daril, Darl, Darly, Daryell, Daryle, Daryll, Darylle, Daroyl

Dasan (Pomo) leader of the bird clan.
Dassan

Dave (Hebrew) a short form of David, Davis.

Davey (Hebrew) a familiar form of David.
Davee, Davi, Davie, Davy

David (Hebrew) beloved. Bible: the first king of Israel. See also Dov.
Daevid, Dai, Daivid, Dav, Dave, Daved, Daven, Davey, Davido, Davon, Davoud, Davyd, Dawud, Dayvid
Foreign forms: Arabic: **Daoud;** *Basque:* **Dabi;** *Czech:* **Davidek;** *Ethiopian:* **Dawit;** *Finnish:* **Taaveti;** *French:* **Davide;** *Hawaiian:* **Havika, Kawika;** *Italian:* **Davidde;** *Polish:* **Dawid;** *Russian:* **Daveed, Dodya;** *Swahili:* **Dauid;** *Welsh:* **Dafydd, Taffy;** *Yiddish:* **Tevel**

Davin (Scandinavian) brilliant Finn.
Daevin, Davinte, Dawin, Dawine
Foreign form: American: **Davon**

Davis (Welsh) son of David.
Dave, Davidson, Davies, Davison

Davon (American) a form of Davin.
Daevon, Davon, Davone,

Davonn, Davonne, Davonte, Dayvon, Devon

Dawson (English) son of David.

Dax (French, English) water.

Dayne (Scandinavian) a form of Dane.

Dayton (English) day town; bright, sunny town.
Daeton, Daiton, Deyton

De (Chinese) virtuous.

Deacon (Greek) one who serves.
Deke

Dean (French) leader. (English) valley.
Deane, Deen, Dene, Deyn
Foreign form: Italian: **Dino**

Deandre (French) a combination of the prefix De + André.
D'andre, D'andré, D'André, D'andrea, Deandrae, Déandre, Deandré, Deandra, De André, Deandrea, De Andrea, Deaundera, Deaundra, Deaundre, De Aundre, Deaundrey, Deondray, Deondre, Deondré

Deangelo (Italian) a combination of the prefix De + Angelo.
Dang, Dangelo, D'Angelo,

Danglo, Deaengelo, Déangelo, De Angelo, Deangleo, Deanglo, Diangelo, Di'angelo

Deanthony (Italian) a combination of the prefix De + Anthony.
D'anthony, Danton, Dianthony

Dearborn (English) deer brook.
Dearbourn, Dearburne, Deerborn

Decarlos (Spanish) a combination of the prefix De + Carlos.
Dacarlos, Decarlo, Di'carlos

Declan (Irish) man of prayer. Religion: Saint Declan was a fifth-century Irish bishop.

Dedrick (German) ruler of the people.
Deadrick, Dederick, Dedric, Dedrix, Diedrich, Diedrick, Dietrich, Detrick

Deems (English) judge's child.

Dejuan (American) a combination of the prefix De + Juan. See also Dajuan.
Dejan, Dejon, Dejun, Dewan, Dewaun, Dewon, Dijaun, D'Juan, Dujuan, D'Won

Dekel (Hebrew, Arabic) palm tree, date tree.

Del (English) a short form of Delbert, Delvin, Delwin.

Delaney (Irish) descendant of the challenger.
Delaine, Delainey, Delainy, Delan, Delane, Delanny, Delany

Delano (French) nut tree. (Irish) dark.
Delayno

Delbert (English) bright as day. See also Dalbert.
Bert, Del, Dilbert

Delfino (Latin) dolphin.

Délì (Chinese) virtuous.

Dell (English) small valley. A short form of Udell.

Delling (Scandinavian) scintillating.

Delmar (Latin) sea.
Dalmar, Dalmer, Delmer, Delmor, Delmore

Delroy (French) belonging to the king. See also Elroy, Leroy.
Delray, Delree, Delroi

Delsin (Native American) he is so.
Delsy

Delvin (English) proud friend; friend from the valley.
Del, Delavan, Delvyn, Delwin

Delwin (English) an alternate form of Delvin.
Dalwin, Dalwyn, Del, Dellwin, Dellwyn, Delwyn, Delwynn

Deman (Dutch) man.

Demarco (Italian) a combination of the prefix De + Marco.
Damarco, D'Marco

Demarcus (American) a combination of the prefix De + Marcus.
Damarcius, Damarcus, Demarkes, Demarkis, Demarkus, D'Marcus

Demario (Italian) a combination of the prefix De + Mario.
Demarreio, Demarrio, Demerrio

Dembe (Luganda) peaceful.
Damba

Demetris (Greek) a short form of Demetrius.
Demeatric, Demeatrice, Demeatris, Demetres, Demetress, Demetric, Demetrice, Demetrick, Demetrics, Demetricus, Demetrik, Demitrez

Demetrius (Greek) lover of the earth. Mythology: a follower of Demeter, the goddess of the harvest and fertility. See also Mimis, Mitsos.
Damitriuz, Demeitrius, Demeterious, Demetreus, Demetrias, Demetrios, Demetrious, Demetris, Demetriu, Demetrium, Demetrois, Demetruis, Demetrus, Demitirus, Demitri, Demitrias, Demitriu, Demitrius, Demitrus, Demtrius, Demtrus, Dimitri, Dimitrios, Dimitrius, Dmetrius
Foreign forms: Italian: Demetrio; Polish: Dymek; Russian: Dimitri

Demichael (American) a combination of the prefix De + Michael.
Dumichael

Demitri (Greek) a short form of Demetrius.
Dametri, Damitré, Demeter, Demetre, Demetrea, Demetri, Demetriel, Demitre, Domotor

Demond (Irish) a short form of Desmond.
Demonde, Demonds, Demone, Dumonde

Demont (French) mountain.
**Démont, Demonta, Demonte,
Demontez, Demontre**

Demorris (American) a combination of the prefix De + Morris.
Demoris, DeMorris, Demorus

Demos (Greek) people.
Demas, Demosthenes

Demothi (Native American) talks while walking.

Dempsey (Irish) proud.
**Demp, Demps, Dempsie,
Dempsy**

Dempster (English) one who judges.
Demster

Denby (Scandinavian) Geography: a Danish village.
**Danby, Den, Denbey, Denney,
Dennie, Denny**

Denham (English) village in the valley.

Denholm (Scottish) Geography: a town in Scotland.

Denis (Greek) an alternate form of Dennis.

Denley (English) meadow; valley.
Denlie, Denly

Denman (English) man from the valley.

Dennis (Greek) Mythology: a follower of Dionysius, the god of wine. See also Dion.
**Den, Denies, Deniz, Dennet,
Denny, Dennys, Deon, Dinis**
*Foreign forms: French: Denis,
Denys, Dione; Hungarian: Dénes,
Dennes; Russian: Denya; Spanish:
Dionis, Nicho*

Dennison (English) son of Dennis. See also Dyson, Tennyson.
**Den, Denison, Denisson,
Dennyson**

Denny (Greek) a familiar form of Dennis.
Den, Denney, Dennie, Deny

Denton (English) happy home.
Dent, Denten, Dentin

Denver (English) green valley. Geography: the capital of Colorado.

Denzil (Cornish) Geography: a location in Cornwall, England.
**Danzel, Danzell, Dennzel,
Dennzil, Dennzyl, Denzel,**

**Denzell, Denziel, Denzill,
Denzyl, Donzell**

Deon (Greek) an alternate form of Dennis. See also Dion.
Deion, Deone, Deonno

Deontae (American) a combination of the prefix De + Dontae.
**D'Ante, Deante, Deonta,
Deonte, Deonté, Deontée,
Deontie, Deontre, Deontrea,
Deontrez, Diante, Diontae,
Diontay**

Dequan (American) a combination of the prefix De + Quan.
**Dequain, Dequan, Dequann,
Dequaun**

Derek (German) ruler of the people. A short form of Theodoric. See also Dirk.
**Darek, Darick, Darrick, Derak,
Dereck, Derecke, Derele,
Derick, Derk, Derke, Derrek,
Derrick, Deryek**

Derick (German) an alternate form of Derek.
**Deric, Dericka, Derico, Deriek,
Derik, Derikk, Derique,
Deryck, Deryk, Deryke,
Detrek**

Dermot (Hebrew) a short form of Jeremiah. (Irish) free from

Dermot (cont.)
envy. (English) free. See also
Kermit.
**Der, Dermod, Dermott,
Diarmid, Diarmuid**

Deron (Hebrew) bird; freedom.
(American) a combination of
the prefix De + Ron.
**Daaron, Daron, Da-Ron,
Darone, Darron, Dayron,
Dereon, Deronn, Deronne,
Derrin, Derrion, Derron,
Derronn, Derronne, Derryn,
Diron, Duron, Durron, Dyron**

Derrek (German) an alternate
form of Derek.
Derrec, Derreck

Derrell (French) an alternate
form of Darrell.
**Derrel, Dérrell, Derriel, Derril,
Derrill**

Derren (Irish) great. An alter-
nate form of Darren.
**Deren, Derran, Derrien,
Derrin, Derryn**

Derrick (German) ruler of the
people. An alternate form of
Derek.
**Derric, Derrik, Derryck,
Derryk**

Derry (Irish) redhead. Geography: a city in Northern Ireland.
Darrie, Darry, Derrie, Derrye

Derryl (French) an alternate
form of Darryl.
Deryl, Deryll

Derward (English) deer keeper.

Derwin (English) an alternate
form of Darwin.
Derwyn

Deshane (American) a combi-
nation of the prefix De +
Shane.
Deshan, Deshayne

Deshawn (American) a combi-
nation of the prefix De +
Shawn.
**Dasean, Dashaun, Dashawn,
Desean, Deshaun, Deshaune,
Deshauwn, Deshawan,
D'Sean, D'shaun, D'Shaun,
D'shawn, D'Shawn, Dusean,
Dushan, Dushaun, Dushawn**

Deshea (American) a combination of the prefix De + Shea.
Deshay

Déshì (Chinese) virtuous.

Deshon (American) an alter-
nate form of Deshawn.
**Deshondre, Deshone,
Deshonte, Deshun**

Desiderio (Spanish) desired.

Desmond (Irish) from south
Munster.
**Demond, Des, Desi, Desmon,
Desmund, Dezmon, Dezmond**

Destin (French) destiny, fate.
Destine, Deston
Foreign form: *American:* **Destry**

Destry (American) a form of
Destin.
Destrey, Destrie

Detrick (German) an alternate
form of Dedrick.
Detric

Devayne (American) an alter-
nate form of Dewayne.
**Devain, Devaine, Devan,
Devane, Devayn, Devein,
Deveion**

Deven (Hindi) for God. (Irish)
an alternate form of Devin.
Deaven, Deiven

Deverell (English) riverbank.

Devin (Irish) poet.
**Deavin, Deivin, Dev, Devan,
Deven, Devlyn, Devy, Dyvon**

Devine (Latin) divine. (Irish) ox.
**Davon, Devinn, Devon, Devyn,
Devyne**

Devlin (Irish) brave, fierce.
Dev, Devland, Devlen, Devlyn

Devon (Irish) an alternate form of Devin.
Deavon, Deivon, Deivone, Deivonne, Devoen, Devohn, Devone, Devonn, Devonne, Devontae, Devontaine, Devontay, Devyn

Dewayne (Irish) an alternate form of Dwayne. (American) a combination of the prefix De + Wayne.
Deuwayne, Devayne, Dewain, Dewaine, Dewan, Dewon, Dewune

Dewei (Chinese) highly virtuous.

Dewey (Welsh) prized.
Dew, Dewi, Dewie

DeWitt (Flemish) blond.
Dewitt, Wit
Foreign form: English: Dwight

Dexter (Latin) dexterous, adroit. (English) fabric dyer.
Daxter, Decca, Deck, Decka, Dekka, Dex, Dextar, Dextor, Dextrel, Dextron

Diamond (English) brilliant gem; bright guardian.
Diamend, Diamenn, Diamont

Dick (German) a short form of Frederick, Richard.

Dic, Dicken, Dickens, Dickenson, Dickerson, Dickie, Dickon, Dickson, Dicky, Dik, Dikerson

Didi (Hebrew) a familiar form of Jedidiah.

Didier (French) desired, longed for. A masculine form of Desiree.

Diedrich (German) an alternate form of Dedrick, Dietrich.
Didrich, Didrick, Didrik, Diederick

Diego (Spanish) a form of Jacob, James.
Diaz, Jago

Dieter (German) army of the people.
Deiter

Dietrich (German) an alternate form of Dedrick.
Deitrich, Deitrick, Deke, Diedrich, Dierck, Dieter, Dieterich, Dieterick, Dietz

Digby (Irish) ditch town; dike town.

Dillon (Irish) loyal, faithful. See also Dylan.
Dil, Dilan, Dill, Dillan, Dillen, Dillie, Dillin, Dillion, Dilly, Dillyn, Dilon, Dilyn

Dilwyn (Welsh) shady place.
Dillwyn

Dimitri (Russian) a form of Demetrius.
Dimetra, Dimetri, Dimetric, Dimetrie, Dimitr, Dimitric, Dimitrie, Dimitrik, Dimitris, Dimitry, Dimmy, Dmitri, Dymitr, Dymitry

Dimitrios (Greek) an alternate form of Demetrius.
Dhimitrios, Dimitrius, Dimos, Dmitrios

Dimitrius (Greek) an alternate form of Demetrius.
Dimetrius, Dimitricus, Dimitrius, Dimetrus, Dmitrius

Dingbang (Chinese) protector of the country.

Dinh (Vietnamese) calm, peaceful.
Din

Dino (German) little sword. (Italian) a form of Dean.
Deano

Dinos (Greek) a familiar form of Constantine, Konstantin.

Dinsmore (Irish) fortified hill.
Dinnie, Dinny, Dinse

Diogenes (Greek) honest. History: an ancient philosopher who searched the streets for an honest man.

Dion (Greek) a short form of Dennis, Dionysus.
Deon, Dio, Dionn, Diontae, Dionte, Diontray

Dionysus (Greek) celebration. Mythology: the god of wine.
Dion, Dionesios, Dionisios, Dionusios, Dionysios, Dionysius
Foreign forms: Basque: **Dunixi;** *Italian/Spanish:* **Dionicio, Dionigi, Dionisio**

Dirk (German) a short form of Derek, Theodoric.
Derk, Dirck, Dirke, Durc, Durk, Dyrk

Dixon (English) son of Dick.
Dickson, Dix

Dmitri (Russian) an alternate form of Dimitri.
Dmitiri, Dmitrik

Doane (English) low, rolling hills.
Doan

Dob (English) a familiar form of Robert.
Dobie

Dobry (Polish) good.

Doherty (Irish) harmful.
Docherty, Dougherty, Douherty

Dolan (Irish) dark haired.
Dolin, Dolyn

Dolf, Dolph (German) short forms of Adolf, Adolph, Rudolf, Rudolph.
Dolfe, Dolfi, Dolphe, Dolphus

Dom (Latin) a short form of Dominic.
Dome, Domó

Domenico (Italian) a form of Dominic.
Domenic, Domicio, Dominico, Menico

Domingo (Spanish) born on Sunday.
Demingo, Domingos

Dominic (Latin) belonging to the Lord.
Demenico, Dom, Domanic, Domenic, Domini, Dominie, Dominitric, Dominy, Domonic, Nick
Foreign forms: Czech: **Domek, Dumin;** *French:* **Dominique;** *Hungarian:* **Deco, Domokos;** *Italian:* **Domenico;** *Polish:* **Dominik, Donek;** *Spanish:* **Chuminga**

Dominick (Latin) an alternate form of Dominic.
Domenick, Domiku, Domineck, Dominick, Dominicke, Dominiek, Domminick, Domnick, Domonick

Dominique (French) a form of Dominic.
Domeniqu, Domenque, Dominiqu, Dominiqueia, Domnenique, Domnique, Domoniqu, Domonique

Don (Scottish) a short form of Donald.
Donn
Foreign form: Hawaiian: **Kona**

Donahue (Irish) dark warrior.
Donohoe, Donohue

Donald (Scottish) world leader; proud ruler.
Don, Dónal, Donall, Donát, Donaugh, Donnie
Foreign forms: Finnish: **Tauno;** *Irish:* **Donal;** *Italian:* **Donaldo;** *Norwegian:* **Donalt;** *Ukranian:* **Bodan, Bogdan, Bohdan**

Donatien (French) gift.
Donathan, Donathon

Donato (Italian) gift.
Dodek, Donatello, Donati, Donatus
Foreign form: French: **Donatien**

Dong (Vietnamese) easterner.
Duong

Donkor (Akan) humble.

Donnell (Irish) brave; dark.
Doneal, Donell, Donelle, Donnelly, Doniel, Donielle, Donnel, Donnelle, Donniel

Donnelly (Irish) an alternate form of Donnell.
Donelly, Donlee, Donley

Donnie, Donny (Irish) familiar forms of Donald.

Donovan (Irish) dark warrior.
Dohnovan, Donavan, Donavin, Donavon, Donavyn, Donevon, Donoven, Donovin, Donovon, Donvan

Dontae, Donté (American) forms of Dante.
Donta, Dontai, Dontao, Dontate, Dontay, Dontaye, Dontea, Dontee, Dontez

Dooley (Irish) dark hero.
Dooly

Doran (Greek, Hebrew) gift. (Irish) stranger; exile.
Dore, Dorin, Doron, Dorran, Dorren, Dory

Dorian (Greek) from Doris, Greece. See also Isidore.

Dore, Dorey, Dorie, Dorien, Dorion, Dorján, Dorrian, Dorrien, Dorryen, Dory

Dorrell (Scottish) king's door-keeper.
Dorrel, Dorrelle, Durrell

Doug (Scottish) a short form of Dougal, Douglas.
Dougie, Dougy, Dugey, Dugie, Dugy

Dougal (Scottish) dark stranger.
Doug, Dougall, Dugal, Dugall, Dughall
*Foreign forms: English: **Dugald**; Irish: **Doyle***

Douglas (Scottish) dark river, dark stream.
Doug, Douglass, Dougles, Dugaid, Dughlas
*Foreign form: Hawaiian: **Koukalaka***

Dov (Hebrew) a familiar form of David. (Yiddish) bear.
Dovid, Dovidas, Dowid

Dow (Irish) dark haired.

Doyle (Irish) a form of Dougal.
Doy, Doyal, Doyel

Drake (English) dragon; owner of the inn with the dragon trademark.
*Foreign form: Italian: **Drago***

Draper (English) fabric maker.
Dray, Draypr

Drew (Welsh) wise. (English) a short form of Andrew.
Drewe, Dru

Dru (English) an alternate form of Drew.
Druan, Drud, Drue, Drugi, Drui

Drummond (Scottish) druid's mountain.
Drummund, Drumond, Drumund

Drury (French) loving. Geography: Drury Lane is a street in London's theater district. Literature: according to a nursery rhyme, Drury Lane is where the Muffin Man lives.

Dryden (English) dry valley.
Dry

Duane (Irish) an alternate form of Dwayne.
Deune, Duain, Duaine, Duana

Duarte (Portuguese) rich guard.

Duc (Vietnamese) moral.
Duoc, Duy

Dudd (English) a short form of Dudley.
Dud, Dudde, Duddy

Dudley (English) common field.
Dudd, Dudly

Duff (Scottish) dark.
Duffey, Duffie, Duffy

Dugan (Irish) dark.
**Doogan, Dougan, Douggan,
Duggan**

Duke (French) leader; duke.
Dukey, Dukie, Duky

Dukker (Gypsy) fortuneteller.

Duncan (Scottish) brown warrior. Literature: King Duncan
was MacBeth's victim in
Shakespeare's play *MacBeth*.
Dunc, Dunn

Dunham (Scottish) brown.

Dunley (English) hilly meadow.

Dunlop (Scottish) muddy hill.

Dunmore (Scottish) fortress on
the hill.

Dunn (Scottish) a short form of
Duncan.
Dun, Dune, Dunne

Dunstan (English) brown-stone
fortress.
Dun

Dunton (English) hill town.

Durand (Latin) an alternate
form of Durant.

Durant (Latin) enduring.
**Duran, Durance, Durand,
Durante, Durontae, Durrant**

Durell (Scottish, English) king's
doorkeeper.
**Dorrell, Durel, Durial, Durreil,
Durrell, Durrelle**

Durril (Gypsy) gooseberry.

Durward (English) gatekeeper.
Dur, Ward

Durwin (English) an alternate
form of Darwin.

Dustin (German) valiant
fighter. (English) brown rock
quarry.
**Dust, Dustan, Dusten, Dustie,
Dustine, Duston, Dusty,
Dustyn**

Dusty (English) a familiar form
of Dustin.

Dustyn (English) an alternate
form of Dustin.

Dutch (Dutch) from the
Netherlands; from Germany.

Duval (French) a combination
of the prefix Du + Val.
Duvall, Duveuil

Dwaun (American) an alternate
form of Dajuan.
**Dwan, Dwaunn, Dwawn,
Dwon, Dwuann**

Dwayne (Irish) dark. See also
Dewayne.
**Dawayne, Dawyne, Duane,
Duwain, Duwan, Duwane,
Duwayn, Duwayne, Dwain,
Dwaine, Dwan, Dwane,
Dwyane, Dywane**

Dwight (English) a form of
DeWitt.

Dyer (English) fabric dyer.

Dyke (English) dike; ditch.
Dike

Dylan (Welsh) sea. See also
Dillon.
Dyllan, Dyllon, Dylon

Dyre (Norwegian) dear heart.

Dyson (English) a short form of
Dennison.
Dysen, Dysonn

Eagan (Irish) very mighty.
Egan, Egon

Earl (Irish) pledge. (English) nobleman.
Airle, Earld, Earle, Earlie Earlson, Early, Eorl, Erl, Erle, Errol

Earnest (English) an alternate form of Ernest.
Earn, Earnesto, Earnie, Eranest

Easton (English) eastern town.
Eason

Eaton (English) estate on the river.
Eatton, Eton, Eyton

Eb (Hebrew) a short form of Ebenezer.
Ebbie, Ebby

Eben (Hebrew) rock.
Eban

Ebenezer (Hebrew) foundation stone. Literature: Ebenezer Scrooge is a character in Charles Dickens's *A Christmas Carol.*
Eb, Ebbaneza, Eben, Ebeneezer, Ebeneser, Ebenezar, Eveneser

Eberhard (German) courageous as a boar.
Eberhardt, Evard, Everard, Everardo, Everhardt, Everhart

Ebo (Fanti) born on Tuesday.

Ed (English) a short form of Edgar, Edsel, Edward.
Edd

Edan (Scottish) fire.

Edbert (English) wealthy; bright.
Ediberto

Eddie (English) a familiar form of Edgar, Edsel, Edward.
Eddee, Eddy

Eddy (English) an alternate form of Eddie.
Eddye, Edy

Edel (German) noble.
Adel, Edelmar, Edelweiss

Eden (Hebrew) delightful. Bible: the earthly paradise.
Eaden, Eadin, Edan, Edenson, Edin, Edyn

Edgar (English) successful spearman.
Ed, Eddie, Edgars
Foreign forms: French: *Edgard;* German: *Medgar;* Italian: *Edgardo;* Polish: *Edek, Garek, Gerik*

Edison (English) son of Edward.
Eddison, Edisen, Edson

Edmond (English) an alternate form of Edmund.
Edmonde, Edmondson
Foreign forms: French: *Esmond;* Italian: *Edmondo;* Russian: *Edmon*

Edmund (English) prosperous protector.
Eadmund, Edmond, *Edmunds*
Foreign forms: Irish: *Aimon, Eamon;* Spanish: *Edmundo, Mundo*

Edric (English) prosperous ruler.
Eddrick, Ederick, Edrice, Edrick

Edsel (English) rich man's house.
Ed, Eddie

Edson (English) a short form of Edison.

Eduardo (Spanish) a form of Edward.
Edvardo, Edwardo

Edward (English) prosperous guardian. See also Audie, Ned, Ted, Teddy.
Ed, Eddie, Edwards, Edwy, Ewart
Foreign forms: Basque: **Edorta;** Czech: **Edko, Edo, Edus;** Danish: **Edvard;** French: **Édouard;** German: **Eduard;** Hawaiian: **Ekewaka;** Italian: **Edoardo;** Polish: **Edik, Edzio, Etzio;** Portuguese: **Duarte;** Spanish: **Eduardo**

Edwin (English) prosperous friend. See also Ned, Ted.
Eadwinn, Edik, Edlin, Edwyn
Foreign form: Italian/Spanish: **Eduino**

Efrem (Hebrew) a short form of Ephraim.
Efe, Efren, Efrim, Efrum

Egan (Irish) ardent, fiery.
Egann, Egen, Egon

Egbert (English) bright sword. See also Bert, Bertie.

Egerton (English) Edgar's town.

Edgarton, Edgartown, Edgerton, Egeton

Egil (Norway) awe-inspiring.
Eigil

Egon (German) formidable.

Ehren (German) honorable.

Eikki (Finnish) ever-powerful.

Einar (Scandinavian) individual-ist.
Foreign forms: Danish: **Ejnar;** English: **Inar**

Ekon (Nigerian) strong.

Elam (Hebrew) highlands.

Elan (Hebrew) tree. (Native American) friendly.
Elann

Elden (English) an alternate form of Alden.
Eldin

Elder (English) dweller near the elder trees.

Eldon (English) holy hill.

Eldred (English) an alternate form of Aldred.
Eldrid

Eldridge (English) an alternate form of Aldrich.

El, Eldred, Eldredge, Eldrege, Eldrid, Eldrige, Elric

Eleazar (Hebrew) God has helped.
Elazar, Eleasar, Eliasar, Eliazar, Elieser, Elizar
Foreign forms: French: **Eléazar;** Greek: **Lazarus;** Spanish: **Elazaro, Eliezer, Elizardo**

Elger (German) an alternate form of Alger.
Elger, Ellgar, Ellger

Elgin (English) noble; white.
Elgan, Elgen

Eli (Hebrew) uplifted. A short form of Elijah, Elisha. Bible: the high priest who trained the prophet Samuel. See also Elliot.
Elie, Elier, Eloi, Eloy Ely

Elias (Greek) a form of Elijah.
Elia, Eliasz, Elice, Ellice, Elyas
Foreign form: English: **Ellis**

Elihu (Hebrew) a short form of Eliyahu.
Elih, Eliu, Ellihu

Elijah (Hebrew) the Lord is my God. An alternate form of Eliyahu. Bible: a great Hebrew prophet. See also Eli, Elisha.
El, Elijuo, Elisjsha, Eliyahu, Ellis

Foreign forms: *Czech:* **Elya;** *English:* **Elian, Elliot;** *French:* **Elie;** *Greek:* **Elias, Ilias;** *Russian:* **Ilya;** *Yiddish:* **Elija;** *Zuni:* **Elia**

Elisha (Hebrew) God is my salvation. Bible: a great Hebrew prophet, successor to Elijah. See also Eli.
Elijsha, Elisee, Elish, Elisher, Elishia, Elishua, Lisha
Foreign forms: *French:* **Elisée;** *Italian/Spanish:* **Eliseo**

Eliyahu (Hebrew) the Lord is my God. The original form of Elijah.
Elihu

Elkan (Hebrew) God is jealous.
Elkana, Elkanah, Elkin, Elkins

Elki (Moquelumnan) hanging over the top.

Ellard (German) sacred; brave.
Allard, Ellerd

Ellery (English) elder tree island.
Ellary, Ellerey

Elliot, Elliott (English) forms of Eli, Elijah.
Elio, Eliot, Eliott, Eliud, Eliut, Elyot, Elyott

Ellis (English) a form of Elias.

Ellison (English) son of Ellis.
Elison, Ellson, Ellyson, Elson

Ellsworth (English) nobleman's estate.
Ellswerth, Elsworth

Elmer (English) noble; famous.
Aylmer, Elemér, Ellmer, Elmir, Elmo

Elmo (Latin) a familiar form of Anselm. (English) an alternate form of Elmer.

Elmore (English) moor where the elm trees grow.

Elonzo (Spanish) an alternate form of Alonzo.
Elon, Élon, Elonso

Eloy (Latin) chosen.

Elrad (Hebrew) God rules.
Rad, Radd

Elroy (French) an alternate form of Delroy, Leroy.
Elroi

Elsdon (English) nobleman's hill.

Elston (English) noble's town.
Ellston

Elsworth (English) noble's estate.

Elton (English) old town.
Alton, Eldon, Ellton

Elvin (English) a form of Alvin. See also Elvis.
El, Elvyn, Elwin, Elwyn, Elwynn

Elvis (Scandinavian) wise. (English) a form of Elwin.
El, Elvys

Elvy (English) elfin warrior.

Elwell (English) old well.

Elwood (English) old forest. See also Wood, Woody.

Ely (Hebrew) an alternate form of Eli. Geography: a river in Wales.
Elya

Emanuel (Hebrew) an alternate form of Emmanuel.
Emaniel, Emanual, Emanuele

Emerson (German, English) son of Emery.
Emmerson, Emreson

Emery (German) industrious leader.
Aimery, Emari, Emerich, Emerio, Emmerich, Emmerie, Emmery, Emmo, Emory
Foreign forms: *Czech:* **Imrich;** *French:* **Emeri;** *Hungarian:* **Imre**

Emil (Latin) flatterer. (German) industrious.
Emilek, Emill, Emils
Foreign forms: French: *Émile;* Italian/Spanish: *Emiliano, Emilio;* Welsh: *Aymil, Emilyan, Emlyn*

Emilio (Italian, Spanish) a form of Emil.
Emilio, Emilios, Emilo

Emmanuel (Hebrew) God is with us. See also Immanuel, Manuel.
Emanuel, Emanuell, Emek, Emmaneuol, Emmanle, Emmanueal, Emmanuele, Emmanuil
Foreign forms: Czech: *Eman;* Hungarian: *Maco;* Spanish: *Mango*

Emmett (German) industrious; strong. (English) ant. History: Robert Emmett was an Irish patriot.
Em, Emitt, Emmet, Emmit, Emmot, Emmott, Emmy

Emory (German) an alternate form of Emery.
Emmory, Emrick

Emre (Turkish) brother.
Emra, Emrah, Emreson

Emrick (German) an alternate form of Emery.
Emryk

Engelbert (German) bright as an angel. See also Inglebert.
Bert, Englebert

Ennis (Greek) mine. (Scottish) an alternate form of Angus.
Eni, Enni

Enoch (Hebrew) dedicated, consecrated. Bible: the father of Methuselah.
Enoc, Enock, Enok

Enos (Hebrew) man.
Enosh

Enrique (Spanish) a form of Henry. See also Quiqui.
Enrigué, Enriqué, Enriquez, Enrrique

Enver (Turkish) bright; handsome.

Enzi (Swahili) powerful.

Ephraim (Hebrew) fruitful. Bible: the second son of Joseph.
Efraim, Efrayim, Ephraen, Ephrem
Foreign forms: Spanish: *Efrem, Efren, Ephrain*

Erasmus (Greek) lovable.
Rasmus
Foreign forms: French: *Érasme;* Italian/Spanish: *Erasmo*

Erastus (Greek) beloved.
Erastious, Ras, Rastus
Foreign form: French: *Éraste*

Erbert (German) a short form of Herbert.
Ebert, Erberto

Ercole (Italian) splendid gift.

Erhard (German) strong; resolute.
Erhardt, Erhart

Eric (German) a short form of Frederick. (Scandinavian) ruler of all. (English) brave ruler. History: Eric the Red was a Norse hero and explorer.
Ehrich, Erica, Erick, Erickson, Ericson, Erik, Erric, Eryc, Eryk, Rick
Foreign forms: Czech/German: *Erich;* French: *Ériq;* Hawaiian: *Elika;* Icelandic: *Erikur;* Italian: *Erico*

Erich (Czech, German) a form of Eric.

Erik (Scandinavian) an alternate form of Eric.
Erek, Eriks, Erikson, Errick

Erin (Irish) peaceful. History: another name for Ireland.
Erine, Erinn, Erino, Eryn, Erynn

Erland (English) nobleman's land.
Erlend

Erling (English) nobleman's son.

Ernest (English) earnest, sincere.
Earnest, Ernestino, Ernie
Foreign forms: Czech: **Arno;** Dutch: **Ernestus;** German: **Ernst;** Hungarian: **Erno;** Spanish: **Ernesto**

Ernesto (Spanish) a form of Ernest.
Ernester, Neto

Ernie (English) a familiar form of Ernest.
Earnie, Erney, Erny

Erol (Turkish) strong, courageous.

Errol (Latin) wanderer. (English) an alternate form of Earl. See also Rollo.
Erol, Erold, Erroll, Erryl

Erskine (Scottish) high cliff. (English) from Ireland.
Ersin, Erskin, Kinny

Ervin, Erwin (English) sea friend. Alternate forms of Irwin.
Earvin, Erv, Erven, Ervyn,

Erwan, Erwinek, Erwinn, Erwyn, Erwynn

Ervine (English) an alternate form of Irving.
Erv, Ervin, Ervince, Erving, Ervins

Esau (Hebrew) rough; hairy. Bible: Jacob's twin brother.
Esaw

Eskil (Norwegian) vessel of god.

Esmond (English) rich protector.

Este (Italian) east.
Estes

Estéban (Spanish) a form of Stephen.
Estabon, Estefan, Estephan

Ethan (Hebrew) strong; firm.
Eathan, Etan, Ethe

Ettore (Italian) steadfast.
Etor, Etore

Euclid (Greek) intelligent. History: the founder of Euclidean geometry.

Eugene (Greek) born to nobility. See also Gene, Gino.
Eoghan, Eugeni
Foreign forms: Czech: **Ezven,**

Zenda; Dutch: **Eugenius;** French: **Eugéne;** German: **Eugen;** Hawaiian: **Iukini, Kini;** Hungarian: **Jenö;** Russian: **Evgeny, Gena, Yevgenyi, Zhek, Zhenya;** Scottish: **Ewan;** Spanish: **Eugenio**

Eustace (Greek) productive. (Latin) stable, calm. See also Stacey.
Eustachius, Eustachy, Eustashe, Eustis, Eustiss
Foreign forms: Dutch: **Eustatius;** French: **Eustache;** German: **Eustasius;** Italian: **Eustazio**

Evagelos (Greek) an alternate form of Andrew.
Evaggelos, Evangelo, Evangelos

Evan (Irish) young warrior. (English) a form of John. See also Bevan.
Ewen, Ev, Evann, Evans, Even, Evens, Evin, Evyn
Foreign forms: Scottish: **Ewan;** Welsh: **Eoin, Owen**

Evelyn (English) hazelnut.
Evelin

Everett (English) a form of Eberhard.
Ev, Evered, Everet, Everette, Everitt, Evert, Evrett

Everley (English) boar meadow.
Everlea, Everlee

Everton (English) boar town.

Ewald (German) always powerful. (English) powerful lawman.

Ewert (English) ewe herder, shepherd.
Ewart

Ewing (English) friend of the law.
Ewin, Ewynn

Ezekiel (Hebrew) strength of God. Bible: a Hebrew prophet. See also Haskel, Zeke.
Ezeck, Ezeeckel, Ezekeial, Ezekial, Ezell, Eziakah
Foreign forms: French: *Ezéchiel;* Italian: *Ezechiele;* Spanish: *Ezequiel, Eziequel*

Ezer (Hebrew) an alternate form of Ezra.

Ezra (Hebrew) helper; strong. Bible: a prophet and leader of the Israelites.
Ezer, Ezri
Foreign forms: French/Spanish: *Esdras;* German: *Esra;* Hawaiian: *Ezera*

Fabian (Latin) bean grower.
Fabayan, Fabe, Fabeon, Fabi, Fabius, Fabiyus, Fabyen, Faybian, Faybien
Foreign forms: English: *Fabyan;* French: *Fabert, Fabien;* German: *Faber;* Italian: *Fabiano, Fabio;* Polish: *Fabek;* Russian: *Fabiyan*

Fabio (Latin) an alternate form of Fabian. (Italian) a short form of Fabiano.

Fabrizio (Italian) craftsman.
Fabrice, Fabrizius

Fadi (Arabic) redeemer.

Fadil (Arabic) generous.

Fagan (Irish) little fiery one.
Fagin

Fahd (Arabic) lynx.
Fahad

Fai (Chinese) beginning.

Fairfax (English) blond.
Fair, Fax

Faisal (Arabic) decisive.
Faisel, Faisil, Faisl, Faizal, Fasel, Fasil, Faysal, Fayzal, Fayzel

Fakhir (Arabic) excellent.
Fahkry

Fakih (Arabic) thinker; reader of the Koran.

Falco (Latin) falconer.
Falcon, Falk, Falke, Falken

Falkner (English) trainer of falcons.
Falconer, Falconner, Faulconer, Faulconner, Faulkner

Fane (English) joyful, glad.
Fanes, Faniel

Farid (Arabic) unique.

Faris (Arabic) horseman.

Farley (English) bull meadow; sheep meadow.
Fairlay, Fairlee, Fairleigh, Fairley, Fairlie, Far, Farlay, Farlee, Farleigh, Farlie, Farly, Farrleigh, Farrley

Farnell (English) fern-covered hill.
Farnall, Fernald, Fernall, Furnald

Farnham (English) field of ferns.
Farnam, Farnum, Fernham

Farnley (English) fern meadow.
Farnlea, Farnlee, Farnleigh, Farnly, Fernlea, Fernlee, Fernleigh, Fernley

Farold (English) mighty traveler.

Farquhar (Scottish) dear.
Fark, Farq, Farquar, Farquarson, Farque, Farquharson, Farquy, Farqy

Farr (English) traveler.
Faer, Farran, Farren, Farrin, Farrington, Farron

Farrell (Irish) heroic.
Farrel, Farrill, Farryll, Ferrell

Farrow (English) piglet.

Faruq (Arabic) honest.
Farook, Farooq, Farouk, Faruqh

Fath (Arabic) victor.

Fatin (Arabic) clever.

Faust (Latin) lucky, fortunate. History: the sixteenth-century German doctor who inspired many legends.
Faustino, Faustis, Faustus
Foreign form: Italian: **Fausto**

Favian (Latin) understanding.

Faxon (German) long haired.

Feivel (Yiddish) God aids.

Felipe (Spanish) a form of Philip.
Feeleep, Felipino, Felo, Filip, Filippo, Filips, Fillip, Flip

Felix (Latin) fortunate; happy. See also Pitin.
Fee, Felic, Feliciano, Felicio, Felike, Felizio, Phelix
Foreign forms: Italian: **Félice;** *Russian:* **Feliks;** *Spanish:* **Félix, Felo, Pitin**

Felton (English) field town.
Felten, Feltin

Fenton (English) marshland farm.
Fen, Fennie, Fenny

Ferdinand (German) daring, adventurous.
Ferd, Ferda, Ferdie, Ferdy, Ferdynand, Nando
Foreign forms: French:

Ferdinánd, Fernand; *Spanish:* **Fernando, Hernando**

Fergus (Irish) strong; manly.
Fearghas, Fearghus, Feargus, Fergie, Ferguson, Fergusson

Fermin (French, Spanish) firm, strong.
Ferman, Firmin, Furman

Fernando (Spanish) a form of Ferdinand.
Ferdinando Ferdnando, Ferdo, Fernandez

Ferran (Arabic) baker.
Feran, Feron, Ferrin, Ferron

Ferrand (French) iron gray hair.
Farand, Farrand, Farrant, Ferrant

Ferrell (Irish) an alternate form of Farrell.
Ferrel, Ferrill, Ferryl

Fidel (Latin) faithful.
Fidelis, Fido
Foreign forms: French: **Fidele, Fidèle;** *Italian:* **Fidelio**

Field (English) a short form of Fielding.
Fields

Fielding (English) field; field worker.
Field

Fife (Scottish) from Fife,
Scotland.
Fyfe

Fifi (Fanti) born on Friday.

Filbert (English) brilliant.
Bert, Philbert
*Foreign forms: French: **Filberte;**
Italian/Spanish: **Filberto***

Filmore (English) famous.
**Fillmore, Filmer, Fyllmer,
Fylmer**

Finian (Irish) light skinned;
white.
**Finnian, Fionan, Fionn,
Phinean**

Finlay (Irish) blond-haired
soldier.
**Findlay, Findley, Finlea, Finlee,
Finley, Finn, Finnlea, Finnley**

Finn (German) from Finland.
(Irish) blond haired; light
skinned. A short form of Finlay.
(Norwegian) from the
Lapland.
Fin, Finnie, Finnis, Finny

Finnegan (Irish) light skinned;
white.
Finegan

Fiorello (Italian) little flower.

Firman (French) firm; strong.
Ferman

Firth (English) woodland.

Fiske (English) fisherman.
Fisk

Fitch (English) weasel, ermine.
Fitche

Fitz (English) son.
Filz

Fitzgerald (English) son of
Gerald.

Fitzhugh (English) son of
Hugh.
Hugh

Fitzpatrick (English) son of
Patrick.

Fitzroy (Irish) son of Roy.

Flann (Irish) redhead.
Flainn, Flannan, Flannery

Flavian (Latin) blond, yellow
haired.
**Flavel, Flavelle, Flavien,
Flawiusz**
*Foreign forms: Italian: **Flavio,
Flavious, Flavius***

Fleming (English) from
Denmark; from Flanders.
**Flemming, Flemmyng,
Flemyng**

Fletcher (English) arrow feath-
erer, arrow maker.
Flecher, Fletch

Flint (English) stream; flint-
stone.
Flynt

Flip (Spanish) a short form of
Felipe. (American) a short
form of Philip.

Florent (French) flowering.
**Florenci, Florencio, Florentin,
Florentino, Florentyn,
Florentz, Florinio, Florino**

Florian (Latin) flowering,
blooming.
**Florien, Florrian, Flory,
Floryan**

Floyd (English) a form of Lloyd.

Flurry (English) flourishing,
blooming.

Flynn (Irish) son of the
red-haired man.
Flin, Flinn, Flyn

Folke (German) an alternate
form of Volker.
Folker

Fonso (German, Italian) a short
form of Alphonso.
Fonzo

Fontaine (French) fountain.

Fonzie (German) a familiar form of Alphonse.
Fons, Fonsie, Fonz

Forbes (Irish) prosperous.
Forbe

Ford (English) a short form of names ending in "ford."

Fordel (Gypsy) forgiving.

Forest (French) an alternate form of Forrest.

Forester (English) forest guardian.
Forrester, Forrie, Forry, Forster, Foss, Foster

Forrest (French) forest; woodsman.
Forest, Forester, Forrie

Fortino (Italian) fortunate, lucky.

Fortune (French) fortunate, lucky.
Fortun, Fortunato, Fortuné
Foreign form: Italian: **Fortunio**

Foster (Latin) a short form of Forester.

Fowler (English) trapper of wild fowl.

Fran (Latin) a short form of Francis.
Franh

Francesco (Italian) a form of Francis.

Francis (Latin) free; from France. Religion: Saint Francis of Assisi was the founder of the Franciscan order.
Fran, France, Frang, Frank, Frannie, Franny, Franscis, Fransis, Franta, Franus, Frencis
Foreign forms: Czech: *Frantisek;* Danish: **Frants;** Hungarian: **Ferenc;** French: **Franchot, François;** German: **Franciskus, Franz;** Italian: **Francesco;** Spanish: **Farruco, Francisco;** Swedish: **Frans**

Francisco (Portuguese, Spanish) a form of Francis. See also Paco, Pancho.
Chilo, Cisco, Franco, Fransisco, Frasco, Frisco

François (French) a form of Francis.

Frank (English) a short form of Francis, Franklin.
Franc, Franck, Franek, Frang, Franio, Franke, Frankie, Franko
Foreign forms: Hawaiian: *Palani;* Spanish: **Pancho**

Frankie (English) a familiar form of Frank.
Franky

Franklin (English) free landowner.
Fran, Francklin, Francklyn, Frank, Frankin, Franklinn, Franklyn, Franquelin

Franklyn (English) an alternate form of Franklin.
Franklynn

Fraser (French) strawberry. (English) curly haired.
Fraizer, Frasier, Fraze, Frazer, Frazier

Frayne (French) dweller at the ash tree. (English) stranger.
Fraine, Frayn, Frean, Freen, Freyne

Fred (German) a short form of Frederick. See also Alfred, Manfred.
Fredd, Fredo, Fredson

Freddie (German) a familiar form of Frederick.
Freddi, Freddy, Fredi, Fredy

Frederic (German) an alternate form of Frederick.
Frédéric, Frederich, Frederric, Fredric, Fredrich

Frederick (German) peaceful ruler. See also Dick, Eric, Rick.
Fred, Fredderick, Freddie, Freddrick, Frederic, Frédérick, Frederrick, Fredrick, Fredricka, Fredwick, Fredwyck, Friedrich, Fritz
Foreign forms: Dutch: *Frederik;* French: *Fréderic;* Hawaiian: *Peleke;* Italian/Spanish: *Federico, Federigo, Fico, Fredo, Frederico, Fredrico, Frederigo;* Polish: *Fredek;* Swedish: *Fredrik*

Freeborn (English) child of freedom.
Free

Freeman (English) free.
Free, Freedman, Freemon, Friedman, Friedmann

Fremont (German) free; noble protector.

Frewin (English) free; noble friend.
Frewen

Frey (English) lord. (Scandinavian) Mythology: god of prosperity.

Frick (English) bold.

Fridolf (English) peaceful wolf.
Freydolf, Freydulf, Fridulf

Friedrich (German) an alternate form of Frederick.
Friedel, Friedrick, Fridrich, Fridrick, Friedrike, Fryderyk

Fritz (German) a familiar form of Frederick.
Fritson, Fritts, Fritzchen, Fritzl

Fulbright (German) very bright.
Fulbert

Fuller (English) cloth thickener.

Fulton (English) field near town.

Fyfe (Scottish) an alternate form of Fife.
Fyffe

Fynn (Ghanian) Geography: another name for the Offin river.

Gabby (American) a familiar form of Gabriel.
Gabbi, Gabbie, Gabi, Gabie, Gaby

Gabe (Hebrew) a short form of Gabriel.

Gábor (Hungarian) God is my strength.
Gabbo, Gabo

Gabriel (Hebrew) devoted to God. Bible: the Archangel of Annunciation.
Gab, Gabe, Gaberial, Gabin, Gabino, Gabis, Gabrail, Gabreil, Gabriël, Gabriele, Gabriell, Gabys, Gebereal, Ghabriel
Foreign forms: American: *Gabby;* Czech: *Gabko, Gabris;* Hungarian: *Gábor;* Italian:

Gabrielli, Gabriello; Russian: Gavril, Gavrilo; Spanish: Riel

Gadi (Arabic) God is my fortune.
Gad, Gaddy, Gadiel

Gaetan (Italian) from Gaeta, a region in southern Italy.
Gaetano, Gaetono
Foreign form: French: **Gatien**

Gage (French) pledge.
Gager

Gair (Irish) small.
Gaer, Gearr, Geir

Gaius (Latin) rejoicer.
Foreign forms: Welsh: **Cai, Caius**

Galbraith (Irish) Scotsman in Ireland.
Galbrait, Galbreath

Gale (Greek) a short form of Galen.
Gael, Gail, Gaile, Gayle

Galen (Greek) healer; calm. (Irish) little and lively.
Gaelan, Gaelen, Galan, Gale, Galin, Gaylen
Foreign form: Spanish: **Galeno**

Gallagher (Irish) eager helper.

Galloway (Irish) Scotsman in Ireland.
Gallway, Galway

Galt (Norwegian) high ground.

Galton (English) owner of a rented estate.
Gallton

Galvin (Irish) sparrow.
Gal, Gall, Gallven, Gallvin, Galvan, Galven

Gamal (Arabic) camel. See also Jamal.
Gamall, Gamil

Gamble (Scandinavian) old.

Gan (Chinese) daring, adventurous. (Vietnamese) near.

Gannon (Irish) light skinned, white.
Gannie, Ganny

Ganya (Zulu) clever.

Gar (English) a short form of Gareth, Garnett, Garrett, Garvin.
Garr

Garcia (Spanish) mighty with a spear.

Gardner (English) gardener.
Gard, Gardener, Gardie, Gardiner, Gardy

Gareth (Welsh) gentle.
Gar, Garith, Garreth, Garth, Garyth

Garett (Irish) an alternate form of Garrett.
Gared, Garet

Garfield (English) field of spears; battlefield.

Garland (French) wreath of flowers; prize. (English) land of spears; battleground.
Garlan, Garlen, Garllan, Garlund, Garlyn

Garman (English) spearman.
Garmann, Garrman

Garner (French) army guard, sentry.
Garnier

Garnett (Latin) pomegranate seed; garnet stone. (English) armed with a spear.
Gar, Garnet, Garnie

Garrett (Irish) brave spearman.
Gar, Gareth, Garett, Garret, Garrette, Gerret, Gerrett, Gerrit, Gerritt, Gerrot, Gerrott
Foreign forms: English: **Garrad, Garred, Garrod, Jarrett**

Garrick (English) oak spear.
Gaerick, Garek, Garick, Garik, Garreck, Garrek, Garrik,

Garrick *(cont.)*
**Garryck, Garryk, Gerreck,
Gerrick**

Garrin (English) an alternate
form of Garry.
**Garran, Garren, Garron,
Garyn**

Garrison (French) troops
stationed at a fort; garrison.
Garris

Garroway (English) spear
fighter.
Garraway

Garry (English) an alternate
form of Gary.
Garrey, Garri, Garrie, Garrin

Garson (English) son of Gar.

Garth (Scandinavian) garden,
gardener. (Welsh) a short form
of Gareth.

Garvey (Irish) rough peace.
**Garbhán, Garrvey, Garrvie,
Garv, Garvan, Garvie, Garvy**

Garvin (English) comrade in
battle.
**Gar, Garvan, Garven, Garvyn,
Garwen, Garwin, Garwyn,
Garwynn**

Garwood (English) evergreen
forest. See also Wood, Woody.
Garrwood

Gary (German) mighty spearman. (English) a familiar form
of Gerald.
Gare, Garey, Gari, Garry
Foreign form: Hawaiian: **Kali**

Gaston (French) from Gascony,
France.
Gascon

Gavin (Welsh) white hawk.
**Gav, Gavan, Gaven, Gavinn,
Gavino, Gavyn, Gavynn,
Gawain**

Gavriel (Hebrew) man of God.
Gav, Gavi, Gavrel, Gavril, Gavy

Gawain (Welsh) an alternate
form of Gavin.
**Gawaine, Gawayn, Gawayne,
Gawen, Gwayne**

Gaylen (Greek) an alternate
form of Galen.
**Gaylin, Gaylinn, Gaylon,
Gaylyn**

Gaylord (French) merry lord;
jailer.
**Gaillard, Gallard, Gay,
Gayelord, Gayler, Gaylor**

Gaynor (Irish) son of the
fair-skinned man.
**Gainer, Gainor, Gay, Gayner,
Gaynnor**

Geary (English) variable,
changeable.
Gearey, Gery

Geffrey (English) an alternate
form of Geoffrey. See also
Jeffrey.
Geff, Geffery, Geffrard

Gene (Greek) born to nobility.
A short form of Eugene.
Foreign form: Polish: **Genek**

Geno (Italian) a form of John.
A short form of Genovese.
Genio, Jeno

Genovese (Italian) from Genoa,
Italy.
Geno

Gent (English) gentleman.
Gentle, Gentry

Genty (Irish, English) snow.

Geoff (English) a short form of
Geoffrey.

Geoffrey (English) divinely
peaceful. A form of Jeffrey. See
also Godfrey, Jeff.
**Geffrey, Geoff, Geoffery,
Geoffre, Geoffry, Geofrey,
Gofery**
Foreign forms: French: **Geffroy,
Geoffroi;** German: **Gottfried;**
Italian: **Giotto;** Rumanian: **Geofrl**

George (Greek) farmer. See also Iorgos.
Georg, Georgas, Georget, Georgi, Georgios, Georgiy, Georgy, Gheorghe, Giorgos, Goerge, Goran, Gordios, Gorge, Gorje, Gorya, Grzegorz
Foreign forms: Arabic: **Gevorak;** Czech: **Durko, Jiri, Jur, Jurik;** Danish: **Jorgen;** Dutch: **Joris;** Ethiopian: **Semer;** Finnish: **Yrjo;** French: **Georges;** German: **Jörg, Jürgen;** Hawaiian: **Keoki, Mahi'ai;** Hebrew: **Yoyi;** Italian: **Georgio, Giorgio;** Japanese: **Joji;** Lithuanian: **Jurgis;** Polish: **Jerzy;** Russian: **Egor, Georgii, Gyorgy, Yegor, Yuri, Zhora;** Scandinavian: **Georg;** Scottish: **Geordie;** Spanish: **Jorge, Jorrín**

Georgios (Greek) an alternate form of George.
Georgious, Georgius

Georgy (Greek) a familiar form of George.
Georgie

Geovanni (Italian) an alternate form of Giovanni.
Geovan, Geovani, Geovannee, Geovanny

Geraint (English) old.

Gerald (German) mighty spearman. See also Fitzgerald, Jerry.
Garald, Gary, Gérald, Gerale, Gerick, Gerold, Gerrald, Gerrell, Gérrick, Gerrild, Gerrin, Gerrold, Gerry, Geryld
Foreign forms: Dutch: **Gerrit;** English: **Jarrell, Jerald;** French: **Geralde, Geraud, Giraud, Girauld;** Hungarian: **Gellert;** Irish: **Gearalt;** Italian/Spanish: **Geraldo, Giraldo;** Russian: **Garold, Garolds, Kharald;** Scandinavian: **Jarell**

Gerard (English) brave spearman. See also Jerry.
Garrard, Garrat, Garratt, Gearard, Gerad, Gerar, Gérard, Geraro, Gerd, Gerrard, Gerrit, Gerry, Girard
Foreign forms: French: **Géraud, Jerard;** German: **Gerhard;** Polish: **Gerek;** Spanish: **Gerardo, Gherardo**

Gerardo (Spanish) a form of Gerard.

Germain (French) from Germany. (English) sprout, bud. See also Jermaine.
Germaine, German, Germane, Germano, Germayn, Germayne
Foreign form: Arabic: **Jamaine**

Geronimo (Greek, Italian) a form of Jerome. History: a famous Apache chief.
Geronemo

Gerry (English) a familiar form of Gerald, Gerard. See also Jerry.
Geri, Gerre, Gerri, Gerrie, Gerryson

Gershom (Hebrew) exiled. (Yiddish) stranger in exile.
Gersham, Gersho, Gershon, Gerson, Geurson, Gursham, Gurshan

Gert (German, Danish) fighter.

Gervaise (French) honorable.
Garvais, Garvaise, Garvey, Gervais, Gervasio, Gervaso, Gervayse, Gervis, Gerwazy
Foreign form: English: **Jervis**

Ghilchrist (Irish) servant of Christ. See also Gil.
Gilchrist, Gilcrist, Gilie, Gill, Gilley, Gilly

Gi (Korean) brave.

Gia (Vietnamese) family.

Gian (Italian) a form of Giovanni, John.
Gianetto, Giann, Giannes, Gianni, Giannis, Giannos, Ghian

Giancarlo (Italian) a combination of John + Charles.
Giancarlos

Gianpaolo (Italian) a combination of Gian + Paul.
Gianpaulo

Gib (English) a short form of Gilbert.
Gibb, Gibbie, Gibby

Gibor (Hebrew) powerful.

Gibson (English) son of Gilbert.
Gibbon, Gibbons, Gibbs, Gibson, Gilson

Gideon (Hebrew) tree cutter. Bible: the judge who delivered the Israelites from captivity.
Gidon
Foreign forms: Bulgarian/French: **Gedeon;** *Italian:* **Gideone;** *Russian:* **Hedeon**

Gidon (Hebrew) an alternate form of Gideon.

Gifford (English) bold giver.
Giff, Giffard, Gifferd, Giffie, Giffy

Gig (English) horse-drawn carriage.

Gil (Greek) shield bearer. (Hebrew) happy. (English) a short form of Gilbert.
Gili, Gill, Gilli, Gillie, Gillis, Gilly

Gilbert (English) brilliant pledge; trustworthy. See also Gil, Gillett.
Gib, Gilburt, Giselberto, Giselbertus
Foreign forms: French: **Guilbert;** *German:* **Giselbert;** *Italian/Spanish:* **Gilberto**

Gilberto (Spanish) a form of Gilbert.

Gilby (Scandinavian) hostage's estate. (Irish) blond boy.
Gilbey, Gillbey, Gillbie, Gillby

Gilchrist (Irish) an alternate form of Ghilchrist.

Gilen (Basque, German) illustrious pledge.

Giles (French) goatskin shield.
Gide, Gilles, Gyles

Gillean (Irish) Bible: Saint John's servant.
Gillan, Gillen, Gillian

Gillespie (Irish) son of the bishop's servant.
Gillis

Gillett (French) young Gilbert.
Gelett, Gelette, Gillette

Gilmer (English) famous hostage.

Gilmore (Irish) devoted to the Virgin Mary.
Gillmore, Gillmour, Gilmour

Gilon (Hebrew) circle.

Gilroy (Irish) devoted to the king.
Gilderoy, Gildray, Gildroy, Gillroy, Roy

Gino (Greek) a familiar form of Eugene. (Italian) a short form of names ending in "gene," "gino."
Ghino

Giorgos (Greek) an alternate form of George.
Georgos

Giovanni (Italian) a form of John. See also Jeovanni, Jiovanni.
Geovanni, Gian, Gianni, Giannino, Giavani, Giovani, Giovannie, Giovanno, Giovanny, Giovany, Giovonathon, Giovonni

Gipsy (English) wanderer.
Gipson, Gypsy

Gitano (Spanish) gypsy.

Giuseppe (Italian) a form of Joseph.
Giuseppino

Gladwin (English) cheerful.
See also Win.
**Glad, Gladdie, Gladdy,
Gladwinn, Gladwyn,
Gladwynne**

Glanville (English) village with
oak trees.

Glen (Irish) an alternate form
of Glenn.

Glendon (Scottish) fortress in
the glen.
**Glenden, Glendin, Glenn,
Glenton**

Glendower (Welsh) from
Glyndwer, England.

Glenn (Irish) a short form of
Glendon.
**Gleann, Glen, Glennie,
Glennis, Glennon, Glenny**
Foreign forms: Scottish: **Glyn,
Glynn**

Glenville (Irish) village in the
glen.

Goddard (German) divinely
firm.
**Godart, Goddart, Godhardt,
Godhart, Gothart, Gotthard,
Gotthart**
Foreign forms: Dutch:
Gotthardt; *French:* **Godard**

Godfrey (German) a form of
Jeffrey. (Irish) God's peace.
See also Geoffrey.
**Godfree, Godfry, Godoired,
Godrey, Gofraidh, Gorry,
Gottfried**
Foreign forms: French:
Godefroi; *Italian:* **Goffredo,
Gofredo;** *Spanish:* **Godofredo;**
Swedish: **Gottfrid**

Godwin (English) friend of
God. See also Win.
**Godwinn, Godwyn, Goodwin,
Goodwyn, Goodwynn,
Goodwynne**
Foreign form: Dutch: **Godewyn**

Goldwin (English) golden
friend. See also Win.
**Goldewin, Goldewinn,
Goldewyn, Goldwyn,
Goldwynn**

Goliath (Hebrew) exiled. Bible:
the giant Phillistine whom
David slew with a slingshot.
Golliath

Gomer (Hebrew) completed,
finished. (English) famous
battle.

Gonza (Rutooro) love.

Gonzalo (Spanish) wolf.
**Goncalve, Gonsalve, Gonzales,
Gonzo**

Gordon (English) triangular hill.
**Gord, Gordain, Gordan,
Gorden, Gordy**
Foreign form: Scottish: **Geordan**

Gordy (English) a familiar form
of Gordon.
Gordie

Gore (English) triangular-
shaped land; wedge-shaped
land.

Gorman (Irish) small; blue
eyed.

Goro (Japanese) fifth.

Govert (Dutch) heavenly
peace.

Gower (Welsh) pure.

Gowon (Tiv) rainmaker.
Gowan

Grady (Irish) noble; illustrious.
**Gradea, Gradee, Gradey,
Gradleigh, Graidey, Graidy**

Graeme (Scottish) a form of
Graham.
Graem

Graham (English) grand home.
**Graeham, Graehame,
Graehme, Grahame, Grahme,
Gram**
Foreign form: Scottish: **Graeme**

Granger (French) farmer.
Grainger, Grange

Grant (English) a short form of Grantland.
Grand, Grantham, Granthem, Grantley

Grantland (English) great plains.
Grant

Granville (French) large village.
Gran, Granvel, Granvil, Granvile, Granvill, Grenville, Greville

Gray (English) gray haired.
Grey, Greye

Grayden (English) gray haired.
Graden

Graydon (English) gray hill.
Gradon, Greydon

Grayson (English) bailiff's son. See also Sonny.
Greydon, Greyson

Greeley (English) gray meadow.
Greelea, Greeleigh, Greely

Greenwood (English) green forest.
Green, Greener

Greg, Gregg (Latin) short forms of Gregory.
Graig, Greig, Gregson

Greggory (Latin) an alternate form of Gregory.
Greggery

Gregory (Latin) vigilant watchman.
Gergely, Gergo, Greagory, Greer, Greg, Gregary, Greger, Gregery, Greggory, Gregori, Grégorie, Gregors, Gregos, Gregrey, Gregroy, Gregry, Greogry, Grzegorz
Foreign forms: Armenian: *Krikor;* Bulgarian: **Grigori;** French: **Grégoire;** German: **Gregorius, Jörn;** Irish: **Greagoir;** Italian/Portuguese **Gregorio;** Russian: **Grisha;** Scottish: **Gregor;** Swedish: **Gries**

Gresham (English) village in the pasture.

Greyson (English) an alternate form of Grayson.
Greyston

Griffin (Latin) hooked nose.
Griff, Griffen, Griffie, Griffon, Griffy, Gryphon

Griffith (Welsh) fierce chief; ruddy.
Griff, Griffie, Griffy, Gryphon

Grimshaw (English) dark woods.

Griswold (German, French) gray forest.
Gris, Griz

Grosvener (French) big hunter.

Grover (English) grove.
Grove

Guilford (English) ford with yellow flowers.
Guildford

Guillaume (French) a form of William.
Guillaums

Guillermo (Spanish) a form of William.

Gunnar (Scandinavian) an alternate form of Gunther.
Gunner

Gunther (Scandinavian) battle army; warrior.
Guenter, Guenther, Gun, Gunnar, Guntar, Gunter, Guntero, Gunthar, Günther

Gurion (Hebrew) young lion.
Gur, Guri, Guriel

Gurpreet (Punjabi) devoted to the guru; devoted to the Prophet.
Gurjeet, Gurmeet, Guruprit

Gus (Scandinavian) a short form of Gustave.
Guss, Gussie, Gussy, Gusti, Gustry, Gusty

Gustave (Scandinavian) staff of the Goths. History: Gustavus Adolphus was a king of Sweden.
Gus, Gustaof, Gustáv, Gustava, Gustaves, Gustavs, Gustavus, Gustus, Gusztav
Foreign forms: Czech: **Gustav, Gustik;** *Dutch:* **Gustaff;** *Finnish:* **Kosti;** *Italian/Spanish:* **Gustavo, Tabo;** *Slavic:* **Tavo;** *Swedish:* **Gustaf**

Gustavo (Italian, Spanish) a form of Gustave.

Guthrie (German) war hero. (Irish) windy place.
Guthrey, Guthry

Guy (Hebrew) valley. (German) warrior. (French) guide.
Foreign forms: English: **Guyon;** *Italian/Spanish:* **Guido**

Guyapi (Native American) candid.

Gwayne (Welsh) an alternate form of Gawain.
Gwaine, Gwayn

Habib (Arabic) beloved.

Hackett (German, French) little woodcutter.
Hacket, Hackit, Hackitt

Hackman (German, French) woodcutter.

Hadar (Hebrew) glory.

Haddad (Arabic) blacksmith.

Hadden (English) heather-covered hill.
Haddan, Haddon, Haden, Hadon, Hadyn

Hadi (Arabic) guiding to the right.

Hadley (English) heather-covered meadow.
Had, Hadlea, Hadlee, Hadleigh, Hadly, Lee, Leigh

Hadrian (Latin, Swedish) dark.
Adrian, Hadrien

Hadwin (English) friend in a time of war.
Hadwinn, Hadwyn, Hadwynn, Hadwynne

Hagan (German) strong defense.
Haggan

Hagen (Irish) young, youthful.

Hagley (English) enclosed meadow.

Hahnee (Native American) beggar.

Hai (Vietnamese) sea.

Haidar (Arabic) lion.

Haig (English) enclosed with hedges.

Haji (Swahili) born during the pilgrimage to Mecca.

Hakan (Native American) fiery.

Hakim (Arabic) wise. (Ethiopian) doctor.
Hakeem, Hakiem

Hakon (Scandinavian) of Nordic ancestry.
Haaken, Haakin, Haakon,

Hakon (cont.)
Haeo, Hak, Hakan, Hako, Haukur

Hal (English) a short form of Halden, Hall, Harold.

Halbert (English) shining hero.
Bert, Halburt

Halden (Scandinavian) half-Danish. See also Dane.
Hal, Haldan, Haldane, Halfdan, Halldor, Halvdan

Halen (Swedish) hall.
Hale, Hallen, Haylan

Haley (Irish) ingenious.
Hailey, Haily, Haleigh, Hayleigh, Hayley
Foreign form: English: *Hale*

Halford (English) valley ford.

Hali (Greek) sea.

Halian (Zuni) young.

Halil (Turkish) dear friend.

Halim (Arabic) mild, gentle.
Haleem

Hall (English) manor, hall.
Hal, Halstead, Halsted

Hallam (English) valley.

Hallan (English) dweller at the hall; dweller at the manor.
Halin, Hallene, Hallin

Halley (English) meadow near the hall; holy.

Halliwell (English) holy well.
Hallewell, Hellewell, Helliwell

Hallward (English) hall guard.

Halsey (English) Hal's island.

Halstead (English) manor grounds.
Halsted

Halton (English) estate on the hill.

Halvor (Norwegian) rock; protector.
Halvard

Ham (Hebrew) hot. Bible: one of Noah's sons.

Hamal (Arabic) lamb. Astronomy: a bright star in the constellation of Aries.

Hamar (Scandinavian) hammer.

Hamid (Arabic) praised. See also Mohammed.
Haamid, Hamadi, Hamdrem, Hamed, Hameed, Hamidi, Hammad, Hammed, Humayd

Hamill (English) scarred.
Hamel, Hamell, Hammill

Hamilton (English) proud estate.
Hamel, Hamelton, Hamil, Hamill, Tony

Hamlet (German, French) little village; home. Literature: one of Shakespeare's tragic heroes.

Hamlin (German, French) loves his home.
Hamblin, Hamelen, Hamelin, Hamlen, Hamlyn, Lin

Hammet (English, Scandinavian) village.
Hammett, Hamnet, Hamnett

Hammond (English) village.

Hampton (English) Geography: a town in England.
Hamp

Hanan (Hebrew) grace.
Hananel, Hananiah, Johanan

Hanbal (Arabic) pure. History: founder of Islamic school of thought.

Hanford (English) high ford.

Hanif (Arabic) true believer.
Haneef, Hanef

Hank (American) a familiar form of Henry.

Hanley (English) high meadow. **Handlea, Handleigh, Handley, Hanlea, Hanlee, Hanleigh, Hanly, Henlea, Henlee, Henleigh, Henley**

Hannibal (Phoenician) grace of God. History: a famous Carthaginian general who fought the Romans. **Anibal**

Hanno (German) a short form of Johann.

Hans (Scanadinavian) a form of John. **Hanschen, Hansel, Hants, Hanz**

Hansel (Scandinavian) an alternate form of Hans. **Haensel, Hansl**

Hansen (Scandinavian) son of Hans. **Hanson**

Hansh (Hindi) god; godlike. Religion: another name for the Hindu god Shiva.

Hanson (Scandinavian) an alternate form of Hansen. **Hansen, Hanssen, Hansson**

Hara (Hindi) seizer. Religion: another name for the Hindu god Shiva.

Harald (Scandinavian) an alternate form of Harold. **Haraldo, Haralds, Haralpos**

Harbin (German, French) little bright warrior. **Harben, Harbyn**

Harcourt (French) fortified dwelling. **Court, Harcort**

Hardeep (Punjabi) an alternate form of Harpreet.

Harden (English) valley of the hares. **Hardin**

Harding (English) brave man's son. **Hardin**

Hardwin (English) brave friend.

Hardy (German) bold, daring.

Harel (Hebrew) mountain of God. **Hariel, Harrell**

Harford (English) ford of the hares.

Hargrove (English) grove of the hares. **Hargreave, Hargreaves**

Hari (Hindi) tawny. Religion: another name for the Hindu god Vishnu. **Hariel, Harin**

Harkin (Irish) dark red. **Harkan, Harken**

Harlan (English) hare's land; army land. **Harland, Harlen, Harlenn, Harlin, Harlon, Harlyn, Harlynn**

Harley (English) hare's meadow; army meadow. **Arley, Harlea, Harlee, Harleigh, Harly**

Harlow (English) hare's hill; army hill. See also Arlo.

Harold (Scandinavian) army ruler. **Hal, Haraldas, Haralds, Harry, Herrick, Herryck** *Foreign forms: Czech:* **Jindra;** *Danish:* **Harald;** *Dutch:* **Herold;** *Polish:* **Heronim;** *Russian:* **Garald, Garold;** *Spanish:* **Araldo, Haraldo, Heraldo**

Haroun (Arabic) lofty; exalted. **Haarun, Harin, Haron, Haroon, Harron, Harun**

Harper (English) harp player.
Harp, Harpo

Harpreet (Punjabi) loves God, devoted to God.
Hardeep

Harris (English) a short form of Harrison.
Haris, Hariss

Harrison (English) son of Harry.
Harris, Harrisen

Harrod (Hebrew) hero; conqueror.

Harry (English) a familiar form of Harold. See also Parry.
Harm, Harray, Harrey, Harri, Harrie
Foreign forms: *Hawaiian:* **Hale;** *Italian:* **Arrigo**

Hart (English) a short form of Hartley.

Hartley (English) deer meadow.
Hart, Hartlea, Hartlee, Hartleigh, Hartly

Hartman (German) hard; strong.

Hartwell (English) deer well.
Harwell, Harwill

Hartwig (German) strong advisor.

Hartwood (English) deer forest.

Harvey (German) army warrior.
Harv, Hervey, Hervy
Foreign form: *French:* **Hervé**

Hasad (Turkish) reaper, harvester.

Hasani (Swahili) handsome.
Hasaan, Hasain, Hasan, Hashaan, Hason, Hassen, Hassian, Husani

Hashim (Arabic) destroyer of evil.
Haashim, Hasheem

Hasin (Hindi) laughing.
Hasen, Hassin

Haskel (Hebrew) an alternate form of Ezekiel.
Haskell

Haslett (English) hazel-tree land.
Haze, Hazel, Hazlett, Hazlitt

Hassan (Arabic) handsome.
Hasan

Hassel (German, English) witches' corner.
Hassal, Hassall, Hassell

Hastin (Hindi) elephant.

Hastings (Latin) spear. (English) house council.
Hastie, Hasty

Hatim (Arabic) judge.
Hateem, Hatem

Hauk (Norwegian) hawk.
Haukeye

Havelock (Norwegian) sea battler.

Haven (Dutch, English) harbor, port; safe place.
Haeven, Havin, Hovan

Hawley (English) hedged meadow.
Hawleigh, Hawly

Hawthorne (English) hawthorn tree.

Hayden (English) hedged valley.
Haden, Haidyn, Haydn, Haydon

Hayes (English) hedged valley.
Hayse

Hayward (English) guardian of the hedged area.
Haward, Heyvard, Heyward

Haywood (English) hedged forest.
Heywood, Woody

Hearn (Scottish, English) a short form of Ahearn.
Hearne, Herin, Hern

Heath (English) heath.
Heathe, Heith

Heathcliff (English) cliff near the heath. Literature: the hero of Emily Brontë's novel *Wuthering Heights*.

Heaton (English) high place.

Hector (Greek) steadfast. Mythology: the greatest hero of the Trojan war.

Hedley (English) heather-filled meadow.
Headley, Headly, Hedly

Heinrich (German) an alternate form of Henry.
Heindrick, Heiner, Heinrick, Heinrik, Hinrich

Heinz (German) a familiar form of Henry.

Helge (Russian) holy.

Helki (Moquelumnan) touching.

Helmer (German) warrior's wrath.

Helmut (German) courageous.
Helmuth

Heman (Hebrew) faithful.

Henderson (Scottish, English) son of Henry.
Hendrie, Hendries, Hendron, Henryson

Hendrick (Dutch) a form of Henry.
Hendricks, Hendrickson, Hendrik, Hendriks, Hendrikus, Henning

Henley (English) high meadow.

Henning (German) an alternate form of Hendrick, Henry.

Henrick (Dutch) a form of Henry.
Heinrick, Henerik, Henrich, Henrik, Henryk

Henry (German) ruler of the household.
Hagan, Harro, Harry, Heike, Heinrich, Heinz, Henery, Henning, Henrry
Foreign forms: American: **Hank**; Bulgarian: **Henrim**; Dutch: **Hendrick, Henrick**; French: **Henri**; Greek: **Enrikos**; Hawaiian: **Hanale**; Irish: **Hanraoi**; Italian: **Arrigo,**

Enrico, Enzio; Polish: **Heniek, Honok**; Portuguese: **Henrique**; Rumanian: **Enric**; Spanish: **Enrique, Kiki**; Yiddish: **Hersz**

Herb (German) a short form of Herbert.
Herbie, Herby

Herbert (German) glorious soldier.
Bert, Harbert, Hebert, Hébert, Herb, Hurbert
Foreign forms: Italian: **Erberto, Heberto**; Spanish: **Heriberto**

Hercules (Greek) glorious gift. Mythology: a famous Greek hero renowned for his twelve labors.
Herakles, Herc, Herculie
Foreign form: French: **Hercule**

Heriberto (Spanish) a form of Herbert.
Heribert

Herman (Latin) noble. (German) soldier. See also Armand.
Herminio, Hermino, Hermon, Hermy, Heromin
Foreign forms: English: **Harmon**; Italian: **Ermanno**; Polish: **Mandek**; Spanish: **Ermano**; Swedish: **Hermann, Hermie**

Hermes (Greek) messenger. Mythology: the messenger for the Greek gods.

Herrick (German) war ruler.
Herrik, Herryck

Herschel (Hebrew) an alternate form of Hershel.
Hersch, Herschell

Hersh (Hebrew) a short form of Hershel.
Hersch, Hirsch

Hershel (Hebrew) deer.
Herschel, Hersh, Hershell, Herzl, Hirschel, Hirshel

Hertz (Yiddish) my strife.
Herzel

Hesperos (Greek) evening star.
Hespero

Hewitt (German, French) little smart one.
Hewe, Hewet, Hewett, Hewie, Hewit, Hewlett, Hewlitt

Hewson (English) son of Hugh.

Hezekiah (Hebrew) God gives strength.

Hideaki (Japanese) smart, clever.
Hideo

Hieremias (Greek) God will uplift.

Hieronymos (Greek) a form of Jerome.
Hierome, Hieronim, Hieronimo, Hieronimos, Hieronymo, Hieronymus

Hieu (Vietnamese) respectful.

Hilary (Latin) cheerful.
Hi, Hilarie, Hilarion, Hil, Hill, Hillary, Hillery, Hilliary, Hillie, Hilly
*Foreign forms: Basque: **Ilari**; Danish/Dutch: **Hilarius**; French: **Hilaire**; Spanish: **Hilario***

Hildebrand (German) battle sword.
Hildo

Hilel (Arabic) new moon.

Hillel (Hebrew) greatly praised. Religion: Rabbi Hillel originated the Talmud.

Hilliard (German) brave warrior.
Hillard, Hiller, Hillier, Hillierd, Hillyard, Hillyer, Hillyerd

Hilmar (Swedish) famous noble.

Hilton (English) town on a hill.
Hylton

Hinto (Dakota) blue.

Hippolyte (Greek) horseman.
Hippolit, Hippolitos, Hippolytus
*Foreign forms: Italian: **Ippolito**; Spanish: **Hipolito***

Hiram (Hebrew) noblest; exalted.
Hi, Hirom, Huram, Hyrum

Hiromasa (Japanese) fair, just.

Hiroshi (Japanese) generous.

Hisham (Arabic) generosity.

Hisoka (Japanese) secretive, reserved.

Ho (Chinese) good.

Hoang (Vietnamese) finished.

Hobart (German) Bart's hill.
Hobard, Hobbie, Hobby, Hobie, Hoebart

Hobert (German) Bert's hill.
Hobey

Hobson (English) son of Robert.

Hoc (Vietnamese) studious.

Hod (Hebrew) a short form of Hodgson.

Hodgson (English) son of Roger.
Hod

Hogan (Irish) youth.

Holbrook (English) brook in the hollow.
Brook, Holbrooke

Holden (English) hollow in the valley.
Holdin, Holdun

Holic (Czech) barber.

Holleb (Polish) dove.
Hollub, Holub

Hollis (English) grove of holly trees.
Hollie, Holly

Holmes (English) river islands.

Holt (English) forest.
Holton

Homer (Greek) hostage; pledge; security. Literature: a renowned Greek poet.
Homere, Homeros
Foreign forms: Dutch/German:
Homerus; *French:* **Homère;** *Italian:*
Omero

Hondo (Shona) warrior.

Honesto (Filipino) honest.

Honi (Hebrew) gracious.
Choni

Honon (Moquelumnan) bear.

Honorato (Spanish) honorable.

Honoré (Latin) honored.
Honoratus, Honorius
Foreign form: Spanish: **Honorio**

Hop (Chinese) agreeable.

Horace (Latin) keeper of the hours. Literature: a famous Latin poet.
Foreign forms: Dutch: **Horats;**
Spanish: **Horacio**

Horatio (Latin) clan name. See also Orris.
Foreign forms: German:
Horatius; *Italian:* **Oratio**

Horst (German) dense grove; thicket.
Foreign forms: English: **Hearst,**
Hurst

Horton (English) garden estate.
Hort, Horten, Orton

Hosea (Hebrew) salvation. Bible: a Hebrew prophet.
Hose, Hoseia, Hoshea,
Hosheah

Houghton (English) settlement on the headland.
Hoho

Houston (English) hill town. Geography: a city in Texas.
Huston

Howard (English) watchman.
Howie, Ward
Foreign form: Hawaiian: **Haoa**

Howe (German) high.
Howey, Howie

Howell (Welsh) remarkable.
Howel

Howi (Moquelumnan) turtle dove.

Howie (English) a familiar form of Howard, Howland.
Howey

Howin (Chinese) loyal swallow.

Howland (English) hilly land.
Howie, Howlan, Howlen

Hoyt (Irish) mind; spirit.

Hu (Chinese) tiger.

Hubbard (German) an alternate form of Hubert.

Hubert (German) bright mind; bright spirit.
Bert, Hobart, Hubbard,
Hubbert, Huber, Hugh,
Hugibert
Foreign forms: Czech:

Hubert *(cont.)*
Hubertek; *English:* **Hubie;** *Italian:* **Uberto;** *Russian:* **Beredei;** *Spanish:* **Huberto**

Hubie (English) a familiar form of Hubert.
Hube, Hubi

Hud (Arabic) Religion: a Muslim prophet.
Hudson

Huey (English) a familiar form of Hugh.
Hughey, Hughie, Hughy

Hugh (English) a short form of Hubert. See also Hewitt, Huxley, Maccoy.
Huey, Hughes
Foreign forms: French: **Hugues;** *Hawaiian:* **Hiu;** *Irish:* **Ea;** *Italian:* **Ugo;** *Latin:* **Hugo;** *Welsh:* **Hew**

Hugo (Latin) a form of Hugh.

Hulbert (German) brilliant grace.
Bert, Hulbard, Hulburd, Hulburt, Hull

Humbert (German) brilliant strength.
Hum
Foreign forms: Italian: **Umberto;** *Portuguese:* **Humberto**

Humberto (Portuguese) a form of Humbert.

Humphrey (German) peaceful strength. See also Onofrio.
Hum, Humfredo, Humfrey, Humfry, Humphery, Humphry, Humphrys
Foreign forms: Dutch: **Humfried;** *English:* **Hump, Humph;** *French:* **Onfroi;** *Italian:* **Onofredo;** *Polish:* **Onufry;** *Spanish:* **Hunfredo, Onofré;** *Swedish:* **Humfrid**

Hung (Vietnamese) brave.

Hunt (English) a short form of names beginning with "Hunt."

Hunter (English) hunter.
Hunt

Huntington (English) hunting estate.
Hunt, Huntingdon

Huntley (English) hunter's meadow.
Hunt, Huntlea, Huntlee, Huntleigh, Huntly

Hurley (Irish) sea tide.
Hurlee, Hurleigh

Husam (Arabic) sword.
Hossam

Hussein (Arabic) little; handsome.
Hossain, Hossein, Husain, Husani, Husayn, Husein, Husian, Hussain, Hussien

Hutchinson (English) son of the hutch dweller.
Hutcheson

Hute (Native American) star. Astronomy: a star in the Big Dipper.

Hutton (English) house on the jutting ledge.
Hut, Hutt, Huttan

Huxley (English) Hugh's meadow.
Hux, Huxlea, Huxlee, Huxleigh, Lee

Huy (Vietnamese) glorious.

Hy (Vietnamese) hopeful. (English) a short form of Hyman.

Hyacinthe (French) hyacinth.

Hyatt (English) high gate.
Hyat

Hyde (English) measure of land equal to 120 acres.

Hyder (English) tanner, preparer of animal hides for tanning.

Hyman (English) a form of Chaim.
Haim, Hayim, Hayvim, Hayyim, Hy, Hyam, Hymie

Hyun-Ki (Korean) wise.

Hyun-Shik (Korean) clever.

Iago (Spanish, Welsh) a form of Jacob, James. Literature: the villain in Shakespeare's play *Othello*.
Jago

Iain (Scottish) an alternate form of Ian.

Ian (Scottish) a form of John.
Iain
Foreign forms: English: **Ean, Eyon**; Irish: **Eion**

Ib (Phoenician, Danish) oath of Baal.

Ibrahim (Arabic) a form of Abraham. (Hausa) my father is exalted.
Ibraham, Ibrahem

Ichabod (Hebrew) glory is gone. Literature: Ichabod Crane was the main character of Washington Irving's story "The Legend of Sleepy Hollow."

Idi (Swahili) born during the Idd festival.

Idris (Welsh) eager lord. Religion: a Muslim prophet.
Idriss, Idriys

Iggy (Latin) a familiar form of Ignatius.

Ignatius (Latin) fiery, ardent. Religion: Saint Ignatious of Loyola was the founder of the Jesuit order. See also Neci.
Iggie, Iggy, Ignac, Ignác, Ignacius, Ignatious
Foreign forms: Basque: **Inigo**; English: **Ignatz**; French: **Ignace**; German: **Ignaz**; Italian: **Ignazio**; Spanish: **Ignacio**

Ihsan (Turkish) compassionate.

Ike (Hebrew) a familiar form of Isaac. History: the nickname of the thirty-fourth U.S. president Dwight D. Eisenhower.
Ikee, Ikey

Ilan (Hebrew) tree. (Basque) youth.

Illan (Basque, Latin) youth.

Ilom (Ibo) my enemies are many.

Immanuel (Hebrew) an alternate form of Emmanuel.
Iman, Imanol, Imanuel, Immanuele, Immuneal

Imran (Arabic) host. Bible: a character in the Old Testament.

Inder (Hindi) god; godlike. Religion: another name for the Hindu god Shiva.
Inderjeet, Inderjit, Inderpal, Indervir, Indra, Indrajit

Ing (Scandinavian) a short form of Ingmar.
Inge

Ingelbert (German) an alternate form of Engelbert.
Inglebert

Inger (Scandinavian) son's army.
Ingemar, Ingmar
Foreign form: Russian: **Igor**

Ingmar (Scandinavian) famous son.
Ing, Ingamar, Ingamur, Ingemar

Ingram (English) angel.
Inglis, Ingra, Ingraham, Ingrim

Ingvar (Scandinavian) Ing's soldier.
Ingevar
Foreign form: Russian: Igor

Iniko (Ibo) born during bad times.

Innis (Irish) island.
Innes, Inness, Inniss

Innocenzio (Italian) innocent.
Innocenty, Inocenci, Inocencio, Inocente, Inosente

Inteus (Native American) proud; unashamed.

Iorgos (Greek) an alternate form of George.

Ira (Hebrew) watchful.

Iram (English) bright.

Irv (Irish, Welsh, English) a short form of Irvin, Irving.

Irvin (Irish, Welsh, English) a short form of Irving. See also Ervine.
Inek, Irv, Irvine

Irving (Irish) handsome. (Welsh) white river. (English) sea friend. See also Ervin, Ervine.
Irv, Irvin, Irvington

Irwin (English) an alternate form of Irving. See also Ervin.
Irwinn, Irwyn

Isaac (Hebrew) he will laugh. Bible: the son of Abraham and Sarah. See also Itzak, Yitzchak.
Icek, Ike, Ikey, Ikie, Isaakios, Isac, Isack, Isak, Isiac, Isiacc, Issca, Issiac, Izak, Izzy
Foreign forms: Arabic: Ishaq; Czech: Izak; German: Isaak; Hungarian: Izsak; Italian: Isacco; Russian: Aizik

Isaiah (Hebrew) God is my salvation. Bible: an influential Hebrew prophet.
Isa, Isai, Isaia, Isaid, Isaih, Isais, Isaish, Ishaq, Isia, Isiah, Isiash, Issia, Issiah, Izaiah, Izaiha

Isam (Arabic) safeguard.

Isas (Japanese) meritorious.

Isekemu (Native American) slow-moving creek.

Isham (English) home of the iron one.

Ishan (Hindi) direction.

Ishmael (Hebrew) God will hear. Literature: the narrator of Melville's novel *Moby Dick*.
Isamail, Ishma, Ishmeal, Ishmel
Foreign forms: Arabic: Ismael, Ismail

Isidore (Greek) gift of Isis. See also Dorian.
Isador, Isadorios, Issy, Ixidor, Izadore, Izidor, Izidore, Izzy
Foreign forms: German: Isidor; Italian: Isidoro; Polish: Izydor; Portuguese/Spanish: Isadore, Isidro, Ysidro

Israel (Hebrew) prince of God; wrestled with God. History: the nation of Israel took its name from the name given Jacob after he wrestled with the Angel of the Lord.
Iser, Isser, Izrael, Izzy, Yisrael

Issa (Swahili) God is our salvation.

Itzak (Hebrew) an alternate form of Isaac.
Itzik

Ivan (Russian) a form of John.
Iván, Ivanchik, Ivanichek, Ivano, Ivas, Vanya

Ivar (Scandinavian) an alternate form of Ivor. See also Yvon.
Iv, Iva

Ives (English) young archer. See also Archer.
Ive, Iven, Ivey
Foreign form: *French:* **Yves**

Ivo (German) yew wood; bow wood.
Ivar, Ives, Ivon, Ivonnie, Yvo
Foreign forms: *Basque:* **Ibon;**
Scandinavian: **Ivor**

Ivor (Scandinavian) a form of Ivo.
Ifor, Ivar, Iver

Iye (Native American) smoke.

Izak (Czech) a form of Isaac.
Ixaka, Izaac, Izac, Izak, Izeke, Izik, Izsák

Izzy (Hebrew) a familiar form of Isaac, Isidore, Israel.
Issy

J (American) an initial used as a first name.
J.

Ja (Korean) attractive, magnetic.

Jaali (Swahili) powerful.

Jabari (Swahili) fearless.
Jabaar, Jabare, Jabbar, Jabier

Jabez (Hebrew) born in pain.
Jabe, Jabes, Jabesh

Jabin (Hebrew) God has created.

Jabir (Arabic) consoler, comforter.
Jabiri, Jabori

Jabulani (Shona) happy.

Jacan (Hebrew) trouble.
Jachin

Jace (American) a combination of the initials J. + C.
JC, J.C., Jacey, Jaice, Jayce, Jaycee

Jacinto (Portuguese, Spanish) hyacinth.
Giacinto, Jacindo, Jacint

Jack (American) a familiar form of Jacob, John.
Jackie, Jacko, Jackub, Jacque, Jak, Jax, Jock, Jocko
Foreign form: *Hawaiian:* **Keaka**

Jackie (American) a familiar form of Jack.
Jacky

Jackson (English) son of Jack.
Jacson, Jakson, Jaxon

Jacob (Hebrew) supplanter, substitute. Bible: son of Abraham, brother of Esau. See also Akiva, Coby, James, Kiva.
Jachob, Jack, Jackub, Jacobb, Jacobe, Jacobi, Jacobis, Jacobs, Jacobus, Jacoby, Jacolby, Jake, Jeks, Jim, Jocoby, Jocolby
Foreign forms: *American:* **Jock;**
Czech: **Jokubas, Kuba;** *Dutch:*
Jaap; *French:* **Jacques;** *German:*
Jakob, Jocek; *Greek:* **Iakobos;**
Italian: **Giacobo, Giacomo,**

Jacob (cont.)
Giacopo; *Lithuanian:* **Jecis, Jeska**; *Polish:* **Jalu, Koby**; *Portuguese:* **Jaco**; *Russian:* **Jasha, Yakov, Yasha**; *Scottish:* **Hamish**; *Slavic:* **Yoakim**; *Spanish:* **Chago, Checha, Diego, Iago, Jacobo, Jaime, Tiago**

Jacques (French) a form of Jacob, James. See also Coco.
Jacot, Jacquan, Jacquees, Jacquet, Jacquez, Jaques, Jarques, Jarquis

Jacy (Tupi-Guarani) moon.
Jaicy, Jaycee

Jade (Spanish) jade, precious stone.

Jadon (Hebrew) God has heard.
Jaden, Jadin, Jaeden, Jaedon, Jaiden, Jaydon

Jadrien (American) a combination of Jay + Adrien.
Jad, Jada, Jadd, Jader

Jaegar (German) hunter.
Jaager, Jagur

Jae-Hwa (Korean) rich, prosperous.

Jael (Hebrew) mountain goat.
Yael

Ja'far (Sanskrit) little stream.
Jafar, Jafari, Jaffar

Jagger (English) carter.

Jago (English) an alternate form of James.

Jaguar (Spanish) jaguar.
Jagguar

Jahi (Swahili) dignified.

Jaime (Spanish) a form of Jacob, James.
Jaimey, Jaimie, Jaimito, Jayme, Jaymie

Jairo (Spanish) God enlightens.
Jairus, Jarius

Jaja (Ibo) honored.

Jajuan (American) a combination of the prefix Ja + Juan.
Ja Juan, Jauan, Jawaun, Jejuan, Jujuan, Juwan

Jake (Hebrew) a short form of Jacob.
Jakie, Jayk, Jayke

Jakeem (Arabic) uplifted.

Jakob (Hebrew) an alternate form of Jacob.
Jakab, Jakiv, Jakov, Jakovian, Jekebs
Foreign forms: *Polish:* **Jakub, Jakubek**

Jal (Gypsy) wanderer.

Jalil (Hindi) god; godlike. Religion: another name for the Hindu god Shiva.
Jahlee, Jahleel, Jahlil, Jalaal, Jalal

Jam (American) a short form of Jamal, Jamar.
Jama

Jamaal (Arabic) an alternate form of Jamal.

Jamal (Arabic) handsome. See also Gamal.
Jahmal, Jahmall, Jahmalle, Jahmel, Jahmil, Jahmile, Jam, Jamaal, Jamael, Jamahl, Jamail, Jamala, Jamale, Jamall, Jamel, Jamil, Jammal, Jarmal, Jaumal, Jemal, Jermal
Foreign form: *American:* **Jamar**

Jamar (American) a form of Jamal.
Jam, Jamaar, Jamaari, Jamahrae, Jamara, Jamarl, Jamarr, Jamarvis, Jamaur, Jarmar, Jarmarr, Jaumar, Jemaar, Jemar, Jimar

Jamarcus (American) a combination of the prefix Ja + Marcus.
Jamarco, Jemarcus, Jimarcus

Jamario (American) a combination of the prefix Ja + Mario.
Jamari, Jamariel, Jamarius, Jemario, Jemarus

Jamel (Arabic) an alternate form of Jamal.
Jameel, Jamele, Jamell, Jamelle, Jammel, Jarmel, Jaumell, Je-Mell, Jimell

James (Hebrew) supplanter, substitute. (English) a form of Jacob. Bible: James the Great and James the Lesser were two of the Twelve Apostles.
Jago, Jaimes, Jamesie, Jamesy, Jay, Jaymes, Jem, Jemes, Jim
Foreign forms: Basque: **Jakome**; English: **Jamie, Jas**; French: **Jacques**; Hawaiian: **Kimo**; Russian: **Jasha, Yasha**; Scottish: **Hamish, Seumas**; Spanish: **Diego, Iago, Jaime, Santiago, Yago**

Jameson (English) son of James.
Jamerson, Jamesian, Jamison, Jaymeson

Jamie (English) a familiar form of James.
Jaimey, Jaimie, Jame, Jamee, Jamey, Jameyel, Jami, Jamian, Jammie, Jammy, Jayme, Jaymee, Jaymie

Jamil (Arabic) an alternate form of Jamal.

Jamiel, Jamiell, Jamielle, Jamile, Jamill, Jamille, Jamyl, Jarmil

Jamin (Hebrew) favored.
Jamian, Jamiel, Jamon, Jarmin, Jarmon, Jaymin

Jamison (English) son of James.
Jamiesen, Jamieson, Jamisen

Jamond (American) a combination of James + Raymond.
Jamod, Jamon, Jamone, Jarmond

Jamsheed (Persian) from Persia.

Jan (Dutch, Slavic) a form of John.
Jaan, Janne, Jano, Jenda, Yan

Janeil (American) a combination of the prefix Ja + Neil.
Janel, Janielle, Janile, Janille, Jarnail, Jarneil, Jarnell

Janson (Scandinavian) son of Jan.
Janse, Jansen, Janssen, Janten, Jantzen, Janzen, Jensen, Jenson

Janus (Latin) gate, passageway; born in January. Mythology: the Roman god of beginnings.
Januario

Japheth (Hebrew) handsome. (Arabic) abundant. Bible: a son of Noah. See also Yaphet.
Japeth, Japhet

Jaquan (American) a combination of the prefix Ja + Quan.
Ja'quan, Jaquin, Jaquon, Jaqwan

Jarah (Hebrew) sweet as honey.
Jerah

Jareb (Hebrew) contending.
Jarib

Jared (Hebrew) descendant.
Jahred, Jaired, Jarad, Jareid, Jarid, Jarod, Jarred, Jarrett, Jarrod, Jarryd, Jerad, Jered, Jerod, Jerrad, Jerred, Jerrod, Jerryd, Jordan

Jarek (Slavic) born in January.
Janiuszck, Januarius, Januisz, Jarrek

Jarell (Scandinavian) a form of Gerald.
Jairell, Jareil, Jarel, Jarelle, Jarrell, Jarryl, Jayryl, Jerel, Jerell, Jerrell, Jharell

Jareth (American) a combination of Jared + Gareth.
Jarreth, Jereth

Jarl (Scandinavian) earl, nobleman.

Jarlath (Latin) in control.
Jarl, Jarlen

Jarman (German) from Germany.
Jerman

Jaron (Hebrew) he will sing; he will cry out.
Jaaron, Jairon, Jaren, Jarone, Jayron, Jayronn, Je Ronn, J'ron

Jaroslav (Czech) glory of spring.
Jarda

Jarred (Hebrew) an alternate form of Jared.
Ja'red, Jarrad, Jarrayd, Jarrid, Jarrod, Jarryd, Jerrid

Jarrell (English) a form of Gerald.
Jarel, Jarell, Jarrel, Jerall, Jerel, Jerell

Jarrett (English) a form of Garrett, Jared.
Jairett, Jaret, Jareth, Jaretté, Jarhett, Jarratt, Jarret, Jarrette, Jarrot, Jarrott, Jerrett

Jarrod (Hebrew) an alternate form of Jared.
Jarod, Jerod

Jarryd (Hebrew) an alternate form of Jared.
Jarrayd, Jaryd

Jarvis (German) skilled with a spear.
Jaravis, Jarv, Jarvaris, Jarvas, Jarvaska, Jarvey, Jarvie, Jarvorice, Jarvoris, Jarvous, Jervey
Foreign forms: English: Javaris, Jervis

Jashawn (American) a combination of the prefix Ja + Shawn.
Jasean, Jashan, Jashon

Jason (Greek) healer. Mythology: the hero who led the Argonauts in search of the Golden Fleece.
Jacen, Jaeson, Jahson, Jaisen, Jaison, Jasan, Jase, Jasen, Jasin, Jasten, Jasun, Jay, Jayson

Jaspal (Punjabi) living a virtuous lifestyle.

Jasper (French) green ornamental stone. (English) a form of Casper. See also Kasper.
Jaspar, Jazper, Jespar, Jesper

Javan (Hebrew) Bible: son of Japheth.
Jaavon, Jahvaughan, Jahvine, Jahvon, JaVaughn, Javen, Javin, Javine, Javion, Javoanta, Javon, Javona, Javone, Javoney, Javoni, Javonn, Jayvin, Jayvion, Jayvon, Jevan

Javaris (English) a form of Jarvis.
Javaor, Javar, Javares, Javario, Javarius, Javaro, Javaron, Javarous, Javarre, Javarrious, Javarro, Javarte, Javarus, Javoris, Javouris

Javas (Sanskrit) quick, swift.
Jayvas, Jayvis

Javier (Spanish) owner of a new house. See also Xavier.
Jabier

Jawaun (American) an alternate form of Jajuan.
Jawaan, Jawan, Jawann, Jawn, Jawon, Jawuan

Jay (French) blue jay. (English) a short form of James, Jason.
Jave, Jeays, Jeyes
Foreign forms: Hindi: Jae, Jai, Jaye

Jayce (American) a combination of the initials J. + C.
JC, J.C., Jaycee, Jay Cee

Jayde (American) a combination of the initials J. + D.
JD, J.D., Jayden

Jaylee (American) a combination of Jay + Lee.
Jaylen, Jaylin, Jaylon, Jaylun

Jayme (English) an alternate form of Jamie.
Jaymes, Jayms

Jaymes (English) an alternate form of James.
Jayms

Jayson (Greek) an alternate form of Jason.
Jaycent, Jaysen, Jaysin, Jayssen, Jaysson

Jazz (American) jazz.
Jazze, Jazzlee, Jazzman, Jazzmen, Jazzmin, Jazzmon, Jazztin, Jazzton

Jean (French) a form of John.
Jéan, Jeannah, Jeannie, Jeannot, Jeanot, Jeanty, Jene

Jeb (Hebrew) a short form of Jebediah.
Jebi

Jebediah (Hebrew) an alternate form of Jedidiah.
Jeb, Jebadia, Jebadiah, Jebidiah

Jed (Hebrew) a short form of Jedidiah. (Arabic) hand.
Jedd, Jeddy, Jedi

Jediah (Hebrew) hand of God.
Jedaia, Jedaiah, Jedeiah, Jedi, Yedaya

Jedidiah (Hebrew) friend of God, beloved of God. See also Didi.
Jebediah, Jed, Jedediah, Jedediha, Jedidia, Jedidiah, Yedidya

Jedrek (Polish) strong; manly.
Jedrik, Jedrus

Jeff (English) a short form of Jefferson, Jeffrey. A familiar form of Geoffrey.
Jefe, Jeffe, Jeffey, Jeffie, Jeffy, Jhef

Jefferson (English) son of Jeff. History: Thomas Jefferson was the third U.S. president.
Jeferson, Jeff, Jeffers

Jeffery (English) an alternate form of Jeffrey.
Jefery, Jeffeory, Jefferay, Jeffereoy, Jefferey, Jefferie, Jeffory

Jefford (English) Jeff's ford.

Jeffrey (English) divinely peaceful. See also Geffrey, Geoffrey.
Jeff, Jefferies, Jeffery, Jeffree, Jeffrery, Jeffrie, Jeffries, Jeffry, Jefre, Jefry, Joffre, Joffrey
Foreign forms: French: **Jeoffroi;** *German:* **Godfrey**

Jeffry (English) an alternate form of Jeffrey.

Jehu (Hebrew) God lives. Bible: a military commander and king of Israel.
Yehu

Jelani (Swahili) mighty.
Jel

Jem (English) a short form of James, Jeremiah.
Jemmie, Jemmy

Jemal (Arabic) an alternate form of Jamal.
Jemaal, Jemael, Jemale, Jemel

Jemel (Arabic) an alternate form of Jemal.
Jemehyl, Jemell, Jemelle, Jemeyle, Jemmy

Jemond (French) worldly.
Jemon, Jémond, Jemonde, Jemone

Jenkin (Flemish) little John.
Jenkins, Jenkyn, Jenkyns, Jennings

Jeovanni (Italian) an alternate form of Giovanni.
Jeovani, Jeovany

Jerad, Jered (Hebrew) alternate forms of Jared.
Jeread, Jeredd

Jerahmy (Hebrew) a form of Jeremy.
Jerahmeel, Jerahmeil, Jerahmey

Jerald (English) a form of Gerald.
Jeraldo, Jerold, Jerral, Jerrald, Jerrold, Jerry

Jerall (English) an alternate form of Jarrell.
Jerai, Jerail, Jeraile, Jerale, Jerall, Jerrail, Jerral, Jerrel, Jerrell, Jerrelle

Jeramie, Jeramy (Hebrew) alternate forms of Jeremy.
Jerame, Jeramee, Jeramey, Jerami, Jerammie

Jere (Hebrew) a short form of Jeremiah, Jeremy.
Jeré, Jeree

Jerel, Jerell (English) forms of Jarell.
Jerelle, Jeril, Jerrail, Jerral, Jerrall, Jerrel, Jerrill, Jerrol, Jerroll, Jerryll, Jeryl

Jereme, Jeremey (Hebrew) alternate forms of Jeremy.
Jarame

Jeremiah (Hebrew) God will uplift. Bible: a great Hebrew prophet. See also Dermot.

Jaramia, Jemeriah, Jemiah, Jeramiah, Jeramiha, Jere, Jereias, Jeremaya, Jeremial, Jerimiah, Jerimiha, Jerimya, Jermiah, Jermija, Jerry, Yirmaya
Foreign forms: Basque: **Jeremi;** Dutch/German: **Jeremias;** English: **Jem, Jeremy;** French: **Jéréme;** Italian: **Geremia, Geremiah;** Russian: **Jeremija, Yeremey;** Swedish: **Jeremia**

Jeremie, Jérémie (Hebrew) alternate forms of Jeremy.
Jerémie, Jeremii

Jeremy (English) a form of Jeremiah.
Jaremay, Jaremi, Jaremy, Jem, Jemmy, Jerahmy, Jeramie, Jeramy, Jere, Jereamy, Jeremee, Jeremey, Jeremie, Jeremry, Jérémy, Jeremye, Jereomy, Jeriemy, Jerime, Jerimy, Jermey, Jeromy, Jerremy

Jeriah (Hebrew) Jehovah has seen.

Jericho (Arabic) city of the moon. Bible: a city conquered by Joshua.
Jeric, Jerick, Jerico, Jerik, Jerric, Jerrick

Jermaine (French) an alternate form of Germain. (English) sprout, bud.
Jarman, Jeremaine, Jeremane, Jerimane, Jermain, Jermane, Jermanie, Jermayn, Jermayne, Jermiane, Jermine, Jer-Mon, Jhirmaine

Jermal (Arabic) an alternate form of Jamal.
Jermael, Jermail, Jermal, Jermall, Jermaul, Jermel, Jermell

Jermey (English) an alternate form of Jeremy.
Jerme, Jermee, Jermere, Jermery, Jermie, Jhermie

Jermiah (Hebrew) an alternate form of Jeremiah.
Jermiha, Jermiya

Jerod (Hebrew) an alternate form of Jarrod.

Jerome (Latin) holy. See also Geronimo.
Jere, Jeroen, Jerom, Jérôme, Jeromo, Jeromy, Jerónimo, Jerrome, Jerromy
Foreign forms: English: **Gerome, Jeron;** French: **Jérome;** Greek: **Hieronymos**

Jeromy (Latin) an alternate form of Jerome.
Jeromey, Jeromie

Jeron (English) a form of
Jerome.
Jéron, Jerone, Jerron, J'ron

Jerrett (Hebrew) a form of
Jarrett.
**Jeret, Jerett, Jeritt, Jerret,
Jerrette, Jerriot, Jerritt, Jerrot,
Jerrott**

Jerrick (American) a combination of Jerry + Derrick.
Jaric, Jarrick, Jerick

Jerry (German) mighty spearman. (English) a familiar form
of Gerald, Gerard.
**Jehri, Jere, Jeree, Jeris, Jerison,
Jerri, Jerrie**
Foreign form: Hawaiian: **Kele**

Jess (Hebrew) a short form of
Jesse.

Jesse (Hebrew) wealthy. Bible:
the father of David. See also
Yishai.
**Jescey, Jesee, Jesi, Jesie, Jess,
Jessé, Jessee, Jessey, Jessi,
Jessie, Jessy**

Jessie (Hebrew) an alternate
form of Jesse.

Jesus (Hebrew) God is my salvation. An alternate form of
Joshua. Bible: son of Mary and
Joseph, believed by Christians
to be the Son of God. See also
Yosu.
Jecho, Josu
Foreign forms: Arabic: **Isa;**
Spanish: **Chucho, Jesús**

Jethro (Hebrew) abundant.
Bible: the father-in-law of
Moses. See also Yitro.
Jeth, Jetro, Jett

Jett (Hebrew) a short form of
Jethro. (English) hard, black
mineral.
Jet, Jetson, Jetter, Jetty

Jevan (Hebrew) an alternate
form of Javan.
**Jevaun, Jevin, Jevohn, Jevon,
Jevonne**

Jim (Hebrew) supplanter, substitute. (English) a short form
of James.
Jimi, Jimmy
Foreign forms: American:
Jimbo; Dutch: **Jaap**

Jimell (Arabic) an alternate
form of Jamel.
Jimel, Jimelle, Jimmil

Jimiyu (Abaluhya) born in the
dry season.

Jimmie (English) an alternate
form of Jimmy.
Jimmee

Jimmy (English) a familiar form
of Jim.
**Jimmey, Jimmie, Jimmyjo,
Jimy**

Jimoh (Swahili) born on Friday.

Jin (Chinese) gold.
Jinn

Jing-Quo (Chinese) ruler of the
country.

Jiovanni (Italian) an alternate
form of Giovanni.
Jio, Jiovani, Jiovanny, Jivan

Jirair (Armenian) strong; hard
working.

Jiro (Japanese) second son.

Jivin (Hindi) life giver.
Jivanta

Jo (Hebrew, Japanese) a form
of Joe.

Joab (Hebrew) God is father.
See also Yoav.
Joaby

Joachim (Hebrew) God will
establish. See also Akim.
**Joacheim, Joakim, Jov,
Yehoyakem**
Foreign forms: Basque: **Jokin;**
Portuguese: **Joaquim;** Russian:
Ioakim; Spanish: **Joaquín**

Joaquín (Spanish) a form of Joachim.
Jehoichin, Joaquin, Jocquin, Jocquinn, Juaquin

Job (Hebrew) afflicted. Bible: a righteous man who endured many afflictions.
Jobe, Jobert, Jobey, Jobie, Joby

Joben (Japanese) enjoys cleanliness.

Joby (Hebrew) a familiar form of Job.

Jodan (Hebrew) a combination of Jo + Dan.
Jodhan, Jodin, Jodon, Jodonnis

Jody (Hebrew) a familiar form of Joseph.
Jodey, Jodi, Jodie, Jodiha, Joedy

Joe (Hebrew) a short form of Joseph.
Jo, Joely, Joey

Joel (Hebrew) God is willing. Bible: an Old Testament Hebrew prophet.
Jôel, Joël, Joell, Joelle, Joely, Jole, Yoel

Joey (Hebrew) a familiar form of Joe, Joseph.

Johann (German) a form of John. See also Hanno, Yohann.
Anno, Joahan, Johan, Johanan, Johane, Johannas, Johannes, Johansen, Johanson, Johanthan, Johatan, Johathan, Johathon, Johaun, Johon, Johonson

John (Hebrew) God is gracious. Bible: name honoring John the Baptist and John the Evangelist. See also Yochanan.
Elchanan, Jack, Jaenda, Jahn, Janak, Jen, Jhan, Jhanick, Jhon, Jian, Joen, Johan, Johne, Johnl, Johnlee, Johnnie, Johnny, Johnson, Jon, Jone, Jones
Foreign forms: Basque: **Iban, Ugutz**; Czech: **Hanus, Honza, Ianos, Janco**; Danish: **Jens, Jensy**; Dutch: **Ioan, Jan, Jantje**; English: **Evan, Zane**; Finnish: **Hannes, Janne, Juhana**; French: **Jean, Jehan**; German: **Handel, Johann**; Greek: **Yanni, Yannis**; Hausa: **Yohance**; Hawaiian: **Keoni**; Hungarian: **Jacsi, János**; Irish: **Keon, Sean**; Italian: **Geno, Gian, Giovanni**; Latvian: **Janis**; Lithuanian: **Jonas**; Polish: **Iwan, Janek, Jas**; Portuguese: **Joáo, João**; Russian: **Ivan, Yan, Yanka**; Scandinavian: **Hans**; Scottish: **Ian**; Slavic: **Jovan**; Spanish: **Juan**; Swedish: **Jonam**; Turkish:

Ohannes; Welsh: **Owen**; Zuni: **Kwam**

Johnathan (Hebrew) an alternate form of Jonathan.
Jhonathan, Johathe, Johnatan, Johnathaon, Johnathen, Johnatten, Johniathin, Johnothan, Johnthan

Johnathon (Hebrew) an alternate form of Jonathon. See also Yanton.

Johnnie (Hebrew) a familiar form of John.
Johnie, Johnier, Johnni, Johnsie, Jonni, Jonnie

Johnny (Hebrew) a familiar form of John.
Jantje, Jhonny, Johney, Johnney, Johny, Jonny
Foreign form: Italian: **Gianni**

Johnson (English) son of John.
Johnston, Jonson

Jojo (Fanti) born on Monday.

Jomei (Japanese) spreads light.

Jon (Hebrew) an alternate form of John. A short form of Jonathan.
J'on, Joni, Jonn, Jonnie, Jonny, Jony

Jonah (Hebrew) dove. Bible: an Old Testament prophet who was swallowed by a large fish.
Jona, Yonah
Foreign forms: Italian: **Giona;** Turkish: **Yunus**

Jonas (Lithuanian) a form of John. (Hebrew) he accomplishes.
Jonelis, Jonukas, Jonus, Jonutis, Joonas

Jonathan (Hebrew) gift of God. Bible: the son of King Saul who became a loyal friend of David. See also Yonatan.
Janathan, Johnathan, Jon, Jonatan, Jonatane, Jonate, Jonatha, Jonathen, Jonathon, Jonattan, Jonethen, Jonnatha, Jonnathan, Jonnattan, Jonothan
Foreign form: Hawaiian: **Ionakana**

Jonathon (Hebrew) an alternate form of Jonathan.
Joanathon, Johnathon, Jonothon, Jounathon, Yanaton

Jones (Welsh) son of John.
Joenns, Jonesy

Jontae (French) a combination of Jon + the letter "t."

Johntae, Jontea, Jonteau, Jontez
Foreign form: American: **Jontay**

Jontay (American) a form of Jontae.
Johntay, Johnte, Johntez, Jontai, Jonte, Jonté, Jontez

Joost (Dutch) just.

Jora (Hebrew) teacher.
Yora, Jorah

Joram (Hebrew) Jehovah is exalted.
Joran, Jorim

Jordan (Hebrew) descending. See also Yarden.
Jared, Jordaan, Jordae, Jordain, Jordaine, Jordany, Jorden, Jordenn, Jordi, Jordie, Jordin, Jordon, Jordy, Jori, Jorrdan, Jory
Foreign forms: French: **Jordyn, Jourdain, Jourdan;** Italian: **Giordano;** Portuguese: **Jordáo**

Jordon (Hebrew) an alternate form of Jordan.
Jeordon, Johordan

Jordy (Hebrew) a familiar form of Jordan.

Jorell (American) he saves. Literature: a name inspired by the fictional character Jor-el,

Superman's father.
Jorel, Jor-El, Jorelle, Jorl, Jorrel, Jorrell

Jorge (Spanish) a form of George.
Jorrín

Jory (Hebrew) a familiar form of Jordan.
Joar, Joary, Jori, Jorie

José (Spanish) a form of Joseph. See also Ché.
Josean, Josecito, Josee, Joseito, Joselito, Josey

Josef (German, Portuguese, Czech, Scandinavian) a form of Joseph.
Joosef, Joseff, Josif, Jozef, József, Juzef

Joseph (Hebrew) God will add, God will increase. Bible: in the Old Testament, the son of Jesse who came to rule Egypt; in the New Testament, the husband of Mary. See also Yosef.
Jody, Joe, Joeseph, Joey, Jojo, Josephat, Josephie, Josephus, Josheph, Jozzepi
Foreign forms: Arabic: **Yusuf;** Basque: **Joseba;** Czech: **Joza, Jozka, Pepa;** Dutch: **Joop, Jopie;** Finnish: **Joosef, Jooseppi;** French: **Josephe;** German: **Josef, Jupp,**

Joseph (cont.)
Sepp; Hawaiian: **Iokepa;**
Hungarian: **Jóska, Jozsi;** Italian:
Beppe, Giuseppe, Peppe, Pino;
Japanese: **Jo;** Latvian: **Jazeps;**
Polish: **Jozio, Juziu;** Portuguese:
Zeusef; Russian: **Iosif, Osip, Osya
Yeska, Yusuf;** Serbian: **Josep,
Josip, Joze, Jozef, Jozhe;** Spanish:
Cheche, Chepe, Jobo, José, Pepe;
Yiddish: **Yousef, Youssel**

Josh (Hebrew) a short form of
Joshua.
Joshe

Josha (Hindi) satisfied.

Joshi (Swahili) galloping.

Joshua (Hebrew) God is my
salvation. Bible: the successor
of Moses who led the Israelites
into the Promised Land. See
also Jesus, Yehoshua.
**Johsua, Johusa, Josh, Joshau,
Joshaua, Joshauh, Joshawa,
Joshawah, Joshia, Joshu,
Joshuaa, Joshuah, Joshuea,
Joshula, Joshus, Joshusa,
Joshuwa, Joshwa, Jousha,
Jozshua, Jozsua, Jushua**
Foreign forms: Dutch: **Jozua;**
French: **Josue;** Italian: **Giosia;**
Rumanian: **Iosua**

Josiah (Hebrew) fire of the Lord.
**Joshiah, Josia, Josiahs, Josian,
Josias, Josie, Yoshiyahu**

Joss (Chinese) luck; fate.
Josse, Jossy

Josue (Hebrew) an alternate
form of Joshua.
**Joshue, Josu, Josua, Josuha,
Jozus**

Jotham (Hebrew) may God
complete. Bible: a king of
Judah.

Jovan (Latin) Jove-like, majestic.
(Slavic) a form of John.
Mythology: Jove, also known
as Jupiter, was the supreme
Roman god.
**Jovaan, Jovani, Jovanic,
Jovann, Jovanni, Jovannie,
Jovannis, Jovanny, Jovany,
Jovenal, Jovenel, Jovi, Jovian,
Jovin, Jovito, Jovoan, Jovon,
Jovonn, Jovonne, Yovan**

Jr (Latin) a short form of Junior.
Jr.

Juan (Spanish) a form of John.
See also Chan.
**Juanch, Juanchito, Juanito,
Juann, Juaun**

Juaquin (Spanish) an alternate
form of Joaquín.
Juaquine

Jubal (Hebrew) ram's horn.
Bible: a musician and a
descendant of Cain.

Judah (Hebrew) praised. Bible:
the fourth of Jacob's sons. See
also Yehudi.
Juda, Judas, Judd, Jude

Judas (Latin) a form of Judah.
Bible: Judas Iscariot was the
disciple who betrayed Jesus.
Jude

Judd (Hebrew) a short form of
Judah.
Jud, Judson

Jude (Latin) a short form of
Judah, Judas. Bible: one of the
Christian apostles and author
of the New Testament book,
The Epistle of Saint Jude.

Judson (English) son of Judd.

Julian (Greek, Latin) an alter-
nate form of Julius.
**Jolyon, Juliaan, Juliano, Julien,
Jullian, Julyan**

Julien (Latin) an alternate form
of Julian.

Julio (Hispanic) a form of Julius.

Julius (Greek, Latin) youthful,
downy bearded. History: Julius
Caesar was a great Roman
emperor.
**Jolyon, Julas, Jules, Julian,
Julias, Julie**
Foreign forms: Basque: **Julen;**

French: **Jule, Jules;** Hispanic: **Julio;** Italian: **Giuliano, Giulio, Guilano;** Polish: **Juliusz**

Jumah (Arabic, Swahili) born on Friday, a holy day in the Islamic religion.
Jimoh, Juma

Jumoke (Nigerian) loved by everyone.

Jun (Chinese) truthful. (Japanese) obedient; pure.
Junnie

Junior (Latin) young.
Jr, Junious, Junius

Juro (Japanese) best wishes; long life.

Jurrien (Dutch) God will uplift.
Jore, Jurian, Jurre

Justin (Latin) just, righteous.
Jobst, Jost, Justain, Justan, Justen, Justice, Justinas, Justine, Justinian, Justinius, Justinn, Justins, Juston, Justton, Justun
Foreign forms: Bulgarian: **Iustin;** Czech: **Jusa, Justyn;** German: **Just;** Italian: **Giustino;** Lithuanian: **Justas, Justukas;** Polish: **Justek;** Russian: **Ustin, Yustyn;** Spanish: **Justino, Justo, Tutu;** Swedish: **Justinus;** Welsh: **Iestyn, Jestin, Yestin**

Justis (French) just.
Justs, Justus

Justyn (Latin) an alternate form of Justin.
Justn

Juvenal (Latin) young. Literature: a Roman satiric poet.
Juvon, Juvone

Juwan (American) an alternate form of Jajuan.
Juwann, Juwaun, Juwon, Juwuan

Kabir (Hindi) History: a Hindu mystic.
Kabar

Kabonero (Runyankore) sign.

Kabonesa (Rutooro) difficult birth.

Kacancu (Rukonjo) firstborn child.

Kacey (Irish) an alternate form of Casey. (American) a combination of the initials K. + C. See also KC.
Kace, Kacee, Kacy, Kaesy, Kase, Kasey, Kasie, Kasy, Kaycee

Kadar (Arabic) powerful.
Kader

Kade (Scottish) wetlands. (American) a combination of the initials K. + D.
Kadee, Kaydee

Kadeem (Arabic) servant.
Kadim, Khadeem

Kadin (Arabic) companion, friend.

Kadir (Arabic) spring greening.
Kadeer

Kado (Japanese) gateway.

Kaelan (Irish) an alternate form of Kellen.
Kael, Kaelen, Kaelin, Kaelyn

Kaemon (Japanese) joyful; right handed.

Kahale (Hawaiian) home.

Kahil (Turkish) young; inexperienced; naive.
Cahil, Kale, Kayle

Kahlil (Arabic) an alternate form of Khalíl.
Kahleel, Kahleil, Kahlill, Kalel, Kalil

Kaholo (Hawaiian) runner.

Kai (Welsh) keeper of the keys. (German) an alternate form of Kay. (Hawaiian) sea.

Kailen (Irish) an alternate form of Kellen.
Kail, Kailan, Kailey, Kailin

Kaili (Hawaiian) Religion: a Hawaiian deity.

Kaipo (Hawaiian) sweetheart.

Kairo (Arabic) an alternate form of Cairo.

Kaj (Danish) earth.
Kai

Kala (Hindi) black; time. (Hawaiian) sun. Religion: another name for the Hindu god Shiva.

Kalama (Hawaiian) torch.
Kalam

Kalani (Hawaiian) heaven; chief.
Kalan

Kale (Arabic) a short form of Kahlil. (Hawaiian) a familiar form of Carl.
Kalee, Kaleu, Kaley, Kali, Kalin, Kayle

Kaleb (Hebrew) an alternate form of Caleb.
Kal, Kalab, Kalb, Kale, Kalev, Kalib, Kilab

Kalen, Kalin (Arabic) alternate forms of Kale. (Irish) alternate forms of Kellen.

Kali (Arabic) a short form of Kalil. (Hawaiian) a form of Gary.

Kalil (Arabic) an alternate form of Khalíl.
Kali

Kalkin (Hindi) tenth. Religion: the tenth incarnation of the Hindu god Vishnu.
Kalki

Kallen (Irish) an alternate form of Kellen.
Kallan, Kallin, Kallon, Kallun, Kalon, Kalun, Kalyn

Kalvin (Latin) an alternate form of Calvin.
Kal, Kalv, Vinny

Kamaka (Hawaiian) face.

Kamakani (Hawaiian) wind.

Kamal (Hindi) lotus. Religion: a Hindu god. (Arabic) perfect, perfection.
Kamaal, Kameel, Kamel, Kamil

Kamau (Kikuyu) quiet warrior.

Kameron (Scottish) an alternate form of Cameron.
Kam, Kamey, Kammy, Kamran, Kamren, Kamron

Kami (Hindi) loving.

Kana (Japanese) powerful; capable. (Hawaiian) Mythology: a god who took the form of a rope extending from Molokai to Hawaii.

Kane (Welsh) beautiful. (Irish) tribute. (Japanese) golden. (Hawaiian) eastern sky. (English) an alternate form of Keene. See also Cain.
Kahan, Kain, Kainan, Kaine, Kainen, Kaney, Kayne

Kange (Lakota) raven.
Kanga

Kaniel (Hebrew) stalk, reed.
Kan, Kani, Kannie, Kanny

Kannan (Hindi) Religion: another name for the Hindu god Krishna.
Kannen

Kannon (Polynesian) free. An alternate form of Cannon.
Kanon

Kanoa (Hawaiian) free. (Chinese) Religion: the Chinese god of mercy.

Kantu (Hindi) happy.

Kanu (Swahili) wildcat.

Kaori (Japanese) strong.

Kapila (Hindi) ancient prophet.
Kapil

Kapono (Hawaiian) righteous.
Kapena

Kare (Norwegian) enormous.
Karee

Kareem (Arabic) noble; distinguished.
Karee, Karem, Kareme, Karim, Karriem

Karey (Greek) an alternate form of Carey.
Karee, Kari, Karry, Kary

Karif (Arabic) born in autumn.
Kareef

Kariisa (Runyankore) herdsman.

Karim (Arabic) an alternate form of Kareem.

Karl (German) an alternate form of Carl.
Kaarle, Kaarlo, Kalle, Kalman, Kálmán, Karcsi, Karlitis, Karlo, Karlos, Karlton, Karlus *Foreign forms: Czech: Karel, Karlik, Karol; Hungarian: Kari; Latvian/Russian: Karlen; Swedish: Kjell*

Karmel (Hebrew) an alternate form of Carmel.

Karney (Irish) an alternate form of Carney.

Karr (Scandinavian) an alternate form of Carr.

Karsten (Greek) anointed.

Karu (Hindi) cousin. Bible: the cousin of Moses.
Karun

Kaseem (Arabic) divided.
Kasceem, Kaseym, Kasim, Kazeem

Kaseko (Rhodesian) mocked, ridiculed.

Kasem (Thai) happiness.

Kasen (Basque) protected with a helmet.

Kasey (Irish) an alternate form of Casey.

Kasim (Arabic) an alternate form of Kaseem.

Kasimir (Arabic) peace. (Slavic) an alternate form of Casimir.
Kasim, Kazimierz, Kazimir, Kazio, Kazmer, Kazmér, Kázmér

Kasper (Persian) treasurer. (German) an alternate form of Casper.
Kaspar, Kaspero

Kass (German) blackbird.
Kaese, Kasch, Kase

Kassidy (Irish) an alternate form of Cassidy.
Kassady, Kassie, Kassy

Kato (Runyankore) second of twins.

Kavan (Irish) handsome.
Cavan, Kavanagh, Kavenaugh

Kaveh (Persian) ancient hero.

Kavi (Hindi) poet.

Kay (Greek) rejoicing. (German) fortified place. Literature: one of the knights of King Arthur's Round Table.
Kai, Kaycee, Kayson

Kayin (Nigerian) celebrated. (Yoruba) long-hoped-for child.

Kayle (Hebrew) faithful dog. (Arabic) a short form of Kahlil.

Kaylen (Irish) an alternate form of Kellen.
Kaylan, Kaylin, Kaylon, Kaylyn

Kazuo (Japanese) man of peace.

KC (American) a combination of the initials K. + C. See also Kacey.
Kc, K.C., Kcee, Kcey

Kealoha (Hawaiian) fragrant.
Ke'ala

Keandre (American) a combination of the prefix Ke + Andre.
Keondre

Keane (German) bold; sharp. (Irish) handsome. (English) an alternate form of Keene.
Kean

Kearn (Irish) a short form of Kearney.
Kearne

Kearney (Irish) an alternate form of Carney.
Kar, Karney, Karny, Kearn, Kearny

Keary (Irish) an alternate form of Kerry.
Kearie

Keaton (English) where hawks fly.
Keaten, Keeton, Keetun

Keawe (Hawaiian) strand.

Keb (Egyptian) earth. Mythology: an ancient earth god, also known as Geb.

Kedar (Hindi) mountain lord. (Arabic) powerful. Religion: another name for the Hindu god Shiva.
Keder, Kadar

Kedem (Hebrew) ancient.

Kedrick (English) an alternate form of Cedric.
Keddrick, Kedric

Keefe (Irish) handsome; loved.

Keegan (Irish) little; fiery.
Kaegan, Keagen, Kegan, Keghan, Kegun

Keelan (Irish) little; slender.

Keeley (Irish) handsome.
Kealey, Kealy, Keelen, Keelian, Keelie, Keely

Keenan (Irish) little Keene.
Keanan, Keanen, Keannan, Keenen, Keenon, Kenan, Keynan, Kienan, Kienen, Kienon

Keene (German) bold; sharp. (English) smart. See also Kane.
Keane, Keen, Keenan

Keiji (Japanese) cautious ruler.

Keir (Irish) a short form of Kieran.

Keitaro (Japanese) blessed.
Keita

Keith (Welsh) forest. (Scottish) battle place.
Keath, Keeth, Keithen, Keithon
Foreign form: Hawaiian: **Kika**

Kekoa (Hawaiian) bold, courageous.

Kelby (German) farm by the spring.
Keelby, Kelbee, Kelbey, Kellby

Kele (Hawaiian) a form of Jerry. (Hopi) sparrow hawk.
Kelle

Kelemen (Hungarian) gentle; kind.
Kellman

Keli'i (Hawaiian) chief.

Kelile (Ethiopian) protected.

Kell (Scandinavian) spring.

Kellen (Irish) mighty warrior.
Kaelan, Kailen, Kalan, Kalen, Kalin, Kallen, Kaylen, Keelan, Keilan, Keillan, Kelden, Kellan, Kelle, Kellin, Kelynn

Keller (Irish) little companion.

Kelly (Irish) warrior.
Kelle, Kellen, Kelley, Kelli, Kely

Kelmen (Basque) merciful.

Kelsey (Scandinavian) island of ships.
Kelcy, Kelse, Kelsie, Kelsy, Kesley, Kesly

Kelton (English) keel town; port.
Kelden, Keldon, Kelson, Kelten, Keltonn

Kelvin (Irish, English) narrow river. Geography: a river in Scotland.
Kelvan, Kelven, Kelvyn, Kelwin, Kelwyn

Kemal (Turkish) highest honor.

Kemp (English) fighter; champion.

Kempton (English) military town.

Ken (Japanese) one's own kind. (Scottish) a short form of Kendall, Kendrick, Kenneth.
Kena, Kenn, Keno

Kendall (English) valley of the river Kent.
Ken, Kendal, Kendale, Kendali, Kendel, Kendell, Kendrall, Kendrell, Kendryll

Kendrick (Irish) son of Henry. (Scottish) royal chieftain.
Ken, Kendric, Kendricks, Kendrik, Kendrix, Kendryck, Keondric, Keondrick

Kenley (English) royal meadow.
Kenlea, Kenlee, Kenleigh, Kenlie, Kenly

Kenn (Scottish) an alternate form of Ken.

Kennan (Scottish) little Ken.
Kenna, Kenan, Kennen, Kennon

Kennard (Irish) brave chieftain.
Kenner

Kennedy (Irish) helmeted chief. History: John F. Kennedy was the thirty-fifth U.S. president.
Kennedey

Kenneth (Irish) handsome. (English) royal oath.
Ken, Keneth, Kennet, Kennethen, Kennett, Kennieth, Kennith, Kennth, Kennyth
*Foreign forms: Russian: **Kenya**; Scottish: **Kenny***

Kenny (Scottish) a familiar form of Kenneth.
Keni, Kenney, Kennie, Kinnie

Kenrick (English) bold ruler; royal ruler.
Kenric, Kenricks, Kenrik

Kent (Welsh) white; bright. (English) a short form of Kenton. Geography: a county in England.

Kentaro (Japanese) big boy.

Kenton (English) from Kent, England.
Kent, Kenten, Kentin, Kentonn

Kentrell (English) king's estate.

Kenward (English) brave; royal guardian.

Kenyon (Irish) white haired, blond.
Kenyan, Kenynn

Kenzie (Scottish) wise leader. See also Mackenzie.
Kensie

Keola (Hawaiian) life.

Keon (Irish) a form of John.
Keeon, Keion, Keionne, Keondre, Keone, Keontae, Keontrye, Keony, Keyon, Kian, Kion

Kerel (Afrikaans) young.

Kerem (Turkish) noble; kind.

Kerey (Gypsy) homeward-bound.
Ker

Kerman (Basque) from Germany.

Kermit (Irish) an alternate form of Dermot.
Kermey, Kermie, Kermy

Kern (Irish) a short form of Kieran.
Kearn, Kerne

Kerr (Scandinavian) an alternate form of Carr.
Karr

Kerrick (English) king's rule.

Kerry (Irish) dark, dark haired.
Keary, Keri, Kerrey, Kerri, Kerrie

Kers (Todas) Botany: an Indian plant.

Kersen (Indonesian) cherry.

Kerwin (Irish) little; dark. (English) friend of the marshlands.
Kervin, Kervyn, Kerwinn, Kerwyn, Kerwynn, Kirwin, Kirwyn

Keshawn (American) a combination of the prefix Ke + Shawn.
Kesean, Keshaun, Keshon

Kesin (Hindi) long-haired beggar.

Kesse (Ashanti, Fanti) chubby baby.
Kessie

Kestrel (English) falcon.
Kes

Keung (Chinese) universe.

Kevan (Irish) an alternate form of Kevin.
Kavan

Keven (Irish) an alternate form of Kevin.
Keve

Kevin (Irish) handsome. See also Cavan.
Keevin, Keevon, Kev, Kevan, Keven, Keveon, Keverne, Kévin, Kevinn, Kevins, Kevion, Kevis, Kevn, Kevon, Kevron, Kevvy, Kevyn

Key (English) key; protected.

Khälid (Arabic) eternal.
Khaled

Khalíl (Arabic) friend.
Kahlil, Kaleel, Kalil, Khalee, Khali, Khalial, Khaliyl

Khaliq (Arabic) creative.
Kaliq, Khalique

Khan (Turkish) prince.
Khanh

Khayru (Arabic) benevolent.
Khiri, Khiry, Kiry

Khoury (Arabic) priest.
Khory

Khristian (Greek) an alternate form of Christian, Kristian.
Khris, Khristin

Khristos (Greek) an alternate form of Christopher, Christos.

Khris, Khristophe, Khristopher, Kristo, Kristos

Kibbe (Nayas) night bird.

Kibo (Uset) worldly; wise.

Kidd (English) child; young goat.

Kiel (Irish) an alternate form of Kyle.

Kiele (Hawaiian) gardenia.

Kieran (Irish) little and dark; little Keir.
Keiran, Keiren, Keiron, Kern, Kernan, Kiernan, Kieron, Kyran

Kiet (Thai) honor.

Kiho (Dutooro) born on a foggy day.

Kijika (Native American) quiet walker.

Killian (Irish) little Kelly.
Kilian, Killie, Killy

Kim (English) a short form of Kimball.
Kimie, Kimmy

Kimball (Greek) hollow vessel. (English) warrior chief.
Kim, Kimbal, Kimbell, Kimble

Kin (Japanese) golden.

Kincaid (Scottish) battle chief.

King (English) king. A short form of names beginning with "King."

Kingsley (English) king's meadow.
King, Kingslea, Kingslie, Kingsly, Kinslea, Kinslee, Kinsley, Kinslie, Kinsly

Kingston (English) king's estate.
King, Kinston

Kingswell (English) king's well.
King

Kinnard (Irish) tall slope.

Kinsey (English) victorious royalty.

Kinton (Hindi) crowned.

Kioshi (Japanese) quiet.

Kipp (English) pointed hill.
Kip, Kippar, Kipper, Kippie, Kippy

Kiral (Turkish) king; supreme leader.

Kiran (Sanskrit) beam of light.

Kirby (Scandinavian) church village. (English) cottage by the water.
Kerbey, Kerbie, Kerby, Kirbey, Kirbie, Kirkby

Kiri (Cambodian) mountain.

Kirk (Scandinavian) church.
Kerk

Kirkland (English) church land.

Kirkley (English) church meadow.

Kirkwell (English) church well; church spring.

Kirkwood (English) church forest.

Kirton (English) church town.

Kit (Greek) a familiar form of Christian, Christopher, Kristopher.
Kitt, Kitts

Kito (Swahili) jewel; precious child.

Kitwana (Swahili) pledged to live.

Kiva (Hebrew) a short form of Akiva, Jacob.
Kiba, Kivi

Kiyoshi (Japanese) quiet;
peaceful.

Kizza (Fanti) born after twins.
Kizzy

Klaus (German) a short form of
Nicholas.
Klaas, Klaes, Klas, Klause

Kleef (Dutch) cliff.

Kleng (Norwegian) claw.

Knight (English) armored
knight.
Knightly

Knowles (English) grassy slope.
Knolls, Nowles

Knox (English) hill.

Knute (Scandinavian) an alternate form of Canute.
Knud, Knut

Kody (English) an alternate
form of Cody.
Kodey, Kodi, Kodie, Koty

Kofi (Twi) born on Friday.

Kohana (Lakota) swift.

Kojo (Akan) born on Monday.

Koka (Hawaiian) Scotsman.

Kolby (English) an alternate
form of Colby.
Kelby, Kole, Kollby

Kolton (English) an alternate
form of Colton.
Kolt, Kolten, Koltin

Konane (Hawaiian) bright
moonlight.

Kondo (Swahili) war.

Kong (Chinese) glorious; sky.

Konnor (Irish) an alternate
form of Connor.

Kono (Moquelumnan) squirrel
eating a pine nut.

Konrad (German) an alternate
form of Conrad.
**Khonrad, Koen, Koenraad,
Kon, Konn, Konney, Konni,
Konnie, Konny, Konrád,
Konrade, Konrado, Kord,
Kort, Kunz**

Konstantin (German, Russian)
a form of Constantine. See
also Dinos.
**Konstancji, Konstandinos,
Konstantinas, Konstantine,
Konstantinos, Konstantio,
Konstanz, Kostantin, Kostas,
Kostenka, Kostya, Kotsos**
Foreign form: *Polish:* **Konstanty**

Korey (Irish) an alternate form
of Corey, Kory.
Kore, Korio, Korria, Korrye

Kornel (Latin) a short form of
Cornelius, Kornelius.
**Kornél, Korneli, Kornelisz,
Krelis, Soma**

Kornelius (Latin) an alternate
form of Cornelius.
**Karnelius, Korneilius, Kornel,
Korneliaus, Kornelious,
Kornellius**
Foreign form: *Dutch:* **Kees**

Korrigan (Irish) an alternate
form of Corrigan.
**Korigan, Korigan, Korrigon,
Korrigun**

Kort (German, Dutch) an alternate form of Cort, Kurt.

Kory (Irish) an alternate form of
Corey.
**Korey, Kori, Korie, Korrey,
Korrie, Korry**

Kosey (African) lion.
Kosse

Kosmo (Greek) an alternate
form of Cosmo.
Kosmy

Kostas (Greek) a short form of
Konstantin.

Kosumi (Moquelumnan) spear fisher.

Kovit (Thai) expert.

Kraig (Irish, Scottish) an alternate form of Craig.
Kraggie, Kraggy

Kris (Greek) an alternate form of Chris. A short form of Kristian, Kristofer, Kristopher.
Kriss, Krys

Krishna (Hindi) delightful, pleasurable. Religion: one of the human incarnations of the Hindu god.
Kistna, Kistnah, Krisha, Krishnah

Krispin (Latin) an alternate form of Crispin.
Krispian, Krispino, Krispo

Kristian (Greek) an alternate form of Christian, Khristian.
Kerstan, Khristos, Kit, Kris, Krist, Kristar, Kristjan, Krists, Krystian, Khrystiyan
Foreign forms: *German:* **Krischan;** *Polish:* **Kristek, Krystek;** *Swedish:* **Krister**

Kristo (Greek) a short form of Khristos.

Kristofer (Swedish) a form of Kristopher.

Kristef, Kristoffer, Kristofor, Kristus

Kristopher (Greek) Christ-bearer. An alternate form of Christopher. See also Topher.
Kit, Kris, Kristfer, Kristfor, Kristophor, Kristos, Krists, Krisus, Krystupas, Krzysztof
Foreign forms: *French:* **Kristophe;** *German:* **Kristoph;** *Hungarian:* **Kristóf;** *Italian:* **Kristoforo;** *Swedish:* **Kristofer**

Kruz (Spanish) an alternate form of Cruz.

Kueng (Chinese) universe.

Kugonza (Dutooro) love.

Kumar (Sanskrit) prince.

Kuper (Yiddish) copper.

Kurt (Latin, German, French) courteous; enclosure. A short form of Kurtis. An alternate form of Curt.
Kort, Kuno

Kurtis (Latin, French) an alternate form of Curtis.
Kurt, Kurtice, Kurtiss

Kwako (Akan) born on Wednesday.

Kwame (Akan) born on Saturday.
Kwamin

Kwan (Korean) strong.

Kwasi (Akan) born on Sunday. (Swahili) wealthy.
Kwesi

Kyle (Irish) narrow piece of land; place where cattle graze. (Yiddish) crowned with laurels.
Kiel, Kilan, Kile, Kilen, Kiley, Ky, Kye, Kyele, Kylan, Kylen, Kylie, Kyrell
Foreign form: *English:* **Kyler**

Kyler (English) a form of Kyle.

Kynan (Welsh) chief.

Kyne (English) royal.

Kyros (Greek) master.

Laban (Hawaiian) white.

Lachlan (Scottish) land of lakes.
Lache, Lachlann, Lachunn, Lakelan, Lakeland

Ladd (English) attendant.
Lad, Laddey, Laddie, Laddy

Lado (Fanti) second-born son.

Lafayette (French) History: Marquis de Lafayette was a French soldier and politician who aided the American Revolution.
Lafaiete, Lafayett

Laird (Scottish) wealthy landowner.

Lais (Arabic) lion.

Lajos (Hungarian) famous; holy.
Lajcsi, Laji, Lali

Lal (Hindi) beloved.

Lamar (German) famous throughout the land. (French) sea, ocean.
Lamair, Lamario, Lamaris, Lamarr, Lamarre, Larmar, Lemar

Lambert (German) bright land.
Bert, Lambard, Lambirt, Lampard, Landbert
Foreign form: Italian: **Lamberto**

Lamond (French) world.
Lammond, Lamondre, Lamund, Lemond

Lamont (Scandinavian) lawyer.
Lamaunt, Lamonte, Lamontie, Lemont

Lance (German) a short form of Lancelot.
Lancy, Lantz, Launce
Foreign forms: Italian: **Lanza, Lanzo**

Lancelot (French) attendant. Literature: the knight who loved King Arthur's wife, Queen Guinevere.
Lancelott, Launcelet, Launcelot
Foreign form: German: **Lance**

Lander (Basque) lion man. (English) landowner.
Landers, Landor

Lando (Portuguese, Spanish) a short form of Orlando, Rolando.

Landon (English) open, grassy meadow.
Landan, Landen, Landin

Landry (French, English) ruler.
Landre, Landré, Landrue

Lane (English) narrow road.
Laney, Lanie, Layne

Lang (Scandinavian) tall man.
Lange

Langdon (English) long hill.
Landon, Langsdon, Langston

Langford (English) long ford.
Lanford, Lankford

Langley (English) long meadow.
Langlea, Langlee, Langleigh, Langly

Langston (English) long, narrow town.
Langsden, Langsdon

Lani (Hawaiian) heaven.

Lanny (American) a familiar form of Lawrence, Laurence.
Lannie, Lennie

Lanu (Moquelumnan) running around the pole.

Lap (Vietnamese) independent.

Laquintin (American) a combination of the prefix La + Quintin.
Laquentin, Laquenton, Laquintas, Laquintiss, Laquinton

Laramie (French) tears of love. Geography: a town in Wyoming on the Overland Trail.

Larkin (Irish) rough; fierce.
Larklin

Larmore (French) armorer.
Larimore, Larmer, Larrimor

Larnell (American) a combination of Larry + Darnell.

Laron (French) thief.
Laran, La'ron, La Ron, Laronn, La Ruan

Larry (Latin) a familiar form of Lawrence.
Larrie, Lary

Lars (Scandinavian) a form of Lawrence.
Laris, Larris, Larse, Larsen, Larson, Larsson, Lasse, Laurans, Laurits, Lavrans, Lorens

LaSalle (French) hall.
Lasalle, Lascell, Lascelles

Lashawn (American) a combination of the prefix La + Shawn.
Lasean, Lashajaun, Lashon, Lashonne

László (Hungarian) famous ruler.
Laci, Lacko, Laslo, Lazlo

Lateef (Arabic) gentle; pleasant.
Latif, Letif

Latham (Scandinavian) barn. (English) district.
Laith, Lathe, Lay

Lathan (American) a combination of the prefix La + Nathan.
Lathaniel, Lathen, Lathyn, Leathan

Lathrop (English) barn, farmstead.
Lathe, Lathrope, Lay

Latimer (English) interpreter.
Lat, Latimor, Lattie, Latty, Latymer

Latravis (American) a combination of the prefix La + Travis.
Latavious, Latraviaus, Latravious, Latrivis

Laughlin (Irish) servant of Saint Secundinus.
Lanty, Lauchlin, Leachlainn

Laurence (Latin) crowned with laurel. An alternate form of Lawrence. See also Renzo.
Lanny, Lauran, Laurance, Laureano, Lauren, Laurentios, Laurentiu, Laurentius, Laurenz, Laurin, Laurits, Laurnet, Laurus, Lurance
Foreign forms: American: **Rance**; Basque: **Laurentzi**; Danish: **Lauritz**; Dutch: **Laurens**; English: **Laurie**; Filipino: **Lauro**; French: **Laurent**; Lithuanian: **Raulas, Raulo**; Russian: **Laurentij, Lavrenti**; Spanish: **Laurencio**; Swedish: **Lauris**

LaValle (French) valley.
Lavail, Laval, Lavalei, Lavalle

Lavan (Hebrew) white.
Foreign forms: American: **Lavaughan, Lavon, Lavonne, Levan, Levaughan, Levaughn**

Lave (Italian) lava. (English) lord.

Lavi (Hebrew) lion.

Lawford (English) ford on the hill.
Ford, Law

Lawler (Irish) mutterer.
Lawlor, Lollar, Loller

Lawrence (Latin) crowned with laurel.
Lanny, Lanty, Larance, Laren, Larian, Larien, Laris, Larrance, Larrence, Larry, Laurence, Law, Lawerance, Lawrance, Lawren, Lawrey, Lawrie, Lawron, Lawry, Lon, Lorne, Lowrance
Foreign forms: Basque: **Loren**; Hungarian: **Lóránt, Lorenca**; Italian: **Lorenzo, Loretto**; Latvian: **Brencis**; Polish: **Laiurenty**; Portuguese: **Laurencho, Lourenco**; Russian: **Labrentsis, Larka, Larya, Lavrenti**; Scandinavian: **Lars**; Spanish: **Chencho, Lencho**

Lawson (English) son of Lawrence.

Lawton (English) town on the hill.
Laughton, Law

Lazaro (Italian) a form of Lazarus.
Lazarillo, Lazarito, Lazzaro

Lazarus (Greek) a form of Eleazar. Bible: Lazarus was raised from the dead.
Lazar, Lázár, Lazaros, Lazarusie
Foreign forms: French: **Lazare**; Italian: **Lazaro**

Leander (Greek) lion-man; brave as a lion.
Ander
Foreign forms: French: **Léandre**; Spanish: **Leandro**

Leben (Yiddish) life.

Lee (English) a short form of Farley and names containing "lee."
Leigh

Lefty (American) left-handed.

Leggett (French) one who is sent; delegate.
Legate, Leggitt, Liggett

Lei (Chinese) thunder. (Hawaiian) a form of Ray.

Leib (Yiddish) roaring lion.
Leibel

Leif (Scandinavian) beloved.
Laif, Lief

Leigh (English) an alternate form of Lee.

Leighton (English) meadow farm.
Lay, Layton, Leigh, Leyton

Leith (Scottish) broad river.

Lek (Thai) small.

Lel (Gypsy) taker.

Leland (English) meadowland; protected land.
Lealand, Lee, Leeland, Leigh, Leighland, Lelan, Lelann, Leyland

Lemar (French) an alternate form of Lamar.
Lemario, Lemarr

Lemuel (Hebrew) devoted to God.
Lem, Lemmie, Lemmy

Len (German) a short form of Leonard. (Hopi) flute.

Lenno (Native American) man.

Lennon (Irish) small cloak; cape.

Lennor (Gypsy) spring; summer.

Lennox (Scottish) with many elms.
Lenox

Lenny (German) a familiar form of Leonard.
Lennie, Leny

Leo (Latin) lion. (German) a short form of Leopold.
Lavi, Lee, Leib, Leibel, Leos, Léocadie, Leosoko, Lion, Lyon
Foreign forms: Czech: **Léo, Leosko;** Hawaiian: **Lio;** Polish: **Leos;** Portuguese: **Leão;** Russian: **Lev**

Leon (Greek, German) a short form of Leonard, Napoleon.
Leo, Léon, Léonce, Leoncio, Leondris, Leonetti, Leoni, Leonirez, Leonizio, Leonon, Leons, Leontios, Leontrae
Foreign forms: Italian: **Leone;** Lithuanian: **Leonas, Liutas;** Polish: **Leonek**

Leonard (German) brave as a lion.
Leanard, Lee, Len, Lena, Lenard, Lennard, Lenny, Leno, Leon, Leonaldo, Leonardis, Leonart, Leonerd, Leonhard, Lernard, Lnard, Londard, Lonnard, Lynnard
Foreign forms: French: **Léonard, Lienard;** Greek: **Leonidas;** Italian/Spanish: **Leonardo, Lon;** Polish: **Linek, Nardek;** Russian: **Leonid, Lonya;** Swedish: **Lennart, Leontes**

Leonel (English) little lion. See also Lionel.

Leonhard (German) an alternate form of Leonard.
Leonhards

Leopold (German) brave people.
Leo, Leorad, Lipót, Luepold, Luitpold, Poldi
Foreign forms: French: **Léopold;** Italian/Spanish: **Leopoldo**

Leor (Hebrew) my light.
Leory, Lior

Lequinton (American) a combination of the prefix Le + Quinton.
Lequentin, Lequenton, Lequinn

Leron (French) round, circle. (American) a combination of the prefix Le + Ron.
Le Ron, Lerone, Liron, Lyron

Leroy (French) king. See also Delroy, Elroy.
Lee, Leeroy, LeeRoy, Leigh, Lerai, Leroi, LeRoi, LeRoy, Roy

Les (Scottish, English) a short form of Leslie, Lester.
Lessie

Leshawn (American) a combination of the prefix Le + Shawn.
Lesean, Leshaun, Leshon

Leslie (Scottish) gray fortress.
Lee, Leigh, Les, Leslea, Leslee, Lesley, Lesly, Lezlie, Lezly

Lester (Latin) chosen camp. (English) from Leicester, England.
Leicester, Les

Lev (Hebrew) heart. (Russian) a form of Leo. A short form of Leverett, Levi.
Leb, Leva, Levka, Levko, Levushka

Leverett (French) young hare.
Lev, Leveret, Leverit, Leveritt

Levi (Hebrew) joined in harmony. Bible: the son of Jacob; the priestly tribe of Israel.
Leavi, Leevi, Lev, Levey, Levie, Levin, Levitis, Levy, Lewi

Levon (American) an alternate form of Lavon.
Leevon, Levone, Levonn, Lyvonne

Lew (English) a short form of Lewis.

Lewin (English) beloved friend.

Lewis (English) a form of Louis. (Welsh) an alternate form of Llewellyn.
Lew, Lewes, Lewie, Lewy

Lex (English) a short form of Alexander.
Lexi, Lexie, Lexin

Lí (Chinese) strong.

Liam (Irish) a form of William.

Liang (Chinese) good, excellent.

Liberio (Portuguese) liberation.
Liberaratore, Liborio

Lidio (Greek, Portuguese) ancient. Geography: an ancient province in Asia Minor.

Liko (Chinese) protected by Buddha. (Hawaiian) bud.
Like

Lin (Burmese) bright. (English) a short form of Lyndon.
Linh, Linn, Linny, Lyn, Lynn

Linc (English) a short form of Lincoln.
Link

Lincoln (English) settlement by the pool. History: Abraham Lincoln was the sixteenth U.S. president.
Linc, Lincon

Lindberg (German) mountain where linden trees grow.
Lindbergh, Lindburg, Lindy

Lindell (English) valley of the linden trees.
Lendall, Lendel, Lendell, Lindall, Lindel, Lyndale, Lyndall, Lyndel, Lyndell

Lindley (English) linden field.
Lindlea, Lindlee, Lindleigh, Lindly

Lindon (English) an alternate form of Lyndon.
Lin, Lindan, Linden

Lindsay (English) an alternate form of Lindsey.
Linsay

Lindsey (English) linden-tree island.
Lind, Lindsay, Lindsee, Lindsy, Linsey, Lyndsay, Lyndsey, Lyndsie, Lynzie

Linford (English) linden-tree ford.
Lynford

Linfred (German) peaceful, calm.

Linley (English) flax meadow.
Linlea, Linlee, Linleigh, Linly

Linton (English) flax town.
Lintonn, Lynton, Lyntonn

Linu (Hindi) lily.

Linus (Greek) flaxen haired.
Linas, Linux

Lionel (French) lion cub. See also Leonel.
Lional, Lionell, Lynel, Lynell, Lyonel
*Foreign form: Italian: **Lionello***

Liron (Hebrew) my song.
Lyron

Lise (Moquelumnan) salmon's head coming out of the water.

Lisimba (Yao) lion.
Simba

Lister (English) dyer.

Litton (English) town on the hill.
Liton

Liu (African) voice.

Liuz (Polish) light.
Lius

Livingston (English) Leif's town.
Livingstone

Liwanu (Moquelumnan) growling bear.

Llewellyn (Welsh) lionlike.
Lewis, Llewelin, Llewellen, Llewelleyn, Llewellin, Llywellyn, Llywelyn

Lloyd (Welsh) gray haired; holy.
Loy, Loyd, Loyde, Loydie
Foreign form: *English:* **Floyd**

Lobo (Spanish) wolf.

Lochlain (Irish, Scottish) land of lakes.
Laughlin, Lochlann

Locke (English) forest.
Lock, Lockwood

Logan (Irish) meadow.
Logen

Lok (Chinese) happy.

Lomán (Irish) bare. (Slavic) sensitive.

Lombard (Latin) long bearded.
Bard, Barr

Lon (Spanish) a short form of Alonzo, Leonard, Lonnie. (Irish) fierce.
Lonn

Lonan (Zuni) cloud.

Lonato (Native American) flint stone.

London (English) fortress of the moon. Geography: the capital of Great Britain.

Long (Chinese) dragon. (Vietnamese) hair.

Lonnie (German, Spanish) a familiar form of Alonzo.
Lonnell, Lonniel, Lonny

Lono (Hawaiian) Mythology: a god of peace and farming.

Lonzo (German, Spanish) a short form of Alonzo.
Lonso

Lorcan (Irish) little; fierce.

Lord (English) noble title.

Loren (Latin) a short form of Lawrence.
Lorin, Lorren, Lorrin, Loryn

Lorenzo (Italian, Spanish) a form of Lawrence.
Larinzo, Lerenzo, Lorenc, Lorence, Lorenco, Lorencz, Lorens, Lorentz, Lorenz, Lorenza, Loretto, Lorinc, Lörinc, Lorinzo, Loritz, Lorrenzo, Lorrie, Lorry, Renzo, Zo

Lorimer (Latin) harness maker.
Lorrie, Lorrimer, Lorry

Loring (German) son of the famous warrior.
Lorrie, Lorring, Lorry

Loris (Dutch) clown.

Loritz (Latin, Danish) laurel.
Lauritz

Lorne (Latin) a short form of Lawrence.
Lorn, Lornie

Lorry (English) an alternate form of Laurie.
Lori, Lorri, Lory

Lot (Hebrew) hidden, covered. Bible: Lot fled from Sodom, but his wife glanced back upon its destruction and was transformed into a pillar of salt.

Lothar (German) an alternate form of Luther.
Lotaire, Lotarrio, Lothair, Lothaire, Lothario

Lou (German) a short form of Louis.

Louie (German) a familiar form of Louis.

Louis (German) famous warrior. See also Aloysius, Clovis.
Lewis, Lou, Louie, Lucho, Ludwig
Foreign forms: *Czech:* **Lude, Ludek, Ludko;** *Finnish:* **Ludirk;** *Gypsy:* **Lash, Lashi, Lasho;** *Hawaiian:* **Lui;** *Irish:* **Lugaidh;** *Italian:* **Ludovici, Luigi;** *Russian:* **Ludis;** *Spanish:* **Aloisio, Luis**

Loudon (German) low valley.
Loudan, Louden, Loudin, Lowden

Lourdes (French) from Lourdes, France. Geography: a town in France. Religion: a place where the Virgin Mary was said to have appeared.

Louvain (English) Lou's vanity. Geography: a city in Belgium.

Lovell (English) an alternate form of Lowell.
Lovel, Lovelle, Lovey

Lowell (French) young wolf. (English) beloved.
Lovell, Lowe, Lowel

Loyal (English) faithful, loyal.
Loy, Loye, Lyall, Lyell

Lubomir (Polish) lover of peace.

Luboslaw (Polish) lover of glory.
Lubs, Lubz

Luc (French) a form of Luke.
Luce

Lucas (German, Irish, Danish, Dutch) a form of Lucius.
Lucassie, Luckas, Lucus

Lucian (Latin) an alternate form of Lucius.
Liuz, Lucan, Lucanus, Lucianus, Lucias, Lucjan, Lukianos, Lukyan
Foreign form: Italian: **Luciano**

Lucius (Latin) light; bringer of light.
Loukas, Lucanus, Lucas, Lucca, Luce, Lucian, Lucious, Luke, Lusio
Foreign forms: French: **Lucien;** *Italian:* **Luca, Lucio;** *Scottish:* **Lucais**

Lucky (American) fortunate.
Luckie, Luckson

Ludlow (English) prince's hill.

Ludwig (German) an alternate form of Louis. Music: Ludwig Van Beethoven was a famous nineteenth-century German composer.
Ludovic, Lutz
Foreign forms: Italian: **Ludovico;** *Polish:* **Ludwik, Lutek;** *Swedish:* **Ludvig, Ludvik**

Luigi (Italian) a form of Louis.
Lui, Luigino

Luis (Spanish) a form of Louis.
Luise, Luiz

Lukas (Greek, Czech, Swedish) a form of Luke.
Loukas, Lukash

Luke (Latin) a form of Lucius. Bible: author of the *Gospel of Saint Luke* and *Acts of the Apostles*—two New Testament books.
Luck, Lucky, Luk, Lukas, Luken, Lukes, Lukus
Foreign forms: French: **Luc;** *Hungarian:* **Lúkács;** *Latvian:* **Lukass;** *Polish:* **Lukasz;** *Russian:* **Luchok, Luka, Lukasha, Lukyan;** *Zuni:* **Lusio**

Luken (Basque) bringer of light.
Luk

Luki (Basque) famous warrior.

Lukman (Arabic) prophet.
Luqman

Lulani (Hawaiian) highest point in heaven.

Lumo (Ewe) born face-downward.

Lundy (Scottish) grove by the island.

Lunn (Irish) warlike.
Lon, Lonn

Lunt (Swedish) grove.

Lusila (Hindi) leader.

Luther (German) famous warrior. History: the Protestant reformer Martin Luther was one of the central figures of the Reformation.
Luthor
Foreign forms: French:
Lothaire; *Spanish:* **Lutero**

Lyall, Lyell (Scottish) loyal.

Lyle (French) island.
Lisle, Ly, Lysle

Lyman (English) meadow.
Leaman, Leeman

Lynch (Irish) mariner.
Linch

Lyndal (English) valley of lime trees.
Lyndale, Lyndall, Lyndel, Lyndell

Lyndon (English) linden-tree hill. History: Lyndon B. Johnson was the thirty-sixth U.S. president.
Lin, Lindon, Lyden, Lydon, Lyn, Lynden, Lynn, Lynton

Lynn (English) waterfall; brook.
Lyn, Lynell, Lynette, Lynnard, Lynoll

Lyron (Hebrew) an alternate form of Leron, Liron.

Lysander (Greek) liberator.
Sander

Mac (Scottish) son.
Macs

Macadam (Scottish) son of Adam.
MacAdam, McAdam

Macallister (Irish) son of Alistair.
Macalaster, MacAlister, McAlister, McAllister

Macario (Spanish) happy; blessed.

Macarthur (Irish) son of Arthur.
MacArthur, McArthur

Macaulay (Scottish) son of righteousness.
Macauley, McCauley

Macbride (Scottish) son of a follower of Saint Brigid.
Macbryde, Mcbride, McBride

Maccoy (Irish) son of Hugh. See also Coy.
MacCoy, Mccoy, McCoy

Maccrea (Irish) son of grace.
MacCrae, MacCray, Macrae, MacCrea, Mccrea, McCrea

Macdonald (Scottish) son of Donald.
MacDonald, Mcdonald, McDonald, Mcdonna, Mcdonnell, McDonnell

Macdougal (Scottish) son of Dougal. See also Douglas.
MacDougal, Mcdougal, McDougal, McDougall, Dougal

Mace (French) club. (English) a short form of Macy, Mason.
Macean, Macer, Macey, Macy

Mack (Scottish) a short form of names beginning with "Mac" and "Mc."
Macke, Mackey, Mackie, Macklin, Macks

Mackenzie (Irish) son of Kenzie.
Mackenxo, Mackenzey, Mackenzi, MacKenzie, Mackenzly, Mackenzy, Mackienzie, Mackinsey, Makenzie, McKenzie

Mackinnley (Irish) son of the learned ruler.
MacKinnley, Mckinnely, Mckinnlee, Mckinnley, McKinnley

Maclean (Irish) son of Leander.
MacLain, MacLean, McLaine, McLean

Macmahon (Irish) son of Mahon.
MacMahon, McMahon

Macmurray (Irish) son of Murray.
McMurray

Macnair (Scottish) son of the heir.
Macknair

Macon (German, English) maker.

Macy (French) Matthew's estate.
Mace, Macey

Maddock (Welsh) generous.
Madoc, Madock, Madog

Maddox (Welsh, English) son of the benefactor.
Madox

Madison (English) son of Maude; good son.
Maddie, Maddison, Maddy, Madisson, Son, Sonny

Magar (Armenian) groom's attendant.
Magarious

Magee (Irish) son of Hugh.
MacGee, MacGhee, McGee

Magen (Hebrew) protector.

Magnus (Latin) great.
Maghnus, Magnes, Mayer
Foreign form: Scottish: Manius

Maguire (Irish) son of the beige one.
MacGuire, McGuire, McGwire

Mahdi (Arabic) guided to the right path.

Mahir (Arabic, Hebrew) excellent; industrious.
Maher

Mahmúd (Arabic) an alternate form of Mohammed.
Mahmed, Mahmood, Mahmoud

Mahomet (Arabic) an alternate form of Mohammed.
Mehemet, Mehmet

Mahon (Irish) bear.

Maimun (Arabic) lucky.
Maimon

Maitland (English) meadowland.

Majid (Arabic) great, glorious.
Majdi, Majed, Majeed

Major (Latin) greater; military rank.
Majar, Maje, Majer, Mayer, Mayor

Makalani (Mwera) writer.

Makani (Hawaiian) wind.

Makarios (Greek) happy; blessed.
Macario, Macarios, Maccario, Maccarios

Makin (Arabic) strong.

Makoto (Japanese) sincere.

Mal (Irish) a short form of names beginning with "Mal."

Malachi (Hebrew) angel of God. Bible: the last canonical Hebrew prophet.

Maeleachlainn, Mal, Malachia, Malachie, Malchija, Malechy *Foreign forms:* Arabic: *Málik;* Irish: *Malachy*

Malcolm (Scottish) follower of Saint Columba, an early Scottish saint. (Arabic) dove.
Mal, Malcolum, Malcom, Malcum, Malkolm

Malden (English) meeting place in a pasture.
Mal, Maldon

Málik (Arabic) a form of Malachi. (Punjabi) lord, master.
Maalik, Malak, Malik, Malikh, Maliq, Malique, Mallik

Malin (English) strong, little warrior.
Mal, Mallin, Mallon

Mallory (German) army coun-selor. (French) wild duck.
Lory, Mal, Mallery, Mallori, Mallorie, Malory

Maloney (Irish) church going.
Malone, Malony

Malvern (Welsh) bare hill.
Malverne

Malvin (Irish, English) an alter-nate form of Melvin.

Mal, Malvinn, Malvyn, Malvynn

Mamo (Hawaiian) yellow flower; yellow bird.

Manchu (Chinese) pure.

Manco (Peruvian) supreme leader. History: a thirteenth-century Incan king.

Mandala (Yao) flowers.
Manda, Mandela

Mandeep (Punjabi) mind full of light.
Mandieep

Mandel (German) almond.
Mandell

Mander (Gypsy) from me.

Manford (English) small ford.

Manfred (English) man of peace. See also Fred.
Manfrid, Manfried, Mannfred, Mannfryd

Manger (French) stable.

Manheim (German) servant's home.

Manley (English) hero's meadow.
Manlea, Manleigh, Manly

Mann (German) man.
Manin

Manning (English) son of the hero.

Mannix (Irish) monk.
Mainchin

Manny (German, Spanish) a familiar form of Manuel.
Mani, Manni, Mannie

Mano (Hawaiian) shark. (Spanish) a short form of Manuel.
Manno, Manolo

Mansa (Swahili) king. History: a fourteenth-century emperor of Mali.

Mansel (English) manse; house occupied by a clergyman.
Mansell

Mansfield (English) field by the river; hero's field.

Man-Shik (Korean) deeply rooted.

Mansūr (Arabic) divinely aided.
Mansoor, Mansour

Manton (English) man's town; hero's town.
Mannton, Manten

Manu (Hindi) lawmaker. History: the writer of the Hindu code of conduct. (Hawaiian) bird. (Ghanian) second-born son.

Manuel (Hebrew) a short form of Emmanuel.
Mannuel, Manolón, Manual, Manue, Manuelli, Manuelo, Manuil
Foreign forms: Hungarian: *Maco;* Russian: *Manyuil;* Spanish: *Mango, Manny, Mano, Minel*

Manville (French) worker's village. (English) hero's village.
Mandeville, Manvil

Man-Young (Korean) ten thousand years of prosperity.

Manzo (Japanese) third son.

Mapira (Yao) millet.

Marc (French) a form of Mark.

Marcel (French) a form of Marcellus.
Marcell, Marsale, Marsel

Marcello (Italian) a form of Marcellus.
Marchello, Marsello, Marselo

Marcellus (Latin) a familiar form of Marcus.
Marceau, Marceles, Marcelin,
Marcelino, Marcelis, Marcelius, Marcelleous, Marcellin, Marcellino, Marcellous, Marcelluas, Marcely, Marciano, Marcsseau
Foreign forms: French: *Marcel;* Hungarian: *Marcilka;* Italian: *Marcello;* Spanish: *Marcelo*

March (English) dweller by a boundary.

Marco (Italian) a form of Marcus. History: Marco Polo was the thirteenth-century Venetian traveler who explored Asia.
Marcko, Marko

Marcos (Spanish) a form of Marcus.
Markos, Markose

Marcus (Latin) martial, warlike.
Marcas, Marcellus, Marcio, Marckus, Marcous, Mark, Markov
Foreign forms: Dutch/German: *Markus;* Italian: *Marco;* Slavic: *Marek;* Spanish: *Marcos*

Maren (Basque) sea.

Mareo (Japanese) uncommon.

Marid (Arabic) rebellious.

Marin (French) sailor.
Marine, Mariner, Marriner

Foreign forms: Dutch: *Marius;* Italian: *Marino, Mario*

Mario (Italian) a form of Marin.
Marios, Marrio

Marion (French) bitter; sea of bitterness. A masculine form of Mary.
Mariano

Mark (Latin) an alternate form of Marcus. Bible: author of the New Testament book, *The Gospel According to Saint Mark.*
Markee, Markel, Markell, Markey, Marque, Marx
Foreign forms: Danish: *Márkus;* Czech: *Marko;* French: *Marc, Martial;* Greek: *Markos;* Hawaiian: *Maleko;* Italian: *Mariano;* Polish: *Marke, Marian;* Russian: *Marek, Markusha*

Markese (French) an alternate form of Marquis.
Markease, Markeece, Markees, Markeese, Markei, Markeice, Markeis, Markice, Markies, Markiese, Markise

Markham (English) homestead on the boundary.

Marko (Latin) an alternate form of Marco, Mark.
Markco

Markus (Latin) an alternate form of Marcus.
Markas, Markcus, Markcuss, Marqus

Marland (English) lake land.

Marley (English) lake meadow.
Marlea, Marleigh, Marly, Marrley

Marlin (English) deep-sea fish.
Marlion

Marlon (French) a form of Merlin.

Marlow (English) hill by the lake.
Mar, Marlo, Marlowe

Marmion (French) small.
Marmyon

Maro (Japanese) myself.

Marques (Portuguese) nobleman.
Markes, Markques, Marquest, Markqueus, Marquez, Marqus

Marquis (French) nobleman.
Marcquis, Marcuis, Markis, Markuis, Marquee, Marqui, Marquie, Marquist

Marr (Spanish) divine. (Arabic) forbidden.

Mars (Latin) bold warrior. Mythology: the Roman god of war.

Marsden (English) marsh valley.
Marsdon

Marsh (French) a short form of Marshall. (English) swamp land.

Marshall (French) caretaker of the horses; military title.
Marschal, Marsh, Marshal, Marshel, Marshell

Marston (English) town by the marsh.

Martell (English) hammerer.
Martel

Martin (Latin) martial, warlike. (French) a form of Martinus. History: Martin Luther King, Jr. led the civic rights movement and won the Nobel Peace Prize.
Maartin, Marinos, Marius, Mart, Martan, Martine, Martinien, Marto, Márton, Marts
Foreign forms: Czech: **Tynek;** Dutch: **Marten, Martijn;** Hungarian: **Marton;** Irish: **Mairtin;** Italian: **Marciano, Martiniano, Martino;** Latvian:

Martins; Lithuanian: **Martinas;** Norwegian: **Morten;** Polish: **Marcin;** Portuguese: **Martinho;** Russian: **Martyn;** Spanish: **Marti, Martinez**

Martinus (Latin) martial, warlike.
Martin

Marty (Latin) a familiar form of Martin.
Martey, Marti, Martie

Marv (English) a short form of Marvin.
Marve, Marvi, Marvis

Marvin (English) lover of the sea.
Marv, Marvein, Marven, Marwin, Marwynn
Foreign form: Irish: **Mervin**

Masaccio (Italian) twin.
Masaki

Masahiro (Japanese) broad minded.

Masamba (Yao) leaves.

Masao (Japanese) righteous.

Masato (Japanese) just.

Maslin (French) little Thomas.
Maslen, Masling

Mason (French) stone worker.
Mace, Maison, Sonny

Masou (Native American) fire god.

Massey (English) twin.
Massi

Massimo (Italian) greatest.
Massimiliano

Masud (Arabic, Swahili) fortunate.
Masood, Masoud, Mhasood

Matalino (Filipino) bright.

Mather (English) powerful army.

Mathew (Hebrew) an alternate form of Matthew.

Mathias (German, Swedish) a form of Matthew.
Mathi, Mathia, Mathis, Matthia, Matthias, Mattia, Mattias
Foreign forms: Czech: Matus; Irish: Maitias; Spanish: Matías

Mathieu (French) a form of Matthew.
Mathie, Mathieux, Mathiew, Matthieu, Matthiew, Mattieu, Mattieux

Mato (Native American) brave.

Matope (Rhodesian) our last child.

Matoskah (Lakota) white bear.

Matson (Hebrew) son of Matt.
Matison, Mattison, Mattson

Matt (Hebrew) a short form of Matthew.
Mat

Matteen (Afghani) disciplined; polite.

Matthew (Hebrew) gift of God. Bible: author of the New Testament book, the Gospel According to Saint Matthew.
Matheson, Mathew, Mathian, Mathieson, Matt, Mattheus, Matthews, Mattmias, Matty
Foreign forms: Basque/Bulgarian Matai; Czech: Matek; Danish: Mads, Matthaeus; English: Mayhew; French: Mathieu; German: Mathe, Matheu, Matthaus, Matthäus; Greek: Matthaios; Hawaiian: Makaio; Irish: Maitiú; Italian: Matteo; Polish: Mateusz, Matyas; Russian: Matfei, Matvey; Scandinavian: Matteus; Scottish: Mata; Spanish: Mateo; Swedish: Mathias, Mats

Matty (Hebrew) a familiar form of Matthew.
Mattie

Maurice (Latin) dark skinned; moor; marshland. See also Seymour.
Maur, Maurance, Maureo, Maurids, Mauriece, Maurikas, Maurin, Maurino, Maurio, Maurise, Maurius, Mauro, Maurrel, Maurtel, Maury, Maurycy, Moore, Morice, Morrel, Morrice
Foreign forms: English: Morrie, Morris; German: Mauritz, Moritz; Hawaiian: Mauli; Italian: Maurizio; Spanish: Mauricio, Morrill; Welsh: Meurig

Mauricio (Spanish) a form of Maurice.
Mauro

Maury (Latin) a familiar form of Maurice.
Maurey, Maurie, Morrie

Maverick (American) independent.
Mavrick

Max (Latin) a short form of Maximilian, Maxwell.
Mac, Mack, Maxe, Maxx, Maxy
Foreign forms: Hungarian: Maks, Miksa

Maxfield (English) Mack's field.

Maxi (Czech, Hungarian, Spanish) a familiar form of Maximilian.
Makszi, Maxey, Maxie, Maxis

Maxime (French) most excellent.
Maxim

Maximilian (Latin) greatest.
Maixim, Maxamillion, Maxemilian, Maxemilion, Maximalian, Maximili, Maximilia, Maximillian, Maximillion, Maxmilian, Maxmillion, Maxon, Maxymilian, Maxymillian, Mayhew
*Foreign forms: Czech: **Maxi**; Dutch: **Maximilianus**; French: **Maxime, Maximilien**; Greek: **Maximos**; Hungarian: **Miksa**; Italian: **Massimiliano**; Polish: **Maksym, Maksymilian**; Russian: **Maksim, Maxim**; Spanish: **Máximo***

Maxwell (English) great spring.
Max, Maxwel, Maxwill, Maxy

Maxy (English) a familiar form of Max, Maxwell.

Mayer (Hebrew) an alternate form of Meir. (Latin) an alternate form of Magnus, Major.
Mahyar, Mayeer, Mayor, Mayur

Mayes (English) field.
Mayo, Mays

Maynard (English) powerful; brave. See also Meinhard.
May, Mayne, Maynhard
*Foreign form: French: **Ménard***

Mayo (Irish) yew-tree plain. (English) an alternate form of Mayes. Geography: a county in Ireland.

Mazin (Arabic) proper.
Mazen, Mazinn

Mbwana (Swahili) master.
Bwana

McGeorge (Scottish) son of George.
MacGeorge

Mckay (Scottish) son of Kay.
Mackay, MacKay, McKay

McKenzie (Irish) an alternate form of Mackenzie.
Mckensey, Mckensie, Mckenson, Mckensson, Mckenzi

Mead (English) meadow.
Meade, Meed

Medwin (German) faithful friend.

Mehetabel (Hebrew) who God benefits.

Mehrdad (Persian) gift of the sun.

Mehtar (Sanskrit) prince.
Mehta

Meinhard (German) strong, firm. See also Maynard.
Meinhardt, Meinke, Meino, Mendar

Meinrad (German) strong counsel.

Meir (Hebrew) one who brightens, shines; enlightener. History: a leading second-century scholar.
Mayer, Meyer, Muki
*Foreign form: English: **Myer***

Meka (Hawaiian) eyes.

Mel (English, Irish) a familiar form of Melvin.

Melbourne (English) mill stream.
Melborn, Melburn, Melby, Milborn, Milbourn, Milbourne, Milburn, Millburn, Millburne

Melchior (Hebrew) king.
Meilseoir, Melker, Melkior

Meldon (English) mill hill.
Melden

Melrone (Irish) servant of Saint Ruadhan.
Maolruadhand

Melvern (Native American) great chief.

Melville (French) mill town. Literature: Herman Melville was a well-known nineteenth-century American writer.
Milville

Melvin (Irish) armored chief. (English) mill friend; council friend. See also Vinny.
Malvin, Mel, Melvino, Melvon, Melvyn, Melwin, Melwyn, Melwynn

Menachem (Hebrew) comforter.
Menahem, Nachman

Menassah (Hebrew) cause to forget.
Menashe, Menashi, Menashia, Menashiah, Menashya, Manasseh

Mendel (English) repairman.
Mendeley, Mendell, Mendie, Mendy

Mensah (Ewe) third son.

Mercer (English) storekeeper.
Merce

Mered (Hebrew) revolter.

Meredith (Welsh) guardian from the sea.
Meredyth, Merideth, Meridith, Merry

Merion (Welsh) from Merion, England.
Merrion

Merle (French) a short form of Merlin, Merrill.
Meryl

Merlin (English) falcon. Literature: the wizard in King Arthur's court.
Merle, Merlen, Merlinn, Merlyn, Merlynn
Foreign form: French: Marlon

Merrick (English) ruler of the sea.
Merek, Meric, Merrik, Meyrick, Myrucj

Merrill (Irish) bright sea. (French) famous.
Meril, Merill, Merle, Merrel, Merrell, Merril, Meryl

Merritt (Latin, Irish) valuable; deserving.
Merit, Meritt, Merrett

Merton (English) sea town.
Murton

Merv (Irish) a short form of Mervin.

Merville (French) sea village

Mervin (Irish) a form of Marvin.
Merv, Mervyn, Mervynn, Merwin, Merwinn, Merwyn, Murvin, Murvyn, Myrvyn, Myrvynn, Myrwyn

Meshach (Hebrew) artist. Bible: one of Daniel's three friends who were rescued from a fiery furnace by an angel.

Mette (Greek, Danish) pearl.
Almeta, Mete

Meyer (Hebrew) an alternate form of Meir. (German) farmer.
Mayer, Meier, Myer

Mhina (Swahili) delightful.

Micah (Hebrew) an alternate form of Michael. Bible: a Hebrew prophet.
Mica, Micaiah, Michiah, Mika, Myca, Mycah

Micha (Hebrew) a short form of Michael.
Michah

Michael (Hebrew) who is like God?
Machael, Mahail, Maichail, Maikal, Makael, Makell, Meikel, Mekal, Mhichael, Micael, Micah, Micahel, Mical, Michaele, Michaell, Michiel, Michoel, Mike, Mychael
Foreign forms: American:
Mychal, Mykal; *Basque:* **Mikel, Mikell;** *Czech:* **Milko;** *English:* **Mick, Mickael, Miles, Mitchell;** *Finnish:* **Micho, Mikko;** *French:* **Michale, Michel;** *Greek/Bulgarian/ Romanian:* **Mihail;** *Hawaiian:* **Mikáele;** *Hungarian:* **Miska;** *Irish:* **Micheal, Mickey, Mikeal;** *Italian:* **Michele;** *Latvian:* **Mikelis, Mihalje, Mychajlo;** *Norwegian:* **Mikkel;** *Polish:* **Machas, Michal;** *Portuguese/Spanish:* **Miguel;** *Russian:* **Michail, Mikhail, Misha;** *Scottish:* **Micheil;** *Swedish:* **Mikael**

Michel (French) a form of Michael.
Michaud, Miche, Michee, Michon

Michelangelo (Italian) a combination of Michael + Angelo. Art: Michelangelo Buonarroti was one of the greatest Italian Renaissance painters.
Michelange, Miguelangelo

Michel (Italian) a form of Michael.

Michio (Japanese) man with the strength of three thousand.

Mickey (Irish) a familiar form of Michael.
Mick, Mickie, Micky, Miki, Mique

Miguel (Portuguese, Spanish) a form of Michael.
Migeel, Migel, Miguelly, Migui

Mika (Hebrew) an alternate form of Micah. (Ponca) raccoon.
Miika

Mikal (Hebrew) an alternate form of Michael.
Mekal

Mikasi (Omaha) coyote.

Mike (Hebrew) a short form of Michael.
Myk

Mikhail (Greek, Russian) a form of Michael.
Mekhail, Mihály, Mikhael, Mikhalis, Mikhial, Mikhos

Miki (Japanese) tree.
Mikio

Mikolas (Greek) an alternate form of Nicholas.
Miklós, Mikolai

Milan (Italian) northerner. Geography: a city in northern Italy.
Milen, Millan, Millen, Mylan, Mylen, Mylon

Miles (Greek) millstone. (Latin) soldier. (German) merciful.
Milas, Milles, Milo, Milson, Myles

Milford (English) mill by the ford.

Mililani (Hawaiian) heavenly caress.

Milko (Czech) a form of Michael. (German) a familiar form of Emil.
Milkins

Millard (Latin) caretaker of the mill.
Mill, Millar, Miller, Millward, Milward, Myller

Miller (English) miller, grain grinder.
Mellar, Millard, Millen

Mills (English) mills.

Milo (German) an alternate form of Miles. A familiar form of Emil.
Mylo

Milos (Greek, Slavic) pleasant.

Miloslav (Czech) lover of glory.
Milda

Milt (English) a short form of Milton.

Milton (English) mill town.
Milt, Miltie, Milty, Mylton

Mimis (Greek) a familiar form of Demetrius.

Min (Burmese) king.
Mina

Miner (English) miner.

Mingo (Spanish) a short form of Domingo.

Minh (Vietnamese) bright.
Minhao, Minhduc, Minhkhan, Minhtong, Minhy

Minor (Latin) junior; younger.
Mynor

Minoru (Japanese) fruitful.

Miron (Polish) peace.

Miroslav (Czech) peaceful glory.
Mirek, Miroslawy

Mister (English) mister.
Mistur

Misu (Moquelumnan) rippling water.

Mitch (English) a short form of Mitchell.

Mitchell (English) a form of Michael.
Mitch, Mitchael, Mitchall, Mitchel, Mitchele, Mitchelle, Mitchem, Mytch, Mytchell

Mitsos (Greek) a familiar form of Demetrius.

Modesto (Latin) modest.

Mogens (Dutch) powerful.

Mohamet (Arabic) an alternate form of Mohammed.
Mehemet, Mehmet

Mohammad (Arabic) an alternate form of Mohammed.
Mahammad, Mohamad, Mohamid, Mohammadi, Mohammd, Mohammid, Mohanad, Mohmad

Mohammed (Arabic) praised. See also Ahmad, Hamid.
Mahammed, Mahmúd, Mohamed, Mohamet, Mohammad, Mohaned, Mouhamed, Muhammad
Foreign form: Turkish: Mahomet

Mohan (Hindi) delightful. Religion: another name for the Hindu god Krishna.

Moises (Portuguese, Spanish) a form of Moses.
Moisés, Moisey, Moisis

Molimo (Moquelumnan) bear going under shady trees.

Mona (Moquelumnan) gathering jimsonweed seed.

Monahan (Irish) monk.
Monaghan, Monoghan

Mongo (Yoruba) famous.

Monroe (Irish) Geography: the mouth of the Roe River.
Monro, Munro, Munroe

Montague (French) pointed mountain.
Montagu, Monte

Montana (Spanish) mountain. Geography: a U.S. state. Culture: name popularized by football player Joe Montana.
Montaine

Montaro (Japanese) big boy.
Montero

Monte (Spanish) a short form of Montgomery.
Montae, Montaé, Montay, Montee, Monti, Montoya, Monty

Montez (Spanish) dweller in the mountains.
Monteiz, Monteze, Montisze

Montgomery (English) rich man's mountain.
Montgomerie, Monty
Foreign form: Spanish: Monte

Montre (French) show.
Montray, Montres, Montrez

Montreal (French) royal mountain. Geography: a city in Quebec.
Montrail, Montrale, Montrall, Montrel, Montrell

Monty (English) a familiar form of Montgomery.

Moore (French) dark; moor; marshland. See also Maurice.
Moor, Mooro, More

Mordecai (Hebrew) martial, warlike. Mythology: Marduk was the Babylonian god of war.
Mord, Mordechai, Mordy, Mort

Mordred (Latin) painful. Literature: the nephew of King Arthur.
Modred

Morel (French) an edible mushroom.

Moreland (English) moor; marshland.
Moorland, Morland

Morell (French) dark; from Morocco.
Moor, Moore, Morill, Morrell, Morrill, Murrel, Murrell

Morey (Greek) a familiar form of Moris. (Latin) an alternate form of Morrie.
Morrey, Morry

Morgan (Scottish) sea warrior.
Morgen, Morgun, Morrgan

Mori (Madi) born before father finished paying wife's dowry.

Morio (Japanese) forest.

Moris (Greek) son of the dark one. (English) an alternate form of Morris.
Morisz, Moriz

Morley (English) meadow by the moor.
Moorley, Moorly, Morlee, Morleigh, Morlon, Morly, Morlyn, Morrley

Morrie (Latin) a familiar form of Maurice, Morse.
Maury, Morey, Morie

Morris (Latin) dark skinned; moor; marshland. (English) a

form of Maurice.
Moris, Moriss, Morriss, Morry, Moss

Morse (English) son of Maurice.
Morresse, Morrie, Morrison, Morrisson

Mort (French, English) a short form of Mortimer, Morton.
Mortey, Mortie, Mortty, Morty

Mortimer (French) still water.
Mort, Mortymer

Morton (English) town near the moor.
Mort

Morven (Scottish) mariner.
Morvien, Morvin

Mose (Hebrew) a short form of Moses.

Moses (Hebrew) drawnout of the water. (Egyptian) son, child. Bible: the Hebrew leader who brought the Ten Commandments down from Mount Sinai.
Moïse, Mosese, Mosiah, Mosie, Moyses
Foreign forms: Arabic: Mousa; Dutch: Mozes; English: Moe, Moss; French/Italian: Moise,

Moses (cont.)
Mose; Lithuanian: **Moze;**
Polish: **Mosze, Moszek;**
Portuguese/Spanish: **Moises;**
Russian: **Moisei, Mosya;** Yiddish:
Moishe

Moshe (Hebrew, Polish) an
alternate form of Moses.
Mosheh

Mosi (Swahili) first-born.

Moss (Irish) a short form of
Maurice, Morris. (English)
a short form of Moses.

Moswen (African) light in
color.

Mouhamed (Arabic) an alternate form of Mohammed.
Mouhamadou, Mouhamoin

Mugamba (Runyoro) talks too
much.

Mugisa (Rutooro) lucky.
Mugisha, Mukisa

Muhammad (Arabic) an alter-
nate form of Mohammed.
History: the founder of the
Islamic religion.
**Muhamad, Muhamet,
Muhammadali, Muhammed**

Muhannad (Arabic) sword.
Muhanad

Muir (Scottish) moor; marshland.

Mujahid (Arabic) fighter in the
way of Allah.

Mukasa (Luganda) God's chief
administrator.

Mukhtar (Arabic) chosen.
Mukhtaar

Mundo (Spanish) a short form
of Edmundo.

Mundy (Irish) from Reamonn,
Ireland.

Mungo (Scottish) amiable.

Mun-Hee (Korean) literate;
shiny.

Munir (Arabic) brilliant;
shining.

Munny (Cambodian) wise.

Muraco (Native American)
white moon.

Murali (Hindi) god. Religion:
another name for the Hindu
god Krishna.

Murat (Turkish) wish come
true.

Murdock (Scottish) wealthy
sailor.
Murdo, Murdoch
Foreign form: Irish: **Murtagh**

Murphy (Irish) sea-warrior.
Murfey, Murfy

Murray (Scottish) sailor.
**Macmurray, Moray, Murrey,
Murry**

Musád (Arabic) untied camel.

Musoke (Rukonjo) born while a
rainbow was in the sky.

Mustafa (Arabic) chosen; royal.
**Mostafa, Mostaffa, Moustafa,
Mustafah, Mustapha**

Muti (Arabic) obedient.

Mwamba (Nyakusa) strong.

Mwanje (Luganda) leopard.

Myles (Latin) soldier. (German)
an alternate form of Miles.

Myo (Burmese) city.

Myron (Greek) fragrant oint-
ment.
**Mehran, Mehrayan, My,
Myran, Myrone, Ron**

Myung-Dae (Korean) right;
great.

Mzuzi (Swahili) inventive.

Nabil (Arabic) noble.
Nabeel, Nabiel

Nachman (Hebrew) a short form of Menachem.
Nachum, Nahum

Nada (Arabic) generous.

Nadidah (Arabic) equal to anyone else.

Nadim (Arabic) friend.
Nadeem

Nadir (Afghani, Arabic) dear, rare.
Nader

Naeem (Arabic) benevolent.
Naim, Naiym, Nieem

Nagid (Hebrew) ruler, prince.

Nahele (Hawaiian) forest.

Nailah (Arabic) successful.

Nairn (Scottish) river with alder trees.
Nairne

Naji (Arabic) safe.
Najee

Najíb (Arabic) born to nobility.
Najib, Nejeeb

Najji (Muganda) second child.

Nakos (Arapaho) sage, wise.

Nam (Vietnamese) scrape off.

Namaka (Hawaiian) eyes.

Namid (Chippewa) star dancer.

Namir (Hebrew) leopard.
Namer

Nandin (Hindi) god; destroyer. Religion: another name for the Hindu god Shiva.

Nando (German) a familiar form of Ferdinand.
Nandor

Nansen (Swedish) son of Nancy.

Nantai (Navajo) chief.

Nantan (Apache) spokesman.

Naoko (Japanese) straight, honest.

Napier (Spanish) new city.
Neper

Napoleon (Greek) lion of the woodland. (Italian) from Naples, Italy. History: Napoleon Bonaparte was a famous nineteenth-century French emperor.
Leon, Nap, Napoléon, Napoleone, Nappie, Nappy

Narain (Hindi) protector. Religion: another name for the Hindu god Vishnu.
Narayan

Narcissus (Greek) daffodil. Mythology: the youth who fell in love with his own reflection. *Foreign form: French: Narcisse*

Nard (Persian) chess player.

Nardo (German) strong, hardy. (Spanish) a short form of Bernardo.

Nasim (Persian) breeze, fresh air.
Naseem

Nasser (Arabic) victorious.
Naseer, Nasir, Nassor

Nat (English) a short form of Nathan, Nathaniel.
Natt, Natty

Natan (Hebrew, Hungarian, Polish, Russian, Spanish) God has given.
Nataneal, Nataniel

Nate (Hebrew) a short form of Nathan, Nathaniel.

Natesh (Hindi) destroyer. Religion: another name for the Hindu god Shiva.

Nathan (Hebrew) a short form of Nathaniel. Bible: an Old Testament prophet who saved Solomon's kingdom.
Naethan, Nat, Nate, Nathann, Nathean, Nathen, Nathian, Nathin, Nathon, Natthan, Naythan

Nathanael (Hebrew) an alternate form of Nathaniel.
Nathanae

Nathanial (Hebrew) an alternate form of Nathaniel.

Nathanie (Hebrew) a familiar form of Nathaniel.
Nathania, Nathanni

Nathaniel (Hebrew) gift of God. Bible: one of the Twelve Apostles.

Nat, Nate, Nathan, Nathanael, Nathanal, Nathaneal, Nathaneil, Nathanel, Nathaneol, Nathanial, Nathanie, Nathanielle, Nathanuel, Nathanyal, Nathanyel, Natheal, Nathel, Nathinel, Nethaniel, Thaniel
Foreign forms: Spanish: **Natanael, Nataniel**

Nathen (Hebrew) an alternate form of Nathan.

Nav (Gypsy) name.

Navarro (Spanish) plains.
Navarre

Navin (Hindi) new, novel.

Nayati (Native American) wrestler.

Nayland (English) island dweller.

Nazareth (Hebrew) born in Nazareth, Israel.
Nazaret, Nazarie
Foreign forms: French: **Nazaire;** Italian: **Nazario**

Nazih (Arabic) pure, chaste.
Nazim, Nazir, Nazz

Neal (Irish) an alternate form of Neil.
Neale, Neall, Nealle, Nealy

Neci (Latin) a familiar form of Ignatius.

Ned (English) a familiar form of Edward.
Neddie, Neddym, Nedrick

Nehemiah (Hebrew) compassion of Jehovah. Bible: a Hebrew prophet.
Nahemiah, Nechemya, Nehemias, Nehmiah, Nemo, Neyamia

Nehru (Hindi) canal.

Neil (Irish) champion.
Neal, Neel, Neihl, Neile, Neill, Neille, Nial, Nialle, Niele, Nyle
Foreign forms: Danish: **Niels;** Finnish: **Nilo;** Russian: **Nil, Nilya;** Scandinavian: **Nels, Nils;** Scottish: **Nealon, Niall**

Neka (Native American) wild goose.

Nellie (English) a familiar form of Cornell, Nelson.
Nell, Nelly

Nelius (Latin) a short form of Cornelius.

Nelson (English) son of Neil.
Nealson, Neilson, Nellie, Nelsen, Nilson, Nilsson

Nemo (Greek) glen, glade. (Hebrew) a short form of Nehemiah.

Nen (Egyptian) ancient waters.

Neptune (Latin) sea ruler. Mythology: the Roman god of the sea.

Nero (Latin, Spanish) stern.
Nerron
Foreign forms: French: **Neron;** Italian: **Nerone**

Nesbit (English) nose-shaped bend in a river.
Naisbit, Naisbitt, Nesbitt, Nisbet, Nisbett

Nestor (Greek) traveler; wise.
Nester

Nethaniel (Hebrew) an alternate form of Nathaniel.
Netanel, Netania, Netaniah, Netanya, Nethanel, Nethanial, Nethaniel, Nethanyal

Neto (Spanish) a short form of Ernesto.

Nevada (Spanish) covered in snow. Geography: a U.S. state.
Navada

Nevan (Irish) holy.

Neville (French) new town.
Nev, Nevil, Nevile, Nevill, Nevyle

Nevin (Irish) worshiper of the saint. (English) middle; herb.
Nefen, Nev, Nevan, Neven, Nevins, Niven

Newbold (English) new tree.

Newell (English) new hall.
Newall, Newel, Newyle

Newland (English) new land.
Newlan

Newlin (Welsh) new lake.
Newlyn

Newman (English) newcomer.

Newton (English) new town.

Ngu (Vietnamese) sleep.
Nguyen

Nhean (Cambodian) self-knowledge.

Niall (Irish) an alternate form of Neil. History: Niall of the Nine Hostages was a famous Irish ruler who founded the clan O'Neill.
Nial

Nicholas (Greek) victorious people. Religion: the patron saint of children. See also Cole, Colin, Colson, Mikolas.
Niccolas, Nichalas, Nichelas, Nichele, Nichlas, Nichlos, Nichola, Nichole, Nicholl, Nicklaus, Nickolas, Nicky, Niclas, Niclasse, Nicoles, Nicolis, Nicoll, Nikhil, Nikili, Nikolas, Nikolos, Nioclás, Niocol, Nycholas
Foreign forms: Dutch: **Nicolaas;** English: **Nick;** Finnish: **Lasse;** French: **Colar, Nicole;** German: **Claus, Klaus, Nikolaus;** Hungarian: **Niki;** Italian: **Cola, Nicolas, Nicolo;** Latvian/Swedish: **Niklas;** Norwegian: **Nicolai, Niklos;** Polish: **Mikolaj, Milek;** Russian: **Nikita, Nikolai, Kolya;** Scottish: **Caelan;** Swedish: **Nils**

Nichols, Nicholson (English) son of Nicholas.
Nicolls, Nickelson, Nickoles

Nick (English) a short form of Dominic, Nicholas.
Nic, Nik
Foreign form: Hungarian: **Micu**

Nicklaus (Greek) an alternate form of Nicholas.
Nicklas, Nickolau, Nickolaus, Nicolaus, Niklaus, Nikolaus

Nickolas (Greek) an alternate form of Nicholas.
Nickolaos, Nickolus

Nicky (Greek) a familiar form of Nicholas.
Nickey, Nickie, Niki, Nikki

Nicodemus (Greek) conqueror of the people.
Nicodem, Nikodema

Nicolas (Italian) a form of Nicholas.
Nico, Nicola, Nicolaas, Nicolás

Nien (Vietnamese) year.

Nigel (Latin) dark night.
Niegel, Nigal, Nigiel, Nigil, Nigle, Nijel, Nye, Nygel

Nika (Yoruba) ferocious.

Nike (Greek) victorious.

Nikiti (Native American) round and smooth like an abalone shell.

Nikolas (Greek) an alternate form on Nicholas.
Nicanor, Nikalus, Nikola, Nikolaas, Nikolao, Nikolaos, Nikolis, Nikolos, Nikos, Nilos, Nykolas

Nikolos (Greek) an alternate form of Nicholas.
Nikolaos, Nikolò, Nikolous, Nikos, Nilos

Nila (Hindi) blue.

Niles (English) son of Neil.
Nilesh

Nimrod (Hebrew) rebel. Bible: a great-grandson of Noah.

Niño (Spanish) young child.

Niran (Thai) eternal.

Nishan (Armenian) cross, sign, mark.

Nissan (Hebrew) sign, omen; miracle.
Nisan, Nissim

Nitis (Native American) friend.
Netis

Nixon (English) son of Nick.
Nixson

Nkunda (Runyankore) loves those who hate him.

N'namdi (Ibo) his father's name lives on.

Noah (Hebrew) peaceful, restful. Bible: the patriarch who built the ark to survive the Great Flood.
Foreign forms: Bulgarian: Noi; Czech/French: Noe, Noé; Dutch: Noach; Swedish: Noak

Noam (Hebrew) sweet; friend.

Noble (Latin) born to nobility.
Nobe, Nobie, Noby

Nodin (Native American) wind.
Knoton, Noton

Noël (French) day of Christ's birth.
Noel, Noél, Nole, Noli
Foreign forms: English: Nowel, Nowell; Spanish: Natal, Natalio

Nolan (Irish) famous; noble.
Noland, Nolen, Nolin, Nollan, Nolyn

Nollie (Latin, Scandinavian) a familiar form of Oliver.
Noll, Nolly

Norbert (Scandinavian) brilliant hero.
Bert, Norberto, Norbie, Norby

Norman (French) norseman. History: a name for the Scandinavians who conquered Normandy in the tenth century, and England in the eleventh century.
Norm, Normen, Normie, Normy
Foreign forms: Spanish: Normand, Normando

Norris (French) northerner. (English) Norman's horse.
Norice, Norie, Noris, Norreys, Norrie, Norry, Norrys

Northcliff (English) northern cliff.
Northcliffe, Northclyff, Northclyffe

Northrop (English) north farm.
North, Northup

Norton (English) northern town.

Norville (French, English) northern town.
Norval, Norvel, Norvell, Norvil, Norvill, Norvylle

Norvin (English) northern friend.
Norvyn, Norwin, Norwinn, Norwyn, Norwynn

Norward (English) protector of the north.
Norwerd

Norwood (English) northern woods.

Nowles (English) a short form of Knowles.

Numa (Arabic) pleasant.

Numair (Arabic) panther.

Nuncio (Italian) messenger.
Nunzio

Nuri (Hebrew, Arabic) my fire.

Nery, Noori, Nur, Nuris, Nurism, Nury

Nuriel (Hebrew, Arabic) fire of the Lord.
Nuria, Nuriah, Nuriya

Nuru (Swahili) born in daylight.

Nusair (Arabic) bird of prey.

Nye (English) a familiar form of Aneurin, Nigel.

Nyle (Irish) an alternate form of Neil. (English) island.

Oakes (English) oak trees.
Oak, Oakie, Oaks, Ochs

Oakley (English) oak-tree field.
Oak, Oakes, Oakie, Oaklee, Oakleigh, Oakly, Oaks

Oba (Yoruba) king.

Obadiah (Hebrew) servant of God.
Obadias, Obed, Obediah, Obie, Ovadiach, Ovadiah, Ovadya

Oberon (German) noble; bear-like. Literature: the king of the fairies in the Shakespearean play *A Midsummer Night's Dream*. See also Auberon, Aubrey.
Oberron, Oeberon

Obie (English) a familiar form of Obadiah.
Obbie, Obe, Oby

Octavio (Latin) eighth. See also Tavey.
Octave, Octavian, Octavien, Octavious, Octavis, Octavius, Octavo, Octavous, Octavus, Ottavio

Ode (Benin) born along the road. (Irish, English) a short form of Odell.
Odey, Odie, Ody

Oded (Hebrew) encouraging.

Odell (Greek) ode, melody. (Irish) otter. (English) forested hill.
Dell, Odall, Ode

Odin (Scandinavian) ruler. Mythology: the chief Norse god.

Odion (Benin) first of twins.

Odolf (German) prosperous wolf.
Odolff

Odom (Ghanian) oak tree.

Ödön (Hungarian) wealthy protector.
Odi

Odysseus (Greek) wrathful. Literature: the hero of Homer's epic *The Odyssey*.

Ofer (Hebrew) young deer.

Og (Aramaic) king. Bible: the king of Basham.

Ogden (English) oak valley. Literature: Ogden Nash was a twentieth-century American writer.
Ogdan, Ogdon

Ogun (Nigerian) Mythology: the god of war.
Ogunkeye, Ogunsanwo, Ogunsheye

OJ (American) a combination of the initials O. + J.
O.J., Ojay

Ojo (Yoruba) difficult delivery.

Okechuku (Ibo) God's gift.

Okeke (Ibo) born on market day.
Okorie

Okie (American) from Oklahoma.
Okee

Oko (Ga) older twin. (Yoruba) god of war.

Ola (Yoruba) wealthy, rich.
Olu

Olaf (Scandinavian) ancestor. History: a patron saint and king of Norway.
Olav, Ole, Olef, Oluf
Foreign forms: Icelandic: **Olaff, Olafur, Olof**

Olajuwon (Yoruba) wealth and honor are God's gifts.
Olajuan, Olajuwan, Oljuwoun

Olamina (Yoruba) this is my wealth.

Olatunji (Yoruba) honor reawakens.

Olav (Scandinavian) an alternate form of Olaf.
Ola, Olave, Olavus, Ole, Olen, Olin, Olle, Olov, Olyn

Ole (Scandinavian) a familiar form of Olaf, Olav.
Olay, Oleh, Olle

Oleg (Latvian, Russian) holy.
Olezka

Olin (English) holly.
Olen, Olney, Olyn

Olindo (Italian) from Olinthos, Italy.

Oliver (Latin) olive tree. (Scandinavian) kind; affectionate.
Nollie, Oliverios, Olivero, Olliver, Ollivor, Olvan
Foreign forms: English: **Ollie;** French: **Olivier;** Hawaiian: **Oliwa;** Irish: **Oilibhéar;** Italian: **Oliviero;** Spanish: **Oliverio**

Olivier (French) a form of Oliver.

Ollie (English) a familiar form of Oliver.
Olie, Olle, Olley, Olly

Olo (Spanish) a short form of Orlando, Rolando.

Omar (Arabic) highest; follower of the Prophet. (Hebrew) reverent.
Omair, Omarr, Omer, Umar
Foreign form: Swahili: **Omari**

On (Burmese) coconut. (Chinese) peace.

Onan (Turkish) prosperous.

O'neil (Irish) son of Neil.
Oneal, O'neal, Oneil, Onel, Oniel, Onil

Onkar (Hindi) pure being. Religion: another name for the Hindu god Shiva.

Onslow (English) enthusiast's hill.
Ounslow

Onofrio (German) an alternate form of Humphrey.
Oinfre, Onfre, Onfrio

Onur (Turkish) honor.

Oral (Latin) verbal, speaker.

Oran (Irish) green.
Odhran, Odran, Ora, Orane, Orran

Ordell (Latin) beginning.
Orde

Oren (Hebrew) pine tree. (Irish) light skinned, white.
Oran, Orin, Oris, Orono, Orren, Orrin

Orestes (Greek) mountain man. Mythology: the son of the Greek leader Agamemnon.
Aresty, Oreste

Ori (Hebrew) my light.

Orien (Latin) visitor from the east.
Orie, Orin, Oris, Orrin

Orion (Greek) son of fire. Mythology: a hunter who became a constellation.
Foreign form: Basque: Zorion

Orji (Ibo) mighty tree.

Orlando (German) famous throughout the land. (Spanish) a form of Roland.
Lando, Olando, Olo, Orlan, Orland, Orlanda, Orlandus, Orlo, Orlondo, Orlondon

Orleans (Latin) golden.
Orlin

Orman (German) mariner, seaman. (Scandinavian) serpent, worm.
Ormand

Ormond (English) bear mountain; spear protector.
Ormon, Ormonde

Oro (Spanish) golden.

Orrick (English) old oak tree.
Orric

Orrin (English) river. Geography: a river in England.
Orin

Orris (Latin) an alternate form of Horatio.
Oris, Orriss

Orry (Latin) from the Orient.
Oarrie, Orrey, Orrie

Orson (Latin) bearlike.
Orsen, Orsin, Orsini
*Foreign forms: English: **Son, Sonny**; French: **Urson**; Italian: **Orscino, Orsino***

Orton (English) shore town.

Orval (English) an alternate form of Orville.

Orville (French) golden village. History: Orville Wright and his brother Wilbur were the first men to fly an airplane.
Orv, Orval, Orvell, Orvie, Orvil

Orvin (English) spear friend.
Orwin, Owynn

Osborn (Scandinavian) divine bear. (English) warrior of God.
Osbern, Osbon, Osborne, Osbourn, Osbourne, Osburn, Osburne, Oz, Ozzie

Oscar (Scandinavian) divine spearman.

Oscar (cont.)
Oskar, Oszkar
Foreign form: Hawaiian: **Oko**

Osgood (English) divinely good.

O'Shea (Irish) son of Shea.
Oshai, O'Shane, Oshaun, Oshay, Oshea

Oskar (Scandinavian) an alternate form of Oscar.
Osker, Ozker

Osman (Turkish) ruler. (English) servant of God.
Osmanek, Osmen, Otthmor, Ottmar

Osmar (English) divine; wonderful.

Osmond (English) divine protector.
Osmand, Osmonde, Osmont, Osmund, Osmunde, Osmundo

Osric (English) divine ruler.
Osrick

Osvaldo (Spanish) a form of Oswald.
Osvald, Osvalda

Oswald (English) God's power; God's crest.
Oswaldo, Oswall, Oswell, Oswold, Oz, Ozzie

Foreign forms: German: **Waldo;** Spanish: **Osvaldo**

Oswin (English) divine friend.
Osvin, Oswinn, Oswyn, Oswynn

Ota (Czech) prosperous.
Otik

Othman (German) wealthy.

Othello (Spanish) a form of Otto. Literature: the title character in the Shakespearean tragedy *Othello.*

Otis (Greek) keen of hearing. (German) son of Otto.
Oates, Odis, Otes, Otess, Ottis, Otys

Ottah (Nigerian) thin baby.

Ottar (Norwegian) point warrior; fright warrior.

Ottmar (Turkish) an alternate form of Osman. History: the founder of the Ottoman Empire.
Otomars, Ottomar

Otto (German) rich.
Otfried, Otho, Oto, Otón
Foreign forms: Czech: **Otik;** Greek: **Othon;** Italian: **Otello, Ottone;** Norwegian: **Odo;** Polish:

Otek, Otton; Spanish: **Othello, Otilio, Otman**

Ottokar (German) happy warrior.
Otokars, Ottocar

Otu (Native American) collecting seashells in a basket.

Oved (Hebrew) worshiper, follower.

Owen (Irish) born to nobility; young warrior. (Welsh) a form of Evan.
Owain, Owens, Owin, Uaine

Owney (Irish) elderly.
Oney

Oxford (English) place where oxen cross the river.
Ford

Oz (Hebrew) a short form of Osborn, Oswald.

Ozzie (English) a familiar form of Osborn, Oswald.
Ossie, Ossy, Ozi, Ozzi, Ozzy

Pablo (Spanish) a form of Paul.
Pable, Paublo

Pacifico (Filipino) peaceful.

Paco (Italian) pack. (Spanish) a familiar form of Francisco. (Native American) bald eagle. See also Quico.
Pacorro, Panchito, Pancho, Paquito

Paddy (Irish) a familiar form of Patrick.
Paddey, Paddie

Page (French) youthful assistant.
Paggio, Payge
*Foreign forms: English: **Padget, Paige***

Paki (African) witness.

Palladin (Native American) fighter.
Pallaton, Palleten

Palmer (English) palm-bearing pilgrim.
Pallmer, Palmar

Panas (Russian) immortal.

Panayiotis (Greek) an alternate form of Peter.
Panagiotis, Panayioti, Panayoti

Pancho (Spanish) a familiar form of Francisco, Frank.
Panchito

Panos (Greek) an alternate form of Peter.
Petros

Paolo (Italian) a form of Paul.

Paquito (Spanish) a familiar form of Paco.

Paramesh (Hindi) greatest. Religion: another name for the Hindu god Shiva.

Paris (Greek) lover. Geography: the capital of France. Mythology: the prince of Troy who started the Trojan War by abducting Helen.
Paras, Paree, Parris

Park (Chinese) cypress tree. (English) a short form of Parker.
Parke, Parkes, Parkey

Parker (English) park keeper.
Park

Parkin (English) little Peter.
Perkin

Parnell (French) little Peter. History: Charles Stewart Parnell was a famous Irish politician.
Nell, Parle, Parnel, Parrnell, Pernell

Parr (English) cattle enclosure, barn.

Parrish (English) church district.
Parish, Parrie, Parrisch

Parry (Welsh) son of Harry.
Parrey, Parrie, Pary

Pascal (French) born on Easter or Passover.
Pascale, Pascalle, Paschal, Paschalis, Pascoe, Pascow
*Foreign forms: English: **Pace**; Italian: **Pasquale**; Spanish: **Pascual***

Pasquale (Italian) a form of Pascal.
Pascuale, Pasquel

Pastor (Latin) spiritual leader.

Pat (English) a short form of Patrick. (Native American) fish.
Pattie, Patty

Patrick (Latin) nobleman. Religion: the patron saint of Ireland. See also Fitzpatrick.
Patric, Patrique, Patryck, Patryk, Pats, Patsy
Foreign forms: English: *Pat, Patrik;* French: *Patrice;* German: *Patrizius;* Hawaiian: *Pakelike;* Irish: *Paddy, Padraic;* Italian: *Patrizio;* Polish: *Patek;* Spanish: *Patricio, Ticho*

Patterson (Irish) son of Pat.
Patteson

Pattin (Gypsy) leaf.
Patrin

Patton (English) warrior's town.
Paten, Patin, Paton, Patten, Pattin, Patty, Payton, Peyton

Patwin (Native American) man.

Paul (Latin) small. Bible: Saul, later renamed Paul, was the first to bring the teachings of Christ to the Gentiles.
Pasko, Pauli, Paulia, Paulis, Pauls, Paulus, Pavlos

Foreign forms: Danish: *Poul;* Finnish: *Paavo;* German/Polish: *Paulin;* Hawaiian/Portuguese/Swedish: *Paulo;* Hungarian: *Pál;* Italian: *Paolo;* Polish: *Pawel;* Russian: *Pasha, Pavel;* Spanish: *Oalo, Pablo, Paulino;* Swedish: *Pal, Pall, Pol*

Pauli (Latin) a familiar form of Paul.
Pauley, Paulie, Pauly

Paulo (Portuguese, Swedish, Hawaiian) a form of Paul.

Pavit (Hindi) pious, pure.

Pax (Latin) peaceful.
Foreign form: Spanish: *Paz*

Paxton (Latin) peaceful town.
Packston, Pax, Paxon, Paxten, Paxtun

Payne (Latin) man from the country.
Paine

Payton (English) an alternate form of Patton.
Paiton, Pate, Payden, Paydon, Peyton

Pearson (English) son of Peter.
Pearsson, Pehrson, Peterson, Pierson, Piersson

Pedro (Spanish) a form of Peter.
Pedrin, Pedrín, Petronio

Pelham (English) tannery town.

Pelí (Latin, Basque) happy.

Pell (English) parchment.
Pall

Pello (Greek, Basque) stone.
Peru, Piarres

Pelton (English) town by a pool.

Pembroke (Welsh) headland. (French) wine dealer. (English) broken fence.
Pembrook

Penley (English) enclosed meadow.

Penn (Latin) pen, quill. (German) a short form of Penrod. (English) enclosure.
Pen, Penna, Penney, Pennie, Penny

Penrod (German) famous commander.
Penn, Pennrod, Rod

Pepin (German) determined; petitioner. History: Pepin the short, an eighth-century king

of the Franks, was the father of Charlemagne.
Pepi, Peppie, Peppy

Percival (French) pierce the valley; pierce the veil of religion mystery. Literature: a name invented by Chrétien de Troyes for the knight-hero of his epic about the Holy Grail.
Parsafal, Parsefal, Parsifal, Parzival, Perc, Perce, Perceval, Percevall, Percivall, Percy, Peredur, Purcell

Percy (French) a familiar form of Percival.
Pearcey, Pearcy, Percey, Percie, Piercey, Piercy

Peregrine (Latin) traveler; pilgrim; falcon.
Peregrin, Peregryne, Perine, Perry

Pericles (Greek) just leader. History: an Athenian statesman and general.

Perine (Latin) a short form of Peregrine.
Perino, Perrin, Perryn

Perkin (English) little Peter.
Perka, Perkins, Perkyn, Perrin

Perry (English) a familiar form of Peregrine, Peter.
Parry, Perrie

Perth (Scottish) thornbush thicket. Geography: a county in Scotland; a city in Australia.

Pervis (Latin) passage.

Pesach (Hebrew) spared. Religion: another name for the Jewish holiday Passover.
Pessach

Pete (English) a short form of Peter.
Peat, Peet, Petey, Peti, Petie, Piet, Pit

Peter (Greek, Latin) small rock. Bible: Simon, renamed Peter, was the leader of the Twelve Apostles. See also Takis.
Panayiotos, Panos, Perren, Petar, Pete, Péter, Peteris, Peterke, Peterus, Petros, Piaras, Piter
Foreign forms: Arabic: **Boutros;** *Bulgarian:* **Petr;** *Dutch:* **Pieter;** *English:* **Peers, Peirce, Perry, Pierce;** *Estonian:* **Peeter;** *French:* **Pierre;** *Hawaiian:* **Pekelo;** *Icelandic:* **Petur;** *Irish:* **Ferris, Peadair;** *Italian:* **Perion, Piero, Pietro;** *Lithuanian:* **Petras;** *Norwegian:* **Petter;** *Polish:* **Pietrek;** *Rumanian:* **Petru;** *Russian:* **Petya, Pyotr;** *Scandinavian:* **Peder;** *Slavic:* **Petruno, Piotr, Pjotr;** *Spanish:* **Pedro, Perico, Peyo, Piti;** *Swedish:* **Per**

Petros (Greek) an alternate form of Peter.
Petro

Peyton (English) an alternate form of Patton, Payton.
Peyt

Pharaoh (Latin) ruler. History: a title for the ancient rulers of Egypt.
Faroh, Pharo, Pharoah, Pharoh

Phelan (Irish) wolf.

Phelps (English) son of Phillip.

Phil (Greek) a short form of Philip, Phillip.
Phill
Foreign form: Polish: **Fil**

Philander (Greek) lover of mankind.

Philbert (English) an alternate form of Filbert.
Philibert, Phillbert

Philemon (Greek) kiss.
Phila, Philamina, Philmon

Philip (Greek) lover of horses. Bible: one of the Twelve Apostles.
Phil, Philippo, Phillip, Phillipos, Phillp, Philp
Foreign forms: American: **Flip,**

Philip (cont.)
Philly; English: **Piers;** French:
Philippe; German: **Philipp;**
Hawaiian: **Pilipo;** Irish: **Pilib;**
Italian: **Felippo, Pippo;** Polish:
Filipek; Russian: **Fillipp, Filya;**
Spanish: **Felipe, Phelipe;** Yiddish:
Fischel

Philippe (French) a form of
Philip.
Philipe, Phillepe

Phillip (Greek) an alternate
form of Philip.
**Phil, Phillipos, Phillipp,
Phillips, Philly**

Phillipos (Greek) an alternate
form of Phillip.

Philo (Greek) love.

Phinean (Irish) an alternate
form of Finian.
Phinian

Phineas (English) a form of
Pinchas.
Phinehas, Phinny
Foreign form: Irish: **Fineas**

Phuok (Vietnamese) good.
Phuoc

Pickford (English) ford at the
peak.

Pickworth (English) woodcutter's estate.

Pierce (English) a form of Peter.
**Pearce, Pears, Pearson,
Pearsson, Peerce, Peers,
Peirce, Piercy, Piers, Pierson,
Piersson**

Pierre (French) a form of Peter.
Peirre, Piere, Pierrot

Pierre-Luc (French) a combination of Pierre + Luc.

Pietro (Italian) a form of Peter.

Pilar (Spanish) pillar.

Pili (Swahili) second born.

Pillan (Native American)
supreme essence.
Pilan

Pin (Vietnamese) faithful boy.

Pinchas (Hebrew) oracle.
(Egyptian) dark skinned.
**Pincas, Pinchos, Pincus,
Pinkas, Pinkus**
Foreign form: American: **Pinky;**
English: **Phineas**

Piñon (Tupi-Guarani)
Mythology: the hunter who
became the constellation
Orion.

Pio (Latin) pious.

Pippin (German) father.

Piran (Irish) prayer. Religion:
the patron saint of miners.
Peran, Pieran

Pirro (Greek, Spanish) flaming
hair.

Pitney (English) island of the
strong-willed man.
Pittney

Pitt (English) pit, ditch.

Placido (Spanish) serene.
Placidus, Placyd, Placydo

Plato (Greek) broad shouldered. History: a famous Greek
philosopher.
Platon

Platt (French) flat land.
Platte

Pollard (German) close-
cropped head.
Poll, Pollerd, Pollyrd

Pollux (Greek) crown.
Astronomy: one of the twins in
the Gemini constellation.
Foreign forms: English: **Polloch,
Pollock**

Polo (Greek) a short form of Apollo. (Tibetan) brave wanderer. Culture: a game played on horseback. History: Marco Polo was a Venetian explorer who traveled throughout Asia in the thirteenth and fourteenth centuries.

Pomeroy (French) apple orchard.
Pommeray, Pommeroy

Ponce (Spanish) fifth. History: Juan Ponce de León of Spain searched for the fountain of youth in Florida.

Pony (Scottish) small horse.
Poni

Porfirio (Greek, Spanish) purple stone.
Porphirios, Prophyrios

Porter (Latin) gatekeeper.
Port, Portie, Porty

Po Sin (Chinese) grandfather elephant.

Powa (Native American) wealthy.

Powell (English) alert.
Powel

Pramad (Hindi) rejoicing.

Pravat (Thai) history.

Prentice (English) apprentice.
Prent, Prentis, Prentiss, Printiss

Prescott (English) priest's cottage. See also Scott.
Prescot, Prestcot, Prestcott

Presley (English) priest's meadow.
Presleigh, Presly, Presslee, Pressley, Prestley, Priestley, Priestly

Preston (English) priest's estate.
Prestin

Prewitt (French) brave little one.
Preuet, Prewet, Prewett, Prewit, Pruit, Pruitt

Price (Welsh) son of the ardent one.
Brice, Bryce, Pryce

Pricha (Thai) clever.

Primo (Italian) first; premier quality.
Preemo, Premo

Prince (Latin) chief; prince.
Prence, Princeton, Prinz, Prinze

Proctor (Latin) official, administrator.
Prockter, Procter

Prokopios (Greek) declared leader.

Prosper (Latin) fortunate.
Prospero, Próspero

Pryor (Latin) head of the monastery, prior.
Prior, Pry

Pumeet (Sanskrit) pure.

Purdy (Hindi) recluse.

Purvis (French, English) providing food.
Pervis, Purves, Purviss

Putnam (English) dweller by the pond.
Putnem

Qabil (Arabic) able.

Qadim (Arabic) ancient.

Qadir (Arabic) powerful.
Qadeer, Quadeer, Quadir

Qamar (Arabic) moon.

Qasim (Arabic) divider.

Qimat (Hindi) valuable.

Quaashie (Ewe) born on Sunday.

Quan (Comanche) a short form of Quanah.

Quanah (Comanche) fragrant.
Quan

Quant (Greek) how much?
Quanta, Quantae, Quantai, Quantay, Quantea, Quantey, Quantez

Qudamah (Arabic) courage.

Quenby (Scandinavian) an alternate form of Quimby.

Quennell (French) small oak.
Quenell, Quennel

Quentin (Latin) fifth. (English) Queen's town.
Qeuntin, Quantin, Quent, Quenten, Quenton, Quientin, Quienton, Quintin, Quinton, Qwentin

Quico (Spanish) a familiar form of many names.
Paco

Quigley (Irish) maternal side.
Quigly

Quillan (Irish) cub.
Quill, Quillen, Quillon

Quimby (Scandinavian) woman's estate.
Quenby, Quinby

Quincy (French) fifth son's estate.
Quincey, Quinn, Quinnsy, Quinsey

Quinlan (Irish) strong; well shaped.
Quindlen, Quinlen, Quinlin, Quinn, Quinnlan

Quinn (Irish) a short form of Quincy, Quinlan, Quinton.

Quintin (Latin) an alternate form of Quentin.

Quinton (Latin) an alternate form of Quentin.
Quinn, Quinneton, Quint, Quintan, Quintann, Quinten, Quintin, Quintus, Quitin, Quiton, Qunton, Qwinton

Quiqui (Spanish) a familiar form of Enrique.
Quinto, Quiquin

Quitin (Latin) a short form of Quinton.
Quiten, Quito, Quiton

Quito (Spanish) a short form of Quinton.

Quon (Chinese) bright.

Raanan (Hebrew) fresh; luxuriant.

Rabi (Arabic) breeze.
Rabbi, Rabee, Rabiah, Rabih

Race (English) race.
Racel

Racham (Hebrew) compassionate.
Rachaman, Rachamim, Rachim, Rachman, Rachmiel, Rachum, Raham, Rahamim

Rad (English) advisor. (Slavic) happy.
Radd, Raddie, Raddy, Radell, Radey

Radbert (English) brilliant advisor.

Radburn (English) red brook; brook with reeds.
Radborn, Radborne, Radbourn, Radbourne, Radburne

Radcliff (English) red cliff; cliff with reeds.
Radcliffe, Radclyffe

Radford (English) red ford; ford with reeds.

Radley (English) red meadow; meadow of reeds.
Radlea, Radlee, Radleigh, Radly

Radman (Slavic) joyful.
Radmen, Radusha

Radnor (English) red shore; shore with reeds.

Radomil (Slavic) happy peace.

Radoslaw (Polish) happy glory.
Radik, Rado, Radzmir, Slawek

Rafael (Spanish) a form of Raphael.
Rafaelle, Rafaello, Rafaelo, Rafal, Rafeal, Rafeé, Rafel, Rafello, Raffael, Raffaelo, Raffeal

Rafe (English) a short form of Rafferty, Ralph.
Raff

Rafer (Irish) a short form of Rafferty.
Raffer

Rafferty (Irish) prosperous, rich.
Rafe, Rafer, Raferty, Raffarty, Raffer

Rafi (Hebrew) a familiar form of Raphael. (Arabic) exalted.
Raffee, Raffi, Raffy

Rafiq (Arabic) friend.
Rafeeq, Rafic, Rafique

Raghib (Arabic) desirous.
Raquib

Raghnall (Irish) wise power.

Ragnar (Norwegian) powerful army.
Ragnor, Rainier
*Foreign forms: Italian: **Ranieri**; Scandinavian: **Rainer, Rayner, Raynor**; Swedish: **Reinhold***

Rago (Hausa) ram.

Raheem (Punjabi) compassionate God.

Rahim (Arabic) merciful.
Raheem, Raheim, Rahiem, Rahiim

Rahman (Arabic) compassionate.
Rahmatt, Rahmet

Rahul (Arabic) traveler.

Raíd (Arabic) leader.

Raiden (Japanese) Mythology: the thunder god.

Raine (English) lord; wise.
Rain, Raines

Rainer (German) counselor.
Rainar, Rainey, Rainor

Rainey (German) a familiar form of Rainer.
Raine, Rainie, Rainy

Raini (Tupi-Guarani) Religion: the Native American god who created the world.

Rajah (Hindi) prince, chief.
Raj, Raja, Rajae

Rajak (Hindi) cleansing.

Rakin (Arabic) respectable.
Rakeen

Raleigh (English) an alternate form of Rawleigh.
Ralegh

Ralph (English) wolf counselor.
Radolphus, Rafe, Ralf, Ralpheal, Ralphel, Ralphie
Foreign forms: French: **Raoul, Raul;** German: **Rolf**

Ralphie (English) a familiar form of Ralph.

Ralston (English) Ralph's settlement.

Ram (Hindi) god; godlike. Religion: another name for the Hindu god Shiva. (English) male sheep.
Rami, Ramie, Ramy

Ramadan (Arabic) ninth month of the Arabic year.
Rama

Ramanan (Hindi) god; godlike. Religion: another name for the Hindu god Shiva.
Raman, Ramandeep, Ramanjit, Ramanjot

Ramiro (Portuguese, Spanish) supreme judge.
Rameriz, Rami, Ramirez, Ramos

Ramón (Spanish) a form of Raymond.
Raimon, Ramon, Remone, Romone

Ramsden (English) valley of rams.

Ramsey (English) ram's island.
Ram, Ramsay, Ramsy, Ramzee, Ramzi

Rance (English) a short form of Laurence, Ransom. (American) a familiar form of Laurence.
Rancel, Rancell, Rances, Rancey, Rancie, Rancy, Ransel, Ransell

Rand (English) shield; warrior.
Randy

Randal (English) an alternate form of Randall.
Randale, Randel, Randle

Randall (English) an alternate form of Randolph.
Randal, Randell, Randy

Randolph (English) shield-wolf.
Randall, Randol, Randolf, Randolfo, Randolpho, Randy, Ranolph

Randy (English) a familiar form of Rand, Randall, Randolph.
Randey, Randi, Randie, Ranndy

Ranger (French) forest keeper.
Rainger, Range

Rangle (American) cowboy.
Rangler, Wrangle

Rangsey (Cambodian) seven kinds of colors.

Rani (Hebrew) my song; my joy.
Ranen, Ranie, Ranon, Roni

Ranjan (Hindi) delighted; gladdened.

Rankin (English) small shield.
Randkin

Ransford (English) raven's ford.

Ransley (English) raven's field.

Ransom (Latin) redeemer. (English) son of the shield.
Rance, Ransome, Ranson

Raphael (Hebrew) God has healed. Bible: one of the archangels. Art: a prominent painter of the Italian Renaissance. See also Rafi.
Raphaél, Raphale, Raphaello, Rapheal, Raphel, Raphello, Rephael
Foreign forms: Italian: Falito, Rafaele; Polish: Rafal; Spanish: Rafael

Rapier (French) blade-sharp.

Rashad (Arabic) wise counselor.
Raashad, Rachad, Rachard, Rachaud, Raeshad, Raishard, Rashaad, Rashaud, Rashaude, Rashid, Rashod, Rashoda, Rashodd, Rhashad, Rhashod, Roushdy
Foreign forms: American:

Rayshard, Rayshod, Reshad, Rishad, Roshad

Rashawn (American) a combination of the prefix Ra + Shawn.
Rashann, Rashaun, Rashaw, Rashon, Rashun, Raushan, Raushawn, Rhashan, Rhashaun, Rhashawn

Rashean (American) a combination of the prefix Ra + Sean.
Rashane, Rasheen, Rashien, Rashiena

Rashid (Arabic) an alternate form of Rashad.
Rasheed, Rasheid, Rasheyd, Rashida, Rashidah, Rashied, Rashieda, Raushaid

Rashida (Swahili) righteous.

Rashidi (Swahili) wise counselor.

Rasmus (Greek, Danish) a short form of Erasmus.

Raul (French) a form of Ralph.

Raven (English) a short form of Ravenel.
Ravin, Ravon, Ravone

Ravenel (English) raven.
Raven, Ravenell, Revenel

Ravi (Hindi) sun. Religion: another name for the Hindu sun god Surya.
Ravee, Ravijot

Ravid (Hebrew) an alternate form of Arvid.

Raviv (Hebrew) rain, dew.

Rawdon (English) rough hill.

Rawleigh (English) deer meadow.
Raleigh, Rawley, Rawly

Ray (French) kingly, royal. (English) a short form of Rayburn, Raymond.
Rae, Raye
Foreign form: Hawaiian: Lei

Rayburn (English) deer brook.
Burney, Raeborn, Raeborne, Raebourn, Ray, Raybourn, Raybourne, Rayburne

Rayhan (Arabic) favored by God.

Rayi (Hebrew) my friend, my companion.

Raymond (English) mighty; wise protector.
Raemond, Raemondo, Ramond, Ramonde, Ray, Rayman, Raymand, Rayment, Raymon, Raymont, Raymund,

Raymond (cont.)
Raymunde, Redmond
Foreign forms: *Dutch:* **Ramone;**
French: **Aymon;** *German:*
Raimund; *Irish:* **Radmond,**
Reamonn; *Italian:* **Raimondo;**
Portuguese/Spanish: **Raimundo,**
Ramón, Raymundo

Raynaldo (Spanish) an alternate form of Renaldo, Reynold.
Raynal, Raynald, Raynold

Raynard (French) an alternate form of Renard, Reynard.

Rayshawn (American) a combination of Ray + Shawn.
Rayshaan, Rayshan,
Rayshaun, Raysheen,
Rayshon, Rayshone, Rayshun,
Rayshunn

Razi (Aramaic) my secret.
Raz, Raziel, Raziq

Read (English) an alternate form of Reed, Reid.
Raed, Raede, Raeed, Reaad,
Reade

Reading (English) son of the red wanderer. Geography: a city in Pennsylvania.
Redding, Reeding, Reiding

Reagan (Irish) little king.
History: Ronald Wilson Reagan

was the fortieth U.S. president.
Raegan, Regan, Reagen,
Reegan, Reegen, Regen

Rebel (American) rebel.
Reb

Red (American) red, redhead.
Redd

Reda (Arabic) satisfied.
Ridha

Redford (English) red river crossing.
Ford, Radford, Reaford, Red,
Redd

Redley (English) red meadow; meadow with reeds.
Radley, Redlea, Redleigh,
Redly

Redmond (German) protecting counselor. (English) an alternate form of Raymond.
Radmond, Radmund, Reddin,
Redmund

Redpath (English) red path.

Reece (Welsh) enthusiastic; stream.
Reese, Reice, Rice

Reed (English) an alternate form of Reid.
Raeed, Read, Reyde

Reese (Welsh) an alternate form of Reece.
Rees, Reis, Rhys, Riess

Reeve (English) steward.
Reave, Reaves, Reeves

Reg (English) a short form of Reginald.

Reggie (English) a familiar form of Reginald.

Reginal (English) an alternate form of Reginald.

Reginald (English) king's advisor. An alternate form of Reynold.
Reg, Reggie, Reggis, Reginal,
Reginale, Reginalt, Reginel
Foreign forms: *French:*
Reginauld, Reginault, Regnauld;
Scottish: **Ronald;** *Spanish:*
Reginaldo, Naldo

Regis (Latin) regal.

Rei (Japanese) rule, law.

Reid (English) redhead.
Read, Reed, Reide, Ried

Reidar (Norwegian) nest warrior.

Reilly (Irish) an alternate form of Riley.
Reilley, Rielly

Reinhart (German) a form of Reynard.
Rainart, Rainhard, Rainhardt, Rainhart, Reinart, Reinhard, Reinhardt, Renke

Remi, Rémi (French) alternate forms of Remy.
Remie, Remmie

Remington (English) raven estate.
Rem, Tony

Remus (Latin) speedy, quick. Mythology: Remus and his twin brother Romulus founded Rome.

Remy (French) from Rheims, France.
Ramey, Remee, Remi, Rémi, Remmy

Renaldo (Spanish) a form of Reynold.
Raynaldo, Reinaldo, Reynaldo, Rinaldo

Renard (French) an alternate form of Reynard.
Ranard, Raynard

Renato (Italian) reborn.

Rendor (Hungarian) policeman.

René (French) reborn.
Renat, Renato, Renatus, Renault, Renee, Renny

Renfred (English) lasting peace.

Renfrew (Welsh) raven woods.

Renjiro (Japanese) virtuous.

Renny (Irish) small but strong. (French) a familiar form of René.
Ren, Renn, Renne, Rennie

Reno (American) gambler. Geography: a gambling town in Nevada.
Renos, Rino

Renshaw (English) raven woods.
Renishaw

Renton (English) settlement of the roe deer.

Renzo (Latin) a familiar form of Laurence. (Italian) a short form of Lorenzo.

Reshawn (American) a combination of the prefix Re + Shawn.
Reshaun, Reshaw, Reshon, Reshun

Reshean (American) a combination of the prefix Re + Sean.
Reshane, Reshay, Resheen, Reshey

Reuben (Hebrew) behold a son.
Reuban, Reubin, Reuven, Rheuben, Rubey, Rubin, Ruby, Rueben
*Foreign forms: English: **Rube**; Spanish: **Ruben***

Reuven (Hebrew) an alternate form of Reuben.
Reuvin, Rouvin, Ruvim

Rex (Latin) king.

Rexford (English) king's ford.

Rexton (English) king's town.

Rey (Spanish) a short form of Reynard, Reynaldo, Reynold.
Reyes

Reyhan (Arabic) favored by God.
Reyham

Reynard (French) wise; bold, courageous.
Raynard, Renard, Rennard, Rey
*Foreign forms: French: **Renaud, Renauld**; German: **Reinhardt**; Italian/Spanish: **Renardo, Reynardo***

Reynold (English) king's advisor.
Rainault, Rainhold, Ranald, Raynald, Renald, Renaldi, Rey, Reynald, Reynaldos, Reynol, Reynolds
Foreign forms: Danish/Swedish: Reinhold; Dutch: Reinold; French: Renauld, Renault; German: Reinald, Reinwald; Italian: Rinaldo; Spanish: Raynaldo, Reinaldo, Reinaldos, Renaldo, Reynaldo

Rhett (Welsh) an alternate form of Rhys. Literature: Rhett Butler was the hero of Margaret Mitchell's novel *Gone with the Wind*.

Rhodes (Greek) where roses grow. Geography: an island off the coast of Greece.
Rhoads, Rhodas, Rodas

Rhys (Welsh) an alternate form of Reece.
Rhett, Rice

Rian (Irish) little king.

Ric (Italian, Spanish) a short form of Rico.
Ricca, Ricci, Ricco

Ricardo (Portuguese, Spanish) a form of Richard.
Racardo, Recard, Ricaldo,

Ricard, Ricardos, Riccardo, Ricciardo, Richardo

Rice (Welsh) an alternate form of Reece. (English) rich, noble.

Rich (English) a short form of Richard.
Ritch

Richard (English) rich and powerful ruler. See also Aric, Dick.
Rich, Richar, Richards, Richardson, Richer, Richerd, Richie, Richshard, Rick, Rickert, Rickey, Ricky, Rihardos, Rihards, Riócard, Risa, Rishard, Ristéard, Ritchard, Rostik
Foreign forms: Dutch: Richart; Estonian: Juku; Finnish: Reku; Hawaiian: Likeke; Irish: Riocard; Lithuanian: Risardas; Polish: Rye, Rysio, Ryszard; Portuguese/Spanish: Ricardo, Rico; Scandinavian: Rikard; Swedish: Rickard

Richart (German) rich and powerful ruler. The original form of Richard.

Richie (English) a familiar form of Richard.
Richey, Richi, Rishi, Ritchie

Richman (English) powerful.

Richmond (German) powerful protector.
Richmon, Richmound

Rick (German) a short form of Richard.
Ric, Ricke, Rickey, Ricks, Ricky, Rik, Rykk
Foreign form: Estonian: Riks

Ricker (English) powerful army.

Rickey (English) a familiar form of Richard, Rick.

Rickward (English) mighty guardian.
Rickwerd, Rickwood

Ricky (English) a familiar form of Richard, Rick.
Ricci, Rickey, Ricki, Rickie, Rikky
Foreign forms: Estonian: Riki, Rikki; Hungarian: Riczi; Spanish: Riqui

Rico (Spanish) a familiar form of Richard. (Italian) a short form of Enrico.
Ric

Rida (Arabic) favor.

Riddock (Irish) smooth field.

Rider (English) horseman.
Ridder, Ryder

Ridge (English) ridge of a cliff.
Ridgy, Rig, Rigg

Ridgeley (English) meadow
near the ridge.
**Ridgeleigh, Ridglea, Ridglee,
Ridgleigh, Ridgley**

Ridgeway (English) path along
the ridge.

Ridley (English) meadow of
reeds.
**Riddley, Ridlea, Ridleigh,
Ridly**

Rigby (English) ruler's valley.

Rigel (Arabic) foot. Astronomy:
one of the stars in the Orion
constellation.

Rigg (English) ridge.
Rigo

Riley (Irish) valiant.
**Reilly, Rilley, Rilye, Rylee,
Ryley, Rylie**

Ring (English) ring.
Ringo

Ringo (Japanese) apple.
(English) a familiar form of
Ring.

Rio (Spanish) river. Geography:
Rio de Janeiro is a seaport in
Brazil.

Riordan (Irish) bard, royal
poet.
Rearden, Reardin, Reardon

Rip (Dutch) ripe, full-grown.
(English) a short form of
Ripley.
Ripp

Ripley (English) meadow near
the river.
Rip, Ripleigh, Ripply

Rishawn (American) a combi-
nation of the prefix Ri +
Shawn.
Rishan, Rishaun, Rishon

Rishi (Hindi) sage.

Risley (English) meadow with
shrubs.
**Rislea, Rislee, Risleigh, Risly,
Wrisley**

Riston (English) settlement
near the shrubs.
Wriston

Ritchard (English) an alternate
form of Richard.
**Ritcherd, Ritchyrd, Ritshard,
Ritsherd**

Ritchie (English) an alternate
form of Richie.
Ritchy

Ritter (German) knight; chival-
rous.
Rittner

Riyad (Arabic) gardens.
Riad, Riyaz

Roald (Norwegian) famous
ruler.

Roan (English) a short form
of Rowan.
Rhoan

Roar (Norwegian) praised
warrior.
Roary

Roarke (Irish) famous ruler.
Roark, Rorke, Rourke, Ruark

Rob (English) a short form of
Robert.
Robb, Robe

Robbie (English) a familiar
form of Robert.
Robie, Robbi

Robby (English) a familiar form
of Robert.
Robbey, Robhy, Roby

Robert (English) famous bril-
liance. See also Dob.
**Bob, Rab, Rabbie, Raby, Rob,
Robars, Robart, Robbie,
Robby, Roberd, Robin,
Roibeárd**

Robert *(cont.)*
Foreign forms: *Czech:* **Bobek,**
Rubert; *French:* **Robers, Robinet;**
German: **Rudbert, Rupert,**
Ruprecht; *Hawaiian:* **Lopaka;**
Irish: **Riobard, Riobart;** *Italian:*
Ruberto, Ruperto; *Lithuanian:*
Rosertas; *Portuguese/Spanish:*
Rober, Roberto

Roberto (Portuguese, Spanish)
a form of Robert.

Roberts, Robertson (English)
son of Robert.
Robertson, Robeson,
Robinson, Robson

Robin (English) a short form of
Robert.
Robben, Robbin, Robbins,
Robbyn, Roben, Robinn,
Robins, Robyn, Roibín

Robinson (English) son of
Robert. An alternate form of
Roberts, Robertson.
Robbinson, Robson, Robynson

Rocco (Italian) rock.
Rocca, Rocky, Roko, Roque

Rochester (English) rocky
fortress.
Chester

Rock (English) a short form of
Rockwell.
Rocky

Rockford (English) rocky ford.

Rockland (English) rocky land.

Rockledge (English) rocky
ledge.

Rockley (English) rocky field.
Rockle

Rockwell (English) rocky
spring. Art: Norman Rockwell
was a well-known twentieth-
century American illustrator.
Rock

Rocky (American) a familiar
form of Rocco, Rock.
Rockey, Rockie

Rod (English) a short form of
Penrod, Roderick, Rodney.
Rodd

Roddy (English) a familiar form
of Roderick.
Roddie, Rody

Roderich (German) an alternate form of Roderick.

Roderick (German) famous
ruler. See also Broderick.
Rhoderick, Rod, Rodderick,
Roddrick, Roddy, Roderic,
Roderich, Roderik, Roderyck,
Rodgrick, Rodric, Rodrich,
Rodrick, Rodricki, Rodrik,

Rodrugue, Rodryck, Rodryk,
Roodney
Foreign forms: *English:* **Rory;**
French: **Rodrigue, Rodrique;**
Italian/Spanish: **Roderigo,**
Rodrigo, Ruy; *Russian:* **Rurik**

Rodger (German) an alternate
form of Roger.
Rodge, Rodgy

Rodman (German) famous
man, hero.
Rodmond

Rodney (English) island clear-
ing.
Rhodney, Rod, Rodnee, Rodni,
Rodnie, Rodnne

Rodolfo (Spanish) a form of
Rudolph.
Rodolpho, Rodulfo

Rodrigo (Italian, Spanish) a
form of Roderick.

Rodriguez (Spanish) son of
Rodrigo.
Rodrigues

Rodrik (German) famous ruler.

Roe (English) roe deer.
Row, Rowe

Roeh (Hebrew) prophet.
Roee

Rogan (Irish) redhead.

Rogelio (Spanish) famous warrior.

Roger (German) famous spearman.
Rodger, Rog, Rogerick, Rogers, Rojelio, Rüdiger
Foreign forms: Dutch: Rutger;
Hawaiian: Lokela; Italian:
Rogiero, Ruggerio;
Portuguese/Spanish: Rogelio,
Rogerio

Rohan (Hindi) sandalwood.

Rohin (Hindi) upward path.

Rohit (Hindi) big and beautiful fish.

Roi (French) an alternate form of Roy.

Roja (Spanish) red.
Rojay

Roland (German) famous throughout the land.
Rolan, Rolanda, Rolland, Rowe, Rowland, Ruland
Foreign forms: English: Rollie,
Rollin, Rollo; French: Rawlins;
Hungarian: Loránd; Italian/
Spanish: Orlando, Rolando;
Polish: Rolek; Swedish: Rolle

Rolando (Portuguese, Spanish) a form of Roland.
Lando, Olo, Roldan, Roldán

Rolf (German) a form of Ralph. A short form of Rudolph.
Rolfe, Rolle, Rolph, Rolphe
Foreign form: Swedish: Rolle

Rollie (English) a familiar form of Roland.
Roley, Rolle, Rolli, Rolly

Rolon (Spanish) famous wolf.

Roman (Latin) from Rome, Italy.
Romman
Foreign forms: French: Romain;
Greek: Romanos; Italian: Romy;
Russian: Roma, Romochka

Romeo (Italian) pilgrim to Rome; Roman. Literature: the title character of the Shakespearean play *Romeo and Juliet.*
Roméo, Romero

Romney (Welsh) winding river.
Romoney

Romulus (Latin) citizen of Rome. Mythology: Romulus and his twin brother Remus founded Rome.
Romolo, Romono, Romulo

Ron (Hebrew) a short form of Aaron, Ronald.
Ronn

Ronald (Scottish) a form of Reginald.
Ranald, Ron, Ronal, Ronney, Ronnie, Ronnold, Ronoldo
Foreign form: Portuguese:
Ronaldo

Rónán (Irish) seal.
Renan, Ronan, Ronat

Rondel (French) short poem.
Rondale, Rondall, Rondeal, Rondell, Rondey, Rondie, Rondrell, Rondy
Foreign forms: American:
Ronel, Ronell, Ronyell

Roni (Hebrew) my song; my joy.
Rani, Roneet, Ronen, Ronit, Ronli

Ronnie (Scottish) a familiar form of Ronald.
Roni, Ronie, Ronney, Ronnie, Ronny

Ronson (Scottish) son of Ronald.
Ronaldson

Ronté (American) a combination of Ron + the suffix -te.
Rontae, Ronte, Rontez

Rooney (Irish) redhead.

Roosevelt (Dutch) rose field. History: Theodore and Franklin D. Roosevelt were the twenty-sixth and thirty-second U.S. presidents, respectively.
Rosevelt

Roper (English) rope maker.

Rory (German) a familiar form of Roderick. (Irish) red king.
Rorey

Rosario (Portuguese) rosary.
Rosendo

Roscoe (Scandinavian) deer forest.
Rosco

Roshean (American) a combination of the prefix Ro + Sean.
Roshan, Roshane, Roshay, Rosheen, Roshene

Rosito (Filipino) rose.

Ross (Latin) rose. (Scottish) peninsula. (French) red.
Rosse, Rossell, Rossi, Rossie, Rossy

Rosswell (English) springtime of roses.
Rosvel

Roswald (English) field of roses.
Ross, Roswell

Roth (German) redhead.

Rothwell (Scandinavian) red spring.

Rover (English) traveler.

Rowan (English) tree with red berries.
Roan, Rowe, Rowen, Rowney

Rowell (English) roe deer well.

Rowland (German) an alternate form of Roland. (English) rough land.
Rowlands, Rowlandson

Rowley (English) rough meadow.
Rowlea, Rowlee, Rowleigh, Rowly

Rowson (English) son of the redhead.

Roxbury (English) rook's town or fortress.
Roxburghe

Roy (French) king. A short form of Royal, Royce. See also Conroy, Delroy, Fitzroy, Leroy.
Roi, Rui, Ruy

Foreign forms: Hawaiian: **Loe;** Spanish: **Rey**

Royal (French) kingly, royal.
Roy, Royale, Royall

Royce (English) son of Roy.
Roice, Roy

Royden (English) rye hill.
Royd, Roydan

Ruben (Hebrew) an alternate form of Reuben.
Rube, Rubin, Ruby

Ruby (Hebrew) a familiar form of Reuben, Ruben.

Rudd (English) a short form of Rudyard.

Rudo (African) love.

Rudolf (German) an alternate form of Rudolph.
Rodolf, Rodolfo, Rudolfo

Rudolph (German) famous wolf. See also Dolf.
Rodolph, Rolf, Rudolphus
Foreign forms: Czech: **Ruda, Rudek;** English: **Rudy;** French: **Raoul, Rodolphe;** Hungarian: **Rezsó;** Italian: **Rudolpho;** Scandinavian: **Rudolf;** Spanish: **Rodolfo, Rudi**

Rudy (English) a familiar form of Rudolph.
Ruddy, Ruddie, Rudey

Rudyard (English) red enclosure.
Rudd

Ruff (French) redhead.

Rufin (Polish) redhead.

Ruford (English) red ford; ford with reeds.
Rufford

Rufus (Latin) redhead.
Rayfus, Rufe, Ruffis, Ruffus, Rufino, Rufo, Rufous

Rugby (English) rook fortress. History: a famous British school after which the sport of rugby was named.

Ruhakana (Rukiga) argumentative.

Ruland (German) an alternate form of Roland.
Rulan, Rulon

Rumford (English) wide river crossing.

Runako (Shona) handsome.

Rune (German, Swedish) secret.

Rush (French) redhead. (English) a short form of Russell.
Rushi

Rushford (English) ford with rushes.

Rusk (Spanish) twisted bread.

Ruskin (French) redhead.
Rush, Russ

Russ (French) a short form of Russell.

Russell (French) redhead; fox colored.
Roussell, Russ, Russel, Russelle, Rusty
Foreign forms: English: **Rush;** Hawaiian: **Lukela**

Rusty (French) a familiar form of Russell.
Rustie, Rustin, Rustyn

Rutherford (English) cattle ford.
Rutherfurd

Rutland (Scandinavian) red land.

Rutledge (English) red ledge.

Rutley (English) red meadow.

Ruy (Spanish) a short form of Roderick.
Rui

Ryan (Irish) little king.
Rhyan, Rhyne, Ryane, Ryann, Ryen, Ryin, Ryne, Ryon, Ryuan, Ryun

Rycroft (English) rye field.
Ryecroft

Ryder (English) an alternate form of Rider.
Rye

Rye (English) a short form of Ryder. A grain used in cereal and whiskey. (Gypsy) gentleman.
Ry

Ryerson (English) son of Rider, Ryder.

Rylan (English) land where rye is grown.
Ryeland, Ryland, Rylin, Rylund

Ryle (English) rye hill.
Ryal, Ryel

Ryman (English) rye seller.

Ryne (Irish) an alternate form of Ryan.

Saber (French) sword.
Sabir, Sabre

Sabin (Basque) ancient tribe of central Italy.
Saben, Sabino

Sabiti (Rutooro) born on Sunday.

Sabola (Ngoni) pepper.

Saburo (Japanese) third-born son.

Saddam (Arabic) powerful ruler.

Sadiki (Swahili) faithful.
Saadiq, Sadiq, Sadique

Sadler (English) saddle maker.
Saddler

Safari (Swahili) born while traveling.
Safa

Safford (English) willow-river crossing.

Sahen (Hindi) above.

Sahir (Hindi) friend.

Sa'id (Arabic) happy.
Saeed, Sa'ied, Sajid, Sajjid, Sayeed, Sayid, Seyed

Saka (Swahili) hunter.

Sakima (Native American) king.

Sal (Italian) a short form of Salvatore.

Salam (Arabic) lamb.

Sálih (Arabic) right, good.
Saleeh, Saleh, Salehe

Salim (Swahili) peaceful.

Salím (Arabic) peaceful, safe.
Saleem, Salem, Saliym
Foreign form: Czech: Salman

Salton (English) manor town; willow town.

Salvador (Spanish) savior.
Salvadore

Salvatore (Italian) savior. See also Xavier.
Sal, Salbatore, Sallie, Sally, Salvator, Salvidor
Foreign form: French: Sauveur

Sam (Hebrew) a short form of Samuel.
Samm, Sammy, Sem, Shem, Shmuel

Samír (Arabic) entertaining companion.

Samman (Arabic) grocer.
Sammon

Sammy (Hebrew) a familiar form of Samuel.
Saamy, Sameeh, Sameh, Samey, Samie, Sammee, Sammey, Sammie, Samy

Samson (Hebrew) like the sun. Bible: a strong man betrayed by Delilah.
Sampson, Shem, Shimshon
Foreign forms: Italian: Sansone; Portuguese: Sansao; Spanish: Sansón

Samuel (Hebrew) heard God; asked of God. Bible: a famous Old Testament prophet and judge.
Sam, Samael, Samaru, Samauel, Samaul, Sameul, Samiel, Sammail, Sammel,

Sammuel, Sammy, Samouel, Samual, Samuello, Samuka, Samule, Sanko, Saumel, Schmuel, Shem, Shmuel, Simuel, Zamuel, Zanvil
Foreign forms: American: *Sambo;* Czech: *Samo;* German: *Zamiel;* Hawaiian: *Kamuela;* Hungarian: *Samu;* Irish: *Somhairle;* Italian: *Samuele;* Japanese: *Samuru;* Lithuanian: *Samuelis;* Portuguese: *Simão;* Slavic: *Samuil, Samvel*

Sanat (Hindi) ancient.

Sanborn (English) sandy brook.
Sanborne, Sanbourn, Sanbourne, Sanburn, Sanburne, Sandborn, Sandbourne

Sancho (Latin) sanctified; sincere. Literature: Sancho Panza was Don Quixote's faithful companion.
Sanchaz, Sanchez, Sauncho

Sandeep (Punjabi) enlightened.

Sander (English) a short form of Alexander, Lysander.
Sandor, Sándor, Saunder

Sanders (English) son of Sander.
Sanderson, Saunders, Saunderson

Sandy (English) a familiar form of Alexander.
Sande, Sandey, Sandie

Sanford (English) sandy river crossing.
Sandford

Sani (Hindi) Saturn.

Sanjiv (Hindi) long lived.
Sanjeev

Sankar (Hindi) god. Religion: another name for the Hindu god Shiva.

Santana (Spanish) History: Antonio Santa Ana was a revolutionary general and president of Mexico.
Santanna

Santo (Italian, Spanish) holy.
Santos

Santon (English) sandy town.

Santonio (Spanish) Geography: a short form of San Antonio, a town in Texas.
Santino, Santon

Santosh (Hindi) satisfied.

Sanyu (Luganda) happy.

Saqr (Arabic) falcon.

Sarad (Hindi) born in the autumn.

Sargent (French) army officer.
Sargant, Sarge, Sarjant, Sergeant, Sergent, Serjeant

Sariyah (Arabic) clouds at night.

Sasha (Russian) a short form of Alexander.
Sacha, Sascha, Sashenka, Sashka, Sashok, Sausha

Sasson (Hebrew) joyful.
Sason

Saul (Hebrew) asked for, borrowed. Bible: in the Old Testament, a king of Israel and the father of Jonathan; in the New Testament, the original name of Saint Paul.
Saül, Shaul, Sol, Solly

Saville (French) willow town.
Savil, Savile, Savill, Savylle, Seville, Siville

Saw (Burmese) early.

Sawyer (English) wood worker.
Sawyere

Sax (English) a short form of Saxon.
Saxe

Saxon (English) swordsman.
History: the Roman name for
Germanic people who fought
with short swords.
Sax, Saxen

Sayer (Welsh) carpenter.
**Say, Saye, Sayers, Sayre,
Sayres**

Sayyid (Arabic) master.
Sayed, Sayid, Sayyad, Sayyed

Scanlon (Irish) little trapper.
Scanlan, Scanlen

Schafer (German) shepherd.
Schaefer, Shaffar, Shäffer

Schmidt (German) blacksmith.
Schmid, Schmit, Schmitt

Schneider (German) tailor.
Schnieder, Snider, Snyder

Schön (German) handsome.
Schönn, Shon

Schuyler (Dutch) sheltering.
**Schuylar, Schylar, Schyler,
Scoy, Scy, Skuyler, Sky, Skylar,
Skyler, Skylor**

Scorpio (Latin) dangerous,
deadly. Astronomy: a southern
constellation between Libra
and Sagittarius resembling a
scorpion. Astrology: the eighth
sign of the zodiac.
Scorpeo

Scott (English) from Scotland.
A familiar form of Prescott.
Scot, Scotto, Scotty

Scotty (English) a familiar form
of Scott.
Scotie, Scottie
Foreign form: Italian: Scotti

Scoville (French) Scott's town.

Scully (Irish) town crier.

Seabert (English) shining sea.
Seabright, Sebert, Seibert

Seabrook (English) brook near
the sea.

Seamus (Irish) a form of James.
Seamas, Seumas

Sean (Hebrew) God is gracious.
(Irish) a form of John.
**Seaghan, Séan, Seán, Seanán,
Seane, Seann, Shaan, Shane,
Shaun, Shawn, Shon, Siôn**

Searle (English) armor.

Seasar (Latin) an alternate form
of Caesar.
**Seasare, Seazar, Sesar, Sesear,
Sezar**

Seaton (English) town near the
sea.
Seeton, Seton

Sebastian (Greek) venerable.
(Latin) revered.
**Bastian, Sabastian, Sabastien,
Sebastin, Sebastion, Sebbie,
Sebestyén, Sebo, Sepasetiano**
*Foreign forms: French:
Sebastien, Sébastien; Italian:
Sebastiano*

Sebastien, Sébastien (French)
forms of Sebastian.
Sebasten

Sedgely (English) sword meadow.
Sedgeley, Sedgly

Seeley (English) blessed.
Sealey, Seely
Foreign form: German: Selig

Sefton (English) village of
rushes.

Seger (English) sea spear; sea
warrior.
Seager, Seeger, Segar

Segundo (Spanish) second.

Seibert (English) bright sea.
Seabert, Sebert

Seif (Arabic) religion's sword.

Seifert (German) an alternate
form of Siegfried.

Sein (Basque) innocent.

Selby (English) village by the mansion.
Shelby

Seldon (English) willow tree valley.
Selden, Sellden, Shelden, Sheldon

Selig (German) a form of Seeley.
Seligman, Seligmann
Foreign form: Yiddish: Zelig

Selwyn (English) friend from the palace.
Selvin, Selwin, Selwinn, Selwynn, Selwynne, Wyn

Sen (Japanese) wood fairy.
Senh

Sener (Turkish) bringer of joy.

Senior (French) lord.

Sennett (French) elderly.
Sennet

Senon (Spanish) living.

Septimus (Latin) seventh.

Seraphim (Hebrew) fiery, burning. Bible: the fiery angels who guard the throne of God.
Saraf, Saraph, Serafim, Serafin, Seraphimus, Seraphin

Foreign form: Portuguese: Serafino

Serge (Latin) attendant.
Seargeoh, Serg, Serguel, Serzh, Sirgio, Sirgios
Foreign forms: German: Sergius; Italian: Sergio, Sergios; Polish: Sergiusz; Russian: Sergei, Sergey

Sergio (Italian) a form of Serge.
Serginio, Serigo, Serjio

Seth (Hebrew) appointed. Bible: the third son of Adam.
Set, Sethan, Sethe, Shet

Séverin (French) severe.
Severan, Severian, Severo, Sevien, Sevrin
Foreign forms: Italian: Severiano; Spanish: Seve, Sevé

Severn (English) boundary. Geography: a river in southern England.

Sevilen (Turkish) beloved.

Seward (English) sea guardian.
Sewerd, Siward

Sexton (English) church offical, sexton.

Sextus (Latin) sixth.
Sixtus

Seymour (French) prayer. Religion: name honoring Saint Maur. See also Maurice.
Seamor, Seamore, Seamour, See

Shabouh (Armenian) king, noble. History: a Persian king.

Shad (Punjabi) happy-go-lucky.
Shadd

Shadi (Arabic) singer.
Shaddy, Shade, Shadee, Shadeed, Shadey, Shadie, Shady, Shydee, Shydi

Shadrach (Babylonian) god; godlike. Religion: another name for Aku, the sun god. Bible: one of Daniel's three companions in captivity.
Shad, Shadrack, Shadrick, Shederick, Shedrach, Shedrick

Shah (Persian) king. History: a title for rulers of Iran.

Shai (Hebrew) a short form of Yeshaya.

Shaka (Zulu) founder, first. History: Shaka Zulu was the founder of the Zulu empire.

Shakir (Arabic) thankful.
Shakeer

Shalom (Hebrew) peace.
Shalum, Shlomo, Sholem, Sholom

Shaman (Sanskrit) holy man, mystic, medicine man.
Shamaine, Shamine, Shamon, Shamone

Shamir (Hebrew) precious stone. Bible: a hard, precious stone used to build Solomon's temple.
Shahmir, Shameer, Shamyr

Shamus (Irish) an alternate form of Seamus. (American) slang for detective.
Seamus, Shemus

Shanahan (Irish) wise, clever.

Shandy (English) rambunctious.
Shandey, Shandie

Shane (Irish) an alternate form of Sean.
Shaine, Shayn, Shayne

Shangobunni (Yoruba) gift from Shango.

Shanley (Irish) small; ancient.
Shannley

Shannon (Irish) small and wise.
Shanan, Shannan, Shannen, Shanon

Shantae (French) an alternate form of Chante.
Shant, Shantell, Shantelle, Shanti, Shantie, Shanton, Shanty

Shap (English) an alternate form of Shep.

Shaquille (Arabic) handsome.

Sharad (Pakistani) autumn.

Sharíf (Arabic) honest; noble.
Shareef, Sharef, Shareff, Shariff, Shariyf, Sharyif

Sharron (Hebrew) flat area, plain. Bible: the area from Mount Carmel south to Jaffa, covered with oak trees.
Sharone, Sharonn

Shattuck (English) little shad fish.

Shaun (Irish) an alternate form of Sean.
Shaughan, Shaughn, Shauna, Shaunahan, Shaune, Shaunn

Shaw (English) grove.

Shawn (Irish) an alternate form of Sean.
Shawen, Shawne, Shawnee, Shawnn, Shawon

Shawnta (American) a combination of Shawn + suffixes beginning with the letter T.
Shawntae, Shawntel, Shawnti

Shavar (Hebrew) comet.
Shavit

Shea (Irish) courteous.
Shae, Shai, Shayan, Shaye, Shey

Sheehan (Irish) little; peaceful.
Shean

Sheffield (English) crooked field.
Field, Shef, Sheff, Sheffie, Sheffy

Shel (English) a short form of Shelby, Sheldon, Shelton.

Shelby (English) ledge estate.
Shel, Shelbey, Shelbie, Shell, Shelley, Shelly

Sheldon (English) farm on the ledge.
Shel, Shelden, Sheldin, Shell, Shelley, Shelly, Shelton

Shelley (English) a familiar form of Shelby, Sheldon, Shelton. Literature: Percy Bysshe Shelly was a British poet.
Shell, Shelly

Shelton (English) town on a ledge.
Shel, Shelley

Shem (Hebrew) name; reputation. (English) a short form of Samuel. Bible: Noah's oldest son.

Shen (Egyptian) sacred amulet. (Chinese) meditation.

Shep (English) a short form of Shepherd.
Shap, Ship, Shipp

Shepherd (English) shepherd.
Shep, Shepard, Shephard, Shepp, Sheppard, Shepperd

Shepley (English) sheep meadow.
Sheplea, Sheplee, Shepply, Shipley

Sherborn (English) clear brook.
Sherborne, Sherbourn, Sherburn, Sherburne

Sheridan (Irish) wild.
Dan, Sheredan, Sheridon, Sherridan

Sherill (English) shire on a hill.
Sheril, Sherril, Sherrill

Sherlock (English) light haired. Literature: Sherlock Holmes was Sir Arthur Conan Doyle's famous British detective character.
Sherlocke, Shurlock, Shurlocke

Sherman (English) sheep shearer; resident of a shire.
Scherman, Schermann, Sherm, Shermann, Shermie, Shermy

Sherrod (English) clearer of the land.
Sherod, Sherrad, Sherrard, Sherrodd

Sherwin (English) swift runner, one who cuts the wind.
Sherwind, Sherwinn, Sherwyn, Sherwynd, Sherwynne, Win

Sherwood (English) bright forest.
Sherwoode, Shurwood, Woody

Shiloh (Hebrew) God's gift.
Shi, Shile, Shiley, Shilo, Shy, Shyle

Shing (Chinese) victory.
Shingae, Shingo

Shipton (English) sheep village; ship village.

Shiro (Japanese) fourth-born son.

Shiva (Hindi) life and death. Religion: the most common name for the god of destruction and reproduction.
Shiv, Shivan, Siva

Shlomo (Hebrew) an alternate form of Solomon.
Shelmu, Shelomo, Shelomoh, Shlomi, Shlomot

Shmuel (Hebrew) an alternate form of Samuel.
Shem, Shemuel, Shmelke, Shmiel, Shmulka

Sho (Japanese) prize.

Shon (German) an alternate form of Schön. (American) a form of Sean.
Shondae, Shondale, Shondel, Shonntay, Shontae, Shontarious, Shouan, Shoun

Si (Hebrew) a short form of Silas, Simon.
Sy

Sid (French) a short form of Sidney.
Cyd, Siddie, Siddy, Sidey, Syd

Siddel (English) wide valley.
Siddell

Siddhartha (Hindi) History: the original name of Buddha.

Siddhartha (cont.)
an Indian mystic and founder
of Buddhism.
**Sida, Sidh, Sidharth,
Sidhartha, Sidhdharth**

Sidney (French) from Saint
Denis, France.
**Cydney, Sid Sidnee, Sidon,
Sydney, Sydny**
Foreign form: Spanish: **Sidonio**

Sidwell (English) wide stream.

Siegfried (German) victorious
peace. Literature: a dragon-
slaying hero.
**Seifert, Seifried, Siegfred, Sig,
Sigfrid, Sigfried Sigfryd,
Siggy, Singefrid, Sygfried**
Foreign forms: American:
Ziggy; French: **Siffre, Sigfroi;**
Hungarian: **Szygfrid;**
Latvian/Russian: **Zigfrid;**
Norwegian: **Sigvard;** Portuguese:
Siguefredo; Spanish: **Sigfredo,
Sigfriedo**

Sierra (Irish) black. (Spanish)
saw toothed. Geography: a
range of mountains with a
jagged profile.
Siera

Sig (German) a short form of
Siegfried, Sigmund.

Siggy (German) a familiar form
of Siegfried, Sigmund.

Sigmund (German) victorious
protector.
**Siegmund, Sig, Siggy,
Sigismund, Sigmond,
Sigsmond, Szygmond**
Foreign forms: American:
Ziggy; Dutch: **Sigismundus;**
French: **Sigismond;** Hungarian:
Zsigmond; Italian: **Sigismondo;**
Polish: **Zygmunt;** Spanish:
Sigismundo

Sigurd (German, Scandinavian) victorious guardian.
Sigurdur, Sjure, Syver

Sigwald (German) victorious
leader.

Silas (Latin) a short form of
Silvan.
Si, Sias, Sylas

Silvan (Latin) forest dweller.
**Silas, Silvanos, Silvanus,
Silvaon, Silvie, Sylvan,
Sylvanus**
Foreign forms: French: **Silvain,
Sylvain;** Italian/Spanish: **Silvano,
Silvio, Sylvio**

Silvester (Latin) an alternate
form of Sylvester.
Silvestr, Silvy
Foreign forms: French:
Silvestre; Italian: **Silvestro**

Simba (Swahili) lion. (Yao) a
short form of Lisimba.
Sim

Simcha (Hebrew) joyful.
Simmy

Simeon (French) a form of
Simon.
Simone

Simms (Hebrew) son of Simon.
Simm, Sims

Simmy (Hebrew) a familiar
form of Simcha, Simon.
**Simmey, Simmi, Simmie,
Symmy**

Simon (Hebrew) he heard.
Bible: in the Old Testament,
the second son of Jacob and
Leah; in the New Testament,
one of the Twelve Disciples.
See also Symington.
**Saimon, Shimon, Si, Sim,
Simen, Simm, Simmon,
Simmonds, Simmons, Simmy
Simonas**
Foreign forms: Arabic: **Samein;**
French: **Simeon;** Greek: **Semon,
Symon;** Irish: **Síomónn;** Italian:
Simone; Polish: **Szymon;**
Portuguese: **Simao;** Slavic: **Simlon,
Simyon;** Spanish: **Ximenes**

Simpson (Hebrew) son of
Simon.
Simonson, Simson

Sinclair (French) prayer.
Religion: name honoring Saint
Clair.
Sinclare, Synclair

Sinjon (English) saint, holy
man. Religion: name honoring
Saint John.
Sinjun, Sjohn

Siraj (Arabic) lamp, light.

Sisi (Fanti) born on Sunday.

Siva (Hindi) an alternate form
of Shiva.
Siv

Sivan (Hebrew) ninth month of
the Jewish year.

Skee (Scandinavian) projectile.
Ski

Skeeter (English) swift.
Skeat, Skeet, Skeets

Skelly (Irish) storyteller.
Shell, Skelley, Skellie

Skelton (Dutch) shell town.

Skerry (Scandinavian) stony
island.

Skip (Scandinavian) a short
form of Skipper.

Skipper (Scandinavian) ship-
master.
Skip, Skipp, Skipple, Skipton

Skule (Norwegian) hidden.

Skye (Dutch) a short form of
Skylar, Skyler, Skylor.
Sky

Skylar (Dutch) an alternate
form of Schuyler.
Skye, Skyelar

Skyler (Dutch) an alternate
form of Schuyler.
Skye, Skyeler, Skylee

Skylor (Dutch) an alternate
form of Schuyler.
Skye, Skyelor, Skylour

Slade (English) child of the
valley.
Slaide, Slayde

Slane (Czech) salty.
Slan

Slater (English) roof slater.

Slevin (Irish) mountaineer.
Slaven, Slavin, Slawin

Sloan (Irish) warrior.
Sloane

Smedley (English) flat meadow.
Smedleigh, Smedly

Smith (English) blacksmith.
**Schmidt, Smid, Smidt, Smitt,
Smitty, Smyth, Smythe**

Snowden (English) snowy hill.
Snowdon

Socrates (Greek) wise, learned.
History: a great ancient Greek
philosopher.
Socratis, Sokrates, Sokratis

Sofian (Arabic) devoted.

Sohrab (Persian) ancient hero.

Soja (Yoruba) soldier.

Sol (Hebrew) a short form of
Saul, Solomon.
Soll, Sollie, Solly

Solly (Hebrew) a familiar form
of Saul, Solomon.
Sollie, Zollie

Solomon (Hebrew) peaceful.
Bible: a king of Israel famous
for his wisdom.
**Salomo, Selim, Shlomo, Sol,
Solamh, Solaman, Solly,
Solmon, Soloman**
*Foreign forms: Arabic:
Sulaiman; Czech: Salamun,
Salman; French: Salaun;
Lithuanian: Solomonas; Polish:
Salamen; Spanish: Salamon;
Yiddish: Shelomah, Zalman*

Solon (Greek) wise. History: a sixth-century Athenian lawmaker noted for his wisdom.

Somerset (English) place of the summer settlers. Literature: William Somerset Maugham was a well-known British writer.
Sommerset, Sumerset, Summerset

Somerville (English) summer town.
Somerton, Summerton, Summerville

Son (Vietnamese) mountain. (Native American) star. (English) son, boy. A short form of Madison, Orson.
Sonny

Songan (Native American) strong.
Song

Sonny (English) a familiar form of Grayson, Madison, Orson, Son.
Sonnie

Sono (Akan) elephant.

Sören (Danish) thunder; war. Mythology: Thor was the Norse god of thunder and war.

Sorrel (French) reddish brown.
Sorel, Sorrell

Soterios (Greek) savior.

Southwell (English) south well.

Sovann (Cambodian) gold.

Spalding (English) divided field.
Spaulding

Spangler (German) tinsmith.
Spengler

Spark (English) happy.
Sparke, Sparkie, Sparky

Spear (English) spear carrier.
Speare, Spears, Speer, Speers, Spiers

Speedy (English) quick; successful.
Speed

Spence (English) a short form of Spencer.
Spense

Spencer (English) dispenser of provisions.
Spence, Spencre, Spenser

Spenser (English) an alternate form of Spencer. Literature: Edmund Spenser was the British poet who wrote *The Faerie Queene*.
Spanser, Spense

Spike (English) ear of grain; long nail.
Spyke

Spiro (Greek) round basket; breath.
Spiridion, Spiridon, Spiros, Spyridon, Spyros

Spoor (English) spur maker.
Spoors

Sproule (English) energetic.
Sprowle

Spurgeon (English) shrub.

Spyros (Greek) an alternate form of Spiro.

Squire (English) knight's assistant; large landholder.

Stacey, Stacy (English) familiar forms of Eustace.
Stace, Stacee

Stafford (English) riverbank landing.
Staffard, Stafforde, Staford

Stamford (English) an alternate form of Stanford.

Stamos (Greek) an alternate form of Stephen.
Stamatis, Stamatos

Stan (Latin, English) a short form of Stanley.

Stanbury (English) stone fortification.
Stanberry, Stanbery, Stanburghe, Stansbury

Stancliff (English) stony cliff.
Stanclife, Stancliffe

Standish (English) stony parkland. History: Miles Standish was a prominent pilgrim in colonial America.

Stanfield (English) stony field.
Stansfield

Stanford (English) rocky ford.
Sandy, Stamford, Stan, Standford, Stanfield

Stanislaus (Latin) stand of glory.
Stanislus, Stannes, Stano
Foreign forms: Czech: **Stana, Stando;** French: **Stanislas;** German: **Stanislau;** Polish: **Stanislaw, Stasio;** Russian: **Slava, Slavik, Stas, Stasik, Tano;** Slavic: **Stane, Stanislav;** Spanish: **Lao, Stanislao**

Stanley (English) stony meadow.
Stan, Stanlea, Stanlee, Stanleigh, Stanly

Stanmore (English) stony lake.

Stannard (English) hard as stone.

Stanton (English) stony farm.
Stan, Stanten, Staunton

Stanway (English) stony road.

Stanwick (English) stony village.
Stanwicke, Stanwyck

Stanwood (English) stony woods.

Starbuck (English) challenger of fate. Literature: a character in Herman Melville's novel *Moby Dick*.

Stark (German) strong, vigorous.
Stärke, Starkie

Starling (English) bird.
Sterling

Starr (English) star.
Star, Staret, Starlight, Starlon, Starwin

Stavros (Greek) an alternate form of Stephen.

Steadman (English) owner of a farmstead.
Steadmann, Stedman, Steed

Steel (English) like steel.
Steele

Steen (German, Danish) stone.
Stein

Stefan (German, Polish, Swedish) a form of Stephen.
Staffan, Staffon, Steafeán, Stefanson, Stefaun, Stefawn, Steffan, Steffon

Stefano (Italian) an alternate form of Stephen.

Stefanos (Greek) an alterante form of Stephen.
Stefans, Stefos, Stephano, Stephanos

Stein (German) an alternate form of Steen.
Steine, Steiner

Steinar (Norwegian) rock warrior.

Steph (English) a short form of Stephen.

Stephan (Greek) an alternate form of Stephen.

Stephan (cont.)
Stephanas, Stephano, Stephanos, Stephanus

Stéphane (French) a form of Stephen.
Stefane, Stepháne

Stephen (Greek) crowned.
Stamos, Stavros, Stefanos, Stepanos, Steph, Stephan, Stephens, Stephenson, Stephfan, Stephin, Stephon, Stephone, Stepven, Steve, Steven, Stevie
Foreign forms: *Basque:* **Estebe;** *Finnish:* **Tapani;** *French:* **Étienne, Stéphane, Tepo, Tiennot;** *German/Swedish:* **Stefan;** *Hungarian:* **István, Pista;** *Irish:* **Stiofan;** *Italian:* **Stefano;** *Norwegian:* **Stefen, Steffen;** *Polish:* **Szczepan;** *Russian:* **Stenya, Stepan;** *Spanish:* **Estéban, Estevao, Teb**

Stephon (Greek) an alternate form of Stephen.
Stefon, Stefone, Stepfon, Stephone

Sterling (English) valuable; silver penny. An alternate form of Starling.
Sterling

Stern (German) star.

Sterne (English) austere.
Stearn, Stearne, Stearns

Steve (Greek) a short form of Stephen, Steven.
Steave, Steeve, Stevie, Stevy

Steven (Greek) crowned. An alternate form of Stephen.
Steevan, Steeven, Steiven, Stevan, Steve, Stevie

Stevens (Greek) son of Steven.
Stevenson

Stevie (English) a familiar form of Stephen, Steven.
Stevey, Stevy

Stewart (English) an alternate form of Stuart.
Steward, Stu

Stig (Swedish) mount.

Stiggur (Gypsy) gate.

Stillman (English) quiet.
Stillmann

Sting (English) spike of grain.

Stockman (English) tree-stump remover.

Stockton (English) tree-stump town.

Stockwell (English) tree-stump well.

Stoddard (English) horse keeper.

Stoker (English) furnace tender.
Stoke, Stokes

Stone (English) stone.
Stoney, Stony

Storm (English) tempest, storm.
Stormi, Stormy

Storr (Norwegian) great.
Story

Stover (English) stove tender.

Stowe (English) hidden, packed away.

Strahan (Irish) minstrel.
Strachan

Stratford (English) bridge over the river. Literature: Stratford-upon-Avon was Shakespeare's birthplace.

Stratton (Scottish) river valley town.

Strephon (Greek) one who turns. Literature: a character in Gilbert and Sullivan's play *Iolanthe*.

Strom (Greek) bed, mattress. (German) stream.

Strong (English) powerful.

Stroud (English) thicket.

Struthers (Irish) brook.

Stu (English) a short form of Stewart, Stuart.
Stew

Stuart (English) caretaker, steward. History: the Scottish and English royal dynasty.
Stewart, Stu, Stuarrt

Studs (English) rounded nail heads; shirt ornaments; male horses used for breeding. History: Studs Terkel, a famous American radio journalist.
Stud, Studd

Styles (English) stairs put over a wall to help cross it.
Stiles

Suck Chin (Korean) unshakable rock.

Sudi (Swahili) lucky.
Su'ud

Sued (Arabic) master, chief.

Suffield (English) southern field.

Suhail (Arabic) gentle.
Sohail, Sohayl, Souhail, Sujal

Sullivan (Irish) black eyed.
Sullavan, Sullevan, Sully

Sully (Irish) a familiar form of Sullivan. (French) stain, tarnish. (English) south meadow.
Sulleigh, Sulley

Sultan (Swahili) ruler.
Sultaan

Sum (Thai) appropriate.

Summit (English) peak, top.
Summet, Summitt

Sumner (English) church officer, summoner.
Summer

Sundeep (Punjabi) light; enlightened.
Sundip

Sunreep (Hindi) pure.
Sunrip

Susano (Hebrew) lily. A masculine form of Susan.

Sutcliff (English) southern cliff.
Sutcliffe

Sutherland (Scandinavian) southern land.
Southerland, Sutherlan

Sutton (English) southern town.

Sven (Scandinavian) youth.
Svein, Svend, Swen, Swenson

Swaggart (English) one who sways and staggers.
Swaggert

Swain (English) herdsman; knight's attendant.
Swaine, Swanson

Swaley (English) winding stream.
Swail, Swailey, Swale, Swales

Sweeney (Irish) small hero.
Sweeny

Swinbourne (English) stream used by swine.
Swinborn, Swinborne, Swinburn, Swinburne, Swinbyrn, Swynborn

Swindel (English) valley of the swine.
Swindell

Swinford (English) swine's crossing.
Swynford

Swinton (English) swine town.

Sy (Latin) a short form of Sylas.
Si

Sydney (French) an alternate form of Sidney.
Syd

Syed (Arabic) happy.

Sying (Chinese) star.

Sylas (Latin) an alternate form of Silas.
Sy

Sylvain (French) a form of Silvan, Sylvester.

Sylvester (Latin) forest dweller.
Silvester, Sly, Syl, Sylverster
*Foreign forms: French: **Sylvain, Sylvestre;** Italian: **Silvestro***

Symington (English) Simon's town, Simon's estate.

Tab (German) shining, brilliant. (English) drummer.
Tabb, Tabbie, Tabby

Tabari (Arabic) he remembers. History: a Muslim historian.
Tabarus

Tabib (Turkish) physician.
Tabeeb

Tabor (Persian) drummer. (Hungarian) encampment.
Tabber, Taber, Taboras, Taibor, Tayber, Taybor, Taver

Tad (Greek, Latin) a short form of Thaddeus. (Welsh) father.
Tadd, Taddy, Tade, Tadek, Tadey

Tadan (Native American) plentiful.

Tadashi (Japanese) honest.

Taddeus (Greek, Latin) an alternate form of Thaddeus.
Taddeusz, Taddius, Tadio, Tadious
*Foreign forms: Czech: **Tadeas, Tades***

Tadi (Omaha) wind.

Tadzi (Carrier) loon.

Taft (English) river.
Taffy, Tafton

Tage (Danish) day.
Tag

Taggart (Irish) son of the priest.

Tahír (Arabic) innocent, pure.
Taheer

Tai (Vietnamese) weather; prosperous; talented.

Taima (Native American) born during a storm.

Taiwan (Chinese) island; island dweller. Geography: a country off the coast of mainland China.
Taywan

Tait (Scandinavian) an alternate form of Tate.
Taite, Taitt

Taiwo (Yoruba) first-born of twins.

Taj (Urdu) crown.
Taji

Tajo (Spanish) day.
Taio

Tajuan (American) a combination of the prefix Ta + Juan.
Tájuan, Tajwan, Taquan, Tyjuan

Takeshi (Japanese) strong and unbending as bamboo.
Takashi, Takeo, Takeyo

Takis (Greek) a familiar form of Peter.
Takius

Takoda (Lakota) friend to everyone.

Tal (Hebrew) dew; rain.
Tali, Talia, Talley, Talor, Talya

Talbert (German) bright valley.

Talbot (French) boot maker.
Talbott, Tallbot, Tallbott, Tallie, Tally

Talcott (English) cottage near the lake.

Tale (Tswana) green.

Talib (Arabic) seeker.

Taliesin (Welsh) radiant brow.
Tallas, Tallis

Taliki (Hausa) fellow.

Talli (Lenape) legendary hero.

Talmadge (English) lake between two towns.

Talmai (Aramaic) mound; furrow. Bible: a king of Geshur and father-in-law of King David.
Telem

Talman (Aramaic) injured; oppressed.
Talmon

Talon (French, English) claw, nail.
Tallin, Tallon

Talor (English) a form of Tal. An alternate form of Taylor.

Tam (Hebrew) honest. (English) a short form of Thomas. (Vietnamese) number eight.
Tama, Tamas, Tamás, Tameas, Tamlane, Tammany, Tammas, Tammen, Tammy

Taman (Slavic) dark, black.
Tama, Tamann

Tamar (Hebrew) date; palm tree.
Tamarr, Tamer, Timur

Tambo (Swahili) vigorous.

Tamir (Arabic) tall as a palm tree.

Tammy (English) a familiar form of Thomas.
Tammie

Tamson (Scandinavian) son of Thomas.
Tamsen

Tan (Burmese) million. (Vietnamese) new.
Than

Tanek (Greek) immortal.
Foreign form: Polish: **Atek**

Taneli (Finnish) God is my judge.
Tanella

Tanguy (French) warrior.

Tani (Japanese) valley.

Tanner (English) leather worker, tanner.
Tan, Tanery, Tann, Tannor, Tanny

Tanny (English) a familiar form of Tanner.
Tana, Tanney, Tannie

Tano (Spanish) camp glory. (Russian) a short form of Stanislaus. (Ghanian) Geography: a river in Ghana.
Tanno

Tanton (English) town by the still river.

Tarell (German) an alternate form of Terrell.
Tarelle, Tarrel, Tarrell, Taryl

Tarif (Arabic) uncommon.
Tareef

Táriq (Arabic) conqueror. History: Tarik was the Muslim general who conquered Spain.
Tareck, Tareek, Tarek, Tarick, Tarik, Tarreq, Tereik

Tarleton (English) Thor's settlement.
Tarlton

Taro (Japanese) first-born male.

Taron (American) a combination of Tad + Ron.
Taeron, Tahron, Tarone, Tarren, Tarun

Tarrant (Welsh) thunder.
Terrant

Tarver (English) tower; hill; leader.
Terver

Tas (Gypsy) bird's nest.

Tass (Hungarian) ancient mythology name.

Tate (Scandinavian, English) cheerful. (Native American) long-winded talker.
Tait, Tayte

Tatius (Latin) king, ruler. History: a Sabine king.
Tatianus, Titus
Foreign form: Italian: *Tazio*

Tau (Tswana) lion.

Taurean (Latin) strong; forceful. Astrology: born under the sign of Taurus.
Tauris, Taurus

Tavaris (Aramaic) an alternate form of Tavor.
Tarvaris, Tarvarres, Tavar, Tavaras, Tavares, Tavari, Tavarian, Tavarius, Tavarres, Tavarri, Tavarris, Tavars, Tavarse, Tavarus, Taveress, Tevaris, Tevarus

Tavey (Latin) a familiar form of Octavio.

Tavi (Aramaic) good.

Tavor (Aramaic) misfortune.
Tarvoris, Tavaris, Tavores, Tavorious, Tavoris, Tavorris, Tavuris

Tawno (Gypsy) little one.
Tawn

Tayib (Hindi) good; delicate.

Taylor (English) tailor.
Tailer, Tailor, Talor, Tayler, Taylour, Teyler

Taz (Arabic) shallow ornamental cup.

Teague (Irish) bard, poet.
Teagan, Teagun, Teak, Tegan, Teige

Tearle (English) stern, severe.

Teasdale (English) river dweller. Geography: a river in England.

Ted (English) a short form of Edward, Theodore.
Tedd, Tedek, Tedik, Tedson

Teddy (English) a familiar form of Edward, Theodore.
Teddey, Teddie

Tedmund (English) protector of the land.
Tedman, Tedmond

Tedrick (American) a combination of Ted + Rick.
Tedric

Teetonka (Lakota) big lodge.

Tekle (Ethiopian) plant.

Telem (Hebrew) mound; furrow.
Talmai, Tel

Telford (French) iron cutter.
Telfer, Telfor, Telfour
Foreign form: Polish: **Telek**

Teller (English) storyteller.
Tell, Telly

Telly (Greek) a familiar form of Teller, Theodore.

Telmo (English) tiller, cultivator.

Tem (Gypsy) country.

Teman (Hebrew) on the right side; southward.

Tembo (Swahili) elephant.

Tempest (French) storm.

Temple (Latin) sanctuary.

Templeton (English) town near the temple.
Temp, Templeten

Tennant (English) tenant, renter.
Tenant, Tennent

Tennessee (Cherokee) mighty warrior. Geography: a state in the American south.
Tennessee, Tennesy, Tennysee

Tennyson (English) an alternate form of Dennison.
Tenney, Tenneyson, Tennie, Tennis, Tenny

Terence (Latin) an alternate form of Terrence.
Teren, Teryn

Terran (Latin) a short form of Terrance.
Teran, Teren, Terin, Terran, Terren, Terrin

Terrance (Latin) an alternate form of Terrence.
Tarrance, Tearance, Tearrance, Terance, Terran

Terrell (German) thunder ruler.
Tarell, Terrail, Terral, Terrale, Terrall, Terreal, Terrelle, Terrill, Terryal, Terryel, Tirel, Tirrell, Turrell
Foreign form: American: **Tyrel**

Terrence (Latin) smooth.
Tarrance, Terence, Terrance, Terren, Torrence
Foreign forms: American: **Tyrease, Tyreese;** English: **Terry;** Spanish: **Terencio**

Terrill (German) an alternate form of Terrell.
Terril, Terryl, Terryll, Tyrill

Terris (Latin) son of Terry.

Terry (English) a familiar form of Terrence.
Tarry, Terrey, Terri, Terrie
Foreign form: Hawaiian: **Keli**

Tertius (Latin) third.

Teva (Hebrew) nature.

Tex (American) from Texas.
Tejas

Thad (Greek, Latin) a short form of Thaddeus.
Thadd, Thadee, Thady

Thaddeus (Greek) courageous. (Latin) praiser. Bible: one of the Twelve Apostles.
Tad, Taddeus, Thad, Thaddaeus, Thaddeau, Thaddeaus, Thaddiaus, Thaddius, Thadeaou, Thadeous, Thadeus, Thadieus, Thadious, Thadius, Thadus
Foreign forms: Italian: **Taddeo, Thaddeo;** Polish/Spanish: **Tadzio, Thaddaus;** Ukranian: **Fadey**

Thady (Irish) praise.
Thaddy

Thai (Vietnamese) many, multiple.

Thaman (Hindi) god; godlike. Religion: another name for the Hindu god Shiva.

Than (Burma) million.
Tan

Thane (English) attendant warrior.
Thain, Thaine, Thayne

Thang (Vietnamese) victorious.

Thanh (Vietnamese) finished.

Thaniel (Hebrew) a short form of Nathaniel.

Thanos (Greek) nobleman; bear-man.
Athanasios, Thanasi, Thanasis

Thatcher (English) roof thatcher, repairer of roofs.
Thacher, Thatch, Thaxter

Thaw (English) melting ice.

Thayer (French) nation's army.
Thay

Theo (English) a short form of Theodore.

Theobald (German) people's prince

Dietbald, Theòbault, Tibalt, Tibold, Tiebold, Tybald, Tybalt, Tybault
Foreign forms: Dutch: **Tiebout;** *French:* **Thebault, Thibault;** *Irish:* **Toiboid;** *Italian/Spanish:* **Teobaldo**

Theodore (Greek) gift of God.
Téadóir, Teador, Ted, Teddy, Tedor, Telly, Teodomiro, Theodors, Theodosios, Theodrekr
Foreign forms: Basque: **Todor;** *Czech:* **Teodus;** *Dutch:* **Theodorus;** *English:* **Theo;** *French:* **Théódore;** *German:* **Tewdor, Theodor;** *Italian/Spanish:* **Teodoro;** *Polish:* **Tedorik, Teos, Tivadar, Tolek;** *Russian:* **Fedya, Feodor, Fyodor;** *Welsh:* **Tudor**

Theodoric (German) ruler of the people. See also Derek, Dietrich, Dirk.
Teodorico, Thedric, Thedrick, Till
Foreign form: French: **Thierry**

Theophilus (Greek) loved by God.
Teofil, Théophile

Theron (Greek) hunter.
Theran, Theren, Therin, Therron

Thian (Vietnamese) smooth.
Thien

Thom (English) a short form of Thomas.
Thomy

Thomas (Greek, Aramaic) twin. Bible: one of the Twelve Apostles. See also Maslin.
Thomason, Thomeson, Thomison, Thomson, Tom, Tomcy, Tomey, Tommy
Foreign forms: Bulgarian/ Russian: **Foma;** *English:* **Tam, Tammy, Thom;** *Estonian:* **Toomas;** *German:* **Thoma, Tomas;** *Hungarian:* **Tomi;** *Irish:* **Tomás, Tomey;** *Italian:* **Tomasso;** *Lithuanian:* **Tomelis;** *Polish:* **Tomek, Tomico, Tomislaw;** *Portuguese:* **Tomaz, Tome;** *Rumanian:* **Toma, Tomik;** *Scottish:* **Tavish, Tevis;** *Spanish:* **Chumo**

Thompson (English) son of Thomas.
Thomison, Thomson

Thor (Scandinavian) thunder. Mythology: the Norse god of thunder and war.
Thorin, Tor
Foreign form: English: **Tyrus**

Thorald (Scandinavian) Thor's follower.

Terrell, Terrill, Thorold, Torald

Thorbert (Scandinavian) Thor's brightness.
Torbert

Thorbjorn (Scandinavian) Thor's bear.
Thorburn, Thurborn, Thurburn

Thorgood (English) Thor is good.

Thorleif (Scandinavian) Thor's beloved.
Thorlief

Thorley (English) Thor's meadow.
Thorlea, Thorlee, Thorleigh, Thorly, Torley

Thorndike (English) thorny embankment.
Thorndyck, Thorndyke, Thorne

Thorne (English) a short form of names beginning with "Thorn."
Thorn, Thornie, Thorny

Thornley (English) thorny meadow.
Thorley, Thorne, Thornlea, Thornleigh, Thornly

Thornton (English) thorny town.
Thorne

Thorpe (English) village.
Thorp

Thorwald (Scandinavian) Thor's forest.
Thorvald

Thuc (Vietnamese) aware.

Thurlow (English) Thor's hill.

Thurmond (English) defended by Thor.
Thormond, Thurmund

Thurston (Scandinavian) Thor's stone.
Thorstan, Thorstein, Thorsten, Thurstain, Thurstan, Thursten, Torsten, Torston

Tiberio (Italian) from the Tibor River region.
Tiberius, Tibius

Tibor (Hungarian) holy place.
Tiburcio

Tiernan (Irish) lord.

Tierney (Irish) lordly.
Tiarnach, Tiernan

Tige (English) a short form of Tiger.
Ti, Tig, Ty, Tyg, Tyge

Tiger (American) tiger; powerful and energetic.
Tige
Foreign form: English: *Tyger*

Tilden (English) tilled valley.

Tilford (English) prosperous ford.

Till (German) a short form of Theodoric.
Thilo, Til, Tillman, Tilman, Tillmann, Tilson

Tilton (English) prosperous town.

Tim (Greek) a short form of Timothy.
Timmie, Timmy

Timin (Arabic) born near the sea. Mythology: sea serpent.

Timmy (Greek) a familiar form of Timothy.

Timon (Greek) honorable. History: a famous Greek philosopher.

Timothy (Greek) honoring God.
Tadhg, Taidgh, Tiege, Tim,

Timothy (cont.)
Timithy, Timkin, Timmathy, Timmothy, Timmoty, Timmthy, Timmy, Timon, Timontheo, Timonthy, Timote, Timothé, Timotheo, Timotheos, Timothey, Timthie, Tomothy
Foreign forms: *Bulgarian:* **Timotei;** *English:* **Tymothy;** *Finnish:* **Timo;** *French:* **Timothée;** *German:* **Timotheus;** *Hawaiian:* **Kimokeo;** *Hungarian:* **Timót;** *Irish:* **Tiomóid;** *Polish:* **Tymon;** *Portuguese/Spanish:* **Timoteo;** *Russian:* **Tima, Timka, Timofey, Timok, Tisha;** *Swedish:* **Timoteus**

Timur (Hebrew) an alternate form of Tamar. (Russian) conqueror.
Timour

Tin (Vietnamese) thinker.

Tino (Greek) a short form of Augustine. (Spanish) venerable, majestic. (Italian) small. A familiar form of Antonio.
Tion

Tinsley (English) fortified field.

Titus (Greek) giant. (Latin) hero. Bible: a recipient of one of Paul's New Testament letters.
Titos

Foreign forms: *French:* **Tite;** *Italian:* **Tito;** *Polish:* **Titek, Tytus**

Tivon (Hebrew) nature lover.

TJ (American) a combination of the initials T. + J.
Teejay, Tj, T.J., T Jae, Tjayda

Tobar (Gypsy) road.

Tobi (Yoruba) great.

Tobias (Hebrew) God is good.
Tobiah, Tobin, Tobit, Toby, Tobyn, Tovin, Tuvya
Foreign forms: *French:* **Tobie;** *Italian:* **Tobia;** *Spanish:* **Tobiás**

Toby (Hebrew) a familiar form of Tobias.
Tobby, Tobe, Tobey

Todd (English) fox.
Tod, Toddie, Toddy

Toft (English) small farm.

Tohon (Native American) cougar.

Toland (English) owner of taxed land.
Tolan

Tolbert (English) bright tax collector.

Toller (English) tax collector.

Tom (English) a short form of Tomas, Thomas.
Thom, Tommey, Tommie, Tommy
Foreign form: *Vietnamese:* **Teo**

Tomas (German) a form of Thomas.
Tom, Tomaisin, Tomcio, Tomo, Tomson

Tombe (Kakwa) northerners. Geography: a village in northern Uganda.

Tomey (Irish) a familiar form of Thomas.
Tome, Tomie, Tomy

Tomi (Japanese) rich. (Hungarian) a form of Thomas.

Tomlin (English) little Tom.
Tomkin, Tomlinson

Tommie (Hebrew) an alternate form of Tommy.
Tommi

Tommy (Hebrew) a familiar form of Thomas.
Tommie

Tong (Vietnamese) fragrant.

Toni (Greek, German, Slavic) a form of Tony.
Tonie, Tonis, Tonnie

Tony (Greek) flourishing. (Latin) praiseworthy. (English) a short form of Anthony. A familiar form of Remington.
Toney
Foreign forms: Czech: **Tonda;** German/Slavic: **Toni;** Polish: **Tonek, Tonik;** Portuguese: **Tonio**

Tooantuh (Cherokee) spring frog.

Topher (Greek) a short form of Christopher, Kristopher.
Tofer, Tophor

Topo (Spanish) gopher.

Topper (English) hill.

Tor (Norwegian) thunder. (Tiv) royalty, king.
Thor

Torin (Irish) chief.
Thorfin, Thorstein

Torkel (Swedish) Thor's cauldron.

Tormey (Irish) thunder spirit.
Tormé, Tormee

Torquil (Danish) Thor's kettle.
Torkel

Torr (English) tower.
Tory

Torrence (Latin) an alternate form of Terrence. (Irish) knolls.
Tawrence, Torance, Toreence, Toren, Torin, Torn, Torr, Torren, Torreon, Torrin, Tuarence, Turance
Foreign form: English: **Tory**

Torrey (English) an alternate form of Tory.
Toreey, Torre, Torri, Torrie, Torry

Toru (Japanese) sea.

Tory (English) a familiar form of Torr, Torrence.
Tori, Torrey

Toshi-Shita (Japanese) junior.
Toshio

Tovi (Hebrew) good.
Tov

Townley (English) town meadow.
Townlea, Townlee, Townleigh, Townlie, Townly

Townsend (English) town's end.
Town, Towney, Townie, Townshend, Towny

Trace (Irish) an alternate form of Tracy.

Tracy (Greek) harvester. (Latin) courageous. (Irish) battler.
Trace, Tracey, Tracie, Treacy

Trader (English) well-trodden path; skilled worker.

Trahern (Welsh) strong as iron.
Traherne, Tray

Travell (English) traveler.
Travelis, Travelle, Trevel, Trevell, Trevelle

Travers (French) crossroads.
Travaress, Travaris, Travarius, Travarus, Traver, Traverez, Travoris, Travorus
Foreign form: English: **Travis**

Travis (English) a form of Travers.
Travais, Traves, Traveus, Travious, Traviss, Travus, Travys, Trevais

Trayton (English) town full of trees.

Tredway (English) well-worn road.
Treadway

Tremaine, Tremayne (Scottish) house of stone.
Tramaine, Tremain, Treymaine, Trimaine

Trent (Latin) torrent, rapid stream. (French) thirty. Geography: a city in northern Italy.
Trente, Trentino, Trento, Trentonio

Trenton (Latin) town by the rapid stream. Geography: a city in New Jersey.
Trendon, Trendun, Trenten, Trentin, Trinton

Trev (Irish, Welsh) a short form of Trevor.

Trevelyan (English) Elian's homestead.

Trevor (Irish) prudent. (Welsh) homestead.
Trefor, Trev, Trevar, Trevares, Trevaris, Trevarus, Trever, Trevoris, Trevorus, Treyvor

Trey (English) three; third.
Trae, Trai, Tray

Trigg (Scandinavian) trusty.

Trini (Latin) a short form of Trinity.

Trinity (Latin) holy trinity.
Trenedy, Trini, Trinidy

Trip, Tripp (English) traveler.

Tristan (Welsh) bold. Literature: a knight in the Arthurian legends who fell in love with his uncle's wife.
Trestan, Treston, Tris, Trisan, Tristen, Tristian, Tristin, Triston, Trystan
Foreign form: Italian: Tristano

Tristram (Welsh) sorrowful. Literature: the title character in Laurence Sterne's eighteenth-century novel *Tristram Shandy*.
Tristam

Trot (English) trickling stream.

Trowbridge (English) bridge by the tree.

Troy (Irish) foot soldier. (French) curly haired. (English) water.
Troi, Troye, Troyton
Foreign form: Hawaiian: Koi

True (English) faithful, loyal.

Truesdale (English) faithful one's homestead.

Truitt (English) little and honest.
Truett

Truman (English) honest. History: Harry S Truman was the thirty-third U.S. president.
Trueman, Trumaine, Trumann

Trumble (English) strong; bold.
Trumball, Trumbell, Trumbull

Trustin (English) trustworthy.
Trustan, Trusten, Truston

Trygve (Norwegian) brave victor.

Trystan (Welsh) an alternate form of Tristan.
Tryistan, Trysten, Trystian, Trystin, Tryston

Tse (Ewe) younger of twins.

Tu (Vietnamese) tree.

Tuan (Vietnamese) goes smoothly.

Tuari (Laguna) young eagle.

Tucker (English) fuller, tucker of cloth.
Tuck, Tuckie, Tucky

Tug (Scandinavian) draw, pull.

Tuketu (Moquelumnan) bear making dust as it runs.

Tulio (Italian, Spanish) lively.

Tullis (Latin) title, rank.
Tullius, Tullos, Tully

Tully (Latin) a familiar form of Tullis. (Irish) at peace with God.
Tull, Tulley, Tullie, Tullio

Tumu (Moquelumnan) deer thinking about eating wild onions.

Tung (Vietnamese) stately, dignified. (Chinese) everyone.

Tupi (Moquelumnan) pulled up.

Tupper (English) ram raiser.

Turk (English) from Turkey.

Turner (Latin) lathe worker; woodworker.

Turpin (Scandinavian) Finn named after Thor.

Tut (Arabic) strong and courageous. History: a short form of Tutankhamen, an Egyptian pharoah.
Tutt

Tuvya (Hebrew) an alternate form of Tobias.
Tevya, Tuvia, Tuviah

Tuyen (Vietnamese) angel.

Twain (English) divided in two. Literature: Mark Twain (the pseudonym of Samuel Clemens) was one of the most prominent nineteenth-century American writers.
Tawine, Twaine, Tway, Twayn, Twayne

Twia (Fanti) born after twins.

Twitchell (English) narrow passage.
Twytchell

Twyford (English) double river crossing.

Ty (English) a short form of Tyler, Tyrone.
Tye

Tyee (Native American) chief.

Tyler (English) tile maker.
Tiler, Ty, Tyel, Tylar, Tyle, Tylee, Tylere, Tyller, Tylor

Tylor (English) an alternate form of Tyler.

Tymothy (English) a form of Timothy.
Tymithy, Tymmothy, Tymoteusz, Tymothee, Timothi

Tynan (Irish) dark.
Ty

Tyquan (American) a combination of Ty + Quan.
Tyquann

Tyree (Scottish) island dweller. Geography: Tiree is an island off the west coast of Scotland.

Tyra, Tyrae, Tyrai, Tyray, Tyre, Tyrea, Tyrée

Tyrel, Tyrell (American) forms of Terrell.
Tyrelle, Tyrrel, Tyrrell

Tyrick (American) a combination of Ty + Rick.
Tyreck, Tyreek, Tyreik, Tyrek, Tyreke, Tyric, Tyriek, Tyrik, Tyriq, Tyrique

Tyron (American) a form of Tyrone.
Tyronn, Tyronna, Tyronne

Tyrone (Greek) sovereign. (Irish) land of Owen.
Teirone, Ty, Tyerone, Tyroney, Tyroon, Tyroun
Foreign forms: American: Terron, Tyron

Tyshawn (American) a combination of Ty + Shawn.
Tyshan, Tyshaun, Tyshinn, Tyshon

Tyson (French) son of Ty.
Tison, Tiszon, Tyce, Tyesn, Tyeson, Tysen, Tysie, Tysne, Tysone

Tywan (Chinese) an alternate form of Taiwan.
Tywon, Tywone

Tzadok (Hebrew) righteous.
Tzadik, Zadok

Tzvi (Hebrew) deer.
Tzevi, Zevi

Udell (English) yew-tree valley.
**Dell, Eudel, Udale, Udall,
Yudell**

Udo (Japanese) ginseng plant.
(German) a short form of
Udolf.

Udolf (English) prosperous
wolf.
Udolfo, Udolph
Foreign form: German: **Udo**

Uku (Hawaiian) flea, insect;
skilled ukulele player.

Ulan (African) first-born twin.

Ulbrecht (German) an alternate form of Albert.

Ulf (German) wolf.

Ulfred (German) peaceful wolf.

Ulger (German) warring wolf.

Ullock (German) sporting wolf.

Ulmer (English) famous wolf.
Ullmar, Ulmar

Ulmo (German) from Ulm,
Germany.

Ulrich (German) wolf ruler;
ruler of all. See also Alaric.
**Uli, Ull, Ullric, Ulrick, Ulrik,
Ulrike, Ulu, Ulz, Uwe**

Ulysses (Latin) wrathful. A form
of Odysseus.
**Ulick, Ulishes, Ulisse, Ulisses,
Ulysse**
Foreign form: Spanish: **Ulises**

Umar (Arabic) an alternate
form of Omar.
Umarr, Umayr, Umer

Umi (Yao) life.

Unai (Basque) shepherd.

Unika (Lomwe) brighten.

Unwin (English) nonfriend.
Unwinn, Unwyn

Upshaw (English) upper wooded area.

Upton (English) upper town.

Upwood (English) upper forest.

Urban (Latin) city dweller;
courteous.
Urvane
Foreign forms: English: **Urbane;**
French: **Urbain, Urbaine;** *German:*
Urbanus; *Italian/Spanish:* **Urbano;**
Russian: **Urvan**

Uri (Hebrew) a short form of
Uriah.
Urie

Uriah (Hebrew) my light. Bible:
the husband of Bathsheba and
a captain in David's army. See
also Yuri.
Uri, Uria, Urias, Urijah

Urian (Greek) heaven.

Uriel (Hebrew) God is my light.
Urie

Urtzi (Basque) sky.

Usamah (Arabic) like a lion.
Usama

Usi (Yao) smoke.

Uwe (German) a familiar form
of Ulrich.

Uzi (Hebrew) my strength.

Uziel (Hebrew) God is my strength; mighty force.
Uzie, Uzziah, Uzziel

Vachel (French) small cow.
Vache, Vachell

Vaclav (Czech) wreath of glory.
Vasek

Vadin (Hindi) speaker.

Vail (English) valley.
Vaile, Vaill, Vale, Valle

Val (Latin) a short form of Valentine.

Valborg (Swedish) mighty mountain.

Valdemar (Swedish) famous ruler.

Valentine (Latin) strong; healthy.
Val, Valenté, Valentyn, Velentino
Foreign forms: Dutch: Valentijn; Italian: Valencio, Valentino; French/Spanish: Valentin

Valerian (Latin) strong; healthy.
Valeriano, Valerio, Valeryn
Foreign forms: Russian: Valera, Valerii

Valin (Hindi) an alternate form of Balin. Mythology: a tyrannical monkey king.

Vallis (French) from Wales, England.

Van (Dutch) a short form of Vandyke.
Vander, Vane, Vann, Vanno

Vance (English) thresher.

Vandyke (Dutch) dyke.
Van

Vardon (French) green knoll.
Varden, Verdan, Verdon, Verdun

Varian (Latin) variable.

Varick (German) protecting ruler.
Warrick

Vartan (Armenian) rose producer; rose giver.

Varun (Hindi) rain god.
Varron

Vashawn (American) a combination of the prefix Va + Shawn.
Vashae, Vashan, Vashann, Vashaun, Vashon, Vishon

Vasilis (Greek) an alternate form of Basil.
Vas, Vasaya, Vaselios, Vashon, Vasil, Vasile, Vasileior, Vasileios, Vasilios, Vasilius, Vasilos, Vasilus, Vasylko, Vasyltso, Vazul
Foreign forms: Russian: Vasily, Vassilij, Vasya

Vasin (Hindi) ruler, lord.

Vaughn (Welsh) small.
Vaughan, Vaughen, Vaun, Von, Voughn

Vegard (Norwegian) sanctuary; protection.

Velvel (Yiddish) wolf.

Vere (Latin, French) true.

Vered (Hebrew) rose.

Vergil (Latin) an alternate form of Virgil.
Verge

Vern (Latin) a short form of Vernon.
Verna, Vernal, Verne, Vernell, Vernine, Vernis, Vernol

Verner (German) defending army.
Varner

Verney (French) alder grove.
Vernie

Vernon (Latin) springlike; youthful.
Vern, Vernen, Verney, Vernin

Verrill (German) masculine. (French) loyal.
Verill, Verrall, Verrell, Verroll, Veryl

Vian (English) full of life. A masculine short form of Vivian.

Vic (Latin) a short form of Victor.
Vick, Vicken, Vickenson

Vicente (Spanish) a form of Vincent.
Vicent, Visente

Victor (Latin) victor, conqueror.
Vic, Victa, Victer, Victoriano, Victorien, Victorin
Foreign forms: French: **Victoir;** German/Slavic: **Viktor;** Hawaiian: **Wikoli;** Italian: **Vittorio;** Polish: **Wiktor, Witek;** Russian: **Vitya;** Spanish: **Victorio, Vitin**

Vidar (Norwegian) tree warrior.

Vidor (Hungarian) cheerful.

Vijay (Hindi) victorious. Religion: another name for the Hindu god Shiva.

Vikas (Hindi) growing.

Vin (Latin) a short form of Vincent.
Vinn

Vinay (Hindi) polite.

Vince (English) a short form of Vincent.
Vence, Vint

Vincent (Latin) victor, conqueror.
Vencent, Vin, Vincence, Vincens, Vincents, Vincenty, Vincien, Vincient, Vinciente
Foreign forms: Czech: **Vinco;** Dutch: **Vincentius;** English: **Binky, Vince, Vinny;** Greek: **Binkentios;** Hungarian: **Vinci;** Irish: **Uinseann;** Italian: **Vicenzo, Vincenzo;** Polish:

Wicent, Wincent; Russian: **Vikent, Vikenti, Vikesha;** Spanish: **Vicente, Vincente**

Vincenzo (Italian) a form of Vincent.
Vincenz, Vincenzio, Vinzenz

Vinny (English) a familiar form of Calvin, Vincent. See also Melvin.
Vinnie

Vinson (English) son of Vincent.
Vinnis

Virgil (Latin) rod bearer, staff bearer. Literature: a Roman poet best known for his epic *Aenid.*
Vergil, Virge, Virgial, Virgie
Foreign form: Spanish: **Virgilio**

Vishnu (Hindi) protector.

Vitas (Latin) alive, vital.
Foreign forms: Spanish: **Vida, Vidal**

Vito (Latin) a short form of Vittorio.
Veit, Vital, Vitale, Vitalis, Vitas, Vitin, Vitis, Vitus, Vytas

Vittorio (Italian) a form of Victor.
Vito, Vitor, Vitorio, Vittore, Vittorios

Vladimir (Russian) famous prince. See also Waldemar, Walter.
Dima, Vimka, Vlad, Vladamir, Vladik, Vladimar, Vladimeer, Vladimire, Vladjimir, Vladka, Vladko, Vladlen, Volodya, Volya, Vova, Wladimir

Vladislav (Slavic) glorious ruler.
Vladik, Vladya, Vlasislava
Foreign forms: Polish: *Wladislav;* Russian: *Slava, Vlas, Vyacheslav*

Volker (German) people's guard.
Folke

Von (German) a short form of many German names.

Wade (English) ford; river crossing.
Wadesworth, Wadie, Waide, Wayde, Waydell

Wadley (English) ford meadow.
Wadleigh, Wadly

Wadsworth (English) village near the ford.
Waddsworth

Wagner (German) wagoner, wagon maker. Music: Richard Wagner was a famous German composer.
Waggoner

Wain (English) a short form of Wainwright. An alternate form of Wayne.

Wainwright (English) wagon maker.

Wain, Wainright, Wayne, Wayneright, Waynewright, Waynright, Wright

Waite (English) watchman.
Waitman, Waiton, Waits, Wayte

Wakefield (English) wet field.
Field, Wake

Wakely (English) wet meadow.

Wakeman (English) watchman.
Wake

Walcott (English) cottage by the wall.
Wallcot, Wallcott, Wolcott

Waldemar (German) powerful; famous. See also Vladimir.
Valdemar, Waldermar, Waldo

Walden (English) wooded valley. Literature: Henry David Thoreau made Walden Pond famous with his book *Walden*.
Waldi, Waldo, Waldon, Welti

Waldo (German) a familiar form of Oswald, Waldemar, Walden.
Wald, Waldy

Waldron (English) ruler.

Waleed (Arabic) newborn.
Waled, Walid

Walerian (Polish) strong; brave.

Wales (English) from Wales, England.
Wael, Wail, Wali, Walie, Waly

Walford (English) Welshman's ford.

Walfred (German) peaceful ruler.

Wali (Arabic) all-governing.

Walker (English) cloth walker; cloth cleaner.
Wallie, Wally

Wallace (English) from Wales.
Wallas, Wallie, Wallis, Wally, Walsh, Welsh
Foreign form: German: Wallach

Waller (German) powerful. (English) wall maker.

Wally (English) a familiar form of Walter.
Walli, Wallie

Walmond (German) mighty ruler.

Walsh (English) an alternate form of Wallace.
Welch, Welsh

Walt (English) a short form of Walter, Walton.
Waltey, Waltli, Walty

Walter (German) army ruler, general. (English) woodsman. See also Vladimir.
Walder, Wally, Walt, Waltli, Walther, Wat
Foreign forms: Czech: Ladislav, Waltr; French: Gaultier, Gautier; Italian: Gualtiero; Lithuanian/Swedish: Valter, Vanda; Russian: Vova; Spanish: Gualberto, Gutierre, Waterio

Walther (German) an alternate form of Walter.

Walton (English) walled town.
Walt

Walworth (English) fenced-in farm.

Walwyn (English) Welsh friend.
Walwin, Walwinn, Walwynn, Walwynne, Welwyn

Wang (Chinese) hope; wish.

Warburton (English) fortified town.

Ward (English) watchman, guardian.
Warde, Warden, Worden

Wardell (English) watchman's hill.

Wardley (English) watchman's meadow.
Wardlea, Wardleigh

Ware (English) wary, cautious.

Warfield (English) field near the weir; fishtrap.

Warford (English) ford near the weir; fishtrap.

Warley (English) meadow near the weir; fishtrap.

Warner (German) armed defender. (French) park keeper.
Foreign form: English: Werner

Warren (German) general; warden; rabbit hutch.
Ware, Waring, Warrenson, Warrin, Warriner, Worrin

Warton (English) town near the weir; fishtrap.

Warwick (English) buildings near the weir; fishtrap.
Warick, Warrick

Washburn (English) overflowing river.

Washington (English) town near water. History: George Washington was the first U.S. president.
Wash

Watford (English) wattle ford; dam made of twigs and sticks.

Watkins (English) son of Walter.
Watkin

Watson (English) son of Walter.
Wathson

Waverly (English) quaking aspen-tree meadow.
Waverlee, Waverley

Waylon (English) land by the road.
Wallen, Walon, Way, Waylan, Wayland, Waylen, Waylin, Weylin

Wayman (English) road man; traveler.
Waymon

Wayne (English) wagon maker. A short form of Wainwright.
Wain, Wanye, Wayn, Waynell
Foreign form: Hawaiian: **Wene**

Wazir (Arabic) minister.

Webb (English) weaver.
Web, Weeb

Weber (German) weaver.
Webner

Webley (English) weaver's meadow.
Webbley, Webbly, Webly

Webster (English) weaver.

Weddel (English) valley near the ford.

Wei-Quo (Chinese) ruler of the country.
Wei

Welborne (English) spring-fed stream.
Welborn, Welbourne, Welburn, Wellborn, Wellborne, Wellbourn, Wellburn

Welby (German) farm near the well.
Welbey, Welbie, Wellbey, Wellby

Weldon (English) hill near the well.

Welford (English) ford near the well.

Wells (English) springs.

Welsh (English) an alternate form of Wallace, Walsh.
Welch

Welton (English) town near the well.

Wenceslaus (Slavic) wreath of honor. Music: "Good King Wenceslaus" is a popular Christmas carol.
Wenceslas, Wenzel, Wiencyslaw
Foreign form: Hungarian: **Vencel**

Wendell (German) wanderer. (English) good dale, good valley.
Wandale, Wendall, Wendel, Wendle, Wendy

Wenford (English) white ford.
Wynford

Wentworth (English) pale man's settlement.

Wes (English) a short form of Wesley.
Wess

Wesh (Gypsy) woods.

Wesley (English) western meadow.
Wes, Weslee, Wesleyan, Weslie, Wesly, Wessley, Westleigh, Westley

West (English) west.

Westbrook (English) western brook.
Brook, West, Westbrooke

Westby (English) western farmstead.

Westcott (English) western cottage.
Wescot, Wescott, Westcot

Westley (English) an alternate form of Wesley.

Weston (English) western town.
West, Westen, Westin

Wetherby (English) wether-sheep farm.
Weatherbey, Weatherbie, Weatherby, Wetherbey, Wetherbie

Wetherell (English) wether-sheep corner.

Wetherly (English) wether-sheep meadow.

Whalley (English) woods near a hill.

Wharton (English) town on the bank of a lake.
Warton

Wheatley (English) wheat field.

Whatley, Wheatlea, Wheatleigh, Wheatly

Wheaton (English) wheat town.

Wheeler (English) wheel maker; wagon driver.

Whistler (English) whistler, piper.

Whit (English) a short form of Whitman, Whitney.
Whitt, Whyt, Whyte, Wit, Witt

Whitby (English) white house.

Whitcomb (English) white valley.
Whitcombe, Whitcumb

Whitelaw (English) small hill.
Whitlaw

Whitey (English) white skinned; white haired.

Whitfield (English) white field.

Whitford (English) white ford.

Whitley (English) white meadow.
Whitlea, Whitlee, Whitleigh

Whitman (English) white haired man.
Whit

Whitmore (English) white moor.
Whitmoor, Whittemore, Witmore, Wittemore

Whitney (English) white island; white water.
Whit, Whittney, Widney, Widny

Whittaker (English) white field.

Wickham (English) village enclosure.
Wick

Wickley (English) village meadow.
Wilcley

Wilbert (German) brilliant; resolute.
Wilberto, Wilburt

Wilbur (English) wall fortification; bright willows.
Wilber, Wilburn, Wilburt, Willbur, Wilver

Wilder (English) wilderness, wild.

Wildon (English) wooded hill.
Wilden, Willdon

Wiley (English) willow meadow; Will's meadow.
Wildy, Willey, Wylie

Wilford (English) willow-tree ford.

Wilfred (German) determined peacemaker.
Wilferd, Wilfrid, Wilfride, Wilfried, Wilfryd, Will, Willfred, Willfried, Willie, Willy
Foreign form: Spanish: **Wilfredo**

Wilfredo (Spanish) a form of Wilfred.
Fredo, Wifredo, Willfredo

Wilhelm (German) determined guardian. The original form of William.
Wilhelmus, Willem

Wilkie (English) a familiar form of Wilkins.
Wikie

Wilkins (English) William's kin.
Wilkens, Wilkes, Wilkie, Wilkin, Willkes, Willkins

Wilkinson (English) son of little William.
Willkinson

Will (English) a short form of William.
Wilm, Wim

Willard (German) determined and brave.

William (English) determined guardian. See also Wilhelm.
Bil, Villiam, Wiliame, Wiliame, Willaim, Willam, Willeam, Williams, Willyam
Foreign forms: Basque: **Gilamu;** Czech: **Vilek, Vilém, Viliam;** Dutch: **Wim;** Finnish: **Viljo;** French: **Guillaume;** German: **Vilhelm, Willem, Willie, Willil;** Hawaiian: **Wiliama;** Hungarian: **Vili;** Irish: **Liam, Uilliam;** Italian: **Guglielmo;** Polish: **Boleslaw, Wilek;** Portuguese: **Guilherme;** Slavic: **Vasyl;** Spanish: **Guillermo;** Swedish: **Ville, Williw;** Welsh: **Gwilym;** Yiddish: **Welfel**

Williams (German) son of William.
Williamson

Willie (German) a familiar form of William.
Wille, Willey, Willi, Willia, Willy, Wily
Foreign form: Hawaiian: **Wile**

Willis (German) son of Willie.
Willice, Wills, Willus

Willoughby (English) willow farm.
Willoughbey, Willoughbie

Wills (English) son of Will.

Wilmer (German) determined and famous.
Willimar, Willmer, Wilm, Wilmar, Wylmar, Wylmer

Wilmot (Teutonic) resolute spirit.
Willmot, Wilm, Wilmont

Wilson (English) son of Will.
Wilkinson, Willson

Wilt (English) a short form of Wilton.

Wilton (English) farm by the spring.
Will, Wilt

Win (Cambodian) bright. (English) a short form of Winston.
Winn, Winnie, Winny

Winchell (English) bend in the road; bend in the land.

Windsor (English) riverbank with a winch. History: the surname of the British royal family.
Wincer, Winsor, Wyndsor

Winfield (English) friendly field.
Field, Winifield, Winnfield, Wynfield, Wynnfield

Winfried (German) friend of peace.

Wing (Chinese) glory.
Wing-Chiu, Wing-Kit

Wingate (English) winding gate.

Wingi (Native American) willing.

Winslow (English) friend's hill.

Winston (English) friendly town; victory town.
Win, Winsten, Winstonn, Winton, Wynstan, Wynston

Winter (English) born in winter.
Winterford

Winthrop (English) victory at the crossroads.

Winton (English) an alternate form of Winston.
Wynten, Wynton

Winward (English) friend's guardian; friend's forest.

Wit (Polish) life. (English) an alternate form of Whit. (Flemish) a short form of DeWitt.
Witt, Wittie, Witty

Witha (Arabic) handsome.

Witter (English) wise warrior.

Witton (English) wise man's estate.

Wolcott (English) cottage in the woods.

Wolf (German, English) a short form of Wolfe, Wolfgang.
Wolff, Wolfie, Wolfy

Wolfe (English) wolf.
Wolf, Woolf

Wolfgang (German) wolf quarrel. Music: Wolfgang Amadeus Mozart was a famous eighteenth-century Austrian composer.
Wolf, Wolfgans

Wood (English) a short form of Woodrow. See also Elwood, Garwood.
Woody

Woodfield (English) forest meadow.

Woodford (English) ford through the forest.

Woodrow (English) passage in the woods. History: Thomas Woodrow Wilson was the twenty-eighth U.S. president.
Wood, Woodman, Woody

Woodruff (English) forest ranger.

Woodson (English) son of Wood.

Woodward (English) forest warden.
Woodard

Woodville (English) town at the edge of the woods.

Woody (American) a familiar form of Woodrow.
Wooddy, Woodie

Woolsey (English) victorious wolf.

Worcester (English) forest army camp.

Wordsworth (English) wolf-guardian's farm. Literature: William Wordsworth was a famous English poet.
Worth

Worie (Ibo) born on market day.

Worth (English) a short form of Woodsworth.
Worthey, Worthington, Worthy

Wrangle (American) an alternate form of Rangle.
Wrangler

Wray (Scandinavian) corner property. (English) crooked.

Wren (Welsh) chief, ruler. (English) wren.

Wright (English) a short form of Wainwright.

Wrisley (English) an alternate form of Risley.
Wrisee, Wrislie, Wrisly

Wriston (English) an alternate form of Riston.
Wryston

Wyatt (French) little warrior.
Wiatt, Wyat, Wyatte, Wye, Wyeth

Wybert (English) battle-bright.

Wyborn (Scandinavian) war bear.

Wyck (Scandinavian) village.

Wycliff (English) white cliff; village near the cliff.
Wycliffe

Wylie (English) charming.
Wiley, Wye

Wyman (English) fighter, warrior.

Wymer (English) famous in battle.

Wyn (Welsh) light skinned, white. (English) friend. A short form of Selwyn.
Win, Wynn, Wynne

Wyndham (Scottish) village near the winding road.
Windham, Wynndham

Wythe (English) willow tree.

Xan (Greek) a short form of Alexander.
Xande, Xander

Xanthus (Latin) golden haired.
Xanthos

Xavier (Arabic) bright. (Basque) owner of the new house. See also Javier, Salvatore.
Xabier, Xaiver, Xavian, Xavon,

Xever, Xizavier, Xzaiver, Xzavaier, Xzaver, Xzavier, Xzavion, Zavier
Foreign forms: German: **Xaver;** Italian: **Saverio**

Xenophon (Greek) strange voice.
Xeno, Zennie

Xenos (Greek) stranger; guest.
Zenos

Xerxes (Persian) ruler. History: a name used by many Persian emperors.
Zerk

Xylon (Greek) forest.

Yael (Hebrew) an alternate form of Jael.

Yagil (Hebrew) he will rejoice.

Yahya (Arabic) living.
Yahiya

Yair (Hebrew) he will enlighten.

Yakez (Carrier) heaven.

Yale (German) productive. (English) old.

Yana (Native American) bear.

Yancy (Native American) Englishman, Yankee.
Yan, Yance, Yancey, Yanci, Yantsey

Yanton (Hebrew) an alternate form of Johnathon, Jonathon.

Yao (Ewe) born on Thursday.

Yawo (Akan) born on Thursday.

Yaphet (Hebrew) an alternate form of Japheth.
Yapheth, Yefat, Yephat

Yarb (Gypsy) herb.

Yardan (Arabic) king.

Yarden (Hebrew) an alternate form of Jordan. Geography: another name for the Jordan River, which flows through Israel.

Yardley (English) enclosed meadow.
Lee, Yard, Yardlea, Yardlee, Yardleigh, Yardly

Yaron (Hebrew) he will sing; he will cry out.
Jaron, Yairon

Yasin (Arabic) prophet. Religion: another name for Muhammed.

Yasir (Afghani) humble; takes it easy. (Arabic) wealthy.
Yasar, Yaser, Yashar, Yasser

Yasuo (Japanese) restful.

Yates (English) gates.
Yeats

Yavin (Hebrew) he will understand.
Jabin

Yehoshua (Hebrew) an alternate form of Joshua.
Yoshua, Y'shua, Yushua

Yehudi (Hebrew) an alternate form of Judah.
Yechudi, Yechudit, Yehuda, Yehudah, Yehudit

Yeoman (English) attendent; retainer.
Yoeman, Youman

Yeshaya (Hebrew) gift. See also Shai.

Yeshurun (Hebrew) right way.

Yigal (Hebrew) he will redeem.
Yagel, Yigael

Yishai (Hebrew) an alternate form of Jesse.

Yisrael (Hebrew) an alternate form of Israel.
Yesarel, Yisroel

Yitro (Hebrew) an alternate form of Jethro.

Yitzchak (Hebrew) an alternate form of Isaac. See also Itzak.
Yitzak, Yitzchok, Yitzhak

Yngve (Swedish) ancestor; lord, master.

Yo (Cambodian) honest.

Yoav (Hebrew) an alternate form of Joab.

Yochanan (Hebrew) an alternate form of John.
Yohanan

Yoel (Hebrew) an alternate form of Joel.

Yohann (German) an alternate form of Johann.
Yohane, Yohannes, Yohn

Yonah (Hebrew) an alternate form of Jonah.
Yonas

Yonatan (Hebrew) an alternate form of Jonathan.
Yonathan, Yonathon

Yong (Chinese) courageous.

Yong-Sun (Korean) dragon in the first position; courageous.

York (English) boar estate; yew-tree estate.
Yorick, Yorke, Yorker, Yorkie, Yorrick

Yosef (Hebrew) an alternate form of Joseph.

Yoseff, Yosif, Yosyf, Yousef, Yusif

Yóshi (Japanese) adopted son.
Yoshiki, Yoshiuki

Yoshio (Japanese) good, respectful.

Yosu (Hebrew) an alternate form of Jesus.

Young (English) young.

Young-Jae (Korean) pile of prosperity.

Young-Soo (Korean) keeping the prosperity.

Yov (Russian) a short form of Yoakim.

Yovan (Slavic) an alternate form of Jovan.
Yovani, Yovanny, Yovany

Yu (Chinese) universe.
Yue

Yudell (English) an alternate form of Udell.
Yudale, Yudel

Yuki (Japanese) snow.
Yukiko, Yukio, Yuuki

Yul (Mongolian) beyond the horizon.

Yule (English) born at Christmas.

Yuli (Basque) youthful.

Yuma (Native American) son of a chief.

Yurcel (Turkish) sublime.

Yuri (Russian, Ukrainian) a form of George. (Hebrew) a familiar form of Uriah.
Yehor, Youri, Yura, Yurchik, Yure, Yurii, Yurij, Yurik, Yurko, Yurochka, Yurri, Yury, Yusha

Yutu (Moquelumnan) coyote out hunting.

Yuval (Hebrew) rejoicing.

Yves (French) a form of Ives.
Yvens, Yvon

Yvon (French) an alternate form of Ivar, Yves.
Ivon

Zac (Hebrew) a short form of Zacharia, Zachary.
Zacc

Zacary (Hebrew) an alternate form of Zachary.
Zac, Zacaras, Zacariah, Zacarias, Zacarious, Zacory, Zacrye

Zaccary (Hebrew) an alternate form of Zachary.
Zac, Zaccaeus, Zaccari, Zaccaria, Zaccariah, Zaccary, Zaccea, Zaccury

Zaccheus (Hebrew) innocent, pure.
Zacceus, Zacchaeus

Zach (Hebrew) a short form of Zacharia, Zachary.

Zachariah (Hebrew) God remembered.
Zacarius, Zacary, Zaccary, Zachary, Zachory, Zachury, Zaquero, Zecharia, Zechariah, Zecharya, Zeggery, Zhachory
Foreign forms: English: **Zeke**; German: **Zachari, Zacharias**; Hungarian: **Zako**; Portuguese/Spanish: **Zacarias**

Zacharie (Hebrew) an alternate form of Zachary.
Zachare, Zacharee

Zachary (Hebrew) God remembered. A familiar form of Zachariah. History: Zachary Taylor was the twelfth U.S. president.
Zacary, Zaccary, Zach, Zacha, Zachaios, Zacharey, Zacharia, Zacharie, Zachaury, Zachery, Zachry, Zack, Zackary, Zackery, Zakary, Zeke
Foreign forms: Danish: **Sakeri**; Russian: **Sachar, Zakhar**

Zachery (Hebrew) an alternate form of Zachary.
Zacherey, Zacheria, Zacherias, Zacheriah, Zacherie, Zacherius

Zachry (Hebrew) an alternate form of Zachary.
Zachre, Zachrey, Zachri

Zack (Hebrew) a short form of Zachariah, Zachary.
Zach, Zak, Zaks

Zackary (Hebrew) an alternate form of Zachary.
Zack, Zackari, Zacharia, Zackariah, Zackarie, Zackery, Zackie, Zackorie, Zackory, Zackree, Zackrey, Zackry

Zackery (Hebrew) an alternate form of Zachery.

Zadok (Hebrew) a short form of Tzadok.
Zaddik, Zadik, Zadoc, Zaydok

Zafir (Arabic) victorious.
Zafar, Zafeer, Zaffar

Zahir (Arabic) shining, bright.
Zahair, Zaheer, Zahi, Zayyir

Zahur (Swahili) flower.

Zaid (Arabic) increase, growth.

Zaide (Hebrew) older.

Zaim (Arabic) brigadier general.

Zakariyya (Arabic) prophet. Religion: an Islamic prophet.

Zakary (Hebrew) an alternate form of Zachery.
Zak, Zakarai, Zakareeyah,

Zakari, Zakaria, Zakarias, Zakarie, Zakariya, Zakariyyah, Zakary, Zake, Zakerie, Zakery, Zaki, Zakir, Zakkai, Zakqary, Zakree, Zakri, Zakris, Zakry

Zaki (Arabic) bright; pure. (Hausa) lion.
Zakia

Zakia (Swahili) intelligent.

Zale (Greek) sea-strength.
Zayle

Zalmai (Afghani) young.

Zamir (Hebrew) song; bird.

Zan (Italian) clown.
Zanni

Zander (Greek) a short form of Alexander.
Zandrae, Zandy

Zane (English) a form of John.
Zain, Zayne

Zanis (Latvian) an alternate form of Janis.
Zannis

Zareb (African) protector.

Zared (Hebrew) ambush.

Zarek (Polish) may God protect the king.

Zavier (Arabic) an alternate form of Xavier.
Zavior, Zayvius, Zxavian

Zayit (Hebrew) olive.

Zeb (Hebrew) a short form of Zebediah, Zebulon.
Zev

Zebediah (Hebrew) God's gift.
Zeb, Zebadia, Zebadiah, Zebedee, Zebedia, Zedidiah

Zebedee (Hebrew) a familiar form of Zebediah.
Zebadee

Zebulon (Hebrew) exalted, honored; lofty house.
Zabulan, Zeb, Zebulen, Zebulun, Zebulyn, Zev, Zevulon, Zevulun, Zubin

Zechariah (Hebrew) an alternate form of Zachariah.
Zecharia, Zekarias, Zeke, Zekeriah

Zed (Hebrew) a short form of Zedekiah.

Zedekiah (Hebrew) God is mighty and just.
Zed, Zedechiah, Zedekias

Zedidiah (Hebrew) an alternate form of Zebediah.

Zeeman (Dutch) seaman.

Zeév (Hebrew) wolf.
Zeévi, Zeff, Zif

Zeke (Hebrew) a short form of Ezekiel, Zachariah, Zachary, Zechariah.

Zeki (Turkish) clever, intelligent.

Zemar (Afghani) lion.

Zen (Japanese) religious. Religion: a form of Buddhism.

Zeno (Greek) cart; harness. History: a Greek philosopher.
Zenan, Zenas, Zenon, Zino, Zinon

Zephaniah (Hebrew) treasured by God.
Zaph, Zaphania, Zeph, Zephan

Zephyr (Greek) west wind.
Zeferino, Zeffrey, Zephram, Zephran

Zero (Arabic) empty, void.

Zeroun (Armenian) wise and respected.

Zeshawn (American) a combination of the prefix Ze + Shawn.
Zeshan, Zeshaun, Zeshon

Zeus (Greek) living. Mythology: the chief god in the Greek pantheon who ruled from Mount Olympus.

Zev (Hebrew) a short form of Zebulon.

Zevi (Hebrew) an alternate form of Tzvi.
Zhvie, Zhvy, Zvi

Zhixin (Chinese) ambitious.
Zhi, Zhihuán, Zhipeng, Zhi-yang, Zhiyuan

Zia (Hebrew) trembling; moving.

Zigor (Basque) punishment.

Zimra (Hebrew) song of praise.
Zemora, Zimrat, Zimri, Zimria, Zimriah, Zimriya

Zimraan (Arabic) praise.

Zion (Hebrew) sign, omen; excellent. Bible: name used to refer to the land of Israel and to the Hebrew people.
Tzion

Ziskind (Yiddish) sweet child.

Ziv (Hebrew) shining brightly. (Slavic) a short form of Ziven.

Ziven (Slavic) vigorous, lively.
Zev, Ziv, Zivka, Zivon

Zohar (Hebrew) bright light.

Zollie, Zolly (Hebrew) alternate forms of Solly.
Zoilo

Zoltán (Hungarian) life.

Zorba (Greek) live each day.

Zorya (Slavic) star.

Zubin (Hebrew) a short form of Zebulon.

Zuhayr (Arabic) brilliant, shining.

Zuka (Shona) sixpence.

Very Best Baby Name Worksheet

Mom's Favorite Names

rating	girls	rating	boys
____	Marisol	____	_____
____	Margarita	____	_____
____	Carmen	____	_____
____	Natasha	____	_____
____	Zoë	____	Sebastian
____	_____	____	Gabriel
____	_____	____	Max

Dad's Favorite Names

rating	girls	rating	boys
____	Alexis	____	_____

Final Choice Worksheet

Girls' Names

rating	first	middle	last
____	Carmen	- Natasha	Montalvo
____	Zoe	- Marisol	
____		Margarita	
____		Alexis	
____		- Elizabeth	
____			
____			

Boys' Names

rating	first	middle	last
____	Xavier	Gregory	Montalvo
____		Sebastian	
____	Sebastian	David	
____	Gabriel		
____			
____			

The 15 things to consider:
namesakes, nationality, religion, gender, number of names, sounds, rhythms, pronunciation, spelling, popularity, uniqueness, stereotypes, initials, nicknames, meanings.

Pregnancy, Childbirth, and the Newborn

by Simkin, Whalley, and Keppler

If you only buy one childbirth guide, this should be the one. It's the most complete—it tells and shows (with over 100 photos, illustrations, and charts) how to prepare yourself for a healthy, positive birth experience. It covers nutrition, exercise, labor comfort measures, anesthesia choices, birth, breastfeeding, and new baby care. Created by the Childbirth Education Association of Seattle, childbirth experts call it their "bible."

Order #1169

The Maternal Journal

by Matthew Bennett

This highly acclaimed pregnancy planner contains what every expectant parent needs to know. Presented in a colorful and easy-to-understand undated calendar format.

Order #3171

Getting Organized for Your New Baby

by Maureen Bard

Here's the fastest way to get organized for pregnancy, childbirth, and new baby care. Busy expectant parents love the checklists, forms, schedules, charts, and hints in this book because they make getting ready so much easier.

Order #1229

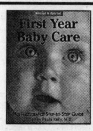

First-Year Baby Care

edited by Paula Kelly, M.D.

Since babies don't come with an "owner's manual" we created one to help you anticipate and handle your new baby's basic needs without worry. This helpful handbook covers feeding, bathing, first aid, health, childproofing, and sleeping (good luck!). Newly revised, this book gives new parents the techniques and confidence they need.

Order #1119

Order Form

Quantity	Title	Author	Order No.	Unit Cost	Total
	35,000+ Baby Names	Lansky, B.	1225	$5.95	
	Baby & Child Emergency First-Aid Handbook	Einzig, M.	1381	$8.00	
	Baby & Child Medical Care	Hart, T.	1159	$9.00	
	Baby Journal	Bennett, M.	3172	$7.95	
	Baby Name Personality Survey	Lansky/Sinrod	1270	$8.00	
	Best Baby Name Book	Lansky, B.	1029	$5.00	
	Best Baby Shower	Cooke, C.	1239	$7.00	
	Dads Say the Dumbest Things!	Lansky, B	4220	$6.00	
	David, We're Pregnant!	Johnston, L.	1049	$6.00	
	Discipline without Shouting or Spanking	Wyckoff/Unell	1079	$6.00	
	Feed Me! I'm Yours	Lansky, V.	1109	$9.00	
	First-Year Baby Care	Kelly, P.	1119	$7.00	
	Familiarity Breeds Children	Lansky, B.	4015	$7.00	
	Gentle Discipline	Lighter, D.	1085	$6.00	
	Getting Organized for Your New Baby	Bard, M.	1229	$9.00	
	Grandma Knows Best	McBride, M.	4009	$6.00	
	Happy Helpful Grandma Guide	Spirson, L.	1290	$8.00	
	If We'd Wanted Quiet/Poems for Parents	Lansky, B.	3505	$12.00	
	Joy of Grandparenting	Sherins/Holleman	3502	$7.00	
	Joy of Parenthood	Blaustone, J.	3500	$6.00	
	Maternal Journal	Bennett, M.	3171	$7.95	
	Moms Say the Funniest Things!	Lansky, B.	4280	$6.00	
	New Adventures of Mother Goose	Lansky, B.	2420	$15.00	
	Pregnancy, Childbirth, and the Newborn	Simkin/Whalley/Keppler	1169	$12.00	
	Practical Parenting Tips	Lansky, V.	1180	$8.00	
	Very Best Baby Name Book	Lansky, B.	1030	$8.00	
				Subtotal	
			Shipping and Handling (see below)		
			MN residents add 6.5% sales tax		
				Total	

YES, please send me the books indicated above. Add $2.00 shipping and handling for the first book and $.50 for each additional book. Add $2.50 to total for books shipped to Canada. Overseas postage will be billed. Allow up to four weeks for delivery. Send check or money order payable to Meadowbrook Press. No cash or C.O.D.'s please. Prices subject to change without notice. **Quantity discounts available upon request.**

Send book(s) to:

Name_____ Phone_____

Address _____

City _____ State _____ Zip _____

Payment via:

❑ Check or money order payable to Meadowbrook Press. (No cash or C.O.D.'s please) Amt. enclosed $ _____

❑ Visa (for orders over $10.00 only) ❑ MasterCard (for orders over $10.00 only)

Account #_____ Signature_____ Exp. Date _____

You can also phone us for orders of $10.00 or more at 1-800-338-2232.
*A **FREE** Meadowbrook Press catalog is available upon request.*
Mail to: Meadowbrook Inc., 18318 Minnetonka Blvd., Deephaven, MN 55391

(612) 473-5400   Toll-Free 1-800-338-2232   FAX (612) 475-0736